MW00823884

Paul Duncan and Jürgen Müller (Eds.)

FILM NOIR

100 All-Time FAVORITES

CONTENTS

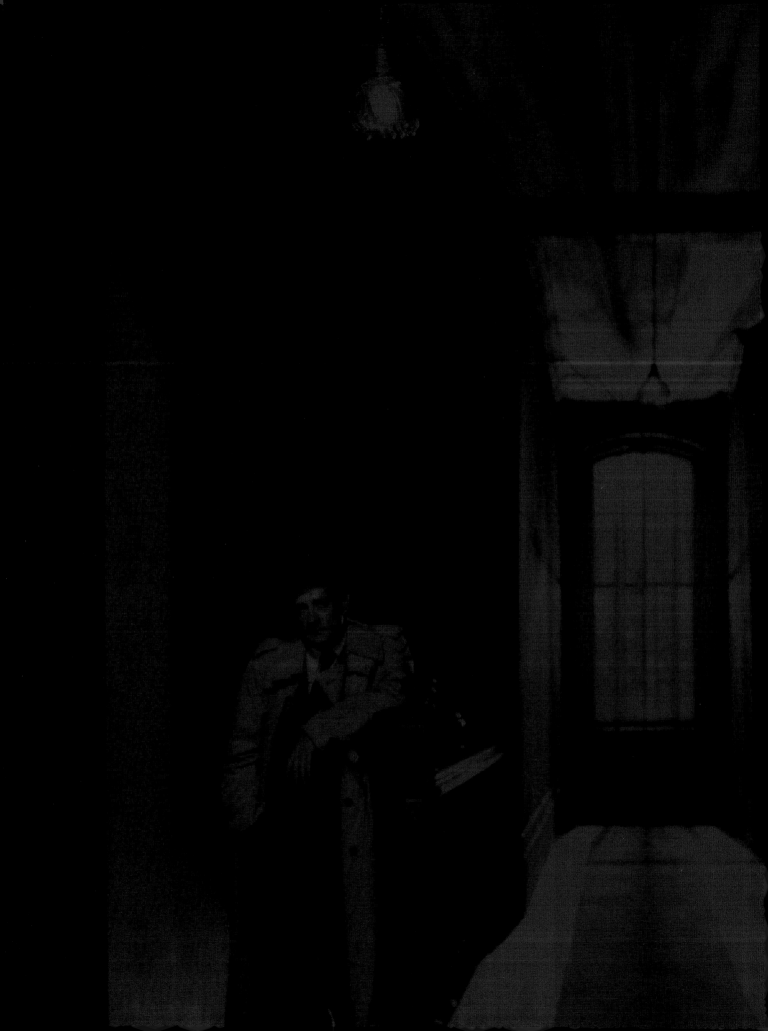

NOTES ON FILM NOIR

by Paul Schrader

In 1946 French critics, seeing the American films they had missed during the war, noticed the new mood of cynicism, pessimism, and darkness which had crept into the American cinema. The darkening stain was most evident in routine crime thrillers, but was also apparent in prestigious melodramas.

The French cineastes soon realized they had seen only the tip of the iceberg: as the years went by, Hollywood lighting grew darker, characters more corrupt, themes more fatalistic, and the tone more hopeless. By 1949 American movies were in the throes of their deepest and most creative funk. Never before had films dared to take such a harsh uncomplimentary look at American life, and they would not dare to do so again for twenty years.

Hollywood's film noir has recently become the subject of renewed interest among moviegoers and critics. The fascination film noir holds for today's young filmgoers and film students reflects recent trends in American cinema: American movies are again taking a look at the underside of the American character, but compared to such relentlessly cynical film noir as *Kiss Me Deadly* or *Kiss Tomorrow Goodbye*, the new self-hate cinema of *Easy Rider* and *Medium Cool* seems naïve and romantic. As the current political mood hardens, filmgoers and filmmakers will find the film noir of the late '40s increasingly attractive. The '40s may be to the '70s what the '30 were to the '60s.

Film noir is equally interesting to critics. It offers writers a cache of excellent, little-known films (film noir is oddly both one of Hollywood's best periods and least known), and gives auteur-weary critics an opportunity to apply themselves to the newer questions of classification and transdirectorial style. After all, what is film noir?

¶ Film noir is not a genre (as Raymond Durgnat has helpfully pointed out over the objections of Higham and Greenberg's *Hollywood in the Forties*). It is not defined, as are the Western and gangster genres, by conventions of setting and conflict, but rather by the more subtle qualities of tone and mood. It is a film "noir," as opposed to the possible variants of film gray or film off-white.

Film noir is also a specific period of film history, like German Expressionism or the French New Wave. In general, film noir refers to those Hollywood films of the '40s and early '50s that portrayed the world of dark, slick city streets, crime and corruption.

Film noir is an extremely unwieldy period. It harks back to many previous periods: Warner's '30 gangster films, the French "poetic realism" of Carné and Duvivier, Von Sternbergian melodrama, and, farthest back, German Expressionist crime films (Lang's *Mabuse* cycle). Film noir can stretch at its outer limits from *The Maltese Falcon* (1941) to *Touch of Evil* (1958), and most every dramatic Hollywood film from 1941 to 1953 contains some noir elements. There are also foreign offshoots of film noir, such as *The Third Man*, *Breathless*, and *Le Doulos*.

Almost every critic has his own definition of film noir, and a personal list of film titles and dates to back it up. Personal and descriptive definitions, however, can get a bit sticky. A film of urban nightlife is not necessarily a film noir, and a film noir need not necessarily concern crime and corruption. Since film noir is defined by tone rather than genre, it is almost impossible to argue one critic's descriptive definition against another's. How many noir elements does it take to make a film noir noir?

Rather than haggle definitions, I would rather attempt to reduce film noir to its primary colors (all shades of black), those cultural and stylistic elements to which any definition must return.

1   Chicago gangster Bull Weed (George Bancroft) has a showdown with the police to save his friends in proto-noir *Underworld* (1927), scripted by Ben Hecht and directed by Josef von Sternberg.

2   *The Public Enemy* (1931) follows the rise to power of vicious killer Tom Powers (James Cagney) and his friend Matt Doyle (Edward Woods) during the Prohibition era.

3   Cesar Enrico Bandello (Edward G. Robinson) hungers for power in director Mervyn LeRoy's adaptation of W. R. Burnett's novel *Little Caesar* (1931), which established the template for the gangster movies of the 1930s.

III   At the risk of sounding like Arthur Knight, I would suggest that there were four conditions in Hollywood in the '40s which brought about the film noir. (The danger of Knight's *Liveliest Art* method is that it makes film history less a matter of structural analysis, and more a case of artistic and social forces magically interacting and coalescing.) Each of the following four catalytic elements, however, can define the film noir; the distinctly *noir* tonality draws from each of these elements.

WAR AND POSTWAR DISILLUSIONMENTS: The acute downer which hit the United States after the Second World War was, in fact, a delayed reaction to the '30s. All through the Depression movies were needed to keep people's spirits up, and, for the most part, they did. The crime films of this period were Horatio Algerish and socially conscious. Toward the end of the '30s a darker crime film began to appear *(You Only Live Once, The Roaring Twenties)* and were it not for the war *film noir* would have been at full steam by the early '40s.

The need to produce Allied propaganda abroad and promote patriotism at home blunted the fledgling moves toward a dark cinema, and the film noir thrashed about in the studio system, not quite able to come into full prominence. During the war the first uniquely film noir appeared: *The Maltese*

Falcon, The Glass Key, This Gun for Hire, Laura, but these films lacked the distinctly noir bite the end of the war would bring.

As soon as the war was over, however, American films became markedly more sardonic – and there was a boom in the crime film. For 15 years the pressures against America's amelioristic cinema had been building up, and, given the freedom, audiences and artists were now eager to take a less optimistic view of things. The disillusionment many soldiers, small businessmen, and housewives / factory employees felt in returning to a peacetime economy was directly mirrored in the sordidness of the urban crime film. This immediate postwar disillusionment was directly demonstrated in films like *Cornered, The Blue Dahlia, Dead Reckoning*, and *Ride the Pink Horse*, in which a serviceman returns from the war to find his sweetheart unfaithful or dead, or his business partner cheating him, or the whole society something less than worth fighting for. The war continues, but now the antagonism turns with a new viciousness toward the American society itself.

POSTWAR REALISM: Shortly after the war every film-producing country had a resurgence of realism. In America it first took the form of films by such producers as Louis de Rochemont *(House on 92nd Street, Boomerang!)*

4

and Mark Hellinger *(The Killers, Brute Force)*, and directors like Henry Hathaway and Jules Dassin. "Every scene was filmed on the actual location depicted," the 1947 de Rochemont-Hathaway *Kiss of Death* proudly proclaimed. Even after de Rochemont's particular *March of Time* authenticity fell from vogue, realistic exteriors remained a permanent fixture of *film noir*.

The realistic movement also suited America's postwar mood; the public's desire for a more honest and harsh view of America would not be satisfied by the same studio streets they had been watching for a dozen years. The postwar realistic trend succeeded in breaking film noir away from the domain of the high-class melodrama, placing it where it more properly belonged, in the streets with everyday people. In retrospect, the pre–de Rochemont film noir looks definitely tamer than the postwar realistic films. The studio look of films like *The Big Sleep* and *The Mask of Dimitrios* blunts their sting, making them seem more polite and conventional in contrast to their later, more realistic counterparts.

THE GERMAN INFLUENCE: Hollywood played host to an influx of German expatriates in the '20s and '30s, and these filmmakers and technicians had, for the most part, integrated themselves into the American film establishment. Hollywood never experienced the "Germanization" some civic-minded natives feared, and there is a danger of overemphasizing the German influence in Hollywood.

But when, in the late '40s, Hollywood decided to paint it black, there were no greater masters of chiaroscuro than the Germans. The influence of expressionist lighting has always been just beneath the surface of Hollywood films, and it is not surprising, in *film noir*, to find it bursting out full bloom. Neither is it surprising to find a large number of Germans and Eastern Europeans working in *film noir*: Fritz Lang, Robert Siodmak, Billy Wilder, Franz Waxman, Otto Preminger, John Brahm, Anatole Litvak, Karl Freund, Max Ophüls, John Alton, Douglas Sirk, Fred Zinnemann, William (Wilhelm) Dieterle, Max Steiner, Edgar Georg Ulmer, Curtis (Kurt) Bernhardt, Rudolph Maté.

On the surface the German expressionist influence, with its reliance on artificial studio lighting, seems incompatible with postwar realism, with its harsh unadorned exteriors; but it is the unique quality of film noir that it was able to weld seemingly contradictory elements into a uniform style. The best noir technicians simply made all the world a sound stage, directing unnatural and expressionistic lighting onto realistic settings. In films like *Union Station*, *They Live by Night*, and *The Killers* there is an uneasy, exhilarating combination of realism and expressionism.

Perhaps the greatest master of noir was Hungarian-born John Alton, an expressionist cinematographer who could relight Times Square at noon if necessary. No cinematographer better adapted the old expressionist techniques to the new desire for realism, and his black-and-white photography in such gritty film noir as *T-Men*; *Raw Deal*; *I, the Jury*, and *The Big*

4   Private investigator Philip Marlowe (Humphrey Bogart) is hired by Vivian Rutledge's (Lauren Bacall) rich family in *The Big Sleep* (1946), a dark, complex, and confusing tale based on Raymond Chandler's 1939 novel.

5   Sam Spade (Ricardo Cortez) disarms Wilmer Cook (Dwight Frye) in the original film version of *The Maltese Falcon* (1931), from Dashiell Hammett's novel.

6   After Dick Powell, Humphrey Bogart, and Robert Montgomery played Philip Marlowe in quick succession, George Montgomery took over the role in *The Brasher Doubloon* (1947), based on the novel *The High Window*.

7   Bradford Galt (Mark Stevens, right) is a private eye framed for murder in *The Dark Corner* (1946). The dark mood is courtesy of cinematographer Joseph MacDonald, who also shot *The Street with No Name* (1948), *Call Northside 777* (1948), and *Pickup on South Street* (1953), among others.

8

9

8   The city is also a character in film noir. In *Cry of the City* (1948) Lt. Candella (Victor Mature, second right) scours New York to find out the truth about his childhood friend Martin Rome.

9   Homicide detective Jimmy Halloran (Don Taylor) is chasing killer Garzah through the streets of New York in *The Naked City* (1948), directed by Jules Dassin.

10 *Boomerang!* (1947) follows the true story of State's Attorney Henry L. Harvey (Dana Andrews) as he defends a man accused of killing a priest. The topology of the Connecticut town is vital to the case.

11 Parole officer Griff Marat (Cornel Wilde) surveys Los Angeles before being seduced by Jenny Marsh. *Shockproof* (1949) was written by Samuel Fuller and directed by Douglas Sirk.

10

Combo equals that of such German expressionist masters as Fritz Wagner and Karl Freund.

THE HARD-BOILED TRADITION: Another stylistic influence waiting in the wings was the "hard-boiled" school of writers. In the '30s authors such as Ernest Hemingway, Dashiell Hammett, Raymond Chandler, James M. Cain, Horace McCoy, and John O'Hara created the "tough," cynical way of acting and thinking which separated one from the world of everyday emotions – romanticism with a protective shell. The hard-boiled writers had their roots in pulp fiction or journalism, and their protagonists lived out a narcissistic, defeatist code. The hard-boiled hero was, in reality, a soft egg compared to his existential counterpart (Albert Camus is said to have based *The Stranger* on McCoy), but he was a good deal tougher than anything American fiction had seen.

When the movies of the '40s turned to the American "tough" moral understrata, the hard-boiled school was waiting with preset conventions of heroes, minor characters, plots, dialogue, and themes. Like the German expatriates, the hard-boiled writers had a style made to order for film noir; and, in turn, they influenced *noir* screenwriting as much as the German influenced *noir* cinematography.

The most hard-boiled of Hollywood's writers was Raymond Chandler himself, whose script of *Double Indemnity* (from a James M. Cain story) was the best written and most characteristically noir of the period. *Double In-*

demnity was the first film which played film noir for what it essentially was: small-time, unredeemed, unheroic; it made a break from the romantic noir cinema of (the later) *Mildred Pierce* and *The Big Sleep*.

(In its final stages, however, film noir adapted then bypassed the hard-boiled school. Manic, neurotic post-1948 films such as *Kiss Tomorrow Goodbye*, *D.O.A., Where the Sidewalk Ends*, *White Heat*, and *The Big Heat* are all post-hard-boiled: the air in these regions was even too thin for old-time cynics like Chandler.)

IV STYLISTICS: There is not yet a study of the stylistics of film noir, and the task is certainly too large to be attempted here. Like all film movements film noir drew upon a reservoir of film techniques, and given the time one could correlate its techniques, themes, and causal elements into a stylistic schema. For the present, however, I'd like to point out some of film noir's recurring techniques.

THE MAJORITY OF SCENES ARE LIT FOR NIGHT. Gangsters sit in the offices at midday with the shades pulled and the lights off. Ceiling lights are hung low and floor lamps are seldom more than five feet high. One always has the suspicion that if the lights were all suddenly flipped on the characters would shriek and shrink from the scene like Count Dracula at noontime.

AS IN GERMAN EXPRESSIONISM, OBLIQUE AND VERTICAL LINES ARE PREFERRED TO HORIZONTAL. Obliquity adheres to the choreography of the city, and is in direct opposition to the horizontal American tradition of Griffith and Ford. Oblique lines tend to splinter a screen, making it restless and unstable. Light enters the dingy rooms of film noir in such odd shapes – jagged trapezoids, obtuse triangles, vertical slits – that one suspects the windows were cut out with a pen knife. No character can speak authoritatively from a space which is being continually cut into ribbons of light. The Anthony Mann / John Alton *T-Men* is the most dramatic but far from the only example of oblique *noir* choreography.

THE ACTORS AND SETTING ARE OFTEN GIVEN EQUAL LIGHTING EMPHASIS. An actor is often hidden in the realistic tableau of the city at night, and, more obviously, his face is often blacked out by shadow as he speaks. These shadow effects are unlike the famous Warner Bros. lighting of the '30s in which the central character was accentuated by a heavy shadow; in film noir, the central character is likely to be standing in the shadow. When the environment is given an equal or greater weight than the actor, it, of course, creates a fatalistic, hopeless mood. There is nothing the protagonist can do; the city will outlast and negate even his best efforts.

COMPOSITIONAL TENSION IS PREFERRED TO PHYSICAL ACTION. A typical film noir would rather move the scene cinematographically around the actor than have the actor control the scene by physical action. The beating of Robert Ryan in *The Set-Up*, the gunning down of Farley Granger in *They Live by Night*, the execution of the taxi driver in *The Enforcer*, and of Brian Donlevy in *The Big Combo* are all marked by measured pacing, restrained anger, and oppressive compositions, and seem much closer to the film noir spirit than the rat-tat-tat and screeching tires of *Scarface* twenty years before or the violent, expressive actions of *Underworld U.S.A.* ten years later.

THERE SEEMS TO BE AN ALMOST FREUDIAN ATTACHMENT TO WATER. The empty noir streets are almost always glistening with fresh evening rain (even in Los Angeles), and the rainfall tends to increase in direct proportion to the drama. Docks and piers are second only to alleyways as the most popular rendezvous points.

THERE IS A LOVE OF ROMANTIC NARRATION. In such films as *The Postman Always Rings Twice*, *Laura*, *Double Indemnity*, *The Lady from Shanghai*, *Out of the Past*, and *Sunset Boulevard* the narration creates a mood of *temps perdu*: an irretrievable past, a predetermined fate, and an all-enveloping hopelessness. In *Out of the Past* Robert Mitchum relates his history with such pathetic relish that it is obvious there is no hope for any future: one can only take pleasure in reliving a doomed past.

A COMPLEX CHRONOLOGICAL ORDER IS FREQUENTLY USED TO REINFORCE THE FEELINGS OF HOPELESSNESS AND LOST TIME. Such films as *The Enforcer*, *The Killers*, *Mildred Pierce*, *The Dark Past*, *Chicago Deadline*, *Out of the Past*, and *The Killing* use a convoluted time sequence to immerse the viewer in a time-disoriented but highly stylized world. The manipulation of time, whether slight or complex, is often used to reinforce a noir principle: the how is always more important than the what.

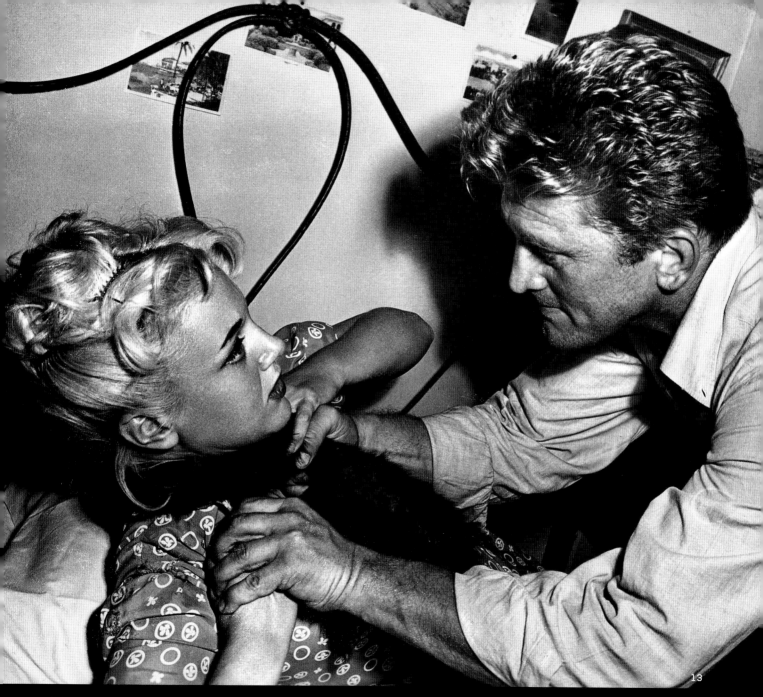

12 Noir villains are often vicious and psychotic. In
Port of New York (1949), Paul Vicola (Yul Brynner)
may look debonair, but when he finds out
girlfriend Toni Cardell (K. T. Stevens) is unreliable
he has no hesitation in disposing of her.

13 Noir antiheroes can also be prone to violence.
In Billy Wilder's *Ace in the Hole* (1951) reporter
Chuck Tatum (Kirk Douglas) assaults Lorraine
Minosa (Jan Sterling) after she makes a pass at
him while her husband is trapped in a cave-in.

14

14   After his wife has been murdered, Det. Sgt. Dave Bannion (Glenn Ford) will take the law into his own hands to bring mob boss Mike Lagana to justice in *The Big Heat* (1953), directed by Fritz Lang and based on a novel by William P. McGivern.

15   Although policemen are supposed to uphold the law, they can also turn noir. Corrupt Det. Sgt. Christopher Kelvaney (Robert Taylor) fights his brother's killer, Joey Langley (Vince Edwards), in *Rogue Cop* (1954).

16   Police Chief Joe Conroy (Sterling Hayden, center) is relieved of his duties when he accuses respected man of the community Al Willis (Gene Barry, right) of murder. Regardless, in *Naked Alibi* (1954) Conroy tails Willis to Border City and takes up the life of a hoodlum.

V THEMES: Raymond Durgnat has delineated the themes of *film noir* in an excellent article in British *Cinema* magazine ("The Family Tree of Film Noir," August, 1970), and it would be foolish for me to attempt to redo his thorough work in this short space. Durgnat divides *film noir* into 11 thematic categories, and although one might criticize some of his specific groupings, he does cover the whole gamut of *noir* production (thematically categorizing over 300 films).

In each of Durgnat's noir themes (whether Black Widow, killers-on-the-run, doppelgangers) one finds that the upwardly mobile forces of the '30s have halted; frontierism has turned to paranoia and claustrophobia. The small-time gangster has now made it big and sits in the mayor's chair, the private eye has quit the police force in disgust, and the young heroine, sick of going along for the ride, is taking others for a ride.

Durgnat, however, does not touch upon what is perhaps the most overriding noir theme: a passion for the past and present, but a fear of the future. The noir hero dreads to look ahead, but instead tries to survive by the day, and if unsuccessful at that, he retreats to the past. Thus film noir's techniques emphasize loss, nostalgia, lack of clear priorities, insecurity; then submerge these self-doubts in mannerism and style. In such a world style becomes paramount; it is all that separates one from meaninglessness. Chandler described this fundamental noir theme when he described his own fictional world: "It is not a very fragrant world, but it is the world you live in, and certain writers with tough minds and a cool spirit of detachment can make very interesting patterns out of it."

VI Film noir can be subdivided into three broad phases. The first, the wartime period, 1941–46 approximately, was the phase of the private eye and the lone wolf, of Chandler, Hammett, and Greene, of Bogart and Bacall, Ladd and Lake, classy directors like Curtiz and Garnett, studio sets, and, in general, more talk than action. The studio look of this period was reflected in such pictures as *The Maltese Falcon*; *Casablanca*; *Gaslight*; *This Gun for Hire*; *The Lodger*; *The Woman in the Window*; *Mildred Pierce*; *Spellbound*; *The Big Sleep*; *Laura*; *The Lost Weekend*; *The Strange Love of Martha Ivers*; *To Have and Have Not*; *Fallen Angel*; *Gilda*; *Murder, My Sweet*; *The Postman Always Rings Twice*; *Dark Waters*; *Scarlet Street*; *So Dark the Night*; *The Glass Key*; *The Mask of Dimitrios*; and *The Dark Mirror*.

The Wilder/Chandler *Double Indemnity* provided a bridge to the postwar phase of *film noir*. The unflinching noir vision of *Double Indemnity* came as a shock in 1944, and the film was almost blocked by the combined efforts of Paramount, the Hays Office, and star Fred MacMurray. Three years later, however, *Double Indemnity*s were dropping off the studio assembly line.

The second phase was the postwar realistic period from 1945–49 (the dates overlap and so do the films; these are all approximate phases for which there are many exceptions). These films tended more toward the problems of crime in the streets, political corruption, and police routine. Less romantic heroes like Richard Conte, Burt Lancaster, and Charles McGraw were more suited to this period, as were proletarian directors like Hathaway, Dassin, and Kazan. The realistic urban look of this phase is seen in such films as *The House on 92nd Street*, *The Killers*, *Raw Deal*, *Act of Violence*, *Union Station*, *Kiss of Death*, *Johnny O'Clock*, *Force of Evil*, *Dead Reckoning*, *Ride the Pink Horse*, *Dark Passage*, *Cry of the City*, *The Set-Up*, *T-Men*, *Call Northside 777*, *Brute Force*, *The Big Clock*, *Thieves' Highway*, *Ruthless*, *Pitfall*, *Boomerang!*, and *The Naked City*.

The third and final phase of film noir, from 1949–53, was the period of psychotic action and suicidal impulse. The noir hero, seemingly under the weight of ten years of despair, started to get bananas. The psychotic killer, who had been in the first period been a subject worthy of study (Olivia de Havilland in *The Dark Mirror*), in the second a fringe threat (Richard Widmark in *Kiss of Death*), now became the active protagonist (James Cagney in *Kiss Tomorrow Goodbye*). There were no excuses given for the psychopathy in *Gun Crazy* – it was just "crazy." James Cagney made a neurotic comeback, and his instability was matched by that of younger actors like Robert Ryan and Lee Marvin. This was the phase of the "B" noir film, and of psychoanalytically inclined directors like Ray and Walsh. The forces of personal disintegration are reflected in such films as *White Heat*, *Gun Crazy*, *D.O.A.*, *Caught*, *They Live by Night*, *Where the Sidewalk Ends*, *Kiss Tomorrow Goodbye*, *Detective Story*, *In a Lonely Place*, *I, the Jury*, *Ace in the Hole*, *Panic in the Streets*, *The Big Heat*, *On Dangerous Ground*, and *Sunset Boulevard*.

The third phase is the cream of the film noir period. Some critics may prefer the early "gray" melodramas, others the postwar "street" films, but film noir's final phase was the most aesthetically and sociologically piercing; the later noir films finally got down to the root causes of the period: the loss of public honor, heroic conventions, personal integrity, and, finally, psychic stability. The third-phase films were painfully self-aware; they seemed

to know they stood at the end of a long tradition based on despair and disintegration and did not shy away from that fact. The best and most characteristically noir films – *Gun Crazy*, *White Heat*, *Out of the Past*, *Kiss Tomorrow Goodbye*, *D.O.A.*, *They Live by Night*, and *The Big Heat* – stand at the end of the period and are the results of self-awareness. The third phase is rife with end-of-the-line noir heroes: *The Big Heat* and *Where the Sidewalk Ends* are the last stops for the urban cop, *Ace in the Hole* for the newspaper man, the Victor Saville–produced Spillane series (*I, the Jury*; *The Long Wait*; *Kiss Me Deadly*) for the private eye, *Sunset Boulevard* for the Black Widow, *White Heat* and *Kiss Tomorrow Goodbye* for the gangster, and *D.O.A.* for the John Doe American.

By the middle '50s film noir had ground to a halt. There were a few notable stragglers: *Kiss Me Deadly*, the Lewis/Alton *The Big Combo*, and film noir's epitaph, *Touch of Evil*, but for the most part a new style of crime film had become popular.

As the rise of McCarthy and Eisenhower demonstrated, Americans were eager to see a more bourgeois view of themselves. Crime had to move to the suburbs. The criminal put on a gray flannel suit and the footsore cop was replaced by the "mobile unit" careening down the expressway. Any attempt at social criticism had to be cloaked in ludicrous affirmations of the American way of life. Technically, television, with its demand for full lighting and close-ups, gradually undercut the German influence, and color cinematography was, of course, the final blow to the "noir" look. New directors like Siegel, Fleischer, Karlson, and Fuller, and TV shows like *Dragnet*, *M-Squad*, *Lineup*, and *Highway Patrol*, stepped in to create the new crime drama.

VII Film noir was an immensely creative period – probably the most creative in Hollywood's history – at least, if this creativity is measured not by its peaks but by its median level of artistry. Picked at random, a film noir is likely to be a better made film than a randomly selected silent comedy, musical, Western, and so on. (A Joseph H. Lewis "B" film noir is better than a Lewis "B" Western, for example.) Taken as a whole period, film noir achieved an unusually high level of artistry.

Film noir seemed to bring out the best in everyone: directors, cameramen, screenwriters, and actors. Again and again, a film noir will make the high point on an artist's career graph. Some directors, for example, did their

17

17 In *Nocturne* (1946), Police Lt. Joe Warne
(George Raft) is driven to solve the murder of
a womanizing composer, even though he has
been told to drop the case.

est work in film noir (Stuart Heisler, Robert Siodmak, Gordon Douglas, Edward Dmytryk, John Brahm, John Cromwell, Raoul Walsh, Henry Hathaway); other directors began in film noir, and it seems to me, never regained their original heights (Otto Preminger, Rudolph Maté, Nicholas Ray, Robert Wise, Jules Dassin, Richard Fleischer, John Huston, André de Toth, and Robert Aldrich); and other directors who made great films in other molds also made great film noir (Orson Welles, Max Ophüls, Fritz Lang, Elia Kazan, Howard Hawks, Robert Rossen, Anthony Mann, Joseph Losey, Alfred Hitchcock, and Stanley Kubrick). Whether or not one agrees with this particular schema, its message is irrefutable: film noir was good for practically every director's career. (Two interesting exceptions to prove the case are King Vidor and Jean Renoir.)

Film noir seems to have been a creative release for everyone involved. It gave artists a chance to work with previously forbidden themes, yet had conventions strong enough to protect the mediocre. Cinematographers were allowed to become highly mannered, and actors were sheltered by the cinematographers to distinguish between great directors and great noir directors.

VIII Film noir's remarkable creativity makes its longtime neglect the more baffling. The French, of course, have been students of the period for some time (Borde and Chaumeton's *A Panorama of American Film Noir* was published in 1955), but American critics until recently have preferred the Western, the musical, or the gangster film to the film noir.

Some of the reasons for this neglect are superficial; others strike to the heart of the noir style. For a long time film noir, with its emphasis on corruption and despair, was considered an aberration of the American character. The Western, with its moral primitivism, and the gangster film, with its Horatio Alger values, were considered more American than the film noir. This prejudice was reinforced by the fact that film noir was ideally suited to the low-budget "B" film, and many of the best noir films were "B" films. This odd sort of economic snobbery still lingers on in some critical circles: high-budget trash is considered more worthy of attention than low-budget trash, and to praise a "B" film is somehow to slight (often intentionally) an "A" film.

There has been a critical revival in the U.S. over the last ten years, but film noir lost out on that too. The revival was auteur (director) oriented, and film noir wasn't. Auteur criticism is interested in how directors are different; film noir criticism is concerned with what they have in common.

The fundamental reason for film noir's neglect, however, is the fact that it depends more on choreography than sociology, and American critics have always been slow on the uptake when it comes to visual style. Like its protagonists, film noir is more interested in style than theme; whereas American critics have been traditionally more interested in theme than style.

American film critics have always been sociologists first and scientists second: film is important as it relates to large masses, and if a film goes awry it is often because the theme has been somehow "violated" by the style. Film noir operates on opposite principles: the theme is hidden in the style, and bogus themes are often flaunted ("middle class values are best"), which contradict the style. Although, I believe, style determines the theme in every film, it was easier for sociological critics to discuss the themes of the Western and gangster film apart from stylistic analysis than it was to do for film noir.

Not surprisingly it was the gangster film, not the film noir, which was canonized in *The Partisan Review* in 1948 by Robert Warshow's famous essay, "The Gangster as Tragic Hero." Although Warshow could be an aesthetic as well as a sociological critic, he was interested in the Western and gangster film as "popular" art rather than as style. This sociological orientation blinded Warshow, as it has many subsequent critics, to an aesthetically more important development in the gangster film — film noir.

IX The irony of this neglect is that in retrospect the gangster films Warshow wrote about are inferior to film noir. The '30s gangster was primarily a reflection of what was happening in the country, and Warshow analyzed this. The film noir, although it was also a sociological reflection, went further than the gangster film. Toward the end film noir was engaged in a life-and-death struggle with the materials it reflected; it tried to make America accept a moral vision of life based on style. That very contradiction — promoting style in a culture which valued themes — forced film noir into artistically invigorating twists and turns. Film noir attacked and interpreted its sociological conditions and, by the close of the noir period, created a new artistic world which went beyond a simple sociological reflection, a nightmarish world of American mannerism which was by far more a creation than a reflection.

Because film noir was first of all a style, because it worked out its conflicts visually rather than thematically, because it was aware of its own identity, it was able to create artistic solutions to sociological problems. And for these reasons films like *Kiss Me Deadly*, *Kiss Tomorrow Goodbye*, and *Gun Crazy* can be works of art in a way that gangster films like *Scarface*, *Public Enemy*, and *Little Caesar* can never be.

OUT OF FOCUS

by Jürgen Müller and Jörn Hetebrügge

OBLIQUE ANGLES, SOFT FOCUS, AND UNSETTLING EFFECTS
IN ORSON WELLES'S *THE LADY FROM SHANGHAI*

The how is always more important than the what. This key sentence from Paul Schrader's "Notes on Film Noir" applies to Orson Welles, the great outsider of American cinema, more than virtually any other filmmaker. Though other directors like Howard Hawks or Robert Siodmak may have been more mainstream, or even have made far more "noirs," no one could rival Welles's stylistic radicalism. And if we are to agree with Schrader's view that film noir should be seen primarily in terms of style, then we can safely describe the brilliant creator of *Citizen Kane* (1941) as its rightful king.

While Welles's legendary debut feature does not actually fall into the category of film noir, it did act as a kind of catalyst for the genre. The film's expressive chiaroscuro aesthetic, its complex narrative structure, and the sensational use of deep focus had a huge influence on the noir style. Welles, however, not only paved the way for film noir; he was also the one to bring it to an end. Almost 20 years after *Kane*, the erstwhile prodigy – who had gained notoriety as a bit of a freak in the intervening years in Hollywood – drew a line under the classic noir period with the bizarre cop film *Touch of Evil* (1958). Between these two seminal dates

Welles directed *The Lady from Shanghai* (1947), a fascinating and impenetrable thriller that is regarded in a formal sense as the epitome of film noir, and hence the reason for our in-depth analysis of this exemplary film in this essay.

There can be no doubt that film noir's enduring fascination is attributable largely to its specific visual qualities. Its flamboyant formal style makes it a dazzling anomaly in the history of Hollywood. At a time when the dream factory was ruled by the dogma of the invisible narrative – designed to allow viewers to immerse themselves effortlessly in a fictional world, as a way of reconciling them with reality and everyday life – the shadowy world of film noir stood in stark contrast. For, instead of disappearing behind the story, form tended to dominate over content in film noir. And, as we will see from *The Lady from Shanghai*, the visual strategies do not make it any easier for the audience to orient themselves either emotionally or in terms of content. Instead, their aim is to unsettle and destabilize the viewer. Film noir, then, renders the coordinates of conventional Hollywood cinema invalid. In doing so, it gives us a sense of the world's complex and

impenetrable nature, as well as a feeling of existential alienation and uncertainty. This is what makes it so refreshingly modern.

"I love movies. But don't get me wrong: I hate Hollywood!" is a quote from Peter Bogdanovich's book of interviews that might equally apply to Orson Welles. His perception of himself as a filmmaker was influenced to a far greater extent by European traditions than by the stark realities of the American entertainment industry. Hence he began his career as a director by trying to assert his artistic independence in the face of the pressures and stale conventions of the studio system. His refusal to compromise cost him his Hollywood career in the end, with the result that he was unable to complete many screen projects, or at least not in the way he envisaged. Even *The Lady from Shanghai*, originally designed as a movie lasting 150 minutes, is now only available in an 87-minute version. This may be a further factor contributing to the film's mysterious aura. Given all the obvious breaks and inconsistencies, it is hardly surprising that Welles felt personally that his work had been ruined. Yet even as a perceived mess, it is still an ambitious movie – a formal experiment, both beautiful and artificial.

Like so many other films noirs, *The Lady from Shanghai* tells the story of a naïve man who becomes embroiled in a deadly intrigue with a *femme fatale*. In New York, Michael O'Hara (Orson Welles) – an Irish sailor with a thirst for adventure who can hold his liquor – meets the mysterious Elsa Bannister (Rita Hayworth), wife of the famous criminal defense lawyer

Arthur Bannister (Everett Sloane). Although he smells trouble, he agrees to working for the couple as a boatswain on a yacht trip through the Caribbean, and they are joined by Bannister's partner, Grisby (Glenn Anders), and a shady associate, Broome (Ted de Corsia). Seeing how unhappy Elsa is with her cynical and apparently impotent husband, Michael starts an affair with her, which does not go unnoticed by Grisby and Broome. Once they reach their destination, San Francisco, Grisby presents Michael with a plan (ostensibly risk free and a safe bet) that will net the young man $5,000 if he carries it out – money that will finance his escape with Elsa. But the plan turns out to be a fiendish trap, and it ends up with Michael in court on a murder charge.

The plot of *The Lady from Shanghai* may seem cliché-ridden at first, but on closer inspection it turns out to be part of an ironic game, as the unfathomable scheme itself suggests. In fact, the plot's credibility is called into question – by the narrator himself, and in a major way – right at the start of the film, when Michael and Elsa first meet at night in Central Park. We hear Michael saying in a voice-over, "Once I'd seen her, I was not in my right mind for quite some time." The film then reflects Michael's memory of events, who admits to being only partially sane through the course of the action. The *mise-en-scène* immediately conveys this unstable narrative perspective by changing from the indirect speech of the voice-over to the direct dialogue between Michael and Elsa, during which even the camera does not take a clear viewpoint. When the sailor

offers the blonde woman a cigarette, it is shot from Michael's perspective: Elsa looks directly at us as she accepts it. But the very next instant, the camera readopts an objective point of view and we see Michael's smiling face in a reaction shot. This first meeting of the two main characters then finishes with Michael's narrative voice confiding in us: "And from that moment on I did not use my head very much, except to be thinking of her." A sentence that only makes his powers of recall seem even less reliable.

Even if the voice-over is absent through long sections of the film, we are nonetheless warned from the outset that in *The Lady from Shanghai* we are dealing with a narrative the veracity of which must be taken with a grain of salt, and that the story line is presented by a narrator who possibly exaggerates, misremembers, or even sets himself up as a hero. While this devalues the content (the what) to a certain extent, the form (the how) becomes increasingly important at the same time. In this way, the actual theme of the movie – the hero's existential aberration – is revealed not least through Welles's elaborate visual strategies. It is obvious that the root of this abnormal behavior is an erotic infatuation. The title itself gives an indication of this, as do the various pinup shots of Rita Hayworth, most of which were apparently added later against the director's wishes; the idea was to make the film more appealing and focus more clearly on the theme of the erotic fixation of the male gaze.

These images leave us in no doubt that *The Lady from Shanghai* is all about the central theme of film noir, the battle of the sexes. And with its *femme fatale*, Welles's film draws on a key character in these pessimistic crime movies. Reference has often been made to the conclusions that can be drawn about the faltering marriage between Rita Hayworth and Orson Welles from the direction of the screen couple Elsa/Michael. The suggestion that Welles turned Hayworth – the vivacious, gorgeous star of *Gilda* with her famous mane of red hair – into an icy, cropped blonde to damage her image and career remains, however, a matter of speculation. In the context of this text, this potential personal angle is less significant than the blatant way this female star is filmed in order to shatter the expectations and viewing habits of the audience.

The Subjectivized Narrative as Nightmare

For the purposes of our formal analysis, however, we return to the start of the film, to the initial meeting mentioned above between Michael and Elsa in Central Park at night. While Michael's voice-over introduces us to the narrative, we see him strolling through the park, which is only sparsely lit by a couple of old-fashioned lanterns; at that point he comes across a coach in which Elsa is being driven around. Unprompted, Michael refers to the beautiful stranger as "princess," as if confirming the fairy-tale quality of the set. Here, Welles seems to be directing the action in a way that makes it difficult to pinpoint it in time: The story could be set just as well in Welles's present-day 1940s as in the late 19th century. This palpable detemporization ends abruptly when the coach emerges unexpectedly into the traffic of New York's metropolis. Yet in a sense the beginning, which seems unreal, influences both the perception and the representation of what will follow. Even though the filmic action is clearly set in the immediate postwar period from that point on, it seems to be divorced from the set rules of an objectified narrative. We experience the plot as something more than simply Michael's memory, which at least pretends to be bound to external reality: It is like a nightmare we live through with the hero, as well as from his perspective.

Interestingly enough, unlike many other film noir directors, Orson Welles dispenses as far as possible with the subjective camera. Michael is

present visually in every sequence, if not in every shot, within the subjective narrative. Welles possibly realized that it not only unsettles the viewer when the camera adopts the protagonist's perspective, but above all distances him as well.

Welles clearly shows Michael's loss of control, which is closely associated with this nightmare, as gradually escalating. Initially, the Irish sailor appears as a figure of authority. In the opening scene in the park he beats up a gang of young men who are molesting Elsa. When her husband, Arthur Bannister, tries to hire him to work on his yacht, the visual composition emphasizes Michael's physical superiority over the puny attorney on crutches. This relationship is reversed, however, in direct proportion to the development of the plot. No sooner has he boarded the yacht than the hero suffers a visible loss of authority. This is conveyed by a very unusual shot that follows directly on, significantly enough, from a voyeuristic sequence that shows Elsa scantily clothed like a mermaid, sunbathing on a rock by the sea (observed through a telescope by Grisby). Smoking a cigarette, the hero enters from screen left, looking across the sea from the deck of the yacht. His shape can be clearly made out in the close-up, but the profile is blurred, as if his face is too close to the camera and thus outside the focal range. The motif of identity loss is directly visualized in this shot.

The soft focus is striking, of course, because cinematographers in the studio era usually took great pains to capture clear images. A film's narrative was thought to be more easily understood if the symbolism was unam-

biguous and transparent – the viewer can then concentrate completely on the story and nothing else, without having to decipher blurred, opaque images. This aspect alone reveals *The Lady from Shanghai* as an unusually experimental film, which jettisons the conventions of feature films more systematically than almost any other film noir, in order to unsettle the viewer and wrest control of the plot from him.

It goes without saying that the convoluted plot adds to the disorienting process: The viewer is constantly misled about the motives of the protagonists, and kept in the dark about the real villain's identity. No one sees immediately through the complex scheme in which the hero/narrator is becoming increasingly entangled. Even at the end it is not absolutely clear why the whole game of betrayal, murder, phony love, and avaricious money-grabbing began in the first place, sucking the sailor into it like a vortex. At the end, as in the very beginning, he settles for the succinct observation that he exits the story a fool – an innocent, if naïve, one. Yet Orson Welles disorients the viewer even more so at the formal and aesthetic level. Rather than clarifying, as was standard in the conventional narrative cinema of his day, his filmic images obscure, by using big close-ups, low angles, and harsh contrasts for facial shots. They unsettle us because these extreme shots gradually erode the authority of the subject who actually constitutes the gaze – Michael. And in the process, the world also loses its objective status. In this way, *The Lady from Shanghai* confirms one specific qualitative difference between film noir and Hollywood's classic cinema of illu-

sion: Welles's movie expands the familiar objectified narrative through expressive moments that mirror the mental state of the male protagonist. In a sense, as a result of this subjectification process his inner self becomes the viewer's "event horizon."

Attraction and Repulsion

The use of short focal lengths favored by Welles since *Citizen Kane* is especially worth mentioning in this context. In contrast to longer focal lengths, the extreme wide-angle lens has not only the advantage of the broader field of vision the term itself conveys; it also creates a greater sense of depth (the depth of the image virtually disappears when a telephoto lens is used). Welles and his cinematographer, Gregg Toland, made sensational use of this effect in *Citizen Kane* by establishing deep focus as the key compositional tool. Another feature of short focal lengths, especially the fish-eye lens, however, is spatial distortion, which is most obvious at close range and at the edge of the frame: Lines are bent, the general appearance of subjects is distorted, and facial features become grotesque. Welles makes deliberate and frequent use of this feature in *The Lady from Shanghai* in order to produce a feeling of unease.

Faces, especially that of Arthur Bannister's partner, Grisby, are often shown in big close-up, mostly as point-of-view shots, which seem to reflect the perspective of the hero, Michael (though they never quite correspond

entirely, as is the case when a subjective camera is used). However, this spatial proximity by no means creates a sense of positive emotional closeness to the character thus depicted, such as sympathy or even identification, in a way that could easily be achieved using a traveling shot (when the camera slowly approaches the actor's face until it fills the entire image). Instead of carefully approaching with a moving camera, Welles uses the shock tactic of an abrupt cut. Michael is taken by surprise and put under pressure – along with the viewer.

Grisby's face leers unpleasantly close to us, not just because we are taken by surprise, but also because it is grotesquely distorted in wide angle. So the physiognomy – not a particularly appealing one, with a thin-lipped, snarling mouth and droopy eyes – is emphasized by the visual effect as well as by the actor reinforcing it through facial expression. This produces more than just distortion, however. For, although the face fills the actual visual space, we can still detect the depth of the hidden area. So the face cuts off our escape route: While we are being sucked into the image by the deep pull of the wide-angle lens, it is, in a manner of speaking, confronting us as well.

This effect is also produced because the face is shown in sharp focus. At such close range we can make out every pore, bead of sweat, and whisker of stubble, and the low angle pushes Grisby's nostrils uncomfortably to the fore. The face becomes disturbingly three-dimensional, affecting us in an almost physical sense (one could argue that the face replaces the scenic

space, becoming the scenic space itself). It almost seems to be bursting out of the screen toward us. And just as Grisby's perplexing, delusional remarks and disturbing laugh pierce our ears acoustically, his breath and sweat are like a visual confrontation. There can be no doubt that Orson Welles is deliberately playing here with the experience of physical repulsion.

To put it bluntly, the face – distorted by the wide angle and shot in deep focus – penetrates the viewer's space. There is even a thematic counterpart to this *mise-en-scène* in one scene in the movie. During the court case the district attorney, Galloway, calls Elsa Bannister, who is observing in the public gallery, to take the stand. He pressurizes her with indiscreet questions about her relationship with Michael until her apparent vulnerability makes her reveal her affair with him (she swallows, unable to withstand his presumptuous glances). Galloway ends his interrogation with a flourish – "No further questions." The verbal violation ends in a big close-up of Galloway, which mirrors the sadistic pleasure in his face with almost terrifying clarity.

The whole trial comes across as chaotic. The defense and prosecution interrupt each other constantly. Along with the judge, they seem more intent on outdoing each other with amusing speeches than finding out the truth. So the cross-examination is more about entertaining the public and jury than establishing the evidence. The public indulges in heckling, the jury whispers in secret, and, in a kind of running gag, one of them frequently interrupts the trial with a sneezing fit. Through all this, the camera constantly changes position, showing the courtroom in an extreme high-angle

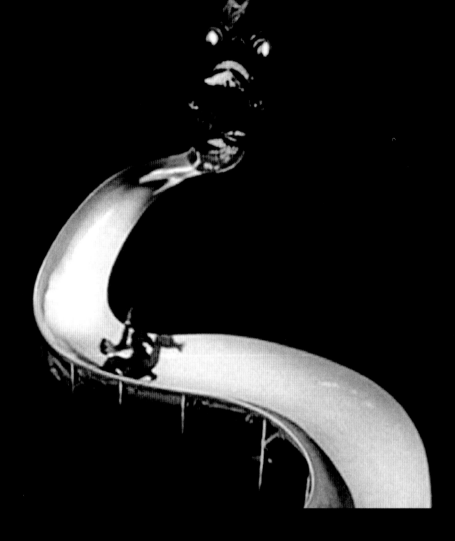

shot, and pointing obliquely up at the faces from the end of the public rows. A nosy old woman jumps up from her chair; another absentmindedly sticks a piece of gum under her seat. During Elsa Bannister's questioning, members of the public lick their lips in eager anticipation of the intimate details. Michael is the only one who is always filmed from the same angle: a cut-in of him, creating, interestingly enough, the same shadowy image in nearly every case. He follows the proceedings with a serious look on his face. The repetition of this image is jarring, an effect heightened by the fact that Michael is lit entirely separately. This static camera perspective suggests that he is locked up in the courtroom as well, where his innocence is actually supposed to be proved.

Another disturbing effect is the constant switch between extreme high- and low-angle shots. They begin in one of the first conversations between Grisby and Michael, when the lawyer asks Michael questions about his past. When Michael fires the revolver in the harbor, we experience this through an extreme low-angle shot, as if he is shooting at us. On one occasion, Welles plays with a miniaturizing effect: We see Michael walking through the cabinet of curiosities in the deserted amusement park. Huge shadows are projected onto the walls, as if foreshadowed by an overwhelming destiny. Added to which, he walks forward in his dream without getting anywhere.

The scene in which Michael signs his murder confession in Grisby's office is also composed of a continuous interplay of high- and low-angle

shots. So, when the conversation begins, the lawyer is sitting in the lower right frame of the picture, with three exotic masks above him diagonally to the left, further emphasizing the demonic side of his character. We then see George in a high shot from screen left, as he walks over to the safe and takes out $5,000 to pay his murderer. Finally, a low-angle shot is also used for the conversation in which Grisby explains the ridiculous legal position to Michael – he will be considered dead if someone admits to murdering him, but the murderer cannot be found guilty if the body is not found. When they have finished talking, Grisby stands right in front of Michael, who is seated with his head thrown back and looking up at him. The camera is placed oppressively close to the two men, so that the viewer's gaze is also directed sharply up to the lawyer and down to Michael. It ends with the lawyer taking a step forward, with half of his face disappearing out of shot. The viewer's final gaze is directed at his mouth, which is contorted in ugly laughter.

However, the most significant means of unsettling the viewer is surely the deconstruction of the spatial context in the film. Welles shows us places without any spatial continuity, where we cannot get our bearings with any certainty, as their appearance appears to change with every shot. One example is the scene in the Chinese theater, when Elsa finds Michael after he has fled from the court. (It should be pointed out, however, that, at the studio's insistence, this scene was later edited radically.) First of all, we see Elsa and Michael sitting together in the stalls, followed by a close-up of

Elsa, evenly lit, and then an extremely shadowy shot of Michael's face. It looks as if Welles has deliberately created a continuity error. For while we start out seeing both characters in exactly the same room, they are then shown as if they are in different rooms with completely different lighting conditions. This can be interpreted in two ways. On the one hand, it basically adds to the strangeness of the imagery, while on the other hand it can be read as the existential expression of a world in which everyone exists only for himself and is left to his own devices, where intersubjectivity seems impossible.

In the same vein, we should also mention the constant alternation between high and low angles, which makes us shrink or grow – in other words, forcing us down on our knees or putting us up on a pedestal. We follow the film from Michael's point of view from the outset. It is his story that is narrated, and he is the person visible from the first to the last shot of the film; yet the more embroiled he becomes in this conspiracy, increasingly becoming a pawn in a game, the more he loses control of the images. Who else but him looks up at his interlocutor from a slightly low angle, when he actually is at least as tall as his opponent? So the image is not an objective representation of the filmic narrative, but the hero's subjective perception: Losing control of the action is inextricably linked with the loss of visual power. The same thing happens in the viewer, who is forced to watch as Michael undergoes this process – experiencing the same loss as the film's character through the narrative perspective.

The hero's growing confusion, which takes place in the course of the subjective narrative, is resolved at the end of the movie after a second de-historicized episode. In the sensational showdown in the amusement park, the film makes a complete break with any objectified representation of time and space. Michael's slide into the hall of mirrors is like a tumble into the abyss. When he ends up as the only person to escape the deadly chaos, he emerges into the open air as if from an air lock. The quiet calm of the deserted park in the morning as he walks through it corresponds to the now obviously distanced gaze of the camera. Like Michael, we too have woken from a nightmare, and the film ends with this awakening as well.

Another visual high point of the film demonstrates the bold way the narrative, which is virtually removed from its moorings in space and time, is used to create an allegorical *mise-en-scène*. Welles chose the Bay Aquarium in San Francisco as the location for this scene, which opens with the long, sinewy arms of an octopus writhing across the image. Michael then enters from screen left, and it cuts to Elsa standing in front of the glass pane of the aquarium. The couple's movements through the set are lit only by the light from the bay. When they talk of their love and eloping together, they stop in front of one of the windows. Suddenly the fish behind the glass are huge. Elsa throws her arms around Michael's neck, and, as they kiss, a class of schoolchildren comes around the corner, only to be herded away by their outraged teacher. The couple walks on, and the fish are back at their normal size. When Michael assures Elsa that she need have no con-

cerns about their future, at that point they are walking past a large sea turtle – a symbol of domesticity and security. They then stop in front of a shark tank, and Michael confesses to Elsa about the murderous plot he has become involved in to secure their future. When he goes on to show her the letter with his confession of guilt that will earn him $5,000, the fish in the background are suddenly disproportionately large again. Their scales are like gleaming metal, while others are chapped and raw, with widely gaping jaws. At the climax of the scene, leopard sharks dart past the couple. The light flickering in the aquarium water gradually becomes brighter, and the faces of the two lovers become silhouetted against it. As they end up in another embrace, the picture fades to black.

According to the rules of classic Hollywood cinema, Orson Welles made basic errors of the trade at this point. But, of course, he did so quite deliberately. It could be argued that he breaks the law governing identification of what is seen, for everyone recognizes in the scene just described that the fish appear far bigger than they actually are. Needless to say, this increase in size is used primarily to create a symbolic *mise-en-scène*: It is certainly no coincidence that we see predatory fish next to the dangerous Elsa – a moray eel to begin with, and then sharks. Even at this stage we are advised of this woman's true nature, and the final kiss apparently seals Michael as her prey. Added to which, the *mise-en-scène* once again emphasizes the nightmarish quality of the narrative. In order to manipulate the proportions in the scene, Welles worked with back projection. In the

interview with Bogdanovich, he explicitly acknowledges the dreamlike effect of the images produced using this technique: "And yet you know, some of that tricking we had to do gave that part of the picture a dreamlike air which I rather like."

Life as a Labyrinth

There is a striking and obvious difference in visual terms between *The Lady from Shanghai* and Welles's masterpiece, *Citizen Kane*: *Kane*'s visual elegance, clarity, and deep focus are formally impressive. According to the film critic André Bazin, deep focus puts the viewer into a relationship with the image that is closer than the one he has with reality. Similarly, a blurred image pushes the viewer away from the screen, forcing him back into his role as passive consumer and leaving him to his own devices. In the case of *The Lady from Shanghai*, the viewer realizes that, along with Michael, his understanding of the story has slipped away from him. His perspective is misaligned. Now he has to find his own way, independently of the hero constructing the story in fact, through the maze of the narrative.

The director manages to play with the notion of the labyrinth several times, impressively realizing this motif, for instance when Elsa is running through a confusing building during the harbor festival in Acapulco. Similarly, the landing stage where Grisby and Michael meet to set up Grisby's murder suddenly becomes a baffling system of girders and walkways, an impression

heightened by a speeded-up tracking shot that gives further expression to Michael's agitation. The nightmarish quality is also brilliantly achieved when Michael keeps on running without escaping from the place, an effect repeated in the scene in the amusement park.

This metaphor is successfully conveyed again when we look down on San Francisco nestling in the valley, as Elsa drives up a mountain in a cabriolet. For a moment she is on the same level as the viewer. It is as if she has just managed to escape from the labyrinthine city. But the next thing the camera pans left, and the automobile is forced back down the hill into the impenetrable warren of streets. The prison where Elsa visits Michael is also like a maze – an effect again achieved because the space appears to be composed of different lighting zones.

The most confusing labyrinth, however, is the hall of mirrors, which expresses the representational nature of reality and simultaneously dissolves the notion of identity through its visual replication process. This hall of mirrors becomes the very essence of paradox, as we can enter it visually, while being denied physical access. This illusion cannot be broken because the mirror itself is concealed in the act of reflection. Such a rational formulation, however, fails to mention that the viewer is repeatedly shot at in this sequence. Our presence is suggested, as much as our complicity in the matter.

We might start off believing that justice will prevail and that the two villains, Elsa and Arthur Bannister, will kill each other in the hall of mirrors.

The reality turns out to be even more absurd. Justice is indeed restored when Michael abandons Elsa as she is dying – a kind of justice indeed, brought about at the price of betraying his love. In this context, it is worth noting the curiously low camera angle at this point. The fish-eye lens allows Welles to place us right next to Elsa's face, as if she is turning more toward the viewer than Michael. At the same time we are judged along with her, and watch Michael anxiously pacing up and down.

The enigmatic quality of the showdown scene in the hall of mirrors lies in the simultaneity of proximity and distance, which prevents us from positioning ourselves in the world. Welles uses dissolves and duplication to dispel any oversimplistic notion of identity. Furthermore, at some point we notice that it is not just the mirrors that are shattered by the gunshots, but that the camera lens has also been fractured. The labyrinth metaphor serves to describe the inability to maintain distance, for we find ourselves in a labyrinth situation when we cannot assume a meta-level in relation to it. The original meaning of "labyrinth," as a complex system of passages, often underground, has been supplemented in modern times with associations with games and puzzles.

Ultimately, all the images that have an unsettling effect on us play with manipulating our experience of space. A cinematic image not only allows us to see objects in that space; the space is simultaneously a device that allows us to move around. The suggestion is that we could move effortlessly in any direction, or even that we cannot leave a specific loca-

tion. Whatever the nature of a particular image, we have assimilated the basic information that affects us as physical beings even before the content has been decoded. There is a sense of non-space in this film. We constantly see images that appear incompatible, measured against the previously prevailing lighting conditions. The space lacks a coherent identity. The camera leaves us high and dry. It refuses to help us orientate ourselves, and instead throws us into a floundering state. The height of the camera changes continuously, showing the characters in high and then low shots alternately, and finally on the same level. The viewer is made to feel dizzy in the cabinet of curiosities, because the images convey a sense of the oblique levels that have to be navigated with care, and disorientation is produced by the lurching camera movements.

Welles's film has traditional roots, reminding us of the Baroque "theater of the world" that tells the tale of the labyrinth of the world and of feelings; and, as Michael says in his closing monologue, only through death can we overcome it all in the end. Nor is the hall of mirrors any more an invention of film noir than the narrator's admission of his own weakness. It is debatable whether Welles intended to deliberately highlight the allegorical nature of the characters. Accordingly, Elsa represents seduction and female power, as well as lies and intrigue. We need only think of her face – quite noticeably heavily made up throughout the film – which we initially interpret as part of her flawlessness. It is only when we see Elsa's face in the Chinese theater alongside the heavily painted actors that we suddenly recognize her masklike quality.

The ending of the movie is particularly revealing in this respect, when the dialogue between Elsa and Michael after the duel in the hall of mirrors reveals that the woman is mad. While she appeared calculating and d6evious right up to the end, her madness and irresponsibility now become crystal clear. Reality has slipped from her grasp at the end and, with it, her responsibility for her actions. But Elsa still has to undergo one final transformation. When she screams that she does not want to die, she becomes a creature clinging to life just like any other.

Toward the middle of the film Michael tells the Bannisters a parable about sharks that eat each other, and go crazy swimming in their own blood. This could be a reference to two well-known sayings: the proverb about big fish eating little fish, and the notion of man as a wolf to his fellow man. In this context, the first name "Michael" is significant, of course, because it alludes to the Archangel Michael, who fights against evil. And it is no coincidence that the boat they are sailing in is called *Circe*, that Elsa is depicted as a siren, and that "Black Irish" (Michael's nickname) represents a man "on life's odyssey." In spite of this obvious stylization, the film maintains a real sense of pathos, especially at the end, when we hear Michael's monologue on the futility of human endeavor. We are naturally tempted to read an existential attitude into this, though the absurdity of existence and human greed are exposed throughout the film; in the words of Camus, *vivre le plus* (living life to the full) is positively celebrated. Another excerpt from the interview with Peter Bogdanovich makes it clear that Welles had alienation and absurdity in mind when he complained about the complete failure of the music

forced on him by the studio: "This sort of music destroys that quality of strangeness which is exactly what might have saved *Lady from Shanghai* from being just another whodunit."

As we have seen, Michael's moral view of the world is deconstructed in Welles's film, while the viewer is unsettled by an elaborate visual game. As the film unfolds, this uncertainty builds up with every new shot. It not only increases, but becomes more powerful as well. Welles clearly intended to present us with an ingenious conspiracy, and to find confusing images for it. The film calls the viewer's authority into question. Since the days of classical antiquity, art has worked on the principle of intelligibility, and rhetoric has developed a sophisticated normative system for facilitating communication. Decorum and internal and external "aptum" (appropriate style) are all governing concepts that are designed implicitly to ensure understanding. In famous writings on rhetoric, it states that art is at its most successful if it appears like nature and sheds all artificiality: Effects would thus appear at their most powerful when their formal construction does not manifest itself.

These claims, as formulated above, might arguably have defined 20th-century mainstream cinema to an extent as well. Equally, it could be said that American cinema of the studio era tried to make form invisible: movies that were not allowed to exceed a certain length for fear of boring people; editing that was meant to be invisible; well-lit scenes and standard camera angles; the absolute no-no of casting movie stars against type. The common feature of all these points is that they are designed to ensure that

form goes unnoticed. If we were to talk of an ideology at this point, then it is one of narrative made absolute. The formal means must not become an end in themselves, but instead be subordinate to the narrative. Only when the formal tools become invisible can the viewer become immersed in the narrative and enjoy the most intense experience of the action.

Although its length was cut by an hour, *The Lady from Shanghai* contradicts this ideal of the Hollywood studio production at just about every level. The characters and figures come over as completely theatrical, and seldom in the studio era has there been a movie with such innovative visual language. What seems so thrillingly excessive to us now made the film's producers feel uneasy: They also resisted showing Rita Hayworth as a fairly short-haired blonde. Not to mention the fact that Welles was forced to reshoot big close-ups of the star to make the film more successful. As Joseph McBride wrote, "Columbia was so horrified at what Welles had done to her image that it held up the film's release for two years and rushed her into several more conventional roles." It was no use, because *The Lady from Shanghai* not only put the brakes on Welles's Hollywood career for ten years, it demolished it completely. The brilliant creator of *Citizen Kane* became an outsider, an outlaw in the film industry.

Abrupt changes in perspective, the use of unusual focal lengths, and the resulting cinema of unsettling effects, soft focus, and oblique angles, as we have demonstrated in a formal aesthetic reading of *The Lady from Shanghai*, can be seen as symbolic of the loss of control over the action – intrinsic to the film and in its external production – and of the search for the central

theme. Soft-focus shots are in this sense not merely the result of inferior technical conditions during takes; they are stylistic features of a film. They serve another function as well – as images of perception. At moments when the composure of the film's protagonist begins to waver – as a result of drunkenness, poisoning, or fainting fits for instance – soft-focus shots are often used to visualize the character's disturbed perceptual state. This effect nearly always comes into its own only when the subjective camera is used; that is, when the gaze of the protagonist coincides with the gaze of the person viewing the film. This means that the disruption of perception within the filmic diegesis – and hence the associated loss of control of the action – is transferred into the movie theater.

AN INTRODUCTION TO NEO-NOIR

by Douglas Keesey

Noir Knows Itself

"I'm a bad girl," says Laure (Rebecca Romijn) in *Femme Fatale*, "real bad – rotten to the heart." Laure *knows* that she's a *femme fatale*. In fact, she just watched *Double Indemnity* on TV and is modeling her behavior after the lovely but lethal Barbara Stanwyck in that film. In *Basic Instinct*, writer Catherine Tramell (Sharon Stone) tells detective Nick Curran (Michael Douglas) that her book is about "a detective. He falls for the wrong woman. She kills him." They both know that this is the plot of many classic film noirs – and *we* know that they know and are intrigued to discover whether their story will turn out the same.

"This isn't going to have a happy ending," Somerset (Morgan Freeman) tells Mills (Brad Pitt) in *Se7en*, for Somerset is conscious of the role they are playing in the kind of noirish tale that almost always has a dark conclusion. ("Film noir" is French for "dark movie" – with "dark" meaning "sinister" and "dreadful" as well as "shadowy," as in Raymond Chandler's great line, "The streets were dark with something more than night.")[1] Contemporary film noir, or neo-noir, is a highly self-conscious genre, keenly aware of the plot conventions, character types, and common techniques associated with past film noirs. Indeed, some neo-noirs are actually about scripting or acting in noir films *(The Singing Detective, Bad Education, Inland Empire)*, while other neo-noirs are remakes of classic film noirs *(The Postman Always Rings Twice)* or "retro-noir" homages set in the period of, and consciously

styled after, past noir films *(Chinatown, Body Heat, L.A. Confidential, The Man Who Wasn't There)*.

The time span of classic film noir is often said to stretch from *The Maltese Falcon* (1941) to *Touch of Evil* (1958). Although they had some growing awareness of genre conventions, the makers of the great '40s and '50s noir movies – *Double Indemnity, Laura, Detour, The Postman Always Rings Twice, D.O.A., Sunset Boulevard, Kiss Me Deadly, The Killing,* and *Vertigo* – did not conceive of them as a single genre of "film noirs." Instead, these movies were known by a variety of different labels, including "crime stories," "suspense pictures," "psychological thrillers," and "melodramas." It was French critics, particularly Raymond Borde and Étienne Chaumeton in their 1955 book, *A Panorama of American Film Noir*, who first popularized the term "film noir," noting that several of these movies were based on the hardboiled detective fiction and crime novels of Raymond Chandler, Dashiell Hammett, and James M. Cain, which had been published in France under the imprint Série Noire (meaning "a dark series of books" but also punning on "a series of bad events").

As the study of this newly recognized genre took off among British and American critics in the 1970s, the roots of film noir were traced to German Expressionist, French Poetic Realist, and Hollywood gangster films of the 1920s and '30s. In addition to these cinematic precursors, the biggest historical influences were identified as World War Two and the ensuing Cold War, with the violence of combat, the threat of nuclear destruction, and the "red

1 Neo-noir often goes retro, harking back to the period and style of the classic noir period. Robert Rodriguez and Frank Miller directed *Sin City* (2005), based on Miller's series of graphic novels, featuring stylized representations of iconic film noir characters and themes. Hartigan (Bruce Willis) is the dedicated cop who will not be corrupted.

2 Based on a graphic novel set in the 1930s, *Road to Perdition* (2002) follows hit man Michael Sullivan (Tom Hanks) as he goes on the run with his son.

3 In *Chinatown* (1974), Jake Gittes (Jack Nicholson, center), pinned by Claude Mulvihill (Roy Jenson), is threatened with the loss of his nose by the man with the knife (director Roman Polanski, left).

4 In *Hollywoodland* (2006) Louis Simo (Adrien Brody) is a low-rent 1950s private investigator who becomes embroiled in the suicide of Superman actor George Reeves, believing it to be a murder.

scares" of McCarthyism spreading paranoia, rage, and disillusionment – all emotions characteristic of film noir. The *femme fatale* – seducer and betrayer of the hapless hero – was also seen as springing from a postwar change in the balance of power between the sexes: male veterans, physically and psychically wounded in the war, came home to find that women had grown in financial and sexual independence from having joined the workforce as part of the home-front war effort. Men found such powerful women both alluring and frightening – the same ambivalence felt for the *femme fatale*. Techniques that have been identified as typical of film noir include dark shadows, particularly those that fall in chiaroscuro patterns like bars or spiders' webs, seeming to entrap the hero; oppressive, angle-down shots and claustrophobic framings; distorting mirrors and unbalanced compositions; and flashbacks and voice-over narration that give visual and aural emphasis to the personal traumas experienced by the disoriented and doomed hero.

And yet, despite the many efforts to describe it, film noir remains the most disputed of all movie genres. Critics disagree about whether there is any one defining element common to all film noirs and about which movies fit and which should be excluded from the genre. As James Naremore points out, "There are many themes, moods, characters, locales, and stylistic features associated with noir, not one of which is shared by all the films that have been placed in the category."[2] Not all noirs have a detective-hero, or a *femme fatale*, or even a tragic ending. Should heist movies, or gangster films, or female Gothic melodramas be categorized as film noirs? Recent critics have argued for an expansive understanding of film noir. According to Wheeler Winston Dixon, "most definitions of noir films are, it seems to me, excessively narrow. The classic archetypes of the lone protagonist in a dark, rainy alley, accompanied by an omnipresent voiceover on the soundtrack, of doomed lovers on the run from the police, or hardboiled detectives unraveling labyrinthine mysteries with cynical assurance represent only one manifestation of this pervasive film genre."[3] Jim Hillier and Alastair Phillips contend that "film noir is as much about a state of mind as a single set of stylistic signs" and that "there is no such thing perhaps as a film noir but rather many forms and variations of a sensibility that alters and shifts according to culture, place and time."[4]

Which brings us to neo-noir. If defining classic film noir is difficult, the challenge only increases with contemporary film noir. Since, as Mark Bould rightly observes, "each additional film noir rethinks, reconstructs and refabricates the genre,"[5] are there any useful generalizations that can be made about films as diverse as *The Crying Game*, *Reservoir Dogs*, *The Matrix*, and *Memento*? My claim is that, in addition to being highly self-conscious of their relation to past noirs, neo-noirs are characterized by blurred boundaries and hybrid genres, and that what is new about neo-noirs can be traced to the influence of contemporary social changes and historical events as well as the latest trends and technological advances in filmmaking.

Blurred Boundaries

Many classic film noirs consist of three character types: the investigator, the villain, and the victim. While even past noirs put some pressure on the boundaries between these types, neo-noir really tends to erode these distinctions. In *The French Connection*, "Popeye" Doyle (Gene Hackman) is a zealous cop whose reckless disregard for the law may help him to catch crooks but also threatens to make him one of them, as this film points to "the thin line between the policeman and the criminal," which is "very often crossed over."[6] In *Manhunter*, Will Graham (William Petersen) is an FBI profiler who must think like the monstrous murderer he seeks – but not too much like him. As the film's tagline warns, "Enter the mind of a serial killer … you may never come back."

The undercover cop (Leonardo DiCaprio) and the gangster mole (Matt Damon) in *The Departed* are affected by their assumed identities and become morally ambiguous characters: "No one knows who they really are, or who anyone else really is."[7] More and more, the difference *between* the investigator and the villain comes to seem like a difference *within* the investigator, who, if he looks hard enough, may find the potential for evil inside himself. "You don't know who you are anymore," Leonard (Guy Pearce) is told in *Memento*. "Maybe it's time you started investigating yourself."

Similarly, a new psychological understanding of the *femme fatale* may reveal that her "evil" is really the result of her having been abused, that she is actually more victim than villain, as can be seen in *Blade Runner*, *The Crying Game*, *Devil in a Blue Dress*, and *Bad Education*. In neo-noir, villainous females can break out of the stereotype to become investigator-heroes (as in *Femme Fatale* and *Inland Empire*), but female investigators can also be morally compromised to the point of villainy (see *Blue Steel* and *demonlover*).

Finally, male investigators are more likely to end up as victims in neo-noir, not only because the villains are too strong for them but because the investigators themselves are morally compromised – so complicit that they have already lost part of the battle. Even in classic film noir, the detective was often beaten up and tempted by sin on the way to solving the case and catching the killer, but the investigations in neo-noir can end in Pyrrhic victory or outright failure, with the hero himself becoming just another victim (see *Chinatown*, *Reservoir Dogs*, *Se7en*, *Following*, and *Basic Instinct 2*).

5

5　Hannibal Lecter, a secondary character in
Manhunter (1986) and *The Silence of the Lambs*
(1991), becomes the focus of Ridley Scott's horror
noir *Hannibal* (2001). Here Hannibal (Anthony
Hopkins) menaces FBI agent Clarice Starling
(Julianne Moore).

Hybrid Genres

Already in the 1940s and '50s, noir was having an influence on other kinds of films, creating hybrid genres such as noir melodramas *(Possessed)*, noir Westerns *(Blood on the Moon)*, noir gangster sagas *(White Heat)*, noir science fiction *(Invasion of the Body Snatchers)*, and even noir musicals *(The Band Wagon)*. But, by the time of neo-noir, it sometimes seems as though noir has spread into virtually all other genres, and with noir has come a troubling of the clear-cut distinctions that used to be maintained within each genre. In the traditional police procedural (such as TV's *Dragnet*), the cops are clearly the good guys tracking down the evildoers, but in the noir-influenced *Dexter*, the man in the crime lab is himself a serial killer, blurring the line between pursuer and pursued, moral and immoral. The antihero of the classic gangster film always inspired a mixture of attraction and repulsion in the viewer, but this is nothing compared to the moral am-

nos, who is psychoanalyzed, leading us to confront both the good and the bad in him. Traditional romances and comedies often take place in idyllic small towns or natural settings, as opposed to classic film noirs, whose terrible events unfold in the big bad city. But in neo-noirs like *Blood Simple*, *Blue Velvet*, *Fargo*, and *The Talented Mr. Ripley*, the city/country distinction breaks down as crime and corruption are shown to be present even in sunny climes ("white noir") and agrarian locales ("country noir"). In "techno-noirs" such as *Blade Runner* and *The Matrix*, noir's pessimism invades science fiction to imagine near futures where the hope for human advancement through science has been turned into a dystopian nightmare. And "superhero noirs" reveal the moral doubts and failings of those who, in earlier incarnations, were simply our saviors. In *The Dark Knight*, a vengeful Batman struggles to differentiate himself from the vengeful Joker, while in *Watchmen*, some of the vigilante superheroes prove hard to distinguish from the villains, leading a fearful populace to wonder, "Who watches the

6   Noir style and story constructs abound in sci-fi and comic-book movies, led by the *Matrix* trilogy. In *The Matrix Reloaded* (2003) Neo (Keanu Reeves) finally meets the Architect of the Matrix.

7   The dark sci-fi chase movie *The Terminator* (1984) spawned three sequels, each featuring the terminator (Arnold Schwarzenegger) – here seen in *Terminator 3: Rise of the Machines* (2003) – or more sophisticated terminators sent from the future to kill a youthful John Connor.

8   Christopher Nolan began a trilogy of films based on the work of comic-book creator Frank Miller with *Batman Begins* (2005), featuring Christian Bale as Batman.

9   In a future totalitarian United Kingdom, V (Hugo Weaving) is a terrorist / freedom fighter in *V for Vendetta* (2005), based on the Alan Moore / David Lloyd graphic novel. V's mask has subsequently been taken up by the Occupy movement and other protest groups.

Contemporary Social Changes and Historical Events

Writer/director Paul Schrader has said that "as a filmmaker you look for rips and tears in the social fabric that can be addressed metaphorically."[8] There are some neo-noirs in which the traumatic impact of contemporary events is not difficult to decode. *Taxi Driver* is about a Vietnam veteran in the urban jungle of New York City who has trouble telling friend from foe and who commits a massacre, destroying a "village" in order to save it. *Chinatown*, though set in the 1930s, reflects the widespread suspicion of rampant corruption among supposedly benign authority figures that followed the Watergate scandal. More recently, the remake of *The Manchurian Candidate* exposes the trumped-up xenophobia manufactured by war-profiteering corporations, while *The Dark Knight* shows a populace tempted to turn against and destroy itself as a result of Bush-era fearmongering about terrorism.

With other neo-noirs, it is less a case of specific historical events and more a matter of larger social changes that have had an influence. The women's movement and the male backlash against it have deepened audience ambivalence toward the *femme fatale*. More women today are empowered in the bedroom and the workplace, and there is a tendency to cheer the *femmes fatales* in *Body Heat*, *Basic Instinct*, and *Bound* as they seek their own pleasure and profit – and often get away with both in the end. But these women also embody male fears of sexually liberated women as castrating predators and of independent career women as out to steal men's money. The abolition of Hays Code censorship restrictions, along with the introduction of an age-appropriate ratings system, has led to a new frankness of female nudity and sexually explicit speech, but here again neo-noir's representation of woman tends to be ambiguous: is her open sexuality to be celebrated or feared as overly aggressive? Is her own desire being encouraged or will she be reduced to an object of the voyeuristic male gaze?

Feminism has also prompted men to question their own investment in machismo, and many neo-noirs are deeply split in their attitude to the "hardboiled hero" – both admiring and critical. In *Le Samouraï*, *Pulp Fiction*, *Ichi the Killer*, and *I'll Sleep When I'm Dead*, being a tough guy is shown to be both cool and self-destructive, while the macho killers in *Fingers*, *The Crying Game*, and *Amores Perros* struggle to find a way to admit their sensitive sides without feeling emasculated. The gay rights and civil rights movements have brought a new complexity to neo-noirs like *Cruising* and *Suture*, where the white hetero hero's struggle turns out to be with his own repressed homosexual side or with the "black brother" whom he has oppressed.

In addition to issues of gender, sexuality, and race, social tensions related to class have had a major impact on contemporary film noir. The "greed is good" mentality of the Thatcher, Reagan, and Bush years can be seen in the selfish scheming of the characters in *Body Heat*, *Blood Simple*, *Fargo*, and *Following*, who are all the more driven to emulate the rapacious greed of the upper classes by the fact that the disparity between the very rich and the very poor has grown ever wider. The satisfaction we may feel in seeing these selfish, low-life characters come to a bad end is complicated by a sense of how unjust it is that they should have so little when others – who are no more deserving – have so much. The materialistic mind-set of our conservative politicians and corporate leaders is also evident in the lust for high-priced commodities which plays such a large part in the desire – and often the downfall – of the characters in *To Live and Die in L.A.*, *The Talented Mr. Ripley*, *The Departed*, and *Basic Instinct 2*. The increasing ability of corporations to use the media as a way of manipulating what we desire as consumers – and even what we believe to be real – has fed the paranoia and pessimism of such techno-noirs as *Blade Runner*, *The Matrix*, *Vanilla Sky*, and *demonlover*.

Trends and Technological Advances in Filmmaking

Stylistically, neo-noir owes a great debt to the film movement known as the French New Wave, exemplified by the late-1950s and early-'60s films of Jean-Luc Godard and François Truffaut, with their mobile camerawork (including handheld tracking shots), experimental editing (freeze frames and jump cuts), outdoor shooting, and (sometimes parodic) self-awareness of genres. Many of these innovative techniques were adopted by New Hollywood directors (Robert Altman, Brian De Palma, Martin Scorsese) and went on to influence the makers of contemporary film noir. Technological advances affecting the look of neo-noir include the development of faster film stock and then of digital video, enabling on-location scenes to be shot in color under low-light conditions (and also allowing high-contrast images with truer blacks to be obtained even on color film). The increasing use of widescreen composition aided in the presentation of neo-noir characters being enveloped by darkness (see *Lost Highway*) or surrounded by a vast emptiness (as in the "white noir" *Point Blank*).

The invention of the Steadicam helped the viewer to move with and physically experience events alongside the neo-noir hero, and the development of digital editing has made it easier to convey that hero's disorientation through accelerated cutting and through flashback images that break in as shock cuts. Multilayered voices and effects on the soundtrack, combined with music that tends toward dissonance and unresolved harmonies, have worked to dramatize the psychological complexity and moral ambiguity of the neo-noir protagonist. And CGI images and other digital effects have presented a neo-noir world that seems ever more threatening and unreliable, constantly morphing under the control of shadowy others – or because of the hero's own unstable mind.

11

10 Noir style and content is endemic worldwide. Bong Joon-ho's *Memories of Murder* (*Salinui chueok*, 2003) follows the search for a serial killer in the South Korean countryside.

11 *Perfume* (*Das Parfum – Die Geschichte eines Mörders*, 2006) is the story of 18th-century French perfumer and serial killer Jean-Baptiste Grenouille (Ben Whishaw).

12 Hong Kong inspector Chan Kwai Bun (Lau Ching-wan) finds killers by reenacting their crimes and getting into their mind-set in *Mad Detective* (*San taam*, 2007), directed by Johnnie To and Wai Ka-fai.

13 In *The Lives of Others* (*Das Leben der Anderen*, 2006), set in East Berlin in 1984, secret police captain Gerd Wiesler (Ulrich Mühe) is ordered to spy on a couple but then becomes obsessed with them.

12

13

14

14 Noir in the modern world. Max (Jamie Foxx) and Annie (Jada Pinkett Smith) try to escape a contract killer in Michael Mann's *Collateral* (2004), filmed all over Los Angeles.

15 *Disturbia* (2007) follows bad boy Kale (Shia LaBeouf) after he thinks he sees a murder at a neighbor's house in this modern retelling of *Rear Window* (1954).

Where Is Film Noir Going in the 21st Century?

It seems fitting to conclude with some discussion of recent developments. One international trend is toward male characters whose increasingly graphic violence threatens to obliterate the line separating them as heroes from the villains they are supposedly fighting. The uncertainty about the noir hero in such films as *Taxi Driver*, *Hardcore*, and *8MM* has now been exacerbated by the hero's more and more extreme acts of violence to the point where we wonder whether there really is any difference between the protagonist and the antagonist. In *Ichi the Killer*, *Irreversible*, *A History of Violence*, *Shutter Island*, *A Serbian Film*, and *Savages*, we may find that our cheering for the hero sticks in our throats as his own acts are revealed to be ever more brutal and appalling. As the unnamed main character (Ryan Gosling) in *Drive* puts it about the bloody vengeance he is about to wreak, "I have to go somewhere and I don't think I can come back." Perhaps because audiences have grown inured to movie mayhem, today's noir directors are upping the ante on violence to shock filmgoers into feeling again and to make them doubt their self-righteous demands for revenge against criminal "others." As director Michael Winterbottom said when he was criticized as immoral for the brutal way in which he depicted a deputy sheriff's violence in *The Killer In-side Me*, "surely what would be immoral would be for the violence to be entertaining or acceptable?"[9]

A related trend in neo-noir is that female characters are also now meeting their dark doubles or doppelgangers more often than before. Such films as *Mulholland Drive*, *Femme Fatale*, *Swimming Pool*, *Don't Look Back*, and *Black Swan* all have heroines who wrestle with the *femme fatale* within themselves. As the lead female (Natalie Portman) in the latter film is told, "I knew the white swan wouldn't be your problem. The real work would be your metamorphosis into her evil twin." Other neo-noirs, including *Raise-moi*, *In the Cut*, *Domino*, and *The Girl with the Dragon Tattoo* (Swedish and American versions), plunge their strong female protagonists into rougher, darker territory than women have heretofore encountered on film. Whether audiences will applaud scenes where female characters anally rape the men who raped them, or wonder about the extent to which the victims have become the violators, remains to be seen.

Another global trend is toward neo-noirs inspired by comic books, manga, graphic novels, and videogames. *From Hell*, *Ichi the Killer*, *Oldboy*, *A History of Violence*, *V for Vendetta*, *Watchmen*, *Inception*, and *The Dark Knight Rises* all spring from a combination of noir fiction and book or video art. Whether it be slicing characters in half with a razor-fitted boot, eating a live octopus, or sinking a meat cleaver into someone's head, these neo-noirs make full use of today's digital effects to depict darker sides of humanity that have never before been visualized so starkly in live-action film. Similarly, motion capture, interpolated rotoscoping, and other recent advances in animation techniques have made possible the distinctive "graphic noir" look of such films as *Sin City*, *Renaissance*, and *A Scanner Darkly*.

But film noir has always been local as well as global, and some of the most intriguing neo-noirs are coming from within indigenous cultural traditions. From Hong Kong, which, especially after the 1997 handover from the U.K. to China, has struggled with a postcolonial anxiety over disappearance and shifting identities, there is *Infernal Affairs I – III*, a trilogy about two men – one a mole in the police department and the other an undercover cop in the mob – who are understandably suffering from an identity crisis. "I just want an identity," the cop pleads; "I want to be a normal man." And *Mad Detective* is about a schizophrenic Hong Kong cop tortured by his uncanny ability to see his suspect's multiple inner personalities. Korea's *Oldboy* follows in the tradition of social criticism often present in Asian gangster noir. Reflecting accounts of kidnappings during the 1997 Asian financial crisis, this film presents a lowly office worker who, after being kidnapped, single-handedly repels an entire gang of thugs using only a hammer and then confronts their capitalist boss in his penthouse, attempting to take revenge on him. Japan's *Ichi the Killer* uses a gangster noir plot to question whether the yakuza practice of bodily self-mutilation as a sign of penance and allegiance to the boss

can become a perverse kind of macho masochism. One character spends much of the film seeking someone who can inflict the greatest possible punishment on him and lamenting that, with most potential sadists, "There's no love in your violence."

The British gangster-film tradition, whose illustrious ancestors include *Get Carter*, *The Long Good Friday*, and *The Krays*, continues strong in the 21st century, following two rather different lines of development. There is the flashy, "laddish," ultraviolent strain, represented by the likes of *Snatch*, *Gangster No. 1*, and *Layer Cake*, and then there are the more subdued character studies meditating on the costs of violence, such as *Sexy Beast*, *I'll Sleep When I'm Dead*, and *In Bruges*. The French tradition of *policier* or *polar* films, following upon *La Balance*, *L.627*, and *La Haine*, is also much in evidence and can perhaps be divided between those crime films that essentially adopt the police perspective – *36 Quai des Orfèvres*, *Le petit lieutenant*, *MR 73* – and those that present events from the standpoint of the criminal "other": *Baise-moi*, *The Beat That My Heart Skipped*, *Mesrine*, *A Prophet*. Director Nicolas Winding Refn explored his native Denmark's criminal underworld of drug dealers and mob bosses in the *Pusher* trilogy, before moving on to helm the rural American noir *Fear X*, the British crime film *Bronson*, and the L.A. noir *Drive*.

Of course, Los Angeles is more than just the location from which Hollywood extends its global reach, spreading its films all over the world. L.A. is also local, with a distinctive history and culture of its own. Continuing

16 Crooked nightclub manager Bobby Green (Joaquin
    Phoenix) tries to save his father and brother, both
    cops, from the Russian mafia in James Gray's *We
    Own the Night* (2007).

17 In Jane Campion's *In the Cut* (2003), Frannie
    Avery (Meg Ryan) has an affair with a police
    detective investigating the murders of young
    women in her neighborhood.

in the tradition of great L.A.-rooted films such as *Point Blank*, *Chinatown*, *Blade Runner*, and *L.A. Confidential*, the neo-noir *Collateral* presents a hit man (Tom Cruise) who, just coasting and killing his way through the city, takes the attitude that "When I'm here, I can't wait to leave. Too sprawled out, disconnected … Nobody knows each other." A taxi driver (Jamie Foxx), whose cab the hit man has commandeered, has also shut himself off from his environs, but in order to save his own life, he is finally forced to connect with the lives around him and is eventually able to say of the city that "It's my home." In *Crank: High Voltage*, Chev Chelios (Jason Statham) has the opposite problem: he is plunged into the heart of multicultural L.A., fearing that his very survival is threatened by the different races and ethnicities that surround him. As Chev attempts to beat, blast, and burn his way to safety, turning himself into a human fireball in the process of destroying all "others," he seems hell-bent on denying one simple truth: neither he nor anyone else in this mixed-race city will survive unless they realize that their lives are interdependent. Like classic film noir, neo-noir plunges us into darkness so that we can see the light.

1 Raymond Chandler, Introduction, *The Simple Art of Murder*, New York: Houghton Mifflin, 1950.
2 James Naremore, *More than Night: Film Noir in Its Contexts*, revised ed., Berkeley: University of California Press, 2008, p. 282.
3 Wheeler Winston Dixon, *Film Noir and the Cinema of Paranoia*, New Brunswick, NJ: Rutgers University Press, 2009, p. 1.
4 Jim Hillier and Alastair Phillips, *100 Film Noirs*, Basingstoke, U.K.: Palgrave Macmillan, 2009, pp. 5, 8.
5 Mark Bould, *Film Noir: From Berlin to Sin City*, London: Wallflower Press, 2005, p. 115.
6 William Friedkin, director's audio commentary, *The French Connection* DVD, Twentieth Century Fox Home Entertainment, 2005.
7 Martin Scorsese in: Ian Christie, "Scorsese: Faith under Pressure," *Sight and Sound*, vol. 16, no. 11 (November 2006), p. 14.
8 Paul Schrader in: Foster Hirsch, *Detours and Lost Highways: A Map of Neo-Noir*, New York: Limelight Editions, 1999, p. 2.
9 Michael Winterbottom in: Hannah McGill, "Inside Out," *Sight and Sound*, vol. 20, no. 6 (June 2010), p. 41.

17

THE CABINET OF DR. CALIGARI

DAS CABINET DES DR. CALIGARI

1920 – GERMANY – 71 MIN.
DIRECTOR ROBERT WIENE (1873–1938)
SCREENPLAY CARL MAYER, HANS JANOWITZ
DIRECTOR OF PHOTOGRAPHY WILLY HAMEISTER
MUSIC GIUSEPPE BECCE
PRODUCTION ERICH POMMER, RUDOLF MEINERT
for DECLA-FILM-GES. HOLZ & CO
STARRING WERNER KRAUSS (Doctor Caligari / Director),
CONRAD VEIDT (Cesare), FRIEDRICH FEHÉR (Francis),
LIL DAGOVER (Jane), HANS HEINRICH VON
TWARDOWSKI (Alan), RUDOLF LETTINGER
(Doctor Olsen, Medical Officer of Health)

"You must become Caligari!"

A slow iris-in shot reveals the narrator, Francis (Friedrich Fehér), sitting in front of a crumbling wall telling his life story to an elderly gentleman. He recalls how he and his friend Alan (Hans Heinrich von Twardowski) once went to a traveling fair in a small town in the northwest of Germany. As the film follows the narrative, they come across Dr. Caligari (Werner Krauss), who displays a 23-year-old somnambulist called Cesare (Conrad Veidt) in a coffin-like box in a sideshow tent. The claustrophobic atmosphere and Cesare's emaciated, chalk-white face and deep black-ringed eyes immediately create

an air of foreboding. Alan is invited to ask the sleepwalker a question, and the terrified young man learns that he will die before dawn. In fact, not only is Alan murdered during the night, but a whole series of crimes are committed in the ensuing weeks. Nothing can be proved against Caligari, who uses the hypnotized Cesare to commit his evil deeds, but when the sleepwalker abducts Francis's sweetheart Jane (Lil Dagover), the intrepid young man conducts his own investigation. After the truth is revealed, Caligari escapes and takes refuge in a mental institution, only to be revealed as the director of the

"The film is set — finally! finally! — in a completely unreal dreamworld...
Veidt stalks thin and unworldly through his confused world: sometimes
with a splendid look, sometimes, like something by Kubin, wandering
ghostly, black and shadowy along a wall. A moon becomes visible —
as shadow play on a gray wall. And demonstrates once again how what
is merely intimated is more horrifying than what is shown outright.
No cinema can compete with our imaginations." *Kurt Tucholsky, in: Die Weltbühne*

1　It seems as though sunlight could never enter this enclosed world of stark shadows. In a famous scene Cesare (Conrad Veidt) abducts the sleeping Jane (Lil Dagover).

2　The movie was made in a studio built of glass at Weissensee, Berlin. The theatrical-looking sets in German Expressionist style were designed and built by the artists Hermann Warm, Walter Reimann, and Walter Röhrig.

3　For the showman (Werner Krauss, right), Cesare is no more than a puppet. For many critics the movie was about state hierarchies and the abuse of power. Siegfried Kracauer saw it in retrospect as anticipating the Nazi era.

GERMAN EXPRESSIONIST CINEMA　The look of film noir can be traced back to the German Expressionist cinema of the 1920s and 1930s. Although the ultimate example of this cinema is Robert Wiene's *The Cabinet of Dr. Caligari* (*Das Cabinet des Dr. Caligari*, 1920), with its surreal settings and caricatured people, it was the emphasis on graphic design, unusual camera angles, montage, forced perspective, subjective camera work, and other technical innovations in films like F. W. Murnau's *The Last Laugh* (*Der letzte Mann*, 1924), G. W. Pabst's *Secrets of a Soul* (*Geheimnisse einer Seele*, 1926), and Josef von Sternberg's *The Blue Angel* (*Der blaue Engel*, 1930) that were to play a major part in the formation of film noir. The films were also preoccupied with the psychology and underlying motivations of the characters, as well as the effect that fate and society had on their lives. Fritz Lang's *M* (*M – Eine Stadt sucht einen Mörder*, 1931), for example, shows us the points of view of police, the criminal underworld, and the child-killer. Many film directors and their creative personnel escaped Hitler's Germany in the 1930s and hotfooted it to Hollywood, including Fritz Lang, Billy Wilder, Robert Siodmak, Fred Zinnemann, and Edgar G. Ulmer – they went on to become some of the leading figures in what was later called film noir.

institution and a specialist in the field of somnambulism. In the end, he is betrayed by entries in his diary. The film then moves to a second surprising conclusion – it turns out that the narrator, Francis, is himself an inmate in an institution. The institution's director (Werner Krauss) does indeed resemble the mysterious Caligari, but it seems that the deranged Francis has seen all the events in a dream.

The Cabinet of Dr. Caligari was one of the best-known silent movies to be made under the Weimar Republic. This horror story clearly refers to the social trauma of World War I. It tells of young men who sleepwalk through a mixture of terror and melancholy, commit murder as if in a trance, or live with the fear of death. At the same time, the film deliberately sets out to show a different level of perception, a symbolic and dreamlike world. The frag-

4   Cesare awakens from his deathlike state: both Werner Krauss (Caligari) and Conrad Veidt were products of the great stage director Max Reinhardt's school of acting.

5   Even the structure of the asylum is somehow dreamlike – but the claim that the back story involving the mental institution was only an afterthought is itself pure myth.

6   "Roll up! Roll up! See, for the first time ever, Cesare, the somnambulist!" At the turn of the 20th century, movies were also shown at traveling fairs and vaudeville theaters.

"Werner Krauss as Caligari resembled a ghostly magician, spinning the lines and shadows through which he trod. And when Conrad Veidt's Cesare brushed along a wall, it was as if the wall itself had exhaled him." *Siegfried Kracauer, From Caligari to Hitler*

7   The director of the asylum is obsessed with an old story; one of his books on somnambulism tells of Dr. Caligari, a mystic who in 1703 traveled through the north of Italy with a sleepwalker named Cesare.

mented typography and ornamentation of the intertitles, and above all the painted backdrops with their shifting perspectives, lopsided doors, over-sized furniture, and sharp, distorted angles all draw on the formal repertoire of Expressionist painting. When it was premiered, the film, shot entirely in the studio, was tinted brownish yellow, bluish green, and pale pink to give powerful visual expression to extreme psychological tension. *The Cabinet of Dr. Caligari* can be interpreted as a metaphor for a modern world of which it has become increasingly difficult to make sense. Reality and illusion are inseparably mixed and the recurring theme of the doppelganger stresses that spec-

tators cannot believe their eyes. In a society dominated by paranoia there is no reliable authority. Of all people, the director of an institution for the insane who should be the most clearheaded is haunted by obsessive notions after reading in an ancient chronicle about Caligari, an 18th-century mystic, and his sinister experiments with sleepwalkers. Disembodied voices tell him: "You must become Caligari." Although at the end of the film everything is explained rationally, the shadowy Expressionistic world lingers on to remind us that our own world could once more turn into a nightmare.

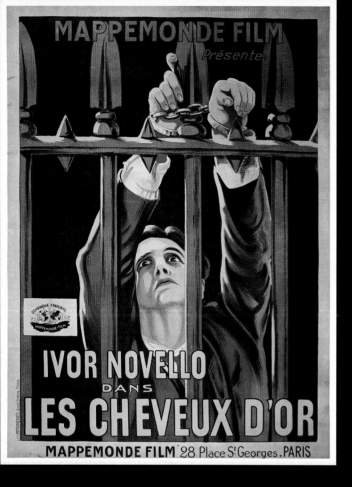

THE LODGER: A STORY OF THE LONDON FOG / THE LODGER

1927 – GREAT BRITAIN – 101 MIN.
(restored version)
DIRECTOR ALFRED HITCHCOCK (1899–1980)
SCREENPLAY ELIOT STANNARD, ALFRED HITCHCOCK,
based on the book of the same name
by MARIE BELLOC-LOWNDES
DIRECTOR OF PHOTOGRAPHY GAETANO DI VENTIMIGLIA
EDITING IVOR MONTAGU PRODUCTION MICHAEL BALCON
for GAINSBOROUGH PICTURES
STARRING IVOR NOVELLO (The Lodger), MARIE AULT
(The Landlady), ARTHUR CHESNEY (Her Husband),
JUNE [= JUNE HOWARD TRIPP] (Daisy),
MALCOLM KEEN (Joe, a Policeman)

"Tonight, Golden Curls."

The "first real Hitchcock film," as Hitchcock himself called it, is also his best silent movie, and at the time of its release was also the best British film to date. Thematically, it offered a variation on the legend of Jack the Ripper. In the London fog, a killer is terrorizing the streets. His victims are all fair-haired women, and he always leaves his calling card at the scene of the crime: "the Avenger." The personal description exactly matches that of the mysterious stranger who one night arrives at the door of a small family. Little by little, clues build up to make the new lodger (Ivor Novello) appear extremely dangerous. And Daisy (June), the landlord's daughter, is blonde...

The Lodger has always held a fascination for Alfred Hitchcock fans. Preferences and structural features of later Hitchcock classics are already

unmistakable, although they appear remarkably underplayed here. The director had a problem with his leading man. The attractive stage actor Ivor Novello, an immensely popular heartthrob, could not possibly be the murderer. As a result, Hitchcock's interests were at odds with those of the audience in the figure of the lodger. Hitchcock's famous suspense is obstructed by this, although the result is a much more interesting film. He does everything he can to make the lodger appear suspicious, as the man has portraits of blonde women removed from his room, leaves the house at exactly the time of the crime, and drives the family into a panic with his strange habits. A number of surprising twists will exonerate him in the end, but until then half the battle is won with Novello's almost schizophrenic expression, the product of his

1

1 With bated breath, Londoners read about the serial killer. Could he be living under our roof? The landlord and his wife have no idea.

2 Suspense: unspoken clues punctuate the game of chess between the lodger (Ivor Novello) and Daisy (June).

3 The lodger isn't the first Hitchcock character to wind up in the hospital.

4 Confusion and suspicion: disturbingly, the lodger has taken down his pictures of blonde women. Daisy is driven to despair by her own misgivings.

ambivalent role. Inadvertently, in addition to the confusion of all the false leads, another of Hitchcock's favorite themes lands in his lap with this film: that of the innocent suspect, as embodied by Cary Grant, for example, in *North by Northwest* (1959). In both films it provides the opportunity for a spectacular escape.

Hitchcock had just returned from Germany, and this was reflected in certain Expressionist lighting effects and a generally oppressive atmosphere. Above all, however, he was now concerned with finding ways to give visual expression to important plot details without having to rely on intertitles. So he had Novello walk up and down over a thick sheet of glass, for instance, instilling fear in his landlords who stare up from beneath it as if mesmerized. Talking with François Truffaut later, he maintained that in a talkie he would

simply have made a chandelier shake, but this search for optical solutions was to become a characteristic feature of Hitchcockian style.

It was his absolute concentration on the plot, however, to which every scene is subordinated, that made this Englishman the inventor of the modern thriller. As the real perpetrator never enters the picture, Hitchcock devotes himself wholly to the immediate surroundings of his victims. The blonde models in the fashion show are seen, half in fun, tucking away black locks under their hats. Daisy's police-inspector fiancé, whose task it is to solve the case of the "Avenger," makes clumsy jokes about the murderer and is obliged to watch, with the audience, as his girlfriend draws closer to the sinister stranger. An ironic handling of the macabre, sexual tensions, the innocent person threatened by an incompetent investigator: it is impossible to imag-

ALFRED HITCHCOCK AND FILM NOIR Alfred Hitchcock's complex relationship with film noir begins with the issue of whether the genre influenced him, or vice versa. In his American films *Rebecca* (1940) and *Shadow of a Doubt* (1943) the classic elements of the noir style are already in evidence: dark shadows, strange camera angles, claustrophobic spaces, and the sense of an ever-present threat. The British-born filmmaker learned much of his trade during his time in Germany, but unlike other leading directors in the genre, he was not an émigré. While the connection between film noir and the thriller director par excellence seems obvious at first glance, the differences soon become apparent. The fatalistic element of film noir also appears in the dark romantic thriller *Notorious* (1946) starring Ingrid Bergman and Cary Grant, in the murder plot co-scripted by Raymond Chandler of *Strangers on a Train* (1951), and in what is possibly its clearest manifestation in *The Wrong Man* (1956), the story of an innocent suspect embroiled in an atmosphere of fear and corruption. However, many of Hitchcock's excursions into film noir rank among his least successful films.

ine Hitchcock's psychological universe without all these elements – not to mention his fatal attraction to blondes. The escape in handcuffs, which almost ends in a lynching, has distinctly fetishistic overtones and was to be repeated in *The 39 Steps* (1935).

Despite the many technical and dramaturgical innovations, the distributors did not know what to do with Hitchcock's work at first. After a few changes, and its eventual release, the film won enthusiastic applause from critics and audiences alike; *The Lodger* had helped to get the young and talented Hitchcock recognized. Last, but not least, this is the first film in which the corpulent director makes a personal appearance – ostensibly merely to fill the picture. PB

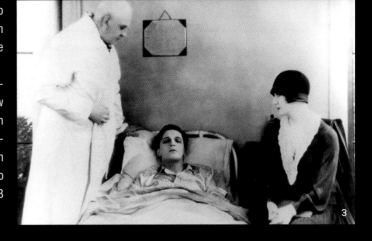

"*The Lodger* established Hitchcock as the Master of Suspense, and almost three quarters of a century later, this dark genesis can still force viewers to feel the chill of bygone London and hear the silent screams of terror." bfi.org.uk

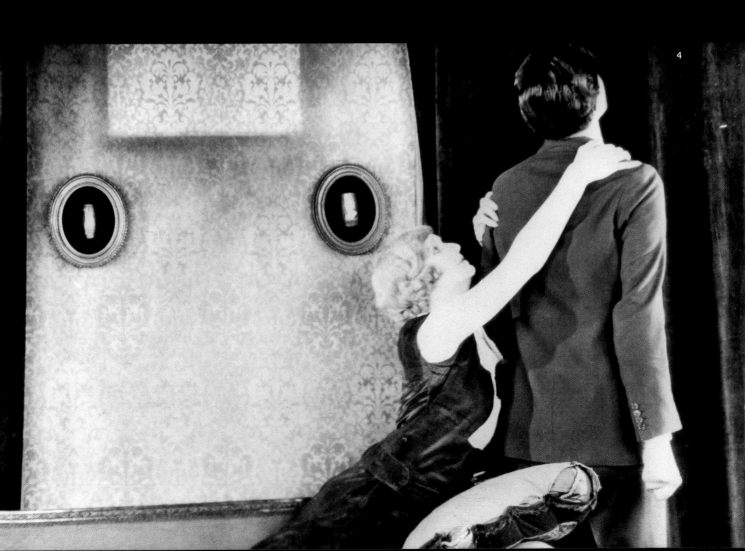

M

M – EINE STADT SUCHT EINEN MÖRDER

1931 – GERMANY – 117 MIN. / 108 MIN.
(restored version)
DIRECTOR FRITZ LANG (1890–1976)
SCREENPLAY THEA VON HARBOU, FRITZ LANG
DIRECTOR OF PHOTOGRAPHY FRITZ ARNO WAGNER
EDITING PAUL FALKENBERG
PRODUCTION SEYMOUR NEBENZAHL and
ERNST WOLFF for NERO FILM AG
STARRING PETER LORRE (Hans Beckert, the Murderer),
ELLEN WIDMANN (Frau Beckmann),
INGE LANDGUT (Elsie Beckmann),
OTTO WERNICKE (Inspector Karl Lohmann),
THEODOR LOOS (Inspector Groeber),
GUSTAF GRÜNDGENS ("Schränker," the Safecracker),
FRIEDRICH GNASS (Franz, the Burglar),
THEO LINGEN (Bauernfänger, the Con Artist),
RUDOLF BLÜMNER (Beckert's Defender),
GEORG JOHN (the Blind Balloon Vendor)

"This monster does not have the right to exist. He must be removed, stamped out, exterminated. Without mercy!"

The city's going mad. A harmless old man is being dragged to the police station by a couple of rough workers; just around the corner, an angry mob is jumping on a fare dodger who's being escorted off the bus by a policeman. What's going on? For the last eight months, someone has been murdering children, and the police still have no idea who he is or where he's hiding. The tension is palpable: everyone is a suspect, and the killer has just struck again, after luring little Elsie Beckmann (Inge Landgut) into an open field with a colorful balloon. He even sends an open letter to the press, announcing that he's not finished yet ...

Inspector Lohmann (Otto Wernicke) gathers his colleagues for an emergency meeting. One idea is to check every patient who has come out of psy-

chiatric care over the last few years, and investigations soon lead the police officers to Hans Beckert (Peter Lorre). Beckert is an unobtrusive lodger who likes to take walks in the city, on the lookout for little girls who will follow him on the promise of some candy or a toy.

But the police aren't the only ones looking for the killer. An underworld organization known as "The Ring" also has an interest in tracking him down, as the heavy police presence is driving business to the wall. While the cops are dithering about how to proceed, "Schränker" (Gustaf Gründgens), the infamous safecracker – "the best man for the job between Berlin and Frisco" – is holding his own crisis session. Soon, all the beggars and drifters in the city are patrolling every corner and alleyway on the lookout for suspicious

characters. Beckert eventually betrays himself with a sign of his pathological compulsiveness – he whistles a particular melody whenever his urge to kill surfaces, and a blind balloon seller (Georg John) identifies him thanks to the haunting tune. Branded with a letter M chalked on the back of his coat, the murderer can no longer elude his pursuers. They corner him in the attic of an office building, and drag him back to their headquarters, where these criminals become his judge and jury.

In *Metropolis* (1927), Fritz Lang had already depicted society – specifically urban society – as a system with strict divisions between the upper and lower classes. That film had shown a privileged, wealthy minority pursuing a life of pleasure in the rooftop gardens of gigantic skyscrapers, while an anonymous mass of laborers languished in bleak, subterranean housing

"It was just a matter of time before someone recognized that there was an undeniably cinematic story to be told in the much-publicized murder trials of names like Haarmann, Großmann or Kürten. What a boon it is that Fritz Lang was the man who braved the waters of this subject matter; for he possessed both the necessary finesse and skill to tackle something this complex." *Filmwelt*

1 The murderer in the mirror: Beckert (Peter Lorre) is horrified to discover that he is a marked man.

2 Playmates and playthings: no one knows his toys like a pervert.

3 Supreme court: Hans is put on trial by the people in this signature Lang tableau.

4 The hot lights: the roof of this office building seemed like a good hiding place – until somebody tripped the switch.

3

compounds. In *M*, a similar social dichotomy is presented in a more realistic, contemporary setting. The city is no longer a futurist construct, but a modern metropolis with all its familiar trappings – tenement houses, factories and industry, dense urban traffic, splendid shopping boulevards, etc. – but here, too, there is an "underworld." Beneath the visible surface of city life lurk criminal organizations; only this time, they happen to share the authorities' interest in capturing a psychopath on the loose. Lang was so inspired by the notion of criminals hunting a murderer in order to curb unwelcome police activity that he lived in constant fear that someone else would beat him to capturing the idea on film. Like *Metropolis*, *M* presents a situation in which the underworld and the "overworld" are compelled to reach an agreement.

For this disturbing film, Lang chose a visual language that emphasizes the model character of his societal construct. Again and again, the camera shows us full-screen street maps, ground plans, fingerprints, and even samples of the murderer's handwriting. These "blueprints" provide novel perspectives on the familiar city, and they are examined meticulously for signs of alien life: Where is the killer hiding? What psychotic traits are expressed in his handwriting? Where is the unique twist in his fingerprint? Fritz Lang's choice of the attic as the disturbed murderer's refuge was no accident: even when Beckert's murderous compulsion is repressed, it remains as physical and real as the forgotten junk in the loft. In this sense, there is an analogous relationship between the body of the killer and the architecture of the city.

7

5   Wall to wall terror: a murderer at the mercy of the masses.

step ahead of the law. Inge Landgut as little Elsie Beckmann.

8   Sign language: baby-faced Peter Lorre adopted some alarming expressions for this star-making role.

6   Slayed in the shade: despite the round-the-clock criminal investigation, Beckert is always one

7   Name that tune: a blind balloon vendor (Georg John) identifies the killer.

> **"This film has got plenty of everything that normally rattles the censors from a mile off. Here, the murderer reaches into his pocket, sharpens his knife and is the epitome of sadism. The government is mocked and organized crime is cheered on."** *Die Weltbühne*

Beckert's "judges" are the assembled denizens of the underworld, and when they charge him with his crimes, the truth erupts: in a gripping monologue, he tells of the inner voices that compel him to kill. Among the assembled listeners are some who can identify with the confessions of this tortured soul, and Beckert's "advocate" (Rudolf Blümner) urges the massed vigilantes to acknowledge the killer's insanity and hand him over to the authorities. Led by the safecracker, the angry mob shouts down his plea.

Shaken by economic crises and political unrest, the Weimar Republic could appeal to no values that were universally acknowledged. In this moral vacuum, a promise of resolute action and "a firm hand" presented a tempting alternative to the protean unpredictability of modern city life. The risk inherent in the freedom of anonymity is that an alienated man can kill without being noticed. Seen from this perspective, *M* is an apt portrayal of German sensibilities on the eve of the Nazis' rise to power. When Beckert is saved from lynching by a last-minute police bust and made to face a proper court of law, Lang's preference for the legal enforcement of justice is unmistakable.

EP

PETER LORRE Born in Hungary in 1904, Ladislav Loewenstein started an apprenticeship as a bank clerk after graduating from high school, but soon dropped out in favor of an acting career. The "Lorre" part of his pseudonym is a wordplay on "Rolle," the German for "role." After a difficult start, he was offered his first theater roles in Vienna and Zurich, and his first, albeit modest appearance on film was in *The Woman Who Disappeared* (*Die verschwundene Frau*, 1929).

Lorre's role as the child murderer Hans Beckert in Fritz Lang's *M* (*M / M – Eine Stadt sucht einen Mörder*, 1931) made him an overnight sensation. Sadly, he was denied a sustained career in German film. Lorre emigrated to the United States. following periods of exile in Austria, France, and Britain, where he played a number of major parts (such as in Alfred Hitchcock's *The Man Who Knew Too Much* in 1934).

In Hollywood, Lorre was predominantly typecast as a psychotic character, a part his diminutive physique, child-like face, and disproportionately large eyes seemed to cut him out for. Mostly playing supporting roles, Lorre brought his unique flair to many movie classics, including *The Maltese Falcon* (1941), *Casablanca* (1942), and *Arsenic and Old Lace* (1944). As agent "Mr. Moto" he even had his own series of B-flicks (1937–1939).

Dissatisfied with the course of his career – Lorre's ambitions lay in serious drama – he returned to Germany in 1949, where he wrote and directed *The Lost One* (*Der Verlorene*, 1951), a passionate and critical examination of the Nazi period in which he also played the lead role. The film did not meet with the acclaim Lorre expected, and he returned to the United States, where he starred in numerous film and television productions until his death in 1964.

PORT OF SHADOWS
LE QUAI DES BRUMES

1938 – FRANCE – 91 MIN.
DIRECTOR MARCEL CARNÉ (1909–1996)
SCREENPLAY JACQUES PRÉVERT, MARCEL CARNÉ,
based on the novel of the same name by
PIERRE MAC ORLAN [= PIERRE DUMARCHAIS]
DIRECTOR OF PHOTOGRAPHY EUGEN SCHÜFFTAN
EDITING RENÉ LE HÉNAFF MUSIC MAURICE JAUBERT
PRODUCTION GREGOR RABINOVITCH for CINÉ-ALLIANCE
STARRING JEAN GABIN (Jean), MICHÈLE MORGAN (Nelly),
MICHEL SIMON (Zabel), PIERRE BRASSEUR (Lucien),
RAYMOND AIMOS (Tramp), ROBERT LE VIGAN (Painter),
EDOUARD DELMONT (Panama), JENNY BURNAY
(Lucien's Girlfriend), RENÉ GÉNIN (Doctor),
MARCEL PÉRÈS (Chauffeur), ROGER LEGRIS (Hotel Page)

"Life's a bitch."

In a grubby dockside bar in Le Havre, a deserter named Jean (Jean Gabin) meets Nelly (Michèle Morgan), a young runaway. He's looking for a ship that will save him by getting him out of France. She wants to get away from her home and her guardian Zabel (Michel Simon), who watches over her jealously. The two of them fall in love, without any prospect of a shared future. Through his relationship with Nelly, Jean gets drawn into the conflict between Zabel and the would-be gangster Lucien (Pierre Brasseur), who suspects the shady old man of being responsible for the disappearance of his buddy Maurice – Nelly's former lover. As matters come to a head, Jean succeeds unexpectedly in gaining a berth on a cargo ship bound for South America. All that remains to the couple is one last night of love in a hotel. Next morning, just as the ship is about to depart, Jean makes a fateful decision: he disembarks, in order to see Nelly one last time.

The deserter, the girl, and the *tristesse* of the docklands: with its atmosphere of melancholy, fatalism, and romance, *Port of Shadows* now seems to embody the essence of French prewar film. This was the country's first cinematic Golden Age, the period of Poetic Realism. Dark melodramas depicted the tragic fates of mainly proletarian heroes, telling tales of man's existential loneliness in a corrupted world, and depicting the futility of all attempts to achieve happiness. Marcel Carné was only 28 when he made *Port of Shadows*, and it established his reputation as a master of these shadowy love dramas. The films that followed – *Hôtel du Nord* (1938) and *Daybreak* (*Le jour*

"It's a thoroughgoing study in blacks and grays, without a free laugh in it; but it's also a remarkably beautiful motion picture from a purely pictorial standpoint and a strangely haunting drama." *The New York Times*

1   When the fog clears: Jean Gabin and Michèle Morgan emerged from the *Port of Shadows* as the premiere romantic pairing of the French screen.

2   Small-minded Zabel (Michel Simon) is consumed with desire for Nelly, and attempts to rape her.

3   The fog of the Le Havre coast represents the uncertain future of the characters, whose lives hang on a knife-edge of heightened emotions.

4　Lost and gone forever: cinematographer Eugen Schüfftan paints a portrait of love that is doomed from the get-go.

5　Director Marcel Carné puts forward the idea that nothing is more important in life than passion.

6　Welcome to our world of toys: Alexandre Trauner's set design shows how lonely it can be when you have to play by yourself.

se lève, 1939) – were no less pessimistic, yet all three of them now come across as the work of a great ensemble working in perfect accord.

The singularly poetic character of *Port of Shadows* is largely due to the tension between everyday realistic elements and a perceptible stylization that removes events from their temporal and spatial context. This is particularly apparent in Jacques Prévert's characteristically sharp dialogue, which moves effortlessly between authentic argot and polished literariness, while Alexandre Trauner's wonderfully artificial sets form a fascinating contrast to the establishing shots filmed on location in the docklands. That the film

retains its integrity as a work of art despite these apparently disparate aesthetic tendencies is due not least to Eugen Schüfftan's camerawork. It bathes the story in a mysterious, diffuse light, so that the film's melancholy atmosphere acquires an attractive and positively sensual quality. All this is supported by Maurice Jaubert's music. Today, *Port of Shadows* affects those who see it as strongly as it did when first released.

But we shouldn't forget that it is also beautifully acted. At the center stands Jean Gabin, at that time the unrivaled star of the French cinema. The character he plays is a man of the people: rough, tough, and easily angered,

"This film is among the few that simply do not age. This ballet of the docklands, this story of a deserted soldier, is as timeless as the fog, as lostness, crime and love. All this is as intertwined and hauntingly present in the landscape of faces violent and beaten, hunted and pure, drunken and dreaming as in the mist-wrapped images of quays and streets." *Der Tagesspiegel*

7   Jean Gabin's tough, romantic image anticipated Humphrey Bogart in *The Big Sleep* and *Casablanca*.

8   Michèle Morgan looks tomboyish in a beret, and the translucent raincoat, which is part of Carné's visual design, alludes to the ephemeral nature of life.

yet vulnerable inside and essentially a very good guy. This made him a cinematic hero of the progressive *Front Populaire* – a man who insists on his dignity in whatever life happens to throw at him. Gabin had already made his name as a tragic lover in Julien Duvivier's *Pépé le Moko* (1937), but it was only after *Port of Shadows* that he truly became an icon of the cinema. This has something to do with the presence and charisma of his co-star Michèle Morgan, who seems immune to the damp shabbiness of her surroundings, and perfectly indifferent to it in her raincoat and beret. With her legendary pale eyes gazing vaguely into the distance, she forms a focal point for Jean's diffuse yearning. Michel Simon, by contrast, embodies the obstacle that blocks their innocent happiness. He lends Zabel the distorted visage of a monstrous petit bourgeois, trapped in bigotry, self-pity, and a kind of joyfully celebrated nastiness. When Jean returns to Nelly, he catches the old man trying to rape her. Senseless with rage, he batters Zabel to death with a brick. Nelly urges her lover to flee, but Jean will never reach the ship: outside on the street, Lucien, the gangster, is waiting with a gun. Jean is shot in the back, and dies in Nelly's arms.

JH

MARCEL CARNÉ Marcel Carné, a carpenter's son, was born in Paris in 1909. From the very start, his film career was classically French: he began as a critic. After working as an assistant director for Jacques Feyder and René Clair, he directed *Jenny*, his first film, in 1936. The script was written by Jacques Prévert, and the two men would become the dream team of Poetic Realism, ushering in a golden age of *French* cinema with such works as *Port of Shadows* (*Le Quai des brumes*, 1938), *Hôtel du Nord* (1938), and *Daybreak* (*Le jour se lève*, 1939). All these films were created in studios, where the director could control every movement. In this peculiarly artificial atmosphere, it was usually raining, and two lonely people had little hope of a happy ending. These movies starred such outstanding actors as Jean Gabin and Arletty [= Léonie Bathiat]. Unfulfilled yearnings are also a feature of Carné's two masterpieces *The Devil's Envoys* (*Les Visiteurs du soir*, 1942) and *Children of Paradise* (*Les Enfants du paradis*, 1945), both of which were made during the German occupation of France. Carné's sudden interest in historical subjects was a result of conditions imposed by the Nazis, who regarded his films as "defeatist." With his melancholy fatalism, Carné stood in opposition to another important representative of French Poetic Realism: Jean Renoir. While the young moviemakers of the *Nouvelle Vague* celebrated Renoir's work, Carné was forgotten – for he wasn't an "auteur" (that was Prévert). After their collaboration ended, Carné made two literary adaptations – *La Marie du port* (1949) and *The Adulteress* (*Thérèse Raquin*, 1953) – and a handful of gangster films that attracted little attention. In 1996, Marcel Carné died in Clamart near Paris.

REBECCA ♙♙

1940 – USA – 130 MIN.
DIRECTOR ALFRED HITCHCOCK (1899–1980)
SCREENPLAY ROBERT E. SHERWOOD, JOAN HARRISON,
based on the novel of the same name by
DAPHNE DU MAURIER
DIRECTOR OF PHOTOGRAPHY GEORGE BARNES
EDITING HAL C. KERN, W. DONN HAYES
MUSIC FRANZ WAXMAN **PRODUCTION** DAVID O. SELZNICK
for SELZNICK INTERNATIONAL PICTURES
STARRING JOAN FONTAINE (The second Mrs. de Winter),
LAURENCE OLIVIER (Maxim de Winter),
GEORGE SANDERS (Jack Favell), JUDITH ANDERSON
(Mrs. Danvers), NIGEL BRUCE (Major Giles Lacy),
GLADYS COOPER (Beatrice Lacy), REGINALD DENNY
(Frank Crawley), C. AUBREY SMITH
(Colonel Julyan), MELVILLE COOPER (Coroner),
FLORENCE BATES (Mrs. Van Hopper)
ACADEMY AWARDS 1940 OSCARS for BEST PICTURE
(David O. Selznick), and BEST CINEMATOGRAPHY
(George Barnes)

"You thought I loved Rebecca? You thought that? I hated her!"

A young woman employed as a travel companion (Joan Fontaine) falls in love with wealthy widower Maxim de Winter (Laurence Olivier) in romantic Monte Carlo. The two marry and retreat to Manderley, the de Winters' familial estate located on the coast of Cornwall. But what starts off as a fairy-tale romance for the new Mrs. de Winter soon spirals into a nightmare when the shadow of her husband's former spouse, Rebecca, begins to tighten its grip on the timid lady of the manor. At the heart of the matter is housekeeper Mrs. Danvers (Judith Anderson), who remains loyal to her previous mistress's memory. Indeed, beyond treating the new madam as an intruder, the servant even goes so far as to insinuate that Maxim de Winter's lingering love for his dead wife is causing him to lapse into trances. Then, one stormy night, the situation is turned on its head as a wrecked ship containing Rebecca's corpse washes ashore and Maxim is suddenly suspected of foul play ...

Rebecca marked the beginning of an exciting eight-year collaboration for director Alfred Hitchcock and legendary Hollywood producer David O. Selznick. The studio executive had originally lured the British filmmaker across the Atlantic with a proposal to adapt the sinking of the Titanic for the screen. However, the financial burden of realizing such a project caused the pair to jump ship for Daphne Du Maurier's best-selling novel. It was to be a change of course with complications of its own as the men's differing visions for the screen version of the story proved to have little in common: whereas Hitchcock saw the manuscript as a starting point to embark on his own interpretation of the story, Selznick was determined to give audiences a picture that was uncompromisingly true to the hit novel, as was the case with his previous and hugely popular cinematic endeavor, *Gone with the Wind* (1939).

2

1   Last night I dreamt I went to Manderley again: home life is horrible for the second Mrs. de Winter (Joan Fontaine), a woman who lives in the shadow of her predecessor, Rebecca.

2   Courting catastrophe: another inquest is ordered after a boat containing Rebecca's body washes ashore near the mansion and foul play is suspected.

3   Bringing down the house: Maxim de Winter and his new bride won't live at Manderley for long if Mrs. Danvers (Judith Anderson) has any say about it.

4   A hairy situation: chills run down Mrs. de Winter's spine as she begins to comprehend that Mrs. Danvers was more in love with Rebecca than Maxim was.

5   Good help is hard to find: horror's favorite housekeeper tries to convince her new mistress to resign, but misses her mark.

Despite being not at all accustomed to production executives meddling in his affairs, Hitchcock found himself with no choice but to concede to Selznick's wishes. *Rebecca*, as a result, breaks dramatically with his previous films. Cast and locale provide for the director's signature British flair, but gone are Hitch's trademark humor and brilliant dramatic irony. Instead, an atmosphere of bewildering darkness and solemnity gradually transforms the psychodrama into a thriller singularly preoccupied with Rebecca's mysterious death. The film rarely leaves the side of its heroine, the story's first-person narrator, who ensures that the audience experiences her character's perpetual state of distress with the same intensity as she does. Little by little, Manderley assumes the character of a prison, as expressive displays of shadow and light imbue the mansion with a horrific life of its own. And by

3

FRANZ WAXMAN   Franz Waxman (1906–1967) was one of Hollywood's busiest and most beloved composers. In fact, he is among the few movie composers whom the United States Postal Service has honored with a stamp. A number of further distinctions also attest to his considerable accomplishments. The man born Franz Wachsmann in Upper Silesia worked his way through music school in Berlin as a pianist with the jazz band The Weintraub Syncopators. Friend and celebrity composer Friedrich Hollaender got the budding musician into the movie industry, hiring him to arrange the score to the smash hit *The Blue Angel* (*Der blaue Engel*, 1930). Shortly thereafter, young Waxman fled to Paris to escape Nazi persecution. It was here that he composed the score to *Liliom* (1934), the first picture Fritz Lang directed in exile. Like so many Jewish artists, Waxman eventually emigrated to the U.S., where he established himself in Hollywood with the horror film *Bride of Frankenstein* (1935). Alfred Hitchcock's eerie romance *Rebecca* (1940) went on to make him a fixture in the industry. From then on, the name Franz Waxman became synonymous with dramatic scores requiring full-scale orchestras. For his work on *Sunset Boulevard* (1950) and *A Place in the Sun* (1951), Waxman made history by becoming the first composer ever to win back-to-back Oscars. In addition, his credits include the unforgettable scores to pictures such as *The Philadelphia Story* (1940), *Suspicion* (1941), *Rear Window* (1954), and *The Nun's Story* (1959).

"What seems to have happened, in brief, is that Mr. Hitchcock, the famous soloist, suddenly has recognized that, in this engagement, he is working with an all-star troupe. He makes no concession to it and, fortunately, vice versa." *The New York Times*

6 Healthy, wealthy, and wise: Worldly Maxim de Winter (Laurence Olivier) falls in love with a woman who lacks the savoir faire of his first wife.

In real life, Olivier thought that actress Joan Fontaine was a touch too green to play the role.

7 Maid of honor: Mrs. Danvers remains true to the spirit of former mistress Rebecca by making the new Mrs. de Winter feel inadequate.

6

"Possibly it's unethical to criticize performances anatomically. Still we insist. Miss Fontaine has the most expressive spine – and shoulders! – we've bothered to notice this season." *The New York Times*

the end of the film, Manderley seems less a place that can be objectively experienced than the very image of a tortured soul.

While the Master of Suspense openly treated *Rebecca* like an unwanted child throughout his career, all the shunning still can not refute the fact that the film ultimately bears his signature. Regardless of how literary the picture's tone may seem to be, it is actually the Hitchcockian visuals that tell the story. To a much greater extent than his British productions, *Rebecca* reveals just how heavily influenced the director was by German silent cinema. More living shadow than human, Mrs. Danvers creeps around Manderley much like Murnau's Nosferatu did in his haunted castle. Nor do the film's similarities with the rest of the master's oeuvre end there. Not only can Mrs. Danvers be seen as a prototype of the many tyrannical mother figures that followed, but the film was weighted with a feeling of doom, arguably unknown

to Hitch's British period, that would eventually reach its culmination in *Psycho* (1960) some 20 years later. Leitmotifs that would gain importance in future masterpieces also make their debut appearance here. One might even say that Mrs. Danvers's worship of her deceased employer nearly resurrects Rebecca as effectively and surreally as *Vertigo*'s (1958) Scottie does Madeleine Elster.

Ironically, for all Hitchcock's eagerness to take artistic license with the original story, the sole moment the movie succeeds in doing so was entirely beyond his control. Instead, it was work of the censors at the Hays Office, who decided that Du Maurier's choice to have Maxim de Winter murder his first wife was unacceptable for viewers. And so, against his better judgment, David O. Selznick allowed for one significant amendment to the original story and had Rebecca lose her life in a tragic fluke accident.   JH

HIGH SIERRA

1941 – USA – 100 MIN.
DIRECTOR RAOUL WALSH (1887–1980)
SCREENPLAY JOHN HUSTON, W. R. BURNETT, based on
a novel of the same name by W. R. BURNETT
DIRECTOR OF PHOTOGRAPHY TONY GAUDIO
EDITING JACK KILLIFER MUSIC ADOLPH DEUTSCH
PRODUCTION HAL B. WALLIS for WARNER BROS.
STARRING HUMPHREY BOGART (Roy Earle), IDA LUPINO
(Marie Garson), JOAN LESLIE (Velma), ALAN CURTIS
(Babe Kozak), ARTHUR KENNEDY (Red Hattery),
HENRY HULL (Doc Banton), HENRY TRAVERS (Pa),
JEROME COWAN (Healy, Reporter),
CORNEL WILDE (Louis Mendoza),
DONALD MACBRIDE (Big Mac)

"All the A-1 guys are gone, or in Alcatraz. All that's left are soda jerks and jitterbugs."

After eight years in jail, Roy Earle (Humphrey Bogart) has only one thing on his mind: pulling off one last heist and settling down to a new life. But times have moved on in the outside world. Earle's boss, Big Mac (Donald MacBride), is now an ailing old man, and all his best "workers" are either dead or behind bars, so when Earle resolves to rob a luxury hotel on the edge of the desert, the best Big Mac can offer in the way of assistance is a couple of inexperienced wise guys: Babe (Alan Curtis) and Red (Arthur Kennedy). It gets worse: these two petty crooks are accompanied by a dame, and a very attractive one at that – Marie (Ida Lupino), who's tired of making a living as a dancer in two-

bit dives. She falls for Earle, but he's planning to wed a poor farmer's daughter, a girl he'd met on his way to California. The girl is lame, and Earle enables her to undergo an expensive operation, but he's soon forced to admit that she doesn't really love him. Then the heist goes disastrously wrong, and Red and Babe are burned to death in the car, along with most of the loot. All Earle can do now is flee – with Marie at his side.

High Sierra is mainly famous for being the film that made Bogart a star. Though he'd been in the business for a decade, first with Fox, then with Warner Bros., he was far from being a top Hollywood actor. As he himself said,

2

moviegoers knew him mainly as the "second banana gangster": the heavy who generally cops a bullet for the star of the show. When it came to *High Sierra*, he wasn't first choice for the role. Only after the role had been turned down by the studio's top gangster stars, George Raft, James Cagney, and Edward G. Robinson did Bogart get the chance to play Roy Earle. And he took it.

Raoul Walsh's film gave Humphrey Bogart his first opportunity to play a more complex and sympathetic character. It also allowed him, finally, to bring his unique personal qualities to a role: the ability to dominate a scene with a minimum of effort, using only a glance, a laconic gesture, or a few well-placed lines. Walsh directs the film efficiently, but it's largely Bogart's powerfully understated performance that makes *High Sierra* more than a piece of melodramatic kitsch. He dominates the film with his portrayal of a hardbitten professional, playing the rest of the cast off the screen. And he radiates a peculiar integrity: Roy Earle is undoubtedly a crook, but he's as unswervingly loyal to his boss as he is to the little dog he adopts, though he knows it's brought its previous owners nothing but bad luck. He also plays it straight with Marie, who is played by Ida Lupino – probably Bogart's strongest film partner – as a kind of female equivalent to Roy Earle.

Behind the mask of cynicism, the gangster is revealed to be an aging moralist. The role of Roy Earle was a kind of template for Bogart's later performances. What distinguishes this particular character is that we also sympathize with him because he is so clearly a victim of a corrupt society. The figure of Earle is said to have been based on the legendary bandit John

IDA LUPINO In the opening titles to *High Sierra* (1941), she got top billing, with her name above Humphrey Bogart's. Yet Ida Lupino was never one of Hollywood's really big stars, which may have had something to do with the fact that she also took an interest in directing. Ida Lupino (1914–1995) was born into a family of vaudeville artistes in London, and she made her first stage appearances as a young girl. In 1931, she made her film debut, and two years later went to Hollywood with a contract from Paramount. Despite some promising starts, her career only really took off when she signed for Warner Bros. in 1940. Under Raoul Walsh's direction, she gave convincing performances in *They Drive by Night* (1940) and *High Sierra*, in both cases playing an energetic and hard-boiled gangster's moll. She also played feisty women in other genres, appearing in Michael Curtiz's adventure movie *The Sea Wolf* (1941) and Vincent Sherman's showbiz drama *The Hard Way* (1943). In real life too, Lupino showed toughness and determination: she left Warner, formed her own production company in 1949, and became one of the first female directors in Hollywood. By 1953, she had directed five full-length features for the cinema. The critic David Thompson has said they were "as tough and as quick as those of Sam Fuller." Then she spent many years working in TV, with credits including episodes of *The Virginian / The Men from the Shiloh* (1962–1971) and *The Rifleman* (1958–1963). She also made numerous guest appearances as an actress in *Bonanza* (1959–1973). In 1966, she directed her last movie, a comedy called *The Trouble with Angels*.
Ida Lupino remained present on the screen over the years, appearing, for example, in Nicholas Ray's *On Dangerous Ground* (1952), Robert Aldrich's *The Big Knife* (1955), and Fritz Lang's *While the City Sleeps* (1956). In *Junior Bonner* (1972), Sam Peckinpah gave her a wonderful role as the wife and mother of two washed-up rodeo riders.

1. Sticking to their guns: escaped convict Roy "Mad Dog" Earle (Humphrey Bogart) and his sweetheart Marie (Ida Lupino) prepare to go out with a bang in *High Sierra*.

2. Turn the other cheek: it'll take more than a closed fist to break Marie Garson's will. Off screen, Ida Lupino, proved herself every bit as assertive as the characters she played and went on to become one of Hollywood's first female directors.

3. Roy Earle visits his old boss Big Mac (Donald MacBride), displaying loyalty and affection, in contrast to his "Mad Dog" nickname.

4. Marie is loyal to Roy, and races to the Sierras only to see him die.

5. Roy Earle lies dead. Stunt performer Buster Wiles plays Earle – he has biscuits in his hand to attract Pard, played by Bogart's own dog, Zero.

"Remember what Johnny Dillinger said about guys like you and him; he said you're just rushing toward death – that's it, you're rushing toward death."

Film quote: Doc Banton (Henry Hull)

"As gangster pictures go, this one has everything – speed, excitement, suspense and that ennobling suggestion of futility which makes for irony and pity. Mr. Bogart plays the leading role with a perfection of hard-boiled vitality... Especially Ida Lupino is impressive as the adoring moll." *The New York Times*

6 *High Sierra* gave Humphrey Bogart a chance to show his vulnerable side. Prior to the picture, Hollywood often typecast him as a cold-blooded killer.

7 Ida Lupino bids Humphrey Bogart a fond farewell as he boards the "Star Bus" and joins the ranks of Hollywood A-listers. Next stop, Casablanca!

8 Blood money: Mad Dog returns to a life of crime to fund Velma's (Joan Leslie) foot operation.

9 Bogart persuaded George Raft to turn down the role of Roy Earle so that Bogart could take it.

6

Dillinger, who achieved a semi-heroic status amongst the impoverished rural population of the United States. Indeed, the film does explain Earle's criminal career as a result of a childhood trauma following his family's eviction from their farm. Walsh's film is thus in the tradition of socially critical gangster movies produced by Warner Bros. in the 1930s. Yet *High Sierra* is also an epilogue to this classical phase of the genre, and its fatalistic mood already anticipates the existential pessimism of film noir. That Earle is heading towards an inexorable fate is indicated in the early scenes, when he drives into the archaic wilderness of the Californian highlands to meet with his accomplices. Walsh stretches out this sequence for a surprising length of time, while both the camerawork and the music conjure an atmosphere of indefinable

unease. Very quietly, a spirit of irrationality enters into the film – a tale of romance that culminates in a somber finale.

Only when he's on the run does Earle realize what he feels for Marie, but by that time it's far too late. This is a couple without a future. As matters come to a head, Earle leaves his lover behind and tries to escape through the mountains alone, but in vain. Earle is encircled by the cops and seeks a hiding place in the rock face. Marie, who has heard through the press that he's on the verge of being captured, hurries to join him, and thereby hastens his end: when the little dog breaks free from her leash and scampers into the line of fire, Roy Earle rushes out to save it – and dies in a hail of bullets.

JH

THE MALTESE FALCON

1941 – USA – 100 MIN.
DIRECTOR JOHN HUSTON (1906–1987)
SCREENPLAY JOHN HUSTON, based on the novel of the same name by DASHIELL HAMMETT
DIRECTOR OF PHOTOGRAPHY ARTHUR EDESON
EDITING THOMAS RICHARDS **MUSIC** ADOLPH DEUTSCH
PRODUCTION HAL B. WALLIS for FIRST NATIONAL PICTURES INC., WARNER BROS.
STARRING HUMPHREY BOGART (Sam Spade), MARY ASTOR (Brigid O'Shaughnessy / Miss Wonderly), GLADYS GEORGE (Iva Archer), PETER LORRE (Joel Cairo), SYDNEY GREENSTREET (Kasper Gutman), JEROME COWAN (Miles Archer), ELISHA COOK JR. (Wilmer Cook), JAMES BURKE (Luke), MURRAY ALPER (Frank Richman), JOHN HAMILTON (Bryan), WARD BOND (Detective Tom Polhaus)

"The stuff that dreams are made of."

The camera pans slowly across San Francisco, gateway to the Orient. Cross fade. At the offices of Sam Spade and Miles Archer, we find ourselves in the hands of two great masters; for soon we will be at the disposal of Humphrey Bogart as he explores a world of intrigue, murder, and betrayal that only legendary filmmaker John Huston could have devised.

The Maltese Falcon was a directorial debut without equal. With this picture, Huston, who later produced cinema classics like The Asphalt Jungle (1950) and Moby Dick (1956), set the standard for all film noir to come. And despite having no industry experience or reputation to fall back on, Huston managed to assemble a cast whose caliber few big-budget films could match: Mary Astor as the foxy Brigid O'Shaughnessy, Peter Lorre as the slippery shyster Joel Cairo, and Sydney Greenstreet as treasure hunter Kasper

Gutman, alias "the fat man." All are determined to get their hands on the elusive black statuette known only as the Maltese Falcon, and are willing to do whatever it takes to make sure the others do not.

Rather than sharing his characters' fixation with the bird, Huston found the stories that unfold in the process of obtaining it to be the most intriguing aspect of Dashiell Hammett's novel of the same name. Much like the critically acclaimed essay "Notes on Film Noir" by screenwriter / director Paul Schrader (Taxi Driver, 1976 – screenplay), The Maltese Falcon contends that the essence of noir lies in giving the *how* greater significance than the *what*.

The web of deceit, double-dealings, and red herrings begins the moment the alluring Miss Wonderly shows up at Sam Spade's office and hires him to rescue her sister from a dangerous character named Floyd

1

2

Thursby. It promises to be the cleanest case the macho detective has ever had, and for once it seems he won't have to hound his client to receive payment. Yet there's something unsettling about the whole affair. Could it be that Miss Wonderly's panic lifted unnaturally when she caught her first glimpse of Spade's partner Miles Archer? Thinking she's got the two detectives eating out of her hand – especially that ladies' man Spade – she spins them a cock and bull story. But rather than following their gut instinct to tell the lady to take her troubles elsewhere, the duo are reeled in by her womanly charms and the generous cash advance. Within 24 hours, Miles Archer is dead, and Sam Spade finds himself up to his neck in a sinister game of cat and mouse.

Not only do the homicide detectives assigned to the Archer case soon suspect Spade of having committed the crime, but the murder leads double-dealing characters to flock to Sam like bees to honey. Conman Joel Cairo shows up in Spade's office from out of nowhere, shedding light on Miss Wonderly's true motives. Her real name is Brigid O'Shaughnessy, and she bated Cairo and his partner, Kasper Gutman, to help her retrieve the precious bird figurine; Spade, it seems, is her next target.

Just when the plot starts adding up, the quest for the ornament takes on more complex dimensions, with the fog surrounding the case gathering more quickly than Spade can lift it. The viewer is always on a level with

"Very clear, even if eccentric, crime entertainment." Kinematograph Weekly

PRIVATE EYES The word "Investigations" on the frosted glass pane, Venetian blinds pulled down tight, a disorderly office with evident traces of alcohol consumption: the trademarks of all good old-fashioned private detectives, from Philip Marlowe to Sam Spade. Much of the film noir of the 1940s and '50s centers around the PI, a jaded, pessimistic outsider whose inquiries regarding seemingly cut-and-dry cases frequently unearth the schemes of a mastermind. And more often than not, a gorgeous woman with a dark past is wrapped up in the whole affair.
Classics of the genre include *The Maltese Falcon* (1941) and *The Big Sleep* (1946). Both films feature Humphrey Bogart ("Bogie") as the hard-boiled detective. Robert Montgomery's *Lady in the Lake* (1947), which he both directed and starred in, experimentally fused the perspective of the camera with that of the detective. Roman Polanski's 1974 box-office smash *Chinatown* proved that life could still be breathed into this genre of yesteryear, and in 1982, Ridley Scott even put a sci-fi spin on detective capers by sending a *Blade Runner* off in pursuit of androids.

1 Fine-feathered friend: a mysterious statuette holds the call of the wild for Sam Spade (Humphrey Bogart) in *The Maltese Falcon*.

2 Daylight desk jobs: but when night falls, Sam Spade and Miles Archer (Jerome Cowan) comb the city's darkest streets for clues.

3 Fraternizing with the enemy: Spade seeks out a contact in law enforcement to get the skinny on his latest case. Ward Bond as detective Tom Polhaus.

4 Beat him to the punch: Joel Cairo (Peter Lorre, center) had better improve his technique if he plans on pursuing a life of crime.

5 Me and my shadow: Spade sniff's out snoop Wilmer Cook (Elisha Cook, Jr.).

"The best private-eye melodrama ever made." *Life Magazine*

"Even today, over fifty years later, the influence of this film is clearly evident in current movies."

Film Quarterly

6 Big Kahuna: the more extensive the underworld, the more formidable its boss. Sydney Greenstreet as fat cat Kasper Gutman.

7 Sealing secrets with a kiss: Brigid O'Shaughnessy (Mary Astor) persuades Spade to help her retrieve the elusive falcon without saying a word.

8 Tricks of the trade: in the blink of an eye, Spade will show our gunman that a pistol isn't always a surefire bargaining chip.

9 Throw them a bone: Spade weasels his way out of an interrogation by giving the coppers a false lead.

Spade, knowing only as much (or rather, as little) as he does. The narrative's deliberately confusing structure is underlined by the low-key lighting as well as the angular and claustrophobic camerawork that literally obscures the bigger picture. But above all else, it is Sam Spade himself who heightens the intensity of the film's shocking climax; the embodiment of the self-assured urban cowboy, this hard-boiled detective is unable to accept that he's been nothing but a patsy in a wild goose chase.

Indeed, our first good look at the film comes at its conclusion, when all the mysteries have been explained and the characters exposed as the culpable fools they are. Nino Frank, the man who coined the term film noir, hit the nail on the head in his 1946 essay on *The Maltese Falcon*: it reveals, he said, a third dimension, in which the magnitude of man's moral decrepitude is mirrored darkly on the surface of the cinema.

BR

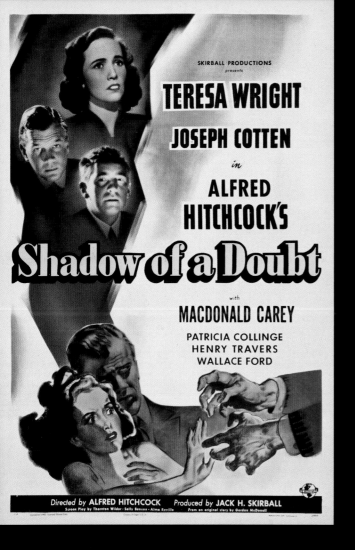

SHADOW OF A DOUBT

1943 – USA – 108 MIN.
DIRECTOR ALFRED HITCHCOCK (1899–1980)
SCREENPLAY THORNTON WILDER, SALLY BENSON,
ALMA REVILLE, based on the story *Uncle Charlie*
by GORDON MCDONELL
DIRECTOR OF PHOTOGRAPHY JOSEPH A. VALENTINE
EDITING MILTON CARRUTH **MUSIC** DIMITRI TIOMKIN
PRODUCTION JACK H. SKIRBALL for SKIRBALL
PRODUCTIONS, UNIVERSAL PICTURES
STARRING TERESA WRIGHT (Charlie), JOSEPH COTTEN
(Uncle Charlie), MACDONALD CAREY (Detective Jack
Graham), HENRY TRAVERS (Joseph Newton),
PATRICIA COLLINGE (Emma Newton), HUME CRONYN
(Herbie Hawkins), WALLACE FORD (Detective Fred
Saunders), EDNA MAY WONACOTT (Ann Newton),
CHARLES BATES (Roger Newton), IRVING BACON
(Station Master), CLARENCE MUSE (Pullman Porter),
JANET SHAW (Louise), ESTELLE JEWELL (Catherine)

"I have a feeling that inside you there's something nobody knows about ... something secret and wonderful. I'll find it out."

Call it women's intuition. Nothing else can describe what's been bugging sheltered niece Charlie (Teresa Wright) about Uncle Charlie (Joseph Cotten) since the moment of his arrival. Indeed, there's more to him than meets the eye. But by the time *Shadow of a Doubt* has come to a close, this charming provincial flower will be wishing she hadn't been so keen on finding out.

At first, Uncle Charlie provides welcome relief from the young lady's drab family life. All that changes, however, when the man's manipulative hand tightens its grip, and she begins to suspect him of the horrible acts we already know him to be guilty of: namely, that he has been targeting wealthy widows on a nationwide murder spree.

The direction of this Hitchcock picture, from the initial encounter of uncle and niece to their final showdown on board a locomotive, seems jar-

ringly casual; but upon closer examination we see the picture for what it really is – a fascinating exercise in subtlety. It follows that *Shadow of a Doubt* is more an in-depth look at small town family life than a classic thriller. More remarkable still is that the British-born filmmaker dared to tread the thin ice of Middle America's inner workings as early as his sixth U.S. production. Despite the film's uncharacteristic subject matter, Hitchcock often referred to *Shadow of a Doubt* as his personal favorite. As his daughter Pat Hitchcock O'Connell divulged in a rare interview, what he loved about the piece was "the prospect of bringing menace into a small town." For extra authenticity, Hitchcock filmed most of the picture on location in Santa Rosa where the story is set. In the master's hands, the moral corruption and misery that lurks just beneath the surface of this sunny Northern California town is soon

2

1   Lady killer: young Charlie's (Teresa Wright) dashing, mysterious Uncle Charlie (Joseph Cotten) isn't above targeting his own flesh and blood.

2   No telling what's out there: the Newtons become gradually more suspicious of a foreign menace weighing upon their lives, but never consider that the newest member of their family might be at the heart of the matter.

3   Indigestion: having eaten from the tree of knowledge, Charlie thinks she might throw up.

4   Somewhere, a place for us: kindred spirits Charlie and Charlie are like two halves of the same whole.

"Thanks in no small part to the precision acting, it's easily as great as other Hitchcock films to which 'masterpiece' status is more colloquially granted." *Movieline*

3

revealed. The relationship between the uncle and the niece is at the heart of this story of decay and fall. The fact that they share the same first name is just a first indication that the apparent opposites are in fact kindred spirits. For as we soon discover, their refusal to submit to routine and mediocrity is infinitely more significant than her being a naïve young creature and him a cultivated and worldly gentleman. At the end of the day, they are both opportunists who demand more out of life than is there for the taking. And it is this common bond that gives Charlie the clue to her uncle's dark secret.

"Not good to find out too much, Charlie," Joseph Cotten says to Teresa Wright. The young lady puts her innocence and naïveté on the line despite the warning; she can neither resist her uncle's mystique, nor the burning sensation that he is her only chance of escaping Santa Rosa's monotonous humdrum.

"A brilliant piece of cynicism that exposes the hypocrisy, moral rot, and guilt that pervades conventional criminals and everyday citizens." *QNetwork*

JOSEPH COTTEN Joseph Cotten was a past master at being in a scene without needing to be seen. From the moment of his cinematic debut in Orson Welles's *Citizen Kane* (1941) it seemed that Cotten (1905–1994) was predestined to play such roles, something that is surely the result of the actor's smooth and rather unassuming facial features. A film critic once said of Cotten that he gives the impression of being "neither villain nor hero." Yet he started off playing the purest of the pure and it was only with the help of Alfred Hitchcock that Cotten became the "man without a face." *Shadow of a Doubt* (1943), in which he bumps off one widow after another as Uncle Charlie, marked his initial pairing with the Master of Suspense. In 1949, he reunited with *Duel in the Sun* director King Vidor to play Dr. Louis Moline in *Beyond the Forest* (1949), a picture in which Bette Davis keeps him on a short chain. Cotten, however, got to give the actress her just desserts in Robert Aldrich's *Hush … Hush, Sweet Charlotte* (1964), driving her character insane by playing dead. In Henry Hathaway's *Niagara* (1952), Cotten butts heads with leading lady Marilyn Monroe or rather with her character who is hell-bent on seeing him dead. His depiction of an American dime novelist in Carol Reed's Viennese postwar drama *The Third Man* (1949) is one of his signature roles. The picture also marked an on-screen reunion with longtime friend Orson Welles, who encouraged Cotten to contribute to *Citizen Kane*'s script back when they first met. Although Cotten more often than not had to settle for playing supporting roles, he was no less brilliant than a leading man, invariably able to make an art form out of playing second best.

5 Poison ivy: Emma Newton (Patricia Collinge) welcomes Charlie into the family with open arms. If only she knew that her clean-cut relative cuts up widows in his spare time.

6 A wolf in grandma's bed: watch out Red Riding Hood – your days are numbered.

"In his stage play, *Our Town*, [Thornton] Wilder celebrated the simple life and the spirit of solidarity that binds ordinary people. *Shadow of a Doubt* examines the dark side of community, casting a cold eye on the black heart of small-town America." *Volker Gunske, in: Lars-Olav Beier/Georg Seeßlen (eds.), Alfred Hitchcock*

Cotten's pompous, happy-go-lucky character thrives on his niece's hero worship. In the eyes of many a Hitchcock fan Uncle Charlie is the Master of Suspense's most insidious fiend. Not to say that the director doesn't grant him a tender moment or two; it's just that Cotten demonstrates neither Robert Walker's boyish charm in *Strangers on a Train* (1951) nor the sensitivity or vulnerability of Anthony Perkins in *Psycho* (1960). Instead, he plays an unscrupulous, cold-blooded killer, whose hedonistic façade is but a thin disguise for sheer brutality.

Cotten's chafing veneer all but crumbles one night during a dinner scene when he makes mention of "fat, greedy widows" – his victims of choice. As Wright voices her objection by saying "they're alive, they're human beings," he responds straight into the camera with a mocking "are they?"

Where other directors might have put the camera back on the right side of the fence, the cynical Hitchcock holds the lens on Cotten, knowing full well that the villain's point of view is the one with more clout – and the heroine is simply the representative of false utopian beliefs. And thus by identifying with the Uncle Charlie character, Hitchcock strengthens the "lasting" impression the role model makes on his niece and on us. While good may appear to triumph over evil at the film's conclusion, small-town life in general has been left unfazed – for better or for worse. However, Charlie's age of innocence has been shattered by the mirror her uncle held to her soul: "At night you used to sleep your untroubled, ordinary little sleep filled with peaceful, stupid dreams … and I brought you nightmares." Words that will no doubt haunt her until the end of her days.   ES

OSSESSIONE

1943 – ITALY – 140 MIN.
DIRECTOR LUCHINO VISCONTI (1906–1976)
SCREENPLAY LUCHINO VISCONTI, MARIO ALICATA,
GIUSEPPE DE SANTIS, ANTONIO PIETRANGELI,
GIANNI PUCCINI, based on the novel *The Postman
Always Rings Twice* by JAMES M. CAIN
DIRECTOR OF PHOTOGRAPHY DOMENICO SCALA, ALDO TONTI
EDITING MARIO SERANDREI MUSIC GIUSEPPE ROSATI
PRODUCTION LIBERO SOLAROLI for INDUSTRIE
CINEMATOGRAFICHE ITALIANE
STARRING CLARA CALAMAI (Giovanna Bragana),
MASSIMO GIROTTI (Gino Costa), JUAN DE LANDA
(Giuseppe Bragana), DHIA CRISTIANI (Anita),
ELIO MARCUZZO (Spagnolo), VITTORIO DUSE
(Detective), MICHELE RICCARDINI (Don Remigio)

"The three of us, together ...
we can't go on living like this."

Luchino Visconti was still working as an assistant to his great role model Jean Renoir when the master handed him a novel. Its author was an American named James M. Cain, and its title, *The Postman Always Rings Twice*. A thriller of the hard-boiled school, written in the style shared by Hammett and Chandler – it hinged on a crime of passion, the classical basis of any film noir. Visconti and writers from the Milanese film magazine *Cinema* enthusiastically went to work adapting it into a screenplay. The result was much more than just another well-made thriller, *Ossessione* became a milestone in the history of European cinema.

The film begins with a truck, driving down a dusty country road in the plains around the river Po. The vehicle halts at a roadhouse, and we catch our first glimpse of the driver. His face is, as yet, invisible; all we can see is his muscular torso, and his two legs, nonchalantly crossed. The man gets out, strolls past the leaseholder, Giuseppe (Juan de Landa), and continues on into

the house. And when Gino (Massimo Girotti) catches sight of Giuseppe's wife Giovanna (Clara Calamai), the story crystallizes in a flash: it's love, or something like it, at first sight. From this moment onwards, they have only one goal in mind: to rid themselves of the old man who stands in their way. Giovanna had only married the lumbering idiot in order to escape a life on the streets anyway. The three of them take a trip together, and the adulterers implement their plan. It all looks like an accident. Their happiness, however, is short-lived: Gino is tormented by his conscience, his feelings for the possessive Giovanna soon begin to cool, and the police are breathing down their necks. The couple flee in a car, and the vehicle careers off the road: Giovanna dies, and Gino is arrested.

It's breathtaking to see how Visconti uses meticulous editing to build up the erotic tension and allow the plot to take its deadly course. The force of desire becomes physically tangible – perhaps precisely because certain

1   One look and hubby's goose is cooked. Clara
    Calamai as Giovanna.

2   A helping hand: the vagrant Gino (Massimo Girotti)
    does odd jobs around landowner Giuseppe's (Juan
    de Landa) farm – with murder free of charge.

3   Coffee, tea or me? It won't be long before Giovanna
    is through taking orders and ready for her own
    piece of the pie.

4   Sun block: the film was initially slapped with a
    ban for its burning depiction of Mussolini's Italy
    and only one copy of the negatives survived. Later
    Luchino Visconti would be hailed as a pioneer of
    Neorealism.

"One look at this couple tells their entire story: she is young, beautiful, and full of passion, married to a man unequal to her in all areas except one: money. Giovanna soon takes a romantic interest in the visitor, discovering the spark that never ignited with her husband. It's a potentially murderous situation … As a portrayal of the conflict between moral conscience and uncontrollable passion, between the need to maintain a secure existence and the desire to remain free of any confining forces, *Ossessione* is a powerful statement, and a remarkable first film from Visconti." *tvguide.com*

scenes are simply not shown. The murder itself is not depicted; and naturally, there could be no question of filming anything resembling the sex scene at the kitchen table in Bob Rafelson's American remake (*The Postman Always Rings Twice*, 1981). Nonetheless, Visconti's film did not escape the censors – not because he was dealing with adultery and murder, but because he had adapted the book so ruthlessly to an Italian milieu. The shabby rooms of the little trattoria, the unwashed dishes, the grim dullness of the Po landscape with its rough, potholed roads: *Ossessione* showed a world of material poverty, where people were thrown back on their most primitive and egotistical instincts. In fascist Italy, this was the real taboo. The cinema was there to provide heroic tales in a tasteful ambience. So Visconti's debut suffered the same fate as most of his later works: what the audience were shown was a

JAMES M. CAIN James M. Cain was born in Maryland in 1892. With his tough, economical style, he is one of the best-known authors of the 'hard-boiled' thriller genre. His novels usually focus on a man's murderous love for a woman, described from the standpoint of the killer – and *The Postman Always Rings Twice* was no exception. It has already formed the basis for six different movies. In *Ossessione* (1943), Luchino Visconti allowed himself certain artistic liberties. For one thing, Cain's name was mentioned nowhere in the credits, for nobody had bothered to inquire after the rights. This error was not repeated in Tay Garnett's *The Postman Always Rings Twice* (1946), starring Lana Turner and John Garfield. Cain even felt that Garnett's movie had improved on his book. Bob Rafelson's remake of 1981 starred Jack Nicholson and Jessica Lange, and it is in fact the version most faithful to the original. For the first time, the male lead did not defang the leading character.
Cain also provided the basis for one of the most important film noirs ever made. In Billy Wilder's *Double Indemnity* (1944), Barbara Stanwyck played the genre-typical *femme fatale*, who persuades her devoted husband to carry out an insurance scam. Though Cain himself had begun as a journalist and scriptwriter, it was Raymond Chandler who was entrusted with the screenplay. Chandler had no very high opinion of his colleague's work – in contrast to such great literati as Thomas Mann or Albert Camus, who admired Cain's writing. In the mid-'40s, James M. Cain was at the height of his fame. Michael Curtiz's adaptation of *Mildred Pierce* (1945) brought Joan Crawford an Oscar for her portrayal of a battling career woman who is swindled out of all she owns. The author's name cropped up again most recently in the HBO miniseries *Mildred Pierce* (2011), this time with Kate Winslet in the starring role. James M. Cain died in Maryland in 1977.

5   The postman always rings twice: lovebirds
    Giovanna and Gino are prepared to bump off
    Giuseppe for their own chance at happiness.

6   Visconti's David: a former competitive swimmer,
    Italian sex symbol Massimo Girotti embodied the
    masculine ideal.

mutilated version of the film he had actually made. The original negatives are still missing.

The few positive reviews included a term that would soon be making the rounds: *il neorealismo*. Filmed while the Fascists were still in power, *Ossessione* was soon being lauded as a forerunner of this movement and the *Cinema* group as its intellectual center. When some members of the group were arrested, Visconti was even held up as a symbol of the anti-Fascist resistance. Yet the director always objected to being placed in such catego-

ries, for he himself stressed his allegiance to the classical realism of Jean Renoir. In fact, *Ossessione* is a film like no other – and, in that, it's a typical Visconti. The movie's theme is the conflict between social morality and unguided passion. Equally striking is its fatalistic pessimism, a stance that would achieve perfect artistic expression in Visconti's later film epics, from *The Leopard* (*Il gattopardo*, 1963) to *Ludwig* (*Ludwig / Le Crépuscule des dieux*, 1972). The stony path to the mad king's palace began on the plains of central Italy.   PB

Visconti's impressive debut is powerfully sensual, exact in its depiction of the chosen milieu and subtly discriminating in its moral judgment. With its numerous scenes filmed on location, and its evident interest in the true state of society, *Ossessione* gave birth to a new style in Italian cinema."

Lexikon des internationalen Films

PHANTOM LADY

1944 – USA – 84 MIN.
DIRECTOR ROBERT SIODMAK (1900–1973)
SCREENPLAY BERNARD C. SCHOENFELD, from the
novel by WILLIAM IRISH [= CORNELL WOOLRICH]
DIRECTOR OF PHOTOGRAPHY ELWOOD BREDELL
EDITING ARTHUR HILTON MUSIC HANS J. SALTER
PRODUCTION JOAN HARRISON for UNIVERSAL PICTURES
STARRING FRANCHOT TONE (Jack Marlow),
ELLA RAINES (Carol "Kansas" Richman),
ALAN CURTIS (Scott Henderson),
AURORA MIRANDA (Estela Monteiro),
THOMAS GOMEZ (Inspector Burgess),
FAY HELM (Ann Terry), ELISHA COOK, JR.
(Cliff Milburn), ANDREW TOMBES, JR. (Bartender),
REGIS TOOMEY (Detective Chewing Gum),
JOSEPH CREHAN (Detective Tom), DORIS LLOYD
(Kettisha), VIRGINIA BRISSAC (Dr. Chase),
MILBURN STONE (Voice of District Attorney)

"No questions, no names ..."

While initial critical reaction to *Phantom Lady* was mixed, even laudatory reviewers noted that its convoluted plot was difficult to follow. In fact, the screenplay had greatly simplified a novel that involved two investigators, one male and one female, being coached by a police detective as they seek information to exonerate a man condemned to death for murdering his wife (with chapter heads that enumerate the days to the execution). Whereas novelist Cornell Woolrich had withheld the revelation of the real killer until the book's conclusion and despite the fact that Universal's trailer (which opens with a hand pulling a hardcover copy from a shelf) had marketed its adaptation as "from the pages of the famous mystery novel" and as "gripping as *The Maltese Falcon*," the filmmakers considerably altered and refocused the narrative into the first film noir (and there are not many) with a woman as both "hero" and lead detective.

Equally remarkable is that *Phantom Lady* was the first project of Joan Harrison, who became the preeminent female producer (again, there weren't many) of classic period noir. Certainly the concept of a woman saving or providing critical assistance to a male protagonist does occur elsewhere in noir, one of the earliest and oddest examples being the 1942 adaptation of *This Gun for Hire* where itinerant chanteuse Ellen Graham (Veronica Lake) ends up helping her kidnapper, hired killer Raven (Alan Ladd). Even more unusual is Harrison's later production with director/star Robert Montgomery of *Ride the Pink Horse* (1947), in which the ostensibly naïve Native American teenager Pila (Wanda Hendrix) provides life-saving assistance to a shady war veteran. Perhaps the most typical of such characters is Lucille Ball's Kathleen Stewart, the resourceful assistant who helps her befuddled boss, private eye Bradford Galt (Mark Stevens), in *The Dark Corner* (1946). As engaged as these and

1 In hopes of getting information to exonerate her condemned boss, Carol "Kansas" Richman (Ella Raines) endures being groped by drummer Cliff Milburn (Elisha Cook, Jr.).

2 Unaware of the psychopath standing behind her, Carol shares information with her boss's friend Jack Marlow (Franchot Tone).

3 Prototypical noir lighting: a guard stands by and the wall clock measures the time left to his execution as Scott Henderson (Alan Curtis) meets with his secretary, Carol.

other female characters in film noir may be in getting men out of "dark corners," none goes farther than Carol "Kansas" Richman (Ella Raines) in *Phantom Lady*. Lucille Ball may have been top-billed in *The Dark Corner*, but Raines (second billed to Franchot Tone) is the actor whose role carries the movie.

In the revelations of Woolrich's penultimate chapter Carol becomes the never-seen phantom lady in order to unmask unhinged artist Jack Lombard – Marlow, in the movie. While Raines's Carol never impersonates the missing woman, as part of the effort to save her boss, Scott Henderson (Alan Curtis), of whom she is clearly enamored, she does adopt other personas. Through them Raines becomes a de facto phantom lady, assuming whatever guise she must to accomplish her mission. In the process, Carol becomes an early example of the empowerment of women that so distinguished the noir movement from standard Hollywood depictions.

The movie opens with a shot of Fay Helm (Ann Terry) seated at a bar in her outlandish feather-topped hat, so the viewer knows that Henderson's "phantom lady" is real. Then when Carol goes to question the bartender (Andrew Tombes, Jr.), the audience who saw him serve drinks to the makeshift couple as the movie began knows that he is lying. Many commentators have cited the "masculine gaze" that Carol focuses on the bartender and uses to unnerve him in the course of her repeated visits to his workplace. In a sequence that would become typical of noir staging, when she ultimately follows him after he leaves work, using the back lot to stand in for New York, director Siodmak and cinematographer Woody Bredell create a maze of glistening highlights and deep shadows. In a bravura *mise-en-scène* with no musical underscore – just the sounds of footsteps and traffic – a raincoated Carol stalks him through the humid night to an el platform, where the sound

"When you've got my gifts you can't afford to let them get away." *Film quote: Jack Marlow (Franchot Tone)*

"We wish we could recommend *Phantom Lady* as a perfect combination of the styles of the eminent Mr. Hitchcock and the old German psychological films, for that is plainly and precisely what it tries very hard to be. It is full of the play of light and shadow, of macabre atmosphere, of sharply realistic faces and dramatic injections of sound. But, unfortunately, Miss Harrison and Mr. Siodmak forgot one basic thing — they forgot to provide their picture with a plausible, realistic plot." *The New York Times*

4

4 More noir staging: low light casts shadows behind the figures of Inspector Burgess (Thomas Gomez), Carol, and Marlow.

5 The exaggerated expressions, as when he serves food, are part of an extremely mannered performance by Franchot Tone as Marlow.

6 Burgess explains to Carol why he now doubts Henderson's guilt: "Only a fool or an innocent man would have stuck to that alibi. A guilty man would have been smarter!"

7 Carol never seems to look back at the right time and catch a glimpse of just how crazy Marlow is.

"An expertly contrived, suspenseful mystery meller developing along usual cinematic lines." *Variety*

5

6

of the approaching train creates the crescendo. Even more stylized and celebrated is Carol's encounter with drummer Cliff Milburn (Elisha Cook, Jr.). With heavy makeup, costume jewelry, and a tight black dress, Carol makes herself into a "hep kitten" to pick up Milburn. Later, as he goes into a frenzied drum riff at an after-hours joint, Siodmak intercuts Milburn with shots of Carol (low-angled and semi-POV) as she laughs and gyrates to drive him to a figurative orgasm that she hopes will make him blurt out the truth.

In a stylistic shift from its literary original, *Phantom Lady* creates a sense of peril and uncertainty for the audience not from what the bartender or Milburn have testified, which they know is false, but from what either man may do after she has egged them on. Because she is empowered, Carol is undeterred by the possibility of being assaulted or raped. The core of that self-reliance is established in the jailhouse meetings between her and Henderson. Permitted physical proximity as they smoke cigarettes together in a barred anteroom, even as a whiny Henderson hangs his head and tells her to forget about him, to abandon him even though he is innocent, her posture and expression confirm that Carol will not give up. It is her determination that will free him, and Siodmak/Bredell situate her in the sequence so that she separates him from the dark bars in the left background and "pushes" him towards the sunlit window, where the bars to freedom are barely visible.

AS

9

8   The demented sculptor Marlow justifies his criminal behavior by saying, "When you've got my gifts you can't afford to let them get away."

9   After Milburn is found dead, Burgess consoles Carol while suggesting that she leave the dangerous work to him.

"With *Phantom Lady*, Siodmak ... established himself as one of the foremost stylists of film noir, creating a somber world of wet streets, dingy offices, low-ceilinged bars, crowded lunch counters and deserted railway platforms, all unified by an atmosphere of heightened realism in which the expressive quality of the image is due entirely to lighting and composition." *Tom Flinn, "Three Faces of Film Noir," in: Film Noir Reader 2*

ROBERT SIODMAK Born in 1900 in Dresden, Germany, Robert Siodmak came to the United States an exile and instantly flourished as a director of Hollywood mysteries duringthe 1940s. Breathing life into pictures like *Phantom Lady* (1944), *The Spiral Staircase* (1945), *The Killers* (1946), and *Criss Cross* (1948), he proved himself a master of film noir, infusing his work with an expressive visual aesthetic and an air of pessimism widely attributed to his German origins. Siodmak first emerged on the directing scene with *People on Sunday* (*Menschen am Sonntag*, 1929), a charming summertime portrait of four young Berliners who spend an ordinary Sunday at the lake. While the film had little in common with Siodmak's later work, one could deem it a precursor to contemporary, independent filmmaking methods that rely on amateur actors and existing locations. Among the famous names directly involved on the project were Siodmak's brother Curt, Billy Wilder, Fred Zinnemann, Eugen Schüfftan, and Edgar G. Ulmer. Traces of the darker aesthetic Siodmak would one day shape into his Hollywood work can be seen in most of his subsequent films, including those he shot for the German UFA Studios and, following the Nazi rise to power, those he made in France. However, one need but view the swashbuckling adventure *The Crimson Pirate*, (1952) to realize that Siodmak's talents weren't limited to film noir. After this film's completion, Siodmak returned to Europe, first resettling in France, then later in Germany. Although *The Devil Strikes at Night* (*Nachts, wenn der Teufel kam*, 1957) was nominated for an Oscar, Siodmak's later pictures hardly live up to the excellence of his earlier work. This may well be a reason why it took so long for his oeuvre to gain the critical acclaim it deserves. Robert Siodmak died in Locarno, in 1973.

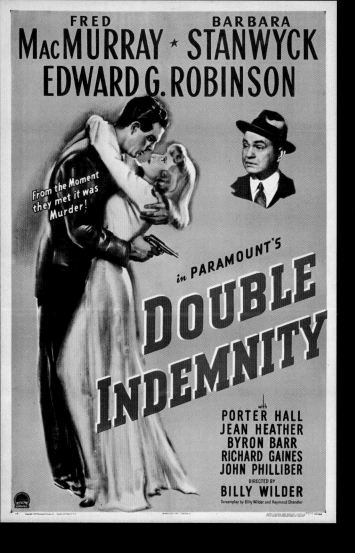

DOUBLE INDEMNITY

1944 – USA – 108 MIN.
DIRECTOR BILLY WILDER (1906–2002)
SCREENPLAY BILLY WILDER, RAYMOND CHANDLER, based
on the novel of the same name by JAMES M. CAIN
DIRECTOR OF PHOTOGRAPHY JOHN F. SEITZ
EDITING DOANE HARRISON MUSIC MIKLÓS RÓZSA
PRODUCTION JOSEPH SISTROM for PARAMOUNT PICTURES
STARRING BARBARA STANWYCK (Phyllis Dietrichson),
FRED MACMURRAY (Walter Neff),
EDWARD G. ROBINSON (Barton Keyes), TOM POWERS
(Mr. Dietrichson), PORTER HALL (Mr. Jackson),
JEAN HEATHER (Lola Dietrichson),
BYRON BARR (Nino Zachetti), RICHARD GAINES
(Mr. Norton), FORTUNIO BONANOVA (Sam Garlopis),
JOHN PHILLIBER (Joe Peters)

"I killed him for the money and the woman, and I didn't get either. Pretty, isn't it?"

A sultry blonde adorned with rings of gold and little else steps into the frame. The light dances on her anklet and wedding band as she strikes a pose in her bath towel from atop the landing, the scent of jasmine trailing down the banister.

Insurance salesman Walter Neff (Fred MacMurray) has caught woman of the house Phyllis Dietrichson (Barbara Stanwyck) at an opportune time – for she's eager to take out an accident insurance policy on her wealthy husband. The problem isn't that Walter can't see right through her diabolical scheme, but rather that murder has never looked this sexy. And thus Phyllis agrees to become Walter's mistress in exchange for a little assistance in what promises to be the perfect crime ...

Film noir reached its zenith with *Double Indemnity*, a picture that made the cinematic transition to the other side of morality a matter of public record. Together with genre great Raymond Chandler, Billy Wilder adapted James M. Cain's identically titled novel for the screen and unleashed a revolutionary,

raw sense of realism that rocked the American cinema. But the real cause for alarm was generated by *Double Indemnity*'s near total disregard of the Production Code's censorship regulations. Infidelity and murder may have been watered down for the mainstream, but their central role in the film's plot caused jaws to drop just the same. Indeed, much of what made the thriller so scandalous was that it dealt with an underworld populated not by gangsters but rather by putatively upstanding citizens who are undone by greed and lust: an insurance salesman and a housewife who conspire to defraud and murder to escape middle-class malaise.

Jarring narrative techniques also kept viewers on edge. Here, the action is prompted by the murderer's recollections shown in flashback. Held at gunpoint in his boss Keyes's (Edward G. Robinson) office, Walter makes an after-hours confession into a Dictaphone. The audience therefore never has the chance to slip into the role of his co-conspirator, because Walter's criminal scheme is one without prospects from the start.

1 Smooth operator: blond, leggy, and cold as ice, femme fatale Phyllis Dietrichson (Barbara Stanwyck) is the ultimate desperate housewife.

2 Tying up the line: Walter (Fred MacMurray) phones Phyllis about her insurance policy to send false signals to boss and confidant Barton Keyes (Edward G. Robinson).

3 Love with a vengeance: Phyllis's loving embrace is just a notch gentler than her death grip.

This subjective telling is made all the more unnerving by Wilder's refusal to idealize his unlikely protagonist. Rather than building him up to be a hopeless romantic or a slave to his heart, the film opts to make him sickeningly conventional. Walter's front of masculinity cannot disguise how limited both his world view and life's horizons are. He's the type of guy who'd never accept a well-paying yet drab desk job simply because he so desperately needs the pathetic sense of spontaneity that the door-to-door business offers; even a little hanky panky with a frustrated housewife is more excitement than Walter usually gets. Which is why when Phyllis turns on the charm, the sales-

man willingly sells her his soul as if he were handing it over to a Hollywood pinup.

John Seitz's cinematography maneuvers us through the characteristic film noir lighting design, heightening *Double Indemnity*'s sense of doom. The stark, expressionist use of light and dark visually imprisons Walter as shadows from the blinds trap him like jail bars; likewise, the camera inhibits his ability to move freely by submersing him in a sea of darkness. If there were any doubts to the contrary, Miklós Rózsa's menacing score assures the viewer that Walter's is not to be a happy ending.

"The darkest film noir of them all." *Neue Zürcher Zeitung*

As director Billy Wilder follows this murderous couple on their blood-stained path, he proves that uncompromising cynicism and black comedy are not mutually exclusive. In fact, their synthesis makes *Double Indemnity*'s skeptical examination of American society all the more effective: apparently unfazed by the police, Phyllis and Walter's secret rendezvous at the super-market has them afraid that ordinary citizens might be on to them. Yet no matter how paranoid this logic, it hits on the idea of being trapped in a sub-urban hell – with the way out losing all appeal once the couple's plan back-fires. *Double Indemnity* is the story of Walter's grand screwup and is thus a portrait of pathos. His delay in coming to his senses only makes his countless flaws that much clearer. Conversely, the conviction with which Phyllis ignores morality altogether gives her character a certain grandeur. And with those merciless eyes that never flinch, Barbara Stanwyck is the unequivocal iron maiden of film noir *femmes fatales.*

JH

4   Don't move a muscle: although apartment doors normally open inward, Wilder takes artistic license to heighten the suspense.

5   That last step is a doozy: Walter ignores the signs and suffers a great fall.

"Along with Orson Welles' *Citizen Kane*, *Double Indemnity* is the boldest, most sinister and most disturbing Hollywood movie of the '40s ... A phantasmagoria of a film; a study of the confusion, desperation and violence that lurks in each and every one of us; a coal-black vision of loneliness, fear and death." *Frankfurter Rundschau*

EDWARD G. ROBINSON   As insurance investigator Barton Keyes, Edward G. Robinson plays a boss who's ready to put in overtime to look out for Walter Neff's (Fred MacMurray) personal welfare in *Double Indemnity* (1944). Robinson's slight stature made him seem like the small American businessman come to life, which gave further credibility to his die-hard efforts at scrimping and saving where insurance claims are concerned.

With his wide mouth and lack of neck, Robinson (1893–1973) bore a more than passing resemblance to a feisty human bulldog. As gangster boss Rico in Mervyn LeRoy's *Little Caesar* (1931), he was the personification of animal aggression; the film itself not only propelled the actor to stardom in the early years of sound, but also launched a wave of Hollywood gangster pictures. Robinson's name soon became synonymous with the genre and expertly nuanced character studies, even in earlier hits like Howard Hawks's *Tiger Shark* (1932) or Roy Del Ruth's *The Little Giant* (1933).

Be that as it may, his real chance to show off his acting range came in the '40s. In addition to his achievement in *Double Indemnity*, he took the screen by storm in Michael Curtiz's *The Sea Wolf* (1941), Fritz Lang's *The Woman in the Window* (1944) and *Scarlet Street* (1945), as well as John Huston's *Key Largo* (1948). Robinson was one of the studio era's leading talents and continued to work in the industry until the end of his life. The Academy of Motion Pictures Arts and Sciences recognized his contribution to film with an honorary Oscar for Lifetime Achievement, awarded posthumously just shortly after his death.

GASLIGHT ♟♟

1944 – USA – 114 MIN.
DIRECTOR GEORGE CUKOR (1899–1983)
SCREENPLAY JOHN VAN DRUTEN, WALTER REISCH,
JOHN L. BALDERSTON, based on the play
Angel Street by PATRICK HAMILTON
DIRECTOR OF PHOTOGRAPHY JOSEPH RUTTENBERG
EDITING RALPH E. WINTERS **MUSIC** BRONISLAU KAPER
PRODUCTION ARTHUR HORNBLOW JR. for MGM
STARRING CHARLES BOYER (Gregory Anton),
INGRID BERGMAN (Paula Alquist), JOSEPH COTTEN
(Brian Cameron), ANGELA LANSBURY (Nancy Oliver),
BARBARA EVEREST (Elizabeth Tompkins),
DAME MAY WHITTY (Miss Thwaites), EMIL RAMEAU
(Maestro Mario Guardi), EDMUND BREON
(Huddleston), TOM STEVENSON (Williams),
HALLIWELL HOBBES (Mr. Muffin)
ACADEMY AWARDS 1944 OSCARS for BEST LEADING ACTRESS
(Ingrid Bergman), and BEST ART DIRECTION /
SET DECORATION (Cedric Gibbons,
William Ferrari, Edwin B. Willis, Paul Huldschinsky)

"They never found out who killed her."

A dark shadow hovers over the house at No. 9 Thornton Square. Years ago, famed singer Alice Alquist was found dead within its walls – murdered in her own London home. Traumatized by the gruesome event, her then adolescent niece Paula (Ingrid Bergman) left British shores to start a new life. But you can't run away from the past forever…

Urged on by her husband, pianist Gregory Anton (Charles Boyer), newlywed Paula decides to face the city of her childhood and the residence she so fears. Before long it becomes clear that darling Gregory is up to no good. Although the growing concern he expresses for Paula's welfare is void of sincerity, his words still manage to convince the staff that Madame isn't well. Objects around the house begin to disappear, allegedly the result of Paula's 'absentmindedness.' Gregory finds one pretense after another to forbid his wife from going outside, and the demons of the past gradually work their magic on her. Unbeknownst to anyone, Paula has become her husband's prisoner and is hanging onto her sanity by a thread. Is someone really pacing around the attic night after night? Why does the gaslight dim every time Gregory leaves the house? Only Scotland Yard official Brian Cameron (Joseph Cotten) suspects the truth, and he decides to reopen the case file on the unsolved murder of Lady Alquist…

Gaslight is based on *Angel Street*, a hit play by Patrick Hamilton which premiered on the London stage in 1939. In 1940, filmmaker Thorold Dickinson brought the first version of *Gaslight* to the British screen, and the crowds went wild. When MGM later obtained the rights for an American production, it attempted to destroy all the prints of the existing piece and market its own as a masterful original.

There is much speculation as to how the second version would have differed had Hitchcock directed it. Rather like *Rebecca* (1940), *Gaslight* focuses on a house that takes possession of its inhabitants – a favorite device in gothic horror. With contemporary audiences sure to unearth Gregory's cruel intentions, the ins-and-outs of 19th-century living present the only real mystery. Still, a diabolical villain is always a welcome guest, and Gregory's determination to get his hands on Aunt Alice's jewel collection doesn't disappoint us in the least; he'd pull the nails out of every floorboard in the attic to get those gems.

"For Cukor, the superficial crime story and the historical setting were merely an excuse for a meticulous study of how one human being gains power over another. It's an act that can only succeed in almost perfect isolation. The film's tension derives from the way in which Gregory Anton spins a net around his unsuspecting wife Paula; as time passes, she is increasingly trapped."

Reclams Filmführer

1 Curling up to a good mystery: all the warm milk in the world can't put Paula's (Ingrid Bergman) mind at ease.

3 Sending chills down her spine: at Gregory's request, Paula's staff works overtime to make sure she loses her marbles.

4 Through the looking glass: as a prisoner in her own home, Paula sees the outside world as a virtual wonderland.

2 Top hat and tales: Gregory (Charles Boyer) sows the seeds of insanity in his wife's head.

But we shouldn't forget that this film is a drama as much as it is a thriller. "Women's director" George Cukor uses his remake to elaborate on the original's examination of married life's everyday horrors. Gregory torments his wife into believing that she's suffering from a "classic case" of hysteria, cutting her off from the outside world while feigning emotional support and undying love. This premeditated conditioning plants the seeds of psychosis, and she becomes increasingly insecure and dependent.

Paula, surprisingly, puts up much less of a fight when it comes to asserting her will than one would have expected with Cukor. That said, the part still won Ingrid Bergman the first of her three Oscars, as the Academy repented snubbing her performance in *Casablanca* (1942) three years earlier. The role allowed her to demonstrate an awe-inspiring intensity that isn't so much rooted in insanity as in the fear of going insane. Bergman spent time at a clinic for the mentally disturbed in order to adopt the physical behavior and facial expressions of a schizophrenic, but more impressive still is the way in which she managed to break free of her obligation to independent producer David O. Selznick and sign up for a project opposite Charles Boyer, who, as the premiere French star of the day, always got top billing. In addition to boasting an impeccable supporting performance from Joseph Cotten, *Gaslight* was the picture that brought the then 18-year-old

PATRICK HAMILTON One of the foremost writers of low-life London of the 1920s and 1930s, Patrick Hamilton's greatest novel is *Hangover Square* (1941), the story of brilliant, schizophrenic composer George Harvey Bone, whose mind slowly disintegrates as he is continually deceived by the woman he desires. John Brahm's 1945 film version has a quite brilliant sequence where, on Guy Fawkes Night, George carries the lifeless body of a prostitute over his shoulder, through the streets, and eventually deposits her on top of an enormous bonfire.
Hamilton (1904–1962) began a quartet of novels about Mr. Ernest Ralph Gorse, beginning with *The West Pier* (1951), followed by *Mr. Stimpson and Mr. Gorse* (1953) (the basis for the 1987 U.K. TV-series *The Charmer*), and *Unknown Assailant* (1955). The fourth book was never completed due to Hamilton's drinking and emotional problems. Gorse uses his charmingly smooth veneer to woo women, seduce them, and then take their money. Although Gorse succeeds in both emotionally and financially destroying his victims, we never see his comeuppance. Hamilton is most famous for two stage plays. *Rope* (1929), filmed by Alfred Hitchcock in 1948 and based on the notorious Leopold-Loeb case, is the story of two students who decide to kill someone to prove their superiority over the rest of the human race. *Gas Light* (1938), filmed by George Cukor in 1944, is the story of a thief who slowly turns his wife insane as he desperately searches the house for the rubies he hid there.

Angela Lansbury to the screen. As Nancy, the chambermaid who does Gregory's evil bidding, Lansbury doesn't bear a trace of her television alter-ego Jessica Fletcher, the ever-so-curious heroine of *Murder, She Wrote* (1984–1996).

Up there with the world-class acting is the austere house on Thornton Square, which becomes a player in its own right. As if caged in by the residence, both mistress and story line rarely venture beyond its walls. Cukor's masterful decoration of the rooms intensifies the plot, with the number of Victorian knickknacks seeming to multiply as Paula becomes more and more oppressed by her memories. A constant reminder of her precarious mental state, the flickering gaslight rises above the London fog like a sinister illusion that has increasingly little to do with reality.　　　　PB

"Ravishingly beautiful, on the verge of madness, and misled in every sense of the term, Ingrid Bergman to some extent becomes Lucia de Lammermoor, the heroine of the opera she had been studying. Shadowy beauties, the two of them. Meanwhile, like Jekyll and Hyde, Joseph Cotten and Charles Boyer embody good and evil, the opposing moral principles. The time was ripe for such black fables, and Cukor deployed his cultural memory to good effect." *Le Monde*

5   Murder, she swept: Nancy the chambermaid (Angela Lansbury) hopes to get promoted by doing the master's dirty work.

6   Can't end on a good note: Gregory plays a concerto that puts his singer wife and her vocal coach (Emil Rameau) at odds.

7   Two can play at that game: Paula tries her own hand at bondage.

"How a young Scotland Yard detective uncovers the real identity of the husband and killer, after the latter has plotted to have his young wife committed to an asylum so that he can have a freer rein in his search of the house, forms an exciting climax." *Variety*

LAURA ♟

1944 – USA – 88 MIN.
DIRECTOR OTTO PREMINGER (1905–1986)
SCREENPLAY JAY DRATLER, SAMUEL HOFFENSTEIN,
ELIZABETH REINHARDT, based on the novel of
the same name by VERA CASPARY
DIRECTOR OF PHOTOGRAPHY JOSEPH LASHELLE
EDITING LOUIS R. LOEFFLER MUSIC DAVID RAKSIN
PRODUCTION OTTO PREMINGER for 20TH CENTURY FOX
STARRING GENE TIERNEY (Laura Hunt), DANA ANDREWS
(Mark McPherson), CLIFTON WEBB (Waldo Lydecker),
VINCENT PRICE (Shelby Carpenter), JUDITH ANDERSON
(Ann Treadwell), DOROTHY ADAMS (Bessie Clary),
JAMES FLAVIN (McEveety), CLYDE FILLMORE (Bullitt),
RALPH DUNN (Fred Callahan), JOHN DEXTER (Artist)
ACADEMY AWARDS 1944 OSCAR for BEST CINEMATOGRAPHY
(Joseph LaShelle)

"I shall never forget the weekend Laura died."

Police detective Mark McPherson (Dana Andrews) has been assigned to investigate the murder of Laura Hunt (Gene Tierney), a *femme fatale* found dead in her New York apartment. No sooner does McPherson make the acquaintance of former suitors Waldo Lydecker (Clifton Webb), an eccentric society journalist who acted as Laura's publicist, and Shelby Carpenter (Vincent Price), her hedonistic fiancé, than the two illustrious men become the case's prime suspects. Solving the crime becomes an obsession, and before he knows it McPherson has fallen captive to the victim's lurid charms. Then, one night, the investigation takes an unexpected turn. Exhausted after yet another fruitless search of the flat, the detective dozes off in an armchair opposite a life-size portrait of the dead woman. When he awakens, Laura is standing before him – in the flesh.

What happened behind the scenes is no less fantastic than the movie's premise. What started off as creative tension between Otto Preminger and studio boss Darryl F. Zanuck escalated into a ringside attraction. Preminger was the project's great champion and eager to direct it, but his talents as a producer inhibited Zanuck from considering the option. When push came to shove a month into filming, Zanuck gave in and filmmaker Rouben Mamoulian was removed from the set. But from that point on, the 20th Century Fox mogul made sure nothing happened during the shoot without his knowing about it. Thus, despite being Otto Preminger's directorial breakthrough, it is not clear how much Mamoulian and Zanuck contributed to the final result. Long regarded as one of film noir's brightest diamonds, the film bears no trace of that artistic conflict. With formal principles as lush and elegant as its deca-

GENE TIERNEY As one of the most striking and sophisticated beauties in 1940s Hollywood, Gene Tierney (1920–1991) made an ideal *Laura* (1944). The actress with raven hair, chiseled features, and a winning smile grew up in an affluent Brooklyn family that didn't spare any expense when it came to young Gene. Her father not only sent her to the best schools, but used his position to help further her theatrical ambitions. Indeed, Mr. Tierney saw to it that his daughter was a Broadway fixture by the age of 19. It was there that she caught the eye of Darryl F. Zanuck, who put her under contract with 20th Century Fox and championed her career. Just months later, Gene Tierney was a Fox headliner.

Initially paired with the leading filmmakers of the age, Tierney produced some of her best work early on in pictures like Fritz Lang's *The Return of Frank James* (1940), John Ford's *Tobacco Road* (1941), Josef von Sternberg's *The Shanghai Gesture* (1941), and Ernst Lubitsch's *Heaven Can Wait* (1943). Of equal caliber are the pictures that made her a Hollywood legend: after her incomparable performance as *Laura*, Tierney played a young widow who falls in love with Rex Harrison's seafaring spirit in Joseph L. Mankiewicz's *The Ghost and Mrs. Muir* (1947). Although the actress's angelic aura often led her to be typecast as the virtuous romantic lead, she also astonished audiences as one of film noir's most venomous *femmes fatales* in John M. Stahl's *Leave Her to Heaven* (1945).

An ongoing battle with depression led Tierney to withdraw from Hollywood and seek full-time psychiatric help. She returned to acting in 1962, but never regained her A-list status. Tierney died in Houston, Texas, in 1991.

1   Dead meet: Laura (Gene Tierney) comes back to life as Detective McPherson's (Dana Andrews) dream girl.

2   Thriller nights: Vincent Price's (left) on-screen interludes with Gene Tierney are even more of a scream than his legendary work in Roger Corman's horror pictures.

3   Center of attention: *Laura*'s narrator, Waldo Lydecker (Clifton Webb), steps out of the shadows and ends up caught between a rock and a hard place.

> ## "First and foremost, *Laura* is a love poem addressed to Gene Tierney, the most beautiful and enigmatic Hollywood actress of her day." *Süddeutsche Zeitung*

dent cast of characters, *Laura* continues to capture the imagination of contemporary viewers. Joseph LaShelle's subtle cinematography submerges the neurotic, borderline necrophiliac romance in a dream logic that suspends the protagonist in an otherworldly realm. At first it's as if the camera were doing the narrator's secret bidding, hanging on his eloquent words and punctuating them with action. Like a brush, the voice — Waldo's voice — paints a portrait of Laura that shimmers with mystery, radiance, and a life of its own; stroke for stroke, McPherson gets to know the journalist's lyric muse and falls in love with her.

Yet the more time the film spends at McPherson's side, the more infrequent the narration. And once Waldo has been lured out of hiding altogether, he is exposed for the leech that he is. Neither omniscient nor almighty, Waldo's blinding jealousy not only causes him to kill a woman he mistakes for Laura, but also ends up costing him his life. The death of the narrator is illogical but not inconsistent. Laura, like Petrarch's eponymous ideal woman, is born of Waldo's memories. She is his creation, his dream girl, and thus her physical return compromises her status as an ideal. She is incapable of living up to his expectations, simply by virtue of being human. And Waldo would rather see her dead than let the imperfections of human existence rob him of his beloved delusion. By concluding with Waldo's death, the film rejects the era's prevailing cinematic constructs of femininity. The moment Laura physically breaks free of Waldo's grip, she symbolically jumps off the pedestal he has created for her and shows, in effect, that she will not be confined to classic Hollywood's subjective view of women.

4   Overexposure: Laura doesn't like the way men in Hollywood have been looking at her.

5   Portrait of a lady: as is so often the case in film noir, McPherson surrenders his heart to a pinup.

6   Characters in search of an author: Lydecker's death at the end of the picture leaves the story without a narrator and is a testament to Otto Preminger's extravagant direction.

7   Her ominous, posh suitors: both these guys have their sights on sampling Laura's earthly delights.

But before it denounces the elitist writer's fantasy as violent, oppressive, and false, Preminger's film explores its seductive potential. Never once do we leave McPherson's side as he succumbs to the idealized Laura, played to perfection by the lovely Gene Tierney. And thus the rude awakening shakes the audience as much as it does McPherson when Laura reveals herself to be alive. The event, however, ultimately marks the film's second coming, with David Raksin's unforgettable score transforming the film from a mystery to a brilliant romance. Laura's miraculous resurrection may be nothing more than a gross display of mistaken identity, yet, without it, love couldn't triumph over death. But as real life grants few such victories, it's hard to be certain whether McPherson woke up at all.

JH

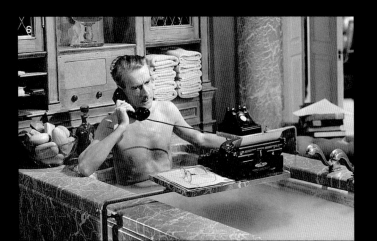

> **"I must say, for a charming, intelligent girl, you certainly surrounded yourself with remarkable collection of dopes."**
>
> *Mark McPherson (Dana Andrews)*

"Producer-director Otto Preminger, screenwriters Sam Hoffenstein, Jay Dratler and Betty Reinhardt, and a good cast, have combined to keep an audience intensely absorbed in a guessing game for 88 minutes, without feeling let down at the end. That's good storytelling." *Variety*

THE WOMAN IN THE WINDOW

1944 – USA – 99 MIN.
DIRECTOR FRITZ LANG (1890–1976)
SCREENPLAY NUNNALLY JOHNSON, based on the novel
Once Off Guard by J. H. WALLIS
DIRECTOR OF PHOTOGRAPHY MILTON KRASNER
EDITING GENE FOWLER JR., MARJORIE JOHNSON
[= MARJORIE FOWLER]
MUSIC ARTHUR LANGE PRODUCTION NUNNALLY JOHNSON
for INTERNATIONAL PICTURES INC.
STARRING EDWARD G. ROBINSON (Professor Richard
Wanley), JOAN BENNETT (Alice Reed),
RAYMOND MASSEY (Frank Lalor), EDMUND BREON
(Doctor Michael Barkstane), DAN DURYEA (Heidt / Tim,
The Bouncer), THOMAS E. JACKSON (Inspector
Jackson), DOROTHY PETERSON (Mrs. Wanley),
ARTHUR LOFT (Claude Mazard / Charlie,
The Coat Check Attendant), FRANK DAWSON (Collins,
The Steward), ROBERT BLAKE (Dickie Wanley)

"The circle's closing in on me!"

Much to the chagrin of the critics but to the relief of the protagonist, the actual woman in the window is, as first suspected, a figment of the hero's imagination. German cinema's favorite son, Fritz Lang (*Metropolis*, 1927; *M* [*M – Eine Stadt sucht einen Mörder*, 1931]), might have opted to stick to the classic film noir formula and not let Professor Richard Wanley off the hook, had he not been a hopeless romantic. The Hollywood censors also factored into the equation, requiring many a Hollywood production to tack on a fairy-tale ending. Thankfully, in this case, even a poor excuse for a Tinseltown Band-Aid can't stop the sting of an hour and a half of nonstop suspense. But let's save the soap box for another occasion: right now, we've got a murder on our hands.

Richard Wanley (Edward G. Robinson), a by-the-book psychology professor, is utterly captivated by the portrait of a lady (Joan Bennett) situated in a storefront window next to the men's club he frequents. In his weekly circle, we eavesdrop on the fears of middle-aged men, whose afternoon conversations cover a range of subjects from impotency to feeling ignored by the opposite sex. On his way home one evening, Wanley stops to admire the woman in the window when a living reflection of the face he so loves sud-

denly appears next to it. At first, the professor believes he is witnessing the woman's genesis, rather than an optical illusion. However, even when he learns that he has, in fact, caught a glimpse of the person who stood for the picture, he can't stop thinking about their mystical encounter. Acting on an encouraging word from his friends at the club, the academic takes advantage of his wife's being away on holiday and gets to know the beauty in black a bit more intimately. The *femme fatale*'s name is Alice, and Wanley all too willingly accepts an invitation up to her apartment – a mistake to say the least. For after a few brief moments alone with her, another man walks in on them and bursts into a jealous rage. Acting in self-defense, Wanley stabs the intruder with the pair of scissors Alice hands him in the nick of time. Yet by warding off his own death, the professor has become a murderer.

In *The Woman in the Window*, psychoanalytic and art historical threads are expertly interwoven into the exposition. We seem to be looking into Wanley's subconscious from the start – evidence that the whole tale is indeed a waking dream. Wanley's lecture about how the modern criminal justice system treats killers comes across as a premonition of his fate, while references to the theories of Sigmund Freud, the Ten Commandments,

3

1 Death catches loan shark Claude Mazard (Arthur Loft) off guard.

2 Opportunity knocks: Heidt (Dan Duryea) puts insider information to good use and blackmails murderess Alice Reed (Joan Bennett) for every cent she's got.

3 Crimes and misdemeanors: Professor Wanley (Edward G. Robinson) commits a traffic violation while trying to dispose of Claude Mazard's body.

4 Tampering with evidence: try though they might, there's no cutting the umbilical cord that links Alice and Prof. Wanley.

"Its rhythm is deliberately, mercilessly, unhurried. With deceptive calm, this film persists in the phase of exposition long after we have come to realize that something terrible is bound to happen." *Filmkritik*

and the Romantic conception of the dual nature of reality accompany the films darkly meandering exploration of the borders between reality and the imagination.

Still, what really grabs our attention is Lang's tight *mise-en-scène*. We struggle to keep up with unlikely murderer Richard Wanley and his accomplice Alice Reed as they dodge the law by fleeing to the underworld, from the disposal of the corpse via the criminal investigation, right up to a run-in with Heidt (Dan Duryea), the gangster bodyguard of the deceased who blackmails the couple in exchange for his silence. The thrills and suspense culminate with Wanley poisoning himself to escape the unbearable pressure.

Nevertheless, the caper remains utterly realistic thanks to Fritz Lang's enthusiasm for modern technology. Dark limousines, wild car chases, high-

"The story fundamentals are not exactly original, but they are paraded with such a fine sense of the dramatic and such careful regard for logic that it acquires a very new, exciting twist." *Kinematograph Weekly*

5 On the cutting edge: when it comes to malice, watch out for Alice.

6 Pretty as a picture: a temptress comes to life and beguiles a man into abandoning a world where nothing ever happens.

> "When the blackmailer (Duryea) makes his move, the fatal suspense becomes a paralyzing numbness – the viscous flow of images grows even more sluggish." *Filmkritik*

impact collisions, mass media, advertising, scientific method, over-the-counter drugs, and even traffic signals all become awe-inspiring phenomena in his hands. Last but not least, a borderline manic fixation with time itself argues for a realistic reading of the film as clocks of every shape and size dominate the screen. We can be certain of only one thing: Wanley's fight for survival is, above all else, a race against time. And when time finally does run out, nothing will ever be the same again ...

BR

FRITZ LANG Fritz Lang (1890–1976) ranks among names like Friedrich Wilhelm Murnau and Georg Wilhelm Pabst as one of the most renowned German-speaking filmmakers. A native of Vienna, he studied painting in his hometown before completing his conservatory education in Munich and Paris. Following a brief military career during World War I, Lang started working as a screenwriter and director with the German production company Decla. His directorial debut came in 1919 with the silent *The Half-Caste (Halbblut)*. In 1921, his picture *Destiny (Der müde Tod – Ein Deutsches Volkslied in sechs Versen)* gave him his first real taste of success. Nonetheless, it was with the seminal *Metropolis* (1927) and *M* (*M – Eine Stadt sucht einen Mörder*, 1931) that Lang left his mark on film history.
His films show clear traces of his roots in architecture, painting, and graphic design. Monumental set pieces, expert lighting design, paintings, and ominous shadows became the insignia of his work. After relocating to Hollywood in the '30s, Lang continued to make films about people surviving against all odds, although he was forced to up the action and sense of realism in his pictures to comply with local tastes. In view of his cinematic predilections, it comes as no surprise that many of the projects he was entrusted with were later grouped under the umbrella of film noir (*Scarlet Street*, 1945; *The Big Heat*, 1953; *Beyond a Reasonable Doubt*, 1956). Lang's retirement from the industry followed a failed attempt to reenter German cinema during the '50s.

MURDER, MY SWEET

1944 – USA – 92 MIN.
DIRECTOR EDWARD DMYTRYK (1908–1999)
SCREENPLAY JOHN PAXTON, based on the novel
Farewell, My Lovely by RAYMOND CHANDLER
DIRECTOR OF PHOTOGRAPHY HARRY J. WILD
EDITING JOSEPH NORIEGA MUSIC ROY WEBB
PRODUCTION ADRIAN SCOTT for RKO
STARRING DICK POWELL (Philip Marlowe),
CLAIRE TREVOR (Velma Valento / Mrs. Helen Grayle),
ANNE SHIRLEY (Ann Grayle), OTTO KRUGER
(Jules Amthor), MIKE MAZURKI (Moose Malloy),
MILES MANDER (Mr. Grayle),
DOUGLAS WALTON (Lindsay Marriott),
DONALD DOUGLAS (Lieutenant Randall),
RALF HAROLDE (Dr. Sonderborg),
ESTHER HOWARD (Jessie Florian)

"You shouldn't kiss a girl when you're wearing a gun. It leaves a bruise."

Contrary to popular belief, there are not many noir films that actually feature private eyes, only about a dozen, and almost half of those are adaptations of hard-boiled writer Raymond Chandler that feature his signature character Philip Marlowe. Although *Farewell, My Lovely* (and *The High Window*) had already been made into films, both early versions were reshaped for other PIs, so *Murder, My Sweet* and its star, Dick Powell, are the first onscreen incarnation of Marlowe. Maybe that's why Chandler himself had a soft spot for Powell over other actors that later portrayed his character. As director Edward Dmytryk saw it, "[Marlowe] can be physically strong, but there's something soft inside about him. That's what makes Dick Powell the best of all the Philip Marlowes. Spade was tough, and that's what was wrong with Bogey doing Marlowe. He made him Spade."

After RKO's radical transformation of Chandler and Marlowe in *The Falcon Takes Over* (1942), hundreds of thousands of paperback copies of Chandler books had been sold (or given away to troops fighting World War II), including more than a million of *Farewell, My Lovely*. So a remake that restored Marlowe as a character was a fiscally sound decision for the studio. For Dmytryk, producer Adrian Scott, and star Powell – who reteamed the next year for the noir *Cornered* (1945) – *Murder, My Sweet* was a career opportunity, a minor A picture with a literary pedigree that guaranteed a built-in following through which crooner Powell and the B-unit filmmakers could redefine their career tracks. Although he "never considered himself a stylist," director Dmytryk in particular seized his chance to make an impression and, in hindsight, took full credit for the results: "As for that style which you've

1 Even as he lights her cigarette, Philip Marlowe's (Dick Powell) expression suggests he has doubts about the sincerity of a coiffed and bejeweled Mrs. Grayle (Claire Trevor).

2 The flashback begins as a blinded Philip Marlowe is questioned by Los Angeles detective Lieutenant Randall (Don Douglas, right) and one of his stolid minions.

3 "Moose. The name is Moose. On account of I'm large." Mike Mazurki as the large "Moose" Malloy towers over both Marlowe and Amthor (Otto Kruger, left).

been talking about as noir, as far as RKO is concerned, I think I had a very definite part in it, [that] honestly we started that style. A cameraman contributes what you ask him to. Before he shot *Murder, My Sweet*, Harry Wild had been doing Westerns and B pictures with pretty flat lighting. I made a low-key cameraman out of him, and after that he did a lot of low-key work."

Dmytryk undeniably succeeded in infusing the film with a noir style and drawing critical attention to his work, which as much as anything involved integrating all the creative resources. That begins with the first frame and the RKO logo, where instead of the regular radio telegraph sounds, the underscore by Roy Webb is heard. The minor key phrasing and the ominous strings are reminiscent of the approach used that same year by Victor Young and Miklós Rózsa at Paramount. In the first sequence (a change from the novel, it opens with Marlowe meeting Moose Malloy), angry voices are heard as the camera pans down from a ceiling fixture to reveal Powell with a bandage around his eyes surrounded by a group of annoyed cops and about to explain what happened. This telling change adds a new level of tension and irony (will Marlowe regain his eyesight?), even as the flashback format compels the viewer to share the character's frame of reference. John Paxton's script retains much of Chandler's dialogue and also incorporates snippets of his first-person prose, which is transformed into voice-over narration, again a "normal" element for the audience in the context of a flashback keyed to a particular person. This conceit permits the filmmakers to inject vocally into *Murder, My Sweet* the colorful and wry commentary for which Chandler was renowned.

When Marlowe interviews Mrs. Florian (Esther Howard) and plies her with liquor, Powell's voice-over notes that she "was a charming middle-aged lady with a face like a bucket of mud. I gave her a drink. She was a gal who'd take a drink, if she had to knock you down to get to the bottle." That's pure Chandler. One of the best-known sequences in the movie uses optical special effects to render a moment when Marlowe is hit with a black jack: "A black pool opened up at my feet. I dived in. It had no bottom. I felt pretty good. Like an amputated leg." Again the surreal visuals here and the expressionistic lighting throughout are justified because they are subjective, externalizations of what Marlowe has seen, heard, and felt.

> **"Plot ramifications may not stand up under clinical study, but suspense is built up sharply and quickly. In fact, the film gets off to so jet-pulsed a start that it necessarily hits a couple of slow stretches midway as it settles into uniform groove. But interest never flags, and the mystery is never really cleared up until the punchy closing."** *Variety*

3

4 & 5 The least sinister relationship in this film noir is between the cynical but chivalrous Marlowe and "good girl" Ann Grayle (Anne Shirley), who is trying to protect her father. Former child star Shirley married producer Adrian Scott and retired from acting after this movie.

6 In a classic denouement *femme fatale* Mrs. Grayle confesses that she was once Moose's girl Velma but plans to send Marlowe to his grave with that information.

7 Before Velma can pull the trigger Ann and her father (Miles Mander, left) arrive at his beach house to discover his treacherous wife, her gun, and Marlowe, once again in need of rescue.

The other A-level actor in *Murder, My Sweet* is Claire Trevor, and her incarnation of the smooth Mrs. Grayle is one of the earliest *femmes fatales* in noir. Character actors with distinctive looks and inflections, from Otto Kruger as the suave and shady doctor Amthor to Mike Mazurki as the giant Moose Malloy, complete the collection of characters that easily transfer from Chandler's hard-boiled universe to the underworld of film noir. Dmytryk overstates a bit when he talks about how "we started that style," but coming as it did early in the classic period, *Murder, My Sweet* indisputably influenced many examples of *femme fatales*, POV, and the atmosphere of paranoia that came later in film noir.

AS

"There's no question that *Murder, My Sweet* started a trend, set a style, that was continued up to the present day. The funny thing was that the original title was *Farewell, My Lovely*. They released it as *Farewell, My Lovely* in New England states, in a few theaters, and everybody thought it was a musical because of Dick Powell and nobody went to see it. That's why we changed the title to *Murder, My Sweet*, so nobody would have any doubt that it wasn't a musical."

Edward Dmytryk, in: Film Noir Reader 3

RAYMOND CHANDLER Although born in Chicago (*1888), Chandler spent his childhood in Great Britain. While in London Chandler hoped to become a poet and worked briefly as a journalist, but became a civil servant to earn a living. Eventually he returned to the U.S. and, after service in the Canadian army during World War I, settled in Los Angeles, where he spent a decade in the financial department of an oil company until his drinking and fraternization with female co-workers got him fired.

Somehow Chandler decided that he could go on the wagon and support himself and his wife by writing pulp fiction. He chose the mystery genre and in another decade had become a well-known if only modestly paid success. When he was hired by Paramount for the lavish sum of $750 per week to co-adapt *Double Indemnity* (1944) with Billy Wilder, Chandler began his love-hate relationship with Hollywood. Already disgruntled over "a contract of almost unparalleled stupidity on the part of my New York agent" that had sold *Farewell, My Lovely* in perpetuity for a mere $2,000, Chandler struggled through contract assignments at the studio and started drinking again. To get the script to *The Blue Dahlia* (1946) out of him, producer John Houseman let Chandler work at home and kept him supplied with liquor. Now making decent money on his latest novel, when Paramount offered him $2,000 per week to renew his contract and write, produce, and even direct anything he wanted, Chandler turned them down flat. He worked for a while at MGM on the script of *Lady in the Lake* (1947), the only adaptation of his own fiction to which he contributed, but quit that also. He moved south to La Jolla, a coastal community to which Chandler compelled Alfred Hitchcock to travel to discuss his work on *Strangers on a Train* (1951), a story that Chandler thought implausible. After the death of his wife Cissy in 1954, Chandler's depression led him to drink, and an attempted suicide, before his death in 1959.

HANGOVER SQUARE

1945 – USA – 77 MIN.
DIRECTOR JOHN BRAHM (1893–1982)
SCREENPLAY BARRÉ LYNDON, based on the novel of
the same name by PATRICK HAMILTON
DIRECTOR OF PHOTOGRAPHY JOSEPH LASHELLE
EDITING HARRY REYNOLDS MUSIC BERNARD HERRMANN
PRODUCTION ROBERT BASSLER for 20TH CENTURY FOX
STARRING LAIRD CREGAR (George Harvey Bone),
LINDA DARNELL (Netta Longdon),
GEORGE SANDERS (Dr. Allan Middleton),
GLENN LANGAN (Eddie Carstairs), FAYE MARLOWE
(Barbara Chapman), ALAN NAPIER
(Sir Henry Chapman), J. W. AUSTIN (Det. Insp. King),
CHARLES COLEMAN (Man at Bonfire),
FRANCIS FORD (Ogilby),
J. FARRELL MACDONALD (Street Vendor),
FREDERICK WORLOCK (Supt. Clay)

"All my life I've had little black moods."

Although his movies, which stretched from 1936 to 1967, have largely been ignored by film historians until recently, director John Brahm nevertheless left a body of work that demonstrates a consistency of style as well as an obsessive fixation on the image of the powerful if conflicted *femme fatale* archetype in film noir. In addition, Brahm, like many of his contemporary noir directors, whether consciously or unconsciously, investigated the issue of feminine power and the ways in which the patriarchy attempts to limit or even destroy that power. Actor Laird Cregar, in collaboration with Brahm and writer Barré Lyndon, forged with *The Lodger* (1944) and its companion piece, *Hangover Square*, two classics of the noir period.

In *Hangover Square*, as Netta (the name invokes the unfaithful wife in the Leoncavallo opera *Pagliacci*), actress Linda Darnell (debuting in this film)

mounts the stage of a seedy Edwardian music hall, where she displays her long legs as she sings an innuendo-laden ditty to an audience of drunken men. Her provocative nature as well as her disdain for the men in the audience infuse her performance onstage and off. As Netta moves to the backstage area to meet her lover / composer, she expresses her contempt for the audience as well as for the mediocre music she is forced to sing. She, like any self-respecting *femme fatale*, has ambition.

That ambition finally finds its tool in the person of the emotionally crippled classical composer George Harvey Bone (played in his last performance with typical sympathy and depth by Laird Cregar). Like a siren, she keeps him in line with promises and brief kisses. And when he begins to stray back to the world of his beloved piano piece, "Concerto Macabro" (an emotionally tor-

1　Actor Laird Cregar, with his soulful eyes, projects the tormented, conflicted nature of the alienated composer George Harvey Bone.

2　Bone is no match for the siren Netta (Linda Darnell) and her languorous legs as she puts the pressure on the classical composer to become her "house" songsmith.

"The late Laird Cregar, brilliant and touching in his embodiment of the hero's anguished, innocent, dangerous confusion, will leave cinema addicts pondering sadly on the major roles he might have played." *Time Magazine*

3   Director John Brahm and cinematographer Joseph LaShelle masterfully re-create the atmosphere of period London as Bone, often in a dreamlike haze, wanders the city streets.

4   Director Brahm uses a moving camera as well as deep focus to set Bone in his milieu, at times high society and at other times, as here, in the underbelly of the city.

5   Netta two-times Bone with a charming theatrical producer, Eddie Carstairs (Glenn Langan), who can offer her more than Bone in advancing her career.

mented concerto written by composer Bernard Herrmann, which Bone is working on throughout the movie), she pulls him back with her prodigious sex appeal. She sits on his piano to obstruct his composing and lures him back into her web with the thinly veiled promise of sex and affection. She even convinces him to cannibalize his beloved concerto as the theme for one of her music-hall ditties.

The ironic twist, of course, is that Bone is a murderer who commits his crimes in a trance, about which he remembers nothing (the crux of Patrick Hamilton's original novel). After killing a shopkeeper at the beginning of the story and setting fire to his store (fire is a motif in the movie, symbolizing Bone's search for purity in his music and life), he wanders the fog-enveloped, chiaroscuro Edwardian streets of London like a lost child. As he did in

"Here Bernard Herrmann gives us the piano concerto over which Cregar's composer-protagonist ceaselessly toils and dies playing at the film's end — a piece that is full of half-suppressed shrieks, an atonal madness struggling to find expression in the still tonal world of upper-class London over a hundred years ago."

Richard Schickel, Film Noir: The Encyclopedia

6

6 Netta promises erotic delights but of course never delivers, keeping the sexually repressed Bone on a leash.

7 Bone's "fiancée," Barbara (Faye Marlowe), the good girl of the piece, is comforted by her father, Sir Henry Chapman (Alan Napier); they represent the uptight high society that Bone aspires towards.

The Lodger, Cregar conveys the depths of this man's torment through the use of his deep, soulful eyes and hulking body language. Cregar's pathos-filled rendering of Bone's responses to cacophony in the form of street noise or discordant music, which send him into these murderous trances, keeps the viewer tied emotionally to his character.

When Netta finally betrays Bone by keeping up an affair with her former lover as well as a new lover, in the person of a theatrical director who can offer her more than George can, he becomes enraged. In one of his trances, he strangles her and disguises her body in a cloak and Guy Fawkes mask (it is coincidentally Guy Fawkes Day). In a visual tour de force Brahm follows in a looping crane shot the disturbed and obviously weary Bone through crowds chanting "Guy, Guy, Guy, stick him in the eye" to the huge bonfire. Slowly and with great difficulty Bone climbs the mountain of debris and deposits his "effigy." As he descends, the crowd sets the pyre ablaze as Bone watches in despair.

The climax is another tour de force for both Brahm and Cregar. Bone has finally finished his concerto as the police close in on him. He plays his masterwork for a society crowd. To finish his concerto, he sets fire to the concert room, allowing everyone to flee as he sits down at the piano and completes his masterpiece. The music rises in emotional waves as the flames engulf the composer at his piano.

JU

JOHN BRAHM Born Hans Brahm in Hamburg, Germany, on August 17, 1893, John Brahm was the son of German actor Ludwig Brahm. Brahm himself was both an actor and a director for such acting troupes as Deutsches Künstler Theater and the Lessing Theater. He was also married to famed stage and screen actress Dolly Haas, whom he would direct in his first feature film, a moody 1936 remake of D. W. Griffith's *Broken Blossoms*. The film was made shortly after Brahm fled the continent for England in response to the rise of Hitler. Brahm then went to America in 1937 to work for both Columbia and 20th Century Fox. Fox head Darryl Zanuck was so impressed with Brahm's ability to make low-budget movies like the proto-noir *Let Us Live* (1939) and the horror film *The Undying Monster* (1942) look stylish, he "wedded" him with actor Laird Cregar to make two classic period noirs – *The Lodger* (1944) and *Hangover Square* (1945). After the success of these films, Brahm made a series of noirs redolent with the Expressionist style he learned in Germany, like *Guest in the House* (1944), *The Locket* (1946), and *The Brasher Doubloon* (1947). Brahm also traveled to Europe to make films with the cult siren Maria Montez, including *Siren of Atlantis* (1949) and *The Thief of Venice* (1950), Montez's last movie. After the collapse of the studio system, Brahm made a smooth transition to television, where he became one of the most sought-after directors for fantasy/horror/sci-fi shows like *The Outer Limits*, *Alfred Hitchcock Presents*, and *Thriller*. Brahm died in Malibu, California, on October 11, 1982.

MILDRED PIERCE 🏆

1945 – USA – 111 MIN.
DIRECTOR MICHAEL CURTIZ (1888–1962)
SCREENPLAY RANALD MACDOUGALL, based on the
novel of the same name by JAMES M. CAIN
DIRECTOR OF PHOTOGRAPHY ERNEST HALLER
EDITING DAVID WEISBART MUSIC MAX STEINER
PRODUCTION JERRY WALD for WARNER BROS.
STARRING JOAN CRAWFORD (Mildred Pierce Beragon),
JACK CARSON (Wally Fay), ZACHARY SCOTT
(Monte Beragon), ANN BLYTH (Veda), JO ANN MARLOWE
(Kay), BRUCE BENNETT (Bert Pierce), EVE ARDEN
(Ida Corwin), MORONI OLSEN (Inspector Peterson),
VEDA ANN BORG (Miriam Ellis),
BUTTERFLY MCQUEEN (Lottie)
ACADEMY AWARDS 1945 OSCAR for BEST LEADING
ACTRESS (Joan Crawford)

"Personally, Veda's convinced me that alligators have the right idea. They eat their young."

Divorce prompts Mildred Pierce (Joan Crawford) to take life into her own hands. We can't blame Bert, (Bruce Bennett), for walking out on his wife and two children: Mildred's undying love for her selfish, snide, and ungrateful daughter Veda (Ann Blyth) left no room for family life. Forced to stand on her own two feet at last, the courageous housewife ventures out of the kitchen and works her way up from lowly waitress to prosperous restaurant owner. She remarries and her new husband, Monte Beragon (Zachary Scott), heir to a fortune in real estate, doubles as her business partner. All the while, it is Mildred's love for Veda, and never her personal ambitions, that drive her to success. But the farther she goes in this life of sacrifice, the more apparent it becomes that a dark shadow has come over her ...

A viewing of the heartbreaking Mildred Pierce can't help but remind one of the countless women's pictures Hollywood produced during the Second World War for wives and mothers on the home front. Joan Crawford, who had been all but written off by the industry, delivers a performance every bit as poignant and heartfelt as those her contemporaries Bette Davis and Olivia de Havilland were regularly turning in. And as well as being a classic melo-

drama about the pitfalls of child-rearing and falling for the wrong men, Mildred Pierce is also a murder mystery.

The film opens on the night of Monte Beragon's death. Mildred's first husband Bert has been charged with the homicide, and so the melodrama, which unfolds in flashback, is covered in ominous shadows right from the start. Structurally speaking, Mildred Pierce is pure film noir, its sole deviation from the formula being that the male characters amount to little more than window dressing. Here, it's a woman who is provoked by a femme fatale to commit the crime, and the latter party is none other than Mildred's own daughter. The viewer is left as dumbfounded as the authorities in what seems for the longest time to be an unsolvable mystery. Then things take a surprising turn halfway through the film, when a second victim materializes unexpectedly.

Possible motives are perpetually refuted before they can be adequately pursued. Whoever is responsible for Beragon's death must have done it with Mildred's interests in mind; for only Veda was more despicable towards her mother than her husband proved to be. Then again, Mildred is a glutton for

1   Roll in the hay: following a little foreplay, Monte Beragon (Zachary Scott) and wife Mildred Pierce (Joan Crawford) go after what they really want.

2   Mildred's husband Monte and her daughter Veda (Ann Blyth, right) start something that will lead to tragedy.

3   Monte is generous when it comes to spending Mildred's money and buys the family a sleek new car.

4   Women's lib: *Mildred Pierce* has all the mystery of film noir without those superfluous male characters to muddle up the story. On the left, Jo Ann Marlowe as Kay – Mildred's other daughter.

"For its control of narrative, its photography of the vanished suburban California of the 1940s, and for its compelling central performance from Joan Crawford, Michael Curtiz's noir thriller is utterly gripping." *The Guardian*

punishment, known for courting the affections of those who'd most readily refuse her.

It is a grand cycle of despair that takes on unforeseen dimensions when we are finally presented with the mystery's solution, and Mildred must pay the price for committing a grave error. The film's original tagline says it all, begging audiences not to "tell anyone what Mildred Pierce did!"

Casablanca director Michael Curtiz collaborated with seasoned cinematographer Ernest Haller to create this classic piece of film noir. Haller's expressionistic use of shadow lends a sophisticated veneer to what would otherwise have been a cinematic soap opera. It is this camerawork that best captures the spirit of James M. Cain's original best-selling novel. Even though the book was a monument to greed, betrayal, and deception – thus

"Joan Crawford's stardom faltered in the mid-1940s, and when her contract with MGM lapsed in 1943 she was out of work until 1945. The consensus was that – with her 40th birthday approaching – her career was over. Then producer Jerry Wald at Warner's found her the role of her life... Adapted from a melodramatic novel by James M. Cain, it is a magnificent blend of film noir and feminine soap, glossily crafted by Michael Curtiz, whose versatile achievements included *Casablanca* and *Yankee Doodle Dandy*." *BBC*

5   The anatomy of a murder: when it comes to mink, Joan Crawford is a serial killer.

6   Get out while the getting's good: Mildred makes her ex-husband Bert (Bruce Bennett) feel invisible shortly before he decides to disappear from her life.

7   Whodunit? Mildred's most recent beau Wally (Jack Carson) isn't on the suspect list for long.

"With this money I can get away from you. From you and your chickens and your pies and your kitchens and everything that smells of grease. I can get away from this shack with its cheap furniture. And this town and its dollar days, and its women that wear uniforms and its men that wear overalls." *Film quote: Veda (Ann Blyth)*

a prime candidate for a genre masterpiece – adapting it for mainstream moviegoers proved problematic due to the intensity of Cain's hard-boiled subject matter. Several authors, including William Faulkner, had a hand in reworking Mildred into a sympathetic figure. In this comeback vehicle, Joan Crawford delivers a rare, understated performance, which garnered the film its sole Oscar. Nevertheless, the behind-the-scenes Crawford was anything but popular, and Curtiz nearly replaced her with Barbara Stanwyck after shooting had commenced.

On a side note, *Mildred Pierce* also won the then 16-year-old Ann Blyth an Oscar nomination for playing one of the most repugnant characters in Hollywood history – a role that incidentally reads like the screen incarnation of a young Joan Crawford.   PB

JOAN CRAWFORD Unlike her contemporaries Greta Garbo and Marlene Dietrich, actress Joan Crawford had no interest in preserving the youthful image that had made her a Hollywood icon. Time and again, she exposed all the battle scars of aging to the camera and turned "revolting" into a mark of style. Among her most poignant later performances – and of her entire career for that matter – was Robert Aldrich's *What Ever Happened to Baby Jane?* (1962), a brutal satire on the flipside of stardom co-starring Bette Davis. Crawford entered show business as a dancing ingenue and exited a striking film diva. All her physical features seemed larger than life – her eyebrows, mouth, shoulders, and even her gestures. It was as if she had been predestined to play self-confident, driven types – like the title role in Michael Curtiz's *Mildred Pierce* (1945), for which she won an Oscar. Born Lucille Fay Le Sueur, Joan Crawford stood before the camera more than 80 times during her 50 years in Hollywood. She made her screen debut in the silent era, before appearing in director Harry Beaumont's *Our Dancing Daughters* (1928) and emerging as a Jazz Age icon. Under contract with MGM Studios, she acted in some of the most prominent films of the '30s like Edmund Goulding's *Grand Hotel* (1932) opposite Greta Garbo; Lewis Milestone's *Rain* (1932) as prostitute Sadie Thompson; and George Cukor's *The Women* (1939). After MGM decided Crawford was box-office poison, she found a new home at Warner Bros., where her star continued to burn up the sky throughout the 1940s. Among her most notable performances of this era was her portrayal of the schizophrenic Louise Howell in Curtis Bernhardt's *Possessed* (1947), for which she received an Oscar nomination. Although she made fewer pictures in the 1950s, they were by no means second-rate. Nicholas Ray's *Johnny Guitar* (1954), featuring Crawford as a tough-as-nails saloon owner, was one of her more ambitious projects of the decade. After her death in 1977, her adopted daughter Christina published *Mommie Dearest: Joan Crawford* (1979), a shockingly candid biography that transformed her public image. In 1981, Frank Perry adapted *Mommie Dearest* for the screen starring Faye Dunaway as a sadistic, megalomaniac Crawford. Crawford was quoted as saying, "If you want to see the girl next door, go next door." And indeed, if there is one indisputable point about the eccentric actress's life, it is that she wasn't ordinary – by any stretch of the imagination.

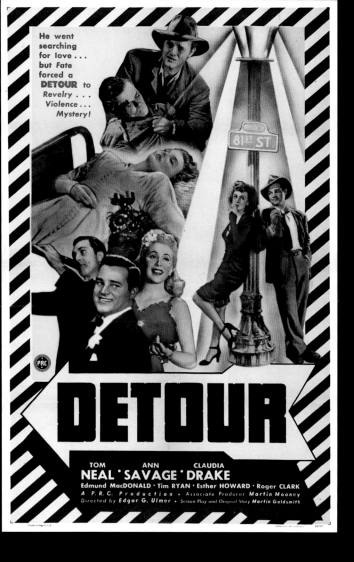

He went searching for love... but Fate forced a **DETOUR** to Revelry... Violence... Mystery!

81ST ST.

PRC

DETOUR

TOM ANN CLAUDIA
NEAL · SAVAGE · DRAKE
Edmund MacDONALD · Tim RYAN · Esther HOWARD · Roger CLARK
A P.R.C. Production · Associate Producer **Martin Mooney**
Directed by **Edgar G. Ulmer** · Screen Play and Original Story **Martin Goldsmith**

DETOUR

1945 – USA – 68 MIN.
DIRECTOR EDGAR G. ULMER (1904–1972)
SCREENPLAY MARTIN MOONEY [uncredited] and
MARTIN M. GOLDSMITH, based on
his novel of the same name
DIRECTOR OF PHOTOGRAPHY BENJAMIN H. KLINE
EDITING GEORGE MCGUIRE MUSIC LEO ERDODY
PRODUCTION LEON FROMKESS for PRC
STARRING TOM NEAL (Al Roberts), ANN SAVAGE (Vera),
CLAUDIA DRAKE (Sue Harvey), EDMUND MACDONALD
(Charles Haskell Jr.), TIM RYAN
(Diner Proprietor), ROGER CLARK (Policeman),
PAT GLEASON (Joe, Trucker)

"Fate, or some mysterious force, can put the finger on you or me for no good reason at all."

Although the first-person narrator was used in many studio noirs, most notably in *Double Indemnity* (1944) and *Criss Cross* (1949), none are more expressive of the noir character's existential angst than the fevered, slang-ridden, and often self-pitying description by hapless pianist Al Roberts (Tom Neal) of his unbelievably tortured trip across America. If there is a telling parallel for Roberts, it is not with other characters, not *Double Indemnity*'s Walter Neff or *Criss Cross*'s Steve Thompson, despite the latter's similar lament: "From the start it all went one way. It was in the cards or it was fate... or whatever you want to call it." Fate catches you unawares, it points its finger or it deals you a hand, and then fate reveals, as it did for Neff, that what you thought were a "nice little pile of blue and yellow chips" from a winning hand are sticks of dynamite that blow up in your face. All the penniless Roberts is trying to do is get from New York to Los Angeles and reunite with his fiancée, Sue (Claudia Drake). First he catches a ride with a well-heeled guy named Haskell (Edmund MacDonald) who drops dead in a manner that could seem like murder. Then he is blackmailed by fellow transient Vera (Ann Savage), who threatens to implicate him unless he does what she wants. All in all quite a series of mischances.

The career of director Edgar G. Ulmer is an intriguing parallel to *Detour*'s sorry tale of a hapless hitchhiker. Before *Detour*, Ulmer cobbled together other remarkable noir films on miniscule budgets for the poverty-row prototype Producers Releasing Corporation: *Bluebeard* (1944) and *Strange Illusion* (1945). For Ulmer such projects were actually a step up from the even smaller budgets on niche movies in Ukrainian or Yiddish such as *The Singing Blacksmith* (1938) or *Cossacks in Exile* (1939). When Roberts muses on how "fate sticks out a foot to trip you," he might be talking about what brought

Ulmer down from directing an A-budget horror at Universal, and about how he fell for the wrong woman, the wife of the studio head's nephew. This is not to characterize Shirley Ulmer as a *femme fatale*, like the scheming women that brought down Walter Neff and Steve Thompson; but no other directors of film noir at any budget have come as close to living the same deterministic nightmare as his or her character as Ulmer did with Al Roberts.

Manipulation of point-of-view is central to *Detour* and many other Ulmer movies. Scenarist Martin M. Goldsmith radically altered his novel by discarding its alternating male and female narrators (both of whom aspire to be successful actors) for the solitary musician Roberts. The dual frames of flashback from and narration by Roberts mean that all events are filtered through a single protagonist. No matter how outlandish the comment, how absurd or alienating the experiences, the audience is compelled to identify with this "hero." Whether the viewer pities him or despises his whiny self-justifications,

there is no escaping Roberts's perspective. Even as he stages his scenes in a straightforward, mostly uncluttered third-person manner, with two-shots in car seats in front of process screens and masters and close-ups inside cheap motel rooms – there was little time on a six-day shooting schedule for moving cameras and anything but the most rudimentary inserts and POVs – Ulmer never breaks from the framing mechanisms. So the unasked and unanswered question must be: are Sue, Vera, and Haskell really as they appear or are they rendered more stereotypically and/or extremely by Roberts in his retelling?

Some commentators, beginning with Andrew Britton in *The Book of Film Noir* (1993), have argued that Roberts only reveals what he wants his audience to hear (and see), that "as a man who lacks all sense of aim and purpose, who is indifferent to everything but what he takes to be his own interests," Roberts manipulates the narrative to mask his own culpability, "instinctively rationalizes his convenience on all occasions, either by absolv-

2

3

1 The hapless Al Roberts (Tom Neal) discovers that he has inadvertently strangled Vera (Ann Savage), while not even in the same room.

2 Z-budget staging: a few extras in the foreground, single stubs of candles at each table, and three dancing couples, while in the back Roberts tickles

the ivories and girlfriend Sue (Claudia Drake) warbles.

3 A typical noir perspective: as Roberts spins deeper into a whirlpool of hopelessness, the audience sees him and Vera's body reflected in the cheap hotel mirror.

4 Fearing that he will be suspected of killing the accidentally dead Charles Haskell (Edmund MacDonald), Roberts takes his first step towards the noir abyss.

ing himself of responsibility for his actions or providing himself with a spurious but flattering account of his motives." Is this the reason why Ann Savage's portrayal of the blackmailing Vera is so furious and pitiless? Is Roberts exaggerating Vera's lack of humanity to justify her ostensibly accidental death? Or is that all a lie? Did Roberts finally have enough of her shrewish manipulation and demeaning remarks and kill her outright?

This key relationship in *Detour* is almost a parody of other fugitive couples in film noir: Vera and Roberts are haters, not lovers, on the run. Tom Neal's performance is as dispirited and empty as Savage's is hyperbolic. In fact, many of the particulars of *Detour* are serio-comic; its snarky remarks and unlikely action – Vera is, after all, strangled by Roberts as he pulls on a telephone cord from the other side of a closed door – are so exaggerated as to be more silly than satirical. In the end, Ulmer merely leaves Roberts in an existential limbo where what's true and what's not lose importance and fate has the last laugh.

AS

B-MOVIE NOIRS From the Anthony Mann / John Alton 1947–1949 series at Eagle-Lion (*T-Men*, *Raw Deal*, *He Walked by Night*, and *Reign of Terror*) to the King Brothers' *Gun Crazy* (1950) to Kubrick's *Killer's Kiss* (1955), many of film noir's "classic" examples were the products of independent producers and filmmakers working on limited budgets. At Eagle-Lion cinematographer Alton also worked on *Hollow Triumph* and *Canon City* (both 1948), then for independent noir producer Benedict Bogeaus on *The Crooked Way* (1949), before rejoining Mann at MGM. One of Bogeaus's later color noirs, *Slightly Scarlet* (1956), starred John Payne, who abandoned softer leading roles at the major studios for tough-guy turns starting with *The Crooked Way* and continuing with *Kansas City Confidential* (1952), *99 River Street* (1953), and *Hell's Island* (1955) for director Phil Karlson and producers Pine/Thomas and Edward Small. Below this B-level whirlpool of talent, whose work was released through Eagle-Lion or United Artists, were Allied Artists, Monogram, and Republic. And at the bottom was PRC, where budgets ran as low as $10,000 and schedules as short as a single week.

At the high end, producers like Walter Wanger and his wife, Joan Bennett, teamed with other A-list actors and director Fritz Lang for *Scarlet Street* (1945) and *Secret Beyond the Door* (1947), distributed through a major studio. Perhaps most remarkable were a short-lived series of B movies from Frank and Maurice King: *When Strangers Marry* (1944), *Dillinger* (1945), *Suspense* (1946), *The Gangster* (1947), *Gun Crazy*, and *Southside 1-1000* (1950). Using talent who had ended a studio contract, fallen on hard times, or been blacklisted, the King Brothers productions epitomized the opportunism and diversity of B-movie film noir.

THE LOST WEEKEND ♙♙♙♙

1945 – USA – 101 MIN.
DIRECTOR BILLY WILDER (1906–2002)
SCREENPLAY CHARLES BRACKETT, BILLY WILDER,
based on the novel of the same name
by CHARLES R. JACKSON
DIRECTOR OF PHOTOGRAPHY JOHN F. SEITZ
EDITING DOANE HARRISON MUSIC MIKLÓS RÓZSA
PRODUCTION CHARLES BRACKETT for
PARAMOUNT PICTURES
STARRING RAY MILLAND (Don Birnam),
JANE WYMAN (Helen St. James)
PHILLIP TERRY (Wick Birnam), HOWARD DA SILVA
(Nat, the Barkeeper), DORIS DOWLING (Gloria),
FRANK FAYLEN (Bim), MARY YOUNG (Mrs. Deveridge),
ANITA SHARP-BOLSTER (Mrs. Foley),
LILLIAN FONTAINE (Mrs. St. James),
LEWIS L. RUSSELL (Charles St. James)
ACADEMY AWARDS 1945 OSCARS for BEST FILM
(Charles Brackett), BEST DIRECTOR (Billy Wilder),
BEST LEADING ACTOR (Ray Milland),
and BEST ADAPTED SCREENPLAY
(Charles Brackett, Billy Wilder)
IFF CANNES 1946 GRAND PRIX for BEST FILM (Billy Wilder),
and AWARD for BEST ACTOR (Ray Milland)

"You know what I'm gonna call my novel? 'The Bottle'!"

The Lost Weekend is a study of two days in the life of an alcoholic writer. The screenplay, based on Charles R. Jackson's popular novel, was written by Billy Wilder and his producer Charles Brackett. The movie was released in 1945 to almost universal acclaim. Though the reviewer from *The New York Times* felt he couldn't quite recommend it to anyone looking for a good night out, he did say that every adult moviegoer should make a point of seeing this "overwhelming drama."

It wasn't just the critics who were unanimous in their praise: the movie even turned out to be a hit at the box office. The following year, its success was crowned with four major Oscars (for Best Film, Director, Screenplay, and Actor). This was quite an achievement, for a movie with an addict as its hero

was far from standard fare at the time. Moreover – although the ending was, perhaps, a little too optimistic – *The Lost Weekend* was an astonishingly unflinching and unsentimental portrayal of alcoholism. From the very first moments of the movie onwards, Don Birnam (Ray Milland) seems to be spiraling helplessly out of control.

A failed writer with very little self-esteem, he simply can't cope with the problems life throws at him. Years of addiction have robbed him of the last dregs of self-respect, and he gets into increasingly humiliating situations. After several failed attempts to beat the bottle, he seems to have given up the struggle for good, lying to his brother Wick (Phillip Terry) and his fiancée Helen (Jane Wyman), and stealing and swindling to buy booze. When sober, he's so

RAY MILLAND Ray Milland was born Reginald Alfred Truscott-Jones in Neath, Wales, in 1907. After college, he served for a time with a cavalry regiment and worked as an amateur stage actor before winning his first small film roles. In 1933, Paramount signed him up, and Ray Milland worked his way up the ranks until he gradually became a leading man. His good looks made him one of the matinee idols of the age; but as the years went by, Hollywood's directors gradually discovered his "dark side." In Fritz Lang's paranoia thriller *Ministry of Fear* (1944), he played a patient released from a mental hospital. Drawn into the sinister intrigues of a Nazi organization, he finds that nothing is as it seems and no one can be trusted; the world outside the clinic walls comes to seem utterly mad. For his performance as the alcoholic writer in Billy Wilder's *The Lost Weekend* (1945), Milland won an Oscar. In *The Big Clock* (1948) directed by John Farrow, with whom he frequently collaborated, Milland played a harried, agitated journalist; and in Alfred Hitchcock's *Dial M for Murder* (1954), he was Grace Kelly's would-be murderous husband. In 1954, Milland signed a contract with the small Republic Studios, for whom he also made several films, including the dark Western *A Man Alone* (1955) and the adventure movie *Lisbon* (1956). Ray Milland survived the collapse of the old studio system relatively unscathed, and carried on working, frequently in splatter movies, until an advanced age. He died in 1986.

tormented by withdrawal symptoms that he begs drinks in a bar and filches a bottle of whiskey from a liquor store. Finally, he suffers a terrifying attack of the DTs and is driven to the verge of suicide.

These stages in a drinker's "career" are punctuated by flashbacks, shameful episodes from Don's past, which he narrates to the barkeeper Nat (Howard Da Silva). And the film also shows us the specific psychological effects of Birnam's addiction: when desperate for a drink, he's boorish and selfish; when slightly drunk, he blossoms into a charming, self-confident raconteur; and when he's smashed, he turns unpleasant again.

The Lost Weekend also gives a very realistic depiction of how Don's alcoholism affects the people closest to him. In their ceaseless endeavors to protect Don from the worst effects of his own self-destructive behavior,

3

1 Hammered: when Don (Ray Milland) falls down and breaks his crown, Helen (Jane Wyman) withholds all tumblers after.

2 Bathtub gin: Don can't remember where he's stashed his booze.

3 Don Quixote: drunk and delusional, Don tells Nat the bartender (Howard Da Silva) about what life looks like from the inside of a bottle.

4 A high-octane existence: when Don's brother Wick (Phillip Terry) stumbles upon yet another bottle of whiskey it looks like the suffering alcoholic will finally have to run on empty.

"This is no picture to serve as sheer entertainment, for herein is what may well be termed the heresy of filmmaking. A picture of doubtful entertainment value? Well, now. *The Lost Weekend* hasn't any laughs. Or gams. Or crackling, smart dialogue. It is startling in its manic depression. It required courage for Paramount to violate cardinal box-office principles to film it." *Variety*

4

Most impressive is the honesty with which it has been made. It seems a case-history documentation in its narrative and photographic style. Mr. Wilder brought his camera and leading players to New York for those scenes which convey the grim relation of the individual to the vast, unknowing mass. " *The New York Times*

5   Ghost writer: lacking the discipline required to pen his memoirs alone, Don asks Helen to help him get his thoughts down on paper.

6   The truth ain't pretty: a nervous breakdown lands Don in the hospital with a cynical nurse (Frank Faylen) whose prognosis is anything but uplifting.

7   Unhappy hour: Don is abandoned by his friend "Jack" and is left to cry into his pillow.

5

both Wick and Helen end up spinning lies to other people. Eventually, Wick loses patience and departs alone on the weekend trip he'd planned taking with his brother. Helen sticks with him, though: "He's a sick person. He needs our help!"

Stylistically, *The Lost Weekend* is notable mainly for the work of cameraman John F. Seitz, a master of "low-key lighting." This is a technique that uses a bright key light without fill or back lights to achieve the kind of strong contrast effects often seen in film noir, with its dark narratives and tormented characters. Unusually for an American movie of the mid-'40s, *The Lost*

Weekend was filmed partly on location. In one dramatic sequence, the camera – clearly hidden at times – accompanies Don through the streets of New York, from one pawnbroker to the next. He's suffering badly from withdrawal symptoms, and he wants to pawn his typewriter; but he's forgotten that today is Yom Kippur, a Jewish holiday, and all the pawnbrokers are closed … Shooting these scenes was a tricky undertaking. As Billy Wilder recalled, the streets couldn't always be cordoned off, and it was very hard to complete the takes before passersby recognized Milland and accosted him to demand an autograph.   LP

"Ray Milland was very good for *The Lost Weekend*. He had no comedy in him, and that was good for the part. There was no laughing in Milland." *Billy Wilder*

THE SPIRAL STAIRCASE

1945 – USA – 83 MIN.
DIRECTOR ROBERT SIODMAK (1900–1973)
SCREENPLAY MEL DINELLI, based on the novel
Some Must Watch by ETHEL LINA WHITE
DIRECTOR OF PHOTOGRAPHY NICHOLAS MUSURACA
EDITING HARRY W. GERSTAD, HARRY MARKER
MUSIC ROY WEBB **PRODUCTION** DORE SCHARY
for DORE SCHARY PRODUCTIONS,
VANGUARD FILMS PRODUCTION, RKO
STARRING DOROTHY MCGUIRE (Helen Capel),
GEORGE BRENT (Professor Warren), ETHEL BARRYMORE
(Mrs. Warren), KENT SMITH (Dr. Parry),
RHONDA FLEMING (Blanche), GORDON OLIVER
(Steve Warren), ELSA LANCHESTER (Mrs. Oates),
RHYS WILLIAMS (Mr. Oates), SARA ALLGOOD
(Nurse), JAMES BELL (Constable)

"And suddenly the shadows began to move."

A young woman, engrossed in a silent movie, doesn't notice that a murder is taking place right above her head. We witness the crime firsthand, through the eyes of a psychopath who targets disabled females. The plot thickens and the suspense builds in great Hitchcockian style. But this is just the beginning…

The bloodcurdling atmosphere, creaking set pieces, and a motley crew of characters scream low-budget horror à la Val Lewton (*Cat People*, 1942; *I Walked with a Zombie*, 1943), only it wasn't Lewton but his partners in crime who actually got this project off the ground. Independent movie producer David O. Selznick had triumphed with mystery before (e.g. Hitchcock's *Rebecca*, 1940), and was eager to produce a star vehicle for his great acting find, Ingrid Bergman. *The Spiral Staircase* would have been that picture, had he not already been committed to *Duel in the Sun* (1946). Lewton's employer, RKO, thus bought the rights from Selznick and signed on Robert Siodmak as the project's director.

Drawing from the best of parlor-room drama and film noir, Siodmak orchestrated the quintessential whodunit, leaving viewers to tread water in a sea of suspense as potential killers are pulled under one by one.

1   Downward spiral: Helen (Dorothy McGuire) descends into a living hell.

2   Deer in the headlights: a serial killer locks eyes with a mesmerizing mute.

3   Helen's ultimate nightmare.

4   A nutty professor? George Brent as the academic Warren son.

5   Stumped or just plain clueless?

Roll film. While New England parts ways with the 19th century, all eyes at the Warren family estate are on Helen (Dorothy McGuire), a mute beauty whose handicap might tempt a killer out of hiding. Indeed, it may already be too late. Home offers little comfort when Helen returns from an evening at the movies, frightened and soaked to the bone. Windows open inexplicably. A draft sends the candles into shivers. And as ominous shadows fall, Helen's face freezes with panic.

But is it an intruder or one of the Warrens who has awakened her utter sense of dread? The bedridden widow Mrs. Warren (Ethel Barrymore) lays down the law as if possessed by the soul of her dear departed husband. Always close at hand are the two Warren sons, the one (George Brent) a sullen, well-off professor, and the other (Gordon Oliver) a happy-go-lucky man about town. Sworn enemies, the brothers compete for the love of Blanche (Rhonda Fleming), the professor's devoted secretary. As in a British film

"The prototype of the 'old dark house, lady in distress' thriller, full of dark corners, flickering candles and featuring a mysterious, menacing killer whose true identity remains hidden until the end." *The New York Times*

comedy, a standard assortment of eccentrics watch intently from the periphery: characters like the knobby-elbowed family housekeeper and her husband the gardener, and a disagreeable live-in nurse who'd give her right arm to save dear mother Warren.

Helen has been in the Warren's care ever since a fire robbed her of both parents and the power of speech. Rather than letting an equally morose fate befall her ward, Mrs. Warren bids the young Dr. Parry (Kent Smith) to look after Helen. Death, however, pays a visit before the good doctor can make his house call: Blanche's body is discovered among the cellar's shadows, where someone she knew left it to rot.

But even when the killer's identity is finally made public, peace is by no means restored to the Warren household. Instead, the revelation sparks a large-scale search for buried family secrets. To the bitter end, *The Spiral Staircase* remains a self-reflexive study in seeing worthy of the introduction sequence in which the viewer's and murderer's perspective first overlap. The film's visual centerpiece is the forbidding spiral staircase itself, a structure that simultaneously gives physical expression to the killer's psychosis and the deviant nature of voyeurism. Step by step, light (and life) disappear into an all encompassing physical darkness as the camera makes its way to the cellar below. Here, in the killer's symbolic lair, perversions of the soul, fear and death have found a home. Murderous beast and audience bystander are joined as one, leaving us to wonder in the end whose eyes we're really looking through …

BR

9

6 A murder plays out on screen as a real murder takes place one floor above the cinema.

7 The film invites the viewer to guess which one is the killer.

8 General practitioner or certified quack? Kent Smith as Dr. Parry.

9 One suspect fewer: Helen finds the Professor's secretary Blanche (Rhonda Fleming) murdered.

NICHOLAS MUSURACA Born in 1892 in Riace (Calabria) Italy, cinematographer Nicholas Musuraca was one of film noir's great pioneers. As director of photography on *Stranger on the Third Floor* (1940), he chiseled the look of the earliest American production considered a part of the genre. It is the first of many impressive professional credits, which include Jacques Tourneur's *Cat People* (1942) and *Out of the Past* (1947), as well as Fritz Lang's *Clash by Night* (1952) and *The Blue Gardenia* (1953). Musuraca got his start in film as a driver and technical employee with J. Stuart Blackton, one of the founders of Vitagraph Studios and the so-called "father of the cartoon." He broke into cinematography during the early 1920s with Westerns and low-budget action flicks. By the end of the 1930s, he had worked his way up the ranks of the Radio Keith Orpheum a.k.a. RKO cameramen. The extraordinarily versatile Musuraca shot his way through genre lines at the studio, overseeing the cinematography of everything from A-pictures to light comedy shorts. In 1949, his work on George Stevens's *I Remember Mama* (1948) was nominated for an Oscar. He shifted gears a bit in 1954, becoming a freelance cameraman, which enabled him to work in television on occasion. Musuraca died in Los Angeles in 1975.

LEAVE HER TO HEAVEN

1945 – USA – 110 MIN.
DIRECTOR JOHN M. STAHL (1886–1950)
SCREENPLAY JO SWERLING, based on the novel of
the same name by BEN AMES WILLIAMS
DIRECTOR OF PHOTOGRAPHY LEON SHAMROY
EDITING JAMES B. CLARK MUSIC ALFRED NEWMAN
PRODUCTION WILLIAM A. BACHER for
20TH CENTURY-FOX
STARRING GENE TIERNEY (Ellen Berent Harland),
CORNEL WILDE (Richard Harland),
JEANNE CRAIN (Ruth Berent), VINCENT PRICE
(Russell Quinton), MARY PHILIPS (Mrs. Berent),
RAY COLLINS (Glen Robie),
GENE LOCKHART (Dr. Saunders),
REED HADLEY (Dr. Mason),
DARRYL HICKMAN (Danny Harland),
CHILL WILLS (Leick Thorne)

"I'll never let you go ... never ... never ... never."

The film that secured actor Gene Tierney's legacy with film noir fans was her tour de force *Leave Her to Heaven* (1945), for which she was nominated for an Academy Award. *Leave Her to Heaven* is Gene Tierney's apotheosis film. As in *The Shanghai Gesture* (1941) and *Laura* (1944), Tierney dominates every scene she is in, both physically, by her beauty, and psychologically, with her emotional intensity. While in von Sternberg's *The Shanghai Gesture* she utilized a consciously stylized hysteria to project the image of a spoiled teenage decadent bent on shocking and then punishing both her repressive father and her libertine mother, in *Leave Her to Heaven* she opts for a more controlled performance that at times veers into the realm of the supernatural.

It is no accident that several of the characters, including her husband, Richard, when speaking of Ellen refer to her psychic abilities or make semi-humorous allusions to the "witches of Salem." There is definitely an other-worldly quality to this controlling woman who, in her mother's words, "loves too much."

The audience first gets a glimpse of this remarkable and imperious woman in a club car on a train heading for New Mexico. There she meets the writer Richard Harland (Cornel Wilde). As soon as she notices him she disconcerts him completely by staring at him without blinking for almost a minute of screen time, as if she is trying to bore into his soul. After he squirms sufficiently, Ellen tells him he resembles her father, a man on whom we later find out she has an Electra-like fixation.

This mesmerizing scene is followed shortly by another revealing and almost mythical one. Richard finds himself staying at the same resort as Ellen and her family. They are there to spread the ashes of her dead father. Early in the morning, as Alfred Newman's melodramatic and almost hyster-

1. The murderous *femme fatale* Ellen (Gene Tierney) lets down her guard for a moment, taking off her dark glasses and revealing her sinister side.

2. Dark glasses back on, Ellen performs her most audacious and shocking act in the film by allowing her husband's clinging brother (Darryl Hickman) to drown.

3. Ellen steamrolls the stupefied Richard (Cornel Wilde) into a love affair and then marriage, simply through the power of her will.

4. The de rigueur "good girl" of the piece, Ruth (Jeanne Crain), who fades into the background every time Ellen appears but conquers in the end by stealing Richard away.

"What's wonderful for me ... is the sense of obsession, of possession that lives beyond the grave." *Martin Scorsese*

ical music score (replete with the cadence-like rhythm of timpani) rises on the soundtrack, Ellen sits ramrod straight on her horse like an Amazon warrior and throws her father's ashes about her, covering both herself and the desert around her, while Richard looks on in awe. After these two key scenes, it is little wonder Richard is left without a will of his own. Ellen proceeds to dump her lawyer fiancé (who, by the way, declares he will always love her anyway – which Ellen calls a "tribute" – and out of devotion is the one who later prosecutes Ruth [Jeanne Crain] for her murder) and announce her marriage to Richard, without his knowledge. As a doctor later on comments, Ellen seems to be able "to will" events.

Intent on possessing Richard fully just as she possessed her father, she gradually begins to whittle away all of Richard's pesky emotional connections

FEMMES FATALES The *femme fatale* is an ancient and quintessential part of our collective imagination, expressed in myths dating back to Lilith and historical figures dating back to Cleopatra. The French phrase "femme fatale" literally means "deadly woman," which understates the human embodiment of lust and peril, that intoxicating allure of sex and death that makes these creatures so fascinating. The *femme fatale* is a sleek and sensuous creature, dangerous either physically or emotionally to her victims. The *femme fatale*'s weapons are often covert and elusive, as opposed to warrior women like the historical/mythical Amazons, who are more likely to pick up a weapon to accomplish their assault on the patriarchy (although *femmes fatales* are not averse to guns, poison, and knives).

In addition, *femmes fatales* are more interested in fulfilling their own personal needs or transgressive desires than in fighting for any ideals. A *femme fatale* slowly drains her victims of their morals, their values, their friends, and often their money. She is sexually insatiable and may even love her victims in her own way, but it doesn't stop her from driving them to obsession. The male's resulting exhaustion leads to confusion and the inability to make sensible or rational decisions. Men who pursue the *femme fatale* risk being cuckolded, humiliated, and driven to poverty and despair in the pursuit of her attention.

The *femme fatale* has many changing forms in literature, history, myth, and art. But she reaches her peak in decadent fin de siècle Europe with writers like Charles Baudelaire and Théophile Gautier and painters like Gustave Moreau. But it could be argued that this lethal lady found her most copacetic home on the silver screen, particularly in American film noir, which both celebrated and decried her growing power during an era rocked by World War II as well as seismic changes to the male-female power dynamic after the war.

5   Ellen plots her revenge while on her deathbed.
    Even after she disappears in the final scenes of the
    film, her presence is still palpable.

6   Ellen's ex-lover, the lawyer Quinton (Vincent Price),
    keeps his promise to the dead Ellen and persecutes
    the hapless Ruth for the murder of Ellen.

7   Ruth responds like any classic noir "good girl" by
    playing the damsel in distress and fainting during
    the anti-climactic trial.

"Stahl is totally in control, his precise pacing and compositions
lending a persuasive dimension of amour fou, while Leon
Shamroy's camerawork makes each image a purring pleasure on
the eye." *Time Out Film Guide*

so he can be hers totally. In a scene rather daring for Production Code
Hollywood, we see Ellen get up from her twin bed and enter her husband's
and play with him, blowing on his face, cuddling up to him, exciting him sexually. The eroticism of the scene is palpable. Today the sequence would have
climaxed (no pun intended) with passionate lovemaking, but bowing to censorship pressures, the director diverts Richard's attention. From another
room he hears the voice of his crippled brother Danny (Darryl Hickman). Ellen
registers her frustration through her disgruntled expression and sets about to
rectify the situation with a murderous sense of purpose.

   Although Ellen tries initially to bend Danny to her will, he does not
respond to her urgings that he attend a boarding school, so in yet another
eerie scene (one of many in this macabre film) she takes him out to the lake

for some physical therapy. Putting on her heart-shaped sunglasses and assuming a masklike expression, she watches as he goes out too far and drowns. Her complete composure during his struggles to stay afloat marks her character as one of the most cold-blooded *femmes fatales* in the history of noir.

Even more shocking, particularly for an audience of the period, is Ellen's self-induced miscarriage. Again, to keep Richard totally to herself, she aborts her own child by staging a fall down the stairs. Richard's reaction to the loss of his child, however, is deeper than she had counted on. Gradually, he begins to draw away from her emotionally and turn to her "good girl" foster sister Ruth (Jeanne Crain).

When Ellen realizes she is losing Richard to Ruth, she commits suicide to separate Richard from his loved one and control him even from the grave. To accomplish that objective, she leaves a letter that implicates her foster sister Ruth in her "murder." With Ellen's death, however, the movie is over. And even though the filmmakers do not have the courage to end the movie there and instead stage a trial that labels Ellen a "monster" and delivers Richard into the arms of the safe and somewhat boring Ruth, it all seems anti-climactic. For Ellen is such a transgressive, powerful figure that all the other characters are little more than silhouettes in Ellen's shadow play, unable to command the audience's attention as Ellen was always able to do.

JU

"I was true to one man once... and look what happened!"

COLUMBIA PICTURES *presents*

Rita HAYWORTH
as
Gilda
with
Glenn FORD

GEORGE MACREADY · JOSEPH CALLEIA

SCREENPLAY BY MARION PARSONNET

Produced by
VIRGINIA VAN UPP
Directed by
CHARLES VIDOR

GILDA

1946 – USA – 110 MIN.
DIRECTOR CHARLES VIDOR (1900–1959)
SCREENPLAY MARION PARSONNET, JO EISINGER,
based on the short story of the same
name by E. A. ELLINGTON
DIRECTOR OF PHOTOGRAPHY RUDOLPH MATÉ
EDITING CHARLES NELSON
MUSIC MORRIS STOLOFF, MARLIN SKILES
PRODUCTION VIRGINIA VAN UPP for COLUMBIA
PICTURES CORPORATION
STARRING RITA HAYWORTH (Gilda), GLENN FORD
(Johnny Farrell), GEORGE MACREADY
(Ballin Mundson), JOSEPH CALLEIA (Obregon),
STEVEN GERAY (Uncle Pio), JOE SAWYER (Casey),
GERALD MOHR (Captain Delgado),
ROBERT E. SCOTT (Gabe Evans), LUDWIG DONATH
(German), LIONEL ROYCE (German),
DONALD DOUGLAS (Thomas Langford),
SAUL MARTELL (Short Guy)

"I hated her so I couldn't get her out of my mind for a minute."

Buenos Aires gambling circuit shark Johnny Farrell (Glenn Ford) is a con with all the right moves. That's at least what he thinks when mafioso Ballin Mundson (George Macready) hires him to be the eyes and ears of his casino. Then in walks Gilda (Rita Hayworth), a woman hotter than the fires of hell and the sensuous smoke that divides the two men. Johnny would give anything to respect the fact that his former girlfriend Gilda is now Ballin's wife – if only she'd let him.

At first Johnny thinks he's become immune to Gilda's charms, but jealousy gets the better of him when he witnesses her make overt advances towards other men. Soon there's just no remaining loyalty to Ballin. Once hubby wises up to the situation, a duel between men spirals into a three-way war fought for love and fueled by unbridled hate.

One of the smash hits of 1946, *Gilda*'s eroticism would later give it a choice spot within the film noir canon. Rita Hayworth was responsible for it

all. The leading lady's legendary striptease, in which she slinks her way to glory while singing "Put the Blame on Mame," knocked the socks off Glenn Ford and the entire world – not bad for just removing a pair of gloves. In this oh-so-ironic display, Gilda cuts men down to size with her unforgettable lyrics, coaxing men to blame the "weaker sex" for all the earth's catastrophes – if they dare.

This musical number is not only one of the most sizzling sensations born of the Old Hollywood studio era; it also brings the picture's subtext to light. In a strapless black dress that matches those dangerously long gloves, Gilda seems like a supernatural floating torso as she sways before a dark stage curtain. Liberating her arms of their apparel, she reveals her body bit by bit, returning it to its original entirety and reclaiming it as her own. More than commenting on the cinema's masculine gaze, Gilda's performance is an avowal of her refusal to be reduced to an object for voyeuristic consumption.

Rather than making excuses for her behavior, Gilda seizes hold of the screen and works her sexuality for all its worth. It follows that her innate confidence and "sense of self" are the real problems that men have with her. Johnny, in particular, vents this internal conflict through his tough-guy façade. Even a convoluted mystery pretext can't disguise how gender dynamics account for the meat of the story. Thrills and suspense are the product of the sexual chemistry and interdependency of the three principles, not of half-baked attempts at world domination that leave us cold. Indeed, the only time the action at the business table truly heats up is when the erotic tension builds between blood rivals Ballin and Johnny, and the love triangle takes on a new dimension.

Still, no matter how racy *Gilda* may have been for its day, it never more than alludes to such sexual taboos. The notorious Production Code forbade the inclusion of anything "unsuitable" for public eyes and forced the studio system to invent a cinematic code language that, while rooted in clichés, hinted at the scandalous. *Gilda* masterfully reappropriates this lingo to poke fun at the film industry's grotesque self-censorship. There is an underlying irreverence as tangible in Gilda's dance numbers as in the way the filmmaker exploits Freudian metaphors. Ballin, for example, takes a "special friend" with him wherever he goes – a cane that transforms into a deadly spear at the push of a button; when he lets Johnny in on his constant companion, the con cheekily inquires as to its gender.

A triumph of innuendo, *Gilda*'s careful layering of eroticism and masterful examination of the cinema's masculine gaze fed the imaginations of male viewers and shaped their image of Hayworth more than any of her other films. It seemed that from then on, all of the actress's admirers were blinded by her Hollywood persona. To put it in the jaded pinup goddess's own words, "men go to bed with Gilda, but wake up with me."   JH

GLENN FORD Quebec native Glenn Ford (1916–2006) transitioned from the stage to the cinema towards the end of the 1930s. His film career got off to a banging start at Columbia pictures, where he became a fixture in shoot-em-up Westerns. However, Ford's real call to stardom came once he returned to North America after serving with the U.S. Marines during World War II. The Bette Davis melodrama *A Stolen Life* (1946) established him as a Hollywood heartthrob and his performance opposite Rita Hayworth in *Gilda* (1946) solidified his reputation. The combination was so magical on screen that Hayworth and Ford were paired together in four further pictures. Soon there was no denying that the leading man had become one of the most popular A-listers in the business.
Ford's more than 100-picture career includes many exceptional performances as tough guys with good, honest values. Whether as cowboys, cops, or the countless military men of his later movies, Ford endowed his characters with a sense of depth often absent in the work of other actors. He even demonstrated his knack for comedy at Marlon Brando's side in Daniel Mann's *The Teahouse of the August Moon* (1956), a satire about the American democratization efforts in postwar Japan. However, Ford took on his most controversial role in Fritz Lang's Hollywood masterpiece *The Big Heat* (1953), delivering a *tour-de-force* performance as a police sergeant fueled by revenge. Glenn Ford died in 2006, age 90, in Beverly Hills.

"*Gilda* is the result of ambrosial Rita Hayworth's desire to prove that she can act. She proves it as well as the next Hollywood girl (unless that girl happens to have specific talent for acting), but mainly, as always before, she proves that she is such a looker that nothing else matters." *Time Magazine*

1 Crowd pleaser: Rita Hayworth removes a glove and struts down the walk of fame.

2 Wheeling and dealing: Johnny (Glenn Ford) walks into a game of Russian roulette when he reenters Gilda's life.

3 A pretty little ditty: Gilda isn't a *femme fatale* in the classic sense. She just treats her suitors as if they were dead.

4 Jackpot: although Rita Hayworth was the film's actual star, Glenn Ford hit the big time with his unforgettable performance.

5 A pair of aces: Rita Hayworth and Glenn Ford's romantic pairing won big with audiences, and the couple went on to star opposite each other in four further films.

Their Love was a Flame that Destroyed!

MGM presents
LANA TURNER
JOHN GARFIELD

THE
Postman
Always
Rings Twice

CECIL KELLAWAY
HUME CRONYN·LEON AMES
AUDREY TOTTER·ALAN REED
SCREEN PLAY BY HARRY RUSKIN AND NIVEN BUSCH
BASED ON THE NOVEL BY JAMES M. CAIN
DIRECTED BY TAY GARNETT
PRODUCED BY CAREY WILSON
A METRO·GOLDWYN·MAYER PICTURE

THE POSTMAN
BOOK

The Book that
Blazed to
Best-Seller Fame!

THE POSTMAN ALWAYS RINGS TWICE

1946 – USA – 113 MIN.
DIRECTOR TAY GARNETT (1894–1977)
SCREENPLAY HARRY RUSKIN, NIVEN BUSCH,
based on the novel of the same name by
JAMES M. CAIN **DIRECTOR OF PHOTOGRAPHY** SIDNEY WAGNER
EDITING GEORGE WHITE **MUSIC** GEORGE BASSMAN
PRODUCTION CAREY WILSON for MGM
STARRING LANA TURNER (Cora Smith),
JOHN GARFIELD (Frank Chambers),
CECIL KELLAWAY (Nick Smith),
HUME CRONYN (Arthur Keats), LEON AMES
(Kyle Sackett), AUDREY TOTTER (Madge Gorland),
ALAN REED (Ezra Liam Kennedy), JEFF YORK (Blair),
CHARLES WILLIAMS (Jimmie White),
CAMERON GRANT (Willie), WALLY CASSELL (Ben)

"*[The tie] is my wedding present to him, but the way he wears it, you'd think it was a noose around his neck.*"

The first "unauthorized" version of James M. Cain's naturalistic noir novel *The Postman Always Rings Twice* was made in France in 1939 as *Le Dernier Tournant* with the powerful Michel Simon as the cuckolded husband Nick. It was banned in the United States and the war interrupted its distribution elsewhere. So it was largely forgotten. The more famous unauthorized adaptation is *Ossessione* (a most appropriate title considering the theme of the novel), directed by the illustrious Italian director Luchino Visconti in 1943. Unfortunately, Visconti, like his French counterpart, never cleared the rights to Cain's work and so any chance of distribution within the United States after the war was squelched by MGM, who owned the rights. In fact MGM had sat on the rights to Cain's Zolaesque novel for over a decade, too timid to take on the formidable Production Code to bring Cain's noir vision of love and death to the screen. It took the phenomenal critical and financial success of Billy Wilder's seminal noir *Double Indemnity* (1944) to inspire MGM to take a dip into Cain's unsettling world.

MGM's version of *The Postman Always Rings Twice* (1946) was more faithful to the novel in plot than Visconti's version (restoring the trial and the first murder attempt, which were absent in the Italian adaptation) and ramped up the star quality of the film by casting the glamorous Lana Turner in the part of Cora. When Frank, played by noir icon John Garfield, first sees Cora she is a blindingly luminous vision in white pumps, a two-piece white outfit, and platinum hair topped by a white turban. He bends down to pick up the lipstick

1 The sexual sparks fly between rough trade Frank (John Garfield) and the anomalously glamorous diner owner Cora (Lana Turner).

2 Sadomasochistic relationships were a trademark of James M. Cain's novels. *The Postman Always Rings Twice* is no exception.

3 The cuckolded Nick (Cecil Kellaway) blithely sings as Frank tries once again to eliminate the main obstacle to his obsessive love for Cora.

"You know, there's something about this that's like, well it's like you're expecting a letter that you're just crazy to get, and you're hanging around the front door for fear you might not hear him ring. You never realize that he always rings twice ..." *Film quote: Frank Chambers (John Garfield)*

she has dropped as it rolls towards him and checks her out from bottom to top, from a submissive position, of course – all shot subjectively so the audience shares his point of view, as she imperially holds out her hand to receive her possession. Although Frank demonstrates his machismo from time to time, it is still Cora who runs the show. She initiates the plot to kill her domineering and suffocating older husband, Nick (Cecil Kellaway), and is the one who punishes Frank for his cowardice in turning against her during the trial (for Nick's murder) and for his infidelities, turning him into a servant as she transforms the failing diner into a success (much like Cain's Mildred Pierce).

Much has been made of the sadomasochistic dimensions of the couple's sexual/romantic relationship. Even in this less explicit version – as opposed to Bob Rafelson's 1981 adaptation, which was free of the heavy

hand of the Production Code office – Turner and Garfield manage to convey with their body language and their eyes the smoldering sexuality of the couple, simultaneously frustrated and stimulated by the presence of Nick, and later, in a post-Nick world, by Cora's justified bitterness at Frank's fickleness. Ultimately, however, their passion wins out and they express their desire against the backdrop of the ominously dark sea.

Although Turner does manage to project some of the working-class desperation and weariness of Cain's original heroine, she is still at the core a movie star (she reportedly only agreed to do the "sordid" role if she could maintain her "style") and as such dominates every frame she appears in. Even though Frank may try to resist this blonde goddess inexplicably "come to earth" in this ramshackle diner ("The Twin Oaks," the first of many exam-

4 Frank, defiant while facing death for yet a second time, only hopes for a reunion with Cora, who has moved beyond life before him.

5 The second half of the movie crystallizes the dominance-submission relationship of Cora and Frank, with Cora as a pillar of strength and Frank wounded and given to moral vacillation.

6 Hapless Nick introduces the transient Frank to his gorgeous and deeply dissatisfied wife.

JOHN GARFIELD Born Jacob Julius Garfinkle in 1913 in New York City, John Garfield was the child of poor working-class Russian Jewish immigrants. Garfield's proletarian background (he was moved around from tenement to tenement after the death of his mother and joined several street gangs) was to infuse not only his acting style but his politics as well. Through the intervention of some caring educators who recognized his talents, Garfield was steered into acting school. In the 1930s he became involved with the revolutionary Group Theatre, largely through the aid of his childhood friend playwright Clifford Odets. Warner Bros., always on the prowl for young talent who suited their proletarian ethos, offered Garfield a contract. Very soon he became one of their prize assets, playing tough but vulnerable noir characters in films like *They Made Me a Criminal* (1939). However, Garfield's integrity and independence led him to refuse projects he considered beneath his talents, and several times he attempted to free himself from his contract with the often authoritarian studio heads. After leaving the grip of the Brothers Warner, Garfield did some of his best work, including *The Postman Always Rings Twice* (1946), *Humoresque* (1946), *Gentleman's Agreement* (1947), *Body and Soul* (1947), *Force of Evil* (1948), and *He Ran All the Way* (1951). With these films Garfield became a true noir icon. Called before HUAC in 1951 for his "Communist" affiliations, he refused to name names and was blacklisted by the studios in their notorious circular Red Channels. In 1952 he died of a heart attack in his beloved New York City.

> **"Throughout *The Postman Always Rings Twice*, we see everything from the viewpoint of the two lovers. They awake considerable audience sympathy and identification. This is true even when they commit crimes. The film is different from many other film noirs in being essentially supportive of the criminals."**
>
> *Michael E. Grost*

5

ples of doubling in both the book and the movie, including the title, of course), and does so at several points (his affair with Madge [Audrey Totter], leaving her twice, and betraying her at the trial), he always comes crawling back to do her bidding, whether as lover, co-conspirator, put-upon handyman, or "henpecked" partner in domesticity (symbolized by the tie she forces him to wear, which she calls his "noose").

The couple's physical attraction may not be as blatant as in the novel, but it still radiates in their magnetic need to be together no matter the cost. They fight, they argue, and they love, but they stay together. They even reach a sort of romantic epiphany, towards the end of the movie, at the beach, where a pregnant Cora waxes poetically about "a new life" ("Kisses that come from life not death"). She even offers to give up her own life, during that famous midnight swim deep into the ocean, to prove her love.

But in the world of noir, fate is rarely generous more than once. And so Cora dies in a car accident with Frank, her lipstick rolling once again onto the ground. But this time Frank cannot pick it up. He is too overwhelmed with grief and shock. In the final irony of the film Frank faces the gas chamber for a murder he did not commit – Cora's (as opposed to the one he did – the husband's). But he accepts his sentence, praying only that he and Cora can be together forever, "no matter where that is." Hell included, one would imagine.   JU

6

> **"Despite complaints of changes in James M. Cain's original story (mostly for censorship purposes), the film packs a real punch and outshines the more explicit 1981 remake."** *Leonard Maltin*

NOTORIOUS

1946 – USA – 101 MIN.
DIRECTOR ALFRED HITCHCOCK (1899–1980)
SCREENPLAY BEN HECHT
DIRECTOR OF PHOTOGRAPHY TED TETZLAFF
EDITING THERON WARTH MUSIC ROY WEBB
PRODUCTION ALFRED HITCHCOCK for RKO
STARRING CARY GRANT (T. R. Devlin), INGRID BERGMAN
(Alicia Huberman), CLAUDE RAINS
(Alexander Sebastian), LOUIS CALHERN
(Paul Prescott), LEOPOLDINE KONSTANTIN
(Anna Sebastian), REINHOLD SCHÜNZEL
(Dr. Anderson), MORONI OLSEN (Walter Beardsley),
IVAN TRIESAULT (Eric Mathis), ALEX MINOTIS
(Joseph), WALLY BROWN (Mr. Hopkins)

"This is a very strange love affair."
"Why?"
"Maybe the fact that you don't love me."

The big-screen romance between Humphrey Bogart and Ingrid Bergman in *Casablanca* (1942) was the breakout role for Bergman. Four years later, Alfred Hitchcock's psychothriller *Notorious* (1946) made it clear that Hollywood's love for Ingrid Bergman was here to stay. Like *Casablanca*, *Notorious* relies on war to provide the backdrop for a tragic love triangle. That, however, is where the resemblance ends, for here Bergman plays Alicia Huberman, the American-born daughter of a Nazi spy.

As her dossier suggests, Alicia is someone who often finds herself caught between two worlds. She agrees to marry someone she does not love for the sake of U.S. secret agent T. R. Devlin (Cary Grant), the man who holds her heart. At Devlin's request, this former party girl is to find out all she can about what goes on in the house of Alexander Sebastian (Claude Rains), a Nazi who has fled to South America.

Alicia's new life down south turns into a death trap when her husband discovers she has unearthed his little sideline in smuggling large quantities of uranium and suspects her of being a double agent. Profoundly disappointed, Alexander begins poisoning his better half with ever-increasing doses of arsenic. But just before he succeeds in ridding himself of Alicia, Devlin saves her life in an eleventh-hour rescue mission.

Notorious is a prime illustration of Hitchcock's "MacGuffin" theory. Here, weapons-grade uranium and its potential for mass destruction casts no cloud over the classic Hollywood love story; the fact that the director's 1944 script, penned one year before the atom bomb was dropped on Hiroshima, tapped into a top-secret war project was pure coincidence.

The film's brilliance is the product of Hitchcockian streamlining, and the drama draws on the structural similarities of spy capers and romances.

INGRID BERGMAN *Notorious* (1946) was the second of three pictures Ingrid Bergman (1915–1982) shot with Alfred Hitchcock, the other two being *Spellbound* (1945), and *Under Capricorn* (1949). She was the first of Hitch's great leading ladies, preceding other famous repeat performers like the icy blondes Grace Kelly and Tippi Hedren. The Master of Suspense was devastated when she declared that their professional collaboration had come to an end, although she maintained her friendship with him until his death. It wasn't just Hitchcock, but rather the whole world that fell at the feet of this extraordinary Stockholm native. Her name was synonymous with natural beauty, noble grandeur, and a unique professionalism. When producer David O. Selznick brought Bergman to Hollywood in 1938, the Swedish starlet was permitted to shoot only one movie a year. The choices she made are astounding, for this was to be an era that included not only *Casablanca* (1942), but also *For Whom the Bell Tolls* (1943) and *Gaslight* (1944). Regrettably, her immaculate reputation became the subject of scandal shortly after she agreed to make *Stromboli* (*Stromboli, terra di Dio*, 1949): she abandoned her husband and children to start a life with the picture's director, Roberto Rossellini. The public shunned Bergman for nearly a decade, and it was only when she received her second Oscar for *Anastasia* (1956) that Hollywood symbolically forgave her the error of her ways. In the years that followed, the actress divided her time between American and European productions. She won further acclaim later on in her career for her work in Ingmar Bergman's *Autumn Sonata* (*Höstsonaten*, 1978) and her portrayal of the Israeli prime minister, Golda Meir, in the made-for-TV *A Woman Called Golda* (1982). Ingrid Bergman died in London at the age of 67. Her daughter, the actress Isabella Rossellini, is one of the greater things born out of her marriage to the Italian director.

1. Take a deep breath: Cary Grant and Ingrid Bergman prepare to dive into Hollywood's longest kiss on record.

2. Pillow talk: Devlin steps in to save Alicia in the nick of time – but the situation might require some mouth-to-mouth resuscitation.

3. Spy versus spy: Devlin convinces Alicia to join the secret service.

> **"Alfred Hitchcock's *Notorious* is the most elegant expression of the master's visual style, just as *Vertigo* is the fullest expression of his obsessions. It contains some of the most effective camera shots in his – or anyone's – work, and they all lead to the great final passages in which two men find out how very wrong they both were."** *Chicago Sun-Times*

General distrust sets the stage for tension time and again, while interludes of deceit and betrayal cross paths with secrets that must be kept at all cost, imbuing the story with intrigue and suspense. These conventions are our only clue as to Devlin's actual feelings for Alicia. Meanwhile, she suffers at the hands of two men. There's Sebastian, the man she sleeps with, who smothers her with his trust and devotion. And then there's the icy Devlin, who repays her patriotism with open sarcasm.

Ingrid Bergman delivers a stunning portrayal of someone held at the mercy of love and duty, a woman coerced into playing a passive role that makes her appear significantly weaker than she is. Grant's Devlin, on the other hand, is as tertiary as a MacGuffin, despite his being the film's alleged romantic lead. Sebastian, the Nazi who genuinely loves Alicia, and who is afflicted by her deceptions all the more for it, does a much better job of winning the audience's compassion. The role exemplifies the complexity Hitchcock gave his villains, as these were often the characters he sympathized with most. Yet the director wasn't the only person who could relate to twisted injustices: to match the physical stature of his Swedish co-star, Claude Rains was forced to act on platforms just like Bogart did in *Casablanca*.

Despite the complexity of the story, the film is told in a relatively transparent manner, although some aspects of the cinematography have entered film history. The camera pairs the various liquids that Alicia drinks with constant state of suffering – from her self-induced alcoholism to the arsenic cocktails she is tricked into nipping. Among the film's finest special effects is a 180° pivoting shot taken from Alicia's point of view, expressing her

4   Spellbound: Alicia is so taken with Devlin that she marries another man at his request.

5   Sworn to secrecy: the CIA pulls Devlin's strings and forces him to feign emotional indifference toward Alicia. Then again, she'd never complete her mission alive if she knew as much as he did.

6   Packs a wallop: Devlin and Alicia go looking for a good vintage and find one that's radioactive.

drunkenness after a long night out with Devlin. The result is one of the few moments when Alicia's love for Devlin doesn't inhibit her from seeing his duplicitous and elusive side. Later on, Hitchcock relocates the main story line to Sebastian's wine cellar where the uranium is hidden, providing the director with an opportune venue to stage the "longest filmed kiss of all time." For three minutes solid, Grant and Bergman are locked in an amorous embrace. Their lips, however, are not. In order to comply with Production Code stipulations, the actual kissing had to be held to intervals of three seconds maximum.

Notorious is undoubtedly the most romantic of all Hitchcock's films. The picture's undercurrent of suppressed sexual tension would turn up time and again in his later works and come to be revered as part of his filmmaking style. This tension is at long last unleashed by a spectacular though inevitable ending that liberates Alicia and Devlin's hearts from a state of imprisonment, leaving the doomed Sebastian with no alternative but to take his own life.

7   We're in this together: Ingrid Bergman appeared in three Hitchcock films, Cary Grant in four. *Notorious* was their only joint venture.

8   Must have been something I ate: Alicia gets sick to her stomach when she thinks about all the wicked things her husband Alex Sebastian (Claude Rains) is up to.

"We do not recall a more conspicuous – yet emotionally delicate – love scene on the screen than one stretch of billing and cooing that the principals play in this film. Yet, withal, there is rich and real emotion expressed by Miss Bergman in her role, and the integrity of her nature as she portrays it is the prop that holds the show." *The New York Times*

THE BIG SLEEP

1946 – USA – 114 MIN.
DIRECTOR HOWARD HAWKS (1896–1977)
SCREENPLAY WILLIAM FAULKNER, JULES FURTHMAN,
LEIGH BRACKETT, based on the novel of the
same name by RAYMOND CHANDLER
DIRECTOR OF PHOTOGRAPHY SID HICKOX
EDITING CHRISTIAN NYBY MUSIC MAX STEINER
PRODUCTION HOWARD HAWKS for FIRST
NATIONAL PICTURES INC., WARNER BROS.
STARRING HUMPHREY BOGART (Philip Marlowe),
LAUREN BACALL (Vivian Rutledge), MARTHA VICKERS
(Carmen Sternwood), JOHN RIDGELY (Eddie Mars),
CHARLES WALDRON (General Sternwood),
SONIA DARRIN (Agnes), REGIS TOOMEY (Bernie Ohls),
ELISHA COOK JR. (Jones), BOB STEELE
(Canino), LOUIS JEAN HEYDT (Joe Brody),
CHARLES D. BROWN (Norris), DOROTHY MALONE
(Acme Bookstore Proprietress), JOY BARLOW
(Taxi Driver), PEGGY KNUDSEN (Mona Mars)

"Such a lot of guns around town and so few brains!"

Old, wealthy, and sick, General Sternwood (Charles Waldron) has a problem on his plate: his loose-living daughter Carmen (Martha Vickers) is being subjected to blackmail. The General hires private eye Philip Marlowe (Humphrey Bogart) to help him out, and before long Marlowe is on the trail of a murderous conspiracy that in some way involves Vivian (Lauren Bacall), Sternwood's second daughter. When Marlowe falls in love with her, he soon finds himself dodging bullets from rival gangsters.

This short synopsis shouldn't deceive anyone into thinking that the plot of *The Big Sleep* is anywhere near intelligible. One famous anecdote tells of Hawks and Bogart arguing on set about how a certain character had actually died: murder, or suicide? Hawks tried to settle the dispute by asking Raymond Chandler, who'd written the novel on which the film was based. But not even the author could help. An earlier version of *The Big Sleep* had included a scene that cast some light on the obscurity of the plot. This scene was cut,

however, because test audiences simply hadn't liked it. As a result, the movie acquired an exceptionally fast narrative tempo, even by Hawks's standards, and the plot is even more labyrinthine than it would otherwise have been. The film seems almost to negate the very idea of objective knowledge, thereby reversing the pattern of the classical whodunit: here, the "story" is not so much a description of how a difficult case is solved, as the atmospheric evocation of a thoroughly criminal cosmos.

Murder, betrayal, perversion: Marlowe makes his way through this bleak film noir landscape with the loneliness of an existential hero. Quick-witted, sure-footed, crafty and tough, he's well-armed for the inhospitable terrain – yet his attractiveness resides not so much in his toughness as in his integrity. Bogart's Marlowe is the ideal screen detective, a man with qualities

"If only somebody had told us – the script-writers, preferably – just what it is that happens in *The Big Sleep*, we might be able to give you a more explicit and favorable report." *The New York Times*

1 Vivian (Lauren Bacall) and Marlowe (Humphrey Bogart) investigate murders, but many of them remain unsolved.

2 Best seller: Dorothy Malone's memorable performance won her many further Hollywood bookings.

3 Weeding through information: General Sternwood's (Charles Waldron, right) conservatory is as ominous

as the concrete jungle where the majority of the film's investigation takes place.

4 Who's got the upper hand? If Marlowe isn't careful Vivian could leave him holding the check.

undreamt of by Sam Spade, the cynical gumshoe in *The Maltese Falcon* (1941). More clearly than Chandler's novel, Hawks's film adaptation of *The Big Sleep* celebrates its hero's incorruptibility, while also establishing that this has at least as much to with an aesthetic attitude as with any real ethical principles. Marlowe is under no illusion that his actions can actually achieve very much, but he knows the power of a beautiful deed – and particularly, its effect on women.

That *The Big Sleep* is such a hugely entertaining movie has less to do with the kind of action scenes we expect from the hard-boiled genre than with a series of witty verbal exchanges between Bogart and a whole host of

self-assured beauties. It's almost worthy of a screwball comedy. Bogart's self-irony about his own star status only serves to make his character even more congenial. "You're not very tall," says the sultry Carmen; "I try to be," replies Marlowe.

In Hawks's film, a woman's weapons include good old-fashioned guns. And indeed, what we're shown is not so much a fight between good·and evil as a battle of the sexes. Not that this tussling for position rules out romance; on the contrary, it can easily provoke it, as is demonstrated by Bogart and Bacall, the dream team at the heart of the film. Just as in Hawks's *To Have and Have Not* (1944), she's easily his match, and the powerful erotic charge

BOGART & BACALL Howard Hawks started the ball rolling. For his movie *To Have and Have Not* (1944), the producer and director was looking for a female co-star who could match up to the male lead, Humphrey Bogart (1899–1957). Hawks's wife found a model named Betty Perske (*1924) on the cover of *Harper's Bazaar* – and Hawks invited her along to the studio. He gave her a new name and arranged some speaking lessons, for the 19-year-old's voice was thin and high-pitched at the time. When Bogart first saw his new partner, his first thought was "she's very tall," for at 5'7'', she was barely shorter than Bogart himself. From the day filming began, Bogart was in love with his co-star, and despite the 25-year age difference, his feelings were soon requited. At the time, Bogart was unhappily married to the actress Mayo Methot (his third marriage), and Hawks worried that he was merely playing with the young girl's feelings. But Bogart was serious. In 1945, he divorced his wife and married Lauren Bacall only eleven days later. The couple made three further films together: *The Big Sleep* (1946 – again directed by Hawks), *Dark Passage* (1947), and *Key Largo* (1948). In 1949, five months after their fourth film as co-stars, Lauren Bacall gave birth to their son Stephen; it was Bogart's first child. Three years later, their daughter Leslie Howard was born. Bacall began making films without Bogey (e.g. *How to Marry a Millionaire*, 1953). The couple never made another movie together, and indeed Bogart's time was running out: in 1957, he died of cancer.

"Brittle Chandler characters have been transferred to the screen with punch by Howard Hawks's production and direction, providing a full load of rough, tense action." *Variety*

5 The big bang: Martha Vickers, an actress in whom Hawks saw powder-keg potential, is simply stunning as the trigger-happy nymphomaniac.

6 Better you than me: the only way for Marlowe to avoid certain death is to remain still while lethal poison is administered to small-time snoop Harry Jones (Elisha Cook Jr., center).

7 Random acts of violence: Eddie Mars (John Ridgely, center) proves to be the culprit behind the wave of crime; his motives, however, remain a mystery.

between them is what holds the film together. When their coolness eventually dissolves, it's always one of the magic moments of the cinema.

Their most remarkable scene together was only added to the movie after filming had been completed. Arguing that too little use had been made of their star potential, the studio bosses pushed Hawks to remedy the deficit.

So Hawks added some dialogue laced with double entendres: "I'm not sure how far you can go," says Bogart; "That depends on who's in the saddle," she answers. In the Hollywood of the '40s, that was as close to explicit sex as it was possible to get.

JH

Vivian: "How did you find her?"
Marlowe: "I didn't find her."
Vivian: "Well then how did you ..."
Marlowe: "I haven't been here, you haven't seen me, and she hasn't been out of the house all evening."

Film quote: Vivian (Lauren Bacall) and Philip Marlowe (Humphrey Bogart)

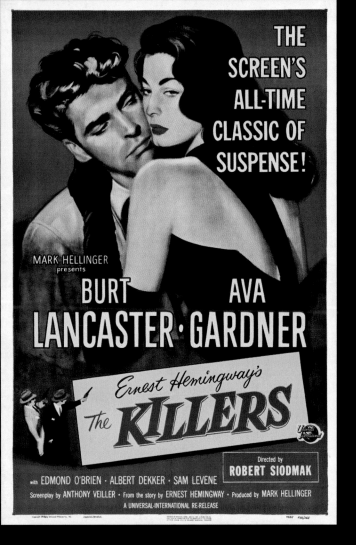

THE KILLERS

1946 – USA – 105 MIN.
DIRECTOR ROBERT SIODMAK (1900–1973)
SCREENPLAY ANTHONY VEILLER, based on the short story
The Killers by ERNEST HEMINGWAY
DIRECTOR OF PHOTOGRAPHY ELWOOD BREDELL
EDITING ARTHUR HILTON MUSIC MIKLÓS RÓZSA
PRODUCTION MARK HELLINGER for MARK HELLINGER
PRODUCTIONS, UNIVERSAL PICTURES
STARRING BURT LANCASTER (Ole "the Swede" Andersen),
AVA GARDNER (Kitty Collins), EDMOND O'BRIEN
(Jim Reardon), SAM LEVENE (Lieutenant Sam Lubinsky),
ALBERT DEKKER (Big Jim Colfax), VIRGINIA CHRISTINE
(Lilly Lubinsky), VINCE BARNETT (Charleston),
JACK LAMBERT ("Dum Dum" Clarke),
CHARLES MCGRAW (Al, Killer #1),
WILLIAM CONRAD (Max, Killer #2)

"Don't ask a dying man to lie his soul into hell."

Ole Andersen (Burt Lancaster), better known as "the Swede," is lying in bed and waiting for death. Two hired guns are on their way to settle a score with him and shut the book on a chapter of his life he had hoped was long done with. Andersen is, nonetheless, ready to pay the piper. He begins to mutter something to a friend about having once done a dumb thing. But before he can elaborate, the assassins cut his story short and disappear into the night.

Ole's few acquaintances are as dumbfounded as we are. Who exactly was the "Swede," and who would want him dead? Why not try and run from death, if he saw it coming? And what was "dumb" enough to die for?

These are the questions Jim Reardon (Edmond O'Brien) asks as he investigates Andersen's case for an insurance company. The professional aspect is minimal. The paltry 2,500 dollar check is just a drop in the bucket for the claims firm. Who this man was proves much more significant. How did a guy go from being a top-ranking prizefighter to a thief, and later die a filling station attendant in a sleepy town? Like the killers themselves, the mystery closes in on Reardon and refuses to let him go. Indeed, it is a secret powerful enough to cost one man his life and consume the curiosity of another.

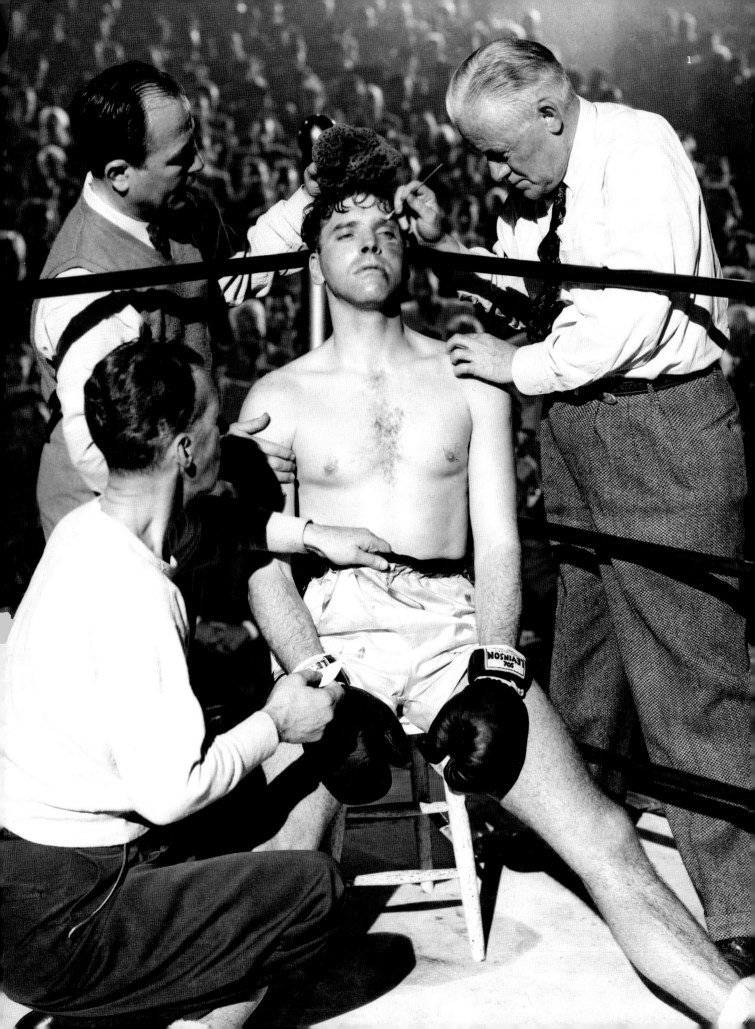

1　Them's the breaks: Ole Andersen's (Burt Lancaster) enemies plan on hitting him when he's down.

2　Always lands on her feet: the lithe Kitty Collins (Ava Gardner) hasn't used up all her lives yet.

3　Your number is up: boxer Ole Andersen, better known as "the Swede," is about to lose the fight against death.

4　A full tank of leaded: the Swede is given the works at his own filling station.

5　Trading places: Ole tries to shield Kitty from being arrested, and Lieutenant Sam Lubinsky (Sam Levene) throws the book at him instead.

A poisonous past, a love that death cannot extinguish, a date with destiny – *The Killers* pulls out all the stops and the result is film noir at its finest. Although the protagonist is fitted for his coffin just moments after we first meet him, director and genre specialist Robert Siodmak doesn't estrange the audience for a second. He contours his hero with humanity, winning our sympathies through flashback sequences of Ole as a strapping young man who simply fell for the wrong woman.

Burt Lancaster's understated performance manifests itself as indifference in the character, making it seem that Ole senses how his story will turn out even before he draws his lot. Such is the case when he willingly surrenders himself to fate at the soirée where he first sees the fiery Kitty Collins (Ava Gardner). And once Cupid's arrow has struck, there's no hope for prim Miss Lilly (Virginia Christine), who silently worships the hunk from afar and makes sad attempts to win his heart with her cooking. Kitty goes on to tighten her hold

"We know what Ava has done to other men. Burt was a hunk of steaming granite, but how could we expect him to have fared any better than Old Blue Eyes? Man is doomed, but it makes for great art, which eases the pain. That's why Sinatra songs sound so good in all-night diners."

The Austin Chronicle

6

on Ole when a boxing injury sends him into a state of crisis. It's just another twist of fate that leaves us wondering if Ole gets a say at all in steering his life.

A near unsolvable crime peppered with psychological and existentialist elements make *The Killers* an unforgettable bit of filmmaking. Ernest Hemingway's story *The Killers* provided Siodmak with the material he needed to create a cinematic exploration of guilt, atonement, and predestination. Piece by piece, Reardon reconstructs Ole Andersen's past, entering his world and becoming acquainted with all its inhabitants. Somehow every aspect of the man's life seems interconnected: Ole's old pal Lieutenant Sam Lubinsky (Sam Levene), the officer who arrested him, took the homely Lilly as his bride.

Darling Kitty, on the other hand, is the one Ole took the fall for in the first place. Today she belongs to Big Jim Colfax (Albert Dekker), a man who once weaseled Ole into robbing a bank.

All of it relates back to some unknown whole that mere piecing together can't explain. Even Ole's time in the slammer seems to be an integral part of the grand scheme, as it means he strikes up a friendship with Charleston (Vince Barnett), an elderly inmate who teaches him astrology. Looking to the stars, things that we'd normally write off as random occurrences suddenly click into a pattern some would call fate. But insights like that usually come too late …

SH

BURT LANCASTER "Deep down inside, I'm really a frustrated opera singer," Burt Lancaster (1913–1994) once said of himself. A thespian and sportsman rolled into one, his athletic build often overshadowed the fact that he was an art and music aficionado, not to mention a skilled character actor. Needless to say, the man born Burton Stephen Lancaster in New York won himself initial fame in action and adventure pictures. A former circus performer without any formal acting training, Lancaster was discovered by a Broadway producer in the early '40s. His first movie, *The Killers* (1946), made him an overnight star. Two years later, he and Harold Hecht started a production company together, which at the time was considered a highly unusual undertaking for an actor. He played opposite Edward G. Robinson in the family drama *All My Sons* (1948). *Criss Cross* (1949) marked his second collaboration with director Robert Siodmak, whom he'd team up with again for *The Crimson Pirate* (1952). Time and again, Lancaster would take on more "serious projects" like *Come Back, Little Sheba* (1952) in an attempt to rid himself of his action-hero image. Fred Zinnemann's *From Here to Eternity* (1953), starring Lancaster, garnered eight Oscars – but its leading man had to make do with a nomination (the statuette went to William Holden for his performance in Billy Wilder's *Stalag 17*, 1953). Nearly ten years later, he finally got to take home an award of his own for his portrayal of a businessman in *Elmer Gantry* (1960). While Lancaster found his work in John Frankenheimer's film the *Birdman of Alcatraz* (1962) to be among his best, his efforts won him another nod from the Academy but no Oscar; that year Gregory Peck's performance in *To Kill a Mockingbird* (1962) had made the Best Actor category an open and shut case. In the years that followed, Lancaster became a favorite character actor with European directors like Luchino Visconti (*The Leopard* / *Il gattopardo*, 1963) although he maintained his image as a death-defying daredevil in pictures like Frankenheimer's apocalyptic thriller *The Train* (*Le Train* / *Il treno*, 1964) and Sydney Pollack's comedy Western *The Scalphunters* (1968). In later years, Lancaster took on more contemplative roles, playing a past-his-prime mafioso in Louis Malle's *Atlantic City* (1980) and an American oil tycoon in Bill Forsyth's tragicomedy *Local Hero* (1982). In 1994, Burt Lancaster died of heart failure in Century City, California.

"Under the expert direction of Robert Siodmak, Burt Lancaster gives his first screen performance (and is startlingly effective). Siodmak also does wonders with Ava Gardner." *Pauline Kael*

6   Emerging constellations: cellmate Charleston (Vince Barnett) is the only person who knows which signs govern Ole's life.

7   Iron maiden: Ole's fate is sealed from the moment he lays eyes on Kitty. But is she really the one hell-bent on torturing him?

BODY AND SOUL 🏆

1947 – USA – 106 MIN.
DIRECTOR ROBERT ROSSEN (1908–1966)
SCREENPLAY ABRAHAM POLONSKY
DIRECTOR OF PHOTOGRAPHY JAMES WONG HOWE
EDITING FRANCIS D. LYON, ROBERT PARRISH
MUSIC HUGO FRIEDHOFER, JOHNNY GREEN
(Song: "Body and Soul")
PRODUCTION BOB ROBERTS for ENTERPRISE PRODUCTIONS
STARRING JOHN GARFIELD (Charlie Davis), LILLI PALMER
(Peg Born), ANNE REVERE (Anna Davis),
HAZEL BROOKS (Alice), WILLIAM CONRAD (Quinn),
JOSEPH PEVNEY (Shorty Polaski), LLOYD GOUGH
(Roberts), CANADA LEE (Ben Chaplin), ART SMITH
(David Davis), VIRGINIA GREGG (Irma)
ACADEMY AWARDS 1947 OSCAR for BEST FILM EDITING
(Francis D. Lyon, Robert Parrish)

"Like a tiger stalking his prey."

Charlie Davis (John Garfield) has a boxer's face, and every scar on it tells a story. The deep groove on his chin is a souvenir of Chicago; the little scratch alongside it he picked up in Philadelphia; the cut on his left eyebrow is a permanent reminder of Boston. His girl Peg (Lilli Palmer) hasn't seen him for a year, and now she kisses each of his wounds in turn. Charlie is proud of his record – 21 fights, 19 KOs, two victories on points. Every one of these triumphs means money in the bank, and Charlie can live like a king; but for his friend and manager Shorty (Joseph Pevney), that's a worrying development. He fears that Charlie's greed and the promoters' deviousness are turning him into a money machine, and that he's losing touch with his friends and family. Shorty tells Peg to marry him as fast as she can, as she's the only one who can still get through to him. But their wedding plans are postponed when Charlie gets the chance to challenge the champ for his world title.

The boxer, we learn, grew up poor as dirt. His parents had run a little store, struggling through the Depression years until a gangster's bullet put paid to their dreams. With his widowed mother on welfare, Charlie saw boxing as his best shot at a lucrative career. Ignoring her protests, he went for it – body and soul.

Like many boxer movies, *Body and Soul* shows an ambitious fighter using his guts and talent to come up from poverty, only to find his sporting integrity threatened by organized crime. What makes this film so exceptional is that it's also a gritty depiction of an authentic real-life milieu. Director Robert Rossen really did grow up poor on New York's Lower East Side, and he shows it the way it was, with burning oil drums, dilapidated streets, low-life dives and smoky, sepulchral pool halls. This is a world populated by sharp young hoods and shady, hard-bitten "businessmen." Rossen's film is no biopic, no hagiography of a local boy made good, and nor is it a mythical representation of some archetypal suffering hero. Here,

a fictional tale of an up-and-coming boxer serves as a credible vehicle for a dramatized social study. With this in mind, it's all the more remarkable that the boxing scenes so successfully captured the audience's imagination. And indeed, the use of a handheld camera lent this movie an unprecedented visual quality, a speed, urgency, and directness that had a lasting influence on the genre.

Like *The Killers* (1946) before it, and *The Set-Up* and *Champion* (both 1949) after, *Body and Soul* is a film noir set in a sporting milieu. The harsh opening sequence sets the tone for the rest of the movie. A bird's-eye view of Charlie's open-air training camp, with a swinging punchbag casting shad-

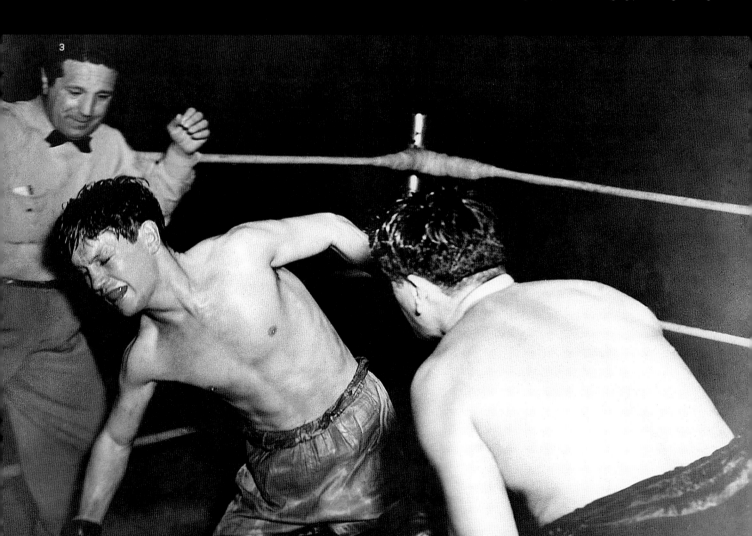

1 Through the meat grinder: like an animal at the slaughterhouse, Charlie (John Garfield) gets backed into a corner with no way out.

2 Taking time out: Charlie often seems dazed and confused between rounds; but these are, in fact, his greatest moments of clarity.

3 Blood, sweat and tears: survival in the ring means rolling with the punches.

4 Cheap blond, cheap shots: Alice (Hazel Brooks) sucker punches when he's at his most vulnerable.

"Everything is addition or subtraction; the rest is conversation." *Film quote: David Davis (Art Smith)*

ows on the ring in the moonlight. On the soundtrack, strings play an ominous staccato. Then the camera abandons its rigid gaze and dives through the branches of a leafless tree to home in on Charlie, whose face, in close-up, is twisted in terror. The boxer's nightmare reveals his inner conflict.

John Garfield was an actor who had actually fought numerous bouts in his youth, and he arrived at the movies after playing a pugilist in a success-ful stage play. In *Body and Soul*, he gave a convincing portrayal of a naïve, instinctive fighter with more heart than brains – a bit like Rocky, in John G. Avildsen's 1976 hit of the same name. The characterization is supported by a "tiger" motif that would come to typify the boxing-movie genre: Peg paints a portrait of Charlie as a boxer with a tiger's legs, and quotes William Blake's famous poem more than once: "Tyger, Tyger burning bright / In the forests of

the night / What immortal hand or eye / Could frame thy fearful symmetry?" It's Peg's way of declaring her love for her man, but it also hints at the destructive potential inherent in his beauty and strength – and at the temp-tation of crime.

Charlie anticipates the obsessive heroes of late film noir. He is also the quintessential Robert Rossen protagonist, bursting with youth and energy yet lacking in self-control and unable to see things as they really are. Even when his friends die as a direct or indirect result of the gangsters' machinations, Charlie refuses to learn his lesson. In his stubborn determination to escape the poverty of his youth, he falls prey to sinister crooks – and to the unscru-pulous Alice (Hazel Brooks). In one of the film's finest sequences, Charlie is training at the punchball, while Alice's shapely legs dangle alluringly in the

5 Foul play: when it comes to fighting at the pool hall, the first guy to sink the other's balls wins.

6 Lofty ideas: Peg Born (Lilli Palmer) invites Charlie back to her apartment and verses him in the ways of modern Bohemian life.

7 TKO: Peg and Charlie don't need to wait for anyone to count to ten to know that their friend will never get up again.

"Nobody is anybody who belongs to somebody."
Film quote: Peg Born (Lilli Palmer)

background. If they're a distraction for the viewer, they make it even harder for Charlie to keep his mind on his job.

Alice is not so much a film noir *femme fatale* as the female counterpart to our ambitious hero. Peg, by contrast – wonderfully played by Lilli Palmer – is an honest, independent woman, with a life of her own as an art student. That's why she retains his mother's approval even when he himself has lost it. Only at the last possible moment – in the final round of the fight that decides everything – does Charlie salvage his personal integrity. By cutting himself free of the mobsters, he finally manages to liberate himself from his past, his social class, and the circumstances that might have crushed him.

It's often been complained that the film's conclusion is none too credible. In fact, Rossen had originally planned to have Charlie die for his convictions. As a result, filming was accompanied by noisy disagreements between the director and his screenwriter Abraham Polonsky, who insisted that moviegoers would want a happy ending. Eventually, two versions were made; and when Rossen had compared them, he agreed to abandon his original finale. The movie was a box-office smash.   OK

JAMES WONG HOWE James Wong Howe was born in China in 1899, under the name Wong Tung Jim. His reputation as the best cameraman of his day was due to his many excellent ideas, and to a stroke of good luck: in 1919, Cecil B. DeMille was looking for a camera assistant … and because there was no one more qualified around, he took on one of the studio's handymen.

Howe had been a passionate photographer since childhood, and he liked to take still pictures around the set just to gain experience. One day, the silent movie star Mary Miles Minter asked him to take some portrait photos of her, and he hit upon a way of making her blue eyes look darker and more intense. Minter was delighted by the results, and asked Howe if he could manage the same thing with a film camera. The young photographer had no idea how he'd done it, but he answered her question in the affirmative. After closely examining the shots, he realized that a piece of black silk had been reflected in Ms. Minter's eyes; and so he went on to film her face in close-up through a hole in a black silk curtain. Soon, word was spreading amongst the stars, of a mysterious Chinese cameraman who could make eyes darker. Howe's career took off.

As the silent era came to an end, though, he was suddenly in trouble. Howe had spent some time abroad, and by the time he came back, the "talkies" were all the rage. He was seen as old-hat and out of touch, and couldn't get anyone to employ him. Soon, though, he had impressed the studios with his speed, his efficiency, and his skillful experimentation with new lenses. In particular, his use of low-contrast lighting in interior shots became his trademark.

During World War II, racial prejudice made Howe's life difficult; and in the McCarthy period that followed, he was suspected of being a Communist sympathizer. In 1956, however, he won an Academy Award for his work on *The Rose Tattoo* (1955), followed by a second in 1963, for *Hud* (1963). Though he didn't get an Oscar for *Body and Soul* (1947), the spectacular boxing scenes and the fine use of light certainly made it one of his best pieces of work. For the close-ups in the fight sequences, there was no room to use a dolly, so Howe stepped into the ring on roller skates and used a handheld camera. He also shook the camera deliberately when filming some of the punches, powerfully evoking the boxers' subjective experience. A further unforgettable highpoint of Howe's career was *Seconds* (1966), in which he used distorting lenses to create some unusually effective representations of drug experiences. For Rock Hudson's disturbing death struggle, he used a fish-eye lens, thereby inspiring a host of imitators in subsequent trash movies. By the early '70s, Howe was swamped with work, but his deteriorating health forced him to leave the film business. James Wong Howe died in Hollywood of cancer in 1976.

NIGHTMARE ALLEY

1947 – USA - 110 MIN.
DIRECTOR EDMUND GOULDING (1891–1959)
SCREENPLAY JULES FURTHMAN, based on the novel
of the same name by WILLIAM LINDSAY GRESHAM
DIRECTOR OF PHOTOGRAPHY LEE GARMES
EDITING BARBARA McCLEAN MUSIC CYRIL J. MOCKRIDGE
PRODUCTION GEORGE JESSEL for 20TH CENTURY FOX
STARRING TYRONE POWER (Stanton "Stan" Carlisle),
JOAN BLONDELL (Zeena), COLEEN GRAY
(Molly / Electra), HELEN WALKER (Lilith),
TAYLOR HOLMES (Grindle), MIKE MAZURKI (Bruno),
IAN KEITH (Pete), JULIA DEAN (Mrs. Peabody),
JAMES BURKE (Marshall)

"Body of a Man, Soul of a Geek."

In the classical Hollywood narrative structure, a man overcomes obstacles to become a success. It is the rags-to-riches story form popularized by Horatio Alger, and the embodiment of the American Dream – obtaining material wealth, the girl, and social status through hard work and endeavor – which is rooted in the American Declaration of Independence, where "all men are created equal" and are "endowed by their Creator with certain inalienable Rights" including "Life, Liberty and the pursuit of Happiness."

Nightmare Alley follows Stanton "Stan" Carlisle's (Tyrone Power) upward mobility from carny hand, to hotshot mentalist at a Chicago Hotel, to would-be spiritualist as he pursues the American Dream. He progresses from entertaining the working class for nickels and dimes, to conning the upper classes for thousands of dollars, yet the marks want to know the same things – will they make money in the future, and are their loved ones who have passed at peace?

Stanton is only able to achieve his success through his relationships with women. His affair with the maternal Zeena (Joan Blondell) nets him the word codes for the mentalist act, but only after the accidental death of her alcoholic husband Pete (Ian Keith) – an accident perpetrated by Stanton. Stanton learns the codes with the aid of young, impressionable Molly (Coleen Gray), who then becomes his partner in the mentalist act as well as in life. Finally, to make the transition from mentalist to spiritualist Stanton begins a working relation with phony psychoanalyst Lilith Ritter (Helen Walker) by using the information she gathers during sessions with patients Mrs. Peabody (Julia Dean) and Ezra Grindle (Taylor Holmes) to fake contact with their dead loved ones.

Yet for all this forward and upward motion, there is a sense of doom and foreboding that permeates the film. The word "Geek" appears on a carny sign in the center of the screen in the first shot of the film, so from the outset the viewer knows that all of Stanton's efforts are predestined to fail. The geek is the lowest form of entertainment in the carny – an alcoholic who bites heads off live chickens in return for a bottle a day and a place to bed down – yet he is also the biggest draw on the midway. "How can a guy get

"If one can take any moral value out of *Nightmare Alley* it would seem to be that a terrible retribution is the inevitable consequence for he who would mockingly attempt to play God." *The New York Times*

1 Stanton "Stan" Carlisle (Tyrone Power) is a likeable carny hand who has an affair with Zeena (Joan Blondell), a married woman.

2 Zeena is drawn to Stan's vitality, but cinematographer Lee Garmes's ominous lighting suggests darker times ahead.

3 Psychoanalyst and business partner Lilith Ritter (Helen Walker) sums up Stan: "You're a perfectly normal human being. Selfish and ruthless when you want something, kind and generous when you've got it."

so low?" Stanton asks. The film shows "how" in a series of recurring visual and aural cues. The night when Stanton accidentally contributes to the death of Pete begins with the word "Geek" hovering on a sign in the background. Feeling guilty about profiting from Pete's death, Stanton hears the screams of the geek during moments of stress, eventually leading him to Lilith's couch, where he reveals his psychological weaknesses, weaknesses Lilith eventually uses to break him.

Stanton is for the most part a rather likeable figure. Despite all his setbacks, Stanton does not blame anyone but himself, and always bounces back with a way forward. He recognizes that he is selfish, but remains unconscious of his motivations. "I don't know why," he tells Zeena. It is one of the best performances of Tyrone Power's career. According to the New York Times, "Mr. Power has a juicy role and sinks his teeth into it, performing with considerable versatility and persuasiveness."

WILLIAM LINDSAY GRESHAM On a visit to the freak show at Coney Island, the young Gresham (1909–1962) became fascinated by a sharply dressed Italian man who had a small headless body hanging out of his stomach. The small body was also impeccably dressed. Learning that the Italian was happily married with five normal children, Gresham began to envy him – all Gresham had was a father afraid of losing his job and a mother always grousing about money.

In November 1937, Gresham went to Spain and fought with the Abraham Lincoln Battalion in the Spanish Civil War. There he met Joseph Daniel "Doc" Halliday, who liked to reminisce about his times in a carnival. It was from him that Gresham learned all about carny culture, the habits, the mentality, the language, and geeks. Immediately, a story idea entered into Gresham's head, about the rise of a carny conman and his subsequent descent into geekdom. When Gresham returned to New York, his first marriage ended in divorce, he took to drink, and, in despair, attempted to hang himself in a closet but the hook came loose and he fell to the ground, gaining consciousness hours later.

After marrying poet Helen Joy Davidman, Gresham began work on his novel, hanging out at the Dixie Hotel, where the carnival workers did their drinking. Nightmare Alley was published in 1946, met with immediate success, sold to Hollywood for $60,000, and became a classic film noir the following year. While he was writing the equally bleak Limbo Tower (1949), Gresham probably believed he was on the road to a successful career as a novelist, but that was not to be the case. The funds began to dry up, he began drinking heavily, and would fly into rages for little or no reason. After his second divorce, Gresham moved to Florida, married Joy's first cousin Renée Rodriguez, and completed three non-fiction books – on carneys, Houdini, and bodybuilding – then discovered he had cancer of the tongue. On September 14, 1962, with no wish for either himself or his family to face a long, ugly death, he checked into the Dixie Hotel, registering as "Asa Kimball, of Baltimore" – the central character of Limbo Tower – and took his own life.

After returning from World War II, Power had tired of playing the romantic lead and was determined to show his considerable acting skills on the silver screen. First he teamed with director Edmund Goulding for the metaphysical (and mega-successful) *The Razor's Edge* (1946), then he bought the rights to William Lindsay Gresham's best-selling novel *Nightmare Alley* with a view to portraying the corrupt central character. Darryl F. Zanuck, head of production at 20th Century Fox, was against it, but Power got his way, working with Goulding again, although much of the novel had to be toned down to adhere to the Production Code. Screenwriter Jules Furthman (*To Have and Have Not*, 1944; *The Big Sleep*, 1946) made Stanton less avaricious, and the class division between the good proletarian carny people and the materialistic, corrupt upper classes was toned down, but the implied power of the Tarot

4   When Zeena predicts bad things using the Tarot cards, Stan dismisses it as "chump stuff," believing that he is in control of his own destiny.

5   After Stan sleeps with Molly (Coleen Gray, right) the carny people force them to marry, then the couple start a mentalist act that becomes successful.

6   Zeena's alcoholic husband, Pete (Ian Keith, center), was once a great man, but is now a loser; he prefigures Stan's fate.

"Stan Carlisle fascinated me. He was such an unmitigated heel. Here was a chance to create a character different from any I had ever played before." *Tyrone Power*

cards was retained. Early in the movie Zeena gives a reading that Pete would "disappear," and it came true because of Stan's actions. Later, Zeena gives another reading and tells Stan that he must not proceed with his new venture (the spiritualism racket), which Stan again ignores because he thinks Tarot cards, spiritualism, and psychoanalysis is "chump stuff." After Stanton's stunt to con Grindle is ruined by Molly, Lilith betrays him, so he has no option but to make a run for it. His road to dissolution and alcoholism is swift and irrevocable. He gets so low, he's happy to take a position as a geek. "Mister, I was made for it," he tells the carny boss. The tacked-on ending, which Zanuck insisted upon, has Stan find Molly again, but their relationship now echoes that of Zeena and Pete at the beginning of the movie, and we all know how that ended.

Zanuck lavished money on sets, even hiring a carnival and sideshow attraction to pitch on the back lot, and assigned Lee Garmes (*Shanghai Express*, 1932; *Scarface*, 1932) to apply some of his "Rembrandt lighting" – i.e., light coming from one major source – to heighten the atmosphere. The end result is somewhat deviant and malevolent, portraying the flipside of the American Dream, where to become successful you must prey on the weaknesses of others.

The film premiered in the U.S. on October 9, 1947, but was not publicized by Zanuck, and failed to recoup its cost. Subsequently, *Nightmare Alley* acquired a cult status, not least because it was unavailable for many years, but is now recognized as one of the most noir of the film noirs of the 1940s.

PD

OUT OF THE PAST

1947 – USA – 97 MIN.
DIRECTOR JACQUES TOURNEUR (1904–1977)
SCREENPLAY DANIEL MAINWARING, FRANK FENTON,
JAMES M. CAIN, based on the novel
Build My Gallows High by GEOFFREY HOMES
[= DANIEL MAINWARING]
DIRECTOR OF PHOTOGRAPHY NICHOLAS MUSURACA
EDITING SAMUEL E. BEETLEY
MUSIC ROY WEBB PRODUCTION WARREN DUFF for RKO.
STARRING ROBERT MITCHUM (Jeff Bailey / Markham),
JANE GREER (Kathie Moffett), KIRK DOUGLAS
(Whit Sterling), VIRGINIA HUSTON (Ann), STEVE BRODIE
(Fisher), RHONDA FLEMING (Meta Carson),
RICHARD WEBB (Jim), PAUL VALENTINE (Joe),
DICKIE MOORE (mute boy), KEN NILES (Leonard Eels)

"You want to just shut the door and forget it?"

Out of the Past starts its story in the purity of sunshine. But the daunting sense of darkness that soon takes hold of this picture needs no physical night to stake its claim.

A stranger named Joe (Paul Valentine) arrives in the sleepy California town of Bridgeport in an effort to reconnect with Jeff Bailey (Robert Mitchum), the owner of the local filling station. Bailey, a Bridgeport transplant, has done his best to adapt to local customs and is enjoying the good life complete with blonde sweetheart and a respectable position in the community. But when Joe shows up, Bailey's past comes crashing down around him.

Like many other film noirs, Jacques Tourneur's *Out of the Past* examines the way the past catches up with the present, of events that refuse to be erased or forgotten. The clock turns back to Bailey's days as a private detective in New York. Gangster Whit Sterling (Kirk Douglas) hires him to track down his runaway lover Kathie (Jane Greer), who has robbed him blind, and bring her home. But instead of completing the job, Bailey falls in love with the steely vixen. They run off together with the intention of never looking back, but a former associate of Bailey's named Fisher (Steve Brodie) finds them out. Before he gets a chance to pull the whistle on them, Kathie shoots the informant dead and makes herself scarce with the stolen cash. Left with few other prospects, Bailey moves to Bridgeport and melts away into the quiet backdrop. Then Sterling's right-hand man Joe shows up like a messenger of death: his boss wants to discuss some unfinished

"A classic film noir, so dark and fatalistic that even the scenes in sunny California and heatstroked Acapulco look like overexposed nightmares." *Süddeutsche Zeitung*

business with Bailey up at his place in Lake Tahoe – and he won't take no for an answer.

That night, while driving up to meet Sterling, Bailey confesses the details of his sordid past to his current girlfriend Ann (Virginia Huston). The fleeting twilight and the deep, soothing cadence of Bailey's voice imbue the flashback sequences that follow with a dreamlike quality, beautifully complemented by a shift in the film's visual aesthetic. Darkness assumes command and with it comes an air of uncertainty, the intangible, and an almost supernatural quality reminiscent of Tourneur's horror movies from the early 1940s. This atmospheric change makes Bailey's encounter with Kathie seem like a stroke of fate. The notion that these two might be doomed to walk to the ends

of the earth together is hinted at again later during a climactic evening rendezvous by the fishing nets on the beaches of Mexico. And indeed when Bailey finally reaches the destination of his drive with Ann, the cast-iron gate to Sterling's estate closes behind him, as if to say that the past has swallowed him up – once and for all. Before the next scene is over, he'll find himself standing face to face with Kathie. But their strange reunion is by no means an indication that their debts have been settled.

The cult status *Out of the Past* has managed to earn itself over the decades is primarily the doing of its leading man. Robert Mitchum plays not only the most laconic, but also the most fatalistic of all film noir protagonists. The embodiment of human melancholy, Bailey knows that his die has been

2

3

1   Holding onto the past: Whit Sterling (Kirk Douglas) reclaims what's rightfully his – the capricious Kathie (Jane Greer).

2   Rear assault: time and time again, Kathie catches Bailey (Robert Mitchum) off guard and stings him with her poisonous allure.

3   On a crash course with destiny: Tourneur uses darkness and light to foreshadow where Kathie and Bailey's destructive relationship is headed.

4   Present company excluded: Meta (Rhonda Fleming) has no involvement in Bailey's past, and seems to love him from afar.

cast long before Sterling comes calling. Even when we see him painting an optimistic picture of the future for sweetheart Ann in one of the film's preliminary scenes, there's an undeniable disillusionment in his face that contradicts everything he says. Later, Bailey's behavior seems strikingly detached as he coolly attempts to foil Sterling's diabolical schemes by playing Kathie against him. It's as if he'd already surrendered himself to fate and only intends to indicate the futility of trying to shape it. This seeming contradiction between taking action and acting with indifference, which Mitchum captures like no other actor, is characteristic of the complex dramatic arcs that move the film along, yet make it so impenetrable: *femme fatale* Kathie reveals a vulnerable side beyond her cold-blooded vamp exterior; Ann drops the good-girl veneer and floors us with unexpected

"Robert Mitchum is magnificently cheeky and self-assured as the tangled 'private eye' consuming an astronomical number of cigarettes in displaying his nonchalance."

The New York Times

4

5   Kirk Douglas and Robert Mitchum established
    themselves as film noir fixtures in the 1940s.

6   Taking their coffee black: no amount of sweetener
    can mask the fact that these three characters will
    all meet with a bitter end.

7   Sit for a spell: the beguiling Kathie hypnotizes the
    men in her life with a set of irresistible doe eyes.

> "Mitchum gives a very strong account of himself. Jane Greer as the charming, baby-faced killer is another source of potent interest." *Variety*

sensuality and a fiery spirit; Sterling, too, proves he possesses a few admirable traits.

Tourneur blurs the black-and-white film noir archetypes that make so many examples of the genre seem cut and dried. This approach to characterization is reflected in the film's look. Whenever cinematographer Nicholas Musuraca, who also served as cameraman for Tourneur's *Cat People* (1942), shrouds the otherwise familiar-looking locations in low-key lighting, we begin to doubt our ABC of Hollywood visuals. Suddenly, sunny Bridgeport looks remarkably less than idyllic. Its deeply conformist inhabitants, to whose eyes Bailey will forever remain an outsider, is a prelude to the fascist atmosphere that would become commonplace in depictions of 1950s suburban life. This town will offer Bailey no sanctuary. No sir, it's simply not in the cards.   JH

JACQUES TOURNEUR   The son of critically acclaimed director Maurice Tourneur, Jacques Tourneur (1904–1977) was literally born into filmmaking. Getting his start in the business as his father's personal assistant, this native Parisian began directing his own projects towards the end of the 1920s. In 1935, he headed for Hollywood, where he shot featurettes and, as of 1939, B movies. *Cat People* (1942) brought him his greatest industry breakthrough. It was to be the first of his legendary three horror-movie collaborations at RKO with producer Val Lewton. The film revolutionized the genre by favoring a suggestive depiction of terror over an explicit one, often simply achieved by expressionistic lighting. *Cat People*, *I Walked with a Zombie* (1943), and *The Leopard Man* (1943) all contributed to Tourneur's reputation as a filmmaker with an unbeatable sense of style. *Berlin Express* (1948) and *Out of the Past* (1947), thrillers reminiscent of his previous work in horror follow in Tourneur's great aesthetic tradition. He spent a great deal of time researching supernatural phenomena and the paranormal, a passion made evident in *The Night of the Demon / Curse of the Demon* (1957) filmed in England. This, however, is not to say that Tourneur's talent was limited, for he was as versatile as they come, and demonstrated a rare feel for color photography that dazzled audiences in a wide range of genres. Tourneur's Western *Wichita* (1955) is as visually stunning as his battling knight epics *The Flame and the Arrow* (1950) and *Anne of the Indies* (1951). He died in Bergerac, France, in December of 1977.

T-MEN

1947 – USA – 92 MIN.
DIRECTOR ANTHONY MANN (1906–1967)
SCREENPLAY JOHN C. HIGGINS, from an unpublished
story by VIRGINIA KELLOGG, based upon
the files of the U.S. Treasury Department
DIRECTOR OF PHOTOGRAPHY JOHN ALTON
EDITING FRED ALLEN MUSIC PAUL SAWTELL
PRODUCTION AUBREY SCHENCK for EDWARD SMALL
PRODUCTIONS, RELIANCE PICTURES,
EAGLE-LION FILMS
STARRING DENNIS O'KEEFE (Dennis O'Brien / "Harrigan"),
ALFRED RYDER (Tony Genaro / "Galvani"), MARY MEADE
(Evangeline), WALLACE FORD (Schemer),
JUNE LOCKHART (Mary, Genaro's wife),
CHARLES MCGRAW (Moxie), JANE RANDOLPH (Diana),
ART SMITH (Gregg), HERBERT HEYES
(Chief Carson), JACK OVERMAN (Brownie),
JOHN WENGRAF (Shiv), JIM BANNON (Lindsay),
WILLIAM MALTEN (Paul Miller)

"They had to know all the answers. Failure to do so would mean a bad grade later on in the shape of a bullet or an ice pick."

T-Men is the first of a half-dozen films made by director Anthony Mann and cinematographer John Alton; theirs is arguably the most important collaboration in film noir's classic period. As a director Mann believed that each setup had only one optimal camera angle and used careful positioning of actors within the decor to discover it. Alton believed in "painting with light," a phrase he used as the title of his 1949 book on cinematography. *T-Men* draws its story from actual case files and introduces its narrative with an on-camera lecture by an official of the Treasury Department about the dangerous work performed by its agents. From that stuffy and stentorian opening the movie follows two such agents as they insert themselves precariously into the noir underworld. The brutality and betrayal they suffer in the dark and deadly landscape of Los Angeles is captured by Mann and Alton in a manner that transforms a modest programmer into a *tour de force* of postwar noir.

The documentary approach of the opening immediately cedes to anonymous action: a nighttime shoot-out where oblique angles capture strained faces momentarily illuminated by the bright flash from gun muzzles. This stark contrast in staging and styles reflects and reinforces the sense of a dark maelstrom that exists on the fringes of normal society, ready to suck in and destroy the unaware. Unlike many hapless noir protagonists, the title figures in this movie, "T-Men" Dennis O'Brien (Dennis O'Keefe) and Tony Genaro (Alfred Ryder), wade voluntarily into the turbulent noir whirlpool. They pose as upstart criminals Harrigan and Galvani to infiltrate counterfeiting rings first in Detroit and then in Los Angeles.

In the context of dual identities and divided loyalties, Mann's work repeatedly probes character psychology across genres. Particularly in his early noir work, the difficult choices come down in the face of deadly peril.

1   For Treasury Agent Dennis O'Brien (Dennis O'Keefe) one of the major downsides of working undercover is being roughed up by suspicious hoodlums.

2   Sometimes the beating is closer to one-on-one as Moxie (Charles McGraw) punches O'Brien (posing as Harrigan), while Brownie (Jack Overman) keeps him upright.

3   From the underworlds of Detroit to L.A. the undercover T-Men spend a lot of time sitting apprehensively while listening to cheap grifters.

4   O'Brien must watch as Moxie, under orders from Shiv (John Wengraf, behind them), prepares to shoot undercover T-man Genaro (Alfred Ryder, right).

To establish credibility, the T-men pose as brash upstarts. After traveling from Michigan to Southern California, O'Brien is caught passing bogus bills and beaten for his trouble by his counterfeiting competitors. This is all part of the plan to convince Schemer (Wallace Ford) that he is an authentic wrongdoer with an illegitimate commodity for sale – in this case high-end plates for printing phony money.

While Alton's lighting reflects the unstable environment that imperils the T-men, Mann uses his performers to create basic tension. For most of the narrative, O'Brien and Genaro remain in their gangster personas. While real felons Schemer, Moxie (Charles McGraw), and Shiv (John Wengraf) initially accept the Treasury agents as cohorts, the audience knows who they really are and can read the irony in their subtle facial expressions and nervous tics. These subtle moments are the only visual confirmation the viewer receives that "Harrigan" is more hero than hoodlum. By forcing the viewer to participate in this overlay of cop and crook, Mann and Alton create a difficult dramatic identification, where the hero's ultimate success depends on deception, on being someone he is not.

Two related sequences in particular epitomize this. In the first, Genaro and Schemer visit a market and encounter a woman whom both the audience and the characters, except for Schemer, know is Genaro's wife. While the lighting is realistic, an angle of figures reflecting in a store window suggests the presence of layers. From a parallel emotional vantage point, Schemer

ANTHONY MANN Native Californian filmmaker Anthony Mann (1906–1967) shot a slew of film noir thrillers prior to devoting himself to the Hollywood Western renaissance of the 1950s. James Stewart, who before his collaboration with Mann was generally known for his work in light comedies, played the antihero on the verge of collapse in the director's *The Naked Spur* (1953) as well as in darker pieces like *Winchester '73* (1950), *Bend of the River* (1951), *The Far Country* (1954) and *The Man from Laramie* (1955). Mann's cinematic work was also characterized by elaborate on-screen acting constellations underscored by the bold visual execution of his subject matter. Shortly after Mann started work on *Spartacus* (1960), producer Kirk Douglas replaced the director with Stanley Kubrick; nonetheless, Mann got his chance at staging wide-screen ancient epics for the American cinema with smash hits like *El Cid* (1961) and *The Fall of the Roman Empire* (1964).

senses that Genaro and the woman are not the strangers they pretend to be. In hopes of ingratiating himself with the menacing Moxie, Schemer confides his suspicions.

In the second, "Harrigan" must tag along as Moxie and his minions go to confront "Galvani." In another ironic use of reflection, Mann and Alton stage the deadly encounter with Genaro backed up against a wall next to a dresser and mirror. This creates a dynamic combination of subjective and objective perspectives in a single frame. The viewer can see the undercover man's apprehension and fear as he faces a likely bullet and slumps against the wall in anticipation of its impact. At the same time, what Genaro sees is visible in the mirror. Moxie holds a gun aimed at him while two expression-less thugs stand behind him. To Moxie's right is O'Brien. Neither Moxie nor

3

> # "An entertaining action film. *March-of-Time* technique in the early reels flavors the footage with pungent realism that builds up to a suspenseful finish at the final fadeout."
> *Variety*

4

5

> **"Early segments include a series of shots introducing Charles McGraw. These show his head emerging from the darkness, then rotating around. He seems like a powerful mechanical object, such as a lighthouse or piston. This image creates a sense of machine-like implacability."** *Michael E. Grost*

5 O'Brien looks over the shoulder of club photographer Evangeline (Mary Meade) as she examines one of his bogus bills.

6 Classic Anthony Mann framing: Schemer (Wallace Ford) on one side of the door and O'Brien / Harrigan on the other cannot see each other, but the audience sees them both.

7 The doomed Schemer realizes that Moxie has locked him inside a steam room where he will die in parboiled agony.

8 When he isn't getting beaten up, O'Brien / Harrigan is hitting the deck and dodging bullets.

his other men can see O'Brien's face. Only Genaro and the audience perceive the look of helplessness and despair.

Whether in this single shot or in the extended sequences of Schemer's murder – he is parboiled in a steam bath – or the climactic confrontation aboard a freighter where a wounded O'Brien still manages to extract vengeance for his dead partner, Mann and Alton meticulously stage and illumi-nate for optimal impact. Using depth of field, character placement at the edges of frames, vectors created by lines in the decor, shafts of light in smoky rooms, and any combinations thereof, Mann and Alton define their own noir grammar to which they will return, working together or with others, in sub-sequent films.

AS

6

7

8

"I told you . . .
you know
nothing
about
wickedness"

COLUMBIA
PICTURES
presents

Rita **HAYWORTH** · Orson **WELLES**
in
The **Lady** from **Shanghai**

with EVERETT SLOANE and GLENN ANDERS · Screenplay and Production by ORSON WELLES

THE LADY FROM SHANGHAI

1947 – USA – 87 MIN.
DIRECTOR ORSON WELLES (1915–1985)
SCREENPLAY ORSON WELLES, based on the novel
If I Die Before I Wake by SHERWOOD KING
DIRECTOR OF PHOTOGRAPHY CHARLES LAWTON JR.
EDITING VIOLA LAWRENCE MUSIC HEINZ ROEMHELD
PRODUCTION ORSON WELLES for COLUMBIA
PICTURES CORPORATION
STARRING RITA HAYWORTH (Elsa Bannister),
ORSON WELLES (Michael O'Hara), EVERETT SLOANE
(Arthur Bannister), GLENN ANDERS (George Grisby),
TED DE CORSIA (Sidney Broome),
ERSKINE SANFORD (Judge), GUS SCHILLING
(Goldfish), CARL FRANK (District Attorney),
EVELYN ELLIS (Bessie), LOUIS MERRILL (Jake)

"When I start out to make a fool of myself, there's very little can stop me!"

"If I'd known where it would end, I'd have never let anything start. If I'd been in my right mind, that is. But once I'd seen her, I was not in my right mind for quite some time." When sailor Michael O'Hara (Orson Welles), affectionately known as "Black Irish" feasts his eyes on the lovely Elsa Bannister (Rita Hayworth), he is overcome by a maddening love for which there is no cure. His otherwise keen instincts, his good sense of judgment – all cast to the wind. But it's no wonder: as Elsa rides through New York's Central Park in a horse-drawn carriage even we are blinded by her radiance. And by the time O'Hara makes his initial approach, coolly asking if she'd care for a cigarette, she's already got him by the tail. His destiny is sealed.

In a day's time Elsa and Black Irish will be charting a course for Mexico aboard a luxury yacht with her wealthy husband, star attorney Arthur Bannister (Everett Sloane), and his business partner George Grisby (Glenn Anders). But rather than enjoying a pleasure cruise, the sailor gets the impression he's been shanghaied as bizarre situations unfold and he eventually stands trial for murder in San Francisco. As if that weren't enough, the day the hearing ends, O'Hara will be staring down the barrel of a gun.

There are films that read like a slice of life: the characters speak in the slang our ears are accustomed to, shooting the breeze against unassuming images of everyday life (Eric Rohmer's lighthearted romantic comedies come to mind). And then there is the other kind: films in which every line of dialogue, every image, and the set up of every shot is calculatingly loaded for maximum impact. *The Lady from Shanghai* clearly falls into the second category. With absolute precision commanding every shot, the film opens with an image of the Hudson River at twilight that a hard cut replaces with Central Park. No sooner do we realize where we are than Elsa lights up the night in her white polka-dot dress. Meanwhile, O'Hara's voice-over leads us through the scene, enveloping it all in a foreboding, fatalistic haze. Every frame, every sound, every pore of this picture is oozing with danger.

This highly mannered and symbolic tone continues throughout the film. A bizarre *menage-à-quatre* between O'Hara, Elsa, her unpredictable crippled husband, and his sleazy confidante gives way to images of repressed sexual desire and outright violence on the high seas. Just where these characters actually stand is anybody's guess. Anecdotes packaged in code are the view-

1

Rita couldn't just turn up as the very well-known pinup girl that she was; she needed a completely new look. So we made her platinum blonde with very short hair. Harry Cohn was the studio boss, and you can imagine how delighted he was when he found out about it!" *Orson Welles*

1. Good housekeeping: Elsa (Rita Hayworth) contemplates sweeping private detective Broome (Ted de Corsia) out of the house with the rest of the dirt.

2. Look at this mesh: from behind this net, sailor Michael O'Hara (Orson Welles) can't help but think he's been shanghaied by a mermaid.

3. Peep show: Bannister's business associate, George Grisby (Glenn Anders, right), gets his jollies watching Elsa and Michael from a safe distance.

4. An inside job: Grisby (right) hires Michael to act as if he's killed him; but Michael reconsiders when his employer turns up dead as a doornail.

5. Legal eagle no more: the lawyer who never lost a case ruins his perfect record and gets Michael (far right) a one-way ticket to Alcatraz. Everett Sloane (standing right) as Arthur Bannister.

er's only lifeline. One of the more telling signals comes from O'Hara, who recounts how sharks gathered around his fishing boat one fateful day and ate each other alive as soon as they smelled blood. Then, as if it were a prophecy, Grisby unexpectedly ups the stakes with fire high above a Mexican village, offering to pay O'Hara if he'll agree to murder him. The way the scene is filmed is equally unnerving, the diagonal overhead shot implying that either man could fall to his death from the cliff on which the bizarre business proposition is made. And the pull from these hellish depths is stronger than O'Hara dare think.

Scenes such as these could have just as easily fallen flat or died of symbolic overkill. But director, screenwriter, producer, and star Orson Welles (*Citizen Kane*, 1941) is such a virtuoso that he need not think twice as he

6

"The most amazing visual effect is the climactic Crazy House / Hall of Mirrors location, which is a wonder of surrealist set design." *TV Guide*

interweaves cinematic stereotypes with the conventions of film noir and gangster flicks. In his hands, *The Lady from Shanghai* emerges as a triumph of grotesque, an alluring, highly artificial display that toys with the medium every chance it gets. Archetypes are turned inside out with champions of the American way revealed as the despicable and ruthless creatures they really are. And Rita Hayworth, the quintessential sex symbol of the 1940s and Welles's wife at the time of shooting (they were divorced in 1947), plays the biggest praying mantis of them all.

The film closes in a bygone San Francisco amusement park called "Playland at the Beach" with a showdown sequence that is as legendary as *Psycho*'s (1960) shower scene. Unable to distinguish between appearance and reality, shards of glass come crashing down as gunfire initially targets reflections rather than flesh. It is only when two of the characters lose their lives that O'Hara comes face-to-face with the shattering truth surrounding *The Lady from Shanghai*.

HJK

ORSON WELLES Born in 1915, actor and director Orson Welles had already made a name for himself by 1938, when he directed a radio adaptation of H. G. Wells's *The War of the Worlds*. It threw the people of New York into a panic. Suddenly, Welles was famous, or notorious; and when he signed the contract with RKO Studios for his first major film, *Citizen Kane* (1941), he was granted a number of unusual privileges. *The Magnificent Ambersons* followed in 1942; but as the box-office returns from *Kane* had proved disappointing, he was not allowed to edit the latter film as he had wished. And so began a series of projects that were completed by other directors, or remained entirely unfinished or suffered mutilation at the hands of studio bosses, like his late noir movie, *Touch of Evil* (1958). Welles responded with various strategies, including a low-budget movie version of his theater production of *Macbeth* (1948). It was followed by two further Shakespeare adaptations; with *Othello* (1952), he won the Grand Prix at Cannes in the same year. From 1948 onwards, he worked repeatedly in Europe, both as a director and as an actor. Filmmakers who employed him included Claude Chabrol, Fred Zinnemann, and Sergei Bondartschuk. Apart from Kane, his most memorable acting role was probably as Harry Lime in Carol Reed's *The Third Man* (1949). Among his many works for cinema and TV in the years after 1960, *F for Fake* (1975) stands out – an eccentric, episodic documentary about great forgers and his own passion for charlatanism. Orson Welles died in Los Angeles in 1985.

6   No more distorting reality: Michael sees the truth from all angles in the hall of mirrors.

7   The mirrors crack'd from side to side: the curse is come upon me cried the lawyer from Shanghai!

THE TREASURE OF THE SIERRA MADRE ♟♟♟

1948 – USA – 126 MIN.
DIRECTOR JOHN HUSTON (1906–1987)
SCREENPLAY JOHN HUSTON, based on the
novel of the same name by B. TRAVEN
DIRECTOR OF PHOTOGRAPHY TED D. MCCORD
EDITING OWEN MARKS **MUSIC** MAX STEINER
PRODUCTION HENRY BLANKE for WARNER BROS.
STARRING HUMPHREY BOGART (Fred C. Dobbs),
WALTER HUSTON (Howard), TIM HOLT (Bob Curtin),
BRUCE BENNETT (James Cody), BARTON MACLANE
(Pat McCormick), ALFONSO BEDOYA (Gold Hat),
JOHN HUSTON (American in a White Suit),
ROBERT BLAKE (Boy with the Lottery Tickets),
JOSÉ TORVAY (Pablo), MARGARITO LUNA (Pancho)
ACADEMY AWARDS 1948 OSCARS for BEST DIRECTOR
(John Huston), BEST SCREENPLAY (John Huston),
and BEST SUPPORTING ACTOR (Walter Huston)

"Bye, mountain, thanks!"

Howard (Walter Huston), old and experienced, has no illusions: "Gold itself ain't good for nothin', except makin' jewelry with, and gold teeth." He's spent his life grubbing around in the dirt, hoping to strike it rich some day, and he's still very far from wealthy. In a lousy dive in Tampico, Mexico, he picks up with Dobbs (Humphrey Bogart) and Curtin (Tim Holt), two washed-up workers who are broke, yet again, after being cheated by McCormick (Barton MacLane), a crooked businessman: "Yeah, I know what gold does to men's souls." Yet Howard's eyes sparkle when he talks about prospecting . . . and that's why he

leaps at the chance when Dobbs and Curtin, in sheer desperation, decide to form a partnership and go off in search of gold. Together, the three of them make their way to the Sierra Madre, a remote, inaccessible corner of Mexico where Howard suspects there are immense riches waiting to be found.

Howard leads the group, for he's the only one with the necessary know-how; yet he's very anxious that everyone should get on well. He knows only too well that the success of their expedition depends on mutual trust, and that as soon as they lose that trust, every gold strike will become a murderous

affair. It's as if the elusive substance were a drug capable of clouding a man's reason and driving him mad. Curtin is the most innocent of the three, but he also has a moral sense. The braggart Dobbs, by contrast, has a tendency to be excessively distrustful. He's been taken for a sucker too often in life not to see a simple, friendly chat between his partners as proof of a plot against him. The three men do eventually find gold – lots of it – and that's when their troubles really start.

The mysterious B. Traven had published the original novel in 1927, and director John Huston (who makes three brief appearances in the film as a rich American dressed in white) had been wanting to film it since before World War II. The arrival of his call-up papers put his professional plans on hold for a while, but shortly after the Allied victory, the project began to take shape

once more. It was important to Huston to make some changes to the literary model: the dialogue seemed too unwieldy, and the plot too loose and overloaded with metaphorical significance. He was mainly interested in exploring how the characters develop, and in depicting the murky depths that open up beneath and within them as they walk the tightrope between trust and suspicion. In Mexico, Huston went looking for suitable locations, as he wanted to film outdoors as much as possible.

The finished product powerfully evokes the sheer physical isolation of the three gold diggers. For months on end, these men are left to themselves and their imaginations. In an environment made up of rocks, dust, heat, and cacti, their clothes grow increasingly tattered and shabby. Huston's father Walter won an Oscar for his performance (while his son carried off two, for

1   24 carats a day, 7 days a week: Curtin (Tim Holt) experiences the round-the-clock burn of gold fever while seeking the mother lode.

2   That's the ticket: Dobbs (Humphrey Bogart) wonders whether buying a lottery number off a young boy is an easier route to fortune.

3   All for one and one for all: when it comes to mining, three musketeers Dobbs, Howard (Walter Huston), and Curtin are inseparable.

4   Thinking with his ass: the ongoing treasure hunt drives Dobbs to the brink of insanity.

5   Still got a ways to go: Curtin and Dobbs sense that age isn't the only respect in which Howard is further along than they are.

"More than a meditation on the vanity of all earthly ambition, it is a hymn to liberty, from John Huston to his father Walter – who plays Bogart off the screen quite effortlessly. The true hero of this film is the film itself." *Le Nouvel Observateur*

Treasure of the Sierra Madre was one of the first American films shot almost completely on location outside the U.S. Tampico, Mexico, was the jumping off point, but Huston wanted his cast as far away from civilization as possible, which to Bogart was any place where you couldn't drive to Mike Romanoff's restaurant for a drink. 'John wanted everything perfect,' he said." *moviediva.com*

6   Holy frijoles! Mexican banditos get ready to
    give themselves something to celebrate this
    Cinco de Mayo.

7   Age before beauty: Dobbs and Curtin would be
    lost without Howard's wisdom. Director John
    Huston cast his father in the role of the old sage,

and both men took home Oscars for their work
that year.

Best Director and Best Screenplay). The director had persuaded his dad to leave out his dentures in the cause of authenticity, yet Walter Huston still spoke his lines at breakneck speed and without fluffing a single one of them. His philosophical excursions on the deadly effects of filthy lucre are worth their weight in gold.

Howard is the most human of the three characters, for he lives according to the principle that he can't expect more from life than it chooses to give him. When the tale has run its course, the gold dust they've sweated to acquire blows away in the wind, leaving not a trace behind, Howard bursts into raucous laughter: "The gold has gone back to where we found it!" Nature knows no morality, yet it doesn't stop Howard from seeing the drama of their terrible loss as a clever comedy penned by a higher power. His laughter liberates and rejuvenates, for it scorns death and puts life before profit. More essential to life than riches is the happiness achievable in a human community based on trust. "Hell is other people," wrote Jean Paul Sartre in *No Exit* (*Huis Clos*, 1944); Huston had directed Sartre's play in New York only shortly before making this film.   SR

B. TRAVEN Who was the mysterious B. Traven? Even the textbooks aren't entirely sure. All we know for certain is that from the time of his earliest literary successes in the early 1930s until his death nearly 40 years later, he craved anonymity. "B. Traven" changed his name several times. The British journalist Woodrow Wyatt claimed to have proven that he was actually Albert Otto Maximilian Feige, a German born in Schwiebus near Frankfurt in 1882. Rolf Recknagel had another theory: in a biography first published in Leipzig in 1966, he argued that Traven was none other than Ret Marut, former publisher of the Munich-based socialist-anarchist journal *Der Ziegelbrenner*. (The name "Ret Marut" was also, it seems, a pseudonym.) What we do know is that Traven fled to Mexico by a roundabout route after the First World War. He did so under the name "Berick T. Torsvan," making good use of the opportunity to abandon his old identity. His career as a writer began in Mexico, where he allegedly became a Mexican citizen in 1941, under the name "Hal Croves." There, he wrote a series of compelling and socially critical novels, such as *Death Ship* (1926), *The Treasure of the Sierra Madre* (1927), and *The Rebellion of the Hanged* (1936). These densely metaphoric works are characterized by a highly idiosyncratic voice, and the social criticism they embody has a decidedly existentialist flavor. They also speak out clearly against violence and inhumanity. While preparing to make his version of *The Treasure of the Sierra Madre* (1948), John Huston arranged to meet Mr. Hal Croves in Mexico. Croves said that he was Traven's agent, but Huston was later convinced he had been dealing with B. Traven himself. After Traven's death on March 26, 1969, Traven's widow Rosa Elena Luján confirmed that he had indeed been none other than the German-speaking anarchist Ret Marut, who had played a significant role in the Munich "Räterepublik" (Council Republic).

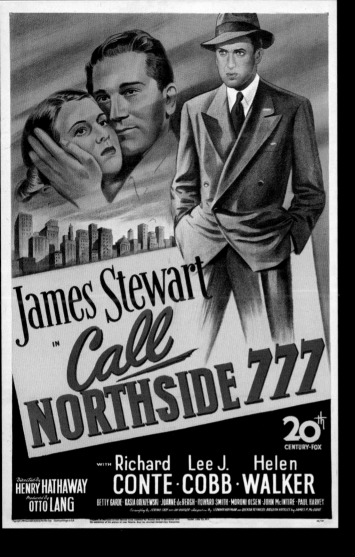

CALL NORTHSIDE 777

1948 – USA – 111 MIN.
DIRECTOR HENRY HATHAWAY (1898–1985)
SCREENPLAY JEROME CADY, JAY DRATLER,
LEONARD HOFFMAN, QUENTIN REYNOLDS, based
on a factual report by JAMES P. MCGUIRE
DIRECTOR OF PHOTOGRAPHY JOSEPH MACDONALD
EDITING J. WATSON WEBB JR. MUSIC ALFRED NEWMAN
PRODUCTION OTTO LANG for 20TH CENTURY FOX
STARRING JAMES STEWART (P. J. McNeal), RICHARD CONTE
(Frank Wiecek), LEE J. COBB (Brian Kelly,
Editor of the Chicago Times), HELEN WALKER
(Laura McNeal), BETTY GARDE (Wanda Skutnik),
KASIA ORZAZEWSKI (Tillie Wiecek), JOANNE DE BERGH
(Helen Wiecek-Rayska), HOWARD SMITH
(K. L. Palmer, Publisher of the *Chicago Times*),
GEORGE TYNE (Tomek Zaleska),
E. G. MARSHALL (Rayska)

"You look nice. Will you marry me?"
"I did."

They call it the "Dream Factory," but the world's most successful film industry was always a little more versatile than that. Glamorous escapism was never all that Hollywood had to offer, and even the major studios occasionally took a walk on the wild side. *Call Northside 777* is one of those naturalistic dramas that let the moviegoer know what it's really like to be a loser. The spare social realism of this movie is balanced by the extraordinary richness of its means and methods: besides borrowing elements from the gangster movie, the courtroom drama, the detective story, and the reporter's tale, it uses semi-documentary strategies to ensure authenticity and credibility. The locations are carefully chosen, while the milieu are drawn with admirable precision and integrated into a historical framework that underscores the

film's aspiration to tell the honest truth. We're told right at the start that this film is based on events that really happened, and we have no trouble believing it.

We're in Chicago, during Prohibition. A policeman is murdered and two Polish immigrants, Frank Wiecek (Richard Conte) and Tomek Zaleska (George Tyne), are convicted of the crime. Their guilt is far from certain, but they both get life terms. Eleven years later, a reporter from the *Chicago Times* takes an interest in the case, eventually clearing their names and securing their freedom. But the road to liberty is long and stony, for nothing in this city is easily come by – least of all truth and justice. It's as though Chicago were populated solely by corrupt cops and lackadaisical lawyers, despairing workers and

1 A run-on sentence: journalist P. J. McNeal (James Stewart) attempts to right the wrongs that have befallen Frank Wiecek (Richard Conte) by taking his case to the public.

2 Standing up to authority: shortly after delving into the Wiecek case, McNeal sets his sights on getting the unjust verdict overturned.

3 Not one for sob stories: Brian Kelly (Lee J. Cobb), editor of the *Chicago Times* has no intention of jeopardizing his paper by letting McNeal open up a can of worms.

4 Witness on the night stand: Laura McNeal (Helen Walker) appeals to her husband to do the right thing.

"As a Chicago reporter assigned to dig up an 11-year-old murder case, Stewart cavorts between a phony cynicism and a sob-sister sentimentalism before emerging as a full-fledged newspaperman." *Variety*

selfish petty crooks. Faced with this human disaster, supercilious reporter P. J. McNeal (James Stewart) rediscovers his heart and finds a mission in life.

In the cinematic representation of this city, the twisted circumstances of its inhabitants' lives are transformed into a visual metaphor. Through the play of light and shade, grids and lattices, strong contrasts, vertical compositions and low camera angles, Joseph MacDonald's cinematography evokes an atmosphere of suffocation and claustrophobia. Here, skyscrapers are monstrous and menacing, corridors are endless, backyards are sepulchral, and the people live in soul-crushing poverty; and amongst it all is a decent woman, fighting for the life and reputation of her child. For years, Tillie Wiecek (Kasia Orzazewski) has worked hard and saved every penny in the hope of proving the innocence of her son Frank. She places an ad in the paper, offer-

"It's an uphill struggle, because everything is apparently against McNeal: the judge died shortly after the verdict, the solicitor disappeared, the woman who picked Frank out of the line-up could not be found, and Frank's wife divorces him." *Monthly Film Bulletin*

5 McNeal probes into dark territory but each potential witness leads to a dead end.

6 Pressed for time: Wiecek is living proof that it takes more than an honest face to convince a jury.

"Henry Hathaway's direction marks a retreat from the documentary form. Instead of consistent realism, he lapses into a hybrid technique with plenty of hokey melodramatic tones." *Variety*

7 The film moves between the myriad cultures and classes of Chicago society.

8 Higher love: Frank and Helen's (Joanne De Bergh) feelings for one another are strong enough to tear down any barrier that comes between them.

9 Dust buster: Tillie Wiecek (Kasia Orzazewski) will not rest until her son's name has been wiped clean.

DOCUMENTARY NOIR In its contemporary review of *T-Men*, *Variety* alludes to its use of a *March-of-Time* technique. This confirms that a style (which actually began in radio news from 1931 through to the end of World War II) had been readily associated with the visuals of a monthly theatrical series, *The March of Time*. The 20-minute newsreels produced in association with *Time* magazine by the de Rochemont brothers, Louis and Richard, combined footage of actual events with interviews and some dramatic reenactments, a method still used in reality television today. Eventually Louis de Rochemont crossed over into feature production at 20th Century Fox. Although his actual noir credits – beginning with *The House on 92nd Street* (1945) and continuing with *Boomerang!* (1947) – were few, the documentary style applied to narratives of criminal investigation quickly spread to other productions at Fox, such as *Call Northside 777* and *The Street with No Name* (both 1948), and then to other studios. The preeminence of cop noir within the feature production of the classic period was relatively short-lived before it made the transition to early television and is perhaps best exemplified by the Mark Hellinger and Jules Dassin feature *The Naked City* (1948). As with *T-Men*, that movie's selection from the "eight million stories in the naked city" was based on real cases and partly inspired by the bodies-in-the-street photojournalism of Arthur Fellig a.k.a. Weegee. The Mann (uncredited) and Alton follow-up to *T-Men*, *He Walked by Night* (1948), opens with a *Naked City*–style mini-recap of police methods based in Los Angeles. Three years later, one of that film's lead actors, Jack Webb, created the most famous of police procedural TV series, *Dragnet* (1951–1959), which in turn spun off a feature of the same name in 1954, one of the last cop noirs of the classic period.

---

ing a reward to anyone who can help her find the true cop-killer. McNeal responds – and finds the woman in a state of sheer desperation. Meanwhile, her innocent son is hardly better off: Frank has even persuaded his wife to divorce him, so that she and their son might have a better life. He himself has long since surrendered to his fate.

Although the *Chicago Times* does its best to expose the truth, McNeal's investigative zeal eventually reaches its limits. When truth and justice come up against egotism and self-interest – when there is no such thing as society – man's last, best hope is technology. In the end, it takes a sophisticated deployment of lie detectors and photographic gear to establish the truth. If hope doesn't die in this remarkable film, it's due in no small part to this almost fetishized technological apparatus.   BR

THEY LIVE BY NIGHT

1948 – USA – 95 MIN.
DIRECTOR NICHOLAS RAY (1911–1979)
SCREENPLAY CHARLES SCHNEE, adapted by
NICHOLAS RAY from the novel *Thieves Like Us*
by EDWARD ANDERSON
DIRECTOR OF PHOTOGRAPHY GEORGE E. DISKANT
EDITING SHERMAN TODD MUSIC LEIGH HARLINE
PRODUCTION JOHN HOUSEMAN for RKO
STARRING CATHY O'DONNELL (Catherine "Keechie"
Mobley), FARLEY GRANGER (Arthur "Bowie" Bowers),
HOWARD DA SILVA (Chickamaw Mobley),
JAY C. FLIPPEN (Henry "T-Dub" Mansfield),
HELEN CRAIG (Mattie Mansfield), WILL WRIGHT
(Keechie's father), MARIE BRYANT (Singer),
IAN WOLFE (Hawkins), WILLIAM PHIPPS
(Young Farmer), HARRY HARVEY (Hagenheimer),
BYRON FOULGER (Lambert)

"Teach me how to kiss."

They Live by Night is almost elegiac as it contrasts the feelings of its young lovers, Bowie (Farley Granger) and Keechie (Cathy O'Donnell), with the insensitivity of the world around them. In a way Nicholas Ray's film is something of a fable. Its characters, with their odd-sounding names – Bowie, Keechie, T-Dub, Chickamaw – exist in a world of grubby garages and cheap motels, cut off from the mainstream, from the ordinary, in an aura that is at once proletarian and mythic. Ray's aerial shot of the speeding car that opens the narrative is pointedly omniscient rather than intimate, alienating rather than engaging.

As its fugitive lovers are still teenagers, the noir irony of *They Live by Night* is strongly underscored by the very youth and innocence of its "outlaw" protagonists. As a title card reads: "This boy and this girl were never properly introduced to the world we live in. To tell their story, they live by night." As a brief prologue also suggests, Bowie and Keechie are not just "thieves like us." Bowie is, in fact, too naïve to survive. It is not merely that he is just a "kid" (the nickname the press gives him to add color to their depiction of his flight) playing at being a man. It is because his lack of sophistication permits real criminals such as T-Dub (Jay C. Flippen) and Chickamaw (Howard Da

Amour fou isolates the lovers, makes them ignore normal social obligations, ruptures ordinary family ties, and ultimately brings them to destruction. This love frightens society, shocks it profoundly. And society uses all its means to separate these lovers as it would two dogs in the street." *Luis Buñuel*

1   Escaped convict Arthur "Bowie" Bowers (Farley Granger) is consoled by Catherine "Keechie" Mobley (Cathy O'Donnell).

2   The disapproval that Keechie has for her felonious uncle Elmo "Chickamaw" Mobley (Howard Da Silva, right) is obvious from her expression.

3   As an anxious Bowie rides in back, Henry "T-Dub" Mansfield (Jay C. Flippen) and Chickamaw flank the young farmer (William Phipps) whose vehicle they have commandeered.

4   Bowie's car accident leads to a confrontation in which Chickamaw shoots a policeman.

"In a way I'm a thief just the same as you are, but I won't sell you hope when there ain't any."

Film quote: Mr. Hawkins (Ian Wolfe)

Silva) to take advantage of him. How else but through his naïveté could they persuade Bowie that the only way to clear himself of an old criminal charge is to get money for a lawyer; and how else to get money for a lawyer than by helping his friends to rob a bank?

Immediately after the adult criminals T-Dub and Chickamaw introduce Bowie to their violent milieu, he is wounded. Although Keechie is initially resentful, almost scornful, of Bowie when the outlaws hide out at her place and she is forced to tend his wounds, Ray uses the intimate action between them to draw the viewer into the expectation of a romantic liaison, as established in the prologue (and in the advertising). Although far from glamorized, the young actors are attractive and vital in aspect, which Ray underscores by framing them together with the worn and battered T-Dub and Chickamaw. Even as they argue, it is clear that Bowie and Keechie are fated to be lovers.

LOVERS ON THE RUN The epitome of amour fou or "mad love" on screen is arguably the noir films that feature lovers on the run. These fugitive couples are outcasts and outlaws, hunted and hopeless, and usually dead or dying by the film's end. In a 15-year span from *You Only Live Once* (1937) to *Where Danger Lives* (1950), the obsessive character of amour fou and the alienated posture of the fugitives in relation to society as a whole meshed with the prototypical themes of film noir. The manner in which the wild passion of the fugitives is portrayed is as significant as the plot points, which keep them on the run. Some are older and more hardened than Lang's seminal couple in *You Only Live Once*, like Roy Earle and Marie in *High Sierra* (1941). Others, like Bowie and Keechie in *They Live by Night* (1948), are quite immature. Some pairings are imbalanced, like the hapless doctor and psychopathic patient in *Where Danger Lives*. There are also "upbeat" examples of the lovers-on-the-run plot. In Douglas Sirk's *Shockproof* (1949) and Felix E. Feist's *Tomorrow Is Another Day* (1951), both couples survive, but the noir sensibility of these pictures is sustained through the madness of their love. The ultimate noir fugitive couple is Bart Tare and Annie Laurie Starr in *Gun Crazy* (1950). Far removed from the innocence of *They Live by Night*, the aura of eroticism that director Joseph H. Lewis builds so intensely into the first part of the movie is, albeit 1950 vintage, anything but subtle. *Gun Crazy*'s association of guns, crime, and passion is most explicit in the celebrated long-take robbery with the camera in the backseat of the car. It climaxes (pun intended) as the couple races away: Annie Laurie looks back, her hands around Bart's neck as if to embrace him and her sustained, breathless smile unmistakably sexual.

5   The newly escaped convicts reach a farmhouse occupied by a young couple and their son from whom they demand assistance.

6   Keechie clearly has her doubts about the help offered by T-Dub's sister-in-law Mattie (Helen Craig).

7   Escapees on the lam, T-Dub and Chickamaw are hampered by Bowie, whose ankle is injured.

> ## "*They Live by Night* has the failing of waxing sentimental over crime, but it manages to generate interest with its crisp dramatic movement and clear-cut types." *The New York Times*

But not even Keechie's common sense can save Bowie from his own ingenuousness. Ultimately, she may succeed in separating him from the influence of T-Dub and Chickamaw, but the couple cannot separate themselves from the constraining influences of society.

Like the doorbell of the wedding broker that plays an off-key wedding march while he hawks a "deluxe ceremony including a snapshot of the happy couple," the real world taints their love with its cheapness and insensitivity. It entices them with the hope of escape like the bungalow of a backwoods motel where they find temporary refuge, where they put up a Christmas tree and buy each other gifts. In the end, because Bowie is guilty, Hollywood standards dictate that he must die; but unlike Fritz Lang in his deterministic prototype *You Only Live Once* (1937), Ray never suggests that the fate of his protagonist is a matter of implacable destiny rather than simple mischance.

8

8   Bowie's notoriety as "the Kid" causes him to be
    recognized and confronted when he and Keechie
    go to a nightclub.

9   In the inevitable conclusion the couple are
    betrayed by Mattie, and Keechie ends up kneeling
    next to Bowie's body.

"Underneath *They Live by Night* is a moving, somber story of hopeless young love. There's no attempt at sugarcoating a happy ending, and yarn moves towards its inevitable, tragic climax without compromise." *Variety*

The fact that Keechie survives creates an alternate prototype for the ending of a fugitive-couple drama. The Christmas tree and the small presents they leave behind when they must flee their bungalow are icons of the hope and kindness that sustained Bowie and Keechie in their brief time together.

It could be argued that the poignancy of the relationships in both *You Only Live Once* and *They Live by Night*, with their links to life mates in the animal world, with poignant wedding chapels and Christmas displays, may seem more romantic than noir. What is darkest about both movies, particularly in the context of mainstream Hollywood, is that one or both halves of each couple perish. And while Lang's couple is young, Bowie and Keechie start out as "this boy and this girl," as little more than children. Obviously one of the motivating factors is the straightforward concept of moral retribution, of the need that is both abstractly dramatic and backed by the dictates of the Hollywood production code for the guilty to die. It is by emphasizing the innocence of their protagonists – literally for Eddie, who is not guilty of the crime for which he is condemned, and emotionally for Bowie, who is ensnared by the older, duplicitous criminals – that filmmakers such as Lang and Ray made films about young lovers on the run even darker and firmly embedded them into the noir cycle.

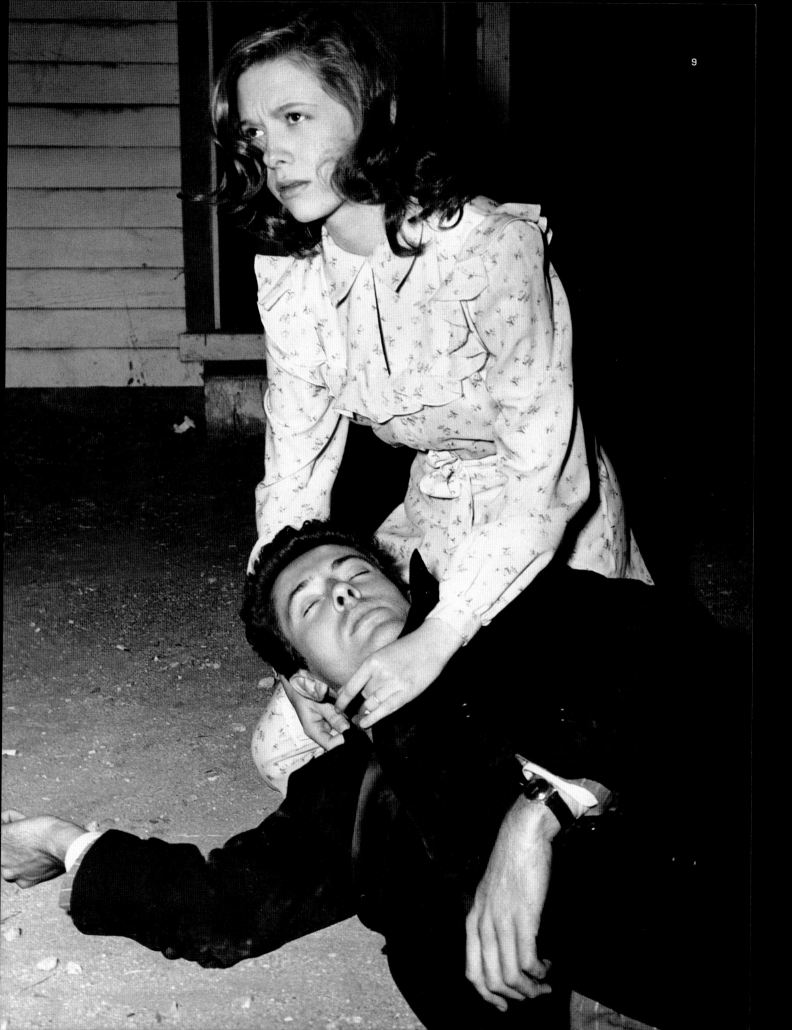

9

FORCE OF EVIL

1948 – USA – 78 MIN.
DIRECTOR ABRAHAM POLONSKY (1910–1999)
SCREENPLAY ABRAHAM POLONSKY, IRA WOLFERT,
based on the novel *Tucker's People* by IRA WOLFERT
DIRECTOR OF PHOTOGRAPHY GEORGE BARNES
EDITING ART SEID MUSIC DAVID RAKSIN
PRODUCTION BOB ROBERTS for MGM
STARRING JOHN GARFIELD (Joe Morse), THOMAS GOMEZ
(Leo Morse), BEATRICE PEARSON (Doris Lowry),
HOWLAND CHAMBERLAIN (Freddie Bauer),
MARIE WINDSOR (Edna Tucker), ROY ROBERTS
(Ben Tucker), PAUL FIX (Bill Ficco),
PAUL MCVEY (Hobe Wheelock), BARRY KELLEY
(Det. Egan), STANLEY PRAGER (Wally)

"What do you mean 'gangsters'?
It's business."

As if fate could be provoked by a movie's title, *Force of Evil* marked the debut of a stellar filmmaking talent in its writer-director Abraham Polonsky, only to trigger a 21-year eclipse of what – in a just world – would surely have become a career to rank among the giants.

John Garfield is Joe Morse, a sharp-dressing, even sharper-witted Wall Street lawyer who thrives on both sides of the law. His top client, Tucker (Roy Roberts), is a kingpin of the "numbers" racket. This illegal but outwardly harmless lottery harvested nickel and dime bets from millions of people in the United States who followed the results in daily newspapers and enjoyed a widespread vogue during the 1930s and 1940s, well before such gambling was widely legalized. These facts are quickly and clearly dramatized in the film's first few minutes. Indeed, it is striking what plentiful moral and emo-

tional ground is covered – and with such a darkly entertaining touch – over the mere 78 minutes that make up this film as a whole.

As he organizes a high-level effort to head off a rackets investigation and legalize these games for Tucker, Joe hopes to protect his older brother Leo (Thomas Gomez), who runs a small numbers operation independent of Tucker. The brothers have long been at bitter odds. Leo's betting profits put Joe through law school. Joe now wants to repay this by helping Leo become wealthy. The catch is, Leo would have to work for Tucker's big syndicate and cease to be his own boss.

Leo: "Tucker's money is no good."
Joe: "Money has no moral opinions!"
Leo: "I find I have, Joe. I find I have."

"*Force of Evil* appears on the surface to be a tightly structured, 78-minute B film, but it has so much more going for it. The moral drama has an almost mythic scale; it displays a corrupted world collapsing from within. In this respect, *Force of Evil* is very different from other film noir. It's not just the individual who is corrupted, but the entire system. It's a political as well as existential vision." *Martin Scorsese*

2

1 Joe Morse (John Garfield) confronts a loving nemesis in Doris Lowry (Beatrice Pearson), who tells him frankly: "I don't wish to die of loving you."

2 Edna Tucker (Marie Windsor), the kingpin's temptress wife. She warns Joe: "You could spend the rest of your life trying to remember what you shouldn't have said."

3 Doris loves the flowers, but is a bit suspicious. "What are you celebrating?" she asks. "A clean conscience," Joe replies. "Oh?" she teases. "Whose?"

The dialogue throughout is so rhythmic and smart that it's been described as blank verse. Certainly, savoring it is one of the great pleasures of discovering this film – especially when flirtation is afoot. "Don't say no when you want to say yes," Joe tells Leo's lovely, conscientious assistant Doris (Beatrice Pearson). "Don't ... maintain a moral superiority over me which doesn't exist." Doris is a wonderfully complex combination of sensuality and rock-ribbed principle, and Joe finds her fascinating. She is just as drawn to his wildness, his vitality – and his honesty, despite his shady dealings. Joe pours on the charm, teasing: "Tell me the story of your life, and maybe I can suggest a happy ending." She challenges him: "Do you love

me?" He refuses to lie: "Not so soon," he replies, "But it would be such a comfort to kiss you right now."

Joe's good intentions put his brother on a tragic collision course with the interests of Tucker and the mob, and the explosion, when it comes, pits Doris against him as well. "If I ever thought of loving you," she tells Joe, "it was to love something rotten and corrupt in myself. I don't wish to love you, or see you, or know you. And I'll try not to remember you." The mixture of intellect and passion, and irony, in those words – especially that hopeless phrase "I'll try" when it comes to forgetting their love – are typical of *Force of Evil* as a whole. Polonsky matched this textual richness with visual work

THE BLACKLIST "Scoundrel Time" was playwright Lillian Hellman's phrase for this dark period in American history – those years between 1947 and 1959 when citizens were called before the U.S. Congress to answer invasive questions – not just about their own beliefs, but of anyone their interrogators judged relevant. This was called "naming names." Refuse to cooperate, anwd opportunities to work would dry up.

This fear-filled practice fed upon anxieties about Soviet expansionism in the aftermath of World War II and was known as the blacklist, a professional kiss of death in Hollywood, where relationships are already fragile. Later studies showed that at least 300 people lost jobs over their refusal to name names, and of these, only 30 were able to resume their careers. Polonsky spent the 21 years between directing assignments churning out scripts under assumed names.

John Garfield, the brilliant star of *Force of Evil* (1948), literally died of the blacklist. Scarlet fever had damaged his heart as a boy. Although politically liberal – an admirer of Franklin Roosevelt – he refused to discuss the political beliefs of his friends and family when Congress called him in, and found himself out of work. He struggled despite having been Oscar-nominated for his work in *Gentleman's Agreement* (1947), and praised to high heaven in *Body and Soul* (1947), which Polonsky wrote. The week he died he was under tremendous pressure to testify again. His already frail heart could not bear the strain. "He defended his street boy's honor," said Polonsky, "and they killed him for it."

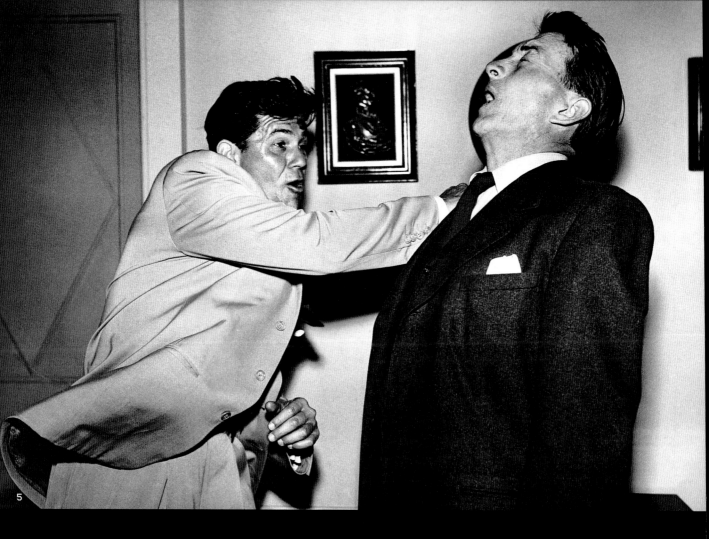

5

"A dynamic crime-and-punishment drama, brilliantly and broadly realized. Out of material and ideas that have been worked over time after time, so that they've long since become stale and hackneyed, it gathers suspense and dread, a genuine feeling of the bleakness of crime and a terrible sense of doom. And it catches in eloquent tatters of on-the-wing dialogue moving intimations of the pathos of hopeful lives gone wrong." *The New York Times*

6

by cinematographer George Barnes, a Hitchcock veteran. He urged Barnes to emulate the work of painter Edward Hopper. ("Ah, single source lighting!" Barnes teased, after they'd visited the museum. "Why didn't you say?") Arthur Seid's cutting and David Raksin's music likewise fuse to powerful effect throughout.

And yet, after this outstanding beginning, Polonsky did not direct another film until he made *Tell Them Williew Boy Is Here* with Robert Redford in 1969. Why? Simple. He was a lifelong Marxist. Despite a record of distinguished service as a U.S. intelligence officer during World War II, fighting the Nazis alongside the French resistance, Polonsky was brought before Congress, where he politely refused to answer questions about anybody's politics but his own, and so was blacklisted.

"I'd like to keep you," studio chief Darryl F. Zanuck told him frankly, as the showdown loomed: "I'll try – but when the pressure gets too tough I'll have to let you go, because I can't take it." Between 1951 and 1967 Polonsky was productive in the shadows. He wrote countless screenplays under a wide variety of pseudonyms. It is unknown how many scripts, under how many names, he actually wrote – he preferred to leave these buried. They kept his family fed. He also wrote critically acclaimed novels: *The World Above*; *A Season of Fear*. But his talent for directing film was as profoundly ingrained as his personal integrity, and that means there are at least two dozen films on the level of *Force of Evil* that never got made. That is a tragic loss – but it derives from a society-wide system of bullying that Polonsky understood only too well. *Force of Evil* teems with that understanding, that wisdom.   FXF

7

4   Betrayed by former allies and now their target, Joe descends the trashy riverbank to where his brother has been left for dead.

5   Belting Ficco (Paul Fix), who lords his advantage over Joe with a phrase U.S. politicians frequently abused in those days: "We need every man's loyalty."

6   Leo (Thomas Gomez) hangs on to his integrity as he confronts his brother Joe: "Even a bankrupt has to put his books in order."

7   Doris tells Joe: "Somehow you're wild and crazy and stuck in a trap, and somehow you won't fight to get out, and somehow I love you."

8   One of Joe's law partners is Chamberlain (Freddie Bauer), a suave Ivy Leaguer descended from generations of old money and polite corruption.

"Abraham Polonsky, along with Charlie Chaplin and Joseph Losey, remains one of the great casualties of the anti-Communist hysteria of the '50s." *Andrew Sarris, The American Cinema*

8

CHAMPION

1949 – USA – 99 MIN.
DIRECTOR MARK ROBSON (1913–1978)
SCREENPLAY CARL FOREMAN, based on a short
story by RING LARDNER
DIRECTOR OF PHOTOGRAPHY FRANZ PLANER
EDITING HARRY W. GERSTAD MUSIC DIMITRI TIOMKIN
PRODUCTION STANLEY KRAMER for UNITED ARTISTS
STARRING KIRK DOUGLAS (Midge Kelly),
MARILYN MAXWELL (Grace Diamond),
ARTHUR KENNEDY (Connie Kelly), PAUL STEWART
(Tommy Haley), RUTH ROMAN
(Emma Bryce), LOLA ALBRIGHT (Palmer Harris),
LUIS VAN ROOTEN (Jerry Harris)

"And now you're king of the world. Winner take all."

Champion opens with Midge Kelly (Kirk Douglas) as "king of the world," or at least champion of it. As the credits roll, he parades down the aisle of a packed arena, through the ropes, and into the ring while fans applaud. A ringside "color" man doing radio commentary belabors the obvious: "They're still cheering ... no question about it, this is the most popular champion in the history of this event." From an elegiac visual, a low angle of Midge smiling back at the spectators, robe parted, hands taped, ready to put the gloves on and give them a show, a spotlight is transformed into the beam of a locomotive and the scene dissolves back to an earlier time. The flashback is into a different world, of homeless drifters and casual violence, a darker world where Midge and his brother Connie (Arthur Kennedy) are unceremoniously beaten and tossed from a box car, the stark underworld of film noir.

Many sports movies use the organized competition as a figurative equivalent of a purely social struggle for success. In the context of film noir, whether it's a racetrack or a fight ring or a tennis court, the unsavory aspects of the game taint the process. Ring Lardner's story was an undiluted indictment of the criminal elements that manipulate boxing. Despite their predilection for focusing on the socially conscious aspects of any drama, both producer Stanley Kramer and screenwriter Carl Foreman understand that Midge Kelly must at least start out as a hero. At first, he is just that: protective of his disabled brother, devoted to his mom, charming with both men and women. Casting Kirk Douglas and permitting frequent displays of his dimpled chin and cheeks underscore that effect. Even when Midge learns that he and Connie have been duped, that the money they thought was invested in a sea-

side diner is now gone, the brothers do not turn to crime. Instead they start waiting tables and washing dishes. Remarkably, the filmmakers expend more than 20 minutes on the proletarian portion of the flashback (the totality of which covers 85 of the 99 minutes of running time), until one begins to wonder, is this film noir or something inspired by Preston Sturges's parody "O Brother, Where Art Thou?" in *Sullivan's Travels* (1941). Not until the diner's owner forces Midge into marriage with his deflowered daughter Emma (Ruth Roman) is Midge's first character blemish revealed.

While *Champion* has its share of process screens and studio sets, the next sequence, as Midge seeks out promoter/manager Tommy Haley (Paul Stewart) and starts to train for the fight game in an actual, seedy Los Angeles gym, introduces a documentary style. Despite the misgivings of both Haley

1　An extremely battered Midge Kelly (Kirk Douglas) still manages to take a fighting stance.

2　Down and out brothers Midge and Connie (Arthur Kennedy) arrive at the Los Angeles gym in search of promoter Tommy Haley.

3　Having brought Midge into the fight game, Haley (Paul Stewart) watches his protégé handle the après-fight encounter with the local press.

4　Midge pummels his latest opponent. Connie Kelly: "I kept thinking you weren't just hitting that guy in the ring. You were hitting a lot of guys, different guys, all the guys that ever hurt you."

"*Champion* is a stark, realistic study of the boxing rackets and the degeneracy of a prizefighter. Fight scenes, under Franz Planer's camera, have realism and impact." *Variety*

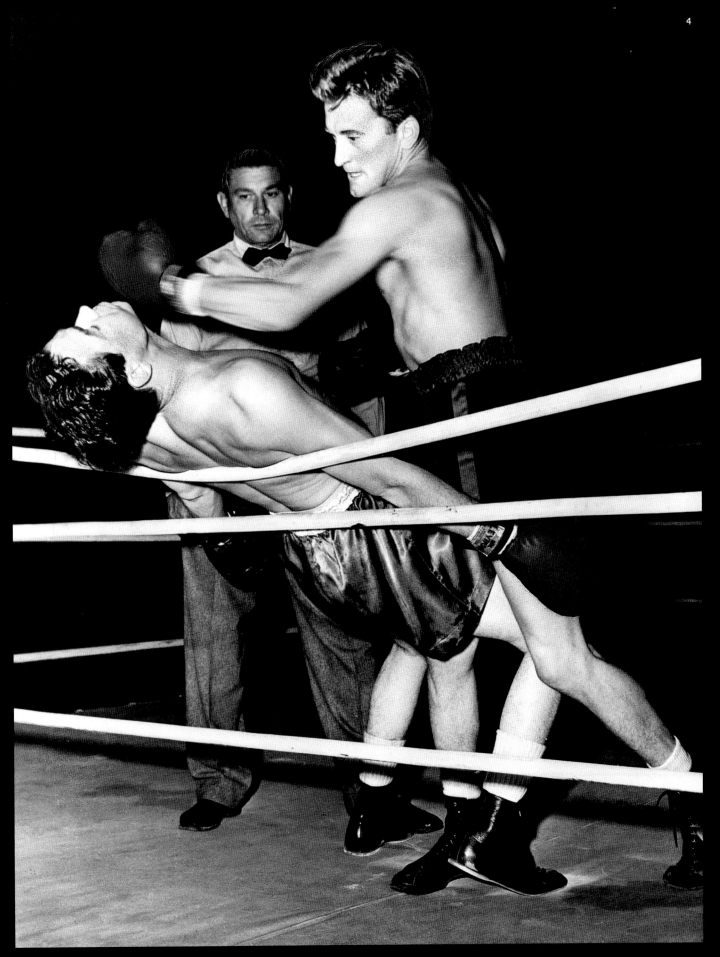

and Connie, Midge's perseverance restores some luster to his hero status. When Connie questions the thrill he gets from "hitting people," Midge's chest-pounding answer is simple: "Did you hear the crowd: for the first time in my life, people were cheering for me. Were you deaf? Didn't you hear them?"

From that point, despite the comic touches in some of the extended montages of Midge's training, the road ahead is one that leads inexorably into darkness, into the world of noir. There is a turn when, after three years Midge is ordered to taking a dive. His protest seems noble enough: "Work like a slave, live like a monk, beat your brains out and then the fat bellies with the big cigars tell you you're still a tramp." A three shot captures Haley and

Connie flanking Midge as he ruefully accepts that "I lose," then punches a table lamp. That throws him into darkness but leaves the others illuminated. Despite this visual metaphor, despite Haley's assurances that "in a year or so you'll get a legitimate shot, that's the deal," Midge refuses to wait, refuses to lose. After he and Connie and Haley are all beaten by thugs, it's clear that Midge's motive for not taking a dive was less about what's right and more about his own impatience in getting his due.

Midge's descent accelerates. He drops Haley and uses the connections of Grace Diamond (Marilyn Maxwell), a former contender's girlfriend, to reinstate himself and get a title shot. Then he dumps Grace for Palmer (Lola Albright), the wife of his new promoter Harris (Luis Van Rooten), until Harris

5

5   Having humiliated her boxer lover in the ring, Midge takes over his high-end girlfriend Grace Diamond (Marilyn Maxwell).

6   Midge poses for Palmer (Lola Albright), the young wife of his new promoter, Jerry Harris, who supports her sculpting hobby but not her dalliances with his clients.

7   The hobbled Connie uses his cane to lash out at Midge, who has once again betrayed his trust.

> # "You're going to be a good little girl, 'cause if you aren't, I'll put you in the hospital for a long, long time."
>
> *Film quote: Midge Kelly (Kirk Douglas)*

literally buys her back by writing off loans to Midge. While the narrative covers many years and the audience can infer that Midge's loss of moral compass is gradual, the actual run time of the movie works against that; and Midge's transformation into antihero is somewhat imbalanced. One semiconstant as Midge struggles to control his destiny is his loyalty to his brother, whose love for Emma Midge accepts and even encourages. In that context, Emma's rape by Midge is hard to understand except as a plot device needed to alienate Connie. The filmmakers try to come full circle and end the flashback with the color man who triggered it; but once skewed, the narrative sputters to a close: Midge wins the last match by literally fighting to his death.

AS

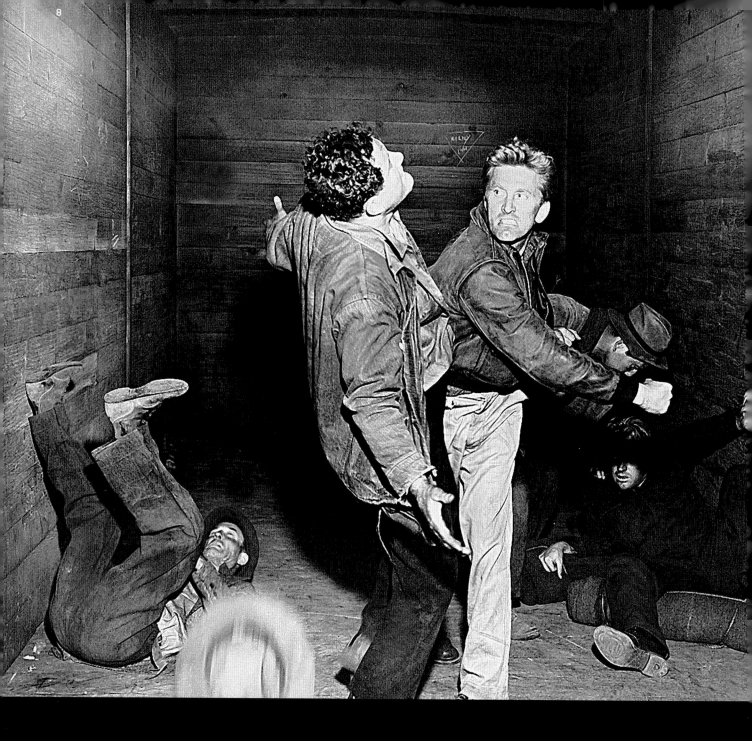

"**Director Mark Robson has covered up story weaknesses with a wealth of pictorial interests and exciting action of a graphic, colorful sort. His scenes in training gymnasiums, managers' offices and, of course, the big fight rings are strongly atmospheric and physically intense.**" *The New York Times*

8 The first of several encounters Midge has outside the ring with multiple opponents.

9 Although he has the raw talent to hold his own for a while, eventually the other men riding the rails toss Midge out of the boxcar and he tumbles down a hill.

BOXING NOIR Professional boxing in the 1940s and 1950s was a natural fit with film noir. Journalistic exposés after World War II revealed a poorly regulated system where corrupt local and state officials conspired with gambling syndicates to control the sport and the considerable profit to be had from bets on the outcome of major bouts. Still the best-known example is the earliest, *Body and Soul* (1947). That picture's writer, Abraham Polonsky; cinematographer, James Wong Howe; and star, John Garfield, were, like *Champion*'s scenarist, Carl Foreman, and activist producer, Stanley Kramer, Hollywood leftists whose careers would soon be threatened by the investigations of the House Un-American Activities Committee. As with *Champion*'s Midge Kelly, Garfield's Charley Davis is swept up in a world of easy money and easy women. As his mother (rather than brother) had warned, Charley faces the same dilemma as most noir protagonists in a universe of moral ambiguity. Released just weeks before Mark Robson's *Champion*, Robert Wise's *The Set-Up* (1949) is based on a narrative poem and retains a pointedly elegiac aspect. Like Midge, an aging and now small-time boxer, Stoker Thompson (Robert Ryan), is supposed to throw a bout but refuses to do so and suffers the consequences.

Much broader in its indictment of the fight game is *The Harder They Fall* (1956), also directed by Mark Robson, with Humphrey Bogart as a down-and-out sportswriter asked to puppet master for a syndicate planning to elevate and bring down a large but raw prospect to produce a gambling windfall. Although it has a less cynical protagonist, this feature, released near the end of the noir period, embraces the overt violence and corruption seen in *Night and the City* (1950), a tale of wrestling in postwar London.

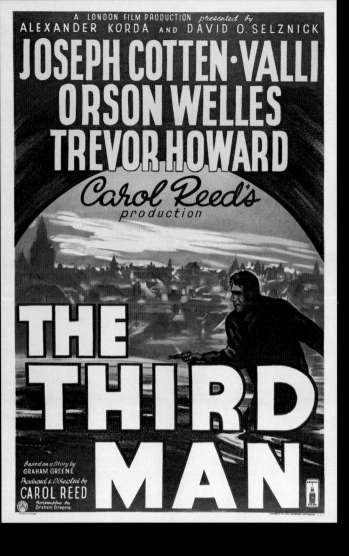

THE THIRD MAN 🏆

1949 – GREAT BRITAIN – 104 MIN.
DIRECTOR CAROL REED (1906–1976)
SCREENPLAY GRAHAM GREENE
DIRECTOR OF PHOTOGRAPHY ROBERT KRASKER
EDITING OSWALD HAFENRICHTER
MUSIC ANTON KARAS
PRODUCTION CAROL REED, ALEXANDER KORDA,
DAVID O. SELZNICK for LONDON FILM
PRODUCTIONS, BRITISH LION FILM CORPORATION
STARRING JOSEPH COTTEN (Holly Martins),
ORSON WELLES (Harry Lime), ALIDA VALLI
(Anna Schmidt), TREVOR HOWARD (Major Calloway),
PAUL HÖRBIGER (Porter), ERNST DEUTSCH
(Baron Kurtz), ERICH PONTO (Doctor Winkel),
SIEGFRIED BREUER (Popescu), BERNARD LEE
(Sergeant Paine), GEOFFREY KEEN (British MP)
ACADEMY AWARDS 1950 OSCAR for BEST
CINEMATOGRAPHY (Robert Krasker)
IFF CANNES 1949 GRAND PRIX for
BEST FILM (Carol Reed)

"Poor Harry!"

A corpse floats belly up in the picturesque blue Danube as a narrator's voice off-handedly remarks that postwar Vienna's black market economy is no place for amateurs. We're not more than a minute into the film, and yet already knee deep in a story that capitalizes on the magic of place and period like no other film ever made. Closely following Graham Greene's script, British director Carol Reed shot *The Third Man* in occupied Vienna against a backdrop of romance and rubble. From these ashes rose a masterpiece of black comedy that is as much a thriller as it is melodrama. With spot-on accuracy, Reed captures the atmosphere of postwar mayhem as displaced persons wheel and deal in a many-tongued chatter, hoping to make a buck and praying to stay alive.

This world of black-market trade and unpredictable police raids couldn't be more foreign to American dime novelist Holly Martins (Joseph Cotten). Before he gets a chance to take in his surroundings, Holly is whisked off to attend the sudden funeral of his good friend Harry Lime (Orson Welles), his sole acquaintance in town. The sordid details Holly unearths while conducting his own impromptu investigation of Harry's allegedly accidental death

unfold on screen in the deliciously macabre style of Alfred Hitchcock's earlier British films. Without warning, the scene flips from one locale to the next: Martins outruns a bloodthirsty mob who suspects him of having killed Lime's porter (Paul Hörbiger), but ends up getting shoved into the back of a taxi waiting for him at the gates of his hotel. When the ride is over, he surfaces as the guest of honor at a meeting of literary enthusiasts only to disappoint them when, as the author of *The Lone Rider of Santa Fé*, he has little to say about James Joyce. No sooner does he exit the function than he is tailed by a pair of hoods, bitten by a parrot, and forced to scale a mountain of rubble. It is a never-ending fight for survival that culminates in a fluke encounter with none other than Harry Lime himself.

No one could paint villainy in as tragic a palette as actor-director Orson Welles, and the unscrupulous penicillin racketeer Harry Lime counts among his greatest roles. Despite a performance confined to the story's end and 15 minutes of screen time, Welles's character never budges from the center of the plot. While his disturbing and prolonged absence holds the audience in an indefinite state of suspense, this by no means eclipses Welles' actual per-

1 The grapes of wrath: Major Calloway (Trevor Howard) is out to give penicillin racketeer Harry Lime a taste of his own medicine.

2 Freeze tag: Harry Lime (Orson Welles) does his best to blend in with the surroundings.

3 The river Stynx: in the labyrinthine tunnels of Vienna's sewer system, Calloway, Paine (Bernard Lee), and Holly Martins (Joseph Cotten) discover that Harry Lime is indeed the scum of the earth.

"The music is particularly original and exciting. Like a leitmotif, the catchy and authentically popular zither melody accompanies the appearances of the mysterious Harry Lime, telling us of his presence even when he remains invisible or is represented only by his proxies and messengers." *Der Tagesspiegel*

> "Top credit must go to Mr. Reed for molding all possible elements into a thriller of superconsequence, and most especially for the brilliant and triumphant device of using a zither as the sole musical background of the film. This eerie and mesmerizing music, which is rhythmic and passionate and sad, becomes, indeed, the commentator – the genius loci – of the Viennese scene." *The New York Times*

4

CAROL REED Carol Reed (1906–1976) was the illegitimate son of British theater producer Sir Herbert Beerbohm. Tall, slender, and always sporting a slicked back hairdo, this British director was the embodiment of elegance. He earned his reputation in film with the postwar drama *The Third Man* (1949), starring Joseph Cotten hot on the heels of penicillin trafficker Harry Lime (Orson Welles). In an atmosphere of perpetual night, *The Third Man* is an elaborately crafted study in shadow and light, a legendary piece of film noir that paints a portrait of the Viennese black market at the end of World War II. Its thrilling chase scenes in labyrinthine sewers are immortalized in the minds of film buffs. Lime's distorted silhouette cast upon the walls of these tunnels – always just a step ahead of his pursuers – is arguably one of the most unforgettable images in cinematic history. In the Dickens adaptation *Oliver!* (1968) the villain, Bill Sikes, played by Carol Reed's nephew Oliver Reed, makes a similar appearance as a sinister figure. The success of *The Third Man* – which, like many of Reed's other films, is a literary adaptation – caused the audience's expectations of him as well as those he placed upon himself to skyrocket. Boasting thespian beginnings, Reed performed in a celebrated stage troupe headed by Edgar Wallace. It was this prolific author and mystery expert who taught him how to recognize a good story. Shot during the final year of the Second World War, *The True Glory*, a documentary about the Allied landing in Normandy, won Reed international critical acclaim and the 1946 Best Documentary Film Oscar. During the war Reed had served as the head of Army Cinematographic Services, which provided him with an opportunity to direct film. The Brits also gave official credence to his greatness when Queen Elizabeth returned him to his aristocratic stature. Other gems among Reed's films include *Night Train to Munich* (1940), *Odd Man Out* (1947), *The Fallen Idol* (1948), and *Our Man in Havana* (1959).

5

formance. In the shadows of an entryway, we see a tomcat seated contentedly beside a man's pant leg. We recognize the animal as the pet of Lime's lover Anna (Alida Valli), who informed us in a prior scene that the cat "only likes Harry." Light shoots in from a window on the opposite side of the street and confirms what we already suspect – from the perspective of a drunken and dumbfounded Holly Martins, we lock eyes with the supposedly dead Harry Lime. His wide-eyed baby face curls into a contemptuous grin that was quintessentially Welles. Then he vanishes. Later, when the smoke has cleared, he'll offer us this flippant justification for his insidious behavior: "In Italy for 30 years under the Borgias, they had warfare, terror, murder, bloodshed; but they produced Michelangelo, Leonardo da Vinci, and the Renaissance. In Switzerland they had brotherly love and 500 years of democracy

4 Fan club: actress Anna Schmidt (Alida Valli) is the only person who believes in Harry's virtue. After all, he is the man responsible for falsifying her identity.

5 The great divide: even in death, Harry Lime gets the last laugh by making Holly and Anna's earthly union impossible.

6 More than he bargained for: dime novelist Holly Martins is suddenly expected to take a stance on matters which are clearly over his head – James Joyce included.

and peace. And what did that produce? The cuckoo clock." Unlike the irresistible bounder he plays in *The Third Man*, Welles's contributions to the film were anything but elusive. Cameraman Robert Krasker's opulent, black-and-white photography works with the same expressionist lighting and camera angles that Welles himself favored as a filmmaker.

As much as Krasker looked to Welles for guidance, the principal characters define themselves and their moral beliefs according to Harry Lime: the British Major Calloway (Trevor Howard), is determined to apprehend Lime in the name of all the children who lost their lives to the racketeer's contam-

inated penicillin; Anna, however, wouldn't denounce him no matter what the extent of his crimes, claiming as she does that "a person doesn't change because you find out more." And then, of course, there's Holly Martins, a man who could never turn his pal over to the authorities, but still bestows the kiss of death upon him during the film's thrilling conclusion in the maze of Vienna's sewers. Beyond all this, Harry Lime's ubiquitous presence lingers in every note of this picture's score. The character has grown inseparable from Anton Karas's zither-based theme, which has found an additional home in popular music. **LP**

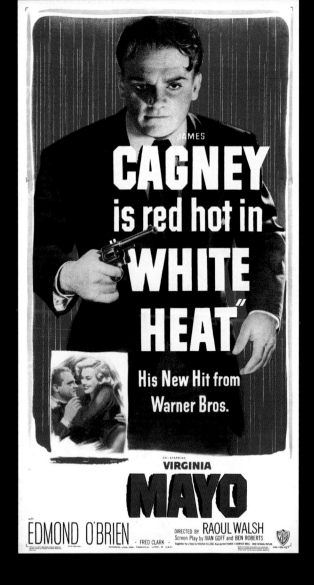

WHITE HEAT

1949 – USA – 114 MIN.
DIRECTOR RAOUL WALSH (1887–1980)
SCREENPLAY IVAN GOFF, BEN ROBERTS, based
on a story by VIRGINIA KELLOGG
DIRECTOR OF PHOTOGRAPHY SID HICKOX
EDITING OWEN MARKS MUSIC MAX STEINER
PRODUCTION LOUIS F. EDELMAN for WARNER BROS.
STARRING JAMES CAGNEY (Arthur "Cody" Jarrett),
VIRGINIA MAYO (Verna Jarrett), EDMOND O'BRIEN
(Hank Fallon alias Vic Pardo), MARGARET WYCHERLY
(Ma Jarrett), STEVE COCHRAN (Big Ed Somers),
JOHN ARCHER (Philip Evans), WALLY CASSELL
(Cotton Valletti), FRED CLARK (Daniel Winston),
FORD RAINEY (Zuckie Hommell),
PERRY IVINS (Doctor Simpson)

"Made it, Ma! Top of the world!"

Cody Jarrett (James Cagney) and his gang kill four people in the course of a train robbery. The police have no proof that he did it but they're hot on his trail, so Cody decides to turn himself in for a lesser offense. By admitting to a hotel burglary that he hadn't even committed, he creates an alibi for himself and evades the electric chair. Cody Jarrett receives a two-year jail sentence and settles in for a spell in the pen. But the cops haven't given up; they smuggle undercover agent Hank Fallon (Edmond O'Brien) into his cell, and Fallon gradually succeeds in gaining Jarrett's trust. Matters come to a head when Jarrett hears that his beloved mother (Margaret Wycherly) has died. She's been leading the gang in his absence, and one of the gang members has murdered her. Furious and distraught, Jarrett breaks out, together with his cellmate Fallon. He's determined to take his revenge – and to wind up "on top of the world," where Ma always said he belonged …

In a career lasting 50 years, Hollywood veteran Raoul Walsh made more than 100 movies – and *White Heat* is undoubtedly one of his best. Walsh was known as a "man's director," and this film demonstrated once again his mastery of the no-frills, straightforward style that shaped Warner Brothers' image during the era of the great studios. Like John Huston's *Key Largo* (1948), Walsh's film is a late example of the classic Warner gangster movies of the '30s. In Huston's movie, Edward G. Robinson had played an aging Mafia boss; here, too, one of the genre's greatest stars appears as a thoroughly anachronistic character.

James Cagney's performance in *The Public Enemy* (1931) had made him a screen idol. *White Heat*, however, was no classical gangster movie about the rise and fall of a charismatic crook, and it's clear from the outset that Cody Jarrett has seen better days. The sheer heavy-handedness of the train robbery is evidence of this – it's like something from the Wild West. The clear-headed, efficient work of the police, which Walsh captures with the dry detachment of a documentary filmmaker, provides an obvious contrast. If Jarrett is a bandit of the old school, the cops are the men of tomorrow. They have car phones and tracking devices, and Cody doesn't like that kind of stuff one bit. In fact he only picks up a telephone once in the whole film – to rip it off the wall. Cody Jarrett is not so much spontaneous as hysterically impulsive. He is ruled entirely by instinct, and his mother is the only human being

"**What distinguishes this picture from beginning to end is the obvious sympathy – devoid of pity or complacency – that Walsh has for the hero of his story. In Jarrett, James Cagney depicted one of the last great criminals of his career, and deploys the full potential of his striking physiognomy.**" *Positif*

1   The end of the road for mentally unstable gangster Arthur "Cody" Jarrett (James Cagney).

2   Atta girl! Verna Jarrett (Virginia Mayo) always was a sucker for a little male chauvinism.

3   They'll never take me alive: chronic headaches bring out the violent side in Arthur Jarrett.

4   You dirty rat: Arthur confronts the thugs of the round table.

5   Mama's boy: Cody's lifelong devotion to his Ma (Margaret Wycherly, center) leaves Verna holding the short end of the stick.

6   Cody Jarrett leads a brutal train robbery that results in four dead railway men, and one of his own.

he trusts. It's she who spurs him on, reminding him constantly that someday he's going to be "on top of the world." And when Cody happens to be incapacitated by one of his terrible recurring headaches, only one thing really helps: a massage from Ma. One piece of camera magic shows how strongly Ma Jarrett dominates her son's thoughts and feelings. In a cross-fade from Cody to his mother, their features melt and mingle; for a brief moment, they are one and the same person. This sequence anticipates the ending of

Hitchcock's *Psycho* (1960), when schizophrenic killer Norman Bates finally "becomes" his own dead mother.

Walsh's film leaves us in no doubt that Cody Jarrett is very sick in spirit. Even the cops know exactly what's bugging him: as a child, he could only gain his mother's attention by simulating headaches. Fallon ruthlessly exploits this psychic defect in order to trap his quarry, and this makes the police's methods look unpleasantly sneaky. It's a striking contrast where

EDMOND O'BRIEN As David Thomson noted, Edmond O'Brien (1915–1985) was one of the few Hollywood stars who managed to break the great unwritten rule: never sweat in front of the camera. He was an unglamorously physical actor. After his first major role as the poet Gringoire in William Dieterle's *The Hunchback of Notre Dame* (1939), he was rarely to be seen as a truly sympathetic character. O'Brien, whose stage experience had included a spell with Orson Welles's Mercury Theater, was not destined to play the heroes or the lovers. In *White Heat* (1949), he embodied an undercover police agent whose life is in constant danger, yet his performance never allowed us to forget that there was something unpleasantly devious about the whole business. In Rudolph Maté's *D.O.A.* (1950), he played a poisoned man determined to catch his would-be murderer; yet the tragedy of the situation was undermined by the fact that O'Brien chose to interpret his character as a paranoid petty bourgeois. Even in the role that brought him an Oscar as Best Supporting Actor he made a peculiarly unpleasant impression: as the press agent in Joseph L. Mankiewicz's *The Barefoot Contessa* (1954), he was Humphrey Bogart's conformist adversary.

In two of the most famous late Westerns, he did play comparatively positive characters: John Ford's *The Man Who Shot Liberty Valance* (1962) saw him as an alcoholic publisher, and in Sam Peckinpah's *The Wild Bunch* (1969) he played the "elder statesman" and conscience of the gang. O'Brien directed two movies himself, and he also acted successfully in TV for many years.

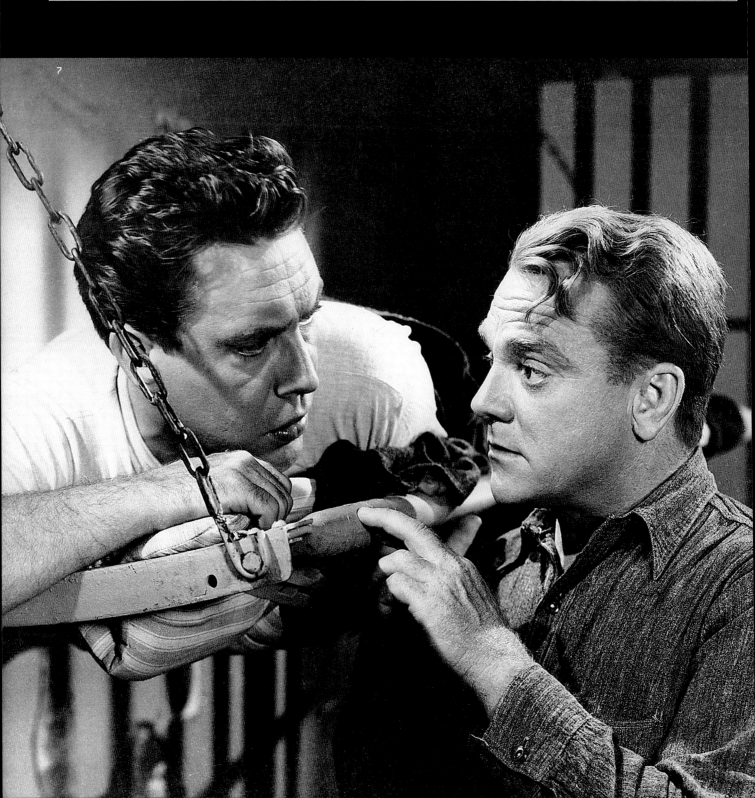

7   Misery loves company: the slammer is the perfect
    place for failed independent felons to regroup.

8   Home away from home: just like in times of war,
    pinups and camaraderie help keep up morale.

9   Old crone or old pro? It's not always easy to
    distinguish between loving mother and masked
    murderer. Margaret Wycherly as Ma Jarrett.

"Betrayed by his wife and friend, the criminal becomes an almost tragic figure. James Cagney's sharp psychological performance as Cody is particularly striking for the weight and credibility it brings to the story. Is it any wonder that Edmond O'Brien is so dislikeable in the role of the stool pigeon?" *Kölner Stadt-Anzeiger*

Cody Jarrett, for all his brutality, seems as innocent as a baby. *White Heat* shows us the diseased heart of the typical Cagney gangster, whose overwhelming vitality is rooted in an unstillable hunger for success, although even in this shocking role Cagney remains an "angel with a dirty face." It's this moral ambivalence – typical of the film noir genre – that makes Walsh's film so gripping right up until the spectacular finale. Surrounded by cops, and desperately seeking refuge in an oil refinery, Jarrett eventually realizes he's been betrayed by Fallon. By the time he's clambered to the top of a gigantic oil tank, it's clear he's reached the end of the road; but little Cody has triumphantly proven just how much he loves his mother. "Made it, Ma! Top of the world!" he roars, his last words as his world ends – in a towering inferno.   JH

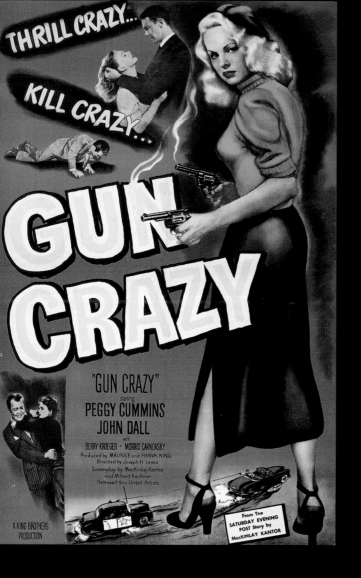

GUN CRAZY /
DEADLY IS THE FEMALE

1950 – USA – 87 MIN.
DIRECTOR JOSEPH H. LEWIS (1907–2000)
SCREENPLAY DALTON TRUMBO [uncredited],
MACKINLAY KANTOR, MILLARD KAUFMAN
[fronting for DALTON TRUMBO], based on a story from
the *Saturday Evening Post* by MACKINLAY KANTOR
DIRECTOR OF PHOTOGRAPHY RUSSELL HARLAN
EDITING HARRY W. GERSTAD MUSIC VICTOR YOUNG
PRODUCTION FRANK and MAURICE KING
for KING BROTHERS PRODUCTIONS
STARRING PEGGY CUMMINS (Annie Laurie Starr),
JOHN DALL (Bart Tare), BERRY KROEGER
(Packett), MORRIS CARNOVSKY (Judge Willoughby),
ANABEL SHAW (Ruby Tare Flagler), HARRY LEWIS
(Deputy Clyde Boston), NEDRICK YOUNG (Dave Allister),
TREVOR BARDETTE (Sheriff Boston),
MICKEY LITTLE (Bart Tare, Age 7), RUSS TAMBLYN
(Bart Tare, Age 14), PAUL FRISON (Clyde Boston,
Age 14), DAVE BAIR (Dave Allister, Age 14),
STANLEY PRAGER (Bluey-Bluey)

"No guts, nothing! I want action!"

Although it was made only a few years later, director Joseph H. Lewis's and writer Dalton Trumbo's *Gun Crazy* (1950) and its couple are far removed from the innocence of other noir fugitive-couple films like Fritz Lang's *You Only Live Once* (1937) and Nicholas Ray's *They Live by Night* (1949). Instead its lethal lovers look forward to the more blatantly sexual fugitive couples of post–Production Code neo-noirs like Arthur Penn's *Bonnie and Clyde* (1967) and Tamra Davis's homage film *Guncrazy* (1992).

But even when compared to those more unfettered films, *Gun Crazy* comes off as quite daring. For instance, when Clyde first shows Bonnie his gun in Arthur Penn's film she casually fondles the barrel and leaves it at that.

As a sexual metaphor such a staging pales in comparison to the meeting of the fugitive couple in *Gun Crazy*.

The first shot of Annie Laurie Starr (Peggy Cummins), the sideshow sharpshooter of the film, is from a low angle, establishing immediately her physical dominance as a correlative for her emotional and psychological dominance over the more submissive Bart. She strides into the frame firing two pistols above her head. A clearly aroused Bart Tare (John Dall), whose childhood love-hate relationship with firearms is shown in the opening scenes, accepts her open challenge to a shoot-off, and soon he and Laurie are firing at crowns of matches.

1 One of the most powerful and complex *femmes fatales* in classic period noir, Annie Laurie Starr (Peggy Cummins), with trademark slanted beret.

2 Bart Tare (John Dall) has a difficult time restraining the energy of his lover Annie, whether that energy is violent or sexual.

3 Even in their final personal holocaust, Bart acts as the voice of reason to his maddened lover.

4 The climax of the movie as the fugitive couple are trapped by the forces of the law and punished for their transgressive amour fou as much as for their criminal acts.

"You can see the quiver in Laurie's lips; and you know what this demon is about to do. This kid hasn't got a chance."

Joseph H. Lewis, in: Film Noir Reader 3

Obsessed, Bart now gets a job at the carnival to be near this erotic icon, and an affair ensues (Laurie: "I'm yours, and I'm real"). But Laurie has other needs besides sexual ones. She wants "things": "Bart, I've been kicked around all my life, and from now on, I'm gonna start kicking back." After being fired by a jealous sideshow manager, Laurie convinces the love-struck Bart to begin a life of crime in order to live the "high life." When he hesitates after a few smaller jobs, she sits on the edge of the bed and coyly slips on her stocking and issues her ultimatum: take it or leave me ("Let's finish it the way we started it – on the level"). Bart, of course, capitulates.

Because they are an attractive couple and, as Bart points out, they "go together. I don't know. Maybe like guns and ammunition go together," the intensity of the budding amour fou is immediate and overt. While Laurie's love for Bart is less obvious at first (she seems, initially, more interested in him as a plaything), she not only marries Bart but pins her hopes on him. At that point, the full madness of amour fou is ready to erupt.

As *Gun Crazy* progresses the lovers' continued physical attraction is keyed, especially for Laurie, to their crime spree. An addiction is building. Laurie's addiction to violence, initially motivated by the desire for "money and all the things it will buy," is now also the need for an adrenaline rush. In feeding her habit, Bart is a typical codependent. Unlike other fugitive couples of the classic period, who flee to save themselves from unjust or exaggerated accusations, Bart and Laurie choose to become criminals.

As they come to depend more and more on each other, the inversion of *They Live by Night* is complete: rather than being innocents whose platonic interdependence becomes a sexual one, Bart and Laurie's purely physical attraction evolved into an emotional and neurotic connection. Laurie's excitement at each of their robberies becomes increasingly palpable as the film moves on inexorably, punctuated with tight close-ups of her face in the throes of sexual excitement. The most famous sequence illustrating this sexual aura occurs at the emotional climax of the movie, immediately after their last job

together. Laurie had planned for them to separate and rejoin later to throw off their pursuers. They drive to a second car and start off in opposite directions. Abruptly and at the same moment they veer around and rejoin each other. They race to each other's arms and embrace in the open street, metaphorically serving notice on society that they will not be separated, then drive off together in one car.

After this extravagant declaration of amour fou it is almost inevitable that they will perish. Driven into a swamp, they die together in the reeds, pursued by Bart's childhood buddies. In a final act of perverse love, he shoots Laurie before she can be cut down by the hunters and then faces the rain of bullets himself.

JU

JOSEPH H. LEWIS Born April 6, 1907, in New York City, Lewis started as an MGM office drone, later became a camera assistant, and then, like his brother Ben, became a film editor at Republic Pictures. He started working second unit and became a full director in 1937. Working mostly in low-budget Western films (including the remarkable Anna May Wong war vehicle *Bombs Over Burma*, 1942), he earned the nickname "wagon-wheel Joe" because editors constantly complained of his predilection for foreground clutter in his in-depth compositions. He broke through to larger-budgeted films at Columbia when he was given the assignment to direct *My Name Is Julia Ross* (1945). He continued to develop in the noir tradition with *So Dark the Night* (1946), *Gun Crazy / Deadly Is the Female* (1950), *Cry of the Hunted* (1953), and *The Big Combo* (1955). After a remarkable collaboration with the blacklisted writer Dalton Trumbo on *Gun Crazy*, they reteamed on the noir Western *Terror in a Texas Town* (1958). Like many noir directors, Lewis moved to television and directed some of the best Western episodic TV in series like *The Rifleman* (1958–1963) and *The Big Valley* (1965–1969, co-created by noir writer A. I. Bezzerides). He retired from movies in the late 1960s and died in Santa Monica, California, on August 30, 2000.

"If you had to select a single film to justify the present enthusiasm for film noir and define its allure, few movies could compete with *Gun Crazy*. The same goes for celebrating the potential of B movies to achieve grade-A flair, excitement, and artistic intelligence."

parallax-view.org

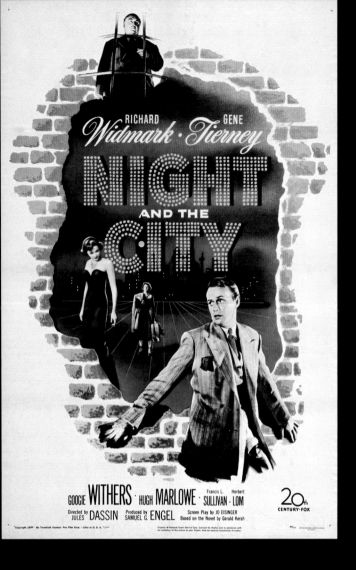

NIGHT AND THE CITY

1950 – USA – 101 MIN.
DIRECTOR JULES DASSIN (1911–2008)
SCREENPLAY JO EISINGER, based on the novel
of the same name by GERALD KERSH
DIRECTOR OF PHOTOGRAPHY MAX GREENE
EDITING NICK DE MAGGIO, SIDNEY STONE
MUSIC BENJAMIN FRANKEL (U.K. Version),
FRANZ WAXMAN (U.S. Version)
PRODUCTION SAMUEL G. ENGEL for
20TH CENTURY FOX
STARRING RICHARD WIDMARK (Harry Fabian),
GENE TIERNEY (Mary Bristol), GOOGIE WITHERS
(Helen Nosseross), HUGH MARLOWE (Adam Dunn),
FRANCIS L. SULLIVAN (Philip Nosseross),
HERBERT LOM (Kristo), STANISLAUS ZBYSZKO
(Gregorius the Great), MIKE MAZURKI (The Strangler),
CHARLES FARRELL (Mickey Beer), ADA REEVE
(Molly the Flower Lady), KEN RICHMOND
(Nikolas of Athens)

"An artist without an art."

A flamboyant, quick-talking figure emerged in Depression-hit 1930s Britain and soon appeared in the fiction and plays of the period before transferring to the silver screen in the 1940s. He was commonly known as a spiv. A spiv was the person who could supply you, for a price, with any item you desired. Out of necessity, to make it easier for you to forget that the goods were stolen, the spiv sold them to you with a wink, a smile, and a lot of charm. There were spiv characters in *Waterloo Road* (1944), *They Made Me a Fugitive* (1947), *It Always Rains on Sunday* (1947), and *Noose / The Silk Noose* (1948), but the final and best films in this cycle were *The Third Man* (1949) and *Night and the City* (1950). In some ways these last two are similar films – both feature a hunt for a spiv through a rubble-strewn city, and the spiv has the love of a good woman – but their treatment is completely different. *The Third Man* sees the hunt for elusive black marketeer Harry Lime (enigmatically played by Orson Welles) from the point of view of his best friend, a pulp writer. *Night and the City* is seen from the point of view of spiv Harry Fabian (Richard Widmark). Fabian is not sympathetic in a single frame or scene of this movie, and

yet he is compelling to watch, which is a tribute to the courage of Widmark's performance – his career best. Although Fabian is dressed well and quick-witted, he is always sweating, has a slimy attitude towards everybody he meets, and seems totally without a conscience. He is a sociopath and ego-centric, but he also has good qualities – a sharp, versatile mind and a tenacious persistence when it comes to achieving his goals.

Night and the City opens with Harry Fabian on the run from an unnamed, unseen man. In fact, throughout the film, Harry is constantly scuttling through the seedy, rain-soaked streets of London's Soho from one rat hole to the next. At one stage he says, "All my life I've been running. From welfare officers, thugs, my father ..." We get another clue to his background when Harry tries stealing from his lover, Mary (Gene Tierney), a fellow American who sings at the Silver Fox nightclub. Mary looks at a photo of them together on a small boat, and remembers the old days, when they were normal people. What happened to Harry to change him from clean-cut college kid to sweating hustler? We never find out.

1   Harry Fabian (Richard Widmark), an American in London, is a low-life hustler and con man, always on the run. Richard Widmark: "I enjoyed the picture; but physically, it was a real tough mother."

2   Fabian meets Silver Fox nightclub owner Phil Nosseross (Francis L. Sullivan) in Trafalgar Square to persuade him to back Fabian's wrestling scheme, unaware that Phil has no intention of financing Fabian.

3   Always owing money, Harry even tries stealing from his lover, Mary (Gene Tierney), the only person who believes in him.

4   At the end, at Harry's lowest ebb, Mary comforts him. It is after this that Harry performs his only unselfish act in the film, and redeems himself.

"Widmark delivers one of his finest portrayals, lending absolute conviction to his role of the hustler who betrays everybody he has any dealings with." *Variety*

Harry is a bundle of energy and ideas, a spontaneous, charming man, a confidence trickster, who has no focus. We see him touting for business, tricking American businessmen into going to the Silver Fox, where luscious, vivacious showgirls will persuade them to buy ludicrously expensive wine and cigarettes. But what is Harry's purpose? Adam (Hugh Marlowe), a toy designer who lives in the same building as Mary (and has designs on her too), describes Harry as being "an artist without an art," who has "no way of expressing himself." Soon afterwards, however, Harry finds his focus at a wrestling bout. Gregorius (Stanislaus Zbyszko), a legendary wrestler, is out-raged at the clowning antics of modern so-called wrestlers. He extols the virtues of proper Greco-Roman wrestling. Harry has a brilliant idea – he persuades Gregorius to help him set up authentic Greco-Roman wrestling in

"If you were brought up in New York, as I was, you know how lost and lonely a boy can feel in a vast, indifferent city. I suppose that city's stayed with me. I try to see man in his background ... The background is mute, indifferent." *Jules Dassin*

London, with Harry as promoter. Since Gregorius is also the father of Kristo (Herbert Lom), a crook and London's biggest wrestling promoter, Harry knows that he will be protected from Kristo.

But Harry needs finance. He gets it through the scheming Helen Nosseross (Googie Withers), wife of fat Phil (Francis L. Sullivan), the owner of the Silver Fox. Helen won't allow Phil to touch her, and is simply waiting for him to die so that she can inherit his money and possessions. Fed up with his advances, Helen asks Harry to get her a license for her own club – in exchange he'll get the money for his wrestlers.

From the opening shot we know Harry and all his plans for life are doomed. The film takes on the aspect of tragedy. It is a descent, a nightmare like the noirest of the film noirs: *Detour* (1945), *Nightmare Alley* (1947), and *Force of Evil* (1948). Phil says at one point, "You've got it all, but you're a dead

"***Night and the City*** is an exciting, suspenseful melodrama which is the story of a double-crossing heel who finally gets his just desserts. In this role, Richard Widmark scores a definite hit." *Variety*

8

5   Crook Kristo (Herbert Lom) is humanized when his father, the legendary wrestler Gregorius (Stanislaus Zbyszko), dies; Kristo blames Fabian.

6   Phil runs the Silver Fox with a rod of iron but is ruled by his desire for his wife, Helen, who refuses to sleep with him.

7   Helen Nosseross (Googie Withers, right) is ambitious and makes sure that the girls in the club, Mary included, encourage the men to buy as much of the overpriced drinks as possible.

8   Helen's ignominious return to the Silver Fox when her own club fails; cinematographer Max Greene shot on over 200 locations around London to give the film its unique look.

man, Harry Fabian. A dead man." Harry has no friends to rely on – "Nobody can help you" – and is blind to the effects his selfish acts have on others. "You're killing me," Mary says, "and you're killing yourself." Then it all goes wrong. Phil withholds the finance. Gregorius the Great dies after a tortuous and gripping fight with The Strangler (Mike Mazurki). In the end, hunted through the night by Kristo's men, Harry, at last, pauses, and reflects, "I was so close, then everything fell apart. I've stopped running." In his final moments, he performs one selfless act, but it's too late. Harry is deluding himself. He was never close to achieving anything – he was always going to die. As soon as he stopped running …

The running metaphor is more poignant when one considers that director Jules Dassin had been given the job by executive producer Darryl F. Zanuck to get Dassin out of America – Zanuck had learned that Dassin was going to be named as a Communist by director Edward Dmytryk. As a consequence of this, when Dassin and screenwriter Jo Eisinger rewrote the script in London in the weeks leading up to the shoot, Dassin imbued the story with the desperation of the hunted. With the ideal lead actor and cinematographer (Max Greene) to play and illustrate this story, it became one of the best film noirs ever made according to modern critics, although it was heavily criticized upon its release.   PD

RICHARD WIDMARK   Born in Sunrise, Minnesota, on December 26, 1914, Richard Weedt Widmark studied acting and became an associate professor of dramatics and speech at Lake Forest University in Illinois before beginning work in radio in 1938. He voiced dramatic roles for *Gang Busters*, *Inner Sanctum Mysteries*, *Suspense*, and other shows, acted on Broadway, then was signed to a seven-year contract with 20th Century Fox in 1947. His first role was as the giggling murderer Tommy Udo in *Kiss of Death* (1947), for which he was nominated for a Best Actor in a Supporting Role Academy Award and won a Golden Globe. Rapidly cast into similar parts, Widmark menaced his co-stars in a series of excellent film noirs: *The Street with No Name* (1948), *Road House* (1948), *Night and the City* (1950), and the racially charged *No Way Out* (1950). As his film persona developed into a menacing, grouchy, single-minded, tough, taciturn man who was basically decent, Widmark took the lead roles in Elia Kazan's *Panic in the Streets* (1950), *Don't Bother to Knock* (1952), and Samuel Fuller's *Pickup on South Street* (1953). Starring in Westerns, war films, dramas, comedies, and epics, Widmark carved out an action-packed career, yet was pro gun control: "I know I've made kind of a half-assed career out of violence, but I abhor violence. I am an ardent supporter of gun control. It seems incredible to me that the United States are the only civilized nation that does not put some effective control on guns." After a career spanning over 60 years, he died on March 24, 2008, aged 93, a week before Jules Dassin, his director on *Night and the City*, also died.

IN A LONELY PLACE

1950 – USA – 94 MIN.
DIRECTOR NICHOLAS RAY (1911–1979)
SCREENPLAY ANDREW SOLT, EDMUND H. NORTH, based on the novel of the same name by DOROTHY B. HUGHES
DIRECTOR OF PHOTOGRAPHY BURNETT GUFFEY
EDITING VIOLA LAWRENCE **MUSIC** GEORGE ANTHEIL, featuring HADDA BROOKS **PRODUCTION** ROBERT LORD for THE SANTANA COMPANY and COLUMBIA PICTURES CORPORATION
STARRING HUMPHREY BOGART (Dixon Steele), GLORIA GRAHAME (Laurel Gray), FRANK LOVEJOY (Det. Sgt. Brub Nicolai), CARL BENTON REED (Capt. Lochner), ART SMITH (Dix's Agent, Mel Lippman), MARTHA STEWART (Mildred Atkinson), JEFF DONNELL (Sylvia Nicolai), HADDA BROOKS (Singer), STEVEN GERAY (Headwaiter), COSMO SARDO (Bartender)

"I was born when she kissed me.
I died when she left me.
I lived a few weeks while she loved me."

Nicholas Ray was a director of rare integrity and sensitivity, especially with actors, yet he never made a finer or deeper film than *In a Lonely Place*. There are indelible, exceptional moments in every one of the two dozen pictures he directed, most famously in *Rebel Without a Cause* (1955), but more than half a century later it is *In a Lonely Place* that most stands apart, that is most fully alive.

Humphrey Bogart plays Dixon Steele, a gifted screenwriter who suffers blacklist status owing to his hard drinking and mean temper. Early in the story he's accused of murder. There isn't enough evidence to arrest him, but he's so good at thinking like a killer, and always so upfront about what he's thinking, that the police are forced to suspect him. "I'll be going now," he tells them, "unless you plan to arrest me for lack of emotion."

Across the courtyard from his apartment lives an actress, Laurel Gray – played by Gloria Grahame. The night of the murder, Laurel saw Dix in the company of the victim, a young woman. She witnessed a bit of their innocu-

ous conversation; they were discussing a project. She later heard her leave, after midnight – and this account serves as his alibi. One of the detectives (Frank Lovejoy) served with Dix in the army and considers him a genius. His rock-hard faith in his friend's innocence against the skeptical protests of the senior detective in the case strengthens Laurel's belief in her own testimony. For there is a slight ambiguity, even in her mind, about whether the murder victim was actually alone when she left Dix's place – but Laurel trusts her intuition, and falls in love.

Dix may be an alienated contrarian when the cops are hounding him, but around Laurel he comes warmly alive, and his transformations, and hers, are the turns around which the story is movingly suspended. The homicide captain remains skeptical and keeps Dix under investigation. This adds a terrible pressure to his psyche, even as his love for Laurel inspires him in his writing. The project that struck him as a sappy romance the night he discussed it with the murder victim has now sprouted wings in his mind.

1   Screenwriter Dixon Steele (Humphrey Bogart) confronts his latest love, Laurel (Gloria Grahame) with evidence of her plans to leave him.

2   Dixon Steele: "I said to myself, 'There she is ... not coy, or cute, or corny. She's a good guy and I'm glad she's on my side.'"

3   Laurel is proud to have such a calming effect on Dix, in the first phase of their passion; he needs her deeply, and communicates this.

"*In a Lonely Place* came to grips with the feeling of malevolence that Bogart had nurtured, and so effectively dropped the knowingness of his 1940s films."

David Thomson, Biographical Dictionary of Film

"Mr. Bogart moves flawlessly through a script which is almost as flinty as the actor himself ... Although Steele can be callous, insulting and vicious in his dark, ugly moods, he can be tender and considerate under the influence of love ... Mr. Bogart plays the role for all it's worth, giving a maniacal fury to his rages and a hard edge to his expressions of sympathy." *The New York Times*

(According to many sources, that signature bit of blank verse of Dix's that begins, "I was born when she kissed me," was not in the script, but contributed by Ray.) Yet there is an abysmal dark side to this tenderness. The same super-vigilant gift that affords Dix such insight into others also renders him paranoid and demonic when there's something he wants, or a motive he suspects, or a lie he's determined to uncover. In love, he falls prey to all three impulses. Laurel gets a taste of this intensity early on as he peppers her with relentless questions. She is then seriously frightened as Dix – agitated by the detectives – erupts in a late-night rage against a motorist who gets in his way. He comes within a hair's breadth of killing this unknown man. Her scream is the only thing that brings him to his senses. After this – although

she still loves him – Laurel begins to plot an escape from Dix. She accepts his marriage proposal – she is too frightened not to – but makes plans to disappear. This is a provocation that, at the climax, causes Dix to lunge and wrap his hands around her throat.

The screenplay by Andrew Solt is so well constructed that as events unfold we are free to reevaluate what we've seen without resorting to flashback. Because we've seen Dix with the doomed woman and remember his gruff kindness toward her (a Bogart specialty) it is possible to feel confident that he is not guilty of any murder. And yet ...? As is true for Laurel, we are not fully certain that the lady left his apartment alone. Dix could be guilty. Laurel and we may well be in denial. Or? We could be trapped inside a trag-

3

"Was Gloria Grahame pretty? Not simply. It was always apparent that her looks might go quickly. Was she sulking seriously, was she gin and wisecrack, or was she as broody as anyone who suspects she is not simply pretty?" *David Thomson, Biographical Dictionary of Film*

4 Laurel has vouched for her new neighbor (and lover) Dix during a murder investigation, but his raw temper has made her skeptical.

5 Ambiguous image: Dix, exploding at Laurel in the film's climax, comes to his senses. Is she dead? Nicholas Ray chooses an unexpected solution.

6 Dix's agent, Mel Lippman (Art Smith), the bartender (Cosmo Sardo), and Paul the headwaiter (Steven Geray) all charm Laurel at Dix's favorite nightspot.

7 As shown, Nicholas Ray shot the ending as written, "because that was my obligation. Then we improvised the ending as it is now."

edy akin to *Othello*. Our hero could be innocent, but his murderous potential is now unleashed. In the novel by Dorothy B. Hughes, Dix does indeed strangle Laurel to death, and Solt's shooting script was true to this.

Yet Ray came to a very different conclusion. "I can't do it," he told colleagues of the impending strangulation. "I just can't do it. Romances don't have to end that way. Marriages don't have to end that way. They don't have to end in violence." He had sound reason to conclude this – he was married to Gloria Grahame, and they quietly separated during shooting. (They go back together later, but that's a whole other disaster story.) Their mixed emotions and shared discretion accorded him the strength to bring off the lovers' more profound breaking apart that gives *In a Lonely Place* its long life. Whether you've had your heart broken, or broken somebody else's heart, Ray has here made room for every heart to relate to this film's haunting outcome.   FXR

NICHOLAS RAY He was immortalized as the man with free-flowing, cotton-white hair, clad in a fur-lined leather coat, and a cowboy kerchief tied around his neck. With a patch over his right eye and a cigarillo dangling from his lips, Nicholas Ray stood before the Manhattan skyline like a supernatural spirit returned from beyond as Derwatt the painter in Wim Wenders's *The American Friend* (*Der amerikanische Freund* / *L'Ami américain*, 1977), a screen adaptation of Patricia Highsmith's thriller *Ripley's Game*. It was a role that also caught Ray in the final stages of cancer, just before he lost his life to the disease in the summer of 1979. His role in this film was an allegory of his own lifework, which encompassed some 30 filmmaking projects: Derwatt, a painter publicly declared dead, sees his artwork go up in value as a result of this media-propagated hoax. At the time, Ray's best directing years were more than a decade behind him, for he virtually withdrew from the movie industry at the beginning of the 1960s. The man born Raymond Nicholas Kienzle in 1911 was Hollywood's filmmaking rebel during the 1940s and '50s, emerging as a force that refused to be tamed by the studio system. He fought vigorously against the sensibilities of big-budget Hollywood, preferring to pursue his strongly narrative and visually overwhelming obsessions that resulted in such unmistakable films as: *Knock on Any Door* (1949), a non-linear social study about a young man whose life goes off track, and *In a Lonely Place* (1950), Ray's scathing critique of Hollywood. His diversity is also exhibited in works like the polarizing city-country drama *On Dangerous Ground* (1952) and the sumptuously colorful Western ballad *Johnny Guitar* (1954). Ray's pictures are distinguished by their excellent sense of color, composition, and supreme mastery of the CinemaScope format. Their power had its greatest impact on voices that would rise to fame in the decade to come: the auteurs of the *Nouvelle Vague*, New British Cinema, and New German Cinema. They took Ray's individualistic, alienated heroes as a model for personal expression in cinema itself. As Jean-Luc Godard said of him, "If cinema hadn't existed, Nicholas Ray could have invented it himself."

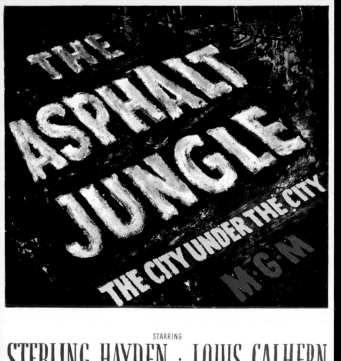

THE ASPHALT JUNGLE

1950 – USA – 112 MIN.
DIRECTOR JOHN HUSTON (1906–1987)
SCREENPLAY BEN MADDOW, JOHN HUSTON, based on the novel of the same name by W. R. BURNETT
DIRECTOR OF PHOTOGRAPHY HAROLD ROSSON
EDITING GEORGE BOEMLER **MUSIC** MIKLÓS RÓZSA
PRODUCTION ARTHUR HORNBLOW JR., for MGM
STARRING STERLING HAYDEN (Dix Handley), LOUIS CALHERN (Alonzo Emmerich), JEAN HAGEN (Doll Conovan), JAMES WHITMORE (Gus Minissi), SAM JAFFE (Erwin "Doc" Riedenschneider), JOHN MCINTIRE (Commissioner Hardy), MARC LAWRENCE (Cobby), BARRY KELLEY (Police Lt. Ditrich), ANTHONY CARUSO (Louis Ciavelli), TERESA CELLI (Maria Ciavelli), MARILYN MONROE (Angela Phinlay), WILLIAM DAVIS (Timmons), DOROTHY TREE (May Emmerich), BRAD DEXTER (Bob Brannom), JOHN MAXWELL (Dr. Swanson)

"One way or another, we all work for our vice."

Despite the exaggerated character types found in his work across many genres, as a filmmaker John Huston has frequently been cited for his naturalism, which is not an adjective often connected with film noir. Huston's association with noir goes back even farther than the consensus commencement of the classic period with his direction of *The Maltese Falcon* (1941). If that picture is not the actual first film noir, it is certainly the boundary line in a cycle of movies that stretches from Huston's adaptation of Dashiell Hammett to Orson Welles's *Touch of Evil* in 1958. As a writer, Huston's initial foray into noir was another adaptation of a novel by W. R. Burnett, *High Sierra* (1941), for director Raoul Walsh.

A decade later Huston's approach as co-writer and director of *The Asphalt Jungle* explores its titled milieu, an urban underworld populated by the same workaday criminals as in *High Sierra*. The literary output of W. R. Burnett (who was also a longtime screenwriter at Warner Bros.), which includes *Little Caesar* (1929) and *Nobody Lives Forever* (1943), was well aligned with Huston's worldview. After the considerable critical and fiscal success of *The Treasure of the Sierra Madre* (1948), Burnett's *The Asphalt Jungle* offered Huston another narrative of greed, paranoia, and mischance, but this time squarely within the confines of noir.

Unlike the title figures of the gangster genre in the 1930s, noir criminals are infrequently larger-than-life. The criminal mastermind of *The Asphalt Jungle*, "Doc" Riedenschneider (Sam Jaffe), enjoys a reputation as a savvy and meticulous schemer. Huston's casting of character actor Jaffe, and Jaffe's quiet but concentrated portrayal of Riedenschneider, is unlikely to

remind the viewer of the flamboyance of Edward G. Robinson as *Little Caesar*'s Rico in 1931, Paul Muni's *Scarface* (1932), or even James Cagney as Tom Powers in *The Public Enemy* (1931).

Nor is Jaffe's character in the same mold as Humphrey Bogart's beaten-down and aging "Mad Dog" Roy Earle in *High Sierra*. Certainly both men are looking for that last big score that could be a ticket to retirement on what passed for easy street in the mid-'20s-century. But while Earle still has the macho to make young punks toe the line with a curled lip and a menacing glare, Riedenschneider is a soft-spoken, cigar-smoking caper leader whose authority comes from his brains not his biceps. Both Earle and Riedenschneider

may have a weakness for young girls, but Doc has the good sense not to mix business with pleasure, not to let emotion influence his judgment. In fact, the only problem with Doc's plan is that he needs financial backing from shady mouthpiece Alonzo Emmerich (Louis Calhern), whose obsession with his concupiscent mistress Angela (Marilyn Monroe) is just the sort of complication that Doc knows can unravel the tightest plans – and it does.

Dix Handley (Sterling Hayden), whom Riedenschneider brings in to be his muscle, is also hoping for a big score that would permit him to go back to his family farm in Kentucky. Hayden's performance is just as solid as Bogart's as Roy Earle, which it also echoes in his harsh/tender relationship with Doll

1   The gang's "muscle," Dix Handley (Sterling Hayden, right), hauls the wounded Louis Ciavelli (Anthony Caruso) away from the scene of the crime.

2   Erwin "Doc" Riedenschneider (Sam Jaffe, right) indulges his vice and watches a very young woman gyrate.

3   The sullen Handley stands ready for trouble as his accomplice Ciavelli drills into the door of the safe.

"*The Asphalt Jungle* is a vivid contrast to Huston's other noir films. He has eliminated the claustrophobic quality found in both *The Maltese Falcon* and *Key Largo*, replacing it with a smooth uncluttered style. However, grotesque characters are still present in *The Asphalt Jungle* although they exist on the periphery of the action rather than residing at the core." *Carl Macek, Film Noir: The Encyclopedia*

STERLING HAYDEN   Born Sterling Walter (1916–1986) and adopted at an early age by the Hayden family of New England, he is perhaps best remembered by modern viewers for his roles as Gen. Jack D. Ripper in Stanley Kubrick's *Dr. Strangelove or: How I Learned to Stop Worrying and Love the Bomb* (1964), the brutal and corrupt New York City police captain McCluskey in Francis Ford Coppola's *The Godfather* (1972), or Roger Wade in Robert Altman's adaptation of Chandler's *The Long Goodbye* (1973). Hayden dropped out of school to become a fisherman and sailor and captained his first vessel at age 22. Although his 6'5" stature and chiseled features landed him work as a model and bit player, Hayden left to join the Marines and spent World War II in Italy and Croatia as "John Hamilton," his identity while working for the OSS, the precursor of the CIA. Returning to Hollywood after the war, Hayden dabbled with Communism (and later named names before HUAC) and believed, as he wrote in his 1963 autobiography, *Wanderer*, that colleagues felt he didn't "give a damn about the loot or the stardom or things like that – something to do with his seafaring, or maybe what he went through in the war." Hayden alternated acting with time at sea on his own boats. That underlying disaffection colored his performances in film noir, which include *Manhandled* (1949), *Crime Wave* (1954), *Suddenly* (1954), and Kubrick's *The Killing* (1956), where Hayden's performance anchors the film's seminal overlapping of perspectives and events.

"In *The Asphalt Jungle* John Huston is certainly committed to debunking certain stereotypes. His finely drawn criminals are not abnormal personages, neither bloodthirsty nor rapacious, but everyday sorts. In its codes of conduct, their underworld hardly differs from legal society." *Raymond Borde and Étienne Chaumeton, A Panorama of American Film Noir*

4

4 Handley carefully hands Ciavelli a vial of "soup," the highly unstable nitroglycerin that will be used to open the safe.

5 "Doc" (left) recaps the upcoming job to his motley crew of accomplices: Handley, Gus Minissi (James Whitmore, standing), and Ciavelli.

6 Doll Conovan (Jean Hagen) is already living on the edge but is unswervingly optimistic and willingly provides Handley a place to stay.

Conovan (Jean Hagen). In *High Sierra*, a cornered Earle "crashes out" on the side of a mountain as his moll Marie (Ida Lupino) watches. In *The Asphalt Jungle*, a fatally wounded Dix Handley falls and dies in a horse pasture with Doll at his side.

However unusual or sensational the acts of his criminal protagonists might be, Burnett's novels were part of a proletarian and realistic tradition in American fiction, so that they ran parallel to both the hard-boiled school of crime literature and mainstream depictions of social turmoil and decay from Dos Passos to Hemingway. In adapting Burnett's work, Huston and co-screenwriter Ben Maddow carried over both his clipped dialogue and sympathetic depictions of small-time crooks. As it was for Earle, the last score of Riedenschneider, Handley, and their confederates is part caper, part ritual of salvation. Whether or not a viewer had read Burnett's book, in the context of film noir, that the plans should all go wrong is hardly unexpected. What dis-

"If I were you, I'd think up a few more charges. You might be able to make one of them stand up … if you get an imbecile jury."

Film quote: Alonzo Emmerich (Louis Calhern)

7   Corrupt lawyer Alonzo Emmerich (Louis Calhern)
    gazes longingly at his vice, his young mistress
    Angela Phinlay (Marilyn Monroe).

8   Emmerich's hired gun Bob Brannom (Brad Dexter,
    seated) gets the drop on Handley while "Doc"
    stands by helplessly.

> "We've got to hand it to the boys, particularly to Mr. Huston: they've done a terrific job! From the very first shot, in which the camera picks up a prowling thug, sliding along between buildings to avoid a police car in the gray and liquid dawn, there is ruthless authority in this picture, the hardness and clarity of steel, and remarkably subtle suggestion that conveys a whole involvement of distorted personality and inveterate crime." *The New York Times*

tinguishes *The Asphalt Jungle* from *The Maltese Falcon* is the emphasis on the mechanics of mischance. That is also a factor in Huston's adaptation of *Key Largo* (1948), but the narrative complexities in that film, set in a single location over a couple of days, are much less broad. Ultimately what gives *The Asphalt Jungle* the same dimensions of existential anguish as so many other film noirs is the style of its performance and visuals. Jaffe, Hayden, and even Calhern, as the pathetic Emmerich hopelessly enmeshed in his own lies and double crosses, are relentlessly realistic in detail and nuance. Huston frames those actors and their actions in a detached and straightforward manner. He situates the events, where the stakes can literally be life-or-death, in an environment that is manifestly everyday and that is also at the heart of film noir.

AS

SUNSET BOULEVARD ♣♣♣

1950 – USA – 110 MIN.
DIRECTOR BILLY WILDER (1906–2002)
SCREENPLAY CHARLES BRACKETT, BILLY WILDER,
D. M. MARSHMAN JR.
DIRECTOR OF PHOTOGRAPHY JOHN F. SEITZ
EDITING ARTHUR SCHMIDT **MUSIC** FRANZ WAXMAN
PRODUCTION CHARLES BRACKETT for PARAMOUNT PICTURES
STARRING GLORIA SWANSON (Norma Desmond),
WILLIAM HOLDEN (Joe Gillis), ERICH VON STROHEIM
(Max von Mayerling), NANCY OLSON (Betty Schaefer),
FRED CLARK (Sheldrake), LLOYD GOUGH (Morino),
JACK WEBB (Artie Green), FRANKLYN FARNUM
(Undertaker), CECIL B. DEMILLE (Himself),
BUSTER KEATON (Himself)
ACADEMY AWARDS 1950 OSCARS for BEST ORIGINAL
SCREENPLAY (Charles Brackett, Billy Wilder,
D. M. Marshman Jr.), BEST MUSIC (Franz Waxman),
and BEST ART DIRECTION (Hans Dreier,
John Meehan, Sam Comer, Ray Moyer)

"I am big.
It's the pictures that got small."

A dead man tells all. A chance encounter with silent-screen legend Norma Desmond (Gloria Swanson) has cost screenwriter Joe Gillis (William Holden) his life. Now he bobs face down in her swimming pool like debris waiting to be fished out by the Hollywood homicide detectives. Welcome to *Sunset Boulevard*, a movie that starts off at the end of the line.

Director Billy Wilder originally staged the above sequence, undoubtedly one of the most chilling openings on film, as a dialogue among corpses at the morgue. Test audiences laughed out loud. Infuriated that moviegoers could mistake his message for black humor, Wilder returned to the drawing board until he achieved the desired result: an unlikely purgatory, where the line separating life from death has been all but erased.

And truly it is in a dimension inhabited by the "living dead" in which Joe Gillis finds himself after successfully outrunning a band of debt collectors. Desmond is in the process of burying her dead monkey – one might deem it a premonition of Gillis's own grim fate. The scene is a spectacle of distilled rage that mirrors the feelings that drove Wilder to shoot this film – hatred of the Hollywood dream factory, where anyone who wishes to survive is obliged to make an ape of himself.

The has-been star and her butler Max von Mayerling (Erich von Stroheim) have made an equally perverse dreamland of the labyrinthine villa that serves as their present surroundings. Here, the screen queen's star continues to flourish and the imagined masses fall at her feet. In her seclusion, she feverishly writes a screenplay about the nubile seductress Salomé and deludes herself that she is on the verge of a comeback performance.

Gillis couldn't have arrived at a more opportune time for all involved. Given that money is no object, the penniless screenwriter is happy to try his hand at making Desmond's incoherent manuscript halfway passable. Despite the young man's initial contempt for the aging movie star, he is reeled into her nostalgic web of glamour and allure. Only when Gillis witnesses his hostess playing cards with the apparitions of other silent film greats like Buster Keaton

and others (all of whom have cameos as themselves) does he realize that he has become an intrinsic part of Desmond's ghostly vortex. Later, when Betty Schaefer (Nancy Olson), Gillis's secret girlfriend and co-writer employed at Paramount, makes a failed attempt at rescuing him, it becomes painfully clear that not even love can get the upper hand over Norma's will. The incident, however, sends the diva into a fit of mania, and she shoots the screenwriter dead to prevent him abandoning her, as everyone else did long ago.

David Lynch, who counts *Sunset Boulevard* among his five all-time favorite films, described it as a "street to another world." The filmmaker was particularly fascinated by the black aura that shrouds the Desmond estate, and used it as a source of inspiration in pictures like *Eraserhead* (1977) and *Blue Velvet* (1986). In its original incarnation, the colossal dilap-

"It is one of those rare movies which are so full of exactness, cleverness, mastery, pleasure, and arguable and unarguable choice and judgment, that they can be talked about, almost shot for shot and line for line, for hours on end." *Sight and Sound*

1 Silent music starts to play: screenwriter Joe Gillis (William Holden) dances with death when he takes up employment with screen legend Norma Desmond (Gloria Swanson).

2 Everything's as if we never said goodbye: Norma informs Cecil B. DeMille that it's time they throw her starved fans a few crumbs.

3 Comeback vehicle: Max von Mayerling (Erich von Stroheim, far left) is Norma's one-man band. By keeping her dreams alive, he supplies the drive she needs to persevere in a world that's forgotten her.

idated mansion was a metaphor for early Hollywood. It recalls a bygone era when the studio system produced screen gods who spoke in a language without words.

Insular in nature, the estate is also symbolic of the human mind and its tendency to create imagined, potentially imprisoning realities. Thus *Sunset Boulevard* can also be seen as a parable about the dark side of imagination. Desmond and von Mayerling are buried alive under their own unstable vision of Shangri-La, and Joe Gillis sells out to them to avoid facing the demands of the outside world. Ironically, he turns his back on his ideals just as things

begin to take shape with Betty Schaefer and success is a mere stone's throw away. As Gillis learns the hard way, there's no return to innocence for those who lose faith in themselves.

This existential reflection about the fear of change also serves as a sharp warning to the representatives of present-day Hollywood. As the film reminds us, the machinery that ran Old Hollywood was still all-powerful in the late 1940s. We need only look at the caricature studio boss set on financial gain, who puffs away at a cigar from atop a cushy sofa, or at the screenwriters he works to the bone. The subtext of Wilder's

BILLY WILDER Wilder was born in 1906 in the Galician town of Sucha Beskidzka, now part of Poland. He cut his teeth working as a journalist in Vienna and Berlin, where he soon gravitated to the movie industry. As an Austrian emigré in Hollywood, he managed an almost seamless transition in his work as a scriptwriter, and his big break came with the comedy *Ninotchka* (1939) directed by his hero, Ernst Lubitsch. The impact of the war – Wilder lost both parents in the Holocaust – made him turn to more serious themes. His fourth excursion as a director, *Double Indemnity* (1944), was a bleak drama about adultery, murder, and betrayal, which became a film noir classic. In addition to Expressionistic lighting he established the voice-over as a dramatic device and his own particular trademark: razor-sharp dialogue, often riddled with double meaning. He created more high points of the genre with an alcoholic's tale *The Lost Weekend* (1945) and *Sunset Boulevard* (1950), a disillusioned account of Hollywood's dream factory. The undisputed master of the modern comedy, he only used style elements of film noir occasionally in his later movies. The taboo subject of adultery, which had presented a challenge to the censors in *Double Indemnity*, also found its way into his biggest hits like *The Seven Year Itch* (1955), *The Apartment* (1960), and *Irma la Douce* (1963). Wilder's view of human weakness became tempered, though no less relevant. In his masterpiece *Some Like It Hot* (1959) featuring cross-dressing, he also satirized the old gangster movies of the 1930s which form the basis of film noir.

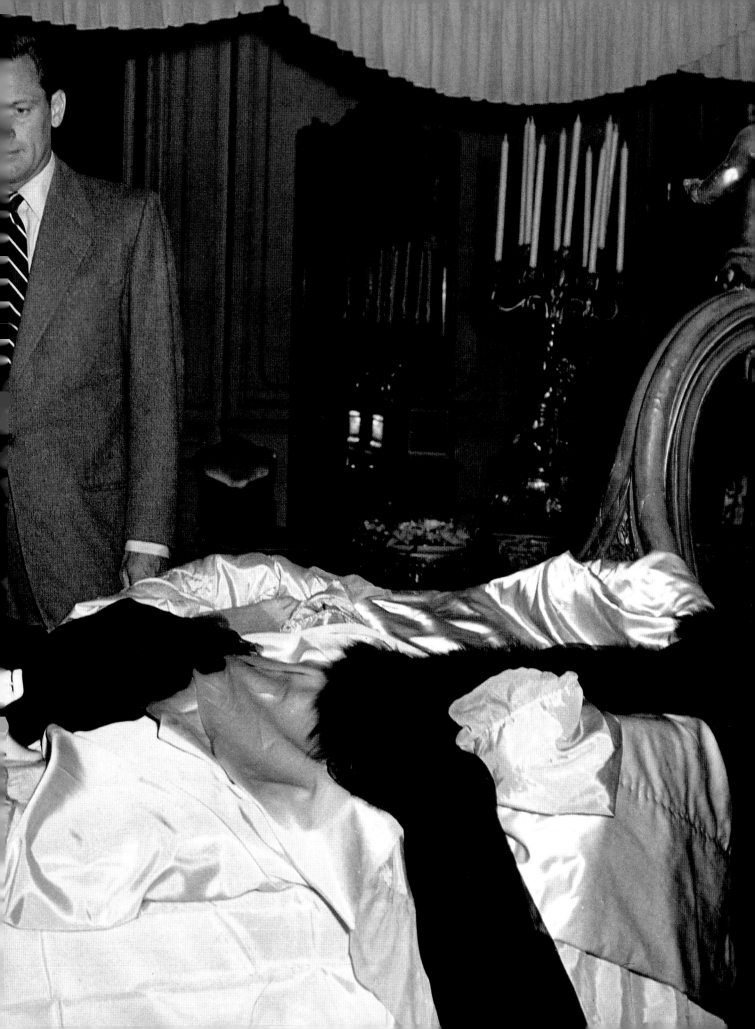

5

intentional typecasting is equally significant: Erich von Stroheim, a film-maker who fell foul of the studios, plays a filmmaker who has been reduced to life as a butler; and silent starlet Gloria Swanson's performance reads like a ghastly self-portrait as both she and her character make a genuine attempt to reenter the spotlight that has shunned her. Their tragic fates are indicative of how the film industry is willing to treat its VIPs when they are suddenly deemed obsolete – never mind that with-out them studios like Paramount wouldn't have existed in the first place, as Desmond states.

Hollywood saw to it that Wilder got his just desserts for dragging the film industry through the mud. Despite being nominated for an astounding eleven Oscars, *Sunset Boulevard* was only awarded three; among them were Best Score, Best Art Direction for a black-and-white film, and Best Original Screenplay. MGM film mogul Louis B. Mayer exited a Paramount screening in an uproar, denouncing Wilder as a "bastard … who should be tarred, feath-ered and chased out of town." But even Mayer eventually had to concede to the fact that the Dream Factory's golden age was a thing of the past – and that the television era was upon him.   SH

THE THIEF

1952 – USA – 85 MIN.
DIRECTOR RUSSELL ROUSE (1913–1987)
SCREENPLAY CLARENCE GREENE, RUSSELL ROUSE
DIRECTOR OF PHOTOGRAPHY SAM LEAVITT
EDITING CHESTER W. SCHAEFFER
MUSIC HERSCHEL BURKE GILBERT
PRODUCTION CLARENCE GREENE for HARRY M. POPKIN
PRODUCTIONS, UNITED ARTISTS
STARRING RAY MILLAND (Dr. Allan Fields), MARTIN GABEL
(Mr. Bleek), RITA GAM (The Girl), HARRY BRONSON
(Harris), JOHN MCKUTCHEON (Dr. Linstrum),
RITA VALE (Miss Philips), REX O'MALLEY (Beal),
JOE CONLIN (Walters)

"86th floor of Empire State.
Woman will carry three books tied with string."

Contemporary reviewers were of mixed opinions about *The Thief*. For many, it was too reliant on its core gimmick, a story told with no dialogue. For some, used to hearing actors speak, there were also performance issues, particularly with Ray Milland's interpretation of Dr. Allan Fields, a physicist who is passing secrets on to agents of an unnamed foreign power. The presumption in 1952, while Julius and Ethel Rosenberg awaited execution for espionage, was that the Soviet Union had somehow convinced Fields to betray his country. Consequently *The Thief* was considered an early Cold War, anti-Communist drama. However, since the film opens in medias res with Fields already engaged in treason, why he is spying is a question that is never asked nor answered.

The movie begins "normally" enough: under the credits the dome of the Capitol Building is visible until a man in hat and trench coat walking right towards the camera gets close enough to blot it out. The strident minor-key underscore by Herschel Burke Gilbert completes the invocation of film noir in a manner somewhat reminiscent of the figure on crutches and title music by Miklós Rózsa that opens *Double Indemnity* (1944). In the first sequence a long take pulls back from a close shot of a ringing telephone to dolly and pan across a room, over to and up along a bed where a solitary figure, a man with a troubled visage, lies dressed and awake listening to the shrill sound. It stops, and the camera retreats slightly when he rolls to the side, turns on a lamp, and lights a cigarette, which a full ashtray reveals is not the first of the day. The invocation is purely noir, without clear indication that the audience will never hear this man answer the telephone and speak into its mouthpiece or to anyone else. Still, the publicity and reviews of *The Thief* made it likely that most viewers knew what its unusual approach would be.

The Thief was also publicized as part of a noir subgroup or anti-Communist propaganda and was bookended by such more traditional examples as *I Was a Communist for the F.B.I.* (1951) and *Pickup on South Street* (1953), where the concepts of paranoia and patriotism are generalizations, and invocations not to betray one's country are woven through the dialogue. In a film, silent or not, with its focus limited to one character through whose viewpoint all events are filtered, whether the criminal is a traitor or some less sensational transgressor – robber, kidnapper, rapist, or simple murderer – the emotional turmoil experienced by the guilty person is always in the foreground. Milland's best-known performance in Billy Wilder's *The Lost Weekend* (1945) involves an even broader range of expression than he brings to the hesitant and morose Fields. If anything, his voiceless portrayal in *The Thief* is underplayed. Without the guidance – or constraint – of the spoken word, the viewers must fill the void with their imaginations, and

some of the thoughts they put into Fields's head may make his distress seem over the top.

A metaphor that underlies *The Thief* from the opening sequence, in which the viewer will discover that the ringing telephone sends wordless instructions, is that in a world without speech the hidden meaning of everyday sounds can be prospicient or foreboding. In his enclosed spy's world only Fields really knows. Since it includes many location exteriors and interiors – most notably the Library of Congress in Washington, D.C., and the Empire State Building in New York City – the visual style of *The Thief* is part of the postwar docu-noir trend. Within that context director Russell Rouse and cinematographer Sam Leavitt also superimpose a noir style: an everyday world full of dark corners and furtive glances. Tension is further enhanced by the use of extended takes. As the film opens, Fields's obvious anxiety and perhaps chagrin over his situation may be read as either regret at his betrayal of

"***The Thief*** (1952) by Russell Rouse, a sound film without dialogue of the type produced in 1929, vainly attempts to dramatize the pangs of guilt of an atomic spy being hunted by the police, through an ingenious use of sound, a chase at the Empire State Building, and Rita Gam's legs."

Raymond Borde and Étienne Chaumeton, *A Panorama of American Film Noir*

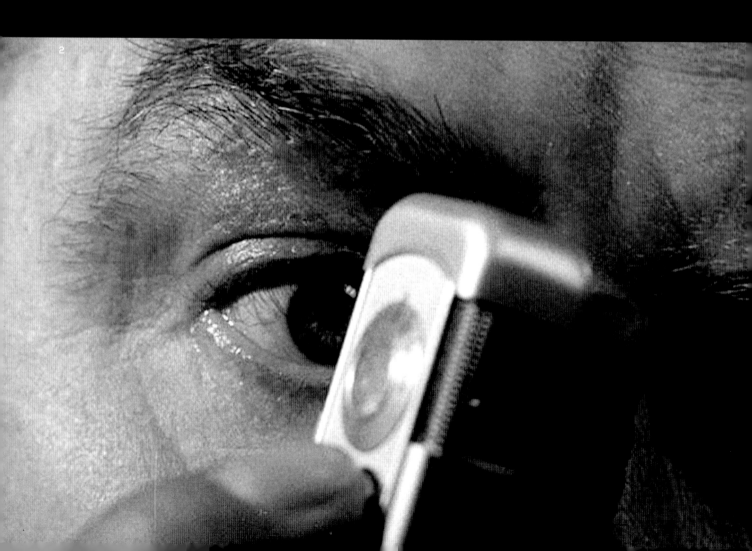

2

1   Throughout this speechless narrative, traitorous physicist Dr. Allan Fields (Ray Milland) is dogged both by actual government agents and by his own demons.

2   Postwar technology on display included the Minox camera, here wielded by an anxious Fields to copy secret documents in a colleague's office.

3   Mr. Bleek (Martin Gabel) is the spymaster for whom Fields usually leaves material in the Library of Congress.

4   In a pre-James Bond world, the other spies are seen fleetingly and, albeit trench-coated, are anything but glamorous.

"The film is not soundless. The busy hum of a city is a cacophonous note, a strident-sounding telephone bell plays an important part and, overall, there's the top-notch musical score by Herschel Gilbert." *Variety*

his fellow citizens or as dread of the consequences that will befall him, or both. Once he realizes that he is under suspicion and being tracked, in the core tradition of noir protagonists, dread and desperation take over. Like other figures of that ilk, Fields sits alone in a dimly lit room of a New York flophouse, nervously puffing on a cigarette and awaiting instructions, while somewhere outside a blinking neon sign sends light and shadow flashing through a window, externalizing the character's emotional paroxysms. There is also the interaction with the young neighbor down the hall as Fields stares through an open door into her boudoir at smooth, bare legs revealed by a parted peignoir. The irony is that this is not about a man brought down by a *femme fatale*. After she notices him in her mirror and gives him a final enigmatic stare, she closes the door.

AS

5

"The moment at the end, as Milland waits despairingly for word of his escape, and the teasingly sexy girl across the hall (Gam) closes her door in his face as she realizes he is watching her, is one Bresson might have been proud of." *Time Out Film Guide*

5 Fields reaches the wharf where a ship to Cairo waits. At the foot of the gangplank, literally on the brink of escape, the guilt-ridden Fields walks away to be arrested.

6 After the botched rendezvous at the Empire State Building, Fields is forced to flee and breaks into the inner recesses of the structure.

7 When his colleague Dr. Linstrum (John McKutcheon) unexpectedly returns for a forgotten item, Fields narrowly avoids being discovered.

8 Fields cannot escape facing the deadly consequences of his behavior when Agent Harris (Harry Bronson) falls to his death.

RUSSELL ROUSE Rouse (1913–1987), the son of a New York–based assistant director, began his career in the film industry by working in the art department at Paramount Studios in the 1930s. After breaking into feature writing on a Laurel and Hardy picture, Rouse first partnered with his usual co-writer (and later producer) Clarence Greene on the PRC comedy *The Town Went Wild* (1944). As the noir movement went into high gear, Rouse and Greene created the story and screenplay for one of the genre's key features, *D.O.A.* (1950). Rouse became a director on *The Well* (1951), a quasi-docu-noir, and continued in that role on *The Thief* (1952) and eight other features, including *Wicked Woman* (1953), *New York Confidential* (1955), and *House of Numbers* (1957). While none of these other features are as unusual in approach as *The Thief* (or as propagandistic), Rouse consistently used moving camera, extended takes, and POV shots from characters in concealed vantage points. Unlike many classic-period independent filmmakers Rouse, who also directed the noirish Western *The Fastest Gun Alive* (1956) and the Hollywood potboiler *The Oscar* (1966), did not do much work in television. A notable exception is the series he created and produced, *Tightrope* (1959–1960), which revolved around an undercover agent who infiltrates criminal enterprises by passing as a gangster.

6

7

POISON IVY
LA MÔME VERT-DE-GRIS

1953 – FRANCE – 97 MIN.
DIRECTOR BERNARD BORDERIE (1924–1978)
SCREENPLAY BERNARD BORDERIE, JACQUES BERLAND,
based on the novel *Poison Ivy* by PETER CHEYNEY
DIRECTOR OF PHOTOGRAPHY JACQUES LEMARE
EDITING JEAN FEYTE MUSIC GUY LAFARGE
PRODUCTION RAYMOND BORDERIE for C.I.C.C.,
PATHÉ CONSORTIUM CINÉMA
STARRING EDDIE CONSTANTINE (Lemmy Caution),
DOMINIQUE WILMS (Carlotta de La Rue),
HOWARD VERNON (Rudy Saltierra), DARÍO MORENO
(Joe Madrigal), MAURICE RONET (Mickey),
GASTON MODOT (Police Inspector), JO DEST
(Harley Chase), JEAN-MARIE ROBAIN (Willie Freen),
GEORGES WILSON (Duncan a.k.a. Melander),
DON ZIEGLER (Director of the FBI),
JEAN-MARC TENNBERG (G.D.B.)

"Is it true that a G-man's brains are all in his revolver?"

After World War II, French publishing house Gallimard launched a new imprint, Série Noire, to publish the English and American hard-boiled novels they were unable to publish during the war. The first two titles were *La Môme vert-de-gris* (originally published as *Poison Ivy* in 1937) and *Cet homme est dangereux* (originally *This Man Is Dangerous*, 1936) by Peter Cheyney. The novels featured Lemuel H. "Lemmy" Caution, a womanizing, hard-drinking, wise-cracking FBI agent; became best sellers; and launched the Série Noire imprint, with each new title assured an initial print run of 30,000 copies. "For a time, the average French reader was convinced that Cheyney was an American author," wrote Étienne Borgers in *The Big Book of Noir* (1998), but in fact Cheyney was a British writer, a former policeman, who emulated and exaggerated the American hard-boiled style.

The French love for the Série Noire went hand-in-hand with their great appetite for the dark crime films they saw for the first time after the war. In 1946 critic Nino Frank coined the phrase "film noir" to categorize these films, and it was not long before the French were making their own versions,

like André Hunebelle's trilogy *Mission in Tangier* (*Mission à Tanger*, 1949), *Méfiez-vous des blondes* (1950), and *Massacre in Lace* (*Massacre en dentelles*, 1952). Based on the first screenplays of Michel Audiard, who would go on to write over 100 films, many of them noirs, this series featured exotic locations appropriate for the French market (Tangier, London, Venice), and followed the adventures of crusading journalist Georges Masse, played by Raymond Rouleau. In their 1955 book, *A Panorama of American Film Noir*, Raymond Borde and Étienne Chaumeton comment, "The film's hero was an investigative journalist partial to whiskey and women. He recalled those easygoing detectives of which William Powell was at one time the prototype."

It was inevitable that the market would welcome an authentic American actor to play an authentic American hero. On November 24, 1952, director Bernard Borderie began filming *Poison Ivy*, starring American-born singer Eddie Constantine as Lemmy Caution. Borderie's wife had spotted Constantine in Victor Stoloff's stodgy but picturesque *Egypt by Three* (1953). "My American gangster persona interested Borderie," Constantine recalled. "He

1 FBI agent Lemmy Caution (Eddie Constantine) flashes a winning smile, but nightclub singer Carlotta de la Rue (Dominique Wilms) is impervious to his charms.

2 As Lemmy Caution watches Carlotta perform he comments, "Any woman that beautiful would be able to sell me an electric chair, I guess. I would gladly buy it."

3 Lemmy breaks into Carlotta's apartment to grill her for information about the killings in the nightclub, but takes time to admire the view.

"Eddie hated Dominique Wilms! Every time they had a love scene, they'd hiss at each other as they said their 'loving' lines! Apparently, they both felt antagonistic towards each other, in spite of the fact that they did several films together and were dynamic on-screen as a couple." *Tanya Constantine*

EDDIE CONSTANTINE Edward Constantine, born Edward Constantinowsky in Los Angeles on October 29, 1917, to Russian and Polish parents, trained for five years as an opera singer in Vienna during his teenage years, then returned to America to pursue a singing career. After failing to impress in the chorus of MGM musicals in Los Angeles, Constantine moved to New York and became part of the men's choir at Radio City Music Hall, but was fired, "because he refused to wear socks of the same color as all the other singers!" his daughter Tanya recalled in an interview with Tim Lucas for *Video Watchdog*. Constantine moved to Paris in the mid-1940s to be with his wife, Hélène, a ballet dancer, then began an affair with Édith Piaf, which led to their starring together in the musical *La Petite Lili*.

After the overnight success of the Lemmy Caution films, beginning with *Poison Ivy* (*La Môme vert-de-gris*, 1953), Constantine became a national celebrity, which did not sit well with his Communist ideals. Tanya remembered, "On one hand, he loved the adulation … he thrived on it. On another, he was in conflict with it … because of guilt. He had a bravado that hid his true vulnerability and, since it wasn't cool to show that side, he kept it hidden from everyone, including himself."

Constantine wanted to get away from the Lemmy persona. "He actually ruined himself by refusing to do any more Lemmy Caution films for several years," his daughter recalled, but in the end he continued to make tough-guy films playing Lemmy, Jeff Gordon, and Nick Carter, while pursuing a parallel singing career. Eventually, adopted by the French and German New Wave, Constantine often played himself, or Lemmy, for directors as diverse as Jean-Luc Godard (*Alphaville*, 1965; *Germany Year 90 Nine Zero* [*Allemagne 90 neuf zéro*, 1991]), Rainer Werner Fassbinder (*Beware of a Holy Whore* [*Warnung vor einer heiligen Nutte*, 1971]), *The Third Generation* [*Die dritte Generation*, 1979]), and Lars von Trier (*Europa*, 1991). He died of a heart attack on February 25, 1993.

4 Eddie Constantine brought a rugged masculinity to the role: "I'm a reaction to the sissyish, beautifully dressed French leading men. When I kiss or slap a dame, a French guy says, 'That could be me.'"

5 Carlotta is nicknamed "The Poison Ivy Kid" because everyone who comes into contact with her is destroyed, but that doesn't deter Lemmy.

decided right away that I had the kind of personality he was looking for." Extensive shooting took place in Casablanca, Tangier, and other photogenic locations in Morocco, as well as at Studios Photosonor, in Courbevoie, northwest of Paris. Filming was completed on February 14, 1953, and the film was released on May 27.

The film opens with a sweeping camera shot – worthy of Orson Welles's later *Touch of Evil* (1958) – around and through the nighttime streets and alleys of Casablanca, into Joe Madrigal's nightclub, through the crowd, and into the backstage area so that we hear the argument that results in the first (of many) deaths that pepper the film. This bravura shot comes courtesy of cinematographer Jacques Lemare, who had worked with Jean Renoir on the intricate *The Rules of the Game* (*La Règle du jeu*, 1939).

On the way to the hospital, a young man talks feverishly about a gold shipment from America, and names the ship that will be carrying it, then dies in the ambulance. He is the brother of nightclub singer Carlotta de la Rue (Dominique Wilms), nicknamed "The Poison Ivy Kid" because she kills every-

one that comes into contact with her. In Washington, FBI agent Lemmy Caution (Eddie Constantine) is ordered to find out who has leaked this confidential information, so he goes undercover as Texan Perry Charles Rice. Upon his arrival in Casablanca, Lemmy's contact Duncan (Georges Wilson) is killed before they can meet, and singer Carlotta's secretary Willie Freen (Jean-Marie Robain) is also shot during Carlotta's performance at the nightclub. Lemmy doesn't need the help of his drunken journalist friend G.D.B. (Jean-Marc Tennberg) to work out that smooth and affable Rudy Saltierra (Howard Vernon) is the baddie and Carlotta is his moll. Lemmy flirts with Carlotta in her bedroom, drinks with Saltierra in a bar, is shot at outside Marrakesh, is betrayed by G.D.B. on a boat, is saved by Carlotta while handcuffed, escapes, tracks down the stolen gold in La Montaigne, allows the mastermind Harley

Chase (Jo Dest) to kill himself, traps Saltierra in Medina, and ends up on a rooftop kissing Carlotta. As Tim Lucas observes in *Video Watchdog*, "Everything about *Poison Ivy* is proto-Bondian, whether it's Lemmy's office flirtations with his FBI superior's Moneypenny-like secretary; his fondness for the good things in life (women and strong drink, especially); his globetrotting; his professional celebrity within the bounds of his professional secrecy; his war of sophistication with his chief adversary; even his cue-end-credits dalliance with the leading lady on the conquered battlegrounds of action while awaiting rescue by helicopter."

Poison Ivy is resplendent with all the accumulated clichés of the film noir genre, with, Borde and Chaumeton assure us, "chases, fistfights, nightclubs, unusual settings," and "knowing winks at the public." It is pure pulp fiction, but it is saved by the winning personality of Eddie Constantine as Lemmy Caution, who cannot pass a woman without making a pass at her, and when offered a drink always replies, "Make it a double." As Tim Lucas confirms, "Constantine's breezy, bullet-proof charisma gave the G-man an extra dimension."

Such was Constantine's success with the role that it led to a 40-year acting and singing career, including 14 more appearances as Lemmy Caution, two of them in unofficial versions directed by Jean-Luc Godard, the most well-known being *Alphaville* (*Alphaville, une étrange aventure de Lemmy Caution*, 1965). Although they had an enormous cultural impact in France and Germany, the Lemmy Caution films were never theatrically released in America and the U.K. and so remain virtually unknown there.   PD

6   At the end of the film, Lemmy and Carlotta shoot it out with Rudy Saltierra's gang in Medina.

7   Lemmy is shot at with a machine gun, beaten up, handcuffed, almost drowned, and repeatedly betrayed, but he remains resilient throughout.

8   *Poison Ivy* made Eddie Constantine an instant star in France, and led to later fame in Germany during his 40-year film career.

"Eddie's Lemmy Caution was a working-class prototype of James Bond, who made his literary debut in Ian Fleming's *Casino Royale* the same year that *Poison Ivy* reached the silver screen."

Tim Lucas, *Video Watchdog*

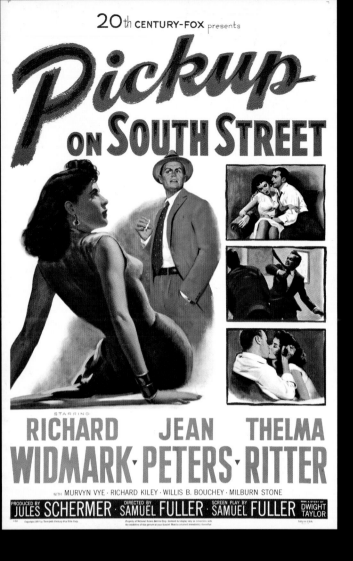

PICKUP ON SOUTH STREET

1953 – USA – 83 MIN.
DIRECTOR SAMUEL FULLER (1912–1997)
SCREENPLAY SAMUEL FULLER, based on an
unpublished story by DWIGHT TAYLOR
DIRECTOR OF PHOTOGRAPHY JOSEPH MACDONALD
EDITING NICK DE MAGGIO MUSIC LEIGH HARLINE
PRODUCTION JULES SCHERMER for 20TH CENTURY FOX
STARRING RICHARD WIDMARK (Skip McCoy),
JEAN PETERS (Candy), THELMA RITTER (Moe Williams),
MURVYN VYE (Captain Dan Tiger), RICHARD KILEY
(Joey), WILLIS B. BOUCHEY (Zara), MILBURN STONE
(Detective Winoki), HENRY SLATE (MacGregor),
JERRY O'SULLIVAN (FBI Agent Enyart),
VIC PERRY (Lightning Louie)

"Sometimes you look for oil, you hit a gusher."

Sam Fuller's reputation for tough and violent characters across a range of Westerns, war movies, and film noir is unquestionably well deserved. Remarkably, however, many of his most brutal protagonists, from the grizzled infantry sergeant – Zack in *The Steel Helmet* and Rock in *Fixed Bayonets!* (both 1951), where even the titles and character names speak volumes – to Kelly, the hard-bitten ex-hooker in *The Naked Kiss* (1964), have a much softer side, which comes from being orphaned/abused children. One of Fuller's most doggedly vengeful characters, Tolly Devlin (Cliff Robertson) in *Underworld U.S.A.* (1961), is an orphan ruthlessly intent on evening the score for his murdered father. Even the consummately cynical pickpocket Skip McCoy (Richard Widmark) in *Pickup on South Street* (1953) turns out to have his soft spots. Like Tolly and other Fuller men, McCoy falls for a girl who's "knocked around a lot."

The unexpectedly patriotic petty criminals of *Pickup on South Street* – pickpocket McCoy, the street walker Candy (Jean Peters), the professional

stoolie Moe (Thelma Ritter) – may seem like anomalies in the underworld of film noir. But in Fuller's even more tightly defined world, there is also an underlying and often overriding moral code, sometimes twisted or off-kilter but always in play, that governs the behavior of his characters. The politics of *Pickup on South Street* may seem simplistic or retrograde from a 21st-century perspective, or when counterpoised to the liberal leanings of most classic-period movies and their makers. Fuller's vision of noir is much more focused on personal conduct, and major transgressions often center around betrayal. In *I Shot Jesse James* (1949) or *House of Bamboo* (1955) the bad faith is among criminals. In *The Crimson Kimono* (1959) police partners fall out over a woman. What Fuller typically adds is a subtle and/or socially conscious twist: the homoeroticism among gang members in *House of Bamboo*, or the repressed racism in *Crimson Kimono*. In *Pickup on South Street*, the not-so-subtle element is the red menace. For Fuller, whose characters

"If *Pickup on South Street* makes any point at all, it's that there is nothing really wrong with pickpockets, even when they are given to violence, as long as they don't play footsie with Communist spies. Since this is at best a thin theme, *Pickup* for the most part falls flat on its face and borders on, presumably unintended, comedy." *Variety*

SAMUEL FULLER The Massachusetts-born Fuller (1912–1997) began his career as an East Coast journalist, moving up from copy boy to crime reporter at the age of 17. He segued to screenwriting in the mid-1930s and did journeyman work for Columbia, Republic, and Fox. His first stint in Hollywood was interrupted by World War II, where Fuller saw extensive action with the U.S. 1st Infantry Division, "The Big Red One," in North Africa, on Omaha Beach during D-Day, and throughout Europe thereafter, for which he received both Bronze and Silver Stars.

When he returned to Hollywood, soldiers were added to journalists as characters about whom Fuller was most comfortable writing. His initial foray into film noir was the screenplay for *Shockproof* (1949), after which he made an arrangement with independent producer Robert Lippert to write three scripts that he would be permitted to direct. Those led to a contract with Fox where the second project was *Pickup on South Street* (1953). As Fuller was shooting that, Columbia released *Scandal Sheet* (1952), its noir adaptation of Fuller's 1944 novel *The Dark Page*. *House of Bamboo* (1955), *The Crimson Kimono* (1959), *Underworld U.S.A.* (1961), the marginally noir *Shock Corridor* (1963), and *The Naked Kiss* (1964) round out Fuller's contributions to the noir movement.

Fuller was one of the few writer/directors of the classic period (and he continued to work into the 1990s) to have captured the attention of both academics and filmmakers of the next generation. Jim Jarmusch, Tim Robbins, Jonathan Demme, Curtis Hanson, Quentin Tarantino, and Martin Scorsese have all praised Fuller's uncompromising individualism. After a dispute with Paramount over his adaptation of the racist-themed *White Dog* (1982), Fuller exiled himself to France. He returned to the US and completed his last script, for the cable movie *Girls in Prison* (1994), shortly before his death.

1   Working girl Candy (Jean Peters) is menaced by her ex-boyfriend Joey (Richard Kiley), a spy who needs his microfilm back.

2   Before he shook her by the shoulders, Joey had tried a softer approach with Candy. Neither worked.

3   After she suffers an assault, Candy is consoled by pickpocket Skip McCoy (Richard Widmark), whose quest for a big score is the cause of her grief.

4   In an earlier clinch, the viewer realizes that, unlike Joey, McCoy has genuine feelings for Candy.

5   In his waterfront squat, a smug McCoy listens to a lecture from Police Capt. Dan Tiger (Murvyn Vye).

"... film is a battleground. Love, hate, violence, action, death ... In a word, emotion." *Samuel Fuller*

across many genres and styles may only be redeemed if they display certain virtues – if they show loyalty to a person or a principle, if they protect the innocent or the weak – *Pickup on South Street* is primarily about that process. The villains here are "commies" and spies, but that is just a cipher for social evil, for figures that in other Fuller movies are enemy combatants, gangsters, child molesters, et cetera.

Within the context of film noir, Fuller and cinematographer Joseph Mac-Donald apply a prototypical visual style. There are many docu-noir sequences, from the opening on the subway as well as amblings and pursuits on the streets of New York City. Daytime interiors in the police bureau, Moe's sparsely furnished room, and the quarters of Candy's ex, Joey (Richard Kiley), are lit without artifice. In contrast, the illumination inside McCoy's waterfront digs is markedly low-key. And the apartment where Candy reports McCoy's intransigence to the other spies is a maze of shadows and wedges of light that leave half the spies' faces in darkness. As he often does, Fuller also uses long takes to subliminally inject tension. At other times, he fills the screen with the faces of his performers. In the very first sequence, Leigh Harline's staccato, jazzy title music briefly carries over to a shot of a subway train streaking diagonally through a dark frame. Inside the car, the editing scheme emphasizes close-ups of Candy, the two federal agents tailing her, and then McCoy, cutting back wide only to establish the cramped and claustrophobic atmosphere at rush hour, when most of the riders must stand and be jostled by those entering and leaving. Fuller frequently captures establishing shots from high angles. Some are motivated, such as POVs when the cops peer down from a high window at the street traffic below. Others, as McCoy returns to his shack

"The climate is so brutish and the business so sadistic in this tale of pickpockets, demireps, informers, detectives and Communist spies that the whole thing becomes a trifle silly as it slashes and slambangs along, and the first thing you know its grave pretenses are standing there, artless and absurd." *The New York Times*

6 Capt. Tiger and FBI Agent Zara (Willis B. Bouchey) try to convince Candy, who did not know what she was carrying for Joey, to help them put the traitor away.

7 Goaded by Joey to track down the man who picked her pocket, Candy turns to professional stool pigeon Moe (Thelma Ritter) for help.

8 In a reverse angle on their tête-à-tête Tiger's expression clearly reveals that he thinks McCoy is a punk.

on the river, are there for pictorial effect only, pointedly to exploit the visual interest in the unusual location.

From a tight shot of McCoy using a microfilm reader at the New York public library and excited when he realizes what he has, Fuller dissolves to a long take. From a mirroring tight shot of the sleepy-eyed Lightning Louie (Vic Perry) rhythmically shoveling Chinese food into his mouth with a pair of greasy chopsticks, the camera pulls back then quickly right to reveal Candy seeking information. As she drops crumpled bills from her purse on the table, Louie scoops them up with the chopsticks. When Candy leans in to protest another demand for payment, Louie almost pokes her in the face with his ever-moving utensils.

The dialogue is clipped and idiomatic, reflecting the hardscrabble life experiences of the characters on the fringe of normal society. There are also many unspoken but pointed reactions from McCoy, Candy, and Moe. In the end, Fuller's staging transforms *Pickup on South Street*, strips away the propagandistic plot and distills from it a gritty, fatalistic noir, where pure chance can bring death to some and permit others to survive.   AS

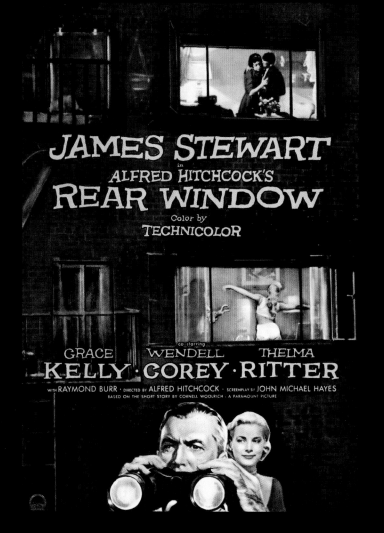

REAR WINDOW

1954 – USA – 112 MIN.
DIRECTOR ALFRED HITCHCOCK (1899–1980)
SCREENPLAY JOHN MICHAEL HAYES, based
on the short story *It Had to Be Murder*
von WILLIAM IRISH [= CORNELL WOOLRICH]
DIRECTOR OF PHOTOGRAPHY ROBERT BURKS
EDITING GEORGE TOMASINI MUSIC FRANZ WAXMAN
PRODUCTION ALFRED HITCHCOCK for PATRON INC.,
PARAMOUNT PICTURES
STARRING JAMES STEWART (L. B. Jeffries),
GRACE KELLY (Lisa Carol Fremont), WENDELL COREY
(Lieutenant Tom Doyle), THELMA RITTER (Stella),
RAYMOND BURR (Lars Thorwald), JUDITH EVELYN
(Miss Lonelyheart), ROSS BAGDASARIAN
(Songwriter), GEORGINE DARCY (Miss Torso),
IRENE WINSTON (Mrs. Thorwald), SARA BERNER
(Woman on the fire escape), FRANK CADY
(Man on the fire escape)

"We've become a race of Peeping Toms."

A heat so thick you could cut it with a knife has taken hold of New York and claimed it as its own. Among those feeling the burn is L. B. Jeffries (James Stewart), a temporarily wheelchair-bound photographer cooped up in his apartment after a spot of bad luck. The shot pans over his right leg, locked in place from hip to toe by a cast, past a broken camera, until finally arriving at a photograph of the disabling incident – a car race that ended in a wreck. Hitchcock's careful arrangement of objects breathes life into the frames of *Rear Window*. Here, shots read like still-life paintings, with another showing a sandwich and an ordinary glass of milk positioned near a large pair of binoculars on top of a table. These are the articles that help Jeffries pass the time now. For in his immobilized state, the photographer keeps his eagle eye in form by indulging in a rather deviant pastime – peering into his neighbors' apartments and their private lives.

The bits of business he observes in his own backyard keep Jeffries' mind occupied and far away from the issue plaguing his soul – namely the question of marriage. Lisa Carol Fremont (Grace Kelly), a fashion designer as affluent as she is attractive, has her sights set on marching him to the altar.

Jeffries, however, has his doubts. He tells himself that she's just too good for him, and doubts whether she can adapt to his lifestyle as a globetrotting photographer. But before long, convalescent Jeffries begins to take a particular interest in an apartment opposite his, and a chain of mysterious events from within distract him and Lisa from the problem at hand.

Just a few windows away, salesman Lars Thorwald (Raymond Burr) and his crabby, bedridden wife (Irene Winston) maintain an unhappy marriage marked by constant bickering. Then one day Mrs. Thorwald isn't there anymore, and hubby starts behaving strangely, sporadically leaving and reentering the apartment one stormy night with an unwieldy looking suitcase. On account of the facts, one can't help but wonder whether Thorwald has conveniently disposed of his wife.

Hitchcock once said that he would have liked to stage one of his movies in a phone booth. Although he personally never followed through on the idea, it has since been adapted for the screen by filmmaker Joel Schumacher (*Phone Booth*, 2002). Hitchcock did, however, direct two pieces that unfold within claustrophobic spaces. *Rope* (1948) plays out entirely within a New

2

CORNELL WOOLRICH Almost 100 movies and television programs have been based on the fiction of Cornell Woolrich, who also published under the pseudonyms William Irish and George Hopley. More film noirs of the classic period were based on his work than on anyone else's. Including *Phantom Lady* (1944) there were 14 movies in a seven-year span: *Street of Chance* (1942), *The Leopard Man* (1943), *The Mark of the Whistler* (1944), *Deadline at Dawn*, *Black Angel*, *The Chase* (all 1946), *Fear in the Night*, *The Guilty*, *Fall Guy* (all 1947), *Night Has a Thousand Eyes*, *I Wouldn't Be in Your Shoes*, *The Return of the Whistler* (all 1948), and *The Window* (1949). In the late 1960s François Truffaut adapted both *The Bride Wore Black* (1968), and *Waltz into Darkness* (as *Mississippi Mermaid*, 1969), the latter remade as *Original Sin* (2001). Perhaps best known of all is Hitchcock's *Rear Window* (1954).

After a childhood in Mexico with his father, Woolrich (1903–1968) lived with his mother in New York while attending Columbia University, from which he later dropped out. He successfully imitated F. Scott Fitzgerald in a series of "Jazz Age" novels, and then concocted "William Irish" for his pulp and detective fiction. Although briefly married (to the daughter of silent filmmaker J. Stuart Blackton), Woolrich was homosexual and had a difficult relationship with his mother while living together in New York City's Hotel Marseilles over two decades. This indirectly informed his fiction, full of hapless heroes and strong women struggling against riptides of mischance and justified paranoia. Although he enjoyed reasonable financial success, Woolrich, who lived in squalid conditions, neglected his health (he lost a leg to gangrene), and drank too much, weighed less than 90 pounds when he died of a stroke.

York apartment's four walls, and *Rear Window*'s format is quite similar. The picture never ventures beyond the housing complex where Jeffries resides, with most of the shots constrained to his interior living space, and only a handful reaching past to the outside world "confronting" him, i.e. the apartments of the tenants across the way.

Hitchcock turns this seemingly straightforward setup into a rich, cinematic investigation that operates on multiple levels at once. Brilliantly acted and deliciously scripted, *Rear Window* emerges as the suspense-filled story of a photographer – a career voyeur if you will – for whom mere observation becomes a life-threatening pastime.

A closer reading of the film reveals clear parallels between the things Jeffries observes and his own life. Indeed, the episodes Jeffries witnesses in

3

"The hero is trapped in a wheelchair, and we're trapped too – trapped inside his point of view, inside his lack of freedom and his limited options." *Chicago Sun-Times*

1   Material witnesses: she's in textiles and he's in traction. James Stewart and Grace Kelly make quite the couple in *Rear Window*.

2   Right in their own backyard: Lisa (Grace Kelly) can't decide whether the wheelchair bound

L. B. Jeffries (James Stewart) is really on to something or just stir crazy.

3   Sticking his foot out: heat, boredom, and incapacitation have turned photographer Jeffries into a regular Peeping Tom and professional busybody.

4   A spotless case: if Jeffries can't convince Lisa and his maid Stella (Thelma Ritter, left) of what he's seen, his neighbor across the way might make a clean sweep of things.

4

5   Chutes and ladders: from togetherness and isolation, to newlyweds and broken families, Jeffries witnesses all of life's highs and lows from the comfort of his own home.

6   Viewfinders: "I just wonder whether it's really all that moral to spy on a guy with a telescope and a pair of binoculars," says Stella the maid, housekeeper and voice of reason.

"Hitchcock often oversold *Rear Window* as an experience of 'delicious terror,' but it's also a subtle romantic comedy. The terror comes as much from the film's claustrophobia ... as its suggestion of the inevitability of incidental invasions of privacy."

San Francisco Examiner

his courtyard are unique vignettes on love which comment on his personal fear of commitment. We see the newlyweds who while away the hours in bed; the scantily clad dancer who receives numerous gentleman callers; and Miss Lonelyheart, who in her eternal solitude sets the table for company she knows isn't coming. And then there are the Thorwalds – at each other's throats often enough to almost warrant Mr. Thorwald doing in the little Mrs.

These manifold tales of loneliness and togetherness, of sharing a life as opposed to merely sharing a living space, are the physical manifestation of the fears racing through Jeffries' mind. And he feels a particular bond to Mrs. Thorwald, who is confined to her bed much in the same way as the photographer is to his wheelchair.

There is also a third story line woven into the movie's fabric that one could describe as a litmus test. By acting as her invalid boyfriend's spy and snooping through the Thorwalds' apartment, Lisa demonstrates just how adventurous she can be. The sophisticated blonde beauty thus proves herself well-suited for a life at go-getter Jeffries's side. It's no fluke that by the end of the picture the one-time proponent of dresses and high heels is seen sporting jeans and sneakers.

HJK

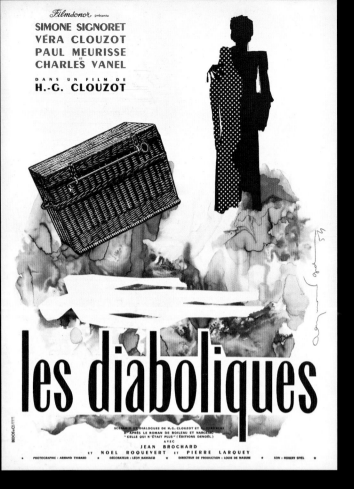

DIABOLIQUE / THE FIENDS

LES DIABOLIQUES

1955 – FRANCE – 114 MIN.
DIRECTOR HENRI-GEORGES CLOUZOT (1907–1977)
SCREENPLAY HENRI-GEORGES CLOUZOT,
JÉRÔME GÉRONIMI, RENÉ MASSON,
FRÉDÉRIC GRENDEL, based on the novel
Celle qui n'etait plus by THOMAS NARCEJAC
and PIERRE BOILEAU
DIRECTOR OF PHOTOGRAPHY ARMAND THIRARD
EDITING MADELEINE GUG MUSIC GEORGES VAN PARYS
PRODUCTION HENRI-GEORGES CLOUZOT for
FILMSONOR S.A., VERA FILMS
STARRING SIMONE SIGNORET (Nicole), VÉRA CLOUZOT
(Christina Delasalle), PAUL MEURISSE (Michel Delasalle),
CHARLES VANEL (Commissaire Fichet),
PIERRE LARQUEY (Drain), JEAN BROCHARD
(Plantiveau), MICHEL SERRAULT (Raimond),
THÉRÈSE DORNY (Madame Herboux),
NOËL ROQUEVERT (Monsieur Herboux),
GEORGES CHAMARAT (Doctor Loisy)

"There should be more to scolding than empty threats."

"Perhaps I'm a little old-fashioned, but when I see a man's wife drying his mistress's tears … no, sir, no, no, no!" In the staffroom of a boarding school in rural France, the hot topic is a love triangle involving the violent and constantly inebriated principal Michel Delasalle (Paul Meurisse), his wife Christina (Véra Clouzot), and the attractive teacher Nicole (Simone Signoret). Michel lives in the pocket of his wealthy spouse, whom he tenderly refers to as "my little ruin" because of her cardiac defect … and then he takes Nicole as his mistress.

Rather than scratching each other's eyes out, the two women join forces, for Michel is quite simply a repulsive man. Sadistic and miserly, he saves money by serving up half-rotten fish to his pupils, and he terrorizes the teaching staff with his stinginess and cynicism. Eventually, his behavior

becomes intolerable, and Christina and Nicole decide it's time to topple the tyrant. They lure him into Nicole's apartment in the city, where a bottle of whiskey is waiting for him, laced with sleeping tablets. Michel concludes the evening unconscious, and he breathes his last breath underwater in the bathtub. The two partners in crime intend to deposit his corpse in the school swimming pool, for no one would be surprised if he had drowned there in the course of one of his nightly binges. But the task is not as simple as it might seem: Nicole's neighbors complain about the late-night racket in the bathroom, and when the body has finally been placed in the truck, a troublesome drunk insists on keeping it company there.

Eventually, they do manage to get the body back to the school, where they dump it in the pool, as planned. It's winter and the water is murky; but

1 Arsenic and old lace: heartless "widow" Christina Delasalle (Véra Clouzot) is driven by the dead to do the darndest things.

2 Partners in crime: accomplices Christina and Nicole (Simone Signoret) wait at the window to see whether hubby will turn up – dead or alive.

in the nature of things, it's only a matter of time before the corpse ascends to the surface and is discovered. Or so the women think. But when Michel stubbornly refuses to rise to the occasion, Christina grows increasingly hysterical. Eventually, she has the water pumped out of the pool … and her ex-husband is nowhere to be seen. A few days later, the cleaners bring his suit – pressed, spotless, and as dry as a bone.

Diabolique is a morality tale and a very black comedy. The film's dubious heroines are subjected to an emotional roller-coaster ride, and the audience follows in their wake. We're constantly made to feel we know more than

Christina and Nicole, only to be wrong-footed again and again. The suspense is intensified by the film's slow pace and its precise evocation of a particular milieu: here, every unforeseen twist has an almost shocking effect.

Henri-Georges Clouzot was always interested in more than just telling a good, gripping yarn, and this adaptation of a novel by the legendary thriller writers Boileau and Narcejac is no exception.

What happens when apparently good people do something evil? Can self-defense ever justify such a cruel crime? Isn't there actually something sadistic about the murder these women commit? Clouzot uses the structure

"I sought only to amuse myself and the little child who sleeps in all our hearts — the child who hides her head under the bedcovers and begs, 'Daddy, Daddy, frighten me!'" *Henri-Georges Clouzot*

3 Losing their faculties: the schoolmaster's icy whims and bouts of rage force the teachers to hold their tongues.

4 Night cap: this really ought to help the schoolmaster rest – in peace.

5 Do as I say, not as I do: teachers these days can be such poor role models. But those who go running to mommy and daddy will get stuck with a punishment far worse than detention.

of a crime story to engage in an existential study of guilt and atonement. The innocence of the schoolchildren makes the corruption and sinfulness of the adult world appear all the more repellent; it verges on a sick joke that these "educators" should be responsible for the ethical development of their students.

The policeman, Commissaire Fichet (Charles Vanel), is a tired old man whose stoical understatement must have inspired countless imitators, from Miss Marple to Columbo. He also appears to be the director's alter ago: an observer with the merciless clarity of true disillusionment. Though time has stripped him of his ideals and convictions, he persists in bringing the truth to light, simply because there is nothing else left for him to do in this world.

SH

"Clouzot's Grand Guignol techniques are so calculatedly grisly that they seem silly, yet they succeed in making one feel queasy and sordid and scared." *Pauline Kael*

6 Not a corpse in sight: where can that man have got to?

7 Police commissioner Fichet (Charles Vanel) isn't interested in the headmistress's ailments, just the facts. Vanel's portrayal inspired an entire generation of big-screen crime fighters.

8 You give me fever: director Delasalle (Paul Meurisse) may be burning up, but these two ladies will burn in hell for what they've done to him.

HENRI-GEORGES CLOUZOT Henri-Georges Clouzot was born in Niort, France, on November 20, 1907. He had already been in the film business for around a decade when he made his directing debut, with *The Murderer Lives at Number 21* (*L'assassin habite … au 21*, 1943). Until then, his shaky health had restricted him to screenwriting. In 1943, he directed *The Raven* (*Le Corbeau*), a study of wartime informers in a small French town; he was then accused of making propaganda for the Nazis and banned from working for six months – regardless of the fact that the Vichy regime had just branded the very same film "anti-French." Though quickly rehabilitated, Clouzot had to wait four years before making his next movie, *Jenny Lamour* (*Quai des Orfèvres*, 1947), for which he was named Best Director at the Cannes Film Festival. His two best-known works are probably the existential adventure movie *The Wages of Fear* (*Le Salaire de la peur*, 1953), which won the Grand Prix in Cannes and the Golden Bear in Berlin, and the somber murder mystery *Diabolique* (*Les Diaboliques*, 1955). Though all of Clouzot's films tell exciting tales, they also share a deeply pessimistic worldview: each of his protagonists struggles against the world, and ultimately – inevitably – fails. *The Mystery of Picasso* (*Le Mystère Picasso*, 1956) must also be counted among his masterpieces. For this portrait of the great Spanish painter – which also received an award in Cannes – he positioned a camera behind the canvas, in order to capture the act of creation as it took place. Henri-Georges Clouzot died in Paris on January 12, 1977.

CORNEL RICHARD BRIAN JEAN
WILDE · CONTE · DONLEVY · WALLACE

Allied Artists presents

THE MOST STARTLING STORY THE SCREEN HAS EVER DARED REVEAL!

THE BIG COMBO

Written by PHILIP YORDAN · Produced by SIDNEY HARMON · Directed by JOSEPH LEWIS

THE BIG COMBO

1955 – USA – 89 MIN.
DIRECTOR JOSEPH H. LEWIS (1907–2000)
SCREENPLAY PHILIP YORDAN DIRECTOR OF PHOTOGRAPHY JOHN ALTON
EDITING ROBERT S. EISEN MUSIC DAVID RAKSIN
PRODUCTION SIDNEY HARMON for SECURITY PICTURES,
THEODORA PRODUCTIONS, and ALLIED ARTISTS
STARRING CORNEL WILDE (Leonard Diamond),
RICHARD CONTE (Mr. Brown), BRIAN DONLEVY
(McClure), JEAN WALLACE (Susan Lowell),
ROBERT MIDDLETON (Peterson), LEE VAN CLEEF
(Fante), EARL HOLLIMAN (Mingo),
HELEN WALKER (Alicia Brown), JAY ADLER (Detective
Sam Hill), JOHN HOYT (Nils Dreyer), TED DE CORSIA
(Ralph Bettini), HELENE STANTON (Rita), ROY GORDON
(Audubon), PHILIP VAN ZANDT (Mr. Jones),
WHIT BISSELL (Doctor), STEVE MITCHELL
(Bennie Smith), BAYNES BARRON (Young Detective),
JAMES MCCALLION (Lab Technician),
TONY MICHAELS (Photo Technician), BRIAN O'HARA
(Attorney Malloy), RITA GOULD (Nurse), BRUCE SHARPE
(Detective), MICHAEL MARK (Hotel Clerk),
DONNA DREW (Miss Hartleby)

"First is first and second is nobody."

Local mob boss Mr. Brown (Richard Conte) has seduced socialite Susan Lowell (Jean Wallace). When Susan is caught up in police detective Leonard Diamond's (Cornel Wilde) relentless pursuit of evidence against Brown, Diamond's judgment as an investigator is compromised by his nascent infatuation with Brown's elegant "moll."

Allegedly, director Joseph H. Lewis infuriated leading man Cornel Wilde because of the explicitly sexual notes that he gave to Wilde's then wife and co-star Jean Wallace. Given that Wilde's Theodora Productions was one of the companies responsible for the project, Lewis was certainly taking a chance with such a directorial tactic; but it got him the performance he wanted. Whether this anecdote is true or not, there is no question that the sexual (and social) dynamics of The Big Combo were far ahead of their time, even for film noir. Since he already has a questionable – for a policeman – relationship with local stripper Rita (Helene Stanton), it should not be unexpected that

Wilde's Det. Diamond falls hard for the glamorous Susan. Less typical is how Diamond's behaviors mirror those of kingpin Brown. As both men are short-tempered and libidinous, as well as obsessive and ruthless, so the distinctions between cop and criminal, Jewish detective and Italian gangster, law enforcer and lawbreaker, are quickly and profoundly blurred.

Underpinning all the twisted relationship – Brown's minions Mingo and Fante are as overtly homosexual a couple as permitted on screen in 1955 and their sadistic and deadly work clearly excites them sexually – is a prototypical noir aura of doom. David Raksin's staccato score and John Alton's frames full of shadows and mist help stylistically to propel the protagonists towards a violent conclusion. For his part, while he romanticizes Susan as victim, despite the fact that her dilemma is self-actuated, and despises Brown as much for his fiscal and physical prowess as for any felonies he might have committed, Diamond might well be seen as overcompensating for his own

1   Susan Lowell (Jean Wallace) is alternately excited and appalled when she is manhandled by the gangster Mr. Brown (Richard Conte).

2   As Det. Sam Hill (Jay Adler) looks on, Lt. Leonard Diamond (Cornel Wilde) realizes that his obsession has cost the life of his girlfriend Rita.

3   Brown's minions Fante (Lee Van Cleef) and Mingo (Earl Holliman) take Susan to their waiting boss.

shortcomings both social and sexual. In much the same way as Lewis's most celebrated noir, *Gun Crazy* (1950), where the fugitive couple of Bart Tare and Annie Laurie Starr are irresistibly pulled towards one another – "like guns and ammunition go together" – the triangle of Diamond, Brown, and Lowell is the emotional core of *The Big Combo*.

As in his other film noirs, director Lewis develops his narrative with dynamic and interconnected set pieces. The most striking are two scenes of Fante (Lee Van Cleef) and Mingo (Earl Holliman) fulfilling Brown's orders. In the latter they betray their former leader Joe McClure (Brian Donlevy), who has become a sort of boss emeritus. McClure is hard of hearing, so in a moment of perverse mercy, the killers take away his hearing aid, so that

neither he nor the viewer can hear the gunshots as McClure dies in a hail of bullets. The hearing aid is also a key prop when Mingo and Fante abduct Diamond and torture him with McClure's device by turning up its amplification and subjecting Diamond to excruciatingly loud sounds.

Equally balanced are the emotional and visual denouements of *The Big Combo*. Diamond uses Rita to ferret out information on Brown, and that gets her killed. Disturbed, but undeterred by his lover's death, Diamond uses jealousy to turn Brown's wife, Alicia (Helen Walker), against her husband.

The noir tour de force of *The Big Combo* is its celebrated conclusion. Brown is cornered in an airplane hangar. As more police close in, he exchanges gunfire with Diamond and is fatally wounded. Now both physically and

JOHN ALTON   Johann Altmann (1901–1996) was born in what was then the Austro-Hungarian Empire. In 1924, during the silent era, Alton went to the United States and broke into the industry as a film lab technician at MGM; in 1927, he was sent to France as first cameraman for director Ernst Lubitsch. Alton also worked in Europe for directors Alan Crosland and Curtis Bernhardt, and at Paramount's Parisian studios, before emigrating to Argentina. After almost a decade there, Alton returned to Hollywood in 1939 and shot low-budget pictures for RKO, Republic, and Eagle-Lion, where he first teamed with director Anthony Mann from 1946 though 1949 on *T-Men* (1947), *Raw Deal* (1948), *He Walked by Night* (1948), and *Reign of Terror* (1949). Eventually Mann took Alton with him back to MGM. Alton continued working with Mann and other directors at the major studios until he had more than a dozen key noir films to his credit, including *Border Incident* (1949); *Mystery Street* (1950); *Devil's Doorway* (1950); *The People Against O'Hara* (1951); *Talk about a Stranger* (1952); *Count the Hours* (1953); *I, the Jury* (1953); and *Slightly Scarlet* (1956). As critic Paul Schrader wrote: "Perhaps the greatest master of noir was Hungarian-born John Alton, an expressionist cinematographer who could relight Times Square at noon if necessary. No cinematographer better adapted the old expressionist techniques to the new desire for realism." In 1949 John Alton described his techniques in his own groundbreaking book, *Painting with Light*, where he noted, "The mood of tragedy is enhanced by a strong contrast of deep blacks and glaring whites – shadows and highlights. In drama we light for mood, we paint poems. Lighting with its ups and downs becomes a symphonic construction paralleling the dramatic sequences." Alton worked in many styles and, ironically, his sole Academy Award was for the Technicolor musical *An American in Paris* (1951).

"Silhouetted figures standing in a rigid position become abstracted Modern Man and Woman. The backlighting of heavy smoke and an ominously circling light visible in the background further abstracts the environment into a modern netherworld." *Janey Place and Lowell Peterson, "Some Visual Motifs of Film Noir," in: Film Noir Reader*

"Fog photographs lighter than it looks to the eye. Actors are dressed in dark wardrobe, so that they stand out against the back haze ... with a remarkable third-dimensional feeling. Fog is particularly suitable for outstanding light effects in the form of shafts of light." *John Alton, Painting with Light*

8

4   The iconic conclusion lit by John Alton: the silhouettes of Susan and Diamond walk out of an airplane hangar into the fog.

5   Fante and Mingo accompany former mob boss McClure (Brian Donlevy), whom they will shortly gun down on orders from Brown.

6   Diamond reacts defensively to another reprimand from his superior Capt. Peterson (Robert Middleton).

7   Although she disapproves of Diamond's mono-maniacal pursuit of Brown, the showgirl Rita (Helene Stanton) agrees to help him.

8   A relentless Diamond taunts and badgers Mrs. Brown (Helen Walker) into betraying her husband.

"Performances are in keeping with the bare-knuckle direction by Joseph Lewis and, on that score, are good. Low-key photography by John Alton and a noisy, jazzy score by David Raksin are in keeping with the film's tough mood." *Variety*

psychologically free from Brown, Susan walks out of the hangar with Diamond. As their two figures are silhouetted against dense fog and a search-light, they are transformed into archetypes: noir man and noir woman. This transformation – and metaphor – at the heart of the image is directly keyed to these surviving characters. By now, the viewer knows who these people are and what they feel but not how their relationship will be resolved. In classical usage, fog enshrouds the passageways between worlds. Clearly Lowell and Diamond are poised on the brink of something new. The fog separates them from the physical reality of the world outside the hangar. Highlights kick

off the edge of the doorway and reinforce this sense of movement towards open space. The movement of Lowell and Diamond towards the shaft of light suggests an elemental behavior: spent by the events of the film, they walk in the direction of the brightest spot at the center of the frame. Although they move at the same time, they are not together, and the distance between them is exaggerated by what cinematographer John Alton called the "third-dimensional feeling." The viewer may assume that, since they are both going to the light, they will rejoin there. But, as the figures disappear into the fog, as they begin the transition, nothing is certain.   AS

RIFIFI

DU RIFIFI CHEZ LES HOMMES

1955 – FRANCE – 120 MIN.
DIRECTOR JULES DASSIN (1911–2008)
SCREENPLAY JULES DASSIN, RENÉ WHEELER,
AUGUSTE LE BRETON
DIRECTOR OF PHOTOGRAPHY PHILIPPE AGOSTINI
EDITING ROGER DWYRE MUSIC GEORGES AURIC,
MICHEL PHILIPPE-GÉRARD, JACQUES LARUE
(Song: "Rififi") PRODUCTION RENÉ GASTON VUATTOUX
for INDUSFILMS, PRIMA FILM,
SOCIÉTÉ NOUVELLE PATHÉ CINÉMA
STARRING JEAN SERVAIS (Tony le Stéphanois),
CARL MÖHNER (Jo le Suedois), ROBERT MANUEL
(Mario Farrati), JANINE DARCEY (Louise),
PIERRE GRASSET (Louis Grutter), JULES DASSIN
(as PERLO VITA) (César le Milanais), MARIE SABOURET
(Mado), ROBERT HOSSEIN (Rémi Grutter),
CLAUDE SYLVAIN (Ida Farrati),
MARCEL LUPOVICI (Pierre Grutter)
IFF CANNES 1955 AWARD for BEST DIRECTOR (Jules Dassin)

"Wake up dog, I want you to be afraid – how does it feel?"

A huge, crudely decorated dummy guitar dominates the room, so that the man standing beside it is almost reduced to an afterthought. He's standing upright, tied to a joist, in the backstage area of a seedy subterranean nightclub. Behind him, the paw of a cardboard tiger; in the semidarkness around him, papier-mâché cacti, palm leaves, a jungle of unidentifiable junk. Bars of light fall on the filthy cellar floor while the man stares calmly into the camera. A shot rings out; his body twitches briefly, and everything dissolves behind a

cloud of black smoke. With no fuss and no nonsense, Jules Dassin has just directed his own execution. The scene was in fact never planned in this form; Dassin had only taken on the role of the Italian safecracker César after the original actor dropped out shortly before filming began.

The killer, Tony le Stéphanois (Jean Servais), is the real hero of the film. His sad eyes practically tell the whole story. After five years in jail, he's lost his girlfriend, he has pneumonia, and he no longer enjoys the respect of his

1 The whole world in his hands: but no amount of wealth can erase the disillusion from his face. Jean Servais as Tony le Stéphanois.

2 Thick as thieves: relying on daredevil acrobatics, the gang pulls off the crime without exchanging a single word.

3 Getting fired up! The gangsters arm themselves for the final showdown like true urban cowboys.

underworld buddies. His friendship with the young crook Jo (Carl Möhner) seems to be the only glimmer of hope in his life – until Tony gathers the strength for one final major coup. Together with Jo, César, and Mario (Robert Manuel), he starts preparing a break-in at the exclusive jewelers Mappin & Webb. Once they have worked out how to disable the alarm system, the heist can begin. It's a gripping sequence: without a word, the four men make their way to the scene of the crime, accompanied by the edgy music of Georges Auric. But when they get to the hallway of the building, the music stops. The men pull on ballet shoes to muffle their footsteps, and they begin to pry open the parquet flooring. The slightest tremor could set off the alarm. For almost a full half-hour, Dassin relies entirely on the strength of the images: there's no music and no dialogue whatsoever. It's a stroke of genius, for in this austere silence, the suspense gradually becomes almost unbearable.

At first, Georges Auric refused to believe the scene could work this way, so he composed a suitable musical soundtrack for the break-in; but when he saw the result, he was happy to dispense with his composition. And so, while Jo removes the flooring in the midst of a terrible silence, the tension rises steadily. Layer by layer, the floor is removed; and as the men tap away softly,

5

4   Underworld highlife: Tony's archenemy owns a
     nightclub where thugs hide out behind bizarre
     backdrops, and buxom beauties sway to the

sounds of Georges Auric chansons. What more
could a gangster movie ask for?

5   Child's play: however, Tony and Jo have no
     enthusiasm for the caper, only the prize.

"It makes the hair on the back of your neck stand on end." *The New York Times*

JULES DASSIN In *Rififi* (*Du rififi chez les hommes*, 1955), director Jules Dassin also played the role of a traitor. In real life, it was Dassin himself who was betrayed. Born in 1911, Dassin was the son of a Jewish hairdresser. At the age of 20, he took a trip around Europe, acting, painting stage sets and studying dramaturgy for a while. After returning to the States, he visited the Jewish Theater in Harlem one evening and soon joined the theater group ARTEF (Arbeter Teater Farband). Meanwhile he took part in various small experimental theater productions and wrote plays for the radio. Soon, he was attracting Hollywood's attention. He worked as an assistant to Alfred Hitchcock before he began making B movies for MGM in the '40s.

He enjoyed a quick commercial success with *The Canterville Ghost* (1944), but his big breakthrough came in the late '40s, with movies such as *The Naked City* (1948) and *Night and the City* (1950). He was now regarded as an American neorealist with a lot of talent, and a successful career was at his fingertips. Then the anti-communist witch-hunters destroyed his future within weeks. Dassin had been a member of the Party for a short time in the '30s, and Edward Dmytryk denounced him as a communist. He was placed on Hollywood's blacklist. From then on, any actor, producer or director who worked with him would have been risking his own career. Dassin hoped to find work abroad, but the long arm of Hollywood reached across the seas, and frightened colleagues often backed out of planned projects at the last minute. Only after three years was he able to make another film – and *Rififi* was a splendiferous success. Dassin's situation remained unaltered, though; again and again, he had to change countries in order to find work. Such conditions made it difficult for him to develop a definite style of his own; his oeuvre is bitty, and it contains numerous mediocre films. In 1964, he made one more American film: the comedy thriller *Topkapi*, a parody of heist films like *Rififi*. Once again, he had landed a big box-office hit. From the end of the '80s, he worked in the theater, and only emerged into the media limelight to receive prizes for his life's work. Jules Dassin died in 2008.

6

6   All in a day's work: César (Jules Dassin) and Mario (Robert Manuel) finetune their safecracking skills and prove that success depends on the pride one takes in the job – no matter how unethical.

7   I got rhythm: whether on the dance floor or in the midst of a heist, no one is suaver than César.

8   Having his way with her: Tony forces ex-girlfriend Mado (Marie Sabouret) to strip, only to beat her to a bloody pulp.

> **"*Rififi* contains a 30-minute sequence of wordless moviemaking that is one of the most engrossing sequences since the invention of the motion picture."** *Time Magazine*

the viewers' nerves are stripped bare. These guys are so careful, and so inventive: it's a joy to see how they prevent the dust from landing on the room below, or how they open the massive safe like a tin can.

When the job's been done, all's right with the world, or so it would seem; but the title song sums up the plot – there's always some kind of trouble in the end. César makes a stupid mistake and betrays the gang's secret. The code of the Mafia demands that Tony kill him. "You know the rules?" he asks. César nods.

The film's presentation of violence was a sensation at the time. Tony forces his ex-lover Mado (Marie Sabouret) to strip off, so that he can beat her with a belt for being unfaithful; meanwhile, Tony's enemy Louis Grutter (Pierre Grasset) treats his junkie brother (Robert Hossein) like a mangy dog. Yet, tough

as it is, the film has the balance and integrity of a work of art. This is due in no small part to the fantastic camerawork of Philippe Agostini. The interiors are skillfully lit, so that the hard world of the criminals is filled with niches of soft darkness. The exteriors have a raw documentary beauty that points towards movies like *The French Connection* (1971), partly because Dassin would only shoot when the sky was overcast. All the while, he makes almost playful use of standard film noir elements, and the obligatory nightclub sequence that accompanies the title song is an unashamed parody, with a mime artist in shadow play, lighting his cigarette from the barrel of a smoking gun.

Rififi's frank treatment of sex and violence didn't stop the Cannes jury from presenting Dassin with the prize for Best Director. In other countries, the film was banned immediately, and was therefore known only to a few until fairly recently. Only at the turn of the century was it released in U.S. cinemas, and the DVD version is now increasingly popular, for *Rififi* is rightly seen as a prototype of the ice-cold thriller. The film is a real shocker. It uses the means of the European cinema to drive the American film noir to its stylistic limits, before the pessimism of the postwar years gives way to the escapist tendencies of the '60s. In particular, it leaves the two-dimensional quality of earlier noir films far behind it. Movie maestros such as Kubrick and Tarantino were inspired by the sheer technical perfection of *Rififi*, but its particular blend of hardness and grace still remains unmatched.

OK

BLOOD-RED KISSES!

WHITE-HOT THRILLS!

Mickey Spillane's LATEST H-BOMB!

PARKLANE PICTURES, Inc. Presents

KISS ME DEADLY

starring RALPH MEEKER

with Albert DEKKER · Paul STEWART · Juano HERNANDEZ

PRODUCED AND DIRECTED BY ROBERT ALDRICH

Screenplay by A. I. BEZZERIDES

Released thru UNITED ARTISTS

KISS ME DEADLY

1955 – USA – 104 MIN.
DIRECTOR ROBERT ALDRICH (1918–1983)
SCREENPLAY A. I. BEZZERIDES, based on the novel
of the same name by MICKEY SPILLANE
DIRECTOR OF PHOTOGRAPHY ERNEST LASZLO
EDITING MICHAEL LUCIANO MUSIC FRANK DE VOL
PRODUCTION ROBERT ALDRICH for PARKLANE PICTURES INC.
STARRING RALPH MEEKER (Mike Hammer),
CLORIS LEACHMAN (Christina), MAXINE COOPER (Velda),
GABY RODGERS (Lily Carver / Gabrielle),
ALBERT DEKKER (Doctor Soberin), PAUL STEWART
(Carl Evello), JUANO HERNANDEZ (Eddie),
WESLEY ADDY (Pat), MARIAN CARR (Friday),
JACK ELAM (Charlie Max)

"Don't open the box!"

Why are all the boys hot on the heels of the woman in the light-colored trench coat? Barefoot, she roams the streets at all hours of the night and the police feel compelled to shut off the streets to arrest her. Does she really present a danger to society? There is something strikingly wrong with this setup, a feeling that sticks with the viewer right up until *Kiss Me Deadly*'s fast and furious finale.

At first glance, the film's premise seems cut and dry. Private investigator Mike Hammer (Ralph Meeker), a gang of thugs, and the police are all trying to locate a missing suitcase with radioactive contents. But nothing is as it appears. The superficially smooth detective turns out to be a big dolt who gets swept up in the events of the case rather than utilizing his powers of deduction; in fact, his machismo altogether prevents him from grasping what's going on. An inordinately large number of women surround Mike and lure the shortsighted crime fighter from locale to locale. First there's the woman from the street, Christina (Cloris Leachman), who catches his curiosity; then there's Velda (Maxine Cooper), his smart and attractive secretary who'd jump through hoops of fire to be near him, but only ends up getting burned; and finally there's the impenetrable Lily (Gaby Rodgers), a game-playing dame

ready to turn the tables on Hammer and seize the stuff that dreams are made of. That would be "the great whatsit," Velda's term for the radioactive material supposedly sniped from the Manhattan Project, the secret atom bomb research project conducted by the U.S. government in the 1940s ...

Kiss Me Deadly succeeds in disorienting its audience by means of its topsy-turvy story and expressive visual style. It is as if we are trapped in the eye of the hurricane and unable to ever see the bigger picture. True, the movie always has us on a par with its protagonist Mike Hammer; trouble is that Mike is always one step behind everybody else. And thus at no time does either he or the viewer know where they stand. Only this much is clear. The mysterious Christina quite literally holds the key to the puzzle, as we realize once it is extracted from her stomach during a medical autopsy. The key leads Hammer to a locker at a posh Hollywood sports club and a suitcase-shaped container housing a mind-boggling mystery. Opening the strange box but a crack, Hammer's eyes are flooded by a blinding light and a piercing screech grabs hold of the soundtrack: the film's underlying eeriness has finally taken

form. Not that it takes a genius to know that this would happen sooner or later. For after all, the way towards this Pandora's box was paved with horrors: fear-struck people, the victims of an abstruse brainchild of modern science that leaves indelible brands on their skin; inexplicable, deadly accidents as unscrupulous killers and an inept police force try to locate the spooky substance with about as much of a game plan as the homme fatale Hammer.

All roads lead to doom as the story's third female character enters the picture. Lily, in truth the wicked Dr. Soberin's (Albert Dekker) assistant Gabrielle, aids the mastermind by supplying him with the dimwitted detective's hard-won clues while she tries to snatch the goods out from under Hammer's nose. Needless to say, the PI is hung out to dry and the radioactive loot lands in the hands of the bad guys. But Gabrielle proves no better than Mike, when at the film's conclusion she too can't help but peek inside the box, letting loose an atomic fireball. In the midst of the resulting apocalyptic tumult Mike Hammer and Velda stagger towards the sea, and therefore back to the origin of all life.

ROBERT ALDRICH Robert Aldrich (1918–1983) had a predilection for the rough and ready. In mysteries, Westerns, sport, and war movies alike, he investigated hermetic, male-dominated spheres that required a hefty dose of stamina from its inhabitants. His main characters, like the policemen in *The Choirboys* (1977), were usually tainted heroes. Pure-hearted souls with promising future prospects were a rarity in his pictures, a point illuminated by the title of his war movie *Too Late the Hero* (1969). This motif, however, does not really do justice to Aldrich's body of work. His figures also included intricately crafted skeptics whose harsh critiques of the Hollywood studio system played central roles in movies such as *The Big Knife* (1955) and *The Legend of Lylah Clare* (1967). Director-producer Aldrich got his start in 1941 with RKO studios as an assistant director, gaining a board-side view of the field from filmmakers like Lewis Milestone, Joseph Losey, and Abraham Polonsky. The film noir wave had a strong impact on Aldrich's initial directing work. A masterpiece in its own right, *Kiss Me Deadly* (1955) expanded and refined the style of the genre. Aldrich's directorial debut was a television piece produced in 1952, and he started working for the big screen just a year after. He often served as producer on many of his projects and even wrote three of the screenplays for his films.

This surreal jigsaw puzzle in the guise of a detective caper ultimately emerges as a '50s farce. Many subjects are touched on and flippantly analyzed, from architecture to common-law marriage to the finer points of music. Underscoring this is the perpetual threat of human annihilation by the wonders of modern science, with unsubtle discussions about the general abuse of technology for purposes like splitting atoms, as well as humanity's inability to responsibly manage the vast technology it has created. But despite the mix of genres, *Kiss Me Deadly* has a striking clarity, and the complex theme of the responsibilities that accompany technological developments and the very real possibility of mankind's end in a nuclear Armageddon are illustrated in gripping cinematic form.   BR

"This pressing need to talk in order to avoid disaster, even death, is a recurrent noir motif, and one that finds its most dramatic statement in *Kiss Me Deadly*." *Journal of Popular Film & Television*

1   Hard-pressed: in his quest for the truth, detective Mike Hammer (Ralph Meeker) falls willingly into the clutches of one conniving woman after another (Marian Carr as Friday, right).

2   Disposing of the evidence: the low-key style, shadows, and angular shots suggest that those gloves have been party to something sinister.

3   Now talk! Mike Hammer puts his powers of persuasion to good use.

4   Mood lighting: tuxedos, cocktail dresses, and a secluded booth for two evoke an air of stifling claustrophobia and mystery in this late noir classic.

5   When the thugs come knocking, Mike Hammer makes a run for the covers.

"This morning we were married ...and now you think I'm going to kiss you, hold you, call you my wife!"

PAUL GREGORY presents
ROBERT MITCHUM
SHELLEY WINTERS
in
THE NIGHT OF THE HUNTER

THE SCENES...THE STORY...THE STARS...BUT ABOVE ALL-THE SUSPENSE!!!!

co starring
LILLIAN GISH
Directed by
CHARLES
LAUGHTON

JAMES GLEASON · EVELYN VARDEN · PETER GRAVES
and Don Beddoe · Gloria Castillo · Billy Chapin · Sally Jane Bruce
Screenplay by JAMES AGEE · Based on the novel by
DAVIS GRUBB · Produced by PAUL GREGORY
Released thru United Artists

THE NIGHT OF THE HUNTER

1955 – USA – 93 MIN.
DIRECTOR CHARLES LAUGHTON (1899–1962)
SCREENPLAY JAMES AGEE, based on the novel of
the same name by DAVIS GRUBB
DIRECTOR OF PHOTOGRAPHY STANLEY CORTEZ
EDITING ROBERT GOLDEN MUSIC WALTER SCHUMANN
PRODUCTION PAUL GREGORY for PAUL GREGORY
PRODUCTIONS, UNITED ARTISTS
STARRING ROBERT MITCHUM (Harry Powell),
SHELLEY WINTERS (Willa Harper), LILLIAN GISH
(Rachel Cooper), EVELYN VARDEN (Icey Spoon),
PETER GRAVES (Ben Harper), BILLY CHAPIN
(John Harper), SALLY JANE BRUCE (Pearl Harper),
JAMES GLEASON (Birdie), DON BEDDOE
(Walt Spoon), GLORIA CASTILLO (Ruby)

"I'll be back, when it's dark."

The actor Charles Laughton directed only one film, and there is nothing else like it. Darkly poetic and deeply moving, *The Night of the Hunter* is a work of horror and enchantment, a hypnotic fairy tale for grown-ups. Laughton's cinematic tableau distills the worst terrors of childhood into a beautiful fable about a brother and sister on the run from a demonic preacher. It's the very stuff of nightmare: two defenseless children pursued relentlessly by an unpredictable and pathologically violent adult.

America is in the grips of the Depression, demoralized and prey to hysterical religiosity. Two rural children, John (Billy Chapin) and his younger sister Pearl (Sally Jane Bruce) watch helplessly as their father is arrested. He had murdered two people for the money to ensure his family's survival. But seconds before the cops catch up with him, he succeeds in handing over the booty to his son John. He makes the boy swear to protect his sister with his own life – and never to talk about the money. It's an almost monstrous burden to place on a child's soul, and it's also the beginning of a nightmarish odyssey for John and Pearl. The father is executed for murder; and a short time later, a sinister wandering preacher appears on the scene. Not content

to woo the widow, he appears to know something about the kids and the carefully hidden loot …

Hollywood's most charismatic bad guy, Robert Mitchum, gives another brilliant performance as the mysterious Harry Powell, serial murderer and itinerant "man of God." With the words LOVE and HATE tattooed on his knuckles, Powell stages bizarre fights between his left and right hands, symbolizing the eternal struggle between Good and Evil. From the very start, he dominates every room he enters, every space he inhabits – an impression reinforced by some powerful and unorthodox framings and camera angles. Harry Powell is practically ubiquitous and seemingly inescapable. *Something wicked this way comes* – on a train, in a car, or on a horse. And to John and Pearl's dismay, it seems Harry Powell is even capable of entering locked rooms. In short, he is a figure of almost mythical power, a manifestation of evil in human form.

And he's irresistible: Harry Powell marries the widowed mother (Shelley Winters) and crushes her spirit with talk of sin and salvation, before murdering her in cold blood to clear his way to her children. To make it look like an

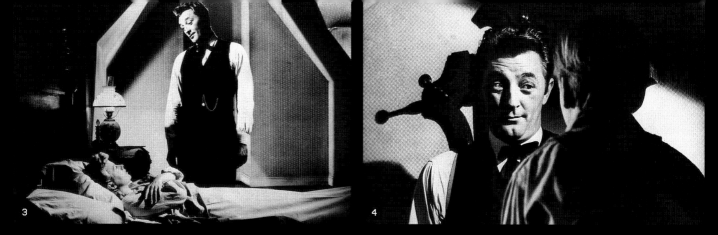

3

4

1 Toying with her affections: Reverend Harry Powell (Robert Mitchum) takes advantage of little Pearl Harper's (Sally Jane Bruce) good nature without a morsel of shame.

2 The self-proclaimed Reverend theatens Pearl Harper while her brother John (Billy Chapin) watches.

3 As I lay dying: Harry Powell pulls an inconceivable con with fatal consequences for the children's mother (Shelley Winters).

"I can hear you whisperin' children, so I know you're down there. I can feel myself gettin' awful mad. I'm out of patience children. I'm coming to find you now." *Film quote: Harry Powell (Robert Mitchum)*

5

6

4   Cheers and sneers: a diabolical mind lies behind this man's bright smile.

5   The little man takes a stand: young John launches a surprise attack on Harry Powell.

6   Bustin' out: the children orchestrate a plan for survival from the confines of their basement.

accident, he places her body in the driver's seat and rolls her car into the river. The underwater sequence that follows has since acquired an almost legendary status. We see the dead woman in the submerged automobile, her loose hair swaying softly above her like seaweed. Poetry and horror, beauty and terror, grace and decay: a fabulously melancholic sequence quite without parallel in the cinema.

Indeed, the whole film is unique in the way it combines an almost mannered expressionist style with motifs from the realms of dream and nightmare. The result is a well-nigh surrealist masterpiece, profoundly strange and subtly frightening. *The Night of the Hunter* gives us a child's-eye view of the world, in which nocturnal terrors become manifest in the person of a monstrous man. At the moment of greatest threat, on the banks of the river, John

and Pearl just manage to escape into a tiny boat; their pursuer, Harry Powell, scrambles after them in the shallows, howling like a beast as the boat drifts away from his grasping hands. The children's ordeal finally ends when they find refuge with Mrs. Cooper, a steadfast and warm-hearted woman who takes in and cares for the waifs and strays that come her way. As Rachel Cooper, the former silent-movie star Lillian Gish is another glory of this film. She is the antithesis of Harry Powell, the light that banishes his darkness, a kind of ideal mother, in fact. And it's Rachel Cooper who finally defeats the evil preacher and hands him over to the police. The circle closes when John, finally freed from his unbearable burden, reveals where the money had been hidden all along: in Pearl's rag doll. By the end of this film, the little girl's doll has come to symbolize far more than a stolen childhood.   BR

SHELLEY WINTERS Shelley Winters was born in East St. Louis, Illinois, in 1922. She once shared an apartment with Marilyn Monroe, and legend has it that it was she who taught Marilyn the "lascivious look." Winters herself picked up the tools of the acting trade at the New York Theatre School, the Actors Studio and with Charles Laughton. She eventually put these tools to good use in over 100 films. After starting her career on Broadway, she had her first screen success in George Cukor's *A Double Life* (1947). Her breakthrough came with the kind of tragic figures that became her specialty. In *A Place in the Sun* (1951), she played a pregnant woman who is murdered by George Eastman (Montgomery Clift) for the sake of the rich and beautiful Angela Vickers (Liz Taylor). This role brought her a first Oscar nomination. In 1955, she gave a brilliant performance alongside Robert Mitchum in *The Night of the Hunter*, the only film ever directed by her former teacher Charles Laughton. For her portrayal of the neighbor in *The Diary of Anne Frank* (1959), she finally won an Academy Award – and her performance as the mother in Stanley Kubrick's *Lolita* (1962) was certainly worthy of one. (At least she was nominated for a Golden Globe.) Just a few years later, she won another Oscar as Best Supporting Actress for her performance as the mother of the blind girl in *A Patch of Blue* (1965). Alongside her Hollywood roles, she also appeared in numerous European productions, such as Roman Polanski's Roland Topor adaptation *The Tenant* (*Le Locataire*, 1976) and Walter Bockmayer's *Looping* (1981). Shelley Winters died in Beverly Hills in 2006.

THE KILLING

1956 – USA – 83 MIN.
DIRECTOR STANLEY KUBRICK (1928–1999)
SCREENPLAY STANLEY KUBRICK, JIM THOMPSON,
based on the novel *Clean Break* by LIONEL WHITE
DIRECTOR OF PHOTOGRAPHY LUCIEN BALLARD
EDITING BETTY STEINBERG MUSIC GERALD FRIED
PRODUCTION JAMES B. HARRIS for UNITED ARTISTS
STARRING STERLING HAYDEN (Johnny Clay),
COLEEN GRAY (Fay), VINCE EDWARDS (Val Cannon),
JAY C. FLIPPEN (Marvin Unger), TED DECORSIA
(Randy Kennan), MARIE WINDSOR (Sherry Peatty),
ELISHA COOK JR. (George Peatty),
JOE SAWYER (Mike O'Reilly), JAMES EDWARDS
(Car Park Attendant), TIMOTHY CAREY (Nikki),
KOLA KWARIANI (Maurice),
JAY ADLER (Leo), JOE TURKEL (Tiny)

"Johnny, you've got to run."
"Yeah. What's the difference?"

Ex-convict Johnny Clay (Sterling Hayden) plans and executes a daring race-track robbery with a group of co-conspirators. The film's strikingly innovative structure, borrowed from the novel, involves overlapping flashbacks as we keep jumping back in time to pick up the story of the robbery from a different character's point of view. So unusual was this structure that pressure was brought to bear on the filmmakers to make it more chronological and less confusing. "Everybody that talked to us said that we should recut the picture as a straight line story," producer James B. Harris noted, but when they tried straightening it out, they decided, "This stinks," and so "we put it back the way we had it." The film's fragmented narrative went on to become a major influence upon future neo-noirs like Tarantino's *Reservoir Dogs* (1992) and *Pulp Fiction* (1994) and Christopher Nolan's *Memento* (2000) and *Inception* (2010).

Johnny, the mastermind of the heist, has plotted out everything like a "jumbled jigsaw puzzle" in which each "single piece" will fit together to form its "predetermined final design." But this is a film noir and so fate intervenes to foil man's best-laid plans. Johnny may stride purposefully from left to right in a series of lateral tracking shots, but at the end of the film, the camera moves in the opposite direction, from right to left, as a baggage cart swerves to avoid a stray poodle, causing Johnny's suitcase to break open and scatter all his money from the robbery to the far winds. That poodle was not part of the puzzle. When Johnny's fiancée, Fay, then urges him to run from the police who are closing in on him, Johnny's reply bespeaks a quintessential noir fatalism: "What's the difference?" Whether he tries to succeed or not, fate will see to it that he fails.

1 Brooding mastermind: Johnny (Sterling Hayden) plans to make a killing from one final heist on what the narrator says "might be the last day of his life."

2 Not a part of the puzzle: this armed guard shows up unexpectedly, so Johnny has to knock him out.

3 Hobo/clown disguise: the mask Johnny dons for the racetrack heist resembles the Halloween masks worn by the Brinks mob during their notorious 1950 robbery.

"The gangster and the artist are the same in the eyes of the masses. They are admired and hero-worshipped, but there is always present an underlying wish to see them destroyed at the peak of their glory." *Film quote: Maurice (Kola Kwariani)*

4   An unsafe bet: like losing tickets littering the
    floor of the racetrack, dead bodies of the "loser"
    characters are strewn about at the end.

5   The eternal sap: every film noir needs a loser, and
    George (Elisha Cook Jr.) may be the most famous
    fall guy in movie history.

But is everyone foredoomed to failure? George (Elisha Cook Jr.), a racetrack cashier who is in on the robbery, complains of stomach pains, and his wife, Sherry (Marie Windsor), says, "Maybe you've got a hole in it." Sherry blabs to her lover Val (Vince Edwards) about the plan for the heist and, after the robbery when Val tries to hold up the gang for their loot, George shoots him dead, getting himself gut-shot in the process. If he hadn't shot at Val, George wouldn't have ended up with a hole in his stomach. It is not fate but George's own desire for revenge that gets him killed.

Similarly, if Sherry had loved George instead of two-timing and double-crossing him to get rich, she wouldn't have ended up with a hole in her stomach, which she gets when George shoots her for her betrayal. "You've got a great big dollar sign where most women have a heart," Sherry is told, and ultimately that dollar sign is replaced by a bullet for her heartlessness. Rather than some predestined doom, it is their own avarice that brings a number of these characters to a vile end. Greed – or their desire to "make a killing" – gets them killed.

6

7

"The style of *The Killing* as a whole can be described in terms of a clash between the 'rational' qualities of its jigsaw-puzzle plot and the 'irrational' qualities of its pulp eroticism and black-comic absurdity." *James Naremore*

8

9

6 Calculated chaos: the riotous violence caused by wrestler Maurice (Kola Kwariani) is actually part of the puzzle – a deliberate distraction from the robbery occurring nearby.

7 The best-laid plans: all of Johnny's money is scattered to the far winds like pieces of the puzzle coming undone.

8 "These 5 Men Had a $2,000,000 Secret Until One of Them Told This Woman!": Sherry (Marie Windsor) seduces George into talking.

9 Poetic justice: after shooting a horse, Nikki (Timothy Carey) finds that a horseshoe punctures his car tire rather than bringing him luck.

But neither fate nor the characters' own actions are necessarily determining. The film's fragmented structure suggests a sense of contingency and open-endedness that flies in the face of any predetermined end. Time confounds space; the narrative isn't an already-completed puzzle but one whose pieces are – or are not – coming together as planned, fitting or ill-fitting in any given moment. Wrestler Maurice (Kola Kwariani) starts a fight to create a diversion so that Johnny can slip unnoticed into the counting room and commit the robbery. That piece of the puzzle fits. But Marvin (Jay C. Flippen), who is bankrolling the heist, is supposed to stay at home and not show up drunk at the racetrack, threatening to ruin everything. Yet this ill-fitting piece actually aids in the completion of a perfect picture, for when something else unexpected happens – Johnny is confronted by a security guard – Marvin bumps into the man, allowing Johnny to escape. Another ill-fitting piece – heavy traffic – unexpectedly delays Johnny's arrival at the gang's hideout, but again this disruption to his own plan saves him from dying along with the rest of his men in the shoot-out between George and Val. And yet the film's final ill-fitting piece – that stray poodle – ends up ruining the entire picture puzzle that Johnny has so painstakingly tried to build piece by piece.

ELISHA COOK JR. Appearing in almost 100 films over seven decades, often playing a petty criminal or a sad-sack loser, Elisha Cook Jr. (1903–1995) was a pint-sized actor with a big presence on screen. There aren't many actors who can rival his noir record. He had roles in two of the very first film noirs, *Stranger on the Third Floor* (1940) and *I Wake Up Screaming* (1941); two of the greatest classics, *The Maltese Falcon* (1941) and *The Big Sleep* (1946); two of the most intriguing noirs, *Phantom Lady* (1944) and *Born to Kill* (1947); along with several noir spoofs and homages, such as *The Black Bird* (1975) and *Hammett* (1982). "Funny, isn't it, that I thought I'd be playing romantic juveniles when I went into movies, and ended up doing pimps, informants, rats, and heels," Cook once commented. "That's okay. I love 'em. They're much more interesting than straight people." Baby-faced Cook's most famous role – as a nervous gunman in *The Maltese Falcon* – is typical: despite his macho bravado ("Keep askin' for it and you're gonna get it – plenty!"), he is disarmed by Sam Spade (Humphrey Bogart) again and again. And when Cook tries to go straight and be a good husband to Sherry in *The Killing*, envisioning her as a future "Mama," it is she who threatens to plug him: "Of course [Mama] may be the last word you ever say, but I'll try to kill you as painlessly as possible."

10

11

10 Bird in a cage: only through death does George escape the cashier's cage of his dead-end job and the "prison bars" of his loveless marriage.

11 A small man with a big gun: the nebbishy George finally emerges with his gun blazing – only to wind up dead in the end.

12 Caged again: as Johnny watches his money blow away and police close in on him, it's as if he's already back in prison.

13 Seductive snooper: Sherry tries to entice Johnny into giving up details about the robbery plan; later she'll say it was he who tried to seduce her.

"The camera watches the whole shoddy show with the keen eye of a terrier stalking a pack of rats." *Time Magazine*

Since a small dog can ruin all of Johnny's big plans, it's no wonder that he concludes, "What's the difference?" But this does not mean that moral decisions and human actions make no difference. When rifleman Nikki (Timothy Carey) – who is tasked with shooting a horse to create a distraction – refuses a lucky horseshoe to get rid of a nosy parking attendant, the discarded horseshoe ends up puncturing Nikki's car tire so he is not able to escape a policeman's bullet. The "poetic justice" of Nikki's demise means that to some extent he makes his own luck – or lack of luck. It's not that his decisions or actions are irrelevant to his fate or that they predetermine it. Instead, they contribute to his fate, adding one piece to the incredibly complicated puzzle that is life – and this film.   DK

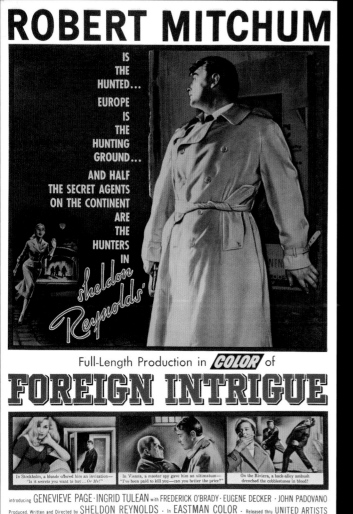

In Stockholm, a blonde offered him an invitation— "Is it secrets you want to buy... *Or Me!*"

In Vienna, a master spy gave him an ultimatum— "I've been paid to kill you—can you better the price?"

On the Riviera, a back-alley ambush drenched the cobblestones in blood!

introducing GENEVIEVE PAGE · INGRID TULEAN with FREDERICK O'BRADY · EUGENE DECKER · JOHN PADOVANO
Produced, Written and Directed by SHELDON REYNOLDS · In EASTMAN COLOR · Released thru UNITED ARTISTS

FOREIGN INTRIGUE

1956 – USA – 95 MIN.
DIRECTOR SHELDON REYNOLDS (1923–2003)
SCREENPLAY SHELDON REYNOLDS, based on his crime story of the same name, HAROLD JACK BLOOM, GENE LEVITT
DIRECTOR OF PHOTOGRAPHY BERTIL PALMGREN
EDITING LENNART WALLÉN **MUSIC** PAUL DURAND
PRODUCTION SHELDON REYNOLDS for MANDEVILLE PRODUCTIONS, UNITED ARTISTS
STARRING ROBERT MITCHUM (Dave Bishop), GENEVIÈVE PAGE (Dominique Danemore), INGRID THULIN (Brita Lindquist), FRÉDÉRIC O'BRADY (Jonathan Spring), EUGENE DECKERS (Pierre Sandoz), INGA TIDBLAD (Mrs. Lindquist), LAURITZ FALK (Jones), FREDERICK SCHREICKER (Karl Mannheim), GEORGES HUBERT (Dr. Thibault), PETER COPLEY (Brown), LILY KANN (Blind Housekeeper), RALPH BROWN (Smith), GILBERT ROBIN (Dodo), JOHN PADOVANO (Tony Forrest)

"Did he say anything before he died?"

In the early 1940s, American radio anthology series like *Crime Doctor* (1940–1947), *Inner Sanctum Mystery* (1941–1952), *Suspense* (1942–1962), and *The Whistler* (1942–1955) broadcast and popularized many mystery, horror, and noir short stories and novels by writers like Cornell Woolrich, Ben Hecht, and Dorothy B. Hughes, which were later adapted for cinema. For example, *Suspense*'s 1943 dramatization of Lucille Fletcher's *Sorry, Wrong Number* was so successful that it was restaged seven times for the show, and a film version was released in 1948 starring Barbara Stanwyck and Burt Lancaster. There were six *Inner Sanctum* mysteries made between 1944 and 1946 starring Lon Chaney Jr., eight films in the Whistler series (1944–1948), and ten in the *Crime Doctor* series (1943–1949).

Likewise, it was not uncommon for TV series of the 1950s to be adapted for the big screen. Although most of the '50s TV series were police procedurals (*Dragnet*, 1951–1959; *Gang Busters!*, 1952; *The Lineup*, 1954–

1960; *M Squad*, 1957–1960), or private eye mysteries (*Martin Kane, Private Eye*, 1949–1954; *77 Sunset Strip*, 1958–1964; *Johnny Staccato*, 1959–1960), one of the most interesting was *Foreign Intrigue* (1951–1955), which followed newspaper reporters in postwar Europe as they investigated the Cold War, the breakdown of society, blackmail, counterfeiting, murder, and espionage. The brainchild of writer/director/producer Sheldon Reynolds, *Foreign Intrigue* was innovative in its use of location (often centered on Vienna, Berlin, Stockholm, Paris, Switzerland, or en route between European destinations), subject matter, and production method (it was filmed at Filmstaden, Råsunda, in Sweden). Running to 156 30-minute episodes over four seasons, the first two seasons followed Robert Cannon (played by Jerome Thor), and sometimes Helen Davis (Sydna Scott), as foreign correspondents of *Consolidated News*, the third season followed Michael Powers (James Daly) and occasionally Patricia Bennett (Anne

1 In Vienna, Dave Bishop (Robert Mitchum) finds lawyer Karl Mannheim dead but is accused of the murder by the residents of the apartment block.

2 Under duress, Bishop agrees to work for the traitor Jones (Lauritz Falk) of the Swedish secret service.

3 Jonathan Spring (Frédéric O'Brady) is both following Bishop and helping him: "A man's got to learn to protect himself in today's world. It's really a jungle, you know."

"The first mark of the talented amateur is that he respects the professional. Au revoir." *Film quote: Jonathan Spring (Frédéric O'Brady)*

Préville) as foreign correspondents of *Associated News*, and the last season had Christopher Storm (Gerald Mohr), owner of the Hotel Frontier in Vienna, aiding those in need like a knight-errant. As well as American directors like Reynolds, Jack Gage, and Steve Previn, there were French (Marcel Cravenne, Eugène Lourié) and Swedish (Lars-Eric Kjellgren, Hans Lagerkvist) directors. Likewise there were many Swedish and French actors in front of the camera, often returning to play different roles; Stig Järrel appeared in six episodes, and Ingrid Thulin in seven. After *Dragnet* produced a successful film based on the TV series in 1954, and *Gang Busters!* did the same the following year, Reynolds shot a film version of *Foreign Intrigue*, which was released July 12, 1956, in America.

Foreign Intrigue begins with the death of mysterious millionaire Victor Danemore in Monte Carlo. His press agent, Dave Bishop (Robert Mitchum), is

repeatedly asked, "Did he say anything before he died?" Even Danemore's widow, Dominique (Geneviève Page), asks the question. Seven years previously, Danemore appeared out of nowhere, with a lot of money but no background. He hired Bishop and bought a wife. As Dominique tells Bishop, "You wrote the dialogue and I was the scenery." A letter from lawyer Karl Mannheim (Frederick Schreicker), who is holding Danemore's documents, leads Bishop to Vienna, but Mannheim is murdered before they talk and Bishop becomes the main suspect.

Bishop is aided by Jonathan Spring (Frédéric O'Brady), who introduces himself as an insurance investigator, but has actually been hired by a rich and powerful man to follow Bishop. Spring, a loveable rogue brought to life by O'Brady's performance, is convinced Danemore was a blackmailer and wants to work with Bishop to uncover the secret documents so that they can profit from the blackmail scheme. After following a lead to Lindquist, a Swedish industrialist in Stockholm who committed suicide, Bishop fails to find out anything useful, but he does fall in love with Lindquist's daughter Brita (Ingrid Thulin). Spring tells Bishop, "Somehow without knowing it we have made tremendous progress, because this morning I was ordered to kill you."

Returning to Vienna, Bishop is picked up by representatives of the Swiss, U.S., U.K., and Swedish counterintelligence services and told that in 1938 Hitler had made contact with men in each country he planned to invade so that they could prepare to take over the reins of power. The men in the U.K., U.S., Sweden, and Switzerland were not used, so remained unknown, and had been blackmailed by Danemore, the Russian sleeper. Bishop agrees to help by playing a double game with Spring, to uncover Spring's boss. In the

4 Bishop "kills" Jones and contacts the authorities, only to find out it was a test of his trustworthiness.

5 Dominique Danemore (Geneviève Page) wants Bishop to join her in the blackmail plot; she killed Mannheim to get her late husband's secret documents.

6 Bishop follows the leads to a house on Hinkel Strasse in Vienna.

"The story of Victor Danemore, Mr. Bishop, is a saga of our times. It is the story, the true story, the world forgot. And the story isn't finished yet." *Film quote: Pierre Sandoz (Eugene Deckers)*

7   Dominique blackmails Mrs. Lindquist (Inga Tidblad, right) and they lock in Brita Lindquist (Ingrid Thulin, left), who is in love with Bishop.

8   When the mysterious Victor Danemore dies, Bishop asks his widow, Dominique, "Wouldn't you like to know who you've been living with for the past seven years?"

9   Bishop falls for Brita, and tells her, "You're fresh in a world that usually sounds stale," but at the end must leave her to continue working undercover.

denouement Dominique tries to entice Bishop into the blackmail plot but is arrested by the secret service, and Brita agrees to wait for Bishop. The final shot shows Bishop walking off into the night with Spring.

Filmed in color by Bertil Palmgren, but with deep, rich shadows, and shot on location in France (Nice, Paris, Versailles), Monaco (Monte Carlo), and Sweden (Stockholm, the Råsunda studio), *Foreign Intrigue* looks and feels like a top-class production. It is linked to the TV series by the presence of series regular John Padovano as newspaperman Tony Forrest (he was also the associate producer), the Hotel Frontier, and barman Dodo, but that is just incidental. The real power of the movie comes from the coolness exuded by Robert Mitchum in the central role, especially in the face of danger. Bishop is not only sly when dealing with Spring, but surprisingly open and humorous in his courtship scenes with Brita.

Like *The Third Man* (1949), *Foreign Intrigue* shows that there are still criminal elements to be cleared up in the wake of World War II.

PD

"Robert Mitchum is the hunted ... all Europe is the hunting ground ... and the continent's ace secret agents are the hunters." *Trailer Commentary*

ROBERT MITCHUM Robert Mitchum (1917–1997) was one of the last great stars of the classic Hollywood cinema. He made his name in the Golden Age of the studio system that dominated the American film industry from the '20s until the late '50s. After the Second World War, a gem of a film brought Mitchum to the attention of a larger public: *Out of the Past* (1947) was originally a B movie, but it established the archetypal Mitchum character, a man whose past will not leave him in peace. Shortly afterwards, he spent a few weeks in jail for possession of marijuana; but he still developed into one of the most popular actors on screen. Mitchum was the ultimate tough guy. In films such as *River of No Return* (1954), *The Night of the Hunter* (1955), and *Cape Fear* (1962) he embodied loners and outsiders – laconically, with understated charm and a kind of nonchalant slothfulness that only increased with age. The characters he played might all have been created by Raymond Chandler; and in *Farewell, My Lovely* (1975), his dry and unflappable detective was the antithesis of the Humphrey Bogart figure. He fulfilled Raymond Chandler's definition of a hero: "… a complete man and a common man, and yet an unusual man." Mitchum's legendary indifference to the art of acting is epitomized in his marginal note to the script of *El Dorado* (1967): NAR (= "no acting required"). His last film was Jim Jarmusch's *Dead Man* (1995), in which he performed alongside Johnny Depp.

BEWARE THESE "GENTLEMEN" OF THE PRESS

"C'mon baby... do it for me, baby... go to him!"

BURT LANCASTER

The world-famed columnist who commands sixty million readers...he can make a star, break a senator or "fix" a politician – in ten words or less!

and this is the kid who had ideas about taking over!

TONY CURTIS

"There's no woman for me Susie, you know that... you're my own sister!"

HECHT, HILL and LANCASTER present "SWEET Smell of SUCCESS"

THE MOTION PICTURE THAT WILL NEVER BE FORGIVEN — OR FORGOTTEN!

Introducing SUSAN HARRISON • Featuring MARTY MILNER • SAM LEVENE • BARBARA NICHOLS • JEFF DONNELL and THE CHICO HAMILTON QUINTET
Screenplay by CLIFFORD ODETS and ERNEST LEHMAN from the Novelette by Ernest Lehman • Directed by ALEXANDER MACKENDRICK • Produced by JAMES HILL

SWEET SMELL OF SUCCESS

1957 – USA – 92 MIN.
DIRECTOR ALEXANDER MACKENDRICK (1912–1993)
SCREENPLAY CLIFFORD ODETS, ERNEST LEHMAN,
based on the novella *Tell Me About It Tomorrow /
Sweet Smell of Success* by ERNEST LEHMAN
DIRECTOR OF PHOTOGRAPHY JAMES WONG HOWE
EDITING ALAN CROSLAND JR. MUSIC ELMER BERNSTEIN,
featuring THE CHICO HAMILTON QUINTET
PRODUCTION JAMES HILL, HAROLD HECHT,
BURT LANCASTER, TONY CURTIS for UNITED ARTISTS
STARRING BURT LANCASTER (J. J. Hunsecker),
TONY CURTIS (Sidney Falco), SUSAN HARRISON
(Susan Hunsecker), MARTIN MILNER (Steve Dallas),
EMILE MEYER (Lt. Harry Kello), BARBARA NICHOLS
(Rita), JEFF DONNELL (Sally), EDITH ATWATER (Mary),
SAM LEVENE (Frank D'Angelo), JOE FRISCO
(Herbie Temple), WILLIAM FORREST (Senator),
AUTUMN RUSSELL (Senator's mistress),
THE CHICO HAMILTON QUINTET (Themselves)

"I'd hate to take a bite out of you. You're a cookie full of arsenic."

Such crackling lines of dialogue, written by Clifford Odets and Ernest Lehman, count among the best in movies, but constitute only part of the dark beauty of *Sweet Smell of Success*. British director Alexander Mackendrick (*Tight Little Island / Whisky Galore!*, 1949; *The Man in the White Suit*, 1951; *The Ladykillers*, 1955) here earned his spurs as an American filmmaker, riding herd on an ensemble of first-rate actors, headed by Burt Lancaster and Tony Curtis, amid the luminous black-and-white cinematography of James Wong Howe. The result is one of the jazziest, most penetrating portraits of New York City on film, not to mention a scalding and still-relevant insight into the power of mass media over the public.

Lancaster is J. J. Hunsecker, a nationally famous newspaper columnist whose power over the worlds of show business and politics make him a man to be feared – and flattered. Curtis is Sidney Falco, the cleverest and most slavish of the many knaves courting his favor. Falco is a smooth-talking press agent who will happily pay any bribe, steal any joke, and pimp any pretty blonde to any man in power if it advances his aims. He will even, as tensions build over the two nights of the story, lower himself to planting criminal evidence to get an innocent man arrested. This last corruption is a line even Falco shies of crossing – but how can he fight it? He covets that aura of power, that "sweet smell of success" that radiates so glamorously, like smoke, from the dreaded J. J.

Even so, he protests: "It's one thing to wear your dog collar," he says. "When it turns into a noose, I'd rather have my freedom." J. J. smiles thinly: "The man in jail is always for freedom." Sidney objects afresh. J. J. stands his ground: "You're in jail, Sidney. You're a prisoner of your own fears, your own greed and ambition." Falco defies this: "You're blind, Mr. Magoo! This is the crossroads for me!" Yet, made an offer he can't refuse, he caves like the self-made prisoner both he and his tormentor know him to be.

2

1   "Match me, Sidney." Sidney Falco (Tony Curtis) is perpetually lighting cigarettes for J. J. Hunsecker (Burt Lancaster), the power broker he is desperate to please.

2   Sidney charms his former girlfriend Rita (Barbara Nichols) into sleeping with another man, to gain an advantage for himself in a world ruled by gossip.

3   J. J.'s younger sister Susan Hunsecker (Susan Harrison) is the one person in his vast circle that he cannot dominate, try as he might.

4   Director Alexander Mackendrick and cinematographer James Wong Howe softened Lancaster's athletic looks and heightened his menace with eyeglasses that masked his eyes in shadow.

> "Sandy Mackendrick was like a mad professor who worked in a world of his own. No matter what you did, no matter how good it really was, it wasn't good enough. He was always reaching for that other dimension beyond an audience's grasp." *Burt Lancaster*

Such nuanced layers of mixed motives grow out of the firsthand observations of Lehman, whose original novella grew directly out of his own experience as a press agent. The dialogue owes its dazzle and intensity to Odets, whose groundbreaking plays (*Awake and Sing!*, 1935, *Golden Boy*, 1937, *Clash by Night*, 1941) had long been distinguished by the all-American "gutter poetry" that was his trademark.

Lehman was originally set to direct his own script, but physical illness growing out of disagreements with the producers (among them Lancaster) drove him to take a restful voyage to Tahiti instead. Mackendrick – who had been hired to develop and direct George Bernard Shaw's play *The Devil's Disciple* (1897) for Lancaster – was pulled from that project and reassigned, and it was he who suggested Odets.

5 "Cat's in the bag, bag's in the river." Sidney is constantly setting traps and sealing fates over the phone.

6 J.J.'s sister Susan is at first suicidal, then turns craftily seductive in her efforts to escape her brother and his creature Sidney.

7 A new day: free of her brother, Susan is free of Sidney too, and leaves him to the ugly fate he has richly earned.

In his book *On Film-Making* (2004), edited by Paul Cronin, Mackendrick recalls that Lehman's screenplay unfolded in talky two-person scenes, in which J.J. would be described as "a man who tells Senators what to do." Odets instead puts a senator in the scene, and shows J.J bossing him around. "What Clifford did in effect was dismantle the structure of every single sequence in order to rebuild situations and relationships that were much more complex, had much greater tension and more dramatic energy." When Mackendrick worried that the dialogue was a bit too poetic, Odets assured him: "Have the actors play it fast, and don't pay attention to the words – just play the actions, and it'll work."

At the center of the tug-of-war between master and slave is J.J.'s sister Susan (Susan Harrison), a fragile ingenue in love with a rising jazz musician (Martin Milner). Sidney notices that J.J. is overprotective to the point of jealous obsession with her, and alertly plays upon this when it suits him. Susan is the one person in J.J.'s life he cannot control. To try and dominate her, he has Sidney plant a smear in a rival column that calls the jazz musician a communist. When that doesn't work, J.J. orders Sidney to plant marijuana on the man – and this provokes Susan to force a violent three-way show-down. Lancaster privately fought off-camera to direct the way his "mad professor" director handled this climax. Mackendrick in turn shot the sequence so cleverly that it could be cut several ways, including the more adventurous way he favored. Traditional Hollywood formulaic logic held that showdowns were between two men – but Mackendrick won. Thus, Sidney flees the scene and the film's final two-person exchange is between Susan and J.J., with the young woman at last dominant. This touch has aged particularly well, and the whole film is alive around it.

FXF

> ## "Clifford Odets came in to clarify the scenes, so the dialogue fit us like a custom-made suit." *Tony Curtis*

7

"There was an enormous difference between Burt Lancaster and Tony Curtis. Tony had a fantastic vanity but no ego. He could act Burt off the screen, but he lacks Lancaster's granite quality of ego. You somehow have to use this to get performances from these deep-sea monsters." *Alexander Mackendrick*

NEWSPAPER NOIR When movies began to talk, the major studios hired playwrights and novelists to write scripts, but in many cases they were outperformed by journalists. As Pauline Kael wrote in *The Citizen Kane Book*: "They were fast, witty writers, used to regarding their work not as deathless prose but as stories written to order for the market, used also to the newspaperman's pretense of putting a light value on what they did – the 'Look, no hands' attitude."

Using a newspaper as a backdrop lends an interesting urgency to a picture. Exposition of characters and their backstories can be tossed off in one-liners, as can be seen in many of the great screwball comedies of the 1930s and 1940s like *The Front Page* (1931), *It Happened One Night* (1934), *His Girl Friday* (1940), and *The Philadelphia Story* (1940). "Fast-talking people," wrote Kael, "who weren't fooled, who were smart and learned their way around."

As the atmosphere changed into the 1940s, reporters became free to act as detectives. Not only did they wrestle with the law, but the newspapermen also considered the morality of their actions in film noirs like *The Stranger on the Third Floor* (1940), *Whispering City* (1947), *Call Northside 777* (1948), *The Big Clock* (1948), *The Underworld Story* (1950), *Ace in the Hole* (1951), *Scandal Sheet* (1952), *The Sellout* (1952), *The Blue Gardenia* (1953), and *While the City Sleeps* (1956). Hollywood was careful not to show a newspaper as the root of evil in a film noir. The ruckus over *Citizen Kane* (1941) proved the wisdom of this. William Randolph Hearst felt so personally insulted that his newspapers refused to run ads for it.

By making *Sweet Smell of Success* (1957), Burt Lancaster, Tony Curtis, and their co-producers were deliberately risking the wrath of the most powerful newspaper columnist in the United States, Walter Winchell. This made the film's sharp bite all the braver, and with such enemies it flopped on its first run. But its truthfulness has paid off – it is now counted by the Library of Congress as one of film history's vital treasures.

ELEVATOR TO THE SCAFFOLD

ASCENSEUR POUR L'ÉCHAFAUD

1958 – FRANCE – 88 MIN.
DIRECTOR LOUIS MALLE (1932–1995)
SCREENPLAY LOUIS MALLE, ROGER NIMIER, based
on the novel of the same name by NOËL CALEF
DIRECTOR OF PHOTOGRAPHY HENRI DECAË
EDITING LÉONIDE AZAR MUSIC MILES DAVIS
(Miles Davis Quintet: Miles Davis, Barney Wilen,
René Urtreger, Pierre Michelot, Kenny Clarke)
PRODUCTION JEAN THUILLIER for
NOUVELLES ÉDITIONS DE FILMS
STARRING JEANNE MOREAU (Florence Carala),
MAURICE RONET (Julien Tavernier), GEORGES
POUJOULY (Louis), YORI BERTIN (Véronique),
LINO VENTURA (Inspector Chérier), JEAN WALL
(Simon Carala), FÉLIX MARTEN (Christian Subervie),
IVAN PETROVICH (Horst Bencker), ELGA ANDERSEN
(Frieda Bencker), CHARLES DENNER
(Inspector Chérier's Assistant)

"I looked for you all night, but I couldn't find you."

Florence (Jeanne Moreau) and her lover Julien (Maurice Ronet) have planned the murder of Florence's husband right down to the last detail. The idea is to make it look as though the man has committed suicide in his office. Hardly has the deed been done when things start to go badly wrong: departing from the scene of the crime, Julien gets stuck in the elevator, and, as he struggles to find a way out, his car is stolen by a couple of kids. Florence, waiting outside for her lover, sees his convertible whizz past and begins to doubt her lover's feelings for her. She wanders the nocturnal streets of Paris in search of Julien, while he, marooned between floors, tries in vain to escape.

Meanwhile, the two joyriders have knocked down and killed a couple of German tourists before fleeing the scene – and the cops have launched a major manhunt for the owner of the car… An adulterous couple, a burdensome spouse, an ingenious murder plan, and the destructive power of accident: it's the stuff of a thousand movies. What was new and exciting about Malle's film was the way he created an existential drama from the ingredients of a classical thriller. *Elevator to the Scaffold* was his directing debut, and he was only 25 years old at the time. Malle himself once said that he had been torn between his desire to emulate Hitchcock and his admiration for the

1 Going up? While Maurice Ronet (1927–1983) was undoubtedly one of the best French actors of his generation, he never achieved the status of A-listers like Alain Delon and Jean-Paul Belmondo.

2 Florence (Jeanne Moreau, right) is left at a loss by what has proven to be a crummy plan.

3 Heavyweight: in 1957, former wrestler Lino Ventura (right) stepped into the acting arena, and ten years later he was knockin' 'em dead as a main attraction.

4 Some actors never fall out of favor. Jeanne Moreau takes an *Elevator to the Scaffold* and remains at the top of French cinema for the rest of her acting career.

"*Elevator to the Scaffold*, a debut film by a 25-year-old director, is so clear and cold that it raises goose bumps. It speaks of loneliness, of the impossibility of happiness and the inexorable logic of accident. This is a French film noir under the cloak of existentialism; a night film." *die tageszeitung*

tant director on *A Man Escaped or: The Wind Bloweth Where It Listeth* (*Un condamné à mort s'est échappé ou Le vent souffle où il veut*, 1956).

In fact, both influences are clearly detectable in Malle's film. After a suspenseful beginning, the plot gradually grinds to an almost complete halt, and Malle subjects his frantic protagonists to a near-clinical examination. While police investigations proceed apace, Florence and Julien seem almost incarcerated in their existential loneliness and despair. Like Bresson, Malle makes repeated use of apt metaphors: Julien is trapped in a kind of prison, but Florence too is lost in the labyrinth that is rain-soaked Paris. In Malle's film, the big city is a symbol of the modern world, and freedom is not what it promises. The surface glitter of the city's storefront windows only serves to emphasize the emotional barrenness of its denizens.

HENRI DECAË Henri Decaë (1915–1987) was one of the major cinematographers of the French New Wave, who freed the camera, and gave the French a new way of looking at the world. His camera starts high to give a superior view of a character, swoops down to pick out a face or an object, and turns 360 degrees to show the world as the characters see it. And all the time, we can feel the delicacy and fragility of the air around us because Decaë worked with natural light. Decaë was able to achieve this immediacy not only because of his genius, but through his training as a photojournalist in the French army during World War II, and his subsequent career making documentaries. He shot Jean-Pierre Melville's first film, *Le Silence de la mer* (1949), but only after Melville had sacked two previous cinematographers. Melville commented later, "Henri Decaë, a young man as sympathetic as he was shy, gifted with great intelligence, and exactly sharing my tastes for all things cinema. The first day we worked together was very pleasant, the second, delightful. From the third day onwards the die was cast." They worked together on six further films, including the noirs *Bob le flambeur* (1955), *Le Samouraï* (1967), and *The Red Circle* (*Le Cercle rouge*, 1970). Decaë also helped make François Truffaut's first film, *The 400 Blows* (*Les Quatre Cents Coups*, 1959); worked with Louis Malle on five films, including *Elevator to the Scaffold* (*Ascenseur pour l'échafaud*, 1958); shot Claude Chabrol's first four movies; and filmed *Purple Noon* (*Plein Soleil* / *Delitto in pieno sole*, 1960) and three other films for René Clément. In the 1970s and 1980s, he shot many comedies, dramas, and action-adventure films in France and the United States, as well as a number of crime films directed by Georges Lautner and written by Michel Audiard.

5

6

> "The debut from Louis Malle, *Elevator to the Scaffold* is a stylish noir-ish crime drama boasting, amongst other things, an improvised Miles Davis soundtrack." *Edinburgh University Film Society*

Although Malle has always taken pains to distance himself from the *Nouvelle Vague*, *Elevator to the Scaffold* was undoubtedly an important source of inspiration for the French *cinéma d'auteur* of the late 1950s. It might be grimmer in tone than anything by Godard or Truffaut, but it evinces the same enthusiasm for American B movies as *Breathless* (*À bout de souffle*, 1960) or *Shoot the Piano Player* (*Tirez sur le pianiste*, 1960). Cameraman Henri Decaë creates a noir Paris in intense black and white, illuminated only by passing headlights and the garish neon of late-night cafés. It's a diffuse and formless environment, an abode of shades in which Florence is soon in danger of losing her soul.

Though Malle takes a strictly detached view of his protagonists, he makes it clear that Florence is in a state of emotional emergency. As the camera focuses on the face of Jeanne Moreau, her beauty ravaged by tension and fatigue, we listen in on Florence's increasingly despairing interior monologue. Miles Davis's now-famous soundtrack makes her uncertainty almost palpable. The jagged aggressiveness of his trumpet transmits the character's anxiety straight to the moviegoer's bloodstream. All in all, *Elevator to the Scaffold* is a deeply pessimistic take on human nature. It now enjoys the status of an uncontested classic.

UB

5 Hanging by a thread: the longer Julien remains trapped in the elevator, the clearer it becomes that there is no such thing as the perfect plan …

6 … no matter how bright the prospects.

7 Disconnected, or no longer in service? In *Elevator to the Scaffold* the telephone is both a means of instant communication and of keeping others at a distance.

8 Slice of life: Louis Malle's detached *mise-en-scène* is reminiscent of mentor Robert Bresson's directing style. No coincidence either, as Malle had assisted Bresson on one of his pictures the year before.

TOUCH OF EVIL

1958 – USA – 95 MIN. / 112 MIN. (Director's Cut)
DIRECTOR ORSON WELLES (1915–1985)
SCREENPLAY ORSON WELLES, based on the novel
Badge of Evil by WHIT MASTERSON
DIRECTOR OF PHOTOGRAPHY RUSSELL METTY
EDITING AARON STELL, VIRGIL VOGEL,
WALTER MURCH (Director's Cut) **MUSIC** HENRY MANCINI
PRODUCTION ALBERT ZUGSMITH for UNIVERSAL PICTURES
STARRING CHARLTON HESTON (Ramon Miguel "Mike"
Vargas), JANET LEIGH (Susan Vargas), ORSON WELLES
(Hank Quinlan), JOSEPH CALLEIA (Pete Menzies),
AKIM TAMIROFF ("Uncle Joe" Grandi), JOANNA MOORE
(Marcia Linnekar), DENNIS WEAVER
(Motel Night Manager), MORT MILLS (Al Schwartz),
MERCEDES MCCAMBRIDGE (Gang Leader),
MARLENE DIETRICH (Tanya)

Quinlan: "Come on, read my future for me."
Tanya: "You haven't got any."
Quinlan: "What do you mean?"
Tanya: "Your future is all used up."

In Los Robles, a small town on the Texan-Mexican border, a limousine explodes. It belongs to a rich construction magnate. One witness to the attack is Vargas (Charlton Heston), a high-ranking Mexican narcotics detective who just happens to be there on his honeymoon. He offers his assistance to the responsible U.S. Sheriff, Hank Quinlan (Orson Welles), but soon realizes that Quinlan is a bigoted racist whose working methods are anything but scrupulous. When Vargas sees Quinlan planting material on a suspect, he resolves to take action. For the Mexican drug baron Grandi (Akim Tamiroff), this means a welcome opportunity to offer Quinlan a business proposition; for after all, they now have an enemy in common – and Vargas, with his young American wife Susan Vargas (Janet Leigh) is an absurdly easy target.

Touch of Evil was Orson Welles's first Hollywood production after a decade in Europe. As things turned out, it was the last movie he ever made in the States. For after the studios had refused to grant him the final cut on

1 Tequila sunrise: in the corrupt border town of Los Robles, Vargas (Charlton Heston) is made to look like a deadbeat scoundrel rather than the lone crusader he actually is.

2 She's a whore who's seen things that weren't meant for human eyes. Marlene Dietrich as Tanya, the Teutonic tramp.

3 Law man Quinlan (Orson Welles) has issued a warrant for Vargas's arrest. His crime – sticking his nose where it don't belong.

4 Quinlan tries to put a lid on Vargas's meddling by working out a deal with Grandi (Akim Tamiroff), a gangster who fronts as a general store owner.

> "A tough and lovely film of stunning beauty. The death-throes of a lion. In the words of Gilles Deleuze, the king of kings in this tale of martyrdom is the story of great cinema itself." *Le Monde*

The Magnificent Ambersons (1942) and *The Lady from Shanghai* (1947) – disfiguring both films in the process, as Welles saw it – he was subjected to the same humiliating treatment yet again.

Shocked by the rough cut, the Universal moguls took the project out of the director's hands, filmed some additional scenes and finally edited the film as they thought fit. Yet even this studio version couldn't completely conceal Welles's signature, and French cineastes in particular hailed the film as a masterpiece. In the U.S. too, it had its fans: Alfred Hitchcock's *Psycho* (1960) would hardly have been possible if he hadn't seen the bizarre motel scenes with Janet Leigh and Dennis Weaver in *Touch of Evil*. In a certain sense, this movie recapitulates the themes of Welles's previous works. As in *Citizen Kane* (1941), he depicts the collapse of a powerful ego-

maniac, who forfeits his integrity as he loses touch with the real world. Welles's Quinlan is a fascinating monster, but we can't ignore the tragedy at the heart of his existence: the painful memory of his murdered wife, whose death has never been avenged.

The almost totalitarian violence of Quinlan's "lawkeeping" is rooted in his conviction that the law can never produce justice. He despises pettifogging judicial abstractions, preferring instead to trust his own infallible instinct. In this way, he manages to keep a tenuous distance from the lurid decay of the Mexican border town, just as he tames his frustrations with endless bars of chocolate. While Quinlan is a massive patriarch, a relic from times past or passing, his younger rival Vargas is streamlined, dynamic, the embodiment of

social progress. Significantly, the Mexican's moral superiority is only once in any doubt: when he himself is under attack. Realizing that Susan is in serious danger, he too resorts to very dubious methods. There's something decidedly hollow about his final victory, as he only prevails by surreptitiously eavesdropping on Quinlan.

With *Touch of Evil*, Welles brought the era of the classical film noir to a worthy end. All of these movies had shared a fundamental doubt about modern man's capacity to understand the world he inhabits. Here, Welles brought this skepticism to a head in a formally spectacular fashion. Extreme camera angles and a distorting wide-angle lens reinforced the eccentric impression made by the film's characters, who seem like parodies at times.

"It was named best film at the 1958 Brussels World Fair (Godard and Truffaut were on the jury), but in America it opened on the bottom half of a double bill, failed, and put an end to Welles' prospects of working within the studio system. Yet the film has always been a favorite of those who enjoy visual and dramatic flamboyance." *Chicago Sun-Times*

6

5 Going through hell in a house of ill repute: Vargas's wife Susan (Janet Leigh) learns the hard way that Quinlan's jurisdiction stretches beyond the borders of law and order.

6 Hostages of the honeymoon suite: Vargas thought his sojourn in Los Robles would be one of wedded bliss. Now, he'll be happy just to get out of this stinking town alive.

7 Justice for the mighty few: Quinlan falsifies evidence whenever he can't seal a conviction with the naked truth.

COP NOIR Normally in film noir the police detective hunts the killer, or hinders the newspaperman, or actively deters the private eye from investigating any further, but sometimes the darker side of the police force is revealed, as in *On Dangerous Ground* (1952), where Robert Ryan is a brutal city cop who finds redemption when his eyes are opened by a blind country woman played by Ida Lupino. Cops can also become obsessive about their work, going further than their superiors, or the law, permit in films like *Nocturne* (1946), *The Hunted* (1948), *Naked Alibi* (1954), or the seminal *The Big Combo* (1955). Even a good cop will seek revenge if he is pushed too far, as can be seen in *The Big Heat* (1953) and *Rogue Cop* (1954), both based on novels by William P. McGivern, where the cop must avenge the deaths in his family. And law keepers can also become lawbreakers, corrupted by the power they wield. In *I Wake Up Screaming* (1941) Victor Mature escapes from jail to prove his innocence, but is pursued by corrupt cop Laird Cregar. Policeman Van Heflin seduces suburban housewife Evelyn Keyes in *The Prowler* (1951), then plots to kill her husband. *Shield for Murder* (1954) stars Edmond O'Brien as a cop who murders a bookmaker, then convinces his bosses it's a legit killing. The ultimate corrupt cop is Hank Quinlan (Orson Welles) in *Touch of Evil* (1958). Quinlan is fascinating because of his moral ambiguity. The more human Welles makes Quinlan, the more interesting he becomes. The theme was explored further in *Clean Slate* (*Coup de torchon*, 1981) and *Bad Lieutenant* (1992).

7

Extremely fast tracking shots and an unusual depth of field make it difficult for the viewer to orientate himself within the frame, and the narrative structure of the movie can only be described as labyrinthine. Any hope of discovering the objective truth seems absurdly misplaced here.

Los Robles, the shabby border town, is a symbol of chaos, of a world in which Good and Evil began to bleed into one another long ago. At the end of the film, Quinlan — lying in the mud and the garbage by the side of the river — is shot dead by his only friend. Under such circumstances, moral judgment seems out of place; and his former lover Tanya (Marlene Dietrich) says the only decent thing possible: "He was some kind of a man."

UB

VERTIGO

1958 – USA – 128 MIN.
DIRECTOR ALFRED HITCHCOCK (1899–1980)
SCREENPLAY ALEC COPPEL, SAMUEL A. TAYLOR,
based on the novel *D'Entre les morts* by
PIERRE BOILEAU and THOMAS NARCEJAC
DIRECTOR OF PHOTOGRAPHY ROBERT BURKS
EDITING GEORGE TOMASINI MUSIC BERNARD HERRMANN
PRODUCTION ALFRED HITCHCOCK for ALFRED J. HITCHCOCK
PRODUCTIONS, INC., PARAMOUNT PICTURES
STARRING JAMES STEWART (John "Scottie" Ferguson),
KIM NOVAK (Madeleine Elster / Judy Barton),
BARBARA BEL GEDDES (Midge Wood), TOM HELMORE
(Gavin Elster), KONSTANTIN SHAYNE (Pop Leibel),
HENRY JONES (Coroner), RAYMOND BAILEY (Doctor),
ELLEN CORBY (Hotel Manager)

"Do you believe that someone out of the past – someone dead – can enter and take possession of a living being?"

The depths of a stairwell beckon from beyond. The ground vanishes, the banister uncoils, and we are overcome by a sense of vertigo. Combining a forward zoom and reverse tracking shot (now sometimes called "contra-zoom" or "trombone shot"), director Alfred Hitchcock creates a dizziness that has gone down as the stuff of legends. As the stairwell springs in and out of proportion, we are thrust into the mind of the protagonist, John "Scottie" Ferguson (James Stewart), a man with a paralyzing fear of heights. A San Francisco police detective, Scottie turns in his badge following a rooftop pursuit that ends in the death of a fellow officer. He blames himself or rather his acrophobia for the incident, convinced that the fatal fall has left him half a man.

Several months pass. Months that for Scottie are a sea of contemplation. Then a phone call promises hope from out of the blue: an old college acquaintance and ship-building tycoon named Gavin Elster (Tom Helmore) wants to meet up and reminisce about old times. However, instead of losing themselves in nostalgic reverie, the businessman offers Scottie a job; Elster's wife, it seems, has been exhibiting signs of psychological instability and needs to be watched. Scottie initially refuses to get involved, but quickly changes his mind upon laying eyes on her: Madeleine Elster (Kim Novak) – a platinum vision of elegance – is supernaturally stunning, and Scottie just can't look away.

And so begins a hypnotic game of cat and mouse. The private detective discreetly follows Madeleine around San Francisco as she goes about her daily business and journeys to the city's furthest enclaves. Guided by music, these are sequences without dialogue and without contact, until one afternoon when Madeleine tries to take her life by jumping into the bay. Scottie

1 The fall of man: Scottie (James Stewart) is head
   over heels for a suicidal dream girl. Kim Novak as
   Madeleine, Hitchcock's ultimate blonde.

2 Image is everything: it's incredible what magic
   a gray dress suit and upswept hair can work when
   you've got all the right moves.

dives in after her, but ultimately cannot abate her suicidal tendencies: just days later, a fit of hysteria sends Madeleine running up the stairs of a church bell tower and out of Scottie's life – for now.

Vertigo is the story of a man stricken by a debilitating handicap that prevents him from seeing clearly at higher elevations. The predicament is confounded when Scottie falls in love with an unattainable woman, and loses all sight of reality and literally the ground below. He's a loner and a dreamer,

qualities we see heightened through his relationship with his pragmatic confidante Midge (Barbara Bel Geddes, later of *Dallas* fame, 1978–1990). And all these things make him the perfect pawn in this masterful Hitchcockian chess game.

It seems almost inconceivable that *Vertigo* met with overall disapproval at the time of its original release. The critics tore it apart and the *New Yorker* branded it "farfetched nonsense." Elements like the Saul Bass title and dream sequences most likely estranged the 1950s moviegoer. Both integrate animation and dissociative color schemes, and qualify as experimental pieces in their own right.

It was only in the '70s that *Vertigo* gained a second lease on life. Critics began to praise the film's sleek story, its beautifully composed shots, and it entered into the canon of great cinema. Although Alfred Hitchcock directed more than his share of masterpieces, *Vertigo* is beyond compare. With an impact as haunting and captivating as ever, the film exhibits all the laudable Hitchcockian themes and calling cards theorists once claimed it lacked: from the master's trademark suspense, where the audience knows more than the characters, via doppelganger motives, voyeurism, guilt complexes embodied by the hero, wry humor, all the way to obsessive love for a blonde woman.

3

"Once this movie is under way, it's off into very deep waters. The desperation of Scottie's need to revive Madeleine is both disturbing and moving, a combination you don't expect from a Hitchcock film." *San Francisco Examiner*

3   Dizzy dame: Scottie follows Madeleine to the most remote corners of the Bay Area and discovers nuts among the Sequoias.

4   On shore and under the covers: Scottie fishes Madeleine out of the bay, but who will fish him out of the sea of delirium that threatens to drown him?

4

7

5   Role playing: Scottie convinces Madeleine to confront her nightmarish visions by acting them out. But she breaks character for a parting kiss in the carriage house.

6   39 steps to psychosis: a legendary scene that left cineastes suffering from acrophobia.

7   Dirty blondes play dirty tricks: she changes her hair color, removes her brassiere and voilà – she's a new woman. Kim Novak as brassy redhead, Judy Barton.

8 & 9   A dead end: Madeleine's grandmother, Carlotta Valdez, has come back from beyond to take possession of what is rightly hers – Madeleine's soul.

10   Scottie wants to transform Judy into the Madeleine he so lovingly remembers.

It is with particular regard to this latter aspect that *Vertigo* emerges as the British filmmaker's magnum opus. As Andreas Kilb argues, it's no secret that Hitchcock was forever molding his vision of the "aloof, mysterious blonde icon," evident in his work with actresses like Ingrid Bergman and Grace Kelly. Yet *Vertigo* takes this single-minded fetish to its zenith. Here, not only Hitchcock, but the characters themselves are doubly driven by the desire to create the perfect blonde. What one can say without robbing the piece of all its mystique is that Madeleine is trained to act as an alluring decoy; and that a woman named Judy turns up in the second half of the film who, apart from her hair color and makeup, is a dead ringer for Madeleine. And so, after losing the love of his life, Scottie is given the chance to recreate her – using Judy.   HJK

8

9

10

JAMES STEWART *It's a Wonderful Life* (1946), *Winchester '73* (1950), and *Rear Window* (1954) are just three of more than 80 feature films starring James Stewart (1908–1997). What these three masterpieces have in common is that their respective directors were instrumental in shaping Jimmy's career: he made three pictures with Frank Capra, eight with Anthony Mann, and four with Alfred Hitchcock. One of the most remarkable actors ever to grace the screen, Stewart very much deserves his own chapter in its history. At 6'3" he made an art form of lankiness and of never quite knowing what to with his long limbs. This, however, didn't stop him from turning up in the musical *Born to Dance* (1936). Indeed, he felt at home in nearly all genres, appearing in comedies, romances, Westerns, war movies, and thrillers alike. He also portrayed a fair share of historical figures, including Glenn Miller and Charles Lindbergh. His list of co-stars is equally impeccable, topped off by names like Edward G. Robinson, John Wayne, Katharine Hepburn, Marlene Dietrich, and a six-foot-three-and-a-half-inch-tall invisible rabbit named *Harvey* (1950). Stewart had an incredible range, always managing to hit on something universal in his acting that was unmarred by histrionics. The son of a Pennsylvania hardware store owner, he got his start in pictures playing shy innocents – usually guys from the countryside – before establishing himself as a leading man in romantic comedies. He freely enlisted in the service during World War II and returned home a highly decorated pilot. From this point on, his screen work took on a darker edge, and his characterizations became more vulnerable and rich with internal conflict. Upon his passing in 1997, the German regional newspaper *Süddeutsche Zeitung* declared him "the last of the cinematic greats … and the greatest among them."

IT HAPPENED IN BROAD DAYLIGHT

ES GESCHAH AM HELLICHTEN TAG / EL CEBO

1958 – WEST GERMANY / SWITZERLAND / SPAIN – 99 MIN.
DIRECTOR LADISLAO VAJDA (1906–1965)
SCREENPLAY FRIEDRICH DÜRRENMATT, HANS JACOBY, LADISLAO VAJDA
DIRECTOR OF PHOTOGRAPHY HEINRICH GÄRTNER
EDITING HERMANN HALLER **MUSIC** BRUNO CANFORA
PRODUCTION LAZAR WECHSLER, ARTUR BRAUNER for PRAESENS-FILM AG, CCC FILMKUNST GMBH, CHAMARTÍN PRODUCCIONES Y DISTRIBUCIONES
STARRING HEINZ RÜHMANN (Commissioner Matthäi), MICHEL SIMON (The Peddler, Jacquier), EWALD BALSER (Professor Manz), GERT FRÖBE (Mr. Schrott), BERTA DREWS (Mrs. Schrott), SIGFRIT STEINER (Detective Feller), SIEGFRIED LOWITZ (Inspector Heinzi), HEINRICH GRETLER (Police Commandant), MARÍA ROSA SALGADO (Frau Heller), ANITA VON OW (Annemarie Heller)

"Such a devil cannot possibly exist."

Child murderers have always been an object of particular revulsion and dread. Sometimes they dominate the headlines for days on end; and sometimes they haunt us for a lifetime. *It Happened in Broad Daylight (Es geschah am hellichten Tag)* is a forgotten classic. A German/Swiss/Spanish co-production, it focuses on Commissioner Matthäi (Heinz Rühmann), a kindly, good-natured police detective who is put in charge of the case of a murdered eight-year-old girl just before his retirement. The main suspect is a peddler (Michel Simon), but Matthäi doesn't believe he's guilty. Then the man hangs himself in his cell in despair, and it looks like an open-and-shut case. But the elderly cop is plagued by doubts, and he decides to pursue his own private investigation. He has promised the parents he will find the culprit, and if Matthäi's suspicions turn out to be well founded, the killer still poses a threat.

The murder, and others like it, took place in Eastern Switzerland. Matthäi rents a gas station on a country road there, and waits. It's a hopeless strategy, but Matthäi believes that sooner or later the nameless monster will put in an appearance. The policeman's only clue is a drawing by the child victim, who, it seems, had met her killer on several occasions: the picture depicts an enormous man with a black car. As this isn't enough to catch the killer, Matthäi hatches a monstrous idea: he hires a housekeeper and uses her little daughter as bait. For months on end he watches and waits, forgetting that it's impossible to keep an eye on a child from dawn till dusk. And when the trap finally snaps shut, it's almost too late …

Sean Penn's remake, *The Pledge* (2000) starred Jack Nicholson and had a very different ending: the murderer dies in a car accident, and the cop descends into madness after years of waiting in vain. Penn was faithful to

"Gert Fröbe plays the murderer like the Kasper character in German puppet theater. The red-haired giant Rübezahl stands in his plushy bedroom; in the sewing basket are the socks his wife has darned for him; jars of marinated fruit line the walls. With a faint smile, he stares almost blissfully at Kasper's stupid, friendly face. Rübezahl does conjuring tricks for children, and under his jacket he always keeps a knife." *Der Tagesspiegel*

1. Trick or treat: child killer Mr. Schrott (Gert Fröbe) has got a heart of gold – when it suits him.

2. Vigilantes hold a midnight vigil: Commissioner Matthäi (Heinz Rühmann) has trouble preventing the outraged villagers from turning into a lynch mob.

3. Traveling salesman Jacquier (Michel Simon) lays low in the forest while devising ways to clear his name of the crimes.

4. Could you run that by me again? Sometimes Inspector Heinzi (Siegfried Lowitz) can't make head or tail of the schemes his boss cooks up.

5. Teasing the killer out of hiding: Inspector Heinzi wins the trust of a little girl who supplies him with the first clue to the killer's identity – a drawing.

the novel by the famous Swiss author Friedrich Dürrenmatt, who had substantially reworked the story line in his final screenplay for the original movie. But *It Happened in Broad Daylight* can hardly be accused of excessive optimism: in one of his few straight roles, Heinz Rühmann, the roly-poly German screen idol, plays a character of deep moral ambiguity. In order to catch the killer, Matthäi abuses the trust of an unsuspecting mother and her child, thereby becoming a kind of ruthless seducer himself. And

as for Gert Fröbe ... he became known as the very archetype of a terrifying sex fiend. And indeed, his performance is every bit as memorable as Peter Lorre's in Fritz Lang's *M* (*M – Eine Stadt sucht einen Mörder*, 1931).

At first, all we're shown of him is a black shadow; then we see his huge fleshy fingers, cramping in panic as his domineering wife humiliates him; finally, this massive man appears full-size – and with his gruesome Punch and Judy Show, he beguiles tiny Annemarie (Anita von Ow), Matthäi's "bait."

FRIEDRICH DÜRRENMATT Swiss author and dramatist Friedrich Dürrenmatt was born January 5, 1921, in Konolfingen. He wanted to provoke and intrigue people with his work, so that they were not just passive receivers of information. He achieved his goal – the opening night of his first play, *It Is Written (Es steht geschrieben)*, in April 1947 resulted in fights and protests amongst the audience. Sometimes Dürrenmatt used the format of the mystery novel to explore his philosophical ideas. In *The Judge and His Hangman (Der Richter und sein Henker*, 1950), Bärlach, a terminally ill master detective on the brink of retirement, takes on the role of judge and jury to force one of his subordinates to execute his nemesis, while in the sequel, *The Quarry (Der Verdacht*, 1951), Bärlach allows his own cancer-ridden body to be put under the knife of Dr. Emmenberger in order to reveal him as an infamous concentration-camp doctor. *The Pledge*, subtitled *Requiem for the Detective Novel (Das Versprechen: Requiem auf den Kriminalroman*, 1958) is based on the film *It Happened in Broad Daylight (Es geschah m hellichten Tag*, 1958), but goes even further by having the obsessive detective Matthäi descend into dissolution and madness in his fruitless quest to catch a child-killer. The horror that lies just beneath the surface of life and authority figures is shown in *A Dangerous Game (Die Panne*, 1956), where a businessman, who is stranded after his car breaks down, is invited to stay for dinner by a former judge, and is made to acknowledge his past guilt. Meanwhile, in the Kafkaesque *The Execution of Justice (Justiz*, 1985), all the facts of a murder are eliminated, so that the case can be tried on purely theoretical grounds. Dürrenmatt died December 14, 1990, in Neuenburg, Switzerland.

6 Giving pointers: to set a trap for the killer, the overly ambitious Matthäi convinces little Annemarie (Anita von Ow) to help him bait

the killer. His plan, however, ends up endangering the girl's life.

7 You should be ashamed of yourself: Annemarie's mother (María Rosa Salgado) is outraged by Matthäi's reckless behavior. And so is he.

"The cast is uniformly excellent. Rühmann gives a thoroughly convincing performance away from his comic parts. Michel Simon in a relatively short role as the peddler is topnotch, and Gert Fröbe impresses as the perverted killer." *Variety*

The role gained Fröbe international recognition, and resulted in his legendary appearance as Bond's nemesis in *Goldfinger* (1964). The subject of the movie is as topical as it ever was, although Sean Penn's treatment is more "modern," as it places the Commissioner's struggle with his conscience in the foreground of the film.

But it's the almost unbearably tense atmosphere of the older movie that makes *It Happened in Broad Daylight* the best German film of the postwar period. Its disturbing effect also has a lot to do with its location: the pristine

world of the Swiss mountains, a kind of Garden of Eden in the sugary German *Heimatfilme* that emerged after the horrors of World War II. Switzerland is the land of alpine horns, chocolate, and Heidi – and the Hungarian director makes cleverly suggestive use of those ambivalent motifs. The music deceptively promises safety where none exists, and the chocolate is used to entice innocent children. In the idyllic picture postcard world of an unspoiled natural paradise lurks the threat of bestial human wickedness. And not even Matthäi will succeed in taming it.

MURDER BY CONTRACT

1958 – USA – 81 MIN.
DIRECTOR IRVING LERNER (1909–1976)
SCREENPLAY BEN SIMCOE, BEN MADDOW (uncredited)
DIRECTOR OF PHOTOGRAPHY LUCIEN BALLARD
EDITING CARLO LODATO MUSIC PERRY BOTKIN
PRODUCTION LEON CHOOLUCK for
ORBIT PRODUCTIONS, COLUMBIA
PICTURES CORPORATION
STARRING VINCE EDWARDS (Claude),
PHILLIP PINE (Marc), HERSCHEL BERNARDI
(George), MICHAEL GRANGER (Mr. Moon),
CAPRICE TORIEL (Billie Williams),
KATHIE BROWNE (Secretary Escort), JOSEPH MELL
(Harry, Hotel Waiter), FRANCES OSBORNE
(Miss Wiley, Ex-Maid), STEVEN RITCH
(Detective Shooting Tear Gas), DAVIS ROBERTS
(Hall of Records Clerk)

"Why would a stranger kill a stranger? Because somebody is willing to pay. It's business, same as any other business."

Filmed in just seven days in February 1958 and released without fanfare the following December, *Murder by Contract* has prevailed against the passing years in high style. Martin Scorsese calls it "the film that has influenced me the most."

Vince Edwards plays Claude, an educated young man who could just as easily have become a lawyer or doctor but instead elects to work as a professional assassin. In the film's first sequence, disguised as a barber, he coldly dispatches a man who dozes as he awaits a shave. Next, wearing hospital whites and a stethoscope, he murders a semicomatose mobster by cutting off his oxygen supply. Finally – all set to the spritely, tiptoeing guitar music of Perry Botkin – he shows up at the door of his employer (Michael Granger) and assassinates him, having just been offered a juicier contract with a rival crime boss.

Director Irving Lerner made his primary career as a film editor, so it follows that these scenes thrive by their energetic, witty cuts. The impending death of the man in a barber's chair is implicit in the rhythm of Edwards's feline movements and the close-ups of that gleaming razor, while the moment of the murder is withheld from us by a perfectly timed fade to black. His intrusion upon his boss follows the similar fade that closes the hospital visit, but the shadowy lighting and Claude's leather jacket suggest the more furtive urgency of his purpose and that perhaps substantial time has passed. For all the brevity of the shooting schedule, Lerner packs a variety of worlds and micro time zones into his narrative. He is greatly helped by the cinematography of Lucien Ballard, who shot Kubrick's *The Killing* (1956), which also featured Vince Edwards, as well as *The Wild Bunch* (1969) and *The Getaway* (1972) for Peckinpah. Each shot is well minted.

1   The house where the intended victim is being
    protected is breached at night by assassin Claude
    (Vince Edwards) through a drainpipe.

2   After many failed tries, Claude confronts his quarry
    Billie Williams (Caprice Toriel), having silently
    killed her bodyguard. "I'm the relief officer," he
    tells her. "I'm new."

3   Wary of female targets because women are
    unpredictable, Claude quizzes this one's former
    maid (Frances Osborne) to get a sense of her
    personal habits.

"Lerner was an artist who knew how to do things in shorthand,
like Bresson and Godard. The film puts us all to shame with
its economy of style, especially in the barbershop murder at the
beginning." *Martin Scorsese, in: Film Comment*

4   The two mobsters supervising the murder scheme, George (Herschel Bernardi) and Marc (Phillip Pine), decide to kill Claude, but he turns the tables by faking a seizure.

5   After a second murder attempt, the newspapers report the death of Billie Williams, but Claude rightly suspects that the woman has survived and that the job is jinxed.

IRVING LERNER Born in New York City and educated at Columbia University, Irving Lerner (1909–1976) majored in anthropology and the social sciences before he turned to filmmaking. His career reflects this at every stage – his first films were documentaries about farming, warfare, and American folk music, and each was attentive to the small worlds created by these workers, soldiers, and artisans, as well as their impact on the world at large. Of these excellent works, *Hymn of the Nations* (1944) and *To Hear Your Banjo Play* (1947) can be found floating about on the World Wide Web. Another, less freely available but well worth hunting for, is *Muscle Beach* (1948) co-directed with Joseph Strick.

A committed Marxist – the world economy crashed as he entered his '20s – Lerner was accused of espionage in 1944 when he was caught taking an unauthorized photograph of the cyclotron in Berkeley, then a major secret of the war effort. The charges didn't stick, but a close associate of his shortly fled to Russia and the scandal left Lerner blacklisted. This hobbled his opportunities as a movie director, for which *Murder by Contract* (1958) remains his finest example – although *Studs Lonigan* (1960), which features a young Jack Nicholson, and *Royal Hunt of the Sun* (1969), about the conquest of the Incas, have over time gathered ardent admirers. The creative bond he formed with star Vince Edwards bore fruit on television – Lerner directed him in a number of episodes of the actor's hit TV series *Ben Casey* (1961–1966).

For the balance of his career Lerner made a living primarily as a film editor. His credits include *Spartacus* (1960) for Stanley Kubrick, and he died while cutting *New York, New York* (1977) for Martin Scorsese, who claims Lerner as a key influence and dedicated that film to his memory.

Ben Maddow, who scripted John Huston's *The Asphalt Jungle* (1950), did an uncredited rewrite on Ben Simcoe's original screenplay. The dialogue has a sharp-edged flare that harmonizes well with the shooting and cutting. "I wasn't born this way," Claude tells the two mobsters assigned to supervise his next big contract: "I train myself. I eliminate personal feeling." The excellence of Vince Edwards as an actor particularly shines in the longer speeches. Pressed to hurry up and get the job done, he replies that cold patience is essential: "You read in the paper about some wife doing away with her husband, a child murderer, a knifing in a tavern brawl. These are crimes of pas-

sion … [These] types eventually get caught. They don't plan. They can't. Even if they did, it'd be no use. The only type of killing that's safe is when a stranger kills a stranger. No motive. Nothing to link the victim to the executioner."

His new employer flies him to Los Angeles to kill a star witness who is heavily guarded under federal protection. This is a challenge, but Claude is equal to it. Where he balks is that the target is also a woman (Caprice Toriel), former mistress of his new boss. The two mobsters flanking him (Herschel Bernardi and Phillip Pine) worry that he's gone soft, but he assures them that – quite the contrary – the problems are purely technical: "I don't like women.

6   7

6   After a final attempt, Claude's escape is foiled by a waiting lawman. Lucien Ballard's elegant cinematography lends visual force to such simple dynamics.

7   No one is safe: Claude pays a visit to murder his first employer, Mr. Moon (Michael Granger), acting on a contract with a rival crime boss.

8   Herschel Bernardi as George sets his sights on removing Claude from the equation in this killing-for-hire.

"A cleanly constructed low-budget suspense picture about a hired killer ... The material is thin, but it has been worked out in visual terms, and the movie is often taut and exciting. Some high-contrast sequences are models of black-and-white atmospheric storytelling." *Pauline Kael, 5001 Nights at the Movies*

They don't stand still. When they move, it's hard to figure out the why or wherefore."

Even so, he's a professional and makes two attempts. The second, a shot taken with a long-range rifle, appears to be successful – but it turns out he has killed a female cop working undercover. Feeling jinxed, he refuses to make a third try and so his two handlers decide to kill him instead. They steer from a busy thoroughfare onto an abandoned film lot – Charlie Chaplin's former studio – an odd but atmospheric choice that, by the way, makes a clever virtue out of a stretched budget. As if inspired by this theatrical touch, Claude turns the tables by faking a seizure and kills his would-be killers. He

then reverses course and make a last try at the female target. His motive is murky – most likely he just wants his money. Yet once he penetrates the ranks of guards surrounding this lady in the dead of night – a well-paced, well-filmed mini-sequence – he hesitates at the very instant she is in his clutches, and his world comes crashing in.

Why hesitate? Perhaps the reason he doesn't want to kill a woman is that, whether for love or hate, to do so violates his professional code against "crimes of passion." Lerner's brilliance as a filmmaker is that he offers no comment – we're left to sort out this final puzzle for ourselves.

FXF

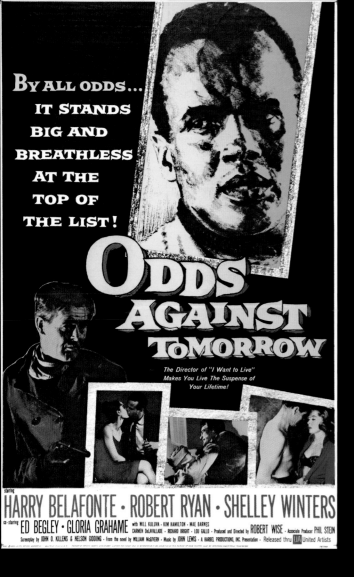

ODDS AGAINST TOMORROW

1959 – USA – 96 MIN.
DIRECTOR ROBERT WISE (1914–2005)
SCREENPLAY NELSON GIDDING, JOHN O. KILLENS
(frontman for ABRAHAM POLONSKY), based on the novel
of the same name by WILLIAM P. MCGIVERN
DIRECTOR OF PHOTOGRAPHY JOSEPH C. BRUN
EDITING DEDE ALLEN MUSIC JOHN LEWIS
PRODUCTION ROBERT WISE for HARBEL PRODUCTIONS
STARRING HARRY BELAFONTE (Johnny Ingram),
ROBERT RYAN (Earle Slater), ED BEGLEY (Dave Burke),
SHELLEY WINTERS (Lorry), GLORIA GRAHAME
(Helen), WILL KULUVA (Bacco), KIM HAMILTON
(Ruth Ingram), MAE BARNES (Annie), CARMEN DE
LAVALLADE (Kittie), RICHARD BRIGHT (Coco)

"Stop – Dead End."

A crisp wind trails through a remote town about 100 miles outside of New York. It is a late autumn afternoon, much like any other. Clusters of clouds fill the sky, interrupted by lone sunbeams that shimmer golden on still river waters. Three New Yorkers, two whites and a black, positioned at three points along the river, idly pass the time. Yet there's something less than idyllic about this scene, as if something dark and threatening were hanging in the air. For the three men, the wait seems endless. For although these guys have next to nothing in common, today they are a unit with a single goal – bank robbery.

In this unlikely piece of film noir, the classic motif of the tragic hero is once again bound up with the inevitable doom of the individual, and the despair so characteristic of the genre is captured in stunning imagery. Scattered bits of newspaper swirl through abandoned streets, steam rises from the gullies, and city lights sparkle in the puddles at nightfall. Director Robert Wise transforms even the suburban corner that the three men traverse en route to the bank into a haunting portrait of solitude.

In truth, none of these men know exactly what they are doing. None of them had ever thought they would be involved in a heist. But happiness has slipped through their fingers one too many times and despair is closing in. Johnny, a black jazz musician (Harry Belafonte), has amassed a gambling debt and needs to get his hands on 7,500 dollars pronto. Estranged from his wife and daughter, he wants nothing more than to be the rich and successful

man his slick threads suggest. But until that moment comes, he's left to sit on the river bank, staring into the dark waters and discovering a child's broken doll among the reeds in the process.

Earle (Robert Ryan), a burly hothead from Oklahoma, is the racist of the group. Recently released from jail after serving time for manslaughter, he has taken up with Lorry (Shelley Winters), a diligent, career-oriented office employee. He sees her independent lifestyle as an affront to his small-mind manhood. Lorry's success only solidifies Earle's image of himself as a born loser. He spends his time at the river loading up his shotgun and firing away at a rabbit.

The third member of the gang is the oldest. Dave (Ed Begley) is a heavy-set crooked cop, thrown off the force and into the slammer for protecting a Mafia ringleader in court. These days he lives with his Alsatian in a run-down motel and couldn't be more ready for a change of pace. As the mastermind behind the heist, he's worked out every last detail of the job and safeguarded against loose ends. But what he hasn't planned on are the personal resentments that plague his partners in crime, and it is just this element that will throw a spanner in the works … Far above the riverbed, Dave sits tight as the lookout, throwing stones at an empty tin can when he should be keeping his eyes peeled for trouble. Like the other men, he's just waiting for six

"The tension builds well to the climax – thanks partly to director Robert Wise, partly to a scriptwriter named John O. Killens, but mostly to actor Ryan, a menace who can look bullets and smile sulphuric acid." *Time Magazine*

1 Gifted jazz musician, Johnny (Harry Belafonte), intends on pulling off a bank heist that would put him on easy street. However, his accomplices prove more of a hindrance than a help.

2 Dave (Ed Begley) tries to smooth things over between Johnny and Earle (Robert Ryan), but only ends up egging on their mutual antagonism.

3 Bringing up baby: Ruth (Kim Hamilton) is the one who's doing it, but Johnny's happy to take the credit for it whenever he's around – every other weekend and on holidays. Still, better that than a deadbeat dad …

2

3

o'clock to roll around – the time their plan will be set into action. That time comes about two-thirds into the picture, launching a 10-minute sequence impressively devoid of plot. The episode is boldly steered by a jazz theme that John Lewis of the Modern Jazz Quartet wrote especially for the movie. What plays out before us is among the most peaceful yet highly anticipated displays ever conceived as an action sequence. Suspense reaches immeasurable heights. Given the intricate back story teeming with expository characters and the conflicts among them, the audience builds up a burning thirst as it counts down to the moment of truth.

Odds Against Tomorrow is an example of how a director can use time as a structural element in cinema. Robert Wise is a virtuoso in his representation of cinematic space, using an extended depth of field to capture the characters' relationships within a single image. Each shot, each second of the sequence made with infrared film, has been carefully calculated to reveal something

particular about the protagonists' states of mind. Once again, Wise shows his mastery of a craft he first learned as a film editor, a line of work he proved his genius in at the cutting table of Orson Welles's *Citizen Kane* (1941).

As the clock of the First National Bank strikes six, Johnny, Earle, and Dave assume their positions in six successively cut shots. The rate at which the plot progresses rapidly approaches real time, and the robbery begins. The preliminary drafts of the script foresaw a happy ending. The animosity between Johnny and Earle would eventually subside, and they'd pull off the job. However, Stanley Kramer's *The Defiant Ones* (1958) with Sidney Poitier and Tony Curtis beat them to the punch the previous year. Thus *Odds Against Tomorrow* couldn't end on a similarly reconciliatory note. A "Stop – Dead End" sign appears in the second to last shot, followed by the camera turning downward into a dark puddle that reflects an unattainable sky.

SR

ROBERT RYAN As a tall, strapping lad, Chicago native Robert Ryan (1909–1973) looked like the parts he was most frequently cast in: elegant, taciturn gentlemen or rugged army officers. But it was in roles as downtrodden individuals that this former Max Reinhardt acting student was at his most brilliant, playing men whom life had passed by, but who continued to wait in vain for their big break. The most memorable of these performances came as boxer Stoker Thompson in *The Set-Up* (1949), directed by Robert Wise, and a burned-out, violent cop in Nicholas Ray's *On Dangerous Ground* (1952). Ryan's sharp facial features seemed tailor-made for such roles. As the ingrained lines became more pronounced over time, Ryan was cast in more nefarious and irredeemable roles, like that of antihero Reno Smith in John Sturges's *Bad Day at Black Rock* (1954). A film critic once said of Ryan's face: it lacks pain as much as it does smoothness. His unusual acting range established him in Hollywood as a perfect "good bad guy" – the more wicked the character, the more Ryan shone in the role. Such was the case when he played James Stewart's nemesis in Anthony Mann's Western *The Naked Spur* (1953). Ryan could run the moral gamut within a single role with the greatest of ease, simultaneously eliciting both the sympathy and disgust of the audience. He did a remarkable job of this in Max Ophüls's *Caught* (1949), in which he plays millionaire Smith Ohlrig, a man who swears his love to a humble department store model only to treat her like a caged animal shortly after marrying her. At the age of 63, Ryan died of cancer in New York, just one year after his wife of many years also lost her life to the disease. He made a total of 77 pictures over the course of his 33-year acting career.

PURPLE NOON

PLEIN SOLEIL / DELITTO IN PIENO SOLE

1960 – FRANCE / ITALY – 116 MIN.
DIRECTOR RENÉ CLÉMENT (1913–1996)
SCREENPLAY RENÉ CLÉMENT, PAUL GÉGAUFF, based
on the novel *The Talented Mr. Ripley*
by PATRICIA HIGHSMITH
DIRECTOR OF PHOTOGRAPHY HENRI DECAË
EDITING FRANÇOISE JAVET MUSIC NINO ROTA
PRODUCTION RAYMOND HAKIM, ROBERT HAKIM
for PARIS FILM, PARITALIA, TITANUS
STARRING ALAIN DELON (Tom Ripley), MAURICE RONET
(Philippe Greenleaf), MARIE LAFORÊT (Marge Duval),
ERNO CRISA (Riccordi), ELVIRA POPESCU
(Mrs. Popova), FRANK LATIMORE (O'Brien),
BILLY KEARNS (Freddy Miles), LILY ROMANELLI
(Housekeeper), AVE NINCHI (Signora Gianna);
NERIO BERNARDI (Agency Director)

"Vous me tuez ... Vous voilà riche."

Why should only others enjoy the good life? What kind of man do you have to be to share the luxurious lifestyle of the rich and beautiful? In the same year that Federico Fellini's *La dolce vita* (1960) conquered the movie theaters, another film approached the topic from its darker side. If Fellini's alter ego Marcello Mastroianni (1924–1996) was in danger of losing his identity amongst the starlets and the pleasures of the senses, Tom Ripley has no identity to lose; and so he takes somebody else's, after murdering the previous owner.

Clément's film is also set in Rome, in and around the Via Veneto. The Americans Philippe Greenleaf (Maurice Ronet) and Tom Ripley (Alain Delon)

enjoy the Italian lifestyle in the most expensive and exclusive cafés. Money is no obstacle, for Philippe's old man, a filthy-rich tycoon, is paying for everything. In fact, Philippe's father has hired Tom to persuade his son to come home. But the good-for-nothing Philippe is having none of it. Tom envies him his monthly checks, his worry-free life and the love of his beautiful girlfriend Marge (Marie Laforêt). When Mr. Greenleaf Sr. declares the mission has failed, what had been a vague idea becomes an actual plan: Tom kills his snobbish companion and takes on his identity. The footloose survival artist Tom Ripley becomes Philippe Greenleaf, the cosmopolitan son of a millionaire.

"Against some sparkling backgrounds of the blue Thyrrhenian Sea, a fishing port on the Gulf of Salerno and the tree-shaded avenues of Rome, French director René Clément has done the incongruous thing of unfolding a murder thriller that is as fascinating as it is dazzlingly beautiful." *The New York Times*

This cold-blooded murder is only a preview to Tom's real task and vocation: the masquerade, which is always on the verge of being uncovered. He imitates Philippe's voice, forges his signature, and types letters on the dead man's typewriter. Further precautions are necessary: Tom has to change hotel constantly, avoid unwanted encounters and commit a second murder – for Philippe's pal Freddy Miles (Billy Kearns) has seen through his little game. Getting rid of the body turns out to be a literally massive problem; but no one will ever pin the murder on Tom Ripley, for everyone knows that the killer was named Philippe Greenleaf.

Mediterranean savoir-vivre, the sun reflected on bronzed bodies, and the music of Fellini's composer Nino Rota: this is the deceptively pleasant face of an exceptionally intense psycho thriller that explores the dark abyss of the human soul. Who is Tom Ripley? Is it narcissism, greed or sheer immorality that drives him to merge his identity with that of another man? Is there a homoerotic element in all this? Certainly, Marge remains a strangely pale and undefined figure in comparison to the two men.

Much more revealing is an embarrassing scene at the start of the film, when Philippe discovers Tom posing in front of a mirror, dressed in Philippe's clothes. It's an intellectual pleasure to compare this movie with Patricia Highsmith's novel and the successful remake, *The Talented Mr. Ripley* (1999). In each movie version, we meet a different Ripley, a different Philippe, a different Marge. In Minghella's version, Matt Damon is a Ripley

1   That glint in his eye: and who should be the wiser?
    In one of his first major roles, Alain Delon commits
    a little murder under the sun.

2   Starboard side: wealthy playboy Philippe Greenleaf
    (Maurice Ronet) and his charming girlfriend Marge
    Duval (Marie Laforêt) make Tom go green with
    envy.

3   The last supper: Philippe initially gets a real kick
    out of Tom's plan, but the fun doesn't stop there.

4   The deed is done: Tom takes command of the
    helm, disposing of the physical evidence and
    assimilates his corpse's lucrative identity upon
    reaching shore.

"Hollywood has forgotten that the creepiest movies are those that quietly crawl under your skin, making you look at your neighbor and nervously wonder what's going on in his head. Modern thrillers are all action and gore, but the 1960 French film *Purple Noon*, which has just been re-released, is a thriller of the old school, its horror unfolding slowly with every quiet conversation." *The Washington Post*

PATRICIA HIGHSMITH Alfred Hitchcock once claimed he had never been able to work well with writers who specialized, as he did, in horror, thrills, or suspense. He was referring in particular to his adaptation of Patricia Highsmith's first novel, *Strangers on a Train* (1951). His scriptwriter Raymond Chandler struggled to make anything of the novel, which he described as silly and lacking in credibility, and was later replaced. Despite this difficult birth, it eventually became one of Hitchcock's best films, focusing on a fatal male friendship and a bizarre theory: two people agree to perform each other's murders. While the Hitchcock film only hinted at possible homoerotic undertones, Anthony Minghella's version of *The Talented Mr. Ripley* (1999) was considerably less hesitant in this respect.

A native Texan, Patricia Highsmith (1921–1995) was always more popular in Europe than in the United States. Many of Highsmith's psychologically insightful novels – there are more than 20 of them – are set in her adopted home country of France. They inspired numerous film adaptations, particularly by French and German directors. Wim Wenders took *Ripley's Game* and made *The American Friend* (*Der amerikanische Freund* / *L'Ami américain*, 1977), with Dennis Hopper playing Tom Ripley. Hans W. Geissendörfer adapted two of her novels: *The Glass Cell* (*Die gläserne Zelle*, 1977) and *Edith's Diary* (*Ediths Tagebuch*, 1983), followed by Claude Chabrol with *Cry of the Owl* (*Le Cri du hibou*, 1987). The Chabrol film was remade in 2009 by Jamie Thraves. Filmmakers clearly loved Patricia Highsmith's work, something she acknowledged with detached amusement. The Queen of Crime died in Locarno in February 1995.

5

6

5   Tom makes sure an eyewitness won't live to see
    the light of day.

6   Erotic yet expendable: in director Clément's hands,
    Marge's character is little more than a hot body.

7   He plays her like a violin: but as a guitar player,
    Marge remains oblivious to Philippe's grim fate.

8   Decanter and deflower her: with the "transforma-
    tion" complete, Tom takes possession of all that is
    rightfully his. And Marge just comes with house.

driven by fears and dark instincts; in *Purple Noon*, Alain Delon's Ripley is cool, unruffled and elegant. Quietly conscious of his own superiority, he can bear with equanimity the humiliations visited upon him by Philippe. And although each of his two murders may have been due to a momentary lapse of self-control, the deceptions that follow are planned right down to the tiniest detail. Highsmith's Ripley was a seductive swindler who simply couldn't be caught — much to the pleasure of her readers, who looked forward to the Ripley novels that would follow. In this respect, René Clément, one of the most celebrated directors of the postwar French cinema, was a little less brave than the novelist. Yet although the ending does disappoint, it is served up with the same almost unbearable suspense as the rest of the film.

PB

PEEPING TOM

1960 – GREAT BRITAIN – 101 MIN.
DIRECTOR MICHAEL POWELL (1905–1990)
SCREENPLAY LEO MARKS DIRECTOR OF PHOTOGRAPHY OTTO HELLER
EDITING NOREEN ACKLAND MUSIC BRIAN EASDALE,
ANGELA MORLEY, FREDDIE PHILLIPS
PRODUCTION MICHAEL POWELL for ANGLO-AMALGAMATED
PRODUCTIONS, MICHAEL POWELL (THEATRE)
STARRING KARLHEINZ BÖHM (Mark Lewis),
MOIRA SHEARER (Vivian), ANNA MASSEY
(Helen Stephens), MAXINE AUDLEY (Mrs. Stephens),
BRENDA BRUCE (Dora), ESMOND KNIGHT
(Arthur Baden), PAMELA GREEN (Milly, the model),
MARTIN MILLER (Doctor Rosan), BARTLETT MULLINS
(Mr. Peters), JACK WATSON (Chief Inspector Gregg)

"Whatever I photograph – I always lose!"

Whenever the movies show us eyes in close-up, we're confronted with questions about the nature of visual perception and filmic representation. When the open razor sliced through the eye in Buñuel and Dalí's *An Andalusian Dog* (*Un Chien andalou*, 1929), it also cut through the audience's habits of perception, which had been formed in the theater at a safe distance from the stage. Many spectators found the notorious sliced-eyeball scene literally impossible to watch, for what they were seeing was their own still-innocent moviegoer's eye, attacked as they wallowed in the cinematic illusion. *Peeping Tom* operates in the same field of visual trespass, although it intrudes on the spectator's senses less harshly than the surrealist shocker.

The film begins with a close-up of a human eye – closed, as if the person it belongs to were dreaming. Then it snaps opens like a camera shutter and stares horror-struck from the screen. This eye is a filmic emblem. It introduces a complex constellation of perceptions, in which the spectator will participate in a highly unusual manner. The eye that fills the screen also stares at the spectator like a camera lens, returning his interested gaze. The watcher is being watched: the spectator – a voyeur, a Peeping Tom – is himself under observation.

In a separate introductory section before the titles sequence, a slow zoom draws the spectator into the lens of a 16-millimeter amateur film camera, half-hidden under a young man's coat. Then the point of view changes: we're now walking towards a prostitute; the camera's crosshairs disfigure the frame. The streetwalker takes us with her to her room. We have become the eye of the camera. And as the woman undresses, the camera moves slowly towards her. Terrified, she raises her hands to her face, and screams. And the camera keeps rolling.

For almost 20 years, critics either ignored *Peeping Tom* or vilified it. From a contemporary perspective, it's hard to understand why. Not until 1979 was the film rehabilitated, when Martin Scorsese and Paul Schrader presented it at the New York Film Festival and placed it on a list of their "guilty pleasures." Better late than never, one might say; but for Michael Powell, it was definitely too late. Since the London premiere of *Peeping Tom* in 1960, his reputation had been ruined. The critics had simply been unable or unwilling to understand the film, ignoring the clear thematic parallels between the eye (of the camera) and the "I" of the killer, the director, and the spectator. "I, the eye": it's this that provides the key to the conflict-ridden personality of Mark

2

1 Make love to the camera: it's about the only thing Mark Lewis (Karlheinz Böhm) shares a tender moment with.

2 Smile for the birdie: Helen Stephens (Anna Massey) is horrified to discover what lies beyond Mark's bashful veneer. Her disgust, however, is tempered by concern.

3 Self-inflicted punishment or just posing? Mark serves as his own stand-in to calculate the perfect angle for photographing mortal fear.

4 Jack the rip-roaring photographer: like most men in his field, Mark only selects a certain type of individual to partake in his art projects – namely, prostitutes, cover girls, and actresses.

"Martin Scorsese once said that this movie, and Federico Fellini's *8 1/2*, 'contain all that can be said about directing.' The Fellini film is about the world of deals and scripts and show biz, and the Powell is about the deep psychological process at work when a filmmaker tells his actors to do as he commands, while he stands in the shadows and watches." *Chicago Sun-Times*

Lewis (Karlheinz Böhm), the shy, film-obsessed assistant cameraman whose traumatic childhood made him a voyeur and a murderer.

The little 16 mm film camera that accompanies Mark everywhere he goes is literally a deadly weapon. When he has found a victim, he moves towards her, filming all the while; then he flips up a leg of the tripod, which he has converted into a deadly stiletto, and stabs. And it's not enough for him to see and film the death struggle of his petrified victims: he also confronts them with their fear by holding up a parabolic mirror, so that the victims can see themselves dying. As he says to Helen (Anna Massey) at one point: "Do

you know what the most frightening thing in the world is?" The answer, we learn, is fear itself.

Helen, a novice author of children's books, is the only human being he can trust. The pathologically shy son of a renowned psychologist, Mark had himself been the victim of an inhuman form of voyeurism, for his father's lust for knowledge had known few limits: in a long series of experiments on fear, he had placed the boy in nightmarish situations and filmed his reactions.

Night after night, Mark watches his own homemade snuff movies, but they cannot solve his conflicts or straighten his twisted soul. The victims' final

5   Mark collapses at Helen's side and dies while she lies unconscious on the floor. If Helen thought Mark was shocking before, she's in for a rude awakening.

6   Neatly partitioned lifestyle: Mark's darkroom and archives are set off from the rest of his apartment. Even though she hasn't seen them yet, Helen senses that Mark's artsier shots might not exactly suit her taste.

7   Needle point: Mark tweaks his tripod to hold his victims in place while "capturing" what he believes is the ultimate in authenticity on film.

CELLULOID PSYCHOPATHS Psychotic killers have served as stock characters in movies since the advent of the motion picture camera and are among the most reliable audience magnets. We could start with Robert Wiene's *The Cabinet of Dr. Caligari* (*Das Cabinet des Dr. Caligari*, 1920), where a homicidal maniac wreaks havoc on the world, causing a shroud of terror to descend upon society. This classic film illustrates just how suitable the device is to blur the borders between reality and the imagination, by visually externalizing the inner dialogue of the protagonists. The condition in which the psychopath finds himself, at least on the big screen, usually involves dealing with a split personality comprised of a dark doppelganger hidden behind an unassuming façade. This lends itself nicely to narrative cinematic devices and allows for plenty of tricks and twists on audience expectations. One could argue that the prototype for the killer who lurks behind the mask of normality is the Norman Bates character (played by Anthony Perkins), from Alfred Hitchcock's *Psycho* (1960). Because all these individuals are dominated by bloodlust as they detach themselves from reality, wild eroticism pairs well with their antisocial behavior. Such was the case in Harold Becker's 1989 picture *Sea of Love*. Lastly, unsavories with eerily voyeuristic tendencies (as in Michael Powell's *Peeping Tom*, 1960) are often found among people who cannot distinguish between reality and fantasy. They might therefore be described as suitable counterparts to cinema spectators.

terror is finally just a sequence of film in a rattling projector. It's never enough. In order to free himself from his trauma and lend some meaning to his life through the medium of his "art," Mark ultimately chooses to kill himself – and to leave a photographic record of his own extinction. He attaches his murderous apparatus to a cupboard and walks towards it.

On the short path to his death, he captures the story of his own life in a series of photos shot with a self-timer: from the abused boy he has always remained to the now-dying adult. And perversely, he's keeping a kind of promise: for Helen had wanted such a series of "magic photos" to illustrate

her first children's book to be accepted for publication. No doubt she had had something rather different in mind.

Peeping Tom is a film that does what it sets out to do, staring unflinchingly into the abyss of the soul and the cinema, and reflecting upon what it sees there. It is neither self-consciously avant-garde nor timidly subject to the dictates of taste, following only its own dramaturgical laws. And as a study of filmmaking itself, *Peeping Tom* has a positively timeless quality.

SR

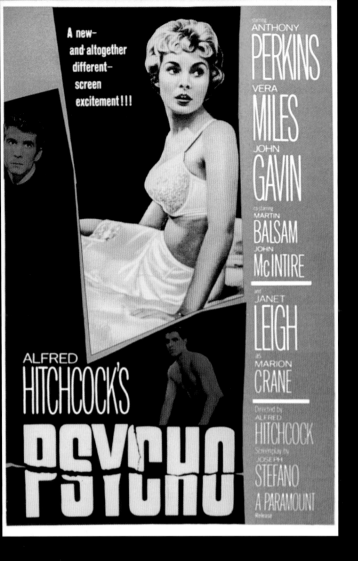

PSYCHO

1960 – USA – 109 MIN.
DIRECTOR ALFRED HITCHCOCK (1899–1980)
SCREENPLAY JOSEPH STEFANO, based on the novel
of the same name by ROBERT BLOCH
DIRECTOR OF PHOTOGRAPHY JOHN L. RUSSELL
EDITING GEORGE TOMASINI
MUSIC BERNARD HERRMANN
PRODUCTION ALFRED HITCHCOCK for
SHAMLEY PRODUCTIONS INC.
STARRING ANTHONY PERKINS (Norman Bates),
JANET LEIGH (Marion Crane), VERA MILES (Lila Crane),
JOHN GAVIN (Sam Loomis), JOHN MCINTIRE
(Al Chambers), MARTIN BALSAM (Milton Arbogast),
LURENE TUTTLE (Mrs. Chambers),
SIMON OAKLAND (Doctor Richmond),
PATRICIA HITCHCOCK (Caroline),
MORT MILLS (Policeman)

"Mother, she's just a stranger!"

It's what you might call a *twisted* fate. Marion Crane's (Janet Leigh) illicit affair with the married Sam Loomis (John Gavin) awakens deviant impulses within her. Entrusted with 40,000 dollars in company funds, she promptly invests in the future, making off with a sum that will allow her to start a new life with Sam. But the cops are on to her, and Marion thinks twice about executing her plan. The choice, however, isn't hers: a storm forces Marion to seek sanctuary at a remote motel, where a relaxing shower ends as a bloodbath. The murderess, it seems, suspected the overnight guest of making advances toward her son, the motel's introverted manager Norman Bates (Anthony Perkins), and decided to nip danger in the bud. Attempting to cover up his mother's regrettable actions, Bates wipes the scene clean, stuffs Marion's corpse into her car, and sinks the vehicle in a swamp – 40 grand and all.

Then the real investigation begins. Despite all their hard work, the gruesome twosome don't get to close shop just yet. Sam, Marion's sister Lila (Vera Miles), and a private detective named Arbogast (Martin Balsam) come in search of the missing woman and the stolen funds. Sticking his nose in the wrong place, Arbogast is also disposed of by the deranged old lady, who apparently resides in the seclusion of the familial estate overlooking the motel. After Sam and Lila wise up to the horrors of the Bates mansion, they are dumbfounded to learn from the authorities that Mrs. Bates has been dead for a good ten years ...

Psycho is undoubtedly Hitchcock's boldest film – although the critical uproar of the time, fixated on a close-up of a toilet bowl, seemed to miss the point. Tauntingly, the master of suspense plays with the viewer's expectations time and again: mercilessly killing off his leading lady in the first third of the picture, and introducing plot elements like the suitcase of money that amount to nothing more than red herrings. Arguably, the entire plot is a network of setups and visual suggestions meant to keep the audience unnerved until the

1 Who? *Moi?* Mama's boy Norman Bates (Anthony Perkins) fears the gaze of foreign eyes – especially when they belong to his attractive hotel guests.

2 Heartbreak hotel: the Bates Mansion, a set-piece replica of an existing building, is among the most readily recognizable homes ever to grace the screen. The original is located in the sixth circle of hell.

3 Behind bars and closed doors: all the conniving Marion Crane (Janet Leigh) ever wanted in life was to run off and elope with lover Sam Loomis (John Gavin). And she would have, had it not been for one little, but fatal, mistake. But then you only get to make one now darling, don't you?

curtain falls. And the seamless manner in which these subversive images undermine the story and suck it into the background makes *Psycho* more reminiscent of an experimental art-house piece than a Hollywood blockbuster. The most striking example of this is the shower scene, where a total of 70 camera shots fill 45 seconds of scream time – the hard cuts between shots and Bernard Herrmann's screeching score viscerally tuning us to each stab of the killer's knife. The scene was so shocking that Hitchcock abstained

from the further inclusion of similarly violent displays in the rest of the film for he clearly already had the audience just where he wanted them.

Equally remarkable is how ingeniously the filmmaker and cinematographer John L. Russell come up with excuses not to reveal the face of Norman's mother until just before the end. We never suspect that Arbogast's stairwell death is shot from a bird's eye for anything other than artistic reasons.

"What makes *Psycho* immortal, when so many films are already half-forgotten as we leave the theater, is that it connects directly with our fears: Our fears that we might impulsively commit a crime, our fears of the police, our fears of becoming the victim of a madman, and of course our fears of disappointing our mothers." *Chicago Sun-Times*

3

GEORGE TOMASINI Together with cinematographer Robert Burks, and composer Bernard Herrmann, editor George Tomasini was one of Alfred Hitchcock's key collaborators. In the decade from 1954 to 1964, George Tomasini (1909–1964) edited nine films for Hitchcock: *Rear Window* (1954), *To Catch a Thief* (1955), *The Man Who Knew Too Much* (1956), *The Wrong Man* (1956), *Vertigo* (1958), *North by Northwest* (1959), *Psycho* (1960), *The Birds* (1963), and *Marnie* (1964). In effect, he edited some of the most iconic sequences in Hitchcock's oeuvre, and brought to life Hitchcock's ideal of "pure cinema," where story, character, and effect are conveyed purely by image and sound, without dialogue. As Paul Monaco wrote in *The Sixties*, "Tomasini's most important work with Hitchcock was the memorable shower scene in *Psycho* (1960). Its aesthetic and dramatic accomplishment was achieved largely through the editor's skill. The completed 45 second sequence that Hitchcock originally storyboarded was compiled by Tomasini from footage shot over several days that utilized a total of over 70 camera setups. From that mass of footage, Tomasini selected 60 different shots, some of them very short, through which he elected to rely heavily on the techniques of 'associative editing.'" It is easy to recall the visceral effect of the shower scene in *Psycho*, or the dust-cropper attack in *North by Northwest*, but it is something else entirely to capture the languid ambiance as James Stewart spies on his neighbors in *Rear Window*, or to show Stewart's lusty obsession in *Vertigo* as he sees the transformed Kim Novak in a hotel room for the first time, or to hold for a few seconds longer on the impenetrable face of Henry Fonda in *The Wrong Man* as his life collapses around him. It is in the latter moments that Tomasini shows the difference between skill and art.

"After Hitchcock's suspense pictures and romantic adventure stories could he come up with a shocker, acceptable to mainstream American audiences, which still carried the spine-tingling voltage of foreign presentations such as *Diabolique*? The answer is an enthusiastic yes. He blended the real and the unreal in fascinating proportions and punctuated his film with several quick, grisly and unnerving surprises."

San Francisco Chronicle

Psycho's narrative takes just as many experimental liberties. Much like in a television drama, lengthy dialogue clarifies plot and subtext. Of prime importance is Norman and Marion's conversation at the motel, in which a bond is established between the killer and his victim. It is here that the viewer learns of Norman's interest in taxidermy, with the stuffed birds themselves acting as an eerie congress of witnesses: no amount of money can make them divulge the grisly acts they've seen. These petrified beasts, and the peephole that Norman uses to spy on Marion as she undresses, are reminders of the camera's voyeuristic nature.

Everywhere we turn, *Psycho* confronts us with visual analogies of watching and being watched: from the eyelike shower drain into which Marion's blood disappears, to the smirking toilet seat that stares us down in one of the final shots. And there is no misunderstanding the accompanying dialogue: "They're probably watching me. Well, let them. Let them see what kind of person I am. I hope they are watching. They'll see. They'll see and they'll know."

It's more than just a coincidental choice of words Hitchcock placed in Bates's mouth. In truth, the soliloquy is as much a personal confession on the part of the director as of its speaker. At the peak of his career, Hitch couldn't have picked a more poignant moment to make it. For beyond the façade of terror, what is *Psycho* if not a great master's artistic manifesto?

SH

4 Drowned out screams: how many cuts does it take to kill Marion Crane? Hitchcock used approximately 70. Urban legend would have you believe that renowned cinema graphic artist, Saul Bass, staged *Psycho*'s shower scene. But it's a bloody lie!

5 Checking in and checking out: Norman is among the few hotel managers who hate having guests.

6 Don't tell mama: Mother will be livid if she finds out who's been sleeping in one of Norman's beds.

SHOOT THE PIANO PLAYER

TIREZ SUR LE PIANISTE

1960 – FRANCE – 82 MIN.
DIRECTOR FRANÇOIS TRUFFAUT (1932–1984)
SCREENPLAY FRANÇOIS TRUFFAUT, MARCEL MOUSSY,
based on the novel *Down There* by DAVID GOODIS
DIRECTOR OF PHOTOGRAPHY RAOUL COUTARD
EDITING CÉCILE DECUGIS, CLAUDINE BOUCHÉ
MUSIC GEORGES DELERUE
PRODUCTION PIERRE BRAUNBERGER for
LES FILMS DE LA PLÉIADE
STARRING CHARLES AZNAVOUR (Charlie Kohler / Edouard
Saroyan), MARIE DUBOIS (Léna), NICOLE BERGER
(Thérésa), MICHÈLE MERCIER (Clarisse), ALBERT REMY
(Chico), CLAUDE MANSARD (Momo), DANIEL
BOULANGER (Ernest), SERGE DAVRI (Plyne), RICHARD
KANAYAN (Fido), JEAN-JACQUES ASLANIAN
(Richard), CLAUDE HEYMANN (Lars Schmeel,
Impresario), BOBY LAPOINTE (Singer), CATHERINE LUTZ
(Mammy), ALEX JOFFÉ (Passerby)

"Scared ... I'm scared. Oh shit, I'm scared."

Pitch-black night. A man rushes through the streets of the city, pursued by the headlights of a car. He crashes into a lamppost and falls to the ground, dazed. A second man approaches him, slaps him a couple of times and helps him to his feet. Suddenly they're engaged in a lively discussion about women, and about the pros and cons of marriage. Eventually, the two men shake hands and go their separate ways – and the fugitive resumes his getaway.

This grotesque opening scene sets the tone for the entire film. In *Shoot the Piano Player*, François Truffaut takes playful delight in disregarding the conventions of the cinema – and it's this quality, perhaps more than

any other, that makes it the most typically *Nouvelle Vague* of all Truffaut's movies.

The figurehead of the New Cinema had good reasons for stating his position so emphatically. His debut, *The 400 Blows* (*Les Quatre Cents Coups*, 1959) had been sensationally successful, and some critics were suggesting that he himself was now part of the establishment. In a clear signal that his second film was directed mainly at a cinematically educated audience, Truffaut reacted by choosing to adapt a noir novel by the former Hollywood screenwriter David Goodis.

1   High notes: Clarisse (Michèle Mercier) strips
    behind a crepe paper dressing shade and fills
    Charlie's sheets with beautiful music in a cheeky
    sequence that plays on cinema's dated con-
    ventions.

2   88 keys: chanson singer Charles Aznavour plays
    Charlie Kohler, the melancholy piano player with
    a cryptic repertoire.

3   Better on stage than at intermission: Thérésa
    (Nicole Berger) is destroyed by her infidelity, even
    though it was all for her husband's career.

The impenetrable darkness and the incredible tempo of the opening are enough to mark out *Shoot the Piano Player* as a homage to the great American B movie. The doomed protagonist is also a kind of film noir antihero: following the suicide of his wife, Charlie Kohler (Charles Aznavour), a once-famous piano virtuoso, has chosen to embrace obscurity and is now working as an anonymous piano player in a seedy Paris dancehall. When the waitress Léna (Marie Dubois) confesses that she loves him, it seems that the shy man is being offered a new beginning, a second chance. But the jealous bar manager is not the only obstacle: there's also a pair of gangsters to deal

with, after Charlie's criminal brother Chico (Albert Remy) takes refuge at the piano player's place.

What attracted Truffaut to Goodis's novel was not just the crime element but the sentimental and personal aspect of the story. To bring this out more clearly, Truffaut drew on other genres — comedy, melodrama, even the Western — and in this way, he cast an ironic light on the clichés of the crime drama. Thus the gangster Momo (Claude Mansard) and his erotomaniac buddy Ernest (Daniel Boulanger) do their best to look seriously dangerous, but the effect is comic, for it seems such a childish pose. First impressions can

DAVID GOODIS The bleakest of the noir fiction writers, David Goodis (1917–1967) hit the big time with *Dark Passage* (1946), about a man who escapes from prison to prove his innocence but, at the end, continues to be a fugitive from justice. It became a best seller, and a Humphrey Bogart / Lauren Bacall film in 1947. Goodis got a gig as a Hollywood screenwriter, then it all went wrong. Goodis had married Elaine Astor in 1943. She left after a year and Goodis could not forget her. She was the erotic obsession that haunted his subsequent novels.

In 1950 Goodis returned to Philadelphia to live with his parents, and began writing the kind of low-life novels for which he has been justifiably praised. The best of these are *The Burglar* (1953), *The Moon in the Gutter* (1953), *Black Friday* (1954), *Street of No Return* (1954), and *Down There* (1956), famously filmed by François Truffaut in 1960 as *Shoot the Piano Player* (*Tirez sur le pianiste*, 1960).

The Goodis central character is hell-bent on self-destruction. There is no redemption for his sins. The squalid environment reflects his interior self-hate and confusion. Goodis's work is respected in France (where there have been at least eight film adaptations), and has gained an increasing number of admirers in America, including film director Paul Thomas Anderson (*Magnolia* [1999]; *There will be Blood* [2007]), who has cited David Goodis as a literary influence.

"Thankfully, Truffaut was not so stuffy as to forget that the best movies can be funny and clever."

Edinburgh University Film Society

3

4   Fans or fanatics? Momo and Ernest (Claude Mansard and Daniel Boulanger, respectively) kidnap Charlie's brother Fido (Richard Kanayan) to get the piano player's attention. Although the gangsters are depicted as comical numbskulls, they are just as deadly as their sly counterparts.

5   And if you're real good, I'll make you feel good: Charlie covers Clarisse's most pleasurables and beats the censors to the punch.

6   A caper born of sweet caresses: the jealous Plyne (Serge Davri) requests a set of fisticuffs from a piano player who is all too happy to oblige.

7   The curtain falls on love: the ticket to Charlie's heart comes at a steep price – death. Marie Dubois as Léna.

"The rules of the genre are sacrificed on the altar of the director's insatiable curiosity about people and things. This is great, great cinema." *Libération*

be deceptive, though. The final showdown takes place outside a mountain cabin in the snow. It looks like a fairy tale, until some very real bullets are fired; and suddenly, Charlie's hopes are stone dead.

As the plot becomes ever more unreal, the film becomes increasingly reflective; and it meditates not only on the cinema, but on loneliness and the way men and women relate to each other. Truffaut himself described *Shoot the Piano Player* as the story of a shy man and his relationship to three very different women. These represent the three *kinds* of woman a man can encounter in his lifetime: there is Léna, the vibrant heroine of the film; Thérésa (Nicole Berger), Charlie's wife, who sacrifices herself for the sake of his career; and Clarisse (Michèle Mercier), a sensuous and self-confident prostitute who really wants nothing more than a home and family. They're the first of many active and attractive female figures who came to typify Truffaut's films.

Here, however, they're more peripheral than central to the movie, for the focus is clearly on Charles Aznavour as Truffaut's alter ego. The piano player has the air of a melancholy outsider, a nowhere man, destined to remain homeless in the world. Charlie is essentially unsavable, for he cannot overcome his anxieties, cannot communicate with the women he loves. As Léna says, "Even when he's with someone, he's on his own." Only at the piano is Charlie capable of exposing his feelings. At the end of the movie, he's back in the bar, playing the same monotonous piece as at the beginning. His sad eyes are staring into empty space. He's playing for himself alone.

JH

CAPE FEAR

1962 – USA – 105 MIN.
DIRECTOR J. LEE THOMPSON (1914–2002)
SCREENPLAY JAMES R. WEBB, based on the novel
The Executioners by JOHN D. MACDONALD
DIRECTOR OF PHOTOGRAPHY SAMUEL LEAVITT
EDITING GEORGE TOMASINI
MUSIC BERNARD HERRMANN PRODUCTION SY BARTLETT
for MELVILLE-TALBOT PRODUCTIONS
STARRING GREGORY PECK (Sam Bowden),
ROBERT MITCHUM (Max Cady), POLLY BERGEN
(Peggy Bowden), LORI MARTIN (Nancy Bowden),
MARTIN BALSAM (Police Inspector Mark Dutton),
JACK KRUSCHEN (Dave Grafton), TELLY SAVALAS
(Charles Sievers), BARRIE CHASE (Diane Taylor),
PAUL COMI (Garner), JOHN MCKEE (Marconi)

"I'm gonna do something to you and your family that you ain't neva gonna forget."

The title sequence makes it pretty clear what kind of man we'll be dealing with: in a pale linen suit and a Panama hat, the cigar-puffing Max Cady (Robert Mitchum) swaggers through the streets of a small town in Georgia, casts a connoisseur's eye over two young women, and enters the courthouse. His passage is accompanied by the ominous music of Bernard Herrmann. Inside the building, he struts past a struggling court employee, ostentatiously indifferent to the lady's losing battle with a pile of law books, and addresses a black janitor as "Daddy." Max Cady is no gentleman, and he doesn't give a damn who knows it. Released after eight years in jail for assaulting a young woman, all he wants now is revenge on Sam Bowden (Gregory Peck), the lawyer who put him behind bars.

Mitchum's sheer physical presence in the role is impressive, and fearsome: for all his languid slowness, Cady never seems harmless or merely stupid. He has the brooding watchfulness of a dangerous wild animal, and his cool insolence is proof of how relaxed he is in his own potent physicality.

In one scene, he's being interrogated at the police station, and the Inspector (Martin Balsam) insists on a body search. Cady is forced to strip to his underpants. It's a procedure that's designed to humiliate and intimidate,

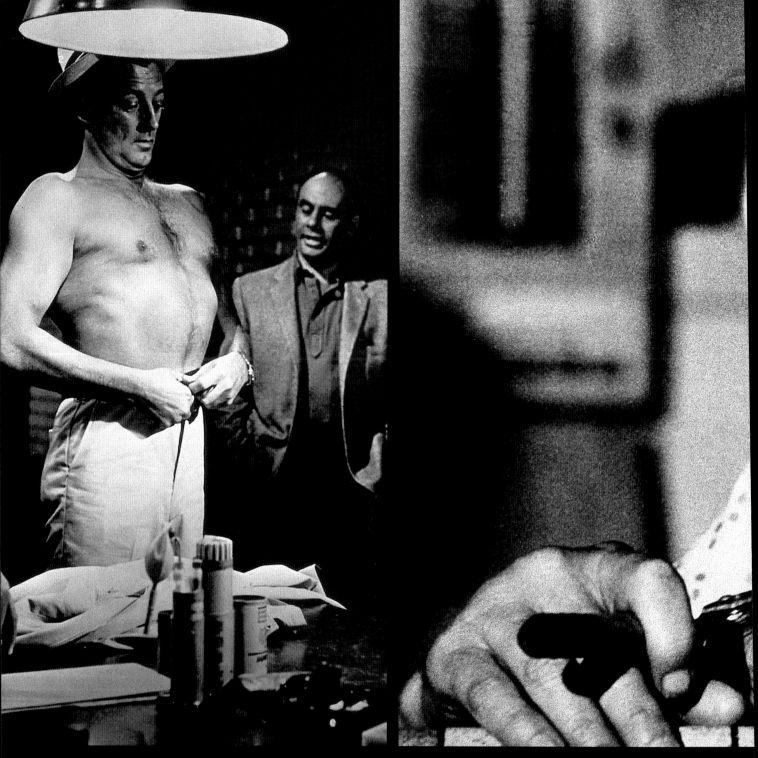

1   The winds of wanton lust: Max Cady (Robert Mitchum) terrorizes Peggy Bowden (Polly Bergen) and her entire family. Twenty years later these two would reunite, starring as husband and wife in Herman Wouk's *Winds of War* and *War and Remembrance* miniseries.

2   Clean as a whistle: a search of Cady's premises unmasks no incriminating evidence. Inspector Dutton (Martin Balsam) simply can't pin a thing on him.

3   Waiting for the fishies to take the bait: Cady knows full well that patience is the key in getting the Bowdens to bite.

"Mr. Thompson has directed in a steady and starkly sinister style. There is no waste motion, no fooling. Everything is sharp and direct. Menace quivers in the picture like a sneaky electrical charge." *The New York Times*

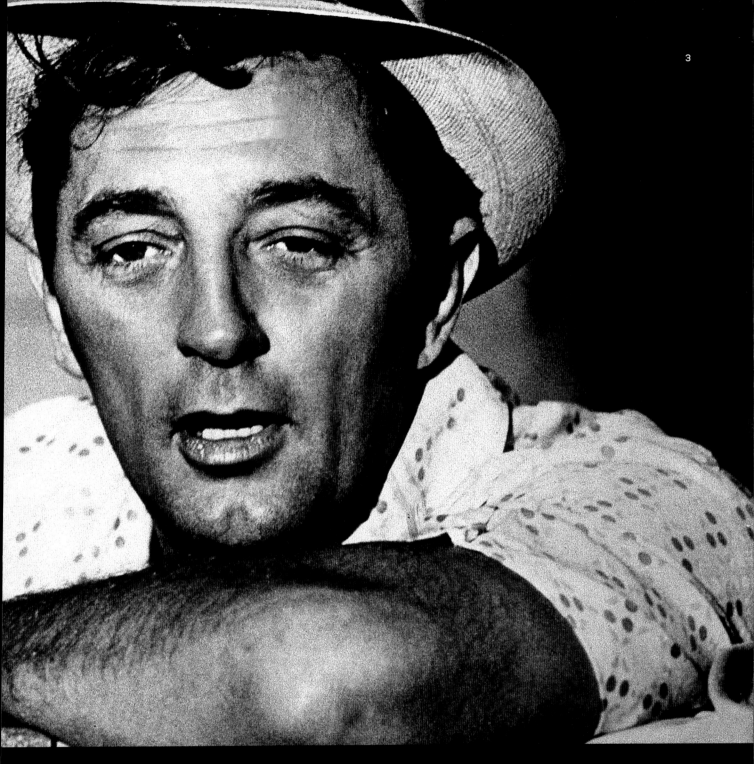

yet he stands there in his boxer shorts without a trace of embarrassment, his hands on his hips, his chest filling the room, and his hat still cheekily perched on his head. He looks twice as big as anyone else, and he appears practically invulnerable.

Cady's revenge on Bowden begins with some relatively unsubtle psychoterror. Simply by *being* there, by turning up in this town again, he unnerves the lawyer increasingly and scares his family witless. Cady is aware of exactly how far he can go; this is one former jailbird who knows the law, and he provokes and menaces his victim without ever doing anything demonstrably criminal.

In a series of tense scenes, director J. Lee Thompson skillfully evokes the growing paranoia of the terrorized family. As Bowden's daughter Nancy (Lori Martin) heads home after school, she catches a glimpse of the ex-jailbird approaching in the distance. Her panic increases until she cracks, runs and hides in the cellar of the school building; yet the man is still behind her, getting closer all the time … Finally, at the last moment, in a state of abject terror, Nancy scrambles out the window. As she races onto the street, we see that her "nemesis" was none other than the innocent janitor; but by this time, she has staggered straight into the arms of Max Cady.

His adversary Sam Bowden is first depicted as an upright, law-abiding citizen. It's a role that Gregory Peck has no trouble embodying to perfection, for he really was the personification of integrity and decent, liberal values. Yet Bowden's façade rapidly begins to crumble. Though the lawyer begins by insisting that a man cannot be locked up for a crime he just *might* possibly

4

"When Hollywood can draw on the most consummate artists available, both in front of and behind the camera, it's capable of producing a film like this: a terrifying depiction of how pitiless violence gradually invades the lives of an average American family." *Frankfurter Allgemeine Zeitung*

5

6

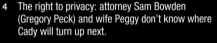
4   The right to privacy: attorney Sam Bowden
    (Gregory Peck) and wife Peggy don't know where
    Cady will turn up next.

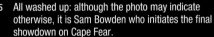
5   All washed up: although the photo may indicate
    otherwise, it is Sam Bowden who initiates the final
    showdown on Cape Fear.

6   Life on the line: Sam's plans to lure Cady into a
    trap have failed and Peggy's left to face the music.

7   Still off the hook: but if Max Cady means no harm,
    why does he trail the Bowden family's every
    move?

commit, he quickly responds to the pressure of Cady's threatening presence by calling the cops to his aid. As a result, Cady's life is made a misery: he's soon being arrested on an almost daily basis, though he's still done nothing to break the law.

In his attempts to free himself from this sadistic nuisance, Bowden deploys more and more dubious methods: he hires a private detective (Telly Savalas), who's ultimately unable to help him; he tries, unsuccessfully, to bribe Cady with money; and eventually, in his desperation, he sends a bunch of thugs to beat him up. In doing so, he risks losing his accreditation from the Bar Association and thereby the very basis of his existence.

Finally, in the dark waters of Cape Fear, the immovable object meets the unstoppable force. It's an explosion of violence, and only one of these men will survive it. The price of this survival is a nauseous recognition that the clear line between good and evil has vanished in a fog of ambiguity.   LP

SAM LEAVITT   Samuel E. Leavitt (1904–1984) served his apprenticeship from 1934 as a camera operator for cinematographer Joseph Ruttenberg at the Biograph Studio in the Bronx, and then later in Hollywood for Harry Stradling on *The Picture of Dorian Gray* (1944) and the film noir *Tension* (1949), among others. His first Hollywood film as director of photography was *The Thief* (1952), which was shot without dialogue and mostly on location in Washington (Library of Congress, Georgetown) and New York City (Central Park, Empire State Building, Times Square). After being nominated for a Golden Globe for *The Thief*, Leavitt found himself working for top directors like Stanley Kramer (*The Defiant Ones*, 1958; *Guess Who's Coming to Dinner*, 1967), and Don Siegel (*Crime in the Streets*, 1956), but worked mostly with Otto Preminger (*The Man with the Golden Arm*, 1955; *Anatomy of a Murder*, 1959). He was not always easy to work with, as he admitted when talking about filming *Crime in the Streets* with Don Siegel: "We had our differences on that picture and other pictures, but they were constructive differences. I don't care who it is, the biggest director or producer, if I have something to say, I talk back to them. That's why I don't get a great many pictures." He won an Oscar for *The Defiant Ones*, and was nominated for *Anatomy of a Murder* (1959) and *Exodus* (1960), but is remembered for his ability to move the camera through complex spaces and find resonant framings, which he did in film noirs like *The Crimson Kimono* (1959), *Seven Thieves* (1960), *Cape Fear* (1962), and *Brainstorm* (1965).

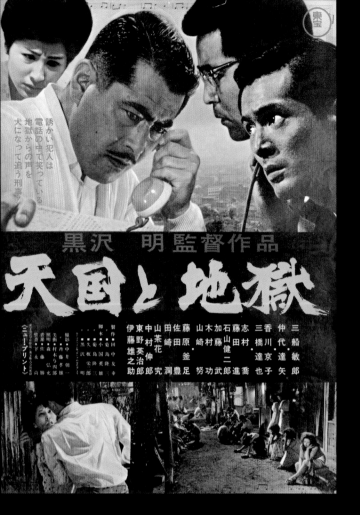

HIGH AND LOW
TENGOKU TO JIGOKU

1963 – JAPAN – 143 MIN.

DIRECTOR AKIRA KUROSAWA (1910–1998)
SCREENPLAY AKIRA KUROSAWA, EIJIRÔ HISAITA,
RYÛZÔ KIKUSHIMA, HIDEO OGUNI,
based on the novel *King's Ransom* by
ED MCBAIN [= SALVATORE LOMBINO]
DIRECTOR OF PHOTOGRAPHY ASAKAZU NAKAI,
TAKAO SAITÔ EDITING AKIRA KUROSAWA
MUSIC MASARU SATÔ PRODUCTION AKIRA KUROSAWA,
RYÛZÔ KIKUSHIMA, TOMOYUKI TANAKA
for TOHO COMPANY
STARRING TOSHIRÔ MIFUNE (Kingo Gondo),
TSUTOMO YAMAZAKI (Ginjirô Takeuchi / Kidnapper),
KYÔKO KAGAWA (Reiko, Gondo's wife),
TAKESHI KATÔ (Detective Nakao), KENJIRÔ ISHIYAMA
(Chief Detective "Bos'n" Taguchi), ISAO KIMURA
(Detective Arai), TAKASHI SHIMURA (Chief of
Investigation Section), TATSUYA MIHASHI
(Kawanishi, Gondo's secretary), YUTAKA SADA
(Aoki, Gondo's chauffeur),
TOSHIO EGI (Jun, Gondo's son)

> *"I could see your house and it was like looking up at heaven.
> I looked up at your house every day and somehow began to hate you.
> After awhile, hating you is what kept me going."*

High and Low, adapted by Akira Kurosawa from the novel *King's Ransom* by Ed McBain, is called *Heaven and Hell* in Japan and is a cinematic poem every bit as rousing as *Seven Samurai* (*Shichinin no samurai*, 1954), though on the surface the two films couldn't be more different. The seven were revealed in pure action – brandishing swords, riding horses, and firing arrows through the glittering torrential rains of a forest monsoon. Here the modern industrialist Kingo Gondo (Toshirô Mifune) must engage in a chess match of wits with an unseen attacker – a pitiless, intelligent kidnapper who has taken his little son. Except, wait a second, the villain grabbed the wrong boy by mistake; he's taken the chauffeur's son. Kingo is faced with gambling his life savings – monies he'd mustered to take charge of his own company, a deal in which timing is critical, without which he faces complete ruin – all to rescue another man's child. What follows is a uniquely structured marvel of moral shadow play.

For the first hour of the film, Kurosawa confines us to Mifune's lavish home. We move from room to room in an increasingly crowded suite of interior spaces – a palatial suite, by turns curtained and uncurtained, with a spectacular view of the city below – while Kingo sweats through the opening moves made by his tormenter. Then we leap – as if from a steaming sauna into ice-cold water – through a vigorous six-minute sequence in real time aboard a bullet train speeding across Yokohama. Somehow the kidnapper has learned exactly how much cash is at stake for Kingo. He has also demanded it be delivered in two briefcases of a size that – as it turns out – can be slipped with smooth precision through the four inches of space afforded by a lavatory window on that train. After, as we catch our breath and the chauffeur's son is safely returned, Kurosawa directs our attention to a sluggish, polluted riverbed in a slum. There we can see Mifune's grand house

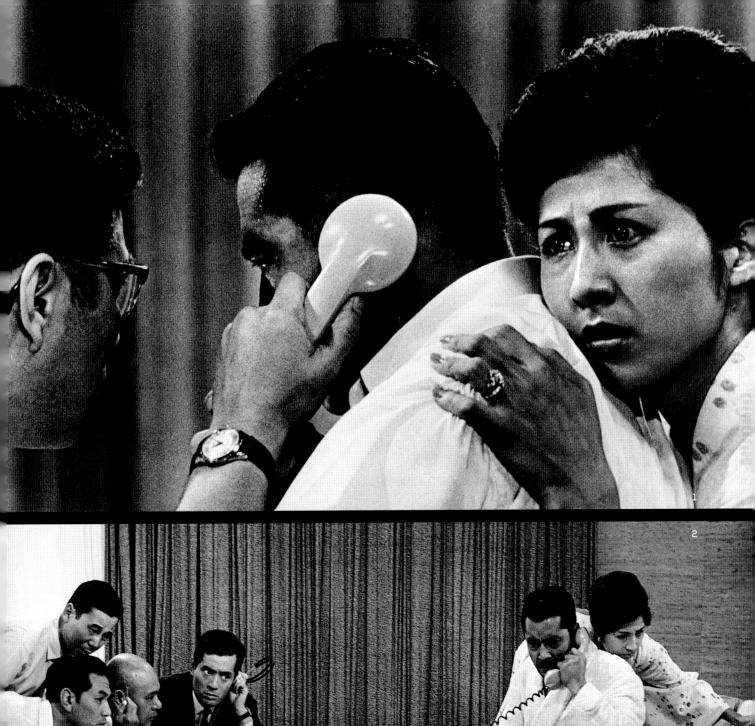

1 & 2   Entrepreneur Kingo Gondo (Toshirô Mifune) and his wife (Kyôko Kagawa) hear their son is kidnapped. Later they learn the victim is their chauffeur's son.

3   The police, led by Detective Nakao (Takeshi Katô, standing), so admire Kingo's sacrifice for another man's son that they go all-out in their search for the kidnapper.

4   "Starting all over already." Kingo, a shoemaker, breaks out his cobbler's tools to adjust the two slim leather briefcases needed for the kidnapper's cash.

"The self that Kurosawa is so eager to affirm cannot be found in any single character but lies in the relationality of the never-ending tension between hero and villain." *Mitsuhiro Yoshimoto, Kurosawa*

> "By losing everything, [Kingo] gains in the end. As he visits the kidnapper in prison, ...both are condemned to pay a price: that of being human." *Martin Scorsese*

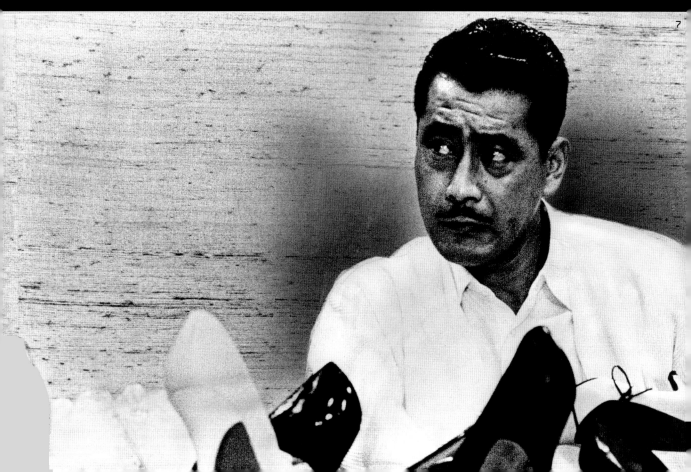

5 After the dazzling sequence on the train, detective "Bos'n" (Kenjirô Ishiyama, center) wrings his hands over the sadistic game the kidnapper is playing.

6 "Why should you and I hate each other?" Kingo is ruined, but sincerely wants to understand this kidnapper, Ginjiro Takeuchi (Tsutomo Yamazaki), caged in the final scene.

7 Prior to the kidnapping, Kingo is a brilliant and prosperous shoe designer on the verge of starting his own company.

reflected upside down in the water's rippling surface. Also mirrored there is the inverted figure of a solitary young man, walking alone. The intensity of his dejection and his visual relation to that house high above him give us a hint to his identity – he is the kidnapper – an inkling that is confirmed in the next sequence of scenes as we get to know and unexpectedly empathize with him.

Kurosawa has in the past attempted – with interesting if lesser results – to fashion an urban thriller (*Stray Dog*, 1949) and plumb psychological depths worthy of Dostoyevsky (*The Idiot*, 1951). In *High and Low* he suc-

ceeds not only at fusing but fulfilling these goals, and he makes it look effortless.

We discover the kidnapper is a medical student who cares little for money. (He is superbly played by Tsutomo Yamazaki, whom Kurosawa discovered for the role.) Although the kidnapper has kept his word and safely returned the chauffeur's son, Kingo has been ruined. The team of detectives – surprised by the wealthy fat cat's unexpected brave sacrifice, and admiring of him – are eager to see justice done. They trace the phone calls; their

"At the other end of the five-foot table, Mr. Kurosawa slowly took off his glasses and sat down. My eyes must have been ugly and impure, but his own eyes slowly and warmly looked back. He was prompting me in a non-judgmental manner ... I passed the audition. I'll never forget his soft eyes. I did it thanks to them." *Tsutomo Yamazaki*

11

8   Detectives Nakao and Bos'n comb the waterfront as the many stray clues knit together and their dragnet tightens.

9   Detectives Arai (Isao Kimura) and Bos'n charge into the kidnapper's seaside hideout, once it's been discovered by Kingo's chauffeur Aoki (Yutaka Sada, right).

10   Having a clue that their quarry is a medical student with access to drugs, the detectives prowl the glittering underworld of a significantly westernized Yokohama.

11   The kidnapper's abandoned car, caked with dust that clung to beads of moisture: it must have been parked seaside on the day of the crime.

search focuses on the slum. They find the dead bodies of the kidnapper's two helpers – both were drug addicts; the young doctor has killed them with a drug overdose – and the dragnet tightens as the detectives logically deduce just who in this world would have ready access to opiates. Kingo joins them in their hunt. At one point, he and the kidnapper even face each other by chance, though he is unaware. The younger man smugly assesses his former target at close range and asks him for a light.

Eventually a trap is sprung. The two enemies at last face each other in full mutual awareness. Kingo is without hatred, but curious. His antagonist is purely hateful – and refuses all compassion. "A death sentence means nothing to me," he declares. "I've been living in my own private hell for a long time. So I'm not afraid of going to hell." As a leaden barrier descends behind the glass wall separating them, Kingo is – in a sublime culminating shot – left alone with his own reflection.

Kurosawa's masterful composition, pace, and physical detail direct us, as the screen fades to black, to meditate alongside his protagonist on tragic mysteries of pride, envy, and a world "below" that he – formerly so high on his hill – once blindly mistook for a beautiful view.   FXF

JAPANESE NOIR When Jean-Luc Godard adopted the tactics of an American crime film for *Breathless* (*À bout de souffle*, 1960), the aim and the pleasure was a feat of style, an entertaining end in itself. When Kurosawa adapted Ed McBain's novel to a Japanese setting four years later, the feeling a viewer was left with cut much deeper. An "American idiom" will inevitably have not just ironic but tragic properties in a nation destroyed and rebuilt during a war with the United States less than 20 years earlier.

As one of Kurosawa's closer analysts, Mitsuhiro Yoshimoto, has put it: "Highways, the bullet train, and the Olympic Stadium are shown as signs of Japan's successful reconstruction and economic development ... at the same time, the persistent appearance of these symbols of economic recovery and technological advancement in Japanese films of the 1960s is also a sign of anxiety and uncertainty." Younger artists such as Seijun Suzuki (*Tokyo Drifter* [*Tôkyô nagaremono*, 1966], *Branded to Kill* [*Koroshi no rakuin*, 1967]) or Takeshi Kitano (*Violent Cop* [*Sono otoko, kyôbô ni tsuki*, 1989], *Sonatine* [1993]) embrace these transformations with an extroverted dash of rock 'n' roll fatalism – a sense of, "If you can't beat them, join them." There is an implicit poignancy and loss in this, despite the lightheartedness. Kurosawa by contrast takes on the inner conflict, the soul profoundly at odds with his or her own society that is the coiled mainspring of film noir. Kingo in *High and Low* (*Tengoku to jigoku*, 1963) hopes against hope to hang onto his hard-earned fortune – but at the same time he is a fascinated onlooker at his own undoing, as if he secretly suspects all along that such wealth is, at its depths, false. There is something movingly undefeated about the cruel young idealist who is working so hard to strip him of such illusions.

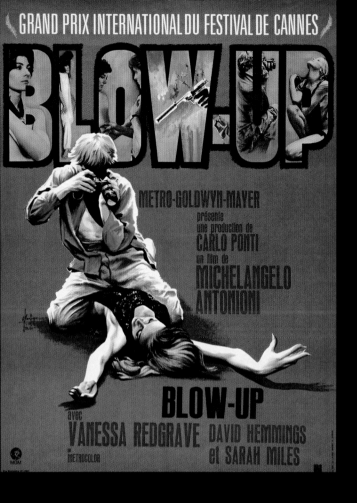

BLOWUP / BLOW-UP

1966 – GREAT BRITAIN – 111 MIN.
DIRECTOR MICHELANGELO ANTONIONI (1912–2007)
SCREENPLAY MICHELANGELO ANTONIONI,
TONINO GUERRA, EDWARD BOND, based on the the
short story *Las babas del diablo* by JULIO CORTÁZAR
DIRECTOR OF PHOTOGRAPHY CARLO DI PALMA
EDITING FRANK CLARKE MUSIC HERBIE HANCOCK,
THE YARDBIRDS PRODUCTION CARLO PONTI for PREMIER
STARRING DAVID HEMMINGS (Thomas),
VANESSA REDGRAVE (Jane), PETER BOWLES (Ron),
VERUSCHKA VON LEHNDORFF (Herself),
SARAH Miles (Patricia), JOHN CASTLE (Bill),
JANE BIRKIN (Teenager), GILLIAN HILLS
(Teenager), THE YARDBIRDS (Themselves)
IFF CANNES 1967 GOLDEN PALM for BEST FILM
(Michelangelo Antonioni)

Thomas: "Don't let's spoil everything, we've only just met."
Jane: "No, we haven't met. You've never seen me."

There's a mystery in these photos. Thomas (David Hemmings), a photographer, strokes his chin while examining some large prints he has hung up in his studio. He moves up closer to scrutinize one particular print, then dashes into his lab and exposes another sheet of paper, hangs this up in place of another print that had been part of the series, and takes a good long look at the entire series of images. Now he has it – the missing link in the chain. That morning, Thomas had got in the way of a murder attempt. Having noticed a couple fooling around in the park, he had started taking snapshots of them, surreptitiously, while hiding in the bushes – until the woman (Vanessa Redgrave) noticed him and vehemently insisted that he hand over the film. Now he knows why: the man was about to be murdered. In the crucial last enlargement, a hand holding a pistol can be seen pointing out from the undergrowth.

If a photograph is "blown up" sufficiently, even the smallest details can become clear. But there is a limit to enlargement: once the image is blown up beyond a certain size, it starts to disappear behind the grainy structure of the photographic material. Eventually, the image will break up into an abstract pattern of grains and blobs, and the motif will become unrecognizable. It's this boundary that fascinates Michelangelo Antonioni in *Blow-Up*. His film is a brilliant essay on the peculiar capacity of pictures to show the surface of things, but not their essence. Perhaps no other movie has examined the relationship between truth and representation so thrillingly or with such subtle complexity.

Thomas, whose life we share for a single day, is himself tormented by this dichotomy between appearance and reality. In the evenings, he takes photos in a shelter for the homeless, searching for life at its most naked and authentic; in the daytime, he works with the trendiest photo models in his beautifully fashionable studio. He commands and directs the girls he photographs, almost penetrating one of his models (Veruschka von Lehndorff) with the lens in his zeal to capture an image that is more than mere surface. For Thomas, photography is a mixture of sex and violence; he rips his pictures from the objects that make them possible. It seems he has no interest whatsoever in his subjects as human beings – neither the homeless people he secretly snaps, nor the beautiful women who writhe on the floor of his studio. In the park, too, he has the appearance of a sex criminal: lurking in the trees like a perverted flasher, he snaps away incessantly, a driven man.

The camera is a deadly weapon, taking shots. Thomas realizes that he has misinterpreted the scene in the park, that his presence did not in fact prevent a murder taking place; for in a further photo, he discovers a cluster of pale points under a bush that look very like a corpse. He drives over to the park once more, and sure enough, he finds a corpse. The next morning, however, after a wild party, everything has disappeared: the pictures have been stolen and the body has vanished – along with any hope of ever knowing for sure what has really taken place.

Blow-Up was the first film Michelangelo Antonioni made outside Italy. In 1967, at the film festival in Cannes, he said that temporary exile in London had put him at a disadvantage, but that the city had stimulated him for that very reason. He spent four months immersing himself in the London scene. With its pop colors, its music, and its sexual freedom – two half-naked women caused a considerable stir at the time – *Blow-Up* can be seen as a reflection of the Swinging Sixties.

But Antonioni's London is no *objet trouvé* – he created it himself. As he put it, he *painted* the landscapes and streets – indeed, he even had whole houses built for the film. And as the actress Sarah Miles said, it's putting the cart before the horse to say that Antonioni was inspired by the Swinging Sixties: for it's truer to say that *Blow-Up* invented them.

1   Exposed: Jane (Vanessa Redgrave) is willing to give up a little something in exchange for the incriminating photos taken in the park.

2   A soul-stealing objective: Thomas (David Hemmings) goes to extremes in the name of photorealism.

3   Set dressing: living dolls wait to be escorted into Thomas's playhouse. *Blow-Up* is a showcase of 1960s fashions and styles, many of which the film was responsible for popularizing.

4   Do you see what I see? *Blow-Up* is a study in image and representation. The script was based on a short story by Argentine novelist Julio Cortázar, whose works often focus on intertwining perspectives.

5   Carrot topless: However, Thomas's skin paled in comparison to Jane's at the time of *Blow-Up*'s cinematic debut. Vanessa Redgrave is reportedly the first woman to bare her boobs in a non-pornographic British film.

6   Modular work spaces: the like of which, according to *Time* magazine, produced an "uptight and vibrantly exciting picture."

7   Grasping at straws: Terence Stamp was originally considered for the role of the photographer, but Antonioni cast the virtually unknown David Hemmings in what proved to be the role of his career.

8   Keep off the grass: Antonioni effortlessly turns manicured park grounds into a sinister locale, where rustling leaves signal blood-curdling clues.

At the end of the film, Thomas watches a troupe of young mime artists playing tennis in the park, with no rackets and no ball. When the imaginary tennis ball flies over the fence, he picks it up and throws it back. We see his face. His tired eyes follow the to-and-fro of the invisible ball; and suddenly we hear sounds: the sounds of a tennis match, the whack of the rackets, the thud of the ball. Thomas gazes at the ground; and then he disappears, like the corpse under the bushes, and like this unfathomable film itself. Despite decades of explication and interpretation, *Blow-Up* has lost nothing of its mystery and its compelling strangeness.

NM

ALIENATION Loneliness was a feeling Nicholas Ray could communicate singularly well as a filmmaker, from his marrow out. This comes through in each of his films and is often the secret ingredient in scenes that on the surface are about very different things. Think of Robert Mitchum as a cowboy coming home in *The Lusty Men* (1952), crawling under the house where he grew up and ferreting out the stash of little toys he once concealed there, ages ago. Think of Peter O'Toole, as an armed trooper stalking Anthony Quinn across the ice in *The Savage Innocents* (1960), and the compassion that grows in his eyes – the only part of him we can see through his winter gear – as he elects to give up the chase. Think of James Dean, Natalie Wood, and Sal Mineo in *Rebel Without a Cause* (1955), lying on their backs in an empty swimming pool, gazing up at the stars – blissful in their shared awareness of having been lonely, until tonight.

The very title *In a Lonely Place* speaks to the heart of film noir. A perilous isolation is implied within most of the titles in this volume. Separate these phrases from the movies they belong to: *Night and the City* (1950), *Out of the Past* (1947), *Point Blank* (1960), *High Sierra* (1941), *Gaslight* (1940), *Ossessione* (1943) – even for non-speakers of Italian that word contains a lonely howl – *The Lodger* (1944), *The Third Man* (1949), *The Woman in the Window* (1944). Take as well the halo of apartness that surrounds such names as Rebecca, or Gilda (*Rebecca* [1940]), (*Gilda*, [1946]).

We are drawn in by the promise of these titles because such films, with their catalogs of crimes, their treacheries, their temporary triumphs and sardonic outcomes, all speak to a lonely awareness that is already within each of us, all through life. We're born as ourselves, and none other. When it comes time to die, there will be no one who can do that for us either. All our love stories, and all our other attempted heists against mortality, will come to the same end – the grave – and all for wildly individual reasons. Yet in this bleak, defiant understanding is also the pleasure and reward of life, and film noir helps us make sense of that.

POINT BLANK

1967 – USA – 92 MIN.
DIRECTOR JOHN BOORMAN (*1933)
SCREENPLAY ALEXANDER JACOBS,
DAVID NEWHOUSE, RAFE NEWHOUSE,
based on the novel *The Hunter* by RICHARD STARK
[= DONALD E. WESTLAKE]
DIRECTOR OF PHOTOGRAPHY PHILIP H. LATHROP
EDITING HENRY BERMAN MUSIC JOHNNY MANDEL
PRODUCTION JUDD BERNARD, ROBERT
CHARTOFF, IRWIN WINKLER for MGM
STARRING LEE MARVIN (Walker),
ANGIE DICKINSON (Chris), JOHN VERNON
(Mal Reese), SHARON ACKER (Lynne),
KEENAN WYNN (Yost), MICHAEL STRONG
(Stegman), LLOYD BOCHNER (Frederick Carter),
JAMES SIKKING (Hired Gun),
CARROLL O'CONNOR (Brewster)

"Walker! You still alive?"

A man lies crumpled in an otherwise empty, gothic prison cell. He's asking himself: "How did I get here?" His wife has betrayed him. His best friend has put a bullet in him. They've both left him for dead. All three were engaged in a heist – robbing a shipment of crime-syndicate cash delivered to San Francisco's island of Alcatraz, where a vast prison stands abandoned.

Lee Marvin is this man, Walker. (If he has a first name, we're never told.) He pulls himself together, staggers out of the cell block, and swims toward the misty city in the distance as an overheard tour guide advises us of the impossibility of escaping Alcatraz by sea. This makes for a startling jump forward in time. It is several months later; Walker has recovered from his wounds, and circles Alcatraz in a tour boat, half-listening to the spiel of this guide from her loudspeaker while giving his attention to a mysterious man named Yost (Keenan Wynn) at his right shoulder. Yost is an expert on the

crime organization now supporting Walker's former best friend (John Vernon) and former wife (Sharon Acker). Is Yost a cop, a criminal, something more shadowy? "You want your $93,000," he tells Walker. "I want the Organization."

Walker then pursues an escalating warpath of revenge in Los Angeles. His echoing footsteps as he strides through L.A. airport are as percussive as a heartbeat. His resurrection is a terrifying surprise for all concerned. His wife bares her soul to him, then takes her own life in remorse. His ex-friend Mal ditched Walker's wife shortly after their return from Alcatraz. Mal is tougher and meaner and harder to dispose of – but likewise topples purely on his own self-destructive momentum. Many critics who first saw the picture in 1967, among them a normally eagle-eyed young Roger Ebert, mistakenly wrote that Walker kills people as he goes. Not true! This is falling into a clever percep-

1 Walker (Lee Marvin) bursts in on ex-wife Lynne (Sharon Acker), who left him for dead on Alcatraz. His resurrection surprises everybody.

2 Walker, seen here suspended high on a prison fence along the bluffs on Alcatraz Island, is an onlooker of his own fate.

3 Walker feels a smoldering attraction for his sister-in-law Chris (Angie Dickinson), yet still he sends her as bait to his treacherous friend Mal (John Vernon).

4 Chris is disappointed that Walker is so cold to her: "You died at Alcatraz, all right." A prophetic insult?

tive trap set by director John Boorman. Walker fires his pistol at an empty bed in one scene, but strictly speaking kills no one. He merely arranges matters, and his victims die by their own misplaced energies. At one point, having triggered a police raid, Walker even listens in shadow — impassive, expressionless — to the ensuing gun battle. He is, as David Thomson puts it so well, "a spectator in his own story."

There is something surreal, even mystical about the all-knowing Yost — and a restless erotic demon motivates Walker's sister-in-law, Chris (Angie Dickinson), with whom he drifts into a half-hazy, half-turbulent romance. His escape from death has been so dreamlike, as is his whole progress through this maze. After awhile a wild possibility suggests itself. Is he dreaming? Verbal hints and visual textures imply there's a strong chance Walker hasn't

"*Point Blank* is the most authentic film made by an Englishman in America."

David Thomson, Biographical Dictionary of Film

left Alcatraz at all and may actually be dying back in that empty cell block. Director Boorman leaves this question hanging in the air beautifully, from one end of the movie to the other. The mystery is never allowed to resolve. We could be witnessing Walker's "death dream." Then again – given the amped-up fugue state which seems to be the lifelong room temperature inside this man's head – we could just as easily be navigating a highly subjective, slightly psychedelic entertainment akin to *North by Northwest* (1959) which fulfills Hitchcock's definition of a good movie as "life with all the dull bits cut out."

John Boorman and Lee Marvin were candidly aware of these parallel possibilities, and play to them, but take care never to tilt the scale too far in either direction. Whether real or imaginary, we are meant to believe what we see. The color palette shifts brilliantly from moment to moment. Grays, greens, blues, reds, and ochres each take turns dominating this or that scene. "The head of the art department complained to the head of the studio," Boorman once recounted. "'There are seven men,' said the memo. They're all wearing green suits, green shirts and green ties. The walls are green and the furniture's green. We're going to be laughed right out of the theater.'" "And yet," smiled Boorman, "If you look at that scene, you're not aware of any uniformity. Some greens grade off into browns, others into black, blue, even white."

> **"The profound unease we feel in identifying with an evil character in a movie is the recognition that we may be capable of such evil. Lee knew from his war experiences the depth of our capacity for cruelty and evil. He had committed such deeds, had plumbed the depths, and was prepared to recount what he had seen down there."** *John Boorman*

5

5   Walker, wife, and friend Mal before the fatal heist. Steven Soderbergh said that he's used stylistic touches from *Point Blank* many times in his filmmaking career.

6   Lynne deserted Walker for his friend Mal, only to be deserted in turn; she takes her own life. Poetic justice is contagious in Walker's world.

7   Lynne judges herself harshly as if seeing herself purely mirrored through Walker's eyes, and how miserably she treated him – is this merely his wish fulfillment?

LEE MARVIN   Marvin (1924–1987) was a direct descendant of Thomas Jefferson; a nephew, at several removes – on both his father's and mother's sides – of George Washington; and a cousin of Robert E. Lee, for whom he was named. As a boy he was a rebel in constant trouble, and found himself kicked out of several exclusive schools. During World War II he enlisted in the Marines and nearly died in the battle of Saipan in 1944, spared by a bullet wound to his backside during the ascent of Mount Tapochau, an action in which most of his unit was killed. After he recovered, he took up acting – as much a surprise to himself as anyone else – and quickly distinguished himself in films, most notably under the direction of Fritz Lang, Stanley Kramer, and Edward Dmytryk, and won an Oscar for his double role in *Cat Ballou* (1965).
Director John Boorman's documentary *Lee Marvin: A Personal Portrait* (1998) illuminates the bond between them that began with *Point Blank*: "Lee and I had long conversations about who our hero Walker should be. I learned a lot about Lee. The critical thing was his World War II experience in the South Pacific. He'd killed people. He'd been badly wounded in an ambush. *Point Blank* was very much about him – about a man who comes back, as it were, from the dead, and tries to connect to normal society. That was what he brought to it. And because Lee had lived it, you felt Walker's internal struggle with peculiar force."

Lee Marvin is essential to this film's power, its eerie gravitas. Again, Thomson – a firm believer in the "death dream" scenario – catches this quality best: Marvin's "expressive somnambulism," he has observed, "is not just a search for vengeance and satisfaction, but the signs of sleep and inertia in a man actually slipping away from the world, defeated by it but inventing a story in which he triumphs as he dies." A portrait of America as a paradise for organized crime also emerges here, one that preserves the light and air of the 1960s in a far more authentic and immediate way than most other movies. One must look to such diverse pictures as *The Manchurian Candidate* (1962) and *Dr. Strangelove* (1964) to find adequate rivals for the darkness, energy, and deadpan humor of *Point Blank*.   FXF

6

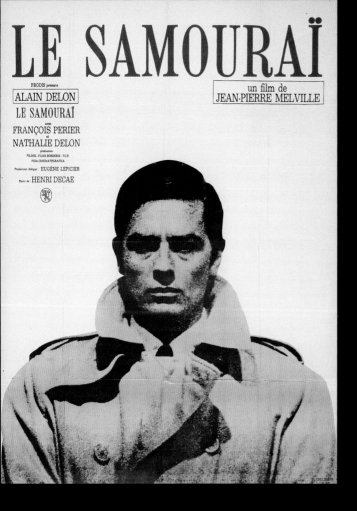

LE SAMOURAÏ

1967 - FRANCE / ITALY - 95 MIN.
DIRECTOR JEAN-PIERRE MELVILLE (1917–1973)
SCREENPLAY JEAN-PIERRE MELVILLE, based on
the novel *The Ronin* by JOAN MCLEOD
DIRECTOR OF PHOTOGRAPHY HENRI DECAË
EDITING MONIQUE BONNOT, YOLANDE MAURETTE
MUSIC FRANÇOIS DE ROUBAIX
PRODUCTION RAYMOND BORDERIE, EUGÈNE LÉPICIER
for FILMEL, C. I. C. C., FIDA
STARRING ALAIN DELON (Jef Costello),
FRANÇOIS PÉRIER (Commissar), NATHALIE DELON
(Jane Lagrange), CATHY ROSIER (Valérie),
MICHEL BOISRAND (Wiener), JACQUES LEROY
(Killer), ROBERT FAVART (Barman),
JEAN-PIERRE POSIER (Olivier Rey),
CATHERINE JOURDAN (Cloakroom Attendant),
ANDRÉ SALGUES (Auto Mechanic)

"I never lose – not really."

The first nine minutes are silent. We see a cheap room, dimly illuminated by the light from two windows; a bird twitters monotonously, and blue smoke curls slowly upwards, indicating the presence of a man smoking in bed (Alain Delon). Eventually he rises, strokes the bars of a birdcage with a handful of folded banknotes, hides the money, dons his trench coat and turns up the collar. He goes to the mirror and puts on his hat, adjusts its brim and leaves the apartment. Out on the street, he climbs into a Citroën DS, lays out a row of ignition keys on the passenger seat, and starts trying them out. When the engine starts, he drives off. In a desolate Parisian suburb, he steers the car into a tiny garage. Immediately a mechanic locks the door, screws on a new license plate, and hands our hero some papers, some money, and – after the driver clicks his fingers – a gun. Our man drives off to an apartment block, gets out and walks up to the door of a flat. A blonde woman (Nathalie Delon) opens the door – and at last we hear the first word: "Jef."

The silent overture has made one thing clear: Jef Costello's *métier* is homicide. The trench coat, the hat, the wad, and the weapon: these are the cinematic trappings of the professional killer. Jean-Pierre Melville's film leads us into the sinister world of its hero with breathtaking efficiency. This is a dehumanized male cosmos with its own rigid rules and mechanisms. Melville's aesthetic is one of reduction; the colors of this movie are as cold as they are artificial, and it's immediately clear to us that *Le Samouraï* is more than a mere variation on the American crime movie. It's a quintessence of the genre, a fascinating abstraction saturated with the pessimistic worldview of its highly idiosyncratic director.

Meville prefaced his film with an invented quote from "The Book of the Samurai": "There is no greater loneliness than that of the samurai, unless it is that of the tiger in the jungle." Costello – the "Samurai" of the title – is almost autistic in his solitary independence, and the caged bird in his apart-

2

3

4

"It almost seems to be an American film dubbed into a French scene to appear American in such things as nightclubs, sordid little hotels, police lineups and the general behavior of the characters." *Variety*

JEAN-PIERRE MELVILLE Those whom the gods love die young. When Jean-Pierre Melville (1917–1973) succumbed to a heart attack in a restaurant, he had made only 13 films, many of which he had also scripted and produced. He liked to call himself a "créateur de cinema," which he felt to be a suitably resonant and imposing designation. The phrase also implies a creative impulse that goes beyond mere directing, and this we can confidently allow him. Melville gives the *form* of his movies more attention than the story alone would demand; his films are carefully constructed pictorial choreographies crafted onto suspense-laden plots. He had a far greater influence on the new French cinema than is generally recognized. One might say that he prepared the ground for the changes in the production system that enabled the *Nouvelle Vague*. Born Jean-Pierre Grumbach, he adopted his new name in honor of his artistic idol, American novelist Hermann Melville, the author of *Moby Dick* and *Billy Budd*. In fact, this French filmmaker was much taken with American archetypes and role models. His films frequently reflect the Hollywood movies of the 1930s; and, off-duty, he sported a magnificent Stetson while tooling around Paris by night in a giant Ford Galaxy, constantly in search of new locations and breathtaking motifs. He enjoyed his greatest successes when working with Jean-Paul Belmondo (*The Finger Man* [*Le Doulos / Lo spione*, 1962]) or Alain Delon (*The Samurai* [*Le Samouraï*, 1967], *Second Breath* [*Le Deuxième Souffle*, 1966]). He made an unforgettable appearance in Godard's *Breathless* (*À bout de souffle*, 1960), as the writer Parvulesco who is interviewed by the Jean Seberg character. When asked to name his dearest desire, he replies: "To become immortal and then die." A statement straight from the heart of a Melville film.

1 Up in smoke: without batting an eye Jef Costello
(Alain Delon) acts as judge, jury, and executioner.
Roles like this established Delon as one of the
French cinema's greatest sex symbols.

2 A no-win situation: lured into a trap by his dubious
employers, Costello finds himself with no hope of
making good. Now all he can do is go out with a
bang.

3 Jane (Delon's then wife Natalie Delon) is the only
person Costello opens up to.

4 Could this be a case of schizophrenia with
a cool veneer? For no matter how grave the
danger, Costello always demonstrates the
same professionalism on a job.

5 Up against the law: the commissioner (François
Périer, standing left of Delon) presents Costello
with a formidable opponent.

ment may well be seen as a metaphor for his own situation. That incompre-
hensible tweeting doesn't just intensify the icy silence that surrounds the
man; it also lends his isolation an obsessive, even pathological quality.
Costello's life seems to consist of nothing but rituals. His gestures seem
inexorable, exhaustively rehearsed, like the movements of an automaton.
When a pretty girl driver stops beside him at the traffic lights, she casts a
flirtatious eye at the killer – but in vain; he stares straight ahead, oblivious
to her charms.

His relationship to his girlfriend Jane (played by Nathalie Delon, the
star's wife at the time) seems to fit into the same pattern. His first appearance
at her apartment is for purely professional reasons: he's being paid to kill
someone, and he needs an alibi. She provides it for him, but she's quite without illusions: "I love it when you come to me; it means you need me."

Costello's job is to kill the owner of an exclusive nightclub, and he performs the task with icy precision. Though the police place him on an identity
parade and put him through an interrogation, his alibi is iron-clad. But the

Samurai is not invulnerable: the Commissar (François Périer) trusts his
instincts and continues to keep an eye on Costello. The killer's boss soon
starts to get worried; and when Costello goes to pick up his blood money, he
doesn't realize he's walking intro a trap. Shots are fired, and Costello manages to escape with a wounded arm. But now he's shut in on both sides.
Pursued by the cops and by the gangsters, he knows there's no way out.

For many film buffs, *Le Samouraï* is still one of the best movies ever
made. And its influence on filmmakers has been considerable, from Paul
Schrader – especially as regards his script for Martin Scorsese's *Taxi Driver*
(1976) – to Michael Mann (*Heat*, 1995). That Melville's film has now acquired
an almost mythical status is due in no small part to the special aura of
Alain Delon, which the director brought out perfectly in the peculiar world of
this film. In Delon's face, apparently so cold and masklike, the spectator
eventually discerns a tragic quality that extends beyond the personal fate of
the killer Costello. As the embodiment of existential solitude, Delon became
an icon of the cinema.   JH

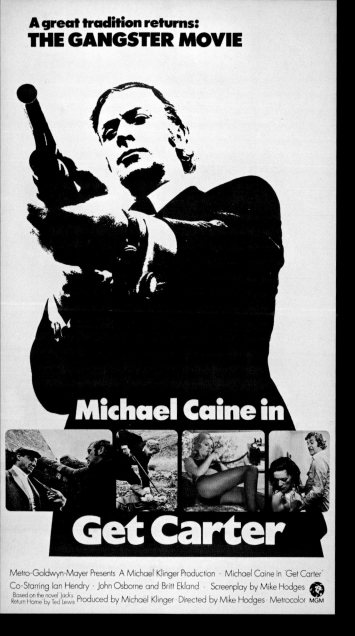

A great tradition returns:
THE GANGSTER MOVIE

Michael Caine in

Get Carter

Metro-Goldwyn-Mayer Presents A Michael Klinger Production · Michael Caine in "Get Carter"
Co-Starring Ian Hendry · John Osborne and Britt Ekland · Screenplay by Mike Hodges
Based on the novel "Jack's
Return Home" by Ted Lewis Produced by Michael Klinger · Directed by Mike Hodges · Metrocolor MGM

GET CARTER

1971 – GREAT BRITAIN – 112 MIN.
DIRECTOR MIKE HODGES (*1932)
SCREENPLAY MIKE HODGES, based on the novel
Jack's Return Home by TED LEWIS
SCREENPLAY WOLFGANG SUSCHITZKY
EDITING JOHN TRUMPER MUSIC ROY BUDD
PRODUCTION MICHAEL KLINGER,
MICHAEL CAINE for MGM
STARRING MICHAEL CAINE (Jack Carter), IAN HENDRY
(Eric Paice), BRITT EKLAND (Anna Fletcher),
JOHN OSBORNE (Cyril Kinnear),
TONY BECKLEY (Peter), GEORGE SEWELL
(Con McCarty), GERALDINE MOFFAT (Glenda),
DOROTHY WHITE (Margaret), ROSEMARIE DUNHAM
(Edna), PETRA MARKHAM (Doreen)

"Remember, they are killers ... Just like you."

Jack Carter (Michael Caine) is back in town. Against the will of his syndicate, the professional killer leaves London and returns to his hometown of Newcastle, where his brother has died in a peculiar road accident. Carter suspects murder, and he wants to find the culprits; but his brother's friends, and girlfriend, are no help at all. Undeterred, and driven by a desire for vengeance, Carter becomes brutal in his persistence; and the king of the local underworld, Kinnear (John Osborne), is standing in his way.

Although many film buffs are fans of his work, the British director Mike Hodges has only made one movie that achieved real popular success: *Flash Gordon* (1980). *Get Carter* is no real exception to this rule. Although it eventually became a cult film in Britain – thanks in no small part to Michael Caine's performance – 30 years elapsed before its (re)discovery by the rest of the world, on the occasion of a Hollywood remake starring Sylvester Stallone.

"There is nobody to root for but the smartly dressed sexual athlete and professional killer (Michael Caine) in this English gangland picture, which is so calculatedly cool and soulless and nastily erotic that it seems to belong to a new genre of virtuoso viciousness. What makes the movie unusual is the metallic elegance and the single-minded proficiency with which it adheres to its sadism-for-the-connoisseur formula." *Pauline Kael*

MICHAEL CAINE Michael Caine once said that he and Harold Lloyd were the only bespectacled actors ever to have made a name for themselves. Indeed, the glasses were not the only disadvantage Caine had to contend with. The son of a cleaner and a fishmonger, Maurice Micklewhite (as he was then known) was born in a working-class area of London on March 14, 1933. From an early age, Caine wanted to become an actor; but although he made his cinematic debut in the mid-'50s, his breakthrough as the laconic secret agent Harry Palmer in *The Ipcress File* (1965), directed by Sidney J. Furie, was still ten years away. He was equally successful in the film's two sequels. In *Alfie* (1966), Caine played a working-class Casanova. The film made him world-famous and earned him his first Oscar nomination. Since then, he has been one of the busiest stars in the English-speaking world. Michael Caine's trademarks are his understated acting style and his distinctive Cockney accent. In the course of his long career, he has won two Academy Awards as Best Supporting Actor for his performances in Woody Allen's *Hannah and Her Sisters* (1985) and in Lasse Hallström's *The Cider House Rules* (1999). In 2000, he received a knighthood from Queen Elizabeth. Sir Michael Caine, even late in life, still appears tirelessly in front of the camera.

1 In the flesh: to this day, Caine excels at everything from rugged working class hero to demented doctor.

2 Local boy gone bad: professional killer Jack Carter (Michael Caine) is back in his hometown to investigate the death of his brother.

3 Sex and Crime: assassin Carter (Michael Caine) knocks 'em all dead.

Get Carter was Hodges's cinematic debut. Up till then, he had spent years working in television, making reports and documentaries. In 1969, he directed *Suspect*, his first TV drama, a thriller about a child murder that took a critical look behind the mask of British society. *Get Carter* is a film with equally few illusions. While charting the course of a private mission of revenge, it also depicts a nation grown squalid, amoral, and violent. Carter cruises the city like a detective. Wherever he happens to land, from the elegant apartments and villas of the decadent elite to the bleak pubs and terraced houses of the working class, he encounters cunning, mistrust, and naked greed. In Hodges's film, we hear the dying echoes of the Swinging Sixties, and all that remains in their wake is a riotous and unconscionable hedonism. Corruption and brutality rule; one rapid sequence combines fast sex and fast cars, but "liberation" is the last word that comes to mind … As if to demonstrate that he was dealing with reality and not just following the conventions of the genre, Hodges filmed on location in the grim and chilly North of England; and he did so with the beady eye of a trained documen-

"You know, I'd almost forgotten what your eyes looked like. Still the same. Pissholes in the snow."

Film quote: Jack Carter (Michael Caine)

6

4 Wherever Carter goes, violence, corruption, and ruin are sure to follow.

5 Rolling with the times: sex is just one more aspect of life that's ruled by greed and brutality.

6 A twisted latter-day *angry young man*: Carter rages against an amoral system that has long since corrupted him too.

> ## "One man against an organization. The courage and naïveté of an individual versus the overwhelming power and sophistication of a system – a perennial theme in the œuvre of that underrated director, Mike Hodges."
>
> *Süddeutsche Zeitung*

tary filmmaker. In this, he is heir to the Free Cinema of the late '50s and early '60s, a period he pays tribute to by casting the dramatist John Osborne as the gangster boss Kinnear.

And in fact we may well see Carter as a twisted, latter-day "angry young man" – an armed proletarian criminal fighting the status quo. In a key scene, he discovers that his niece has been abused for a shabby porn film; as he watches the images on screen, he loses his distance and his icy façade melts into tears. The professional assassin runs amok, slaughtering men and women alike, driven by hatred and the pain of his own loss of innocence.

Even in his rage, Carter kills only the guilty; yet he knows he's no better than his victims. He too is part of the system. The film's inner logic can offer him no new beginning, merely a permanent ending. The final showdown takes place on the beach – one of the mythical places of the cinema. Death takes the form of a precision shot from the rifle of a contract killer. On the marksman's signet ring, we see the letter "J." Like Jack Carter, he's a master of his trade; but unlike Carter, he still has the necessary professional distance from the job he's paid to do.

JH

THE GETAWAY

1972 – USA – 122 MIN.
DIRECTOR SAM PECKINPAH (1925–1984)
SCREENPLAY WALTER HILL, based on the novel of the
same name by JIM THOMPSON
DIRECTOR OF PHOTOGRAPHY LUCIEN BALLARD
EDITING ROBERT L. WOLFE **MUSIC** QUINCY JONES
PRODUCTION MITCHELL BROWER, DAVID FOSTER for
SOLAR PRODUCTIONS, DAVID FOSTER PRODUCTIONS,
FIRST ARTISTS, NATIONAL GENERAL PICTURES
STARRING STEVE MCQUEEN (Carter "Doc" McCoy),
ALI MACGRAW (Carol Ainsley McCoy),
BEN JOHNSON (Jack Benyon),
SALLY STRUTHERS (Fran Clinton), AL LETTIERI
(Rudy Butler), SLIM PICKENS (Cowboy),
RICHARD BRIGHT (Thief), BO HOPKINS (Frank Jackson),
JACK DODSON (Harold Clinton), DUB TAYLOR (Laughlin)

"Only in God I trust."

Carter "Doc" McCoy (Steve McQueen) is about as tough as they come. A criminal as unscrupulous as he is intelligent, Doc enters into an illegal bargain with his lawyer Benyon (Ben Johnson) as a means of getting released early from his ten-year sentence in a maximum security Texas penitentiary. Benyon, it so happens, is the head of a mafia-like organization in Texas and agrees to get McCoy out on the condition that he pulls off a bank robbery for him. Only after the deed has been done, does McCoy discover that Benyon's brother is the chairman of the board at the target bank, and that the heist was staged to cover up an embezzlement scheme.

Aided by two accomplices, McCoy makes the final preparations for the robbery. His wife Carol (Ali MacGraw) will drive the getaway car. Little does he know that Carol agreed to let Benyon have his way with her as part of the deal to get McCoy out of prison. The three men pull off the robbery, but then quickly attempt to do away with each other, leaving one of the accomplices dead. Doc and Carol manage to make their way to Benyon and plan on giving him his share of the loot. However, as Benyon insinuates to McCoy that Carol was also part of the booty he was entitled to, Carol snaps and blows the crooked attorney away. With a bang, the couple start on a race across Texas. To survive, they'll not only have to dodge the authorities, but Benyon's bloodhounds and the accomplice who's still alive.

This sordid band of bounty hunters gets closer and closer to Doc and Carol with each minute that passes. On numerous occasions, the couple rely on daredevil driving maneuvers and split-second decision-making to escape the clutches of the police. They finally make it to their destination, a hotel they believe to be safe in El Paso just north of the Mexican border. Unfortunately, the ex-accomplice is already there, and Benyon's henchmen arrive shortly afterwards. In an extended action sequence, there is a frenetic exchange of shots between all the characters in the hotel rooms and along the corridors. McCoy and his wife escape unscathed and, at gunpoint, convince an unpleasant-looking junk collector to drive them across the border in his beat-up truck. Once there, McCoy buys the vehicle from its owner, and disappears into the Mexican sunset with wife and cash.

The Getaway was the first movie released by the newly established production company First Artists, a group founded that same year by Steve

McQueen, Paul Newman, Sidney Poitier, Barbra Streisand, and Dustin Hoffman. The film portrays urban institutions such as state penitentiaries, bars, and factories, as bloody, amoral, and anarchic setups. The film depicts the flip side of the extreme mobility of American society, and the impact of modern-day violence on the individual. Sam Peckinpah's unmistakable signature has divided audiences into two camps since *The Wild Bunch* (1969) and *Straw Dogs* (1971). There are those who cheer him on and those who are appalled. This was also the case with *The Getaway*. Although the director shows restraint in the images of violence by using a slow-motion camera and operatic choreography, his characters are quite the contrary: they have no limits whatsoever. All social interactions and ties, right down to the most intimate, are dictated by power plays of one sort or another. It is a corrupt world, with

no system of justice. The film's message is not, however, a direct commentary on Nixon's Watergate, and its plot culminates in a classic knock 'em down style, a saloon shoot-out complete with plenty of bullets, smashed furniture, and a wagonload of casualties.

As always, Steve McQueen plays the morally ambivalent gangster to a tee. He is, on the one hand, in full control, impenetrable, a veritable rock. On the other hand, he is a sensitive, no-nonsense kind of guy, who wears his short cut prison do like a wound that begins to heal with the taste of freedom. Only at the film's conclusion does the "every man for himself" mentality begin to disappear. We witness the change only briefly in the promised land of Mexico, as Doc McCoy spares the life of the old cowboy in the pickup and does his first square deal of the film: exchanging goods for money.   RV

1 Sharp eyes and sharp shooting: Steve McQueen as Carter "Doc" McCoy.

2 Great balls of fire: action movies are primarily concerned with extreme situations.

3 & 4 Love and death in Texas: the stars' on-screen marriage proved almost as complicated as their real-life one.

"*Getaway* is pure action, exhilarating and wonderfully sure-footed, a wild but controlled dance amidst a hail of bullets." *Süddeutsche Zeitung*

STEVE McQUEEN The definition of an actor's job means different things at different times. Today, two styles dominate the U.S. cinema. Thespians like Dustin Hoffman, Robert De Niro, and Al Pacino belong to the first school characterized by an ability to slip into a wide range of roles and to take on traits foreign to their actual personality. The second school of thought believes that the actor is a mirror of the current zeitgeist, trends, and desires prevalent in society. Entertainers like Michael Douglas readily fall into this category. One could even make the distinction between "actor" and "performer" down these lines. Steve McQueen was certainly among the greatest of these Hollywood "performers." He was the quintessential adventuresome playboy, the rugged rebel, the fighter. Defeat could look him straight in the eye and McQueen still wouldn't give up. His stoicism seems almost philosophical. His performances certainly benefited from his real-life actions. The man was an avid race car driver, pilot, and an ardent individualist.

Born Terence Steven McQueen in 1930 in a suburb of Indianapolis – home of the Indianapolis 500 – he was the son of a "Top Gun" military pilot. He worked a number of odd jobs as a teenager until John Sturges, famous for directing Westerns, discovered McQueen and cast him in *The Magnificent Seven* (1960) and *The Great Escape* (1963). Both pictures were smash hits at the box office. Further roles in films like *The Cincinnati Kid* (1965) and *Bullitt* (1968) made him one of the most popular screen personalities of all time. It was during the shooting of *The Getaway* (1972), that the strong, silent, competitive McQueen fell in love with leading lady and wife-to-be Ali MacGraw. Less than a year before he died he married for a third time, to model Barbara Minty. In 1980, at just 50 years of age, the King of Cool, as he was known to many fans, died of cancer.

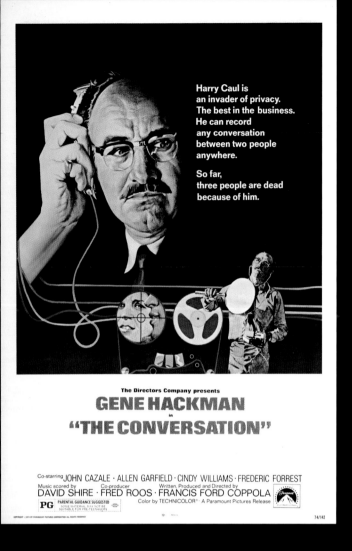

THE CONVERSATION

1974 – USA – 113 MIN.
DIRECTOR FRANCIS FORD COPPOLA (*1939)
SCREENPLAY FRANCIS FORD COPPOLA
DIRECTOR OF PHOTOGRAPHY BILL BUTLER
EDITING RICHARD CHEW MUSIC DAVID SHIRE
PRODUCTION FRANCIS FORD COPPOLA for AMERICAN
ZOETROPE, THE COPPOLA COMPANY,
THE DIRECTORS COMPANY, PARAMOUNT PICTURES
STARRING GENE HACKMAN (Harry Caul), JOHN CAZALE
(Stanley), ALLEN GARFIELD (Bernie Moran),
FREDERIC FORREST (Mark), CINDY WILLIAMS (Ann),
MICHAEL HIGGINS (Paul), ELIZABETH MACRAE
(Meredith), TERI GARR (Amy), HARRISON FORD
(Martin Stett), PHOEBE ALEXANDER (Lurleen)
IFF CANNES 1974 GOLDEN PALM for BEST FILM
(Francis Ford Coppola)

"I don't care what they're talking about. All I want is a nice fat recording."

A bright, sunny day in downtown San Francisco. Union square is bursting with life. Passersby soak up live jazz as a clown parades about the plaza, imitating the people he encounters. The initial camera shots observe the peaceful action from overhead, when, like a bolt from the blue, a disturbance shatters this blissful portrait. Static interference muffles every sound. Seconds later, the calm is fully restored, or so it seems. Yet as the camera moves in on the city dwellers and holds on an inconspicuous guy in a rain poncho, wearing a hearing device and carrying a shopping bag, we begin to see that there's more to this scene than meets the eye. Soon the clown approaches the mysterious man, who quickly turns away – all the while incessantly tailed by the camera.

Our xenophobic friend's name is Harry Caul (Gene Hackman), a professional audio surveillance expert and one of the best in the business. He and his expert team happen to be carrying out a routine assignment. They are to eavesdrop on the conversation of a young couple strolling guilelessly about the square. The jarring audio feedback we hear is caused by his hidden microphone. Much like the enlarged snapshots in Michelangelo Antonioni's

film *Blow-Up* (1966), the reel-to-reel tape recordings of *The Conversation* also contain more information than intended. Caul goes over these tapes countless times. Something just isn't quite right about them. When the pieces at last seem to click into place, he is overcome with dread. Caul not only suspects that the couple could be in grave danger, but also that he has been made an accessory to murder. With this, the thriller begins.

Behind the veil of professional distance that this audio trapper exhibits towards his job and his human targets lies a deep-seated sense of shame. Years ago, Caul's stereo snooping was responsible for the deaths of several innocent people. To stop history from repeating itself, he puts his foot down and withholds the last reels from his client in the hopes of foiling a potential murder plot.

Francis Ford Coppola filmed *The Conversation* between the first two installments of his *Godfather* trilogy (1972, 1974, 1999). He had, in fact, been toying with the idea since the late '60s. Had *The Conversation* been made a few years earlier, it might have been written off as far-fetched hogwash by audiences and critics alike. Nonetheless, when the shoot began in November

1973, the Watergate scandal, which eventually led to the resignation of President Nixon, had turned mere academic theory and speculation into blinding truth. Every U.S. American was confronted with the reality of a government not only capable of invading the private sphere by means of audio surveillance, but also not opposing it. Still *The Conversation* is much more than a political thriller. It is as much a portrait of human fears as it is an intimate drama about a police informant who cracks when he himself becomes the target of undercover surveillance.

Although the leading role was originally intended for Marlon Brando, no one could have delivered a more convincing performance as the scruffy, quirky and utterly alone audio-nark than Gene Hackman. His Harry Caul embodies the average Joe more than he'd like to admit. He is someone who

FRANCIS FORD COPPOLA Francis Ford Coppola (born April 7, 1939 in Detroit) enjoyed a sheltered middle-class childhood in a suburb of New York. His father Carmine was a composer and musician who would later write the music to some of his son's films. Coppola at first studied theater at the Hofstra University, then film at UCLA. While still a student, he worked as an assistant director to Roger Corman, who also produced his first feature film, *Dementia 13* (1963). Coppola made his breakthrough at the early age of 31, when his screenplay to *Patton* (1969) was awarded the Oscar.

A short time later, he was also world-famous as a director – and as the Boy Wonder of the New Hollywood: the Mafia saga *The Godfather* (1972) became one of the biggest hits in movie history and won three Oscars, including Best Film. Two years later, he topped even this: *The Godfather – Part II* (1974) scooped six Academy Awards – including Best Director. In the meantime, Coppola had also made an outstanding movie about an alienated surveillance expert: *The Conversation* (1974), which carried off the Golden Palm at the Cannes Festival.

In 1976, Coppola began work on the Vietnam film *Apocalypse Now* (1979), which he produced himself, and which came very close to ruining him. But after four years in production, that film also won the Golden Palm and two Oscars, and even recouped the huge sum that had been spent making it. Only two years later, however, the failure of the love story *One from the Heart* (1981) drove him into such horrendous debt that he was forced to sell his production company, American Zoetrope. Though he has since directed other films, such as *The Cotton Club* (1984), and *The Godfather – Part III* (1990), none have been as successful as his huge hits of the '70s.

1   Clogged reception? Harry Caul (Gene Hackman) will have things up and running in no time.

2   Bug extermination: in an act of emancipation, Caul rids himself of all hidden surveillance devices by destroying his own apartment.

3   Remixed and remastered: *The Conversation* understandably hit a nerve with post-Watergate America.

4   They're all crowding that other booth: much like that year's Oscars, the cast of *The Conversation* sees someone else cashing in on the accolades. Not to fret, as it was Coppola's other picture *The Godfather – Part II* that took home six golden statuettes.

"Wedded to secrecy as a moral principle, he's the kind of man who lies down to neck with his shoes on – an acutely repressed solitary who insists that he's not responsible for the outcome of his work." *Variety*

constantly intrudes on the privacy of others, but regards his quarry with a distanced abstraction: "I don't care what they're talking about. All I want is a nice fat recording." When the shoe's on the other foot, however, he freaks out like a wild animal that suddenly realizes it's been caged. Our first taste of this comes when his landlady drops off a birthday present in his well-secured apartment while Harry is out.

Walter Murch provided the audio mixes, essential to this film's subject matter. He first collaborated with Coppola on *The Rain People* (1969) and would work as his sound designer again on subsequent productions such as

The Godfather – Part II (1974) and *Apocalypse Now* (1979). In *The Conversation*, every manifestation of sound is more than just a means of underscoring the visuals. Here, the audio track becomes an autonomous entity that not only steers the plot but also generates a sinister smokescreen for the protagonist and spectators alike. We hear only that which Caul hears. Yet, as someone who exclusively focuses on sounds and background noise, making every effort to isolate each distinct thread, he loses sight of the *actual content* of the recorded dialogue – what is really being said. *The Conversation* is a "talkie" at the highest level of introspection.   APO

CHINATOWN †

1974 – USA – 131 MIN.
DIRECTOR ROMAN POLANSKI (*1933)
SCREENPLAY ROBERT TOWNE
DIRECTOR OF PHOTOGRAPHY JOHN A. ALONZO
EDITING SAM O'STEEN **MUSIC** JERRY GOLDSMITH
PRODUCTION ROBERT EVANS for LONG ROAD,
PENTHOUSE, PARAMOUNT PICTURES
STARRING JACK NICHOLSON (J. J. "Jake" Gittes),
FAYE DUNAWAY (Evelyn Cross Mulwray), JOHN HUSTON
(Noah Cross), PERRY LOPEZ (LAPD Lieutenant
Lou Escobar), JOHN HILLERMAN (Russ Yelburton),
DARRELL ZWERLING (Hollis I. Mulwray),
DIANE LADD (Ida Sessions), ROY JENSON (Claude
Mulvihill), ROMAN POLANSKI (Man with the knife),
RICHARD BAKALYAN (LAPD Detective Loach)
ACADEMY AWARDS 1974 OSCAR for BEST ORIGINAL
SCREENPLAY (Robert Towne)

"I'm just a snoop."

Los Angeles, 1937. When private detective J. J. Gittes (Jack Nicholson) is hired to keep tabs on an unfaithful husband, he assumes it's going to be just another routine job. But the investigation takes an unexpected turn. The guy he's been keeping an eye on, a high-ranking official for the city's water and power department, is bumped off. His attractive widow Evelyn (Faye Dunaway) retains Gittes's services to find out whodunit. Before he knows it, Gittes stumbles unexpectedly onto a foul smelling real estate scheme, and soon finds himself entangled in one sordid affair after another. Gittes has several bloody run-ins with thugs determined to put an end to his work on the case, and uncovers clues pointing to the involvement of influential power-players in the sinister dealings. Even Gittes's alluring employer Evelyn seems to know more about the matter than she's letting on …

Chinatown is considered by many film critics to be not only one of the greatest films of the '70s, but of all time. How the movie came to be illus-

trates, like so many other similar moments in Hollywood history, that masterpieces can still be born within the framework of the imperious big studios. Chinatown was simply one of those rare instances when the perfect combination of people came together at just the right time. Prominent "script doctor" Robert Towne wrote the original screenplay as a starring vehicle for friend Jack Nicholson, who at the time was not a solid "A-list" star. When he got wind of the project, Robert Evans, who was head of production at Paramount, wanted to try his hand at producing a film himself. He finalized an agreement with the writer and actor and secured Roman Polanski, with whom he had collaborated previously on Rosemary's Baby (1968), as the picture's director. (Understandably, Polanski had been working in his native Europe following the brutal death of his wife Sharon Tate [1943–1969] in their Los Angeles home.) When Faye Dunaway was cast as the female lead, yet another star known not easy to deal with was added to the mix. As one

Chinatown was seen as a Neo-Noir when it was released — an update on an old genre. Now years have passed and film history blurs a little, and it seems to settle easily beside the original noirs. That is a compliment." *Chicago Sun-Times*

1 Portrait of a lady: *femme fatale* Evelyn (Faye Dunaway) awakens men's dreams and inspires them to action.

2 In her clutches: the private eye (Jack Nicholson) has lost all professional distance from his seductive client.

3 Masterful execution: veteran director John Huston plays a brutal patriarch who holds all the cards.

4 Mack the knife: Polanski in a striking cameo as the "nose-slitter."

3

might expect, the shoot was not exactly plain sailing. Evans dubbed the verbal fireworks between Towne and Polanski "World War III." The problem probably had something to do with the fact that this was the first project Polanski directed without writing it himself. The product was, nonetheless, an international smash. *Chinatown* reeled in a total of 11 Oscar nominations, although Robert Towne was the sole person who ended up taking a statuette home.

Yet what makes *Chinatown* truly fascinating, and the reason it attained its instant status as an uncontested masterpiece, is by and large the film's grace in evoking the Golden Age of 1930s–1940s Hollywood, without losing itself in the nostalgia of the era or wturning the production into just another stiffly stylized homage. Naturally, Polanski's film draws heavily on classic Bogart characters like detective Philip Marlowe from Howard Hawks's *The Big Sleep* (1946) or his more cynical counterpart Sam Spade from *The Maltese Falcon* (1941), directed by Hollywood legend John Huston. Huston himself plays a pivotal role in *Chinatown* as a ruthless and sickeningly sentimental patriarch, who seems to be the key to the entire mystery. Unlike Bogart, Nicholson's character is only capable of being a limited hero. Although J. J. "Jake" Gittes is a likeable small-time snoop, with a weakness for smutty jokes, the charming sheister fails miserably as a moralist and suffers terribly as a result. The scene featuring Polanski as a gangster who slits open Nicholson's nose is absolutely priceless. The Gittes character also lacks the romantic potential of a Bogart hero. Gittes doesn't embody desires, instead he falters on them. Yet his greatest weakness is Chinatown, the place where his career as a cop came to an end and a synonym for all the irresistible,

4

6

5 Just the facts Ma'am: *Chinatown* evokes classic Hollywood cinema without ever romanticizing it.

6 Still nosing around: J. J. Gittes (Jack Nicholson), bloody but unbowed.

exotic dangers of the urban jungle. This same sweet taboo seems to echo in Faye Dunaway's character. In the end, Chinatown presents Gittes with a double-edged defeat. Although Towne had originally written a happy ending, the film's final sequence, which just screams Polanski, sees Gittes inadvertently aiding the forces of evil and losing the love of his life at the same time.

Another great accomplishment of the piece is Polanski and cinematographer John A. Alonzo's triumph in achieving the impact of a black-and-white film noir piece with brilliant color photography. It is uncanny how little the city feels like a movie lot and how convincing the topography looks. Unlike in so many other so-called revisionist noir films, in *Chinatown*, L.A. is not a black, smoldering hell's kitchen but rather a vast, often sunny countryside metropolis still in the early stages of development. The imagery lets the viewer sense

that the city and its surrounding valleys exist in spite of the imposing desert. We are also made aware of the colossal pipeline, supplying the city with water, its artificial lifeblood. Water is, in fact, the major resource being manipulated in the story's diabolical real estate venture, a scandal with genuine historical roots in the region. Robert Towne based his screenplay on non-fictional accounts dating back to early 20th-century Southern California.It was a time when the foundations for the future riches of the world's movie capital were in construction. The location was chosen primarily on account of the area's year-round sun, ideal for filming, and its affordable purchase price. The boom ushered in a wave of land speculators, corruption and violence. It is a grim bit of earth that the City of Angels and Hollywood rests upon. A tale that unfolds in *Chinatown*. JH

JACK NICHOLSON Wily, devious, and even lecherous at times, Jack Nicholson still possesses all the qualities required to portray characters driven by animal instincts rather than intellect. His caustic mimicry, gestures, and trademark sneer vitalize rebels (*One Flew Over the Cuckoo's Nest*, 1975), psychopaths (*The Shining*, 1980), career killers (*Prizzi's Honor*, 1985), and hard-boiled PIs alike (*Chinatown*, 1974; *The Two Jakes*, 1990). Some might even regard the sinister, eternally grinning "Joker" in Tim Burton's *Batman* (1988) as the culminating fusion of his classic roles. Hard to believe that for many years it seemed that the movie star born in Neptune, New Jersey, in 1937 was not destined to make it big as an actor. In the late 1950s, he joined the team of legendary exploitation film director/producer Roger Corman, performing bit roles in his horror flicks and wannabe rockumentaries, as well as writing screenplays. His screenwriting credits include Monte Hellman's Western *Ride in the Whirlwind* (1965) and Corman's exploration in LSD entitled *The Trip* (1967). The turning point in his career came with his role as a perpetually inebriated lawyer in *Easy Rider* (1969). Dennis Hopper's drama about the disappearance of the American Dream quickly attained cult status and earned Nicholson his first of many Oscar nods. His rise to superstardom reached its inevitable height in the 1970s. Among his many credits and honors, Nicholson has been awarded three Oscars, not to mention the projects he has directed himself. Still very much alive in the business, his more recent movies often feature him as stubborn, eccentric types. He likewise proved his formidable skills as an actor in *About Schmidt* (2003) and *The Departed* (2006). *The Bucket List* (2010), a tragicomedy directed by Rob Reiner, however, was considered a flop by most critics.

THE PASSENGER

PROFESSIONE: REPORTER / PROFESSION: REPORTER

1975 – ITALY / FRANCE / SPAIN / USA – 125 MIN.
DIRECTOR MICHELANGELO ANTONIONI (1912–2007)
SCREENPLAY MARK PEPLOE, PETER WOLLEN,
MICHELANGELO ANTONIONI
DIRECTOR OF PHOTOGRAPHY LUCIANO TOVOLI
EDITING MICHELANGELO ANTONIONI, FRANCO ARCALLI
MUSIC IVAN VANDOR PRODUCTION CARLO PONTI for
CIPI CINEMATOGRAFICA S. A., COMPAGNIA
CINEMATOGRAFICA CHAMPION,
LES FILMS CONCORDIA, MGM
STARRING JACK NICHOLSON (David Locke),
MARIA SCHNEIDER (The Girl), IAN HENDRY (Martin
Knight), JENNY RUNACRE (Rachel Locke),
CHUCK MULVEHILL (Robertson), STEVEN BERKOFF
(Stephen), AMBROISE BIA (Achebe), JOSÉ MARÍA
CAFFAREL (Hotel Owner), ÁNGEL DEL POZO
(Police Inspector), MANFRED SPIES (Stranger)

"People disappear every day." – "Every time they leave the room."

"No family, no friends – just a couple of obligations and a weak heart." This is how the arms dealer Robertson (Chuck Mulvehill) sums up his life. British journalist David Locke (Jack Nicholson) encounters his compatriot in a hotel in the middle of the Sahara desert, and a few hours later, he finds him dead in his room. With hardly a second thought, Locke assumes the dead man's identity – partly for professional reasons, and partly (as the viewer gradually discovers) because he has become as estranged from his own life as from his profession as a war reporter. The ink isn't dry on the famous journalist's obituaries before Locke has arranged to meet with Robertson's contractors – a group of African freedom fighters. Clearly, Robertson had be-

lieved in what he was doing; and as conviction is precisely what Locke's life has been lacking, he uses the dead man's calendar to pick up where Robertson had left off.

It seems, at first, that the change of identity has gone off without a hitch. Soon, however, there's a bunch of people pursuing the imposter: not just Robertson's business partners, but his enemies too; and – last, not least – the "widow" of David Locke … In flight from his own past and another man's future, the journalist is clearly in mortal danger.

Locke is joined by a young student (Maria Schneider), who is fascinated by his radical self-erasure and "rebirth." Yet he knows he'll have to come

2

clean eventually, and his attempts to evade his pursuers are half-hearted. The journey ends in a Spanish no-man's-land, a kind of wilderness like the African desert in which it began.

For director Michelangelo Antonioni, the thriller plot of *The Passenger* is a vehicle for reflections on human identity. From the bits and pieces available to him, Locke tries desperately to reconstruct Robertson's life, but the attempt ends in failure. The arms dealer remains a phantom, for Robertson has no reality apart from the complex network of relationships that constituted his unique existence. Even in his new identity, Locke falls victim to the contradictions inherent in his own profession. Antonioni shows us the journalist as a man doomed to passivity, even in his most active moments. Fragments of interviews from Locke's journalistic past reveal the roots of his crisis. Whether his subject was a magician or a dictator, the actual person, the real significance, always remained hidden. What we see is what we get, but we only ever

"I don't have anything to say but perhaps something to show."

Michelangelo Antonioni, in: The Architecture of Vision. Writings and Interviews on Cinema

MICHELANGELO ANTONIONI Antonioni was born in Ferrara in 1912, and died in Rome in 2007. He began his career as a writer of short stories and as a contributor to the Italian film journal *Cinema*, the cradle of neorealism. After making several short documentaries, Antonioni retreated from the view that the cinema should serve a political agenda, and his first feature, *Story of a Love Affair* (*Cronaca di un amore*, 1950) broke with conventional narrative techniques. Until the mid-'60s, Antonioni's great theme was "the sickness of feelings," depicted in films such as *The Night* (*La notte*, 1960), *The Eclipse* (*L'eclisse*, 1962), and *Red Desert* (*Il deserto rosso*, 1964). In his later works, *Blow-Up* (1966), *Zabriskie Point* (1969), and *The Passenger* (*Professione: reporter / Profession: reporter*, 1975), he examined the emotional and existential rootlessness of modern humanity. These films also express Antonioni's distrust of superficial appearances. To him, the essential nature of a thing is forever hidden beneath its visible surface, and no image or representation can alter this fact. In Antonioni's work, landscapes, buildings, gestures, and sounds are the symbols of interior realities; he creates what has been termed a "dramaturgy of the fragmentary," where "the form swallows the content." (Thomas Christen in *du* Magazin 11/1995). At times, his style is almost mannered, perhaps too much in love with effects. Yet his considered use of technical means – like the slow-motion explosion in *Zabriskie Point* or the closing sequence of *The Passenger* – stands in striking contrast to his intuitive working methods, exemplified by his frequent changes to the dialogue during filming. Unlike most of his Italian or American counterparts, Antonioni seems to approach his subjects tentatively, watchfully, as if waiting for an opening, a way into their deeper meaning. As he put it himself: "I know what I have to do. Not what I mean."

1   Lost for words: as gunrunner Robertson, David
    Locke (Jack Nicholson) loses his grip on reality.

2   Who did you say you were? Despite their unbridled
    intimacy, Locke and his nameless companion
    (Maria Schneider) never really get close.

3   One corpse and a fake ID: Locke is surprised how
    easy it is to become someone else.

4   Ticket to ride: on the road to nowhere, in flight
    from the unknown.

see what we want to see – or the little we're shown. In a sense Locke is the director's alter ego, for he too is lumbered with perceivable reality, the only material available to him. As the plot dissolves into a plethora of locations and narrative levels, *The Passenger* emerges as a thesis on the possibility or impossibility of visual representation per se. A recurring metaphor: doors and windows that reveal only a portion of the past or the present. Whatever the image, the camera lingers a little longer than necessary, as if waiting for the magical moment when the visible world will finally yield up its secrets.

The seven-minute final sequence is a final reminder that we wait in vain for revelation. Locke is recumbent on his bed in a hotel room, but the camera angle makes him invisible to the audience; through the window, we see the village square, and the bullring beyond it; a car drives past; a boy throws rocks at a beggar; and the girl converses with various people.

In the midst of these barely decipherable details, the true drama remains hidden, indicated only by the vague sound of a single shot. The camera passes through the barred window, describes a broad curve around the square and comes back round to gaze through the window once more: At the end of his aimless journey, David Locke has arrived at the only inevitable destination.

SH

TAXI DRIVER

1976 – USA – 113 MIN.
DIRECTOR MARTIN SCORSESE (*1942)
SCREENPLAY PAUL SCHRADER
DIRECTOR OF PHOTOGRAPHY MICHAEL CHAPMAN
EDITING TOM ROLF, MELVIN SHAPIRO,
MARCIA LUCAS MUSIC BERNARD HERRMANN
PRODUCTION JULIA PHILLIPS, MICHAEL PHILLIPS
for BILL/PHILLIPS PRODUCTIONS,
COLUMBIA PICTURES CORPORATION
STARRING ROBERT DE NIRO (Travis Bickle),
CYBILL SHEPHERD (Betsy), JODIE FOSTER (Iris),
HARVEY KEITEL (Sport), ALBERT BROOKS (Tom),
PETER BOYLE (Wizard), MARTIN SCORSESE
(Passenger), STEVEN PRINCE (Andy
the Gun Dealer), DIAHNNE ABBOTT
(Candy Saleswoman), VICTOR ARGO (Melio)
IFF CANNES 1976 GOLDEN PALM for
BEST FILM (Martin Scorsese)

"You talkin' to me?"

The restless, metallic strokes of the musical theme in the opening sequence say it all: this film is a threat. A rising steam cloud hangs over the street and covers the screen in white. As if out of nowhere, a yellow cab penetrates the eerie wall of steam and smoke, gliding through in slow motion. The background music abruptly ends atonally; the ethereal taxi disappears, the cloud closing up behind it. Two dark eyes appear in close up, accompanied by a gentle jazz theme. In the flickering light of the colorful street lamps they wander from side to side, as if observing the surroundings. They are the eyes of Travis Bickle (Robert De Niro), a New York taxi driver who will become an avenging angel.

Even at the premiere in 1976, *Taxi Driver* split the critics. Some saw the main character as a disturbed soul who revels in his role as savior of a young prostitute, for whom he kills three shady characters in an excessively bloody rampage, an act for which the press fetes him as a hero. Others looked more closely and detected a skillfully stylized film language in the melancholy images and a common urban sociopath behind the figure of the madman Travis Bickle: "On every street, in every city, there's a nobody who dreams of being somebody," reads one of the film posters.

Travis can't sleep at night. To earn a few cents he becomes a taxi driver. He'll drive anytime and anywhere, he says in his interview. He will

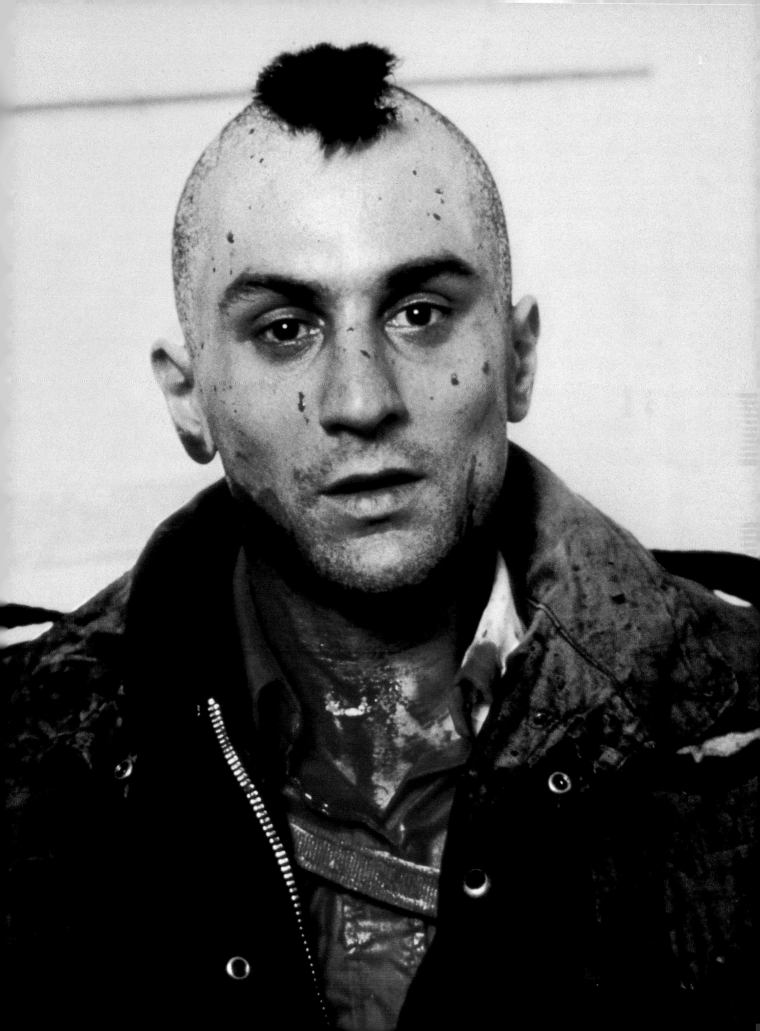

even enter the neighborhoods his colleagues avoid at all costs – the districts with either too little or too much light, in which street gangs loiter around and teenage prostitutes wait for johns under bright neon lights. Travis is given the job. He and his taxi become one and the catastrophe takes its course. Like Travis, the audience gazes out of the driving taxi into the night. Rarely was New York depicted as impressively. The camera style switches between half-documentary and subjective takes. Bernard Herrmann's suggestive music, which accompanies the film, lends it an acoustic structure, creating a unique combination of image and sound. The taxi driving becomes nothing less than a metaphor of film.

Travis's attempt to build a romantic relationship with campaign assistant Betsy (Cybill Shepherd) fails. He can neither express himself, nor his feel-

1   Travis Bickle (Robert De Niro) in the midst of battle.

2   Soldier of fortune at a buck a mile: ex-Marine Travis Bickle, at war with New York.

3   Talk to the hand: Travis helps stamp out violent crime.

4   This screen ain't big enough for the two of us: both pimp (Harvey Keitel) and taxi driver are used to getting their own way.

"Martin Scorsese's *Taxi Driver* is a homage to home from a homeless man; a New York Western, with a midnight cowboy cruising the canyons in a shabby yellow cab." *Der Spiegel*

"An utterly strange, disturbing, alarming and fascinating film. Syncretic and glamorous, it is a lurking reptile that changes color like a chameleon; a synthetic amalgam of conflicting influences, tendencies and metaphysical ambitions, raised to the power of a myth: comical, edgy, hysterical." *Frankfurter Rundschau*

5

5   Jodie Foster as the child prostitute, Iris. Nonethe-
    less, it was Foster's older sister who stood in as
    her body double for the more mature shots.

6   Election campaigner Betsy (Cybill Shepherd) is the
    object of Travis's desire.

ngs, which is why in the end he turns to the gun. Isolated and aimless, he wanders through the city. Travis's story resembles the yellow taxi cab that sliced through the cloud of smoke in the opening sequence. He too emerges out of nowhere, briefly appears in the night light of the city, and vanishes again into nothingness. Travis is no hero, even if many applauded the brutal rampage at the premiere. Violence is naturally an important theme of the film, but the violence is not merely physical, but social. Travis embodies a person who has lost himself in the big city. Robert De Niro gave this type a face and an unmistakable body.

Scorsese is known for creating his films on paper. He draws them like sketches in a storyboard, and time and again he shows that images are his true language. The screenplay was the work of Paul Schrader, and marked the first close collaboration between these two film-obsessed men. The scene in which Travis stands before the mirror shirtless, clutching his revolver and picks a fight with himself is unforgettable: "You talkin' to me? Well I'm the only one here. Who do you think you're talking to?" The scene has been cited over and over, but the original remains unattainable. It is a modern classic.   SF

MARTIN SCORSESE A concert film (*The Last Waltz*, 1978), a musical (*New York, New York*, 1977), a gambling film (*The Color of Money*, 1986), a costume film (*The Age of Innocence*, 1993) – director Martin Scorsese has never committed himself to a specific genre. Born on November 17, 1942, the son of Sicilian immigrants in New York, Scorsese grew up in the Catholic neighborhood of Little Italy and originally intended to join the priesthood. Although he dropped his ecclesiastical ambitions to begin studying at the New York University Film School, religious themes with stories of damnation and redemption run through many of his films. In *The Last Temptation of Christ* (1988) and the Buddhist film *Kundun* (1997) he directly addressed religious motifs. Scorsese's personal style had already established itself by his third feature film. *Mean Streets* (1973) – a story about friendship, loyalty, repentance, and atonement – has a documentary-like touch, with Robert De Niro and Harvey Keitel in leading roles. Scorsese achieved his breakthrough with *Taxi Driver* (1976), a masterpiece about a psychopath (Robert De Niro) who feels he has been chosen to combat big city scum. De Niro became his most important leading actor, portraying Jake LaMotta in *Raging Bull* (1980) and dominating Scorsese's two epic Mafia films, *GoodFellas* (1990) and *Casino* (1995). In his more recent films – *Gangs of New York* (2002), *The Departed* (2006), and *Shutter Island* (2010) – his leading actor of choice has been Leonardo DiCaprio. Scorsese also received his first Oscar for *The Departed*, finally, after five nominations. Scorsese's 3-D film *Hugo* (2011), his declaration of love to cinema itself, was nominated in 11 categories, and ultimately awarded five Oscars. Key members of the Scorsese film clan include screenplay author Paul Schrader, editor Thelma Schoonmaker, and cameraman Michael Ballhaus. Scorsese is not only a gifted stylist, but also a profound student of film. He made two documentaries about the American and the Italian cinema: *A Personal Journey with Martin Scorsese Through American Movies* (1995) and *My Voyage to Italy* (*Il mio viaggio in Italia*, 1999), both of which are sweeping cinematic panoramas, as knowledgeable as they are passionate.

To break the driver, the cop was willing to break the law.

THE DRIVER

A LAWRENCE GORDON PRODUCTION **RYAN O'NEAL · BRUCE DERN · ISABELLE ADJANI** in **"THE DRIVER"**
Co-Starring RONEE BLAKLEY · Associate Producer FRANK MARSHALL · Produced by LAWRENCE GORDON
Written and Directed by WALTER HILL · Music MICHAEL SMALL · A Twentieth Century-Fox / EMI Films Presentation
AVAILABLE IN PAPERBACK FROM BALLANTINE BOOKS   COLOR BY DeLUXE ®   **R** RESTRICTED

THE DRIVER

1978 – USA – 91 MIN.
DIRECTOR WALTER HILL (*1942)
SCREENPLAY WALTER HILL
DIRECTOR OF PHOTOGRAPHY PHILIP H. LATHROP
EDITING TINA HIRSCH, ROBERT K. LAMBERT
MUSIC MICHAEL SMALL PRODUCTION LAWRENCE GORDON
for EMI FILMS LTD., 20TH CENTURY FOX
STARRING RYAN O'NEAL (The Driver), BRUCE DERN
(The Detective), ISABELLE ADJANI (The Player),
RONEE BLAKELY (The Agent), MATT CLARK
(Red Plainclothesman), FELICE ORLANDI
(Gold Plainclothesman), JOSEPH WALSH (Glasses),
RUDY RAMOS (Teeth), DENNY MACKO
(Exchange Man), WILL WALKER (Fingers),
SANDY BROWN WYETH (Split)

"I respect a man who's good at what he does. I'll tell you something else: I'm very good at what I do."

The streets and the garages are his turf. Director Walter Hill wastes no time in getting to the point in the very first scene of *The Driver*: cars are the calling of his hero – his manifest destiny. The Driver (Ryan O'Neal), an experienced getaway gangster, enters an underground parking garage. He inspects his surroundings, walks confidently to a car and jimmies the lock in a matter of seconds. After a quick look at the steering wheel, he starts the engine. The Driver was put on this Earth for one reason only: to drive. The audience need know no more about this man, and true enough we do effectively learn nothing else about him in the 90 minutes still to come. He has no name, no past, and carries no emotional baggage. He has found his place in life in the

driver's seat. He looks out of place in the cheap hotel rooms in which he disappears after his jobs. His nemesis, the Detective (Bruce Dern), remains equally indistinct. What connects the two men is the obsession with which they follow their goals. They seldom laugh, and are almost fanatically driven, a characteristic that will unite them in the end.

The plot of *The Driver* is as minimalist as its characterization: the Driver commits crimes for which the Detective tries to nab him. The duel that develops from this constellation, though it provides for several twists and turns, can be reduced to a game of cat and mouse between two men. This game is the springboard for the entire story – even extending

1   Cloak and dagger: the detective (Bruce Dern) will catch the driver if it kills him, and it just may.

2   A game of cat and mouse: poker-faced player (Isabelle Adjani) doesn't give anything away.

4   Four eyes on the target: gangster Glasses (Joseph Walsh) arouses the driver's wrath.

3   All revved up with nowhere to go: the driver (Ryan O'Neal) earns a living driving getaway cars.

to the ambiguous relationship both men have with the same woman (Isabelle Adjani). Nothing distracts from the game: the scenery – streets, garages, warehouses, and bars – almost all are set in the desolate, nocturnal metropolis, and remain just as abstract as the characters. The dramatization renounces fancy camerawork and clever editing, and the spartan dialogue matches the tight-mouthed style of its protagonists, who never waste or mince their words. During their encounters, the Detective calls the Driver a cowboy, a comparison that astutely picks up on the Western-like plot and style of this Walter Hill big city ballad. And true to the best of the West, the piece culminates in a classic showdown between the rival gunslingers, as their two cars face off with one another before they race to the finish.

"By the end of *The Driver* you can almost smell the rubber burning." *Variety*

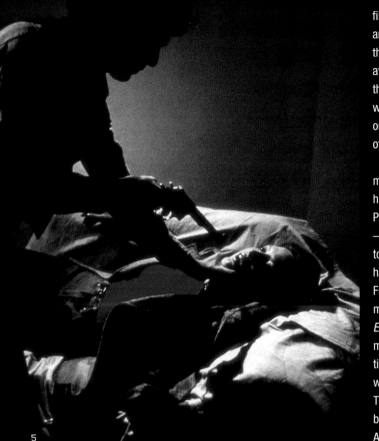

Hill skillfully combines these stylistic elements with components from film noir and the thriller – just as he would later do with *Streets of Fire* (1984) and *Last Man Standing* (1996): manipulation and bold tactical moves govern the game on both sides. The Driver understands the risks he takes. He is fully aware that the Detective will set a trap for him. That he ultimately agrees to the duel is a question of honor: the Detective openly challenges him: "If you win, you'll get some money. If I win, you'll get 15 years." To emerge victorious you not only have to be a real gambler, you've got to be in full command of the game.

Part of this game are the breathtaking chases: legions of faceless policemen appear on the street from nowhere and pursue the Driver, fail to match his driving skills, and vanish into nothingness. As a director's assistant on Peter Yates' *Bullitt* (1968), Walter Hill attentively peered over his shoulder and – together with stunt coordinator Everett Creach – used what he learned to choreograph several chase sequences in *The Driver*. These sequences heavily influenced the genre and are still cited today in movies like John Frankenheimer's *Ronin* (1998). Hill's stylistic and dramatic ambition is unmistakably present in films like *Vanishing Point* (1970) and *The Sugarland Express* (1974), where the spiritual home of the hero was always an automobile. But despite such sensational action sequences, and scattered eruptions of violence (which however are always necessary: the Driver kills only when he is left with no other choice), *The Driver* is a calm, easygoing film. The adversaries secretly observe one another, and the audience follows suit by observing how the characters are forced to react under extreme pressure. And as witnesses, the audience also becomes part of the game.　　　ES

5

5　A criminal constitution: bullets provide an exit when there's no way out.

6　Recovery ward: between jobs the driver recuperates in dreary motel rooms. And like a true outlaw he has no past, no friends, and no home.

"There's a nightmarish thrill to the chase sequences and the claustrophobic underworld of subterranean parking lots." *film-dienst*

WALTER HILL Walter Hill, born January 10, 1942, in Long Beach, California, is considered a solid craftsman among Hollywood's mainstream filmmakers. But this does director, author, and producer Walter Hill only partial justice. Walter Hill belongs to the small group of action film virtuosos who made their mark on the genre in the 1970s and 1980s. After he got his foot in the film industry door, among other jobs as the second directorial assistant for *The Thomas Crown Affair* (1968), Hill wrote screenplays, including the script for Sam Peckinpah's *The Getaway* (1972). He made his directorial debut in 1975 with the action drama *Hard Times / The Streetfighter*. His two subsequent films, *The Driver* (1978) and the street gang drama *The Warriors* (1978) helped form his visual and narrative style. Hill straightforwardly dramatized his bitter stories of broken men with no frills. His characters are not big talkers, they are defined by their actions – a tradition from which he deviated only in buddy movies like *48 Hrs.* (1982), in which Nick Nolte doesn't shoot anywhere near as quickly as Eddie Murphy runs his mouth.
Otherwise Walter Hill dramatized brilliant, taciturn, and brutal "guy movies" that only seldom offered women a main role: *Southern Comfort* (1981) is his answer to John Boorman's *Deliverance* (1972), *Streets of Fire* (1984) a fascinating symbiosis of Western myths and big city ballad, and *Extreme Prejudice* (1987) a macho Western in modern dress. Hill displayed his proclivity for the most American of all film genres in the Westerns *The Long Riders* (1980), *Geronimo: An American Legend* (1993), and *Wild Bill* (1995). And his final masterpiece, *Last Man Standing* (1996), a remake of Akira Kurosawa's *Yojimbo* (1961), also breathes the spirit of the stoic Western hero. In 1989 Walter Hill exhibited a much more humorous side for a television project: he was one of the producers of the self-consciously ironic horror series *Tales from the Crypt*.

DIVA

1981 – FRANCE – 117 MIN.
DIRECTOR JEAN-JACQUES BEINEIX (*1946)
SCREENPLAY JEAN-JACQUES BEINEIX, JEAN VAN HAMME,
based on the novel of the same name by
DELACORTA [= DANIEL ROBERT ODIER]
DIRECTOR OF PHOTOGRAPHY PHILIPPE ROUSSELOT
EDITING MARIE-JOSÈPHE YOYOTTE, MONIQUE PRIM
MUSIC VLADIMIR COSMA
PRODUCTION IRÈNE SILBERMAN for GREENWICH FILM
PRODUCTIONS, FILMS A2, LES FILMS GALAXIE
STARRING FRÉDÉRIC ANDRÉI (Jules), WILHELMENIA
WIGGINS-FERNANDEZ (Cynthia Hawkins), RICHARD
BOHRINGER (Gorodish), THUY AN LUU (Alba),
JACQUES FABBRI (Jean Saporta), DOMINIQUE PINON
(Le curé), GÉRARD DARMON (L'Antillais),
JEAN-JACQUES MOREAU (Krantz), ANNY ROMAND
(Paula), CHANTAL DERUAZ (Nadja, an ex-prostitute)

"There is no such thing as innocent pleasure."

Jules (Frédéric Andréi), a young Parisian postman, loves opera with a passion. He is particularly devoted to the singer Cynthia Hawkins (Wilhelmenia Wiggins-Fernandez), a true diva who flatly refuses to make records, much to the annoyance of her manager. When she gives a concert in Paris, Jules succeeds in making a top-quality bootleg recording of her performance. His achievement doesn't go unnoticed; from now on, the naïve fan will be pursued everywhere he goes by two shady "businessmen" from the Taiwanese pirate-music mafia. As if the situation weren't dangerous enough, Jules is soon the hapless recipient of a second tape, bearing proof that the chief of

the Parisian police is also running a drugs-and-prostitution ring. In next to no time, a team of killers are hot on Jules's heels.

Like many a cult film, *Diva* flopped when first released. The French critics were decidedly sniffy about Jean-Jacques Beineix's directing debut, describing it as glossy but hollow, and moviegoers initially also showed little interest. Only after the film received an enthusiastic reception at American festivals did *Diva* begin to attract a mainly young audience in Europe. It gradually became one of the biggest hits of the '80s. *Diva* ran and ran … and what's more, its influence was considerable: it marked the beginning of

the French "neon cinema," an anti-intellectual counterblast to the dominant *cinema des auteurs* of the older generation. Beineix and Luc Besson were to be the leading lights of this brash new movement.

Diva is undeniably a film that likes to be looked at. It's a fairy-tale thriller that focuses entirely on overwhelming visual effects, at the expense of narrative and character development. So while it's fair to say that Beineix's film is superficial, it cannot be denied that it also functions brilliantly at this surface level. For one thing, the film is edited so superbly that sheer tempo makes the holes in the plot seem negligible. Philippe Rousselot's camerawork is particularly outstanding. The artificiality of the film's imagery constitutes an all-but-independent cosmos, a synthetic parallel world consisting entirely of spectacular locations, and intersecting only tangentially with the

"A designer fairy tale, in which a decked out pad and Revox stereo are more significant than the protagonist's innermost thoughts." *Süddeutsche Zeitung*

1 Sleek and chic: *Diva* marked the advent of 1980s French Neon Cinema – a movement that basked in artificiality rather than the realism of the auteurs.

2 Skin-deep: Beineix's characters luxuriate in superficiality, but fail to fathom deeper waters.

3 Prima Wilhelmenia: a set of powerhouse pipes turned Wiggins-Fernandez into a screen icon.

4 Projection room: lackluster Jules's (Frédéric Andréi) voyeuristic fixation on the singer win him the hearts of the crowd.

5 Golden opportunity: from the wings of the supporting cast, dashing Bohemian Gorodish (Richard Bohringer) suddenly emerges as the film's true hero.

5

JEAN-JACQUES BEINEIX Jean-Jacques Beineix (*1946 in Paris) originally studied medicine, before beginning his film career as an assistant to directors as famous as René Clément and Claude Berri. He was 34 by the time he came to make his first film, *Diva* (1981), which got off to a poor start in France before being enthusiastically received on the American festival circuit. Word spread back to Europe, and it eventually became one of the most successful films of the '80s, establishing Beineix's reputation as a cult director. The public enjoyed *Diva*'s visual brilliance and its characteristic fairy-tale atmosphere, qualities that also marked Beineix's later work and had a lasting influence on the "neon cinema" of the '80s. The critics, however, accused him of superficiality, and his subsequent films failed to mollify them. *The Moon in the Gutter* (*La Lune dans le caniveau*, 1983) was a naïve love story about a longshoreman and a rich girl; *Betty Blue* (*37°2 le matin*, 1985) – Beineix's second big box-office hit – was a fashionable adaptation of Philippe Dijan's best seller; and *Roselyne and the Lions* (*Roselyne et les lions*, 1989) was a somewhat unhappy circus film. After *IP 5* (*IP 5: L'île aux pachydermes*, 1992), noted mainly for the fact that Yves Montand died shortly after the film was completed, Beineix withdrew from the cinema, devoted his time to painting, and made a few documentary films. He attempted a comeback with the surrealistic thriller *Mortal Transfer* (*Mortel transfert*, 2001), but was unable to repeat the success he had enjoyed in the '80s.

real city of Paris. The slow-moving camera draws us in, as if we were dreaming Jules's dreams. And these are the daydreams of an overgrown boy who's built a fantastic playpen in his factory flat, complete with clapped-out luxury limousines, sultry Pop art paintings and a hi-tech beast of a sound system. Safe in this pubertal paradise, Jules can indulge in fantasies of a thrilling existence… until reality intervenes, forcing him to endure a series of perilous adventures before he can win the heart of his opera diva. The lady in question is played by Wilhelmenia Wiggins-Fernandez, and the scenes in which Jean-Jacques Beineix captures her wonderful voice are undoubtedly the high points of the film.

Jules, the gawky hero, would hardly have survived without the support of two guardian angels: Gorodish (Richard Bohringer), a master of the art of living, and his Vietnamese companion Alba (Thuy An Luu). At the time,

many felt that the eccentric Gorodish was the real hero of the film; not just because he freed Jules from every fine mess he got himself into, and kept his cool while doing so, but because he embodied the essential attitudes of the age. This was a generation that had turned its back on ideological struggle and accepted the fact that the world is corrupt. Thus the '80s witnessed a collective retreat from the public to the private sphere, and lifestyle became indistinguishable from life itself. Gorodish was equally at home in a loft or a lighthouse, and happy behind the wheel of a hoodlum's white Citroën; he could conjure up cars like Felix the Cat, and he smoked fine cigars to the music of the spheres while soaking in a freestanding bathtub. The man was almost heroic in his hedonism, and a perfect paragon of '80s style.

JH

BLOW OUT

1981 – USA – 108 MIN.
DIRECTOR BRIAN DE PALMA (*1940)
SCREENPLAY BRIAN DE PALMA
DIRECTOR OF PHOTOGRAPHY VILMOS ZSIGMOND
EDITING PAUL HIRSCH MUSIC PINO DONAGGIO
PRODUCTION GEORGE LITTO for BRIGHTON PRODUCTIONS,
FILMWAYS PICTURES, CINEMA 77
STARRING JOHN TRAVOLTA (Jack Terri), NANCY ALLEN
(Sally Bedina), JOHN LITHGOW (Burke), DENNIS FRANZ
(Manny Karp), PETER BOYDEN (Sam), CURT MAY
(Frank Donahue), JOHN AQUINO (Detective Mackey),
JOHN MCMARTIN (Lawrence Henry), LORI-NAN
ENGLER (Sue), DEBORAH EVERTON (Prostitute)

"It's a good scream."

In the dead of night, a careening car swerves from the road, crashes through the barrier of a bridge, and plunges into the water below. Sound technician Jack Terri (John Travolta), who is coincidentally in the area recording nocturnal sounds for a film soundtrack, jumps in after the car and is just able to save young cosmetics saleswoman Sally Bedina (Nancy Allen) from drowning. Later, in the hospital, Jack learns that presidential candidate George McRyan was behind the wheel and that he was killed in the accident. Apparently he picked Sally up at a party, a detail that his advisers are intent on concealing from the press to prevent his good reputation from being posthumously sullied.

Unconvinced by the official explanation of the cause of the accident – a tire that was supposed to have blown out – Jack listens to his recordings from the fateful night again. Having unintentionally documented the noises of the accident, he discovers that the unmistakable crack of a gunshot can be heard directly before the sound of the exploding tire. Regarded as a

self-important idiot by the police, Jack's only supporter is a television journalist who wants to use the spectacular recording to increase viewer ratings.

Together with Sally, Jack is determined to uncover exactly what happened. But it becomes clear that Sally is much more deeply involved in the situation than she initially acknowledged. In fact, she was being paid to hit on the politician to allow photographer Manny Karp (Dennis Franz) to take compromising pictures. Using this same tactic in the past, the two had managed to dupe countless unfaithful husbands. But Sally suspects that this time, her employer intended her to die as well. And indeed, the would-be assassin (John Lithgow) who fired the shot at the car is planning to murder Sally to prevent her impending testimony.

Pretending to be a reporter interested in Jack's recordings, he calls Sally and arranges a meeting to make the exchange. Jack remains skeptical, particularly after his studio is broken into and all of his tapes are erased. He makes Sally wear a wire so that he can follow her meeting with the

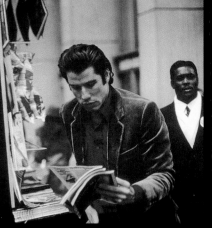

"Writer-director Brian De Palma saw another side to Travolta, casting him as Jack Terri. *Blow Out* may have expanded Travolta's range, but it didn't change his prospects." *Entertainment Weekly*

1 Tricks of the trade: Brian De Palma swings his characters and the audience into a duplicitous reality, underscored by the constant buzzing of a recording studio and cinematic sleights of hand. John Travolta as Jack Terri.

2 Dreaming of a better life leads Sally Bedina (Nancy Allen) to her death.

3 The magazine image of a car accident is just one of the many pieces in this multimedia jigsaw puzzle.

4 The truth that Jack Terri tries to unearth in celluloid and audiotape only entangles him further.

5 The contract killer (John Lithgow) is so sly and flawless in his trade that his actions are soon beyond the control of those who hire him.

reporter from a distance. Quickly realizing that she is in danger, he takes up the chase, but his search is slowed when he finds himself in the midst of the Liberty Day Parade. When he finally finds them, the assassin has already drawn his knife. Under the glow of the ceremonial fireworks, Jack wrestles the blade from his hands and stabs him. But help comes too late for Sally: she is already dead.

Adhering to the aesthetics of the early '80s – choppy camera, rhythmically accentuated music, and heavy makeup for John Travolta – Brian De Palma combines themes of a political thriller with a complex critique of the media. The film begins with a dramatic clip from a "slasher movie" Jack is working on: a heavy-breathing psychotic killer sneaks into a house full of libidinous young women and slowly approaches a showering girl with his raised knife. The woman's scream is so implausible that the producer immediately stops the take. At the end of the film we see the scene once again, but this time the bloodcurdling scream is entirely convincing. Jack used the recording of Sally's authentic scream, which he captured over the radio while she was being murdered.

In addition to addressing media cynicism and strategies, the reality of the pictures is also emphasized. Both the sounds that Jack recorded and the photos, taken with entirely different intentions by Manny Karp, contain fortuitous clues to the events surrounding the crime. This demands an abundance of deciphering work. First, Jack has to cut out Karp's photos, which are printed in a magazine, and then, much like making a flicker book, patch them together to make a moving picture to accompany his own background recordings, eventually revealing the entire truth.

De Palma falls back on photographic and audio-related themes that had already been invoked: the former by Antonioni's *Blow Up* (1966) and the latter by Coppola's *The Conversation* (1974). This tendency to repetition or lack of originality is also discernible in his subsequent films and has attracted criticism. But *Blow Out* does succeed in demonstrating that the combination of somewhat hackneyed themes can produce something entirely new, and is a good a recipe as any to build up nerve-wracking suspense.

MS

BRIAN DE PALMA Like his contemporaries Martin Scorsese and Francis Ford Coppola, Brian De Palma finds much inspiration for his films in a comprehensive knowledge of cinematic history. But unlike his aforementioned friends and colleagues, he's never been showered with praise: his critics often criticize him for being little more than a technically competent Hitchcock disciple. Inspired by the French *Nouvelle Vague*, he made a series of short films before the '70s, when he achieved great commercial success with such thrillers as *Sisters* (1973) and the film adaptation of Stephen King's novel *Carrie* (1976). He was eventually nominated for an Oscar for *The Untouchables* (1986). His last box-office smash was the spy thriller, *Mission: Impossible* (1996), with Tom Cruise. The sci-fi film *Mission to Mars* (2000) was a commercial flop, as was his homage to film noir *The Black Dahlia* (2006). His thriller *Femme Fatale* (2002) was also panned by the critics but now enjoys cult status.

PRINCE OF THE CITY

1981 – USA – 167 MIN.
DIRECTOR SIDNEY LUMET (1924–2011)
SCREENPLAY JAY PRESSON ALLEN, SIDNEY LUMET,
based on the novel by ROBERT DALEY
DIRECTOR OF PHOTOGRAPHY ANDRZEJ BARTKOWIAK
EDITING JOHN J. FITZSTEPHENS MUSIC PAUL CHIHARA
PRODUCTION BURTT HARRIS for ORION PICTURES
STARRING TREAT WILLIAMS (Daniel Ciello), JERRY ORBACH
(Gus Levy), RICHARD FORONJY (Joe Marinaro),
DON BILLETT (Bill Mayo), KENNY MARINO (Dom Bando),
CARMINE CARIDI (Gino Mascone), TONY PAGE
(Raf Alvarez), BOB BALABAN (Santimassino),
NORMAN PARKER (Rick Cappalino),
STEVE INWOOD (Mario Vincente)

"I'm gonna spend the rest of my life lying!"

"City of New York. Police Department. Daniel Ciello. Detective." The film opens with a shot of a service badge. Danny (Treat Williams) and his four fellow officers are introduced in a no-nonsense manner to the audience, as I.D. papers flash across the screen. The five of them work for the S.I.U., a special investigative unit that targets drug traffickers. They enjoy many perks not afforded to regular officers. They operate independently of the department, choosing their own hours and the cases they take on. These men are seasoned professionals who've seen it all. They'll hook up their junkie informants with drugs in return for dirt on the big dealers. One day Danny is approached by Rick Cappalino (Norman Parker) from the special division on police corruption, the so-called Chase Commission. He singles Danny out and begins to ask him some questions. There are no official charges being brought against him, he just wants to "chat." The two investigators start meeting regularly and Danny displays obvious interest in Cappalino's work; he hopes to be able to work with Cappalino in the near future. Bugged with a wireless microphone, Danny is instructed to gather incriminating evidence against corrupt police officers. Although he is quick to ask that his partners be given total immunity, he soon realizes that he is no longer in a position to call the shots.

The nervous intensity at the top of this picture is reminiscent of the police dramas of the 1970s, full of New York street scenes and raw location footage filmed with a handheld camera. As the film progresses, these images are gradually replaced by a predominance of reduced, dark interior shots of ever-increasing intensity. These later shots reflect Danny's own isolation. His partners turn against him and the drug cartel puts his name at the top of its hit list, forcing him and his family to join the witness protection program. *Prince of the City* is by no means a film about heroes with badges; it is a psychological drama about one man who departs from what turns out to be a not so heroic life. A decision he is forced to pay for dearly.

Initially, Sidney Lumet's film does not necessarily read as a psychological thriller. Danny's motivation for working with internal affairs is only gradually revealed. A scene showing the cops during a major drug bust,

behaving like gangsters in a barbershop with scotch and cigars provides us with an early clue. But by the time a drug addict calls Danny out of bed and intimidates him into hooking him up with his next fix, it's abundantly clear why he wants out. Danny and his compatriots are in up to their necks. However, the film itself makes no extra point of condemning its protagonists, who consistently incriminate themselves with their "ends justify the means" philosophy.

Danny's partners fall from grace, but no one falls as far as Danny himself. He is severely punished for his honesty and must fear for his own life and those of his family, while enduring a seemingly endless series of humil-iating interrogations and legal indictments. The people he answers to on the other hand, namely Cappalino and district attorney Paige (Paul Roebling) are given promotions.

Prince of the City takes its story line from a fact-based novel by author Robert Daley about the life of Robert Leuci, a police detective who actually worked for the Chase Commission in 1971. Screenwriter Jay Presson Allen, who produced screenplays like Alfred Hitchcock's *Marnie* (1964) and the musical *Cabaret* (1972), and director Sidney Lumet put together a fascinating script which, in combination with a superb performance from Treat Williams, makes for a gripping film.   HJK

1 Under the bridge, downtown: special narcotics unit investigator Danny Ciello (Treat Williams) knows practically every corner and inch of this town, not to mention every single drug dealer and junkie.

2 & 3 "Undoubtedly someone familiar with police tactics has been associated with the film because the details seem so authentic."
Motion Picture Guide

4 In this dirty business, it's not always easy for drug-busting Danny to keep his hands clean.

5 It used to be that Danny and his buddies went after criminals; now everyone is going after him.

"A fanfare of endlessly varied verbal bravado filmed with the same panache and certitude as Coppola's *Godfather* trilogy, at the expense of a remarkable piece of casting and direction." *Positif*

SIDNEY LUMET Sidney Lumet (1924–2011) was a latecomer to the cinema, but he burst onto the scene. In 1957, at the age of 33, he shot his first feature film, a courtroom drama called *Twelve Angry Men* (1957) that immediately became a classic of the genre. Lumet received an Oscar nomination and was deemed a specialist in courtroom drama from then. This was not entirely unfounded. Lumet revisited this genre many times with films like *The Verdict* (1982) and *Guilty as Sin* (1993).
Still, his accomplishments are not limited to these films alone. His comprehensive body of work covers many film genres including: *The Pawnbroker* (1964), a psychological drama about a concentration camp survivor; *Network* (1976), a bitter satire about the media; not to mention *Garbo Talks* (1984), an enchanting, lighthearted comedy. Throughout his career he continually returned to police thrillers, and in films like *Serpico* (1973) and *Night Falls on Manhattan* (1997) he dealt specifically with police corruption. Shortly after receiving a well-deserved Honorary Oscar in 2005, he made an illustrious comeback with the crime thriller *Before the Devil Knows You're Dead* (2007). The master craftsman's personal memoirs of the film industry are recorded in his book *Making Movies*.

It's a hot summer.
Ned Racine is waiting for
something special to happen.

And when it does...

He won't be ready
for the consequences.

BODY
HEAT

*As the temperature rises,
the suspense begins.*

"BODY HEAT" WILLIAM HURT   KATHLEEN TURNER
and RICHARD CRENNA Written and Directed by LAWRENCE KASDAN
Produced by FRED T. GALLO PANAVISION® TECHNICOLOR®
A LADD COMPANY RELEASE

BODY HEAT

1981 – USA – 113 MIN.
DIRECTOR LAWRENCE KASDAN (*1949)
SCREENPLAY LAWRENCE KASDAN
DIRECTOR OF PHOTOGRAPHY RICHARD H. KLINE
EDITING CAROL LITTLETON MUSIC JOHN BARRY
PRODUCTION FRED T. GALLO for THE LADD COMPANY
STARRING WILLIAM HURT (Ned Racine),
KATHLEEN TURNER (Matty Walker), RICHARD CRENNA
(Edmund Walker), TED DANSON (Peter Lowenstein),
J. A. PRESTON (Oscar Grace),
MICKEY ROURKE (Teddy Lewis), KIM ZIMMER
(Mary Ann), JANE HALLAREN (Stella),
LANNA SAUNDERS (Roz Kraft),
CAROLA MCGUINNESS (Heather Kraft)

"Matty was the kind of woman who could do what was necessary. Whatever was necessary."

Hollywood loves clichés: things must be black or white, good or evil, and characters heroes or villains. More than other professionals, attorneys are consistently portrayed according to stereotypes. If they really were the way they are in the movies, there would only be two types of lawyers: staunch crusaders of justice, the "legal eagles," and shrewd, conniving vultures, who'd sell their mother for a pastrami sandwich. Hollywood tends to group the majority with the latter. They are seldom shown to be everyday people with human strengths and weaknesses.

Ned Racine (William Hurt), the attorney protagonist of Lawrence Kasdan's *Body Heat*, could probably be grouped with the second bunch of unsavories. He's not too bright, likes to chase skirts, drinks too much, and hates his job. Nonetheless, these are precisely the sort of attributes his latest conquest, Matty Walker (Kathleen Turner in her feature film debut), is looking for in a man: "You're not too smart, are you? I like that in a

man." Before he knows what's hit him, he's well over his head in a heated love affair with the married Matty and plotting to kill her husband. Only when it is too late does Ned suspect that he has fallen prey to a lethal scheme.

If this sounds familiar, it's because *Body Heat* was greatly inspired by one of Billy Wilder's American film noir masterpieces (*Double Indemnity*, 1944), which, in turn, was based on James M. Cain's novel of the same name. Written for the screen by Billy Wilder and Raymond Chandler, *Double Indemnity*, shot in flashback, tells the tale of an insurance salesman and a housewife who meet, fall in love, and murder her husband to collect on the insurance money. *Body Heat* takes place in the fictitious city of Miranda Beach, Florida, where the air is so heavy you could cut it with a knife. Nothing good blooms in this subtropical climate, which serves as a metaphor for burning passion, carnal lust, and moral depravity.

Body Heat was Lawrence Kasdan's directorial debut. Until then, Kasdan had been a scriptwriter, working on legendary blockbusters like George Lucas's science fiction film *Star Wars: Episode V – The Empire Strikes Back* (1980) and Steven Spielberg's action-adventure *Raiders of the Lost Ark* (1981), directed by Irvin Kershner. He cast actors in the leading roles of *Body Heat* who were virtually unknown at the time. William Hurt had only previously appeared in Ken Russell's *Altered States* (1980) and Kathleen Turner was an entirely new face at the box office.

The American film critic Pauline Kael scorned the film and its main actress in particular for all too obviously retracing the footsteps of her predecessors who had played similar roles. Kael went on to say that Turner couldn't fill these women's shoes. But not everyone agreed. *Body Heat* cannot simply be written off as a remake, because it is clearly aware of the films it pays homage to.

Kathleen Turner's face becomes a canvas onto which we can project such classic screen vixens as Barbara Stanwyck or Lauren Bacall. Turner, with her raw, seductive voice and cool, calculated composure, was so on target in her portrayal of the ice fox that for years after she was considered the consummate *femme fatale*. Kasdan, who also wrote the *Body Heat* screenplay, was right on the money with his curt and snappy one-liners. The dialogue resurrects the spirit of film noir classics, yet is firmly grounded in the style of the '80s. APO

"In her film debut, Turner registers strongly as a hard gal with a past. Her deep-voiced delivery instantly recalls that of young Lauren Bacall without seeming like an imitation." *Variety*

NEO FILM NOIR After Roman Polanski's *Chinatown* (1974) and Martin Scorsese's *Taxi Driver* (1976), film noir became one of the central film-historical reference points in '80s cinema. Films such as *Blade Runner* (1982), *The Terminator* (1984), *Subway* (1985), *Blue Velvet* (1986), *Angel Heart* (1986), and *Frantic* (1987) picked up the tradition of '40s and '50s film noir, and developed its subject matter and aesthetic position in widely differing ways. The fascination exerted by these tales of hopelessness derives from their "existentialist" atmosphere combined with their disorienting and disturbing pictorial compositions. The serial killer is one of the most unsettling newcomers to the neo film noir repertory, making prominent appearances in *The Silence of the Lambs* (1991), *Se7en* (1995) and *L.A. Confidential* (1997). David Fincher is among the most skilled directors of the genre.

1   Tipping their hats to Billy Wilder: *Body Heat*'s plot is a tribute to *Double Indemnity*. Both then and now, an icy vixen takes center stage, spinning a lethal web of deceit for her unsuspecting prey. Matty (Kathleen Turner) has little difficulty in making Ned Racine (William Hurt) fall head over heels in love with her.

2   Flashback: Kasdan's screen images are saturated in film noir. The dialogue could have been written by Raymond Chandler himself.

3   Ned Racine is not the only one who's been dealt a bum hand.

4   Flames of passion: not the only thing that is being fanned into a blaze in *Body Heat*. A devilish scheme is simultaneously being cooked up on the same fire.

4

BERTRAND TAVERNIER

COUP DE TORCHON

JEAN AURENCHE
BERTRAND TAVERNIER
d'après un roman publié sous le titre
"1275 ÂMES"
de Jim Thompson

EDDY MITCHELL
GUY MARCHAND
STEPHANE AUDRAN

CLEAN SLATE
COUP DE TORCHON

1981 – FRANCE – 128 MIN.
DIRECTOR BERTRAND TAVERNIER (*1941)
SCREENPLAY JEAN AURENCHE, BERTRAND TAVERNIER,
based on the novel *Pop. 1280* by JIM THOMPSON
DIRECTOR OF PHOTOGRAPHY PIERRE-WILLIAM GLENN
EDITING ARMAND PSENNY MUSIC PHILIPPE SARDE
PRODUCTION HENRI LASSA, ADOLPHE VIEZZI for LES FILMS
DE LA TOUR, FILMS A2, LITTLE BEAR
STARRING PHILIPPE NOIRET (Lucien Cordier), ISABELLE
HUPPERT (Rose), JEAN-PIERRE MARIELLE
(Le Péron / Brother), STÉPHANE AUDRAN (Huguette
Cordier), EDDY MITCHELL (Nono), GUY MARCHAND
(Chavasson), IRÈNE SKOBLINE (Anne), JEAN CHAMPION
(Priest), FRANÇOIS PERROT (Colonel Tramichel),
MICHEL BEAUNE (Vanderbrouck)

"Aren't we, too, more or less lifeless?"

French West Africa, 1938. In Bourkassa, a dusty village on the edge of the desert, there's not much evidence of *La Grande Nation*. The white colonial rulers are themselves ruled by their basest instincts, and spend most of their time drinking, whoring, and indulging in various excesses. They treat the Africans with contempt, and when dysentery carries them off, their bodies are unceremoniously dumped in the river, and even used for target practice. Police chief Cordier (Philippe Noiret) observes these goings-on, and does nothing. He is quite aware of the fact that nobody takes him seriously, least of all his wife Huguette (Stéphane Audran), who is carrying on with her alleged brother Nono (Eddy Mitchell). Cordier in turn, is having an affair with Rose (Isabelle Huppert), the ever-willing wife of a bad-tempered merchant. Meanwhile, the two village pimps take pleasure in humiliating him. It's all water off a duck's back – or so it seems. But Cordier is beginning to have his doubts about the life he leads. He seeks advice from his superior, Chavasson

(Guy Marchand), who tells him he has to pay his tormentors back in spades; but what finally awakens Cordier from his lethargy is his encounter with the idealistic teacher Anne (Irène Skobline). He proceeds to murder the pimps and frame Chavasson – and this is only the first coup to be landed by this apparent no-hoper. For Cordier is now a man with a mission ...

Since his debut with *The Clockmaker (L'Horloger de Saint-Paul)* in 1973, Bertrand Tavernier has frequently confirmed his reputation as the humanist among French filmmakers – most recently with *It All Begins Today (Ça commence aujourd'hui*, 1999), in which a head teacher battles against the desolate state of the educational system on behalf of its neglected children. In *Clean Slate* the schoolteacher is equally a positive figure – indeed, the only one in the whole film. Yet not even she can be regarded as a figure of hope, for in the final analysis she merely props up the existing power structure. And although she's mainly responsible for Cordier's metamorphosis, she certainly

1   Stars of the French screen since the 1960s: Stéphane Audran and Philippe Noiret.

2   The thick-skinned cowboy is ill at ease: Cordier's (Philippe Noiret) dubious traits come to the fore.

3   *Clean Slate*'s pessimism is reminiscent of pre-war French cinema. Cordier with mistress Rose (Isabelle Huppert).

JIM THOMPSON   The root idea for the hometown, sadistic cops in Jim Thompson's novels *The Killer Inside Me* (1952) and *Pop. 1280* (1964) came from Thompson's father (an unreliable sheriff who embezzled) and from a meeting with a cop who implied that he could kill the young Thompson without getting caught. The cop told Thompson (as recounted in the autobiographical *Bad Boy*, 1953), "There ain't no way of telling what a man is by looking at him. There ain't no way of knowing what he'll do if he has a chance." Jim Thompson's characters are the most vicious, the most unsympathetic, the most amoral you will come across in noir fiction. They are trapped by women, by society, but mostly by themselves, by the "sickness" inside them that makes them the way they are. Thompson (1906–1977) hit his stride in the early 1950s with a series of novels that included *Savage Night* (1953, narrated by a tiny, consumptive hit man), *The Criminal* (1953, the effect of a schoolgirl rape/murder with multiple points of view), and *A Hell of a Woman* (1954, a salesman in lust), then worked on film scripts for Stanley Kubrick (*The Killing*, 1956; *Paths of Glory*, 1957), before delivering his last great novels (*The Getaway*, 1959; *The Grifters*, 1963; *Pop. 1280*). Thompson's self-destructive behavior ruined his health – he seemed to have his own "sickness" to contend with. When he died on April 7, 1977, none of his books were in print in America, but the 1980s saw a revival of his work and many film adaptations, the finest of which were Bertrand Tavernier's version of *Pop. 1280*, *Clean Slate* (1981), and Michael Winterbottom's *The Killer Inside Me* (2010).

"In fact what is best about *Coup de torchon* is its often mordantly funny scripting and eccentric personages, which hark back to the French cinema of the 1930s." *Variety*

hasn't turned him into a good guy – for it becomes increasingly apparent that the "new" Cordier is a monster. His faith in his mission is the madness of a *petit-bourgeois* unchained, and his behavior becomes increasingly fascistic. The film's cynical undertone (unusual for Tavernier) stems from the book on which it is based, a thriller by the American writer Jim Thompson. However, parallels may certainly be drawn with the films of Claude Chabrol, and their vitriolic attacks on the French bourgeoisie.

Tavernier's attitude is just as critical, and he manages to find a highly entertaining form for this critique. *Clean Slate* is no mere historical drama, but a burlesque black comedy, and it contains many long and wonderfully choreographed scenes reminiscent of the work of Jean Renoir. The director's

style is easy, fluent, and never obtrusive, supporting the development of the plot and preparing the ground for some pretty meaty acting. Isabelle Huppert and Stéphane Audran – two of Claude Chabrol's favored actresses – are wonderful in their shameless vulgarity, while Guy Marchand delivers another of his delightfully ridiculous machos.

Philippe Noiret, however, towers above them all. With his powerful, flabby physique, his screen presence is that of a lethargic rhino. But his brilliant performance makes it abundantly clear that Cordier is anything but an impervious pachyderm. Behind the policeman's amiable gaze, we see his doubt, his deep pain – and the perilous abyss at the heart of the man.

JH

| 4 | Angelic indifference: Rose remains unmoved by her husband's death. | 5 | Bloodstained vaudeville: Guy Marchand (center) provides comic relief as Cordier's sleazy higher-up. | 6 | Caught off guard, the townsfolk show a fascist streak: Cordier begins his mission. |

"Shooting with the Steadicam allows Tavernier to direct his sequence shots and camera movements in a way that is absolutely astonishing in its frenzy ..."

Le Monde

5

6

MAN HAS MADE HIS MATCH
...NOW IT'S HIS PROBLEM

BLADE RUNNER

1982 – USA – 117 MIN.
DIRECTOR RIDLEY SCOTT (*1937)
SCREENPLAY HAMPTON FANCHER, DAVID PEPLOES,
based on the novel *Do Androids Dream of
Electric Sheep?* by PHILIP K. DICK
DIRECTOR OF PHOTOGRAPHY JORDAN CRONENWETH
EDITING MARSHA NAKASHIMA, TERRY RAWLINGS
MUSIC VANGELIS PRODUCTION MICHAEL DEELEY for
THE LADD COMPANY, BLADE RUNNER PARTNERSHIP
STARRING HARRISON FORD (Rick Deckard),
RUTGER HAUER (Roy Batty), SEAN YOUNG (Rachael),
EDWARD JAMES OLMOS (Gaff), M. EMMET WALSH
(Bryant), DARYL HANNAH (Pris), WILLIAM SANDERSON
(Sebastian), BRION JAMES (Leon), JOE TURKEL
(Eldon Tyrell), JOANNA CASSIDY (Zhora),
MORGAN PAULL (Holden)

"You're so different. You're so perfect."

Los Angeles, 2019. Earth-toned high-rise temples soar up into smog-covered skies. Factory towers spit fire, and acid rain collects between the neon-illuminated fissures that separate the mammoth buildings. The city has become a mutant hybrid, a futuristic yet archaic urban leviathan. The L.A. streets are home to an exotic blend of races, while whites are housed in forbidding, monolithic skyscrapers. Everyone who can afford it has relocated to one of the "off world colonies." To make this prospect even more enticing, the Tyrell Corporation has designed humanoids called replicants to be used as slave labor on the foreign planets. These synthetic beings are virtually indistinguishable from real humans, but the law forbids them from setting foot on Earth.

Yet some of these androids manage to slip through the net, and it is the job of the "blade runners" to hunt them down and "decommission" them. Is this an allusion to the Day of Judgment, where only the innocent can escape

the confines of hell? Perhaps. Nothing in this film rich with philosophical and theological admonishments would seem to indicate the contrary.

Rick Deckard (Harrison Ford) used to work as a blade runner. Now a disillusioned ex-cop, he roams the damp streets with a chip on his shoulder like a film noir crusader. He was the best in the business, which is why the bureau want to reactivate him when a band of four rogue androids, two men and two women, makes their way into L.A. Their "life expectancy" has been programmed to four years. Now, they want to know how much time they have left to live, and they'll do anything to prolong it.

Roy Batty (Rutger Hauer), the leader of these humanoid bandits, is blond, buff, and demonic. Meeting his maker Eldon Tyrell (Joe Turkel), a futur-istic Dr. Frankenstein, proves an existential disappointment for Roy. Tyrell lives in a pyramid-shaped structure reminiscent of that of the ancient Mayans and sleeps in a bed like the pope's. Unfortunately, the great creator is in no

position to grant the android a new lease of life, and the fallen angel kills his maker in a dual father-God assassination.

Blade Runner is based on the novel *Do Androids Dream of Electric Sheep?* (1968) by Philip K. Dick, who also wrote the story that inspired *Total Recall* (1990). The film bombed at the box office, but is nonetheless seen as a milestone in sci-fi. It is a dismal, philosophical fairy tale with mind-boggling sets, sophisticated lighting design, and a grandiose score by Vangelis. Alongside *Liquid Sky* (1982) and *The Hunger* (1983), *Blade Runner* is among the most significant '80s New Wave films. One could label it "postmodern" or attribute its power to the director's eclecticism. Scott's mesmerizing *layering* technique showcases his knack for integrating architectural elements, the intricacies of clothing articles, and symbols originating from a wide array of cultures and eras.

The film makes productive use of astoundingly diverse codes, synthesizing their Babylonian confusion into a compact means of communication on the L.A. city streets. In a mélange of Fritz Lang's *Metropolis* (1927), film noir, the imagery of Edward Hopper, and the comic book sketches of Moebius, Ridley Scott creates a wildly driven piece that demands its audience to consider the essence of human identity. The film's subtext gradually unfolds throughout its story, raising issues of the conscious and subconscious. The homonymic link between protagonist Deckard and mathematician Descartes is only part of the rich body of motifs that hint at the film's underlying philosophy. Also not to be overlooked are the variations on the "eye" motif throughout the picture. Here, too, the film synthesizes a word's homonymic potential, alluding to the "I" inherent in the word "eye." The eye is a universal symbol

1   The other, that's who I am: Rachael (Sean Young), attractive and unapproachable like a film noir vamp. She doesn't know that she's a replicant. Even her memories are just implants.

2   More human than human: Roy Batty (Rutger Hauer) is the *Übermensch* in the Nietzschean sense of the word. The blond beast and yet a slave who suffers and shows compassion.

3   Harrison Ford plays blade runner Deckard. In hot pursuit of renegade replicants, although perhaps he's one himself.

"*Blade Runner* was the science fiction of the '80s. The gritty gray counterpart to Kubrick's *2001.*"

epd Film

of recognition and a sense of self-awareness "unique" to humans. Yet in *Blade Runner*, the androids are also equipped with this level of consciousness. "We're not computers, Sebastian, we're physical," Batty declares at one point, laying claim to his humanity as well as his body and physicality, one of the most important topics of the '80s.

For their bodies are precisely what make the androids indistinguishable from their human counterparts. Upon first meeting, Rachael (Sean Young), Eldon Tyrell's secretary, reminds Deckard of the dangers of his occupation when she asks him whether he has ever killed a human by mistake. Her question sensitizes the viewer to the predicament at hand; sometimes the fine line between humans and their replicas is intangible. Rachael herself has sat on both sides of the fence. Although she has always believed herself

to be human, at one point in the film she is forced to confront the reality that she too is an android. There is, however, something "unique" about her. Rachael is the product of an experiment and has been programmed with the memories of Tyrell's niece, which she latches on to as her own. Her memories are rooted in photos. Likewise, it is photos that help Deckard zero in on the whereabouts of the renegade androids. He uses a picture of an empty hotel room as only a 21st-century detective would, or at least, as we might have imagined him to from an '80s perspective. Aided by a contraption known as an Esper machine, he enlarges segments of the photo onto a monitor. This provides him with a sort of X-ray vision that allows him to travel into the depths of the image's two-dimensional space. He soon discovers a woman's reflection from within a mirror. The detective embarks on an

4

4   What does it mean to be human? A question the film puts forth in an aesthetically brilliant framework. The film set the standard for 1980s style.

5   Artificial humans are a recurrent phenomenon in both literature and film – from the Greek myth of Pygmalion, E. T. A. Hoffmann's doll Olympia in *The Sandman*, to Fritz Lang's *Metropolis* and

Spielberg's *A.I.*, to name but a few. Here, the manner-isms of replicant Pris (Daryl Hannah) almost make her seem like a china doll.

> **"At first the villain of the piece, he suddenly becomes its mythic, emphatic center. Batty turns Frankenstein's monster to Biblical Adam; Deckard veers from hunter to homomorph."** *Film Comment*

RIDLEY SCOTT Alan Parker dubbed him "the greatest visual stylist working today." With a deep-rooted love for Hollywood, the films of English director Ridley Scott have played an enormous role in determining Tinseltown's film aesthetics for more than 20 years. Whether he is working in sci-fi thrillers like *Alien* (1979) and *Blade Runner* (1982) (a film which would enjoy cult status ten years later with the release of its director's cut), or a feminist road movie like *Thelma & Louise* (1991), Scott's films are a triumph with critics and audiences alike. A graduate of the London Royal College of Art, the *auteur* got his start working for the BBC and then went on to shoot advertising spots with his own production company.

Born in 1937, his first feature film, *The Duellists* (1977) won the prize for best directorial debut at Cannes. Ridley Scott has also enjoyed tremendous success as a producer. Together with his brother Tony Scott (*Top Gun*, 1985), he purchased the Shepperton Studios in 1995. Neither genre nor quality links the resulting films. Fantasy flick *Legend* (1985), featuring a young Tom Cruise, met with a more modest reception; thriller *Someone to Watch Over Me* (1987) was a veritable grand slam, and *Black Rain* (1989) with Michael Douglas, a film on the Japanese Yakuza, is certainly worth seeing. Clearly, in addition to the numerous hits, Scott has also had his share of misses. Columbus-glorifying *1492: Conquest of Paradise* (1992) as well as *G.I. Jane* (1997) starring Demi Moore bombed at the box-office and were panned by critics. In 2000, Ridley Scott landed himself another smash hit with *Gladiator*, the first big budget Hollywood production about ancient Rome in more than 30 years. His most recent successes have been the biopic drama *American Gangster* (2007), the spy thriller *Body of Lies* (2008) and the *Alien* prequel *Prometheus* (2012).

6

The sun doesn't rise here anymore: bathed in neon light, the streets of L.A. are ruled by a gangland mix of Chinese, Mexicans and punks.

"We used a lot of real punks for the street scenes in *Blade Runner*. Because I had so much 'crowd,' it was better to save time and money by recruiting a huge number of extras: 200 punks, 100 Chinese, another 100 Mexicans." *Ridley Scott, in: Film Comment*

7   Harrison Ford's laconic and somewhat cynical portrayal of Deckard brings many a film noir protagonist to mind. Not only the visual aesthetics and characters evoke elements of film noir, but also the voice-over narrative technique, later eliminated in the director's cut, is typical of the genre.

investigation, which takes the audience on a course through the history of Western art. Ridley Scott cites various paintings in this scene, including Jan van Eyck's *The Arnolfini Wedding* (1434), a piece which, though focused on its two main subjects, also allowed the spectator to see the artist and his assistant peering out from a mirror. Scott's knack for turning cultural paradigms on their heads undoubtedly contributes to the intriguing fabric of the film, many of whose images have become ingrained in our collective visual memories. One such example shows Deckard chasing exotic snake dancer Zhora through the chaotic, mazelike L.A. streets, inundated with people. He finally shoots her dead, causing her to fall in slow motion through a store window. One could argue that these shards of glass signify the shattered reality brought about by the role reversals at the film's conclusion. The blade

runner becomes the bounty, and the android Batty is revealed as a compassionate, "selfless" individual.

It is indeed Batty who saves the blade runner's life in the nick of time and who dies in the end. The moral disparity between android and human no longer exists. This holds even truer if one accepts the hypothesis that Deckard is himself an android. There is some proof in the original version to favor this ongoing debate. The director's cut, released in 1992, has no voice-over and no happy ending, differences that make this theory even more probable. In July 2000, Scott went on record as saying that Deckard definitively was a replicant. An outraged Harrison Ford countered that while making the film, Scott had sworn the opposite. And so the debate goes on …

KK

A Federal Agent is dead.
A killer is loose.
And the City of Angels
is about to explode.

The director of
"The French Connection"
is back on the street again.

TO LIVE AND DIE IN L. A.

1985 – USA – 115 MIN.
DIRECTOR WILLIAM FRIEDKIN (*1939)
SCREENPLAY WILLIAM FRIEDKIN, GERALD PETIEVICH, based
on the novel of the same name by GERALD PETIEVICH
DIRECTOR OF PHOTOGRAPHY ROBBY MÜLLER
EDITING M. SCOTT SMITH MUSIC WANG CHUNG
PRODUCTION IRVING H. LEVIN for SLM PRODUCTION GROUP
STARRING WILLIAM PETERSEN (Richard Chance),
WILLEM DAFOE (Eric Masters), JOHN PANKOW
(John Vukovich), DEBRA FEUER (Bianca Torres),
JOHN TURTURRO (Carl Cody), DARLANNE FLUEGEL
(Ruth Lanier), DEAN STOCKWELL (Bob Grimes),
STEVE JAMES (Jeff Rice), MICHAEL GREENE (Jim Hart)

"You want bread? Then go fuck a baker."

Life in free fall: policeman Richard Chance (William L. Petersen) jumps off bridges in his free time and approaches his job with a similar reckless abandon, never shrinking from risks. He and his partner Jim Hart (Michael Greene) are on the trail of a group of counterfeiters in Los Angeles. When Hart is murdered two days before his retirement, Chance has only one goal: to hunt down the forger Eric Masters (Willem Dafoe), even if it means becoming a criminal himself in the process.

While Chance's kamikaze style initially makes his new partner John Vukovich (John Pankow) uneasy, he too gets sucked in to this dangerous ride. But just when they are about to commence an undercover operation that could provide the final piece of evidence against Masters, the police authorities withdraw the finances necessary for the sting. Chance, who is aware of an illicit transaction, persuades his partner to help him rob the courier so that they can use the cash as bait for Masters. Just when things

2

appear to have fallen into place, the plan turns sour. The two are ambushed by an army of men and the courier is shot in the back. In the subsequen chase through the Los Angeles traffic, director Friedkin once again proves his talent for filming spectacular sequences, just as he did in *The French Connection* (1971).

Eventually it becomes clear that the supposed courier was in fact an FB agent. The emotionally unstable Vukovich threatens to lose his cool, bu Chance is more convinced than ever that he must put a stop to Masters's depravity.

In the opinion of many critics, Los Angeles is the true theme of the film Friedkin depicts the city as a place that remains strangely faceless. In the introductory sequence, the silhouettes of high-rises, bungalows, and factory chimneys merge together into a glowing red mist; there is not a soul to be found on the streets. This is L.A. – the city of highways and cars. Friedkin inserts date and time at the start of several scenes, and although superflu ous to the plot, the information heightens the sense of uncertainty. The char acters of the film fit in with this theme: in this merciless game they exis merely within the boundaries of their roles. Their private lives are reduced to rendezvous in glowing neon clubs and bars, their interpersonal relationship to sex in places characterized by ice-cold '80s design.

Against this background, the line that separates law and crime, good and evil, which is the central theme in all of Friedkin's films, is almost dissolved One central scene accompanied only by music shows an artist forger at work The highly aestheticized portrayal of this occupation – a real counterfeiter wa made available to the film team and real plates were created with the specia

1   According to Eric Masters (Willem Dafoe), there's only a fine line between art and crime.

2   To live and die in the sea of lights that is L.A.: the film's main focus is alienation in the city of cars and freeways.

3   A macho and self-absorbed scoundrel. Richard Chance (William Petersen) is among the most unappealing heroes ever to grace the silver screen.

4   The color of money: director Friedkin shoots a day in the life of a forger as a scorching video segment.

5   Without even knowing it, a hunter becomes the prey.

"The real focus of all my pictures is the fine line between cops and robbers – and the fine line between good and evil." *William Friedkin, in: steadycam*

permission of the authorities – turns the crime into an artistic act. Art and duty, crime and justice – all demand uncompromising devotion, a fanaticism that leads only to destruction. Or, as Friedkin suggests in the poignant scene in which Vukovich adopts Chance's role, the associations and relationships are

interchangeable – experiences are repeated over and over and one begets the other. Friedkin's L.A. is a microcosm of a world out of control, where mora bearings and all solid footing have disappeared.

SH

WILLIAM FRIEDKIN   Born in Chicago in 1939, Friedkin was at his peak in the 1970s. *The French Connection* (1971) and *The Exorcist* (1973) were regarded as milestones in their respective genres. But Friedkin is infamous for his perfectionism and his sometimes despotic behavior with actors – rumors of boxing ears and other abusive behavior during filming have constantly circulated in Hollywood. He strengthened his reputation as an arrogant, individual player with *Sorcerer* (1977), his remake of the classic *Wages of Fear* (*Le Salaire de la peur*, 1953). The fact that Henri-Georges Clouzot's original was regarded a masterpiece was no hindrance. But after *Cruising* (1980) and *To Live and Die in L.A.* (1985), his fame began to wane. Friedkin's later films were patently unable to recapture the atmospheric density of his earlier work.

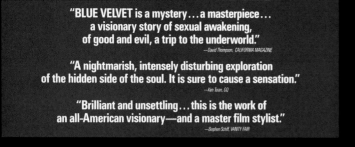

BLUE VELVET

1986 – USA – 120 MIN.
DIRECTOR DAVID LYNCH (*1946)
SCREENPLAY DAVID LYNCH
DIRECTOR OF PHOTOGRAPHY FREDERICK ELMES
EDITING DUWAYNE DUNHAM
MUSIC ANGELO BADALAMENTI
PRODUCTION FRED CARUSO for DE LAURENTIIS
ENTERTAINMENT
STARRING KYLE MACLACHLAN (Jeffrey Beaumont),
ISABELLA ROSSELLINI (Dorothy Vallens),
DENNIS HOPPER (Frank Booth), LAURA DERN
(Sandy Williams), HOPE LANGE (Mrs. Williams),
DEAN STOCKWELL (Ben), GEORGE DICKERSON
(Detective Williams), BRAD DOURIF
(Raymond), FRANCES BAY (Aunt Barbara),
JACK HARVEY (Mr. Beaumont)

"I'll bet a person could learn a lot by getting into that woman's apartment. You know, sneak in and hide and observe."

The camera sweeps over Lumberton, U.S.A., a charming American small town, with white picket fences, tulip-filled gardens, and amiable people. Jeffrey Beaumont (Kyle MacLachlan) is on the way to hospital to visit his father, who suffered a heart attack while watering his lawn. While walking home across a field, he pauses to throw rocks at some bottles. He is soon stopped in his tracks – partially hidden by the grass at his feet lies a milky-looking, rotting human ear, covered with crawling ants. The ear is a completely foreign object in this American small-town idyll, and becomes a mesmerically compelling object. Little does he realize that it is to become his entry ticket into another world. For the moment, he brings the ear to the police.

In Sandy (Laura Dern), the blonde daughter of the investigating detective, Jeffrey finds a hesitant, but eventually more and more curious accomplice and partner. She informs him of a clue in the case that leads to the nightclub singer Dorothy Vallens (Isabella Rossellini). He decides to sneak into her apartment. The thought of forcing his way into this woman's private sphere arouses him more than he will admit to himself, let alone to Sandy.

Blue Velvet is a film about seeing and about the camera as an eye. Jeffrey observes more than he would like to in Dorothy Vallens's apartment. When Dorothy unexpectedly returns, rips the closet door open and orders him out, the boundless terror in his eyes exposes him as a Peeping Tom caught

1

> **"As wicked and contradictory as it may seem to be, *Blue Velvet* is quite clearly one of the few great films of the Eighties, perhaps even the most sensational film since *Last Tango in Paris*. No film has blown me away like this for years."** *L A Weekly*

2

red-handed. When Dorothy threatens him and even calls him by name, the object has suddenly become the subject, the subject the object.

The voyeur experiences arousal, pleasure, and power. Director David Lynch plays with these phenomena and makes the viewer an accomplice, but then turns the tables. In Lynch's film, the voyeur is degraded and ultimately becomes the helpless witness of a brutal act. The scene in which Dorothy is brutally raped by the perverted Frank Booth (Dennis Hopper) is just as shocking and disturbing as the shower murder scene in Hitchcock's *Psycho* (1960). And *Blue Velvet* is as important for 1980s cinema as *Psycho* was for film of the early '60s.

The following day, his experience in Dorothy's apartment truly seems like a bad dream to Jeffrey. For just as it would be in a dream, he was alter-nately observer and participant, and Frank was the representation of the dark side of his soul.

Towards the end of *Blue Velvet*, when the worst is over, the camera shows a close-up of an ear, but this time, it is Jeffrey's own ear. The fissures in the perfect world are apparently sealed, and Jeffrey's journey into the dark depths of the soul is over. But is it entirely over for good, or is this just a temporary respite . . .

While *Blue Velvet* was initially met with much controversy at the time of its release, its status as one of the best American films of the '80s is indisputable. The film established David Lynch as a visionary of modern cinema, marked the well-deserved comeback of the incomparable Dennis Hopper, and shattered the constricting perception of Isabella Rossellini as merely the flawless daughter of the great Ingrid Bergman. RF

1   Mysterious nightclub singer Dorothy Vallens (Isabella Rossellini) is suspicious of an unannounced visitor.

2   Jeffrey Beaumont (Kyle MacLachlan) is about to drive into the unknown depths of his soul.

3   Under duress: Dorothy forces Jeffrey to take his clothes off and make love to her. Suddenly, there is a knock at the door.

DAVID LYNCH CHAMPION OF MYSTERY   From his underground debut *Eraserhead* (1974) through the movies *Blue Velvet* (1986), *Wild at Heart* (1990), *Lost Highway* (1997), and *Mulholland Drive* (2001) to TV series *Twin Peaks* (1989–1991), David Lynch has always made disturbing films about the dark side of the human soul – visually striking films with somber, distressing sound montages that maintain an essentially unresolved element of mystery. In 1999, he directed the surprisingly accessible and sensitive road movie *The Straight Story*. *Inland Empire* (2006), the story of an aging actress hopeful for a comeback who lands herself in a horror trip, combines once again all of the classic Lynch motifs: a journey into darkness, a blurring of reality and dream world, exuberant filmic references, and a rejection of comprehensible narrative.

The multitalented Lynch, long successful also as a painter and photographer, has in recent years increasingly devoted himself to music. After years of working on the soundtracks of his films, he taught himself guitar in his mid-50s and ultimately released the CDs *Crazy Clown Time* (2011) and *The Big Dream* (2013) – celebrated by critics as the soundtracks to unrealized David Lynch films.

"*Blue Velvet* is a big film about the innocence and perversion that characterizes childhood." *David Lynch*

4 Shutter speed: Jeffrey bears witness to a bizarre scene from inside Dorothy's closet.

5 Dorothy sings "Blue Velvet" at the Slow Club: Lynch composer Angelo Badalamenti at the piano.

6 Sandy (Laura Dern) is appalled by Dorothy Vallens's morbid power over Jeffrey. Yet Sandy's romantic feelings compel her to help him.

7 "Mommy… Baby wants to fuck!" With her family in his clutches, Frank Booth (Dennis Hopper) strokes Dorothy Vallens with blue velvet.

HOUSE OF GAMES

1987 – USA – 102 MIN.
DIRECTOR DAVID MAMET (*1947)
SCREENPLAY JONATHAN KATZ, DAVID MAMET
DIRECTOR OF PHOTOGRAPHY JUAN RUIZ ANCHÍA
EDITING TRUDY SHIP MUSIC ALARIC JANS
PRODUCTION MICHAEL HAUSMAN for FILMHAUS
STARRING LINDSAY CROUSE (Margaret Ford),
JOE MANTEGNA (Mike), MIKE NUSSBAUM (Joey),
LILIA SKALA (Dr. Littauer), J. T. WALSH
(The Businessman), WILLO HAUSMAN (Girl with Book),
KAREN KOHLHAAS (Patient), STEVEN GOLDSTEIN
(Billy Hahn), JACK WALLACE (Bartender),
RICKY JAY (George / "Vegas Man"), G. ROY LEVIN
(Poker Player), BOB LUMBRA (Poker Player)

"Don't trust nobody."

Successful psychologist Margaret Ford (Lindsay Crouse) sees her career as more than just a profession. It's her calling. Although her book *Driven*, a treatise on compulsive behavior, rose to the top of the best-seller list, Dr. Ford continues to devote herself to working with the psychologically disturbed. When one day a young patient walks into her office and threatens to shoot himself because he can't pay his gambling debts, Margaret promises to help him sort things out. She makes her way over to "The House of Games," a shady, illegal gambling operation, to convince Mike (Joe Mantegna), the creditor, to reconsider his position. Mike is charismatic, suavely masculine, and always has the upper hand. When it comes to professional gambling, Mike wrote the book, but he's willing to cut Margaret a deal. He'll clear her patient's tab if she'll help him outsmart a truly formidable opponent.

House of Games marked David Mamet's directorial debut for the silver screen. Mamet, who had already earned his reputation as a playwright and screenwriter, collaborated on the film project with old friends and trusted colleagues. Lindsay Crouse (his wife at the time), Joe Mantegna, Mike Nussbaum and, in a cameo, William H. Macy, had all performed in Mamet's plays and were cast in the picture. Familiar with Mamet's pointed dialogue as well as his characters' poignantly stylized and aggressive manner of speaking, the ensemble was perfectly suited to bring this blend of theatricality meets laconic film noir antihero to movie audiences. The film's cinematography, loaded with highly artificial images, also plays a crucial role in uniting these distinct dimensions. After she accepts Mike's offer, the camera follows Margaret's surreal plunge into in an unfamiliar urban jungle that exists only at

1   Psychologist as head case: Margaret (David Mamet's then wife Lindsay Crouse) cultivates a taste for crime.

2   Nothing is as it seems: those who give in to Mamet's imagery have already joined the pawns.

"Usually the screenwriter is insane to think he can direct a movie. Not this time. *House of Games* never steps wrong from beginning to end, and it is one of this year's best films." *Chicago Sun-Times*

night, as if in a parallel universe. It is a world full of traps, riddled with masterful con artists. Captivated, Margaret asks Mike to verse her in the lore of his trade. Mike concedes to her request, secure in the knowledge that Margaret's interest is not restricted to professional curiosity nor driven by scientific obligation.

House of Games tells of repressed appetites and concealed objectives. It is a journey into the subversive realm that lurks behind the façade of propriety. Margaret, a passionate psychoanalyst, is herself a nervous wreck, full of behavioral ticks. Her uptight presence and masculine manner are more indicative of stunted sexuality than professional objectivity. It is of course particularly ironic that the heroine is a psychologist, a choice that clearly indicates Mamet's disillusioned view of American society. The true joy of

watching this film is in savoring its fine appreciation of a good game, or spectacular "set up": Mike professes to make Margaret his partner in crime, while Mamet turns the viewer into a willing accomplice; Mike tells Margaret that observation of detail is the key to understanding the game, and Mamet duly sows these "seeds" throughout the movie in seemingly clear-cut constellations and unambiguous images. But what these signals actually mean is only revealed to us later on in the film. According to Mike, "you can't bluff someone who's not paying attention," a maxim which holds true for the film as a whole. One has to be ready and willing to play in order to be duped. Mamet wins our trust and then pulls the wool over our eyes, thereby teaching us an invaluable lesson in filmmaking.

JH

3   The oldest trick in the book: Mike (Joe Mantegna) lets Margaret in on his hand.

4   The professional: Joe Mantegna embodies masculinity without saying a word.

5   A score that can't be settled: Mike meets his master and his maker.

DAVID MAMET Equally successful as a playwright, screenwriter, and director, David Mamet is an anomaly in American film and theater. He was born the son of a teacher and a lawyer in 1947 in Chicago. In the 1970s, Mamet was already among the most celebrated Off-Broadway writers. His fame skyrocketed in the 1980s when he won the Pulitzer Prize for his drama *Glengarry Glen Ross*. His career as a screenwriter began with *The Postman Always Rings Twice* (1981). Shortly thereafter, Mamet earned himself an Oscar nod for *The Verdict* (1982). His directorial debut for the screen came with *House of Games* (1987). The film starred Joe Mantegna who would take leading roles in later Mamet productions such as *Things Change* (1988) and *Homicide* (1991). Despite the fetching and sharp-witted dialog characteristic of his films, it is Mamet's gift for devising brilliant plots full of unpredictable chutes and ladders that makes his work what it is. His film *Heist* (2001) serves viewers a hearty portion of the total Mamet experience. In 2004, *Spartan* appeared in theaters, a film about the kidnapping of the U.S. president's daughter and the sometimes shady dealings of the secret service. In *Redbelt* (2008), a sports drama of deceit and betrayal, Mamet's delight for lies and deception is realized with a sharp pen and brought impressively to the screen.

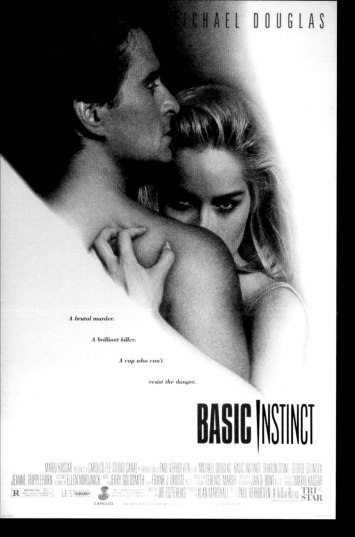

MICHAEL DOUGLAS

A brutal murder.

A brilliant killer.

A cop who can't

resist the danger.

BASIC INSTINCT

BASIC INSTINCT

1992 – USA – 127 MIN.
DIRECTOR PAUL VERHOEVEN (*1938)
SCREENPLAY JOE ESZTERHAS
DIRECTOR OF PHOTOGRAPHY JAN DE BONT
EDITING FRANK J. URIOSTE
MUSIC JERRY GOLDSMITH
PRODUCTION MARIO KASSAR for
CAROLCO PICTURES, LE STUDIO CANAL+
STARRING MICHAEL DOUGLAS (Detective Nick Curran),
SHARON STONE (Catherine Tramell),
JEANNE TRIPPLEHORN (Dr. Beth Gardner),
GEORGE DZUNDZA (Gus), DENIS ARNDT
(Lt. Walker), LEILANI SARELLE (Roxy),
BRUCE A. YOUNG (Andrews), CHELCIE ROSS
(Captain Talcott), DOROTHY MALONE
(Hazel Dobkins), WAYNE KNIGHT
(John Correli)

"She's the fuck of the century."

Sweaty bodies, rough sex, an ice pick, and lots of blood – from the opening shot of the movie, Paul Verhoeven makes it clear what the audience should expect for the next two hours. The director's tenth film appeals to our animal nature, although it's unclear whether the "basic instinct" of the title is a reference to hunting or the reproductive instinct. The story unfolds in a totally macho world where there is no place for weakness. Unfortunately, the hero, disillusioned cop Nick Curran (Michael Douglas), is powerless to resist temptation of any kind. Hot-tempered and partial to provocative women, he's also burdened with a past he would rather forget: ever since killing two innocent bystanders as part of a raid, he has struggled with an alcohol problem and had to endure the jibes of his colleagues. Douglas plays the role with his jaw clenched, but behind the foul temper and tough exterior lies a deeply insecure character whose private and professional life are constantly on the verge of breakdown, He comes across as thoroughly unlikeable, but Curran's weaknesses make him into a character with whom the audience can sympathize.

Despite his personal problems, he's given the job of investigating the murder shown so memorably at the beginning of the movie. The trail of clues leads him to Catherine Tramell (Sharon Stone), a crime writer who is as sexy as she is mysterious, who seems to have already anticipated the brutal act in one of her books. Could she have turned her evil imagination into reality? That solution is a little too obvious even for the police department. No one could be so stupid as to advertise a murder they were planning in a book in advance. Unless of course that is exactly what the murderer wanted the detectives to think.

1   Is she or isn't she? The public were more interested in whether or not Sharon Stone was wearing panties in this scene than they were in working out the whodunit.

2   Detective Nick Curran (Michael Douglas) does battle with alcohol, nicotine, and sharp-tongued women writers.

3   Why would a woman who has everything commit such a senseless murder?

4   Intelligent, beautiful, and – lethal? Catherine Tramell (Sharon Stone) is always a few steps ahead of the investigators.

2

3

"The film is like a crossword puzzle. It keeps your interest until you solve it. Then it's just a worthless scrap with the spaces filled in."

Chicago Sun-Times

Catherine Tramell certainly seems to be capable of such a calculating trick. Breathtakingly seductive, uncompromising in her search for sexual satisfaction and rolling in money, she is a monstrous combination of male wish-fulfillment and castration anxiety: a sex-hungry feminist and man-murdering vamp, intellectually far superior to the men who surround her.

The fearless detectives are helpless in the face of their provocative prime suspect. When they take her in for questioning at the police station, in what is undoubtedly the film's most famous moment and one of the main reasons for its success, she totally confuses them by crossing her legs and letting her skirt ride right up. The pressing question as to whether Catherine murdered her partner during sex is effectively overshadowed by the even more pressing one as to whether Stone was wearing panties during this

scene. Debate raged in the press, and there were even claims that during the love scenes, viewers were witnessing unsimulated sex. Such bizarre slippage of the boundaries between cinema and reality, between actual events and their interpretations is typical of Verhoeven's movies and ultimately part of their attraction.

Appropriately, given this double game with reality, there is also a female psychologist in *Basic Instinct*, in what seems to be the last straw for the beleaguered male characters. Dr. Beth Gardner (Jeanne Tripplehorn) plays a large part in the undoing of Curran. Her job is to test his psychological fitness for active police service, but he becomes hopelessly entwined in a labyrinth of sex, lies, and psycho trickery when he tries to use sexual humiliation to get his own back for this professional degradation. Eventually the inevitable

5

6

happens and Curran succumbs to the charms of the prime suspect. Needless to say this does him no good whatsoever either as far as his resolve to give up smoking and drinking is concerned, or in his professional judgment. It is also highly dangerous, and to the very end the audience is kept guessing which trap the hero will finally fall into.

Sharon Stone's striking presence as woman and as actress makes Joe Eszterhas's plot seem more complex to the viewer than it actually is. Verhoeven's strength – as his first two Hollywood films *RoboCop* (1987) and *Total Recall* (1990) show – lies in the calculated exaggeration of stereotypes; men crash through his films as city cops steaming with an excess of testosterone. They swill whiskey, slap each other on the back and always have a pithy remark on their lips. His women are the complete opposite: unfathomable, and, when there is no "real" man to be had, lesbians. They

invariably spell disaster for the men. Verhoeven's characters are artificial figures that fall apart when confronted with the complexity of reality, precisely because they are nothing but clichés. They are either figures to identify with, helpless prey of their own appetites like Curran, or they are victims like Curran's dumb colleague Gus (George Dzundza). Gus spends the whole film shooting his mouth off before he is forced to a direct, physical realization that reality is much more complicated than he imagined. Verhoeven plays the double game even further, and behind the cool superficiality of his cinematic world there are always threatening depths. In a world of sex and violence, voyeurism becomes the most genuine form of perception, but at the same time – as in the scene at the police headquarters – the pleasure of seeing is revealed to be a complex trap. Verhoeven's movies are reflections on filmmaking. They do not just portray pleasurable illusions, but are themselves

"In Hollywood it's all down to nerve, not originality." *epd Film*

5   Nick Curran has more than the current case on his
     mind – he's a man preoccupied by his past.

6   Weak in the face of temptation of any kind.
     Catherine Tramell turns Detective Curran's head.

7   An ice pick is a useful implement if you like
     drinking cocktails. But it has other uses too.

8   After his fall from grace, Curran is hard-pressed
     to keep a cool head.

7

8

illusion as films. Verhoeven ensures that this self-reflexive level doesn't get lost in all the sex and violence by peppering his movies with allusions and quotations from the entire history of cinema. In *Basic Instinct*, for instance, Michael Douglas's role can be taken as an ironic commentary on the prototype of the good cop he played in younger years in *The Streets of San Francisco* (1972–1977).

Above all, Verhoeven quotes from Alfred Hitchcock's movies, so much so that *Basic Instinct* is almost a homage to the great director, with long drives along coastal roads, dialogues inside cars interspersed with meaningful glances in the rear-view mirror – these all nice touches taken from the master. Hitch is also present in the Freudian motives and explanations that give the film an unexpected comic aspect – above all in the home-baked, slap-dash psychology of Dr. Beth Gardener, a cardboard cutout psychologist

if ever there was one. Verhoeven is not however the kind of director to create such an effect unintentionally.

Besides all that, he shows his mastery of the art of suspense. The audience may feel that they are a couple of steps ahead of the hero all the time but the real danger is always unpredictable.

Some critics saw *Basic Instinct* as a mere glorification of sex and violence, but that fails to do it justice. Verhoeven and Eszterhas clearly intended to do much more than that: Catherine Tramell is presented as a highly intelligent woman who would be unlikely to describe in her books crimes she intended to commit. If the makers of *Basic Instinct* had really only been interested in serving their animal natures, they would have used their craftsmanship and knowledge of film history to conceal it far more skillfully. Unless of course, that was what they wanted film critics to think … SH

PAUL VERHOEVEN Born in Amsterdam in 1938, Verhoeven first indulged his liking for explicit scenes of sex and violence in Dutch movies like *Keetje Tippel* (*Katie Tippel*, 1975) and *De vierde man* (*The Fourth Man*, 1983). His first international production, *Flesh + Blood* (1985), which was set in the Middle Ages, continued the trend. Verhoeven then made his name in Hollywood with the sci-fi spectaculars *RoboCop* (1987) and *Total Recall* (1990). In both movies, he uses action cinema stereotypes to reflect on the voyeurism of the film industry and its inherent imbalance of illusion and reality. After *Basic Instinct* (1992) he came up with a flop slated by the critics, *Show Girls* (1995), which has since become a cult film for the gay scene. In *Starship Troopers* (1996) Verhoeven portrays a grim parody of a future totalitarian regime. His most politically committed film is the historical drama *Black Book* (2006), which shows the suffering of a Jewish woman in the Netherlands during the German Occupation.

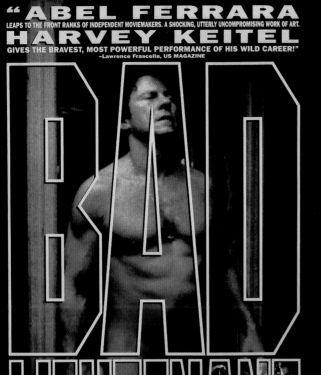

BAD LIEUTENANT

1992 – USA – 96 MIN.
DIRECTOR ABEL FERRARA (*1952)
SCREENPLAY ABEL FERRARA, ZOË LUND
DIRECTOR OF PHOTOGRAPHY KEN KELSCH
EDITING ANTHONY REDMAN MUSIC JOE DELIA
PRODUCTION EDWARD R. PRESSMAN for
BAD LT. PRODUCTIONS
STARRING HARVEY KEITEL (The Lieutenant),
VICTOR ARGO (Bet Cop), ZOË LUND (Junkie),
PAUL CALDERON (Cop One), LEONARD L. THOMAS
(Cop Two), ROBIN BURROWS (Ariane), FRANKIE
THORN (Nun), PEGGY GORMLEY (Wife),
ANTHONY RUGGIERO (Lite), VICTORIA BASTEL
(Bowtay), PAUL HIPP (Jesus)

"Forgive me, please! Forgive me, Father!"

The Lieutenant in question (Harvey Keitel) lives with his wife and children in a suburb of New York. He's a man who can't find peace – and has long been part of the urban hell of violence, drug dealing, and prostitution in which he works every day. As a corrupt, competitive junkie cop, he thinks nothing of abusing his power. He's a cheat and a bully, and has given up fighting against temptation of any kind. He is inextricably enmeshed in a life of gambling, drug taking, and sexual excess. When a nun (Frankie Thorn) is raped and the Catholic Church offers a high reward to anyone who tracks down the perpetrators, the Lieutenant sees a final chance to pay off his debts to the mafia. Although the nun remains silent, she knows who did it. She has forgiven her rapists – an act of mercy which the cynical cop cannot even begin to understand.

Bad Lieutenant is a journey into the darkness of existential despair. Like Martin Scorsese's *Taxi Driver* (1976), Abel Ferrara's movie presents New York as an inferno where ideas like justice or the difference between right and wrong have no place. A world abandoned by God, where the anonymous protagonist – a "fuckin' Catholic" as he describes himself – has lost all faith and where there is no hope of redemption. The lieutenant suffers terribly. He is a driven man who tries to deaden his despair through sex, drugs, and gambling. The lower he sinks, the more he seems to disappear into the gloomy chaos of the city, in the hysterical tumult of a techno disco, or in dark back rooms and stairwells. Increasingly he feels like an alien in the comfortable bourgeois world of his family, and he staggers through the clean sterility of his home in a daze. The coldness of his family life makes it clear that they can never help

2

3

1   Confession of a sinner: face to face with the capacity to forgive, the lieutenant acknowledges his guilt (Frankie Thorn and Harvey Keitel).

2   The film has a clearly religious dimension: a Christ figure (Paul Hipp) appears to the shattered cop.

3   Acting that reaches the limits of self-revelation: Harvey Keitel's performance makes the lieutenant's existential despair almost physically tangible.

4   A nightmare-like sequence: director Abel Ferrara stages the rape of the nun in video-clip style.

5   A showpiece role for Harvey Keitel: the corrupt cop as a mirror image of a violent society.

HARVEY KEITEL   After training at the famous Actors Studio in New York and appearing in various theater productions Off Broadway, Harvey Keitel, who was born in New York in 1939, made his film debut in Martin Scorsese's *Who's That Knocking at My Door* (1968). He went on to make four more films with Scorsese, including *Taxi Driver* (1976). Keitel had long been considered an excellent character actor, thanks to numerous appearances in American and European films, when the '90s heralded the beginning of a new era in his career. Roles in a series of spectacular artistic successes finally made him a star, including Abel Ferrara's *Bad Lieutenant* (1992), Ridley Scott's *Thelma & Louise* (1991), Quentin Tarantino's *Reservoir Dogs* (1992) and *Pulp Fiction* (1994), Jane Campion's *The Piano* (1993), James Mangold's *Cop Land* (1997), and István Szabó's *Taking Sides* (2001).

4

5

> "Make no mistake, Ferrara and his *Bad Lieutenant* are on a trip that's nothing to do with transport; out of phase, rude but by no means routine, their philosophy of cinema is one of borderline aesthetic and human experience. They're playing with fire, by turns unsettling and inspiring, and it's a pleasure to see." *Cahiers du cinéma*

him, and that they are in fact one of the reasons for his fall. The few moments of real warmth and intimacy he experiences are elsewhere, with prostitutes and a junkie friend (Zoë Lund). Ferrara directs the story in uncompromising, almost documentary-style pictures which he only interrupts when the nun appears or when the cop experiences religious visions under the influence of drugs and his moral crisis. The rape of the nun uses the artificiality of a video clip as though it were just one more of the cop's nightmare hallucinations. The appearance of Jesus shortly before the end of the movie is made in the same way. Here, the religious dimension hinted at at various points of *Bad*

Lieutenant is made visible: the nun heralds the divine principle against which the Lieutenant has sinned and without which he has no hope of forgiveness. Only when he realizes this can he find redemption.

The movie's provocative intensity comes above all from Harvey Keitel's outstanding acting, without which the powerful directness of Ferrara's production would not be possible. Keitel's grotesque howl when faced with his own guilt is so overwhelmingly heartfelt that it seems laden with all the tragedy of our human existence.

JH

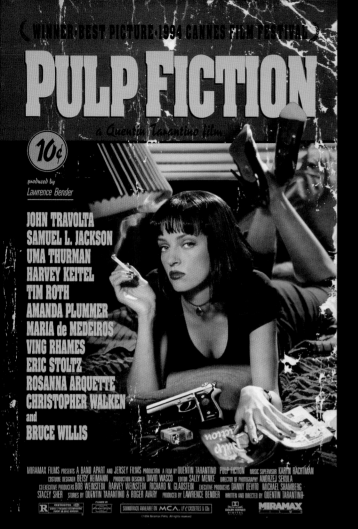

PULP FICTION ⚱

1994 – USA – 154 MIN.
DIRECTOR QUENTIN TARANTINO (*1963)
SCREENPLAY QUENTIN TARANTINO, ROGER ROBERTS AVARY
DIRECTOR OF PHOTOGRAPHY ANDRZEJ SEKULA
EDITING SALLY MENKE MUSIC VARIOUS SONGS
PRODUCTION LAWRENCE BENDER for JERSEY FILMS,
A BAND APART, MIRAMAX FILMS
STARRING JOHN TRAVOLTA (Vincent Vega),
SAMUEL L. JACKSON (Jules Winnfield), UMA THURMAN
(Mia Wallace), HARVEY KEITEL (Winston Wolfe),
VING RHAMES (Marsellus Wallace),
ROSANNA ARQUETTE (Jody), ERIC STOLTZ (Lance),
QUENTIN TARANTINO (Jimmie), BRUCE WILLIS
(Butch Coolidge), MARIA DE MEDEIROS (Fabienne),
CHRISTOPHER WALKEN (Koons), TIM ROTH (Ringo/
Pumpkin), AMANDA PLUMMER (Yolanda / Honeybunny).
ACADEMY AWARDS 1994 OSCAR for BEST ORIGINAL SCREENPLAY
(Quentin Tarantino, Roger Roberts Avary)
IFF CANNES 1994 GOLDEN PALM for
BEST FILM (Quentin Tarantino)

"Zed's dead, baby. Zed's dead."

After his amazing directorial debut, *Reservoir Dogs* (1992), Quentin Tarantino had a lot to live up to. The bloody studio piece was essentially a purely cinematic challenge, and such an unusual movie seemed difficult to beat. But Tarantino surpassed himself with *Pulp Fiction*, a deeply black gangster comedy. Tarantino had previously written the screenplay for Tony Scott's uninspired gangster movie *True Romance* (1993) and the original script to Oliver Stone's *Natural Born Killers* (1994).

At the beginning of his own movie, he presents us with another potential killer couple. Ringo and Yolanda (Tim Roth and Amanda Plummer), who lovingly call each other Pumpkin and Honey Bunny, are sitting having breakfast in a diner and making plans for their future together. They are fed up with robbing liquor stores whose multicultural owners don't even understand simple orders like "Hand over the cash!" The next step in their career plan is to expand into diners – why not start straight away with this one? This sequence, which opens and concludes *Pulp Fiction* serves as a frame-

work for the movie's other three interwoven stories, which overlap and move in and out of chronological sequence. One of the protagonists is killed in the middle of the movie, only to appear alive and well in the final scene, and we only understand how the stories hang together at the very end.

The first story is "Vincent Vega and Marsellus Wallace's Wife." Vincent and Jules (John Travolta and Samuel L. Jackson), are professional assassins on their way to carry out an order. Their boss Marsellus Wallace (Ving Rhames) wants them to bring him back a mysterious briefcase. A routine job, as we can tell from their nonchalant chitchat. Their black suits make them look as if they have stepped out of a '40s film noir. Vincent is not entirely happy, as he has been given the job of looking after Marsellus's wife Mia (Uma Thurman) when the boss is away. In gangster circles, rumor has it that Vincent's predecessor was thrown out of a window on the fourth floor – apparently for doing nothing more than massaging Mia's feet.

2

"Hoodlums Travolta and Jackson — like modern-day Beckett characters — discuss foot massages, cunnilingus and cheeseburgers on their way to a routine killing job. The recently traveled Travolta informs Jackson that at the McDonald's in Paris, the Quarter Pounder is known as 'Le Royal.' However a Big Mac's a Big Mac, but they call it 'Le Big Mac.'" *The Washington Post*

"The Golden Watch," the second story in the film, is the story of has-been boxer Butch Coolidge (Bruce Willis). He too is one of Marsellus's "niggers" as the gangster boss calls all those who depend on him. Butch has accepted a bribe and agreed to take a dive after the fifth round in his next fight. At the last minute, he decides to win instead and to run away with the money and his French girlfriend Fabienne (Maria de Medeiros).

In the third story, "The Bonnie Situation," a couple of loose narrative strands are tied together. Jules and Vincent have done their job. However, on the way back, Vincent accidentally shoots his informer who is sitting in the back of the car. The bloody car and its occupants have to get off the street as soon as possible. The two killers hide at Jim's (Quentin Tarantino), although

his wife Bonnie is about to get back from work at any moment, so they have to get rid of the evidence as quickly as possible. Luckily they can call upon the services of Mr. Wolfe (Harvey Keitel), the quickest and most efficient cleaner there is.

To like *Pulp Fiction*, you have to have a weakness for pop culture, which this film constantly uses and parodies, although it never simply ridicules the source of its inspiration. Quentin Tarantino must have seen enormous quantities of movies before he became a director. The inside of his head must be like the restaurant where Vincent takes Mia; the tables are like '50s Cabrios, the waiters and waitresses are pop icon doubles: Marilyn Monroe, James Dean, Mamie van Doren and Buddy Holly (Steve Buscemi in a cameo appearance). Vincent and Mia take part in a twist competition. The way the saggy-cheeked, aging John Travolta dances is a brilliant homage to his early career and *Saturday Night Fever* (1977).

With his tongue-in-cheek allusions to pop and film culture, Tarantino often verges on bad taste: in one scene from "The Golden Watch," a former prisoner of war and Vietnam veteran (Christopher Walken) arrives at a children's home to give the little Butch his father's golden watch. The scene begins like a kitsch scene from any Vietnam movie, but quickly deteriorates into the scatological and absurd when Walken tells the boy in great detail about the dark place where his father hid the watch in the prison camp for so many years.

Tarantino has an excellent feel for dialogue. His protagonists' conversations are as banal as in real life, they talk about everything and nothing, about potbellies, embarrassing silences, or piercings. He also lays great value on those little details which really make the stories, for example the toaster which together with Vincent's habit of long sessions in the bathroom will cost him his life – as he prefers to take a detective story rather than a pistol into the lavatory.

Tarantino's treatment of violence is a theme unto itself. It is constantly present in the movie, but is seldomly explicitly shown. The weapon is more important than the victim. In a conventional action movie, the scene where Jules and Vincent go down a long corridor to the apartment where they will kill several people would have been used to build up the suspense, but in Tarantino's film Vincent and Jules talk about trivial things instead, like two office colleagues on the way to the canteen.

One of the movie's most brutal scenes comes after Vincent and Mia's restaurant visit. The pair of them are in Mia's apartment, Vincent as ever in the bathroom, where he is meditating on loyalty and his desire to massage

QUENTIN TARANTINO Tarantino had just turned 31 when he won the most important trophies in the movie business for *Pulp Fiction* (1994): the Golden Palm at Cannes and an Oscar for the screenplay. The movie where killers shoot people as casually as they eat hamburgers caused a veritable outbreak of "Tarantinomania," with several directors trying to copy that special Tarantino touch. There was a sudden rash of gangsters dropping cool wisecracks against a backdrop of as much bloodshed as possible and a shameless parade of quotations from other films. Tarantino's formidable knowledge of films didn't come from any university, but from his job in a video shop in Los Angeles. To pass the time, he wrote film scripts. After the unexpected success of his first movie, *Reservoir Dogs* (1992), a gangster story about a bungled bank robbery, the scripts he had in his bottom drawer suddenly became very desirable: Oliver Stone bought the rights to *Natural Born Killers* (1994) and Tony Scott filmed *True Romance* (1993). After writing and starring in *From Dusk Till Dawn* (1996) Tarantino made the surprisingly calm *Jackie Brown* (1997), paying homage to the Blaxploitation cinema of the '70s. Things became crazier again with the two parts of *Kill Bill* (2003, 2004), doffing his cap to '70s kung fu movies among others, and the Nazi satire *Inglourious Basterds* (2009), which brought Christoph Waltz the Oscar for Best Supporting Actor. More recently he has even made the shift to politically committed filmmaker with his controversial Spaghetti Western homage *Django Unchained* (2012) which deals with the theme of slavery.

4

5

1 Do Mia's (Uma Thurman) foot massages turn into an erotic experience?

2 The Lord moves in mysterious ways: Jules (Samuel L. Jackson) is a killer who knows his Bible by heart.

3 Completely covered in blood: Vincent (John Travolta) after his little accident.

4 Everything's under control: as the "Cleaner" Mister Wolfe (Harvey Keitel) takes care of any dirty work that comes up.

5 In his role as Major Koons Christopher Walken plays an ex-Vietnam prisoner of war as he did in *The Deer Hunter* (1978).

6 Echoes of *Saturday Night Fever* (1977): Mia and Vincent risk a little dance.

"Tarantino's guilty secret is that his films are cultural hybrids. The blood and gore, the cheeky patter, the taunting *mise-en-scène* are all very American – the old studios at their snazziest." *Time Magazine*

Mia's feet. In the meantime Mia discovers his supply of heroin, thinks it is cocaine and snorts an overdose. Vincent is then forced to get physical with her, but not in the way he imagined. To bring her back to life, he has to plant an enormous adrenaline jab in her heart.

Pulp Fiction also shows Tarantino to be a master of casting. All the roles are carried by their actors' larger-than-life presence. They are all "cool": Samuel L. Jackson as an Old-Testament-quoting killer, and Uma Thurman in a black wig as an enchanting, dippy gangster's moll. Bruce Willis drops his habitual grin and is totally convincing as an aging boxer who re-fuses to give up. Craggy, jowly John Travolta plays the most harmless and good-natured assassin imaginable. If *Pulp Fiction* has a central theme run-ning through it, then it's the "moral" which is present in each of the three

6

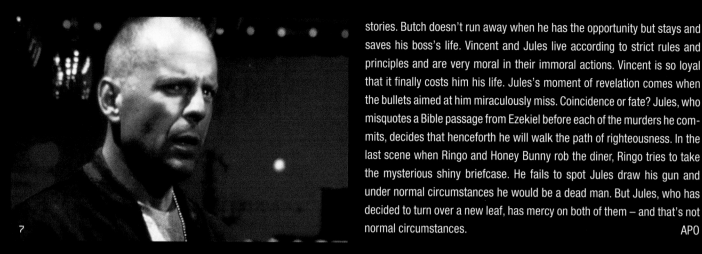

stories. Butch doesn't run away when he has the opportunity but stays and saves his boss's life. Vincent and Jules live according to strict rules and principles and are very moral in their immoral actions. Vincent is so loyal that it finally costs him his life. Jules's moment of revelation comes when the bullets aimed at him miraculously miss. Coincidence or fate? Jules, who misquotes a Bible passage from Ezekiel before each of the murders he commits, decides that henceforth he will walk the path of righteousness. In the last scene when Ringo and Honey Bunny rob the diner, Ringo tries to take the mysterious shiny briefcase. He fails to spot Jules draw his gun and under normal circumstances he would be a dead man. But Jules, who has decided to turn over a new leaf, has mercy on both of them – and that's not normal circumstances.   APO

7

7   Will his pride desert him? Boxer Butch (Bruce Willis) gets paid every time he loses in the ring.

8   You gotta change your life! Jules and Vincent talk about chance and predestiny.

9   Hand over the cash! Yolanda (Amanda Plummer) carries out …

10   … the plan that she and Ringo (Tim Roth) hatched a few moments before.

"Split into three distinct sections, the tale zips back and forth in time and space, meaning that the final shot is of a character we've seen being killed 50 minutes ago." *Empire*

8

9

10

SE7EN

1995 – USA – 125 MIN.
DIRECTOR DAVID FINCHER (*1964)
SCREENPLAY ANDREW KEVIN WALKER
DIRECTOR OF PHOTOGRAPHY DARIUS KHONDJI
EDITING RICHARD FRANCIS-BRUCE
MUSIC HOWARD SHORE **PRODUCTION** ARNOLD KOPELSON,
PHYLLIS CARLYLE for ARNOLD KOPELSON
PRODUCTIONS (NEW LINE CINEMA)
STARRING MORGAN FREEMAN (William Somerset),
BRAD PITT (David Mills), KEVIN SPACEY (John Doe),
GWYNETH PALTROW (Tracy Mills), JOHN C. MCGINLEY
(California), RICHARD ROUNDTREE (Talbot),
R. LEE ERMEY (Chief of Police), JULIE ARASKOG
(Mrs Gould), REGINALD E. CATHEY (Dr. Santiago),
JOHN CASSINI (Officer Davis)

"Detective, the only reason that I'm here right now is that I wanted to be."

One cop tries to pit his idea of order against the chaos of the world. After 34 years of service, disillusioned detective William Somerset (Morgan Freeman) is about to retire but he is still not hardened to the job. He fights against decay and decadence with pedantry: the coffee jug is always rinsed out before he goes to work and his utensils for the endless grind in the urban jungle are tidily arrayed on the chest of drawers. The first ritual actions we see in this movie are Somerset carefully tying his tie and picking a piece of fluff off his jacket, but before long the movie is dominated by rituals of quite a different kind. When the first corpse of the day is found, Somerset registers the circumstances of the crime with a mixture of routine efficiency and mute fatalism.

Despite his outward appearance, Somerset's new colleague David Mills (Brad Pitt) is not made out of such stern stuff. The newcomer is shown the ropes as he is to be Somerset's successor. Pitt plays Mills with concentrated energy, giving us a character that is an apparently confident go-getter. But Mills is soon forced to admit that both his older colleague and the murderer

are his superiors. The audience also soon realizes that the new arrival in this anonymous, permanently rainy city is not as clever as he makes out; the elevated railroad rumbles every quarter of an hour over the apartment he has been talked into taking. Tracy (Gwyneth Paltrow), is waiting for him there. She has been with him since high school.

This uneven pair, familiar from innumerable police films, the wise old veteran and the enthusiastic greenhorn, have to catch a serial killer who commits appalling crimes with missionary zeal, taking gluttony, greed, sloth, lust, pride, envy, and wrath – the seven deadly sins – as his pattern. The self-appointed avenger is also a familiar figure of the genre; he believes he has been chosen by a higher power to turn the sins of the world against the sinners. But there is more at stake in *Se7en* than simple character studies.

The killer (Kevin Spacey) works under the nom de guerre of John Doe – the name American authorities routinely give to unidentified male corpses. His readings in the great works of Western literature (Thomas Aquinas, Dante

4

Alighieri, Geoffrey Chaucer) have inspired him to send a warning to the world. The first deadly sin he punishes is that of gluttony, when he forces a hugely fat man to literally eat himself to death. This extraordinary opening crime begins a series of murders which all feature sophisticated hidden hints left for the investigating cops. The indispensable minimum of shock effects and horrific images needed in a serial killer movie is delivered in an almost off-hand manner during the fat man's autopsy as if to fulfill an unavoidable obligation.

It soon becomes clear that director David Fincher is only marginally interested in the usual thrills and kicks, and that he is not concerned at all with any kind of guessing game as to who has committed the bizarre murders. Fincher has a message to proclaim, like his diabolically precise and brutal killer. It is delivered with shattering clarity and goes like this: the urban

spaces of our civilization are in dangerous decline. In this miserable setting, the murderer's crimes are merely the culmination of the general fear and alienation which creeps like a poison through the movie's stylized images from the very first moment. We see random pictures of a gloomy, dirty gray cityscape, where the constant rain can't wash away the filth, and people slink between the houses, bowed, anxious, and filled with latent aggression that threatens to break out into violence at every moment.

Although the visual aspects of *Se7en* are often compared to Ridley Scott's *Blade Runner* (1982), Fincher's movie is a far cry from the overloaded metaphorical structure of that earlier movie with its visual symbols of a mythical past and a threatening future. Everything that happens here in the way of hidden codes and numbers serves almost exclusively to further the development of the plot.

DAVID FINCHER When the dark third part of the *Alien* series was released in 1991, it left both critics and audiences puzzled. It seemed that the Hollywood career of music video and commercial director David Fincher had ended before it had properly begun. But *Se7en* (1995) marked quite a comeback. His manhunt thriller *The Game* (1997) and satire on capitalism *Fight Club* (1999) also reveal a profoundly pessimistic world view. Fincher's films are often extremely impressive visually; he uses apocalyptic settings to tell stories so dark they would probably have been unthinkable ten years before. *Zodiac* (2007), the biopic about a serial killer, and the adaptation of Stieg Larsson's *The Girl with the Dragon Tattoo* (2011) were also marked by the same gloomy Fincher atmosphere. Born in 1962, Fincher moved into lighter territory on two occasions, with literary epic *The Curious Case of Benjamin Button* (2008) and Facebook drama *The Social Network* (2010).

1   Cop David Mills (Brad Pitt) tries to uncover a system behind the murders. But common sense isn't enough to understand the psychopath's atrocities.

2   An end to terror: police officer William Somerset (Morgan Freeman) has the killer in his sights.

3   A gruesome discovery: the investigators catch their breath at the scene of the crime.

4   Seeking reassurance: Mills shortly before the final confrontation.

5   Nerve-wracking police work: Somerset and Mills study photos of the crime scenes.

"If you want people to listen to you, tapping them on the shoulder isn't enough. You have to hit them with a sledgehammer."

Film quote: John Doe (Kevin Spacey)

The clues written in blood that the killer leaves at the second scene of crime leave the cops no doubt as to the serial nature of the murders. They are on the defensive and feel helpless, as all they know is that they can expect five further corpses in as many days. As the two detectives put together the first pieces of the fiendish mosaic and, in keeping with the rules of the genre, quickly become friends in the process, their methods and thoughts become inextricably intertwined with those of the killer. Early on, we begin to suspect that the finale will be a personal affair. However, when John Doe saunters into the police headquarters after the fifth murder has been discovered and gives himself up, the chase comes to an abrupt end thereby breaking all the conventions of the genre.

Se7en's main quality is its meditation on cultural pessimism. All three of the protagonists have failed in the face of modern civilization, in the long tradition of archetypal American (anti)heroes, and they all touch a raw nerve in our souls. Somerset is bowed with age and at odds with society, he wants to escape but he doesn't know where to, while his youthful partner barely hides his violent tendencies behind the rules of his job. The serial killer, that familiar institution in popular culture, escapes from his identity crisis and the perversion and madness of the world in a closed, cruelly logical system of thought and action but in the end wants only to die. *Se7en* is full of striking images. The opening sequence has become famous, and is visually so revolutionary that it is often copied in commercials. UVB

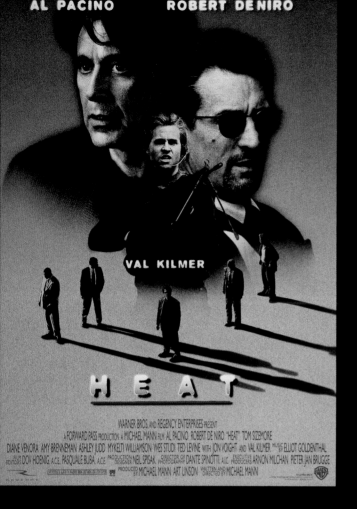

HEAT

1995 – USA – 172 MIN.
DIRECTOR MICHAEL MANN (*1943)
SCREENPLAY MICHAEL MANN
DIRECTOR OF PHOTOGRAPHY DANTE SPINOTTI
EDITING PASQUALE BUBA **MUSIC** ELLIOT GOLDENTHAL
PRODUCTION MICHAEL MANN, ART LINSON for
FORWARD PASS PRODUCTION,
REGENCY ENTERPRISES, LION BRAND FILM
STARRING ROBERT DE NIRO (Neil McCauley),
AMY BRENNEMAN (Eady), AL PACINO (Vincent Hanna),
DIANE VENORA (Justine Hanna),
VAL KILMER (Chris Shiherlis), ASHLEY JUDD
(Charlene Shiherlis), JON VOIGHT (Nate),
TOM SIZEMORE (Michael Cheritto),
MYKELTI WILLIAMSON (Drucker),
WES STUDI (Casals), KEVIN GAGE (Waingro),
DANNY TREJO (Trejo)

"I'm alone, I'm not lonely."

Neil McCauley (Robert De Niro) and his team – Chris, Cheritto, and Trejo – are preparing their next strike. They need a fifth man to make sure it all goes smoothly. They take on a guy by the name of Waingro (Kevin Gage), who messes up the job. The team manages to escape with the loot but now they are wanted for robbery and murder, and the police are on their trails. Waingro shot one of the guards dead just for fun, and it's not too long till we realize that he is a psychopath and a serial killer too. When McCauley tries to get rid of him, he has vanished without trace.

Michael Mann depicts McCauley's gang as a close-knit group of conspirators who are absolute professionals at what they do. The armored car robbery is carried out with the utmost precision, and they use extreme brutality whenever it's necessary.

A new detective, Vincent Hanna (Al Pacino), is assigned to the investigation of the case. One tiny detail and a seemingly crazy story told by an informer puts Hanna on the trail of gang member Cheritto, and he unwittingly leads him to the others. As he has no proof, he has all of them shadowed.

During a break-in, McCauley realizes he is being watched. He sets a trap for his pursuer to find out who he is up against. The team pretend to prepare a new heist and lead Hanna and his men to an abandoned part of the harbor where they make their escape and then observe their pursuers at their leisure.

In *Heat*, Michael Mann is concerned with much more than a simple game of cat and mouse. He shows us single combat between two equally matched opponents and does not shrink from drama and emotions in the depiction of his heroes.

Heat also tells the story of three relationships. McCauley falls in love with the shy graphic designer Eady, Vincent and Justine Hanna's marriage breaks down and almost destroys the life of their daughter Lauren, and Chris

2

1 Ready to take life as it comes: break-in specialist Neal McCauley (Robert De Niro) knows that plans can go wrong and that lives can be ruined.

2 A great moment in film history: Al Pacino as police officer Vincent Hanna ...

3 ... and Robert De Niro as burglar sit at the same table for the first time.

"We're sitting here like a couple of regular fellas. You do what you do. I do what I gotta do."

Film quote: Vincent Hanna (Al Pacino)

and Charlene Shiherlis's marriage is put to a test where there is no second chance. One of the most memorable and understated scenes is the McCauley team family dinner. It looks for all the world like a normal dinner party where couples enjoy sharing an evening with friends. This quiet moment forms a shocking contrast with the violence of the other side of their lives.

McCauley and his team want to carry out a last robbery with which they will make enough to be able to retire, even though they know that the police are hot on their heels. *Heat* is great actors' cinema. McCauley and Hanna are outsiders. They live according to their own principles and follow their own code of honor. McCauley repeats over and over that he cannot afford to have any ties in his job, but his actions tell a different story. When he chooses to go back and avenge his friends rather than escape to safety

at the end of the movie, he is fully conscious of the danger he is in. His main motivation is loyalty.

One of the earliest mentions of the *Heat* project can be found in an interview with Michael Mann (*Film Comment*, 1983) which he gave shortly after the completion of his horror movie *The Keep* (1983). He talks about a screenplay called *Heat* that he wrote and loves, but doesn't want to direct himself. Clearly Mann decided that the project as too important to hand on to someone else and he eventually made two film versions of the same story.

The first work based on the *Heat* screenplay was a television film called *L.A. Takedown* (1989) which was made as a pilot for *Made in L.A.*, a television series that was never made. *L.A. Takedown* is like an early sketch for the feature film as we know it. The basic structure of the movie is already there and

4

4   Jon Voight as Nate, the man in the background.
The character was designed to pay homage to the
writer Edward Bunker, who earned his living in the
1960s by planning break-ins.

5   Wherever his gaze turns, it always lights upon
himself: Val Kilmer as burglar Chris Shiherlis.

6   The street as battlefield. McCauley and Chris
Shiherlis shoot their way to freedom after a
holdup.

EDWARD BUNKER   Author and bit part actor Edward Bunker (1933–2005) first became known to a wider cinema audience as Mr. Blue in Quentin Tarantino's *Reservoir Dogs*
(1992). A serious criminal with many convictions to his name, Bunker had been known to crime fiction fans since the publication of his extraordinary debut novel *No Beast
so Fierce* in 1973. Bunker was still in prison at the time. When this masterpiece of prison literature was filmed five years later by Ulu Grosbard as *Straight Time* (1978),
Bunker not only made his acting debut but was also criminal advisor to the production. This is a role he has played for many prison films since then, including Andrei
Konchalovsky's Oscar-nominated *Runaway Train* (1985), for which Bunker also co-wrote the screenplay. Edward Bunker also worked in an advisory capacity on Martin Bell's
American Heart (1992) and Michael Mann's *Heat* (1995). His final screen appearance, soon after which he died during a cancer operation, was in *The Longest Yard* (2005)
with Adam Sandler.

many key scenes are already well developed, including the famous café
scene where Al Pacino meets Robert De Niro. But the earlier version doesn't
have the emotional depth of the feature film, nor the uncomfortable feeling
that we are watching extraordinary people caught up in an oppressively
ordered world. Six years later work on the actual movie started. Spurred on
by the worldwide success of his film of James Fenimore Cooper's *The Last
of the Mohicans* (1992), Mann began work on his magnum opus.

Mann's production is emotional and dramatic without being exaggerated. The scene where the dying and the living reach out their hands to each
other at the end of the movie is one of cinema's truly great moments.

OM

"A guy once told me, don't let yourself get attached to anything you're not willing to walk out on, if you feel the heat around the corner in 30 seconds flat."

Film quote: Neil McCauley (Robert De Niro)

L.A. CONFIDENTIAL ♟♟

1997 – USA – 138 MIN.
DIRECTOR CURTIS HANSON (*1945)
SCREENPLAY CURTIS HANSON, BRIAN HELGELAND based on
the novel *L.A. Confidential* by JAMES ELLROY
DIRECTOR OF PHOTOGRAPHY DANTE SPINOTTI
EDITING PETER HONESS **MUSIC** JERRY GOLDSMITH
PRODUCTION CURTIS HANSON, ARNON MILCHAN,
MICHAEL G. NATHANSON for REGENCY ENTERPRISES
STARRING RUSSELL CROWE (Bud White), KEVIN SPACEY
(Jack Vincennes), GUY PEARCE (Ed Exley),
KIM BASINGER (Lynn Bracken), DANNY DEVITO
(Sid Hudgeons), JAMES CROMWELL (Dudley Smith),
DAVID STRATHAIRN (Pierce Patchett), RON RIFKIN
(D. A. Ellis Loew), MATT MCCOY (Brett Chase),
PAUL GUILFOYLE (Mickey Cohen)
ACADEMY AWARDS 1997 OSCARS for BEST SUPPORTING ACTRESS
(Kim Basinger), and BEST ADAPTED SCREENPLAY
(Curtis Hanson, Brian Helgeland)

"Why did you become a cop?"
"I don't remember."

Sun, swimming pools, beautiful people: "Life is good in L.A., it's a paradise …" That Los Angeles only exists in commercials. In *L.A. Confidential* – set in the early '50s – the city looks quite different, and is a morass of crime and corruption. Three policemen try to combat this with varying dedication and varying motives. Ambitious young police academy graduate Ed Exley (Guy Pearce) is a champion of law and order, and his testimony against his colleagues in an internal police trial catapults him straight to the top of the station house hierarchy. Bud White (Russell Crowe) is a hardened cynic who is prepared to extract confessions with force, but cannot stand violence against women, and Jack Vincennes (Kevin Spacey) is nothing more than a corrupt phony who uses his police job to get in with the entertainment indus-

try. He is advisor to the television series *Badge of Honor* and sets up stories for Sid Hudgeons (Danny DeVito), slimy reporter on the gossip magazine *Hush-Hush*.

Exley's first case is a spectacular bloodbath in the Nite Owl bar. Five lie dead in the bathroom, killed with a shotgun. Three black youths seen near the scene of the crime are swiftly arrested, and with his brilliant interrogation technique, Exley gets them to admit to having kidnapped and raped a Mexican girl. While White frees the victim and shoots her captor, the three suspects escape from police custody. Exley hunts them down and shoots them dead. He is hailed as a hero and awarded a medal, and it would seem that that is the end of the case. But it doesn't seem to quite add up, and Exley,

1

2

3

> ## "It's striking to see how the elegance and lightness of touch in the atmosphere of *L.A. Confidential* seem both to derive from and influence the actors."
> *Cahiers du cinéma*

4

1 He may have deserved it much more for this film, but Russell Crowe didn't win an Oscar until 2001 for *Gladiator*.

2 Bud White (Russell Crowe) doesn't waste any time with the kidnapper of the Mexican girl.

3 Kim Basinger's Oscar for the part of Lynn Bracken brought her long-overdue universal acclaim.

4 A Christmas angel: Lynn out on business until late in the evening with her employer.

5 A few moments of melancholy apart, Bud White doesn't let the corruptness of the world get to him.

6 Brief moments of happiness: is there a future for Bud and Lynn's love?

7 Lynn the prostitute's little trick: she does herself up to look like 1940s glamour star Veronica Lake.

White and Vincennes continue their investigations until they discover a conspiracy which reaches up into the highest echelons of police and city administration, involving drugs, blackmail, and a ring of porn traders.

L.A. Confidential is a reference to the first and perhaps most brazen American gossip magazine *Confidential* (1952–1957), and Hudgeons, the reporter played by Danny DeVito (who is also the off-screen narrator) is an alter ego of Robert Harrison, its infamous editor. Hudgeons gets his kicks from filth and sensationalism, and typifies the moral decadence that seems to have infected the entire city. The police make deals with criminals, the cops who uncover the conspiracy are far from blameless and even the naïve greenhorn Exley loses his innocence in the course of the film.

Director Curtis Hanson conjures up the brooding atmosphere of the film noir crime movies of the '40s and '50s, but *L.A. Confidential* is far more than a throwback or a simple nostalgia trip. Cameraman Dante Spinotti shoots clear images free from any patina of age and avoids typical genre references like long shadows. The crime and the corruption seem even more devastating when told in pictures of a sunny, crisp Los Angeles winter. The plot is complex and difficult to follow on first viewing, but Hanson does not emphasize this so much as individual scenes which condense the city's amorality into striking images, like Vincennes saying he can no longer remember why he became a cop. Above all, the director focuses on his brilliant ensemble. Australians Russell Crowe and Guy Pearce, who were virtually unknown before the movie was made, make a great team with the amazing Kevin Spacey. Kim Basinger is a worthy Oscar winner as prostitute and Veronica Lake look-alike Lynn.

HJK

5

6

> "When I gave Kevin Spacey the script, I said I think of two words: Dean Martin."
>
> *Curtis Hanson, in: Sight and Sound*

JAMES ELLROY: L.A.'S INDEFATIGABLE CHRONICLER His own life sounds like a crime story. James Ellroy was born in Los Angeles in 1948. When he was ten, his mother fell victim to a sex killer, a crime he works through in his 1996 book *My Dark Places*. The shock threw Ellroy completely off the rails: drugs, petty crime, and 50 arrests followed, and he came to writing relatively late. His first novel, *Brown's Requiem*, was published in 1981 and made into a movie with the same name in 1998. He then wrote a trilogy focusing on the figure of the policeman Lloyd Hopkins. The first of this series, *Blood on the Moon* (1984), was filmed in 1988 as *Cop*. Ellroy's masterpiece is the L.A. quartet, four novels on historical crimes from the period 1947 through 1960. Brian De Palma made the first volume in the series, *The Black Dahlia*, into a film with the same title in 2006. *L.A. Confidential* (1997) was based on the third volume in the series; it took director Curtis Hanson and coauthor Brian Helgeland a whole year and seven different versions to adapt this complex novel into a screenplay.

8 Tabloid reporter Sid Hudgeons (Danny DeVito) loves digging up other people's dirt.

9 Officer Vincennes (right) likes to take Hudgeons and a photographer along to his arrests.

10 Vincennes (Kevin Spacey) makes sure that first and foremost he's looking after number one.

11 Officer Ed Exley (Guy Pearce) earns praise from the press and from his boss Dudley Smith (James Cromwell, right).

9

FIREWORKS
HANA-BI

1997 – JAPAN – 103 MIN.
DIRECTOR TAKESHI KITANO (*1947)
SCREENPLAY TAKESHI KITANO
DIRECTOR OF PHOTOGRAPHY HIDEO YAMAMOTO
MUSIC JOE HISAISHI EDITING TAKESHI KITANO,
YOSHINORI ÔTA PRODUCTION KAZUHIRO FURUKAWA,
HIROSHI ISHIKAWA, MASAYUKI MORI, TAKIO YOSHIDA,
YASUSHI TSUGE for OFFICE KITANO, BANDAI VISUAL
STARRING TAKESHI KITANO (Yoshitaka Nishi),
KAYOKO KISHIMOTO (Miyuki, Nishi's Wife),
REN ÔSUGI (Horibe), SUSUMU TERAJIMA
(Nakamura), TETSU WATANABE
(Tesuka), HAKURYU (Yakuza Hitman),
YASUEI YAKUSHIJI (Criminal), TARÔ ITSUMI
(Kudo), KENICHI YAJIMA (Doctor)
IFF VENEDIG 1997 GOLDEN LION (Takeshi Kitano)

"Thank you. Thank you for everything."

Many friends believe Takeshi Kitano's film *Sonatine* (1993), infused with sui-cidal imagery, was director/actor/writer Takeshi Kitano's dry run for his own attempted suicide in 1994, when he ran his motorcycle into a railroad divid-er. He suffered brain contusions and multiple skull fractures and went through a series of surgeries that left him with altered features and nervous tics that are in evidence in his subsequent performances. Kitano, however, used this traumatic incident to reevaluate his life and develop his more personal aes-thetic talents, including painting and writing.

The result of this period of self-examination and aesthetic development was *Fireworks*. As in his first noir yakuza film, *Violent Cop* (*Sono otoko, kyôbô ni tsuki*, 1989), Kitano is on the side of the "law" in its battle against the yaku-

za gangs. The film centers on the psychological and physical toll these vio-lent and brutal confrontations take on the police themselves. Kitano plays Nishi, an ex-cop who is not only haunted by the deaths and near-deaths of his cohorts but by the demise of his child and the imminent death of his wife from cancer. Unlike his former films, in which the actor Kitano was, for the most part, able to hide his suffering behind a mask, here the scars and facial twitches from his surgeries work to externalize the depths of sorrow this character feels but is unable to verbalize.

Throughout the film Nishi tries to make reparations for the damage done to others around him. He borrows money from the local yakuza boss and eventually even robs a bank to support the widow of a cop killed by a

yakuza thug (the assassination sequence is seen several times in flashback and in slow motion) and to aid his close friend Horibe (Ren Ôsugi),
who was crippled by a yakuza bullet and is now suicidal. (Parenthetically,
Kitano has projected his own struggle with recovery onto the character of
Horibe. Like Kitano, Horibe takes up painting to reignite his interest in life.
Kitano's own paintings act as decor not only for the titles but for much of
the film.)

In the second half of the movie Kitano shifts gears and grafts on a noir
fugitive-couple theme to the gangster-film structure. After the bank robbery,
Nishi and his wife, Miyuki (Kayoko Kishimoto), buy a van and take off into the
country while being pursued by yakuzas as well as police. During the flight
they find the love that they had buried under all their sorrow. They share
moments of whimsy and happiness while playing games (an element in most
Kitano films, which gives his work a childlike innocence amidst all the violence and corruption). They reconnect with the spirit of their original love by

immersing themselves in nature. But as in most fugitive-couple films, from
You Only Live Once (1937) to Gun Crazy (1950), fate is never far behind. In a
clear homage to François Truffaut's fugitive-couple film Mississippi Mermaid
(1969), the pair end up hiding out in the snow-packed mountains where Nishi
dispatches the yakuzas sent to retrieve him.

Predictably for a Kitano film, the pursuit ends at the edge of the sea (the
ocean is a primal symbol in Kitano's films, representing the desire to return
to the womb, to slip into that "final sleep"). Nishi's cop pals find them at last.
In a poignant final scene, Nishi loads two bullets into his gun and asks his
comrades for "a little time." They, of course, agree. Nishi returns to his wife,
and as they embrace, she thanks him for his new tenderness. As the camera
pans discreetly away to the blue expanse of the "mother ocean," two shots
are heard. The camera then cuts to a little girl who has been flying a kite on
the beach as she stares in shock at what she can see but what Kitano refuses to show the audience. It is a moment of horror, like the other violent acts

TAKESHI KITANO Takeshi Kitano was born in Tokyo in 1947. After working at odd jobs in vaudeville-style venues, he became a comedy performer in the 1970s, using the
name he still sports as an actor – "Beat" Takeshi. His often transgressive and surreal comedy style made him one of the stars of manzai (stand-up comedy). He appeared
on numerous TV shows, including hosting the outrageous Takeshi's Castle (Fûun! Takeshi Jô, 1986–1989) in the 1980s.
He broke into the movies with his performance as the brutal POW officer in Nagisa Ôshima's Merry Christmas Mr. Lawrence (1983), starring David Bowie. He also brought
his quirky performances to other international hits like Johnny Mnemonic (1995), Ôshima's Taboo (Gohatto, 1999), and Kinji Fukasaku's Battle Royale (Batoru rowaiaru, 2000).
His debut as a movie director, however, was entirely accidental as he took over the helm of his starring vehicle Violent Cop (Sono otoko, kyôbô ni tsuki, 1989) when the
director fell ill. From that point on Kitano continued to help revitalize the yakuza (gangster) genre with films like Sonatine (1993), Fireworks (Hana-Bi, 1997), Brother (2000),
and Outrage (Autoreiji, 2010). Kitano has brought his own idiosyncratic aestheticism to the Japanese noir/yakuza genre. His films are steeped in alienation and violence but
also punctuated with bursts of comedy. After a motorcycle "accident," Kitano turned more inward, concentrating on painting and writing while making films that featured a
more contemplative, painterly dimension, including non-yakuza masterworks like Dolls (2002) and The Blind Swordsman: Zatôichi (Zatôichi, 2003).

3

1 Takeshi Kitano's bloodied, scarred face crystallizes the violent ethos of his movies, a mixture of sadism and sentimentality.

2 Children's games like flying kites play a major role in Kitano's movies, evoking lost innocence.

3 The guilt-ridden cop Nishi (Takeshi Kitano) lets his most violent nature take over after the death and crippling of his cop buddies by local yakuza.

4 Nishi's wife, Miyuki (Kayoko Kishimoto), becomes more and more withdrawn after the death of her child and being diagnosed with cancer. She is the heart of the movie.

"I know you are going to wonder about the meaning of these works. Don't. Just enjoy." *Takeshi Kitano*

in the movie, but, unlike those other acts, so tender and emotional that Kitano cannot bear to show it to his audience.

Like *Sonatine*, *Fireworks* was a worldwide critical success, helping to give the yakuza genre new credibility in the eyes of world cinema. It won the Grand Prix at the prestigious Venice Film Festival. It also garnered the top award of the French Syndicate of Cinema Critics. Kitano's brilliant examination of death, love, violence, and creativity has had a deep impact on Japanese cinema. Kitano himself underplays its importance in interviews and instead concentrates on what he considers the essence of the movie: "The protagonist is willing to confront death face-to-face in order to accept responsibility for his friends and family."   JU

4

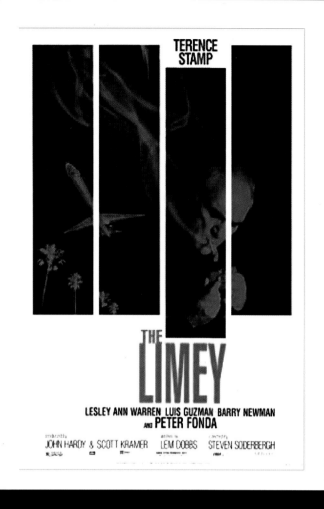

THE LIMEY

1999 – USA – 90 MIN.
DIRECTOR STEVEN SODERBERGH (*1963)
SCREENPLAY LEM DOBBS
DIRECTOR OF PHOTOGRAPHY EDWARD LACHMAN
EDITING SARAH FLACK MUSIC CLIFF MARTINEZ
PRODUCTION JOHN HARDY, SCOTT KRAMER for
ARTISAN ENTERTAINMENT
STARRING TERENCE STAMP (Wilson), LESLEY ANN
WARREN (Elaine), LUIS GUZMÁN (Ed),
BARRY NEWMAN (Avery), JOE DALLESANDRO
(Uncle John), NICKY KATT (Stacy), PETER FONDA
(Terry Valentine), AMELIA HEINLE (Adhara),
MELISSA GEORGE (Jennifer),
MATTHEW KIMBROUGH (Tom)

"Do you understand half the shit he says?"
"No, but I know what he means."

The English are not fond of talking. Americans, on the other hand, most definitely are. In his film *The Limey*, American cinema prodigy Steven Soderbergh concentrates on showing rather than saying. A newspaper clipping with the information that a woman has been killed on the Mulholland Highway, a photograph of the young woman, a man sitting pensively in an airplane: images take the place of words in setting up the story. The name of the man in the airplane is Wilson (Terence Stamp), and he is investigating the mysterious circumstances surrounding the car accident in which his daughter Jenny died. As in the best examples of film noir, Wilson has already reached a kind of ending as the story begins. The aeroplane scene takes place after the mystery has been solved and Wilson has finished his savage vendetta against his

daughter's killers. He is on his way home, returning to his private life in England. He didn't kill media promoter Terry Valentine (Peter Fonda) who had been having an affair with his daughter. Instead, he forced him to talk, and, in a strange sense, saw his own mirror image. Jenny, he learned, was killed accidentally in a fistfight. She loved Valentine and she was trying to stop him committing more crimes by betraying him to the police. When she was a child, she had once threatened to do the same to her criminal father. Now, all Wilson has left are his memories. Silent, blue-toned images of his daughter playing on the beach are shown again and again. A flash of light dances over her features. There is poetry in this repose, a stillness that contrasts with the other hectic and agitated images of the film. Wilson starts to be extremely

1   With stony features and iron determination Wilson (Terence Stamp) tracks down his daughter's murderers.

2   Organized crime lives high above the roofs of the metropolis: Peter Fonda plays music producer Terry Valentine.

3   Beauty, elegance, and crime make an unholy trinity.

"Soderbergh's style evokes the memory of John Boorman's *Point Blank*, which in its time was misunderstood because of its similarly complex narrative style and which also dealt with revenge taken by a determined loner." *epd Film*

depressed in the face of his failure and his loss. In casting Terence Stamp, Soderbergh made a first-class choice. The British actor's stony-faced style seems the perfect medium for expressing both the brutal and the tragic sides of Wilson's character. The director plays with this interaction between emotion and cold detachment: in one scene, Wilson enters a warehouse, and a handheld camera follows him in. His questions are followed by a fistfight, and Wilson is brutally beaten and thrown out. He picks himself up and goes back in, but this time the camera stays outside. Shots are fired. The camera films calmly from a safe distance. There are flashes of light and screams, and one man escapes from the warehouse and runs past the camera. Wilson

returns. Agitated, the camera picks up and closes in on him. He calls: "Tell him, I'm coming." Soderbergh's sequencing of shots disrupts the chronology of events and their chain of causality. The spectators only discover the plot connections bit by bit, as they gradually piece together the story. Often they have to rely on assumptions. This process of mystification is intensified by the separation of action and sound: a figure is shown, we hear him talking, but his lips are not moving. Image and tone are not synchronized again until the next shot. In addition, Soderbergh integrates images from a totally different film. Scenes from Ken Loach's debut movie *Poor Cow* (1967) – also starring Terence Stamp – are incorporated as flashbacks into Wilson's happier past.

In fact *The Limey* is also a homage. Parts of it look exactly like Jean-Luc Godard's first film *Breathless* (*À bout de souffle*, 1960), thanks to the handheld cameras, the jump cuts, and the seemingly improvised gangster story. But Wilson is quite different to Michel Poiccard, the small-time crook played by Jean-Paul Belmondo in the Godard film. Wilson is a professional, an expert criminal who is taking care of business, and nothing can stand in his way. Terry Valentine in his white suit and Wilson in black are like two sides of the same coin, each the embodying a different lifestyle, one American and the other English. And yet they have much more in common than they would care to admit. For that reason, although Terry has Wilson's daughter quite literally on his conscience, Wilson lets him live.   BR

STEVEN SODERBERGH Steven Soderbergh was born on January 14, 1963, in Atlanta, Georgia, and grew up in Baton Rouge, Louisiana, where he started shooting movies on Super 8 at the ripe old age of 13. Four years later, he was working as an editor for an NBC TV show. He gained film experience by directing short films, commercials, and music videos. A documentary film about the band Yes called *Yes: 9212 Live* came out in 1986. He then filmed his feature film *Sex, Lies and Videotape* (1989) in Baton Rouge in the summer of 1988. In addition to winning a Golden Palm at Cannes, the film earned him an Oscar nomination for the Best Original Screenplay.
Subsequent films, such as *Kafka* (1991), *King of the Hill* (1993), and *The Underneath* (1995), seemed to indicate that Soderbergh might not live up to the expectations held of him. But then the film adaptation of Elmore Leonard's best-selling crime novel *Out of Sight* (1998) with George Clooney and Jennifer Lopez catapulted him into the upper echelon of Hollywood directors. His next two films, *Erin Brockovich* (2000) and *Traffic* (2000), were both nominated for Academy Awards for Best Picture and earned him a double Oscar nomination for Best Director in 2001. That year, Soderbergh did indeed take home the golden statue, which he won for his direction of *Traffic*. Since then he has systematically used the commercial success of star-studded mainstream movies like *Ocean's Eleven* (2001), and its two sequels to fund more ambitious projects like the sci-fi remake *Solaris* (2002), and the call-girl story *The Girlfriend Experience* (2009) with porn star Sasha Grey. *Behind the Candelabra*, a film about flamboyant pianist Liberace, was released in 2013, which Soderbergh himself stated is his last film for the time being.

4   The smart ruler of the underworld.

5   Gangsters together: the showdown leads to self-knowledge.

MEMENTO

2000 – USA – 113 MIN.
DIRECTOR CHRISTOPHER NOLAN (*1970)
SCREENPLAY CHRISTOPHER NOLAN, based on the short story
Memento Mori by JONATHAN NOLAN
DIRECTOR OF PHOTOGRAPHY WALLY PFISTER
EDITING DODY DORN MUSIC DAVID JULYAN
PRODUCTION SUZANNE TODD, JENNIFER
TODD, CHRIS J. BALL for NEWMARKET,
SUMMIT ENTERTAINMENT
STARRING GUY PEARCE (Leonard Shelby),
CARRIE-ANNE MOSS (Natalie),
JOE PANTOLIANO (Teddy Gammell),
MARK BOONE JUNIOR (Burt),
STEPHEN TOBOLOWSKY (Sammy Jankis),
HARRIET SANSOM HARRIS (Mrs. Jankis),
CALLUM KEITH RENNIE (Dodd), LARRY HOLDEN
(Jimmy G), JORJA FOX (Leonard's Wife)

"Where was I?"

To begin in the middle – as good a place as any – we find Leonard (Guy Pearce) running at breakneck speed through a parking lot while a shadowy man runs parallel, dodging abreast on the far side of a row of vehicles. "Okay, so what am I doing?" Leonard asks himself. "I'm chasing this guy." Suddenly the shadowy man veers and fires a shot at Leonard, who corrects himself: "No. He's chasing me."

Memento was justly hailed as an instant classic on its first release, because writer/director Christopher Nolan takes all the familiar elements of film noir but freely applies them to a conflict and an outcome that feel altogether new. Leonard is – like all classical noir heroes – a levelheaded Everyman in exceptional jeopardy. Three minutes into the story he is established with a gun in his hand, a body on the floor, and a lost woman he is being true

to. The fresh twist is that beyond this basic information, he knows as little about his immediate situation as we do.

"I know who I am," he explains – for what may be the first or thousandth time – to the nearest willing listener. "I know all about myself. I just can't make new memories." Leonard suffers from memory blindness. Every hour or so his brain hits a restart button and he must orient himself afresh, owing to a blow on the head he received once upon a time when failing to rescue his late wife from the rapist who killed her. He can remember everything about her and his life prior to this atrocity. Otherwise he's at the mercy of whomever is standing in front of him, be it the motel clerk (Mark Boone Junior) who accepts double payments and even books him extra rooms because Leonard can't remember paying the first time around, or the beau-

tiful, enigmatic bartender Natalie (Carrie-Anne Moss) who needs him to do something for her, or perhaps un-do something. Every relationship is tricky – or is it?

This is the question that drives the story's suspense. Leonard is determined to find and kill his wife's attacker. The liveliest, meanest, and most puzzling of the guides and tormentors he works with is Teddy (Joe Pantoliano), a fast-talking know-it-all whom Leonard puts to death in the opening sequence. Why? The next sequence partly explains by jumping us back in time, one hour. We are with Leonard as he matches up new clues he has received with the data in his carefully maintained bundle of files, Polaroid snapshots, and – most fascinatingly – the tattoos covering his torso. Together these offer new but conclusive proof that Teddy was behind his wife's rape and murder. The scene ends as Teddy shows up for their meeting, unaware of what Leonard has discovered. Next we jump back yet another hour, to a meeting with Natalie in

which she hands Leonard the conclusive proof that Teddy is the killer he seeks. And so on, in perpetual backwards motion, so that we put together the puzzle pieces of this complex mystery in ways the characters never can, Leonard especially. We also move through a series of memories that unfold in black and white from his life prior to the injury – reliving a set of cold-blooded choices Leonard made when he was a hot-shot insurance adjuster, fighting the claim of a memory-blind man he regarded skeptically and inadvertently destroyed. That self-inflicted wound to his conscience adds an extra layer of tragic awareness to his current plight. "Poetic justice," he admits.

What makes *Memento* so exceptional – a thematic as well as dramatic thriller – is that it not only appeals to but also trusts our intelligence. We're invited to play an intricate game, yet Nolan deals the cards fairly. We're given unreliable information but never false information. The talents of editor Dody Dorn, cameraman Wally Pfister, composer David Julyan, and production

1   Leonard (Guy Pearce) is armed with information in the form of snapshots and tattoos in his never-ending battle with his memory blindness.

2   Leonard in his bleak shadow world: the superb production design by Patti Podesta creates intense atmospheric effects out of a variety of distressed urban environments.

3   Notes to self: Leonard leaves permanent reminders on his own skin of the few things he knows about his wife's killer, and how to proceed.

CHRISTOPHER NOLAN / PLAYING WITH TIME   "I spent months banging my head against a wall," Christopher Nolan recalled, "trying to come up with a notion of just how do you give an audience the experience of not being able to remember things?"

Nolan, who grew up commuting between Britain and the United States, was a video cameraman in London when, for $6,000, he wrote and directed his first feature, *Following* (1998), a debut acclaimed for the intelligence of its nonlinear structure. This approach amplified not long thereafter when he asked his brother Jonathan – a fiction writer – for the rights to *Memento Mori*, a short story he'd written about memory blindness. Nolan was particularly delighted by the idea of a man recording his memories in a series of tattoos – but the greatest challenge was the question of how to structure the piece, how to convey memory loss on film, in the first person.

"One day I was struck by a notion. What if you withhold from the audience the information that is withheld from the protagonist? Structure it backward." An executive who read an early draft of the script joked that it was like reading stereo instructions, but Nolan persisted. "There is no way to know the truth in life," he once told the *New York Times*, "but we look to films to give us the satisfaction of a controlled world with an objective truth. With *Memento* I wanted to go outside that predictably linear process to make something a bit more elastic, a bit more real."

4   Of the many ghoulish hangers-on that Leonard is
    forced to deal with, Teddy (Joe Pantoliano, here at
    gunpoint) is the most aggressive, and mysterious.

5   "She has lost someone," Leonard writes of Natalie
    (Carrie-Anne Moss): "She will help you out of pity."

6   "I can't remember to forget you," Leonard
    murmurs of his murdered wife (Jorja Fox). She
    forms the beating heart of the few memories
    he possesses.

"*Memento* is like an existential crossword puzzle, or a pungent '50s B thriller with a script by Jorge Luis Borges."

The New York Times

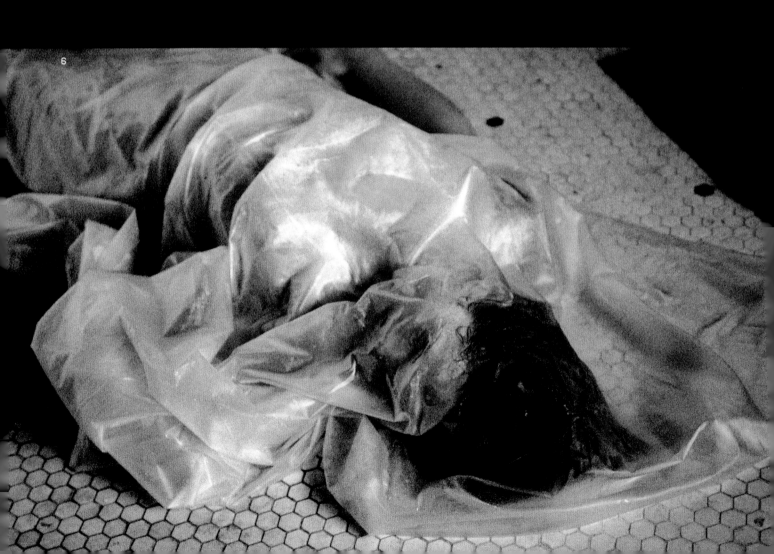

7　"I've seen the movie five times," actress Carrie-Anne Moss said, "and each time I feel differently about what it's about."

8　Is Natalie Leonard's ally, or is she manipulating him too? The question outlives the movie, and is one of its abiding pleasures.

"I wasn't that familiar with Guy's work, or at least, I didn't realize that I was. I hadn't really put together the Guy of *Priscilla, Queen of the Desert*, with the Guy of *L.A. Confidential.*" *Christopher Nolan*

designer Patti Podesta merge in such elegant rhymed cues and artful repeats of staging that we're never lost. There is a steady current of underlying logic by which the hero and we can navigate.

What is Natalie's relation to Teddy? Is her information real, or is she manipulating Leonard to do her bidding, as it appears Teddy has been doing to Leonard for some time now, perhaps years? Pantoliano, Moss, and Pearce strengthen these questions in triplicate with each succeeding scene – or should we call them receding scenes?

"I have to believe in a world outside my own mind," Leonard tells himself. His words express the moral core that persistently operates under all of Nolan's best work. "I have to believe my actions still have meaning, even if I can't remember them."　FXF

"Turn the right corner in Sin City and you can find anything."

Sin City is a wicked place, marked by violence, crime, corruption, and prostitution. It is a product of Frank Miller's fertile imagination. The influential artist created 13 stories between 1991 and 2000 about life in the dark alleys of Sin City, in stories that more or less interweave. Inspired by film noir, his drawing style relies on strong black-and-white contrasts and dispenses almost totally with color. Robert Rodriguez managed to transpose this striking signature style to celluloid in an empathetic way. According to him, it was not so easy to get Miller to join the project; the artist was not convinced it would be possible to convey the visual qualities of his comics to the filmic medium. But a test screening featuring the opening scene of *Sin City* persuaded him, and he came on board as co-director. The result is a visually stunning movie that really does look like a comic that's been brought to life. *Sin City* tells three of the thirteen stories from Miller's books: "The Hard Goodbye"; "The Big Fat Kill"; and "That Yellow Bastard." We see hulk-like Marv (Mickey Rourke) embarking on a bloody personal campaign to avenge the murder of Goldie (Jaime King), the woman he loved. In the process, he comes up against serial killer Kevin (Elijah Wood), who murders silently and with feline speed; and, in spite of Marv's immeasurable physical strength, it is only with great difficulty that he overcomes Kevin. We see Dwight (Clive Owen), a killer with his heart in the right place, going into battle for the prostitutes of Old Town. This is the only way that

2

1 Sin City in the background – with nasty surprises lurking everywhere. But Becky (Alexis Bledel) is not as naïve and alone as she first appears.

2 The movie opens with a seductive woman (Marley Shelton) and a view over the city. What is she running from? We never find out.

3 Dwight (Clive Owen) is around when there's trouble. He especially takes care of dirty work, without batting an eyelid.

4 The Roarks' run-down farm – angel of death Kevin (Elijah Wood) reads the Bible while Hartigan tries to free Nancy.

5 Partner Bob (Michael Madsen) behind him: aging cop Hartigan (Bruce Willis) suspects they are playing with marked cards.

"Other comic adaptations should really cease to exist after this movie, for *Sin City* gives a whole new meaning to the term 'comic adaptation.'"

filmszene.de

a long, bloody feud can be averted. For the truce between prostitutes, police, and mafia is under threat, after notorious police officer Jackie Boy (Benicio del Toro) is tricked and killed in the city's autonomous red-light district. The third story line is a tale in two parts. Bruce Willis plays aging cop Hartigan, who manages to save young Nancy (Makenzie Vega) from the clutches of a child molester who turns out to be the Senator's son, Roark Jr. (Nick Stahl). Although Hartigan shoots him down, he survives badly wounded, and Hartigan ends up in the joint instead. The second part of the story takes place eight years later. Hartigan has been released from jail. Nancy Callahan is now a grown woman (Jessica Alba). A love story begins to unfold, but his old adversary Roark Jr. is lying in wait. The lifesaving medical treatment has mutated him into a foul

yellow monster intent on revenge. But Hartigan manages to save Nancy a second time and on this occasion he kills Roark Jr.

What is striking is that all three stories feature male heroes who have to fight, not only against their adversaries, but also their own shortcomings. Marv is violent and erratic: he is on medication to keep his fantasies under control. Pugnacious Dwight may act cool, but he starts to hallucinate in stressful situations: dead Jackie Boy talks to him when he is trying to dispose of the corpse. Hartigan, on the other hand, has an age-related heart condition and is fighting as much against his own body as against crime. Miller uses a simple narrative device: during long sequences, we hear what the protagonists are thinking as voice-overs. So we see the world through their eyes

6   Nancy Callahan (Jessica Alba) has grown up.
    She turns male heads in Sin City with her skimpy
    cowgirl costume, but her heart belongs to
    one man.

7   Little Miho (Devon Aoki) is deadly – the Old Town
    prostitutes go to war and samurai warrior Miho is
    their most lethal weapon.

8   Marv (Mickey Rourke) seeks revenge for the
    woman he loves, Goldie (Jaime King). The sheer
    strength of his massive body shrugs off serious
    wounds as if they were scratches.

> ## "*Sin City* is a dessert from hell, an intense reduction of certain urban pop culture traditions into a creme brulee of brilliant artificiality." *The Washington Post*

while simultaneously being privy to their emotional instability, which opens the door to the larger-than-life world of sex and crime.

The film was made almost entirely in front of a "green screen" – a process that allows the backgrounds to be keyed in at post-production stage. This was the only way to capture the look of the comic-based storyboards. Countless scenes were taken directly from Miller's books. Like the drawings, the film keeps mainly to monochrome, though Rodriguez further increases the iconic effect of the comics through the specific use of color to emphasize important features of characters and objects. Red blood, blond hair, blue eyes and yellow skin become concentrated symbols of toughness, eroticism, and violence. We look into a world where there are no values, only archetypal qualities – quite simply, a comic in moving images.   JDM

9   Roark Jr. (Nick Stahl) has mutated into a foul
     yellow monster. Now he wants to avenge himself
     on Nancy and Hartigan.

10   Marv is framed for Goldie's murder but just
     manages to elude the police. His parole officer,
     Lucille (Carla Gugino), treats his wounds. They

help each other, but do not become romantically
involved. She is a lesbian and Marv only has
thoughts for his lover.

FRANK MILLER Frank Miller became famous in the 1970s and 1980s for finding new ways of telling comic stories. Born in 1957, the graphic artist was influenced by film noir. His stories of murky heroes are told in high-contrast black-and-white images. While he gave a new look to the icons of the big comic publishers like Marvel or DC, as in the case of Batman, he created a universe of its own with the "Sin City" stories. The film industry soon paid attention to his characters as well. He also made a name for himself as a screenwriter for *RoboCop 2* (1990) and *RoboCop 3* (1993).

Though his stories were used for a whole series of movies, for a long time Miller was reluctant to agree to a film version of *Sin City*. It only happened in 2005, when Robert Rodriguez persuaded him that it could be done and involved him as co-director. This in turn led to Miller trying his own hand at directing in *The Spirit* (2008), working with similar effects to those previously used in *Sin City*. Zack Snyder's surprise hit movie *300* (2006) was also based on one of Frank Miller's comic books.

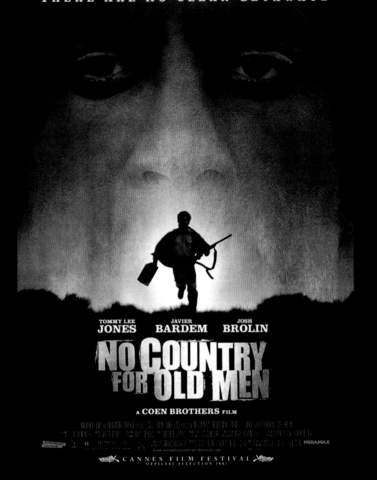

THERE ARE NO CLEAN GETAWAYS

NO COUNTRY FOR OLD MEN ♟♟♟♟

2007 – USA – 122 MIN.
DIRECTORS ETHAN COEN (*1957), JOEL COEN (*1954)
SCREENPLAY JOEL and ETHAN COEN, from the novel of the
same name by CORMAC MCCARTHY
DIRECTOR OF PHOTOGRAPHY ROGER DEAKINS
EDITING RODERICK JAYNES [= JOEL and ETHAN COEN]
MUSIC CARTER BURWELL **PRODUCTION** JOEL and ETHAN COEN,
SCOTT RUDIN for PARAMOUNT VANTAGE,
MIRAMAX FILMS, SCOTT RUDIN PRODUCTIONS,
MIKE ZOSS PRODUCTIONS
STARRING TOMMY LEE JONES (Sheriff Ed Tom Bell),
JAVIER BARDEM (Anton Chigurh), JOSH BROLIN
(Llewelyn Moss), WOODY HARRELSON (Carson Wells),
KELLY MACDONALD (Carla Jean Moss),
GARRET DILLAHUNT (Deputy Wendell), RODGER BOYCE
(Sheriff Roscoe Giddens), TESS HARPER (Loretta Bell),
BARRY CORBIN (Ellis), BETH GRANT (Carla Jean's Mother)
ACADEMY AWARDS 2007 OSCARS for BEST PICTURE
(Joel and Ethan Coen, Scott Rudin), BEST DIRECTOR
(Joel and Ethan Coen), BEST ADAPTED SCREENPLAY
(Joel and Ethan Coen), and BEST ACTOR
IN A SUPPORTING ROLE (Javier Bardem)

"Do you have any idea how crazy you are?"

In the gruesome world of *No Country for Old Men*, anyone leaving a trace is lost. Close to the Mexican border, Vietnam veteran Llewelyn Moss (Josh Brolin) shoots an antelope and its bloody tracks lead him to the scene of a drug deal gone wrong. He takes a bag of money, which contains a tracking device. At the same time, contract serial killer Chigurh (Javier Bardem) strangles a policeman, leaving marks of the brutal fight on the police station floor that are reminiscent of an avant-garde painting. It is not just the camera that registers these violations of normalcy with a clinical eye: Sheriff Ed Tom Bell (Tommy Lee Jones) follows the tracks of both fugitives, mainly to protect the harmless Moss from madman Chigurh, who is now pursuing the fortunate

finder on the desert highways of Texas. Moss demonstrates both ingenuity and caution in stashing the money in the air vent of a motel room; but there, too, scratches are left on the sheet metal behind the grille. And Chigurh's receiver is emitting increasingly frantic signals.

The icy killer with the peculiar name and the most ridiculous haircut in cinema history never leaves any traces. Chigurh comes from nowhere, and will disappear back there. Even in the wacky world of director brothers Joel and Ethan Coen, he is a weird creation: a devil / angel of destiny who kills using a gas canister gun, after allowing his victims to toss a coin – and when he does spare someone's life, it is somehow even creepier. With

Javier Bardem's sardonic poker face, tight-fitting clothes, and striking coiffure, the *New York Times* dubbed him a "Beatle from Hell." The Coens ventured into their first literary adaptation with *No Country for Old Men*. They won an Oscar for this process, as well as for Best Direction and Best Film. Cormac McCarthy's novel, which they adapted virtually word for word, allowed them to revisit their dark movies like *Blood Simple* (1984) and *Miller's Crossing* (1990). McCarthy turns the desert into a primordial site of violence, weaving a new myth of killing and dying into American legend. Here, all human emotion is punished, while every hope of security turns to sand. It is a new world, which gives Sheriff Bell nightmares. The Coens set the stage for this anxious state in majestic fashion, with menacingly quiet shots of the landscape. Before, they tended to make their mark with com-

1 Chigurh, the most enigmatic killer in film history, hasn't finished yet. Javier Bardem won an Oscar for his performance.

2 Sheriff Ed Tom Bell (Tommy Lee Jones) doesn't understand the world any more. This is no country for old men – if it ever was.

3 Clues in the sand: the aftermath of a drug deal gone wrong sets Bell on the right track. But he always gets there too late.

4 Beatle from Hell: with his ridiculous haircut and an even more absurd weapon, Chigurh turns the desert into a battlefield.

"The Coens are back with a vengeance, showing their various imitators and detractors what great American film-making looks like." *The Guardian*

5

6

5 The loot doesn't bring Llewelyn Moss (Josh Brolin) any luck. After a shoot-out in the hotel, he flees over the Mexican border.

6 Looking the devil in the eye: Llewelyn's wife, Carla Jean (Kelly Macdonald), is one of the few people to see Chigurh's face.

7 Myth of eternal life and death: the western desert becomes the poisoned, primordial seedbed of violence in the Coens' tale.

"*No Country for Old Men* is purgatory for the squeamish and the easily spooked. For formalists – those moviegoers sent into raptures by tight editing, nimble camera work and faultless sound design – it's pure heaven." *The New York Times*

JOEL AND ETHAN COEN Brothers Joel and Ethan Coen are famous for their unmistakably eccentric style, wild plays on genre and unconventional division of labor; they do everything together, or so they say. Just for form's sake Joel, born in 1954, appears as director, while Ethan, who is three years his junior, is credited as producer. They use a pseudonym when it comes to editing, for legal reasons. The brothers from Minneapolis grew up far enough away from Hollywood to be free of conventions: most of their movies, to some degree, contain elements of film noir and kooky comedy, with a postmodern, eclectic compositional style that always surprises.

While Joel gravitated to the film industry from the start, Ethan began by studying philosophy and went on to publish short stories. Even their first movie, however, the neo-noir *Blood Simple* (1984), was the result of a screenplay they wrote together. After the crazy fantasy comedy *Raising Arizona* (1987) and cynical gangster movie *Miller's Crossing* (1990), their breakthrough came with *Barton Fink* (1991): the surreal story with overtones of Kafka and Polanski about a screenwriter with writer's block won three top awards at the Cannes Film Festival. From the outset, they were artistically independent, their creative energies flourishing in the comedies that followed. The snow-set film *Fargo* (1996) was populated with blundering killers and inept insurance fraudsters, while in the splendid '70s detective story *The Big Lebowski* (1998) – with Jeff Bridges in the classic hippie role "The Dude" – mischief-making German nihilists complicate the action further. What was striking in these highly artificial films was also the meticulous eye for regional and temporal peculiarities: the assumption that the only reality the Coens know is their films is refuted at least on occasion by their elaborately crafted characters. Then again, the mythical American odyssey *O Brother, Where Art Thou?* (2000) consisted almost exclusively of films from the Depression and the comedies of Preston Sturges. The noir homage shot in black and white, *The Man Who Wasn't There* (2001), revealed a minimalist side to their visual flamboyance. It was followed initially by an artistic low; only the Coens themselves are in a position to overplay their own excessive style. They only recovered their previous form by adapting other writers' material, albeit at the expense of originality: they swiftly won four Oscars for their literary adaptation *No Country for Old Men* (2007), a crime thriller set in the Texan desert. Their remake of the Western *True Grit* (2010) received ten nominations, but they came away empty-handed. The allusion-rich musical comedy *Inside Llewyn Davis*, screened at Cannes in 2013 and awarded the Grand Prix by the jury, shows in best Coen brothers style the breakdown of fictitious folksinger Llewyn Davis in the early '60s.

edies; there, too, the narrative they created of America primarily as myth is indicative of their supreme confidence.

The Oscars came far too late for fans of these visionary jesters. Maybe it was the joke that worked: the one about the Coens making a serious film just for a laugh, and it made it big! Even that venerable institution, the Academy of Motion Picture Arts and Science, must have noticed the underlying humor. Like all the other Coen movies, its almost obsessive craftsmanship and precision are compulsive. As is often the case, the focus is on physical activities: unscrewing the air vent, loading a gun, or sweeping a crime scene for the tiniest traces. Yet what happened quickly and was filmed in slapstick style in films like *Fargo* (1996) is now tantalizingly slow

and heavily laden with meaning – only those new to the Coens, and who are likely to stay that way, will fail to notice the irony in all this.

The fear factor lies precisely in the blend of comic and serious elements. In Chigurh's hands, life becomes a joke. He is the shadow in the back of a car, the assassin creeping around in his socks, his feet appearing at a crack in a door. Like death itself, no one can escape him. With *No Country for Old Men*, the Coens have also established a metaphysical superstructure for the rest of their work that infuses their surreal observations about life with existential depth, with the exception perhaps of *Burn After Reading* (2008), their next and by far their wackiest movie. Traces soon disappear.   PB

WELCOME TO A WORLD WITHOUT RULES.

CHRISTIAN MICHAEL HEATH CARY AARON MAGGIE and MORGAN
BALE CAINE LEDGER OLDMAN ECKHART GYLLENHAAL FREEMAN

THE DARK KNIGHT

JULY 18

THE DARK KNIGHT 🏆🏆

2008 – USA / UK – 152 MIN.
DIRECTOR CHRISTOPHER NOLAN (*1970)
SCREENPLAY JONATHAN NOLAN, CHRISTOPHER NOLAN,
from a story by CHRISTOPHER NOLAN and
DAVID S. GOYER, based on characters by BOB KANE
DIRECTOR OF PHOTOGRAPHY WALLY PFISTER **EDITING** LEE SMITH
MUSIC JAMES NEWTON HOWARD, HANS ZIMMER
PRODUCTION CHRISTOPHER NOLAN, CHARLES ROVEN,
EMMA THOMAS, LORNE ORLEANS for LEGENDARY
PICTURES, DC COMICS, SYNCOPY, WARNER BROS.
STARRING CHRISTIAN BALE (Bruce Wayne / Batman),
HEATH LEDGER (The Joker), AARON ECKHART
(Harvey Dent /Two-Face), MICHAEL CAINE
(Alfred Pennyworth), MAGGIE GYLLENHAAL
(Rachel Dawes), GARY OLDMAN
(Jim Gordon), MORGAN FREEMAN (Lucius Fox),
MONIQUE GABRIELA CURNEN (Detective Anna Ramirez),
ERIC ROBERTS (Salvatore „Sal" Maroni), CHIN HAN
(Yinglain Lau), CILLIAN MURPHY (The Scarecrow)
ACADEMY AWARDS 2008 OSCARS for BEST SUPPORTING ACTOR
(Heath Ledger, posthumous award), and BEST SOUND
EDITING (Richard King)

"Why so serious?"

Batman – or "the bat man" as his opponent the Joker disparagingly refers to him – is one of the most enduring of comic superheroes. Like the citizens of Gotham City, each generation of cinemagoers has been given their own Batman. The darkest, most pessimistic, and morally complex Batman movie of all time was, however, the most welcome. After months of anticipation, the release of *The Dark Knight* broke all box office records. It took over a billion dollars worldwide, making Christopher Nolan's most sinister action spectacle one of the most successful movies in cinema history.

Bruce Wayne (Christian Bale), the playboy billionaire behind the dark knight's mask, is also a superhero – although one without superpowers. This noble character for a post-heroic age is, to put it simply, very rich and highly traumatized. In fact, Nolan's *Batman Begins* (2005) had already covered pre-

cisely the same psychological background in impressive style, but in *The Dark Knight* – the sequel to the restart of the series, following several flops – the perspective is instead turned toward the outside world. The avenger, armed with some heavy-duty technology, is no longer fighting his own demons but a society gone crazy. The old standards of good and evil appear null and void. Thus Batman himself is suddenly less a part of the solution and more of the problem.

This new situation is down to the demonic actions of the Joker (Heath Ledger). After a series of brutal bank robberies, he terrorizes Gotham City with death threats communicated via video. With the local mob involved, he demands that Batman be handed over; if not, each day that goes by will see some people being murdered. Fundamentally for the Joker, however, it is nei-

Heath Ledger is not a straightforward bad guy. He is a monster, Mephisto and punk, Marlon Brando and Sid Vicious, an animal and force of nature, everyone's worst nightmare. If Jack Nicholson's Joker in the 1989 Batman movie was an artist of death, then Heath Ledger is the God of Chaos."

Der Tagesspiegel

ther about money nor his attempts to kill the man fighting for justice and order. The anarchic clown with the smile slashed into his face is having too much fun with his opponent. He enjoys watching the powerless reactions of Batman and responds to them with ever more innovative and horrific mind-games. As well as police lieutenant Jim Gordon (Gary Oldman), Batman has allied himself with district attorney Harvey Dent (Aaron Eckhart), whose desire for a new sense of justice is not hidden behind a mask. The dilemma is who to save first: Dent, wired with dynamite, or his fiancée Rachel (Maggie Gyllenhaal), Bruce Wayne's former love. Batman falls right into the Joker's trap. Rachel dies, and a horribly disfigured Dent turns into the crazed vigilante "Two-Face." As Wayne's butler (Michael Caine) tries to explain: "Some men just want to watch the world burn." More importantly, however, the Joker wants to be the one holding the match.

Heath Ledger immortalized himself in this role shortly before his tragic death. The feverish expectation of the public was informed by the shock of his loss, but his masterly acting performance will endure for much longer. His Joker – seedy, teeth-licking, and sardonically slurping – harks back to punk culture, but more than anything it is his own, one-off creation. His enjoyment of everything immoral, including other people's suffering, exudes literally from every pore and has an infectious effect on the viewer as well, who no doubt secretly applauds his perversely lethal pencil trick. Posh Batman is bound to look stale by comparison.

Otherwise, *The Dark Knight* has little in common with a classic comic book adaptation. In times of uncertainty, when great subjects were viewed with suspicion, superhero movies were the life assurance of the big studios. *X-Men* (2000), *Spider-Man* (2002), *Hulk* (2003), *Fantastic Four* (2005) and

1 Christian Bale slips on the Batman gear for the second time. He also has the wheels to match his status, with his new Batpod.

2 Action fans are indulged too, thanks to a successful blend of special effects and real stunts.

3

4

3 Heath Ledger excels in his disturbing portrayal of clown, devil, and punk combined. He was awarded a posthumous Oscar for his performance, the best in his short career.

4 Terrorizing Gotham City: the Joker is the fantasy element in a largely realistic setting.

5 A cold world of steel and glass: IMAX technology is also used to good effect in filming Batman's struggle against evil.

6 Dictated by the series: Rachel Dawes (Maggie Gyllenhaal) still doesn't suspect the secret identity of playboy millionaire Bruce Wayne (Christian Bale).

7 Batman's world lies in ruins – the reference to 9/11 is obvious.

8 The delightful grimace of violence: Heath Ledger epitomizes the anarchic spirit of the Joker in every scene.

"Ledger seems to make the film grow larger whenever he's onscreen."

The Village Voice

CHRISTIAN BALE Much to the surprise of many, the independent actor whose performances were always somewhat morose has turned into an all-action hero. Christian Bale was not particularly renowned for his physique until his first, well publicized method acting stunt when he lost over 66 lb. / 30 kg for *The Machinist* (2003). Bale plays men on the edge of a nervous breakdown, his trademark being his painstaking control of every muscle in his body. Only on one occasion did he use this obsession with control to humorous effect, in what, of all things, was his best known role for a time: the perverse murderer of women in Mary Harron's film adaptation *American Psycho* (1999). Born in Wales in 1974, the actor comes from an artistic family, whose travels took him as a child to places like Portugal and the United States. At the age of 13, he had his first lead role, in Steven Spielberg's *Empire of the Sun* (1987). Minor movies like *Swing Kids* (1993), *Little Women* (1994), and *Velvet Goldmine* (1998) only raised his profile slightly. Since *American Psycho*, however, Bale has been regarded as an outstanding character actor who brings credibility to big-budget productions and star appeal to indie films. For *Batman Begins* (2005), *The Dark Knight* (2008), and *The Dark Knight Rises* (2012) he slipped into the costume of the famous superhero. At the same time, he was committed to ambitious art-house films. In Werner Herzog's *Rescue Dawn* (2006) he played German American navy pilot Dieter Dengler, shot down over Laos in 1965, while in *I'm Not There* (2007) by Todd Haynes he was one of the six Bob Dylans. In 2008, he unfortunately gained another type of fame for an outburst of rage on the set of *Terminator Salvation* (2009) that was widely distributed over the Internet. After his thrilling appearance in Michael Mann's gangster epic *Public Enemies* (2009) Christian Bale – who is very serious about his work – won the Oscar for Best Supporting Actor in the realistic boxing drama *The Fighter* (2010).

9

9   All hopes are now pinned on Harvey Dent (Aaron Eckhart). But an encounter with the Joker turns him into a crazed vigilante.

10   The smile is wiped off the Joker's face. But his stay in police custody is short-lived.

"Dark as night and nearly as long, Christopher Nolan's new Batman movie feels like a beginning and something of an end. Pitched at the divide between art and industry, poetry and entertainment, it goes darker and deeper than any Hollywood movie of its comic-book kind." *The New York Times*

Iron Man (2008) together with their various sequels offered lightweight blockbuster entertainment. Even Tim Burton's excellent *Batman* (1989) was still completely in thrall to the world of comics, with the playful treatment of color and Gothic elements that characterized the series. Its pleasurable frisson is dissipated in Nolan's version by a brighter, more realistic setting. The new Gotham City (shot in Chicago) is a cold world of glass and uninhabited tower block structures; the frozen corpse of failed investors' dreams. This is our world, whose darkness is not a matter of light, but one of moral ambivalence.

Dent and Batman, the white and black knights, are unable to conquer evil using legitimate means. Batman assumes the guilt for the collateral damage caused by his vigilantism, and is outlawed. Yet the serious way in which

their moral dilemma is debated appears somewhat theoretical. *The Dark Knight* is not so much an authentic testimony to the paranoid mood of the "war against terror" as a carefully controlled movie about controversial issues. Fortunately, we have the Joker, who turns the pained attempts at explanation around – including on himself – with the ludicrous question: "Why so serious?"

This comic movie for grown-ups is entirely convincing, mainly because of its wonderful special effects. Six action sequences filmed with IMAX cameras, including a somersaulting heavy goods transporter and powerful explosions, are given scope to develop to their full effect. And Batman has a new motorcycle: the Batpod. This, at least, continues to provide him and his faithful audiences with fun – in trumps.

"AN EXTRAORDINARY. INTOXICATING MASTERPIECE"

ACADEMY AWARD® NOMINEE

NATALIE **PORTMAN** VINCENT **CASSEL** MILA **KUNIS**

BLACK SWAN

FROM THE DIRECTOR OF THE WRESTLER AND REQUIEM FOR A DREAM

BLACK SWAN 🏆

2010 – USA – 108 MIN.
DIRECTOR DARREN ARONOFSKY (*1969)
SCREENPLAY MARK HEYMAN, ANDRES HEINZ,
JOHN J. MCLAUGHLIN
DIRECTOR OF PHOTOGRAPHY MATTHEW LIBATIQUE
EDITING ANDREW WEISBLUM **MUSIC** CLINT MANSELL
PRODUCTION SCOTT FRANKLIN, MIKE MEDAVOY,
ARNOLD MESSER, BRIAN OLIVER,
JOSEPH P. REIDY, JERRY FRUCHTMAN for
20TH CENTURY FOX, PROTOZOA PICTURES,
PHOENIX PICTURES, CROSS CREEK PICTURES
STARRING NATALIE PORTMAN (Nina Sayers),
VINCENT CASSEL (Thomas Leroy), MILA KUNIS (Lily),
BARBARA HERSHEY (Erica Sayers), WINONA RYDER
(Beth MacIntyre), BENJAMIN MILLEPIED (David),
KSENIA SOLO (Veronica), KRISTINA ANAPAU (Galina)
ACADEMY AWARDS 2010 OSCAR for BEST LEADING
ACTRESS (Natalie Portman)

"I just want to be perfect."

It begins with a dream. A ballerina is dancing the White Swan from Tchaikovsky's *Swan Lake* in a beam of bright light – the lifelong wish of Nina Sayers (Natalie Portman), a dancer in the world-famous New York City Ballet. The new production of this classic is to be the highlight of the season. Whoever wants to dance the coveted role must, however, be able to play the Black Swan as well. Star choreographer Thomas (Vincent Cassel) indeed sees innocent Nina as the perfect casting for the White Swan, but he cannot find the dark, seductive side in her that constitutes the essence of the Black Swan. When he tries to kiss Nina, however, and she bites his lip, Thomas knows that she does in fact have this dark side deep inside her. To her own astonishment, she gets the challenging dual role. Yet the price she has to pay for it is high. The harder and harder she strives to transform herself into the Black Swan, the more she loses grip on reality and ends up being the victim of her own schizophrenia. Her dream did come true, however: "I was perfect." Aronof-

sky's films are about lone individuals, and in *Black Swan* this is presented through the world of ballet. Each ballerina is driven by the enormously competitive pressure to be better than all the rest – simply the best. Surrounded on all sides by mirrors, Nina is constantly confronted with her own image, forcing her to continually examine and control herself, becoming a critic of her own body. This mixture of vanity and self-hatred leads almost inevitably to schizophrenia. We clearly see the consequences in her mother (Barbara Hershey), who was once an ordinary ballet dancer and now has countless self-portraits hanging on her mirror, their harrowing features sad testament to her own failure. Yet even a prima ballerina like Beth MacIntyre (Winona Ryder) cannot cope with the end of her career, resorting to the destructive act of self-mutilation.

As a result, *Black Swan* is anything but a standard ballet movie. Here, it is not about the effortlessly light qualities of dance, but about the extreme

physical and psychological burdens of professional ballet. The film focuses sharply on the fragility of the human body: cracking joints, broken toenails, scratched and bleeding skin. Close-ups of small, everyday injuries (which make them all the more intimate) produce a feeling of deep unease in the viewer. These self-destructive aspects of the pursuit of perfection are translated by Aronofsky into metamorphoses that can only be explained in terms of Nina's warped perception. But instead of a transformation from ugly duckling to beautiful swan, we see a lovely young woman assuming increasingly inhuman features as she almost literally tears herself apart, bends and breaks. These brief, though fiercely intense, sequences are at times torturous for the viewer. In the process, Black Swan comes very close to "body horror" David Cronenberg–style, while also reminding us of Charles Burns's comic-

1   The transformation is complete: Nina (Natalie Portman) has become Odile, the black swan from Tchaikovsky's *Swan Lake*.

2   Vincent Cassel plays top choreographer Thomas Leroy. He alone decides who is to dance the coveted lead role.

3   The methods of the top choreographer Thomas Leroy are immoral and effective in equal measure. He challenges Nina to discover her own sexuality.

"Part tortured-artist drama, *Black Swan* looks like a tony art-house entertainment ... But what gives it a jolt is its giddy, sometimes sleazy exploitation-cinema savvy." *The New York Times*

4   The masterpiece is complete. The premiere of the
    new *Swan Lake* is the high point of the film. In the
    threatening red light of the stage, it will become
    clear whether Nina is up to the demanding
    dual role. She has finally left her pink, girlish
    bedroom behind.

book classic *Black Hole* and its exaggerated depiction of the corporeal experiences of American teenagers.

It is easy to read *Black Swan* as a coming-of-age movie as well.
Although Nina is already on the wrong side of 20, her life at the beginning is
like that of a 12-year-old, mainly because her mother is a control freak. Erica
Sayers wants to protect her daughter from the mistakes she made, keeping
her safe in a pink-tinged world of innocence and youth. Nina's escape from
this naïve, musical-box world is inevitable. She has her rival Lily (Mila Kunis),

of all people, to thank for her sexual awakening; in her uncomplicated zest
for life, Lily is the polar opposite of the driven perfectionist, lightening the
heavy atmosphere of the film to some extent.

Ultimately, however, *Black Swan* is about women who fail. The film
challenges the images of femininity in popular culture and, in so doing,
exposes the problems of not only the obsession with youth to which Beth and
Erica fall victim, but also the conflicting roles demanded of women. The perfect synthesis of Madonna and whore will never work. According to Aronofsky,

5

DARREN ARONOFSKY Darren Aronofsky's career gives his critics and fans headaches similar to those suffered by the protagonists in his films. Born in Brooklyn in 1969, he studied film at Harvard and became an early prodigy with his major thesis movie *Supermarket Sweep* (1991). With *Pi* (1998), an avant-garde black-and-white film about a schizophrenic mathematician crazy about numbers, he became internationally famous. The combination of hallucinatory editing techniques and trance-inducing sounds made him the David Lynch of the impending cyber age. The sequel, *Requiem for a Dream* (2000), still enjoys cult status. This film adaptation of a novel by Hubert Selby Jr. is one of the most visually impressive depictions of drug addiction and the false dreams that make people's lives hell. With unusual camera angles, truly explosive editing, and exhausting time-lapse montage sequences, Aronofsky was once again leading the way. Then, however, time overtook him as well, and ambitious avant-garde work was seen as no more than pretentious art-house cinema. A creative break that was far too lengthy, not to mention artistic turkey *The Fountain* (2006), were to blame. Following the approach of Tarkovsky and Kubrick, the techno-ascetic had embarked on an esoteric search for meaning that only a few wanted to follow. In the meantime, successors with a similar outlook but who were more compatible with mainstream cinema, such as Christopher Nolan, had appeared on the scene: the latter realized one of Aronofsky's dream projects with *Batman Begins* (2005). It was only the independent film *The Wrestler* (2008) – produced with minimal resources – that brought Aronofsky back into the ring. Directed with restraint and with Mickey Rourke brilliantly cast as the has-been ex-champion, this wrestling drama won the Golden Lion in Venice followed by two Oscar nominations, for Rourke and his co-star Marisa Tomei. Aronofsky's comeback seems to be long term: his lavish thriller set in the world of ballet, *Black Swan* (2010), was received with equal enthusiasm two years later at the Venice Film Festival, and won the Oscar for its leading actress, Natalie Portman.

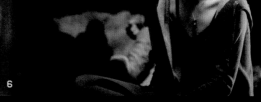

6

7

5 Her rival eliminated, the mirror broken: Nina may have won, but she ends up paying a high price.

6 Erica (Barbara Hershey) sees the opportunity in her daughter that she missed herself.

7 Rival and role model: Lily (Mila Kunis) represents the dark side lacking in Nina, and not just physically.

8 The ballet world is characterized by the ubiquitous mirror mazes, which also serve as a metaphor for Nina's inner turmoil.

Black Swan and its predecessor *The Wrestler* (2008) form a diptych. Both films feature artists who use and exploit their physical beings for others' entertainment; they are about people whose only capital is their own bodies. Losing their mind, however, goes hand in hand with this extreme obsession with physicality. With her role in *Black Swan*, Natalie Portman takes her place in a long line of cinematic doppelgangers, conveyed by one film reference in particular: the movie's ending is very like the fatal conclusion of the silent classic *The Student of Prague* (*Der Student von Prag*, 1913 and 1926; a.k.a. *A Bargain with Satan*, 1913 and *The Man Who Cheated Life*, 1926). Just as the student Balduin is forced to acknowledge that, in shooting at the mirror, he has killed not just his double but himself as well, Nina also realizes that she has inflicted a fatal wound on herself. Her ambition has triumphed, but she has lost her life.

CZ

8

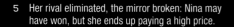

THERE ARE NO CLEAN GETAWAYS

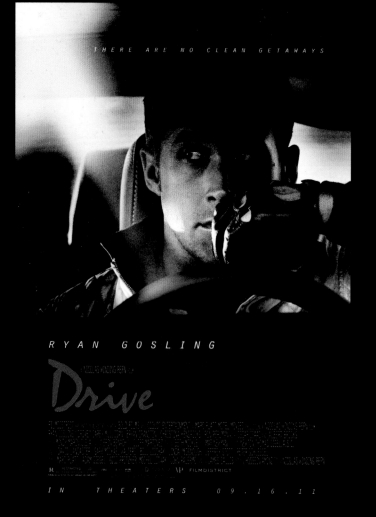

RYAN GOSLING

Drive

IN THEATERS 09.16.11

DRIVE

2011 – USA – 100 MIN.
DIRECTOR NICOLAS WINDING REFN (*1970)
SCREENPLAY HOSSEIN AMINI, based on
the novel *Driver* by JAMES SALLIS
DIRECTOR OF PHOTOGRAPHY NEWTON THOMAS SIGEL
EDITING MATTHEW NEWMAN MUSIC CLIFF MARTINEZ
PRODUCTION MARC PLATT, ADAM SIEGEL,
GIGI PRITZKER, MICHEL LITVAK,
JOHN PALERMO for BOLD FILMS,
ODDLOT ENTERTAINMENT, MARC PLATT
PRODUCTIONS, MOTEL MOVIES
STARRING RYAN GOSLING (Driver),
CAREY MULLIGAN (Irene), BRYAN CRANSTON
(Shannon), CHRISTINA HENDRICKS (Blanche),
RON PERLMAN (Nino), OSCAR ISAAC
(Standard), ALBERT BROOKS (Bernie Rose),
KADEN LEOS (Benicio), JEFF WOLFE
(Tan Suit), JAMES BIBERI (Cook),
RUSS TAMBLYN (Doc)

"This light is not for those men still lost in an old black shadow."

The anonymous Driver (Ryan Gosling) works as a car mechanic and a movie stunt driver by day, while at night he drives a getaway car for thieves. A budding romance between Driver and a neighbor, Irene (Carey Mulligan), is cut short when her husband Standard (Oscar Isaac) gets out of prison. Driver agrees to serve as a wheelman for Standard, who is being forced to rob a pawnshop to pay off some debts, but the heist goes bad and Standard is shot dead. When a hit man then goes after Irene in an elevator, Driver kicks the man's face to a bloody pulp. Taking revenge on the gangster Nino (Ron Perlman), who double-crossed Standard, Driver rams his car into Nino's, pushing it off a cliff, and then drowns the man in the ocean. Driver then attempts to pay off another mobster, Bernie (Albert Brooks). However, Bernie stabs Driver in the chest and Driver knifes Bernie in the throat.

Raymond Chandler once described the detective in a noir tale as a knight out to rescue a damsel in distress. Driver in his satin jacket is like a white knight in a suit of armor, and his car is his steed; he does battle with the dark forces to protect his lady, Irene. Or at least that is the way Driver wants to see himself. Ryan Gosling has described the character he plays as "psychotic": "I think he's somebody who's seen too many movies. He's confusing his life for a film, and he's made himself the hero of his own action film. He's just kind of lost in the mythology of Hollywood." The stunt driver who doubles for the star of an action movie begins to confuse this role with real life, imagining that he is an all-good, all-powerful superhero. Before car "jousting" with the villainous Nino, Driver goes to a movie trailer and dons the latex mask he wears as a stunt driver, as if he were putting on his superhero

1

2

| 1 | "You're doubling for the star": Driver (Ryan Gosling) as stunt driver – and hero of the movie in his head. | 2 | Newton Thomas Sigel: "It was as if the car was an extension of Driver, like he was part man, part machine." | 3 | Driver gaining info on an enemy. Nicolas Winding Refn: "I always set out to make films about women, and I always end up making them about violent men." |

face. (To add to this confusion between film and reality, visible behind Driver are three prosthetic heads of actress Christina Hendricks, who plays a character who gets shot in the head in *Drive*, the very movie we are watching!)

In the elevator scene, Driver shares a dreamy slow-motion kiss with Irene before smashing the hit man's face and crushing his skull, as presented in a series of quick, violent cuts. In Driver's mind, the violence is fully justified to rid the world of this demon threatening his idealized maiden, but Irene looks at him in fear and horror. "He's enacting these movie fantasies on her as though she's some kind of damsel that needs to be rescued. It obviously doesn't go very well," says Gosling. Adds cinematographer Newton Thomas Sigel, "When Irene walks out of the elevator and looks back at Driver,

this wild animal, you realize it's over between them." Driver isn't the only one mistaking a movie role for reality. Although Nino imagines himself to be an Italian gangster, he is actually a Jewish man named Izzy. And Bernie, with his penchant for Chinese food and his knives in an ornate case, seems to think that he's a knife expert in an Asian crime film. When Bernie and Driver meet at a Chinese restaurant at the end, the increasingly shallow focus and tight framing distances them from other diners. The two imagine themselves to be larger-than-life movie characters in a mythic confrontation. Their joint smiles are crosscut with their future stabbing of each other, for having cast themselves in certain roles, they must die the way those characters would die in a movie. Their movie madness, or "psychosis," proves fatal.

NICOLAS WINDING REFN Expelled from an arts academy for throwing a classroom desk against a wall, Nicolas Winding Refn (*1970) has made the violence committed by men a central part of his films. In addition, with a cinematographer for a mother and a film editor as a father, Refn is very conscious of his film heritage and of the influence other directors have had on his work. His Pusher trilogy (1996, 2004, 2005) explores drug addicts and gangsters in a style reminiscent of Martin Scorsese and Quentin Tarantino. *Bronson* (2008) looks at "Britain's most violent criminal" through the lens of Stanley Kubrick's *A Clockwork Orange* (1971), while *Valhalla Rising* (2009) takes a metaphysical approach to Viking violence in a manner influenced by Andrei Tarkovsky. A dyslexic who didn't learn to read until age 13, Refn imbues his films with graphic visuals such as a screwdriver stabbing in *Pusher II*, a disemboweling in *Valhalla Rising*, and the face smashing in *Drive*. (For the latter, Refn sought advice from Gaspar Noé, who had so memorably shown a man's face beaten to a pulp in *Irreversible* [*Irréversible*, 2002].) Because Refn is color blind, his films have very contrasting colors, including a lot of red. But all Refn's films tend to show violent bloodletting as self-defeating, with macho characters destroyed by even more vicious men (the Pusher films) or partly redeemed through a kind of "feminine" self-sacrifice *(Valhalla Rising, Drive)*. *Bronson* is a pivotal film in this regard because its lead character at least tries to find an outlet for his rebellious energies in art – much as Refn attempts to do in film – before falling back into brute aggression. As Refn has said about his own trajectory, "In the beginning, you use art as a destructive medium. It's there to hurt people. But then I went bankrupt and had my first child, and I realized that art was not to hurt but to inspire."

4   Cold Driver yearns for warm Irene (Carey Mulligan). Nicolas Winding Refn: "I'm color blind so I can only see contrast colors, so everything in the film has to have that contrast."

5   Send a shark to kill a shark. Driver: "My hands are a little dirty." Bernie (Albert Brooks): "So are mine."

6   Driver's "code" during the robberies: "I don't sit in while you're running it. I don't carry a gun. I drive."

"I don't have a driver's license, but I've always been fascinated by speed, and I also have a fetish for curves, so I wanted to shoot the cars how I would see them sexually. I'm very much a fetish filmmaker." *Nicolas Winding Refn*

7　Cartoon wisdom: Driver: "There're no good sharks?" Benicio (Kaden Leos): "No. I mean, just look at him. Does he look like a good guy to you?"

8　Like "father," like "son"?: Benicio wears Driver's jacket for protection – but the boy also dons a scary mask like the one Driver uses when killing.

"Driver is essentially a person who doesn't know how to deal with the real world. Once it becomes real, his dogmatic approach to things gets difficult and he makes mistakes by believing that this is the best way to protect. He's a man of violence." *Nicolas Winding Refn*

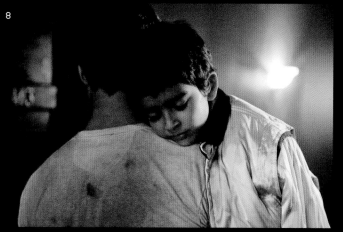

8

But what about the fact that Driver, motionless and unblinking after being stabbed, suddenly seems to come to life and drive away in the end? Some – perhaps Driver himself – may see this as his heavenly reward for having fought so valiantly to save the damsel Irene. But is Driver still benighted in thinking that he's some kind of superhero character on a movie screen, when in fact his vengeful, extreme violence was no different from the villainous Bernie's? In the last shot we see of Driver, his face floats as a reflection in the rear-view mirror, and he is still driving in the dark along a road that is seen through the car's windshield (or windscreen). We recall that Travis Bickle (Robert De Niro), who also justified his own violence as heroic, was similarly still driving and visible in the rear-view mirror at the end of *Taxi Driver* (1976). DK

9   Too soft?: Standard (Oscar Isaac), loving husband and family man, will get gunned down.

10 Too hard?: Driver "doubles" for Standard, trying on the role of husband and father, but becomes a vicious killer.

11 "I don't eat; I don't sleep; I do nothing but think of you": Irene is spellbound by Driver.

"I got connected to [Driver]. When I was a kid and I first saw *First Blood*, it kind of put a spell on me and I thought I was Rambo. I went to school the next day [with] all of my mother's steak knives and I threw them at all the kids at recess." *Ryan Gosling*

INDEX

All those involved in a film's production are mentioned. The production companies are indicated in italics. Numbers in bold refer to a sidebar text.

1000 FILM NOIRS

This is a list of 1000 film noirs and neo-noirs from around the world released between 1920 and 2012

1920
The Cabinet of Dr. Caligari
    Das Cabinet des Dr. Caligari

1927
The Lodger: A Story of the London
    Fog a.k.a. The Lodger
Metropolis
Underworld

1928
The Racket

1929
Blackmail
Thunderbolt

1931
The Big Gamble
City Streets
Isn't Life a Bitch? La Chienne
Little Caesar
M
The Maltese Falcon
The Public Enemy
The Secret Six

1932
The Beast of the City
I Am a Fugitive from a Chain Gang
Payment Deferred
Scarface a.k.a. Scarface, the
    Shame of the Nation
Two Seconds

1934
Crime Without Passion

1935
The Glass Key
A Notorious Gentleman
The Scoundrel

1936
Fury
Sabotage

1937
Pépé le Moko
San Quentin
You Only Live Once

1938
Algiers
La Bête Humaine
Port of Shadows Le Quai des
    brumes
They Drive by Night

1939
Blind Alley
Daybreak Le jour se lève
Invisible Stripes
King of the Underworld
The Last Turn Le Dernier Tournant
Let Us Live
Pièges
Rio
The Roaring Twenties

1940
Angels Over Broadway
City for Conquest
Foreign Correspondent
Girl in 313
The Letter
Michael Shayne: Private Detective
Night Train to Munich
Rebecca
Stranger on the Third Floor
They Drive by Night

1941
Among the Living
Blues in the Night
Citizen Kane
Dressed to Kill

High Sierra
I Wake Up Screaming
Johnny Eager
Ladies in Retirement
The Maltese Falcon
Out of the Fog
Rage in Heaven
The Shanghai Gesture
Suspicion
A Woman's Face

1942
Crossroads
The Glass Key
Kid Glove Killer
Moontide
The Pay Off
Quiet Please, Murder
Saboteur
Street of Chance
This Gun for Hire

1943
Calling Dr. Death
Le Corbeau: The Raven Le Corbeau
The Fallen Sparrow
Journey into Fear
The Leopard Man
Obsession Ossessione
The Seventh Victim
Shadow of a Doubt
Whispering Footsteps

1944
Bluebeard
Christmas Holiday a.k.a.
    W. Somerset Maugham's
    Christmas Holiday
Dark Waters
Destiny
Double Indemnity
Experiment Perilous
Gaslight
Guest in the House

To Have and Have Not a.k.a.
    Ernest Hemingway's To Have
    and Have Not
Laura
The Lodger
The Mark of the Whistler a.k.a.
    The Marked Man (U.K.)
The Mask of Dimitrios
Ministry of Fear
Murder, My Sweet
Phantom Lady
Shadows in the Night
Silent Partner
Strangers in the Night
The Suspect
Voice in the Wind
When Strangers Marry
The Woman in the Window

1945
Bewitched
The Caribbean Mystery
Circumstantial Evidence
Conflict
Cornered
The Crime Doctor's Warning a.k.a.
    Doctor's Warning (U.K.)
Danger Signal
Detour
Dillinger
Escape in the Fog
Fallen Angel
Hangover Square
The Hidden Eye
The House on 92nd Street
Jealousy
Johnny Angel
The Lady Confesses
Lady on a Train
Leave Her to Heaven
The Lost Weekend
Mildred Pierce
My Name Is Julia Ross
Scarlet Street
Sensation Hunters
Spellbound
The Spider
The Spiral Staircase

The Hidden Room (U.S.)
Port of New York
The Reckless Moment
Red Light
Rope of Sand
Scene of the Crime
The Set-Up
Shockproof
The Story of Molly X
Strange Bargain
Take One False Step
Tension
Thieves' Highway
The Third Man
The Threat
Too Late for Tears
Trapped
Under Capricorn
The Undercover Man
Undertow
Whirlpool
White Heat
The Window
Without Honor
The Woman on Pier 13
A Woman's Secret

1950
Armored Car Robbery
The Asphalt Jungle
Backfire
Between Midnight and Dawn
Black Hand
Borderline
Born to Be Bad
The Breaking Point
Caged
The Capture
Convicted
Cry Murder
Customs Agent
The Damned Don't Cry
Dark City
Destination Murder
Dial 1119
D.O.A.
Edge of Doom
The File on Thelma Jordon
Gambling House
Guilty Bystander
Gun Crazy a.k.a Deadly Is the
    Female
Gunman in the Streets
Highway 301
House by the River
Hunt the Man Down
In a Lonely Place

Johnny One-Eye
The Killer That Stalked New York
Kiss Tomorrow Goodbye
A Lady Without Passport
The Lawless
Lonely Heart Bandits
The Man Who Cheated Himself
Mystery Street
Night and the City
No Man of Her Own
No Way Out
Once a Thief
One Way Street
Outrage
Outside the Wall
Paid in Full
Panic in the Streets
Quicksand
The Second Woman
The Secret Fury
711 Ocean Drive
Shadow on the Wall
Shakedown
Side Street
The Sleeping City
The Sound of Fury
Southside 1-1000
Stage Fright
State Penitentiary
The Sun Sets at Dawn
Sunset Boulevard
The Tattooed Stranger
This Side of the Law
The Underworld Story
Union Station
Walk Softly, Stranger
Where Danger Lives
Where the Sidewalk Ends
Woman in Hiding
Woman on the Run

1951
Ace in the Hole
Another Man's Poison
Appointment with Danger
The Basketball Fix
The Big Night
Cause for Alarm!
Cry Danger
Danger Zone
The Dark Man
Detective Story
The Enforcer
The Fat Man
Fourteen Hours
The Girl on the Bridge
He Ran All the Way

His Kind of Woman
Hollywood Story
The Hoodlum
House on Telegraph Hill
I Was a Communist for the F.B.I.
Iron Man
Lightning Strikes Twice
The Long Dark Hall
M
The Man with My Face
The Mob
No Questions Asked
The People Against O'Hara
Pickup
A Place in the Sun
The Prowler
The Racket
The Raging Tide
Roadblock
Roaring City
The Scarf
Sirocco
St. Benny the Dip a.k.a.
    Escape If You Can (U.K.)
Storm Warning
Strangers on a Train
The Strip
The 13th Letter
Three Steps North
Tomorrow Is Another Day
Two-Dollar Bettor a.k.a.
    Beginner's Luck (U.K.)
Two of a Kind
Under the Gun
The Unknown Man
The Well

1952
Affair in Trinidad
Beware, My Lovely
Captive City
Casque d'or
Clash by Night
Deadline – U.S.A.
Don't Bother to Knock
The Green Glove
Hoodlum Empire
Kansas City Confidential a.k.a.
    The Secret Four (U.K.)
The Las Vegas Story
Loan Shark
Macao
The Narrow Margin
Night Without Sleep
On Dangerous Ground
Ruby Gentry

Scandal Sheet a.k.a.
    The Dark Page (U.K.)
The Sellout
The Sniper
The Steel Trap
Strange Fascination
Stranger on the Prowl Imbarco a
    mezzanotte
Sudden Fear
Talk About a Stranger
The Thief
This Woman Is Dangerous
The Turning Point
Without Warning!

1953
Angel Face
Bad for Each Other
Beat the Devil
The Big Heat
The Blue Gardenia
A Blueprint for Murder
City That Never Sleeps
Count the Hours a.k.a.
    Every Minute Counts (U.K.)
Cry of the Hunted
Dangerous Crossing
The Fake
Girls in the Night a.k.a.
    Life After Dark (U.K.)
The Glass Wall
The Glass Web
The Hitch-Hiker
I Confess
I, the Jury
Jennifer
Jeopardy
The Limping Man
The Man Between
Man in the Attic
Man in the Dark
Murder Without Tears
Niagara
99 River Street
No Escape
One Girl's Confession
Pickup on South Street
Poison Ivy a.k.a. Gun Moll
    La Môme vert-de-gris
The System
36 Hours a.k.a. Terror Street (U.S.)
Vicki
The Wages of Fear Le Salaire de
    la peur
Wicked Woman

1954

Beautiful Stranger *a.k.a.*
   Twist of Fate *(U.S.)*
Black Tuesday
Black Widow
Crime Wave *a.k.a.*
   The City Is Dark *(U.K.)*
Cry Vengeance
Dial M for Murder
Down Three Dark Streets
Drive a Crooked Road
Forbidden (U.S.) Proibito
Hell's Half Acre
Highway Dragnet
Human Desire
The Human Jungle
Jail Bait
The Long Wait
Loophole
Make Haste to Live
Murder by Proxy *a.k.a.*
   Blackout *(U.S.)*
Naked Alibi
The Other Woman
Playgirl
Private Hell 36
Pushover
Rear Window
Riot in Cell Block 11
Rogue Cop
Shield for Murder
The Sleeping Tiger
Suddenly
Touchez Pas Au Grisbi
Witness to Murder
World for Ransom

1955

Before I Wake *a.k.a.*
   Shadow of Fear *(U.S.)*
The Big Bluff
The Big Combo
The Big Knife
A Bullet for Joey
Cell 2455, Death Row
Chicago Syndicate
Crashout
The Crooked Web
Desperate Hours
Diabolique Les Diaboliques
Dial Red O
The Fast and the Furious
Female Jungle
Female on the Beach
Finger Man
5 Against the House
Gang Busters

Hell on Frisco Bay
Hell's Island
Hold Back Tomorrow
House of Bamboo
I Died a Thousand Times
Illegal
Killer's Kiss
Kiss Me Deadly
Mad at the World
The Man with the Golden Arm
Mr. Arkadin *a.k.a.* Confidential
   Report *(U.K.)*
Murder Is My Beat
The Naked Street
New York Confidential
Night Freight
The Night Holds Terror
The Night of the Hunter
No Man's Woman
Pete Kelly's Blues
The Phenix City Story
Queen Bee
Rififi Du rififi chez les hommes
Six Bridges to Cross
Storm Fear
Sudden Danger
Tight Spot
Track the Man Down
The Trouble with Harry
The Wicked Go to Hell Les salauds
   vont en enfer
Women's Prison

1956

Accused of Murder
Behind the High Wall
Beyond a Reasonable Doubt
The Boss
Calling Homicide
The Come On
Crime Against Joe
Crime in the Streets
A Cry in the Night
Death of a Scoundrel
Foreign Intrigue
The Harder They Fall
Inside Detroit
The Intimate Stranger *a.k.a.*
   Finger of Guilt *(U.S.)*
Julie
The Killer Is Loose
The Killing
A Kiss Before Dying
Man in the Vault
The Man Is Armed
Miami Exposé
Nightmare

Outside the Law
Over-Exposed
Please Murder Me
Portrait of Alison *a.k.a.*
   Postmark for Danger *(U.K.)*
The Price of Fear
Section des disparus
Slightly Scarlet
The Steel Jungle
Strange Intruder
Terror at Midnight
Timetable
The Unguarded Moment
Walk the Dark Street
While the City Sleeps
The Wrong Man

1957

Affair in Havana
Affair in Reno
Appointment with a Shadow
Baby Face Nelson
The Brothers Rico
The Burglar
Chain of Evidence
Chicago Confidential
Crime of Passion
The Crooked Circle
Edge of the City *a.k.a.*
   A Man Is Ten Feet Tall *(U.K.)*
Escapade
Footsteps in the Night
The Garment Jungle
Hell Drivers
Hit and Run
House of Numbers
Kill Me Tomorrow
Interpol *a.k.a.* Pickup Alley *(U.S.)*
Lizzie
The Long Haul
A Man Is Ten Feet Tall
My Gun Is Quick
The Night Runner
Nightfall
Plunder Road
The Shadow on the Window
Short Cut to Hell
Slander
Slaughter on Tenth Avenue
Sweet Smell of Success
The Tattered Dress
The Unholy Wife
Valerie

1958

The Bonnie Parker Story
The Case Against Brooklyn
Cop Hater
Cry Terror!
Edge of Fury
Elevator to the Scaffold a.k.a.
   Frantic *(U.S.)* Ascenseur pour
   l'échafaud
Gang War
I Want to Live!
It Happened in Broad Daylight Es
   geschah am hellichten Tag
Johnny Rocco
The Lineup
Lonelyhearts
The Midnight Story
The Mugger
Murder by Contract
Party Girl
Screaming Mimi
Step Down to Terror
Touch of Evil
Vertigo

1959

The Beat Generation
The Big Operator
City of Fear
Crime and Punishment, U.S.A.
The Crimson Kimono
Cry Tough
Edge of Eternity
The Great St. Louis Bank Robbery
The Last Mile
Man in the Net
North by Northwest
Odds Against Tomorrow
The Purple Gang

1960

Breathless A bout de souffle
The Criminal *a.k.a.* The Concrete
   Jungle *(U.S.)*
Murder, Inc.
Peeping Tom
Psycho
Purple Noon Plein Soleil
Shoot the Piano Player Tirez sur le
   pianiste

1961

Blast of Silence
Underworld U.S.A.

1962
Cape Fear
Doulos – The Finger Man Le Doulos
Experiment in Terror
The Manchurian Candidate
The Trial Le Procès

1963
High and Low Tengoku to jigoku

1964
Blood and Black Lace Sei donne per
  l'assassino
The Killers
The Naked Kiss
Night Must Fall

1965
Alphaville Alphaville, une étrange
  aventure de Lemmy Caution
Brainstorm
The Money Trap
Pierrot le fou
The Third Day

1966
Blowup *a.k.a.* Blow-Up
Le Deuxième Souffle
Harper

1967
Branded to Kill Koroshi no rakuin
In Cold Blood
Point Blank
Robbery
Le Samouraï
Violated Angels Okasareta hakui

1968
The Bride Wore Black La mariée
  était en noir
Bullitt
The Detective
Lady in Cement
Madigan
Night of the Following Day
The Split

1969
Marlowe

Mississippi Mermaid La Sirène du
  Mississipi
They Shoot Horses, Don't They?
The Unfaithful Wife La Femme
  infidèle

1970
The Bird with the Crystal Plumage
  L'uccello dalle piume di cristallo
The Butcher Le Boucher
Le Cercle rouge
Performance

1971
The Burglars Le Casse
Dirty Harry
The French Connection
Get Carter
Klute
Straw Dogs

1972
And Hope to Die La Course du lièvre
  à travers les champs
Chandler
Champs
Deliverance
Un flic
Frenzy
The Getaway
Hickey & Boggs
The Outside Man Un homme
  est mort
Pulp

1973
Battles Without Honor and Humanity
  Jingi naki tatakai
The Friends of Eddie Coyle
The Long Goodbye
The Outfit
Serpico

1974
Bring Me the Head of Alfredo
  Garcia
Chinatown
The Conversation
Death Wish
The Parallax View
Thieves Like Us

1975
Deep Red Profondo rosso
Dog Day Afternoon
The Drowning Pool
Farewell, My Lovely
French Connection II
Graveyard of Honor Jingi no hakaba
Hustle
Night Moves
The Passenger Professione:
  reporter
Three Days of the Condor
The Yakuza

1976
The Killer Inside Me
The Killing of a Chinese Bookie
Taxi Driver

1977
The American Friend
  Der amerikanische Freund
Rolling Thunder

1978
The Big Sleep
The Driver

1979
Hardcore
Last Embrace
The Onion Field
Série noire

1980
Atlantic City
The First Deadly Sin
The Long Good Friday
Union City

1981
Blow Out
Body Heat
Clean Slate Coup de torchon
Diva
Ms. 45
Prince of the City
Sharky's Machine
The Postman Always Rings Twice
Thief
True Confessions

1982
Blade Runner
The Border
Dead Men Don't Wear Plaid
48 Hours
Hammett
I, the Jury
Still of the Night

1983
Bad Boys
Breathless
The Fourth Man De vierde man
The Moon in the Gutter La Lune
  dans le caniveau
Sudden Impact

1984
Against All Odds
Blood Simple
Body Double
Fear City
The Hit
Mike's Murder
Street of the Damned Rue Barbare
The Terminator
Tightrope

1985
The Falcon and the Snowman
Jagged Edge
To Live and Die in L.A.
The McGuffin
Witness
Year of the Dragon

1986
At Close Range
Blue Velvet
Descente aux enfers
8 Million Ways to Die
52 Pick-Up
Manhunter
The Morning After
Murphy's Law
No Mercy

1987
Angel Heart
The Bedroom Window
Best Seller
The Big Easy
Black Widow

Fatal Attraction
House of Games
Lethal Weapon
No Way Out
P.I. Private Investigations
Slam Dance
Someone to Watch Over Me
Suspect
White of the Eye

1988
Betrayed
Cop
Criminal Law
D.O.A.
Frantic
Stormy Monday
Tequila Sunrise

1989
Black Rain
Blue Steel
Cat Chaser
Dead-Bang
Johnny Handsome
Kill Me Again
The Kill-Off
Prime Suspect
Sea of Love
Street of No Return
Violent Cop Sono otoko, kyôbô
   ni tsuki

1990
After Dark, My Sweet
Another 48 Hrs.
Bad Influence
Boiling Point 3–4 x jûgatsu
Desperate Hours
La Femme Nikita Nikita
Goodfellas
The Grifters

The Hot Spot
Internal Affairs
Jezebel's Kiss
King of New York
The Krays
Miami Blues
Miller's Crossing
Narrow Margin
Pacific Heights
Presumed Innocent
Q & A
Revenge
State of Grace
The Two Jakes

1991
Cape Fear
The Dark Wind
Dead Again
Deceived
Delusion
Diary of a Hitman
Femme Fatale
Homicide
A Kiss Before Dying
The Last Boy Scout
Liebestraum
Mortal Thoughts
New Jack City
Point Break
Rush
Shattered
The Silence of the Lambs
Sleeping with the Enemy
Thelma & Louise
V.I. Warshawski

1992
Bad Lieutenant
Basic Instinct
Deep Cover
Final Analysis
Guncrazy

The Hand That Rocks the Cradle
Illicit Behaviour
Night and the City
Reservoir Dogs
Thunderheart
To Kill For
White Sands

1993
Red Rock West
Sonatine

1994
Léon: The Professional Léon
Natural Born Killers
Pulp Fiction

1995
Heat
Se7en
Underneath
The Usual Suspects

1996
Fargo

1997
Fireworks (U.S.) Hana-Bi
Jackie Brown
L.A. Confidential

1998
Out of Sight

1999
Fight Club
The Limey
The Matrix

2000
Memento

2005
A History of Violence
Sin City *a.k.a.* Frank Miller's Sin
   City

2006
The Departed

2007
Eastern Promises
No Country for Old Men
Zodiac

2008
The Dark Knight

2010
Black Swan

2011
Drive

2012
Killing Them Softly

Ulrich von Berg (UVB), degree in American and Media Studies. Many years' experience as a movie journalist in all branches of the media. Editor and author of various books on film. Lives in Berlin.

Ulrike Bergfeld (UB) studied Art. Numerous publications on art-related subjects. Lives in Berlin.

Philipp Bühler (PB) studied Political Science, History, and British Studies. Film journalist. Writes for various regional German publications. Lives in Berlin.

Paul Duncan (PD) has edited 50 film books for TASCHEN, including the award-winning *The Ingmar Bergman Archives*, and authored *Alfred Hitchcock* and *Stanley Kubrick* in the Film Series.

F. X. Feeney (FXF) is an L.A.-based filmmaker and critic. He coproduced *Z Channel: A Magnificent Obsession* (2004) for director Xan Cassavetes, and his screenwriting credits include *The Big Brass Ring* (1999), adapted from a story by Orson Welles. He is also the author of a dozen TASCHEN titles, most notably *Roman Polanski* and *Michael Mann*.

Robert Fischer (RF), filmmaker and film historian, published numerous film books, essays, and articles as author, editor, and translator. Lives in Vaterstetten near Munich.

Steffen Haubner (SH) studied Art History and Sociology. Author of many academic and press articles. Runs a press office in Hamburg, the city he lives in.

Jörn Hetebrügge (JH) studied German Literature. Author and journalist; many articles on film. Lives in Berlin.

Douglas Keesey (DK) is the author of the TASCHEN books *Clint Eastwood*, *The Marx Brothers*, *Jack Nicholson*, *Paul Verhoeven*, and *Erotic Cinema*. His other publications include *Catherine Breillat*, *Don DeLillo*, *Peter Greenaway*, *Neo-Noir*, and *Contemporary Erotic Cinema*. A selection of his essays can be found at http://works. bepress.com/dkeesey/doctype.html#article. He is a professor of film and literature at California Polytechnic State University.

Katja Kirste (KK), studied Literature and Film in Kiel; works for the The Independent State Board for Broadcasting (ULR) in Schleswig-Holstein and the broadcaster Sky; project leader of a film research project; director of press and PR with Discovery Channel; lectures at the University of Kiel and Passau, and the Media College in Stuttgart; currently freelance journalist and communications consultant. Lives in Munich.

Heinz-Jürgen Köhler (HJK), Film & TV journalist; author of many academic and press articles. Lives in Hamburg.

Oliver Küch (OK) studied English Literature and British History; works for Frauenhofer SIT (Sichere Informationstechnologie) in Darmstadt, head of PR and Marketing. Author of various articles on film, television, and IT themes. Lives in Darmstadt.

Petra Lange-Berndt (PLB), Lecturer / Assistant Professor, History of Art department, University College London. Publications on art and science, animal studies, history, and the history and theory of materiality and mediality. Writings include a book on animal art, and she has coedited a book on the artist Sigmar Polke. Lives in London and Dresden.

Jan-David Mentzel (JDM) studied Art History and Philosophy in Dresden and Florence. Research areas: North European art in the early modern age and the development of genre painting. Currently works at collaborative research center "Transcendence and Public Spirit" at the TU Dresden. Lives in Dresden.

Nils Meyer (NM) studied German Literature and Politics, trainee at the Evangelische Journalistenschule in Berlin, research assistant in Dresden, editor in Bremen. Articles for print, radio, and television. Works as a public relations officer. Lives in Hanover.

Olaf Möller (OM) author, translator, program curator. Film journalist, writes for the national and international press. Lives in Cologne.

Eckhard Pabst (EP) PhD, lectures at Institute for Contemporary German Literature and Media in Kiel. Publications on film and television include a book on images of the city in two German TV series. Lives in Rendsburg, near Kiel.

Lars Penning (LP) studied Journalism, Theater Studies, and General and Comparative Literature. Freelance film journalist. Writes for, among others, *tip* and *taz*. Author of books on Cameron Diaz and Julia Roberts, as well as many critical articles on film history for various publications. Lives in Berlin.

Anne Pohl (APO) active as a journalist since 1987. Author of numerous academic articles. Lives near Hamburg.

Stephan Reisner (SR) studied Literature and Philosophy. Many articles on film, photography, art, and literature. Lives and works as a freelance writer in Berlin.

Burkhard Röwekamp (BR) PhD, media scholar and lecturer at the Institute for Media Studies at the Philipps University in Marburg. Author of books on film aesthetics, history and theory. Specialist areas: the militarization of perception in AV media; the aesthetics, theory and history of film; media pragmatics. His most recent work is on the antiwar film. Lives in Marburg.

Alain Silver (AS) recently published, with James Ursini, *Film Noir Graphics: Where Danger Lives* (2012). They also cowrote *Film Noir* for TASCHEN and *The Noir Style* and coedited *Film Noir: The Encyclopedia*, *Film Noir: The Directors*, the *Film Noir Reader* series, and other genre and director studies. Their latest DVD commentary is on the Mann/Alton film *He Walked by Night*. Silver has also produced, written, and directed many independent features, most recently *Nightcomer* (2013).

Eric Stahl (ES) German Studies graduate, specializing in communication science. Film journalist and cultural editor, wrote many articles in various journals. Eric Stahl died in 2009 at the age of 43.

Markus Stauff (MS) PhD, media scientist, teaches at the Media Studies department of the University of Amsterdam. Key research areas are digital television, media, sports, and cultural studies. Author of many academic articles and several books. Lives in Amsterdam.

James Ursini (JU) has cowritten or coedited over 20 books with Alain Silver, including their *Film Noir Reader* series, which established them as two of the foremost authorities on film noir. Ursini has also written for various film magazines and supplied the commentary for numerous classic film noir DVDs. He has a doctorate in motion pictures studies and lectures on filmmaking in the Los Angeles area.

Rainer Vowe (RV) historian, teaches at the Institute for Film and Television Studies at the Ruhr University in Bochum. Numerous articles on the history of cinema and television. Lives in Bochum.

Christoph Ziener (CZ) studied Art History and Medieval History. Main research areas: film history and North European art of the early modern age. Lives in Dresden.

Cover: In *The Spiral Staircase* (1945), Helen (Dorothy McGuire) descends into a living hell.

Page 1: Tough homicide cop Mike Conovan (Van Johnson) must track down a cop killer in *Scene of the Crime* (1949).

Page 2: The world of charming gambler Johnny O'Clock (Dick Powell) is collapsing around him, in *Johnny O'Clock* (1947).

Pages 6/7: In *Woman on the Run* (1950) Eleanor Johnson (Ann Sheridan) is looking for her husband, unaware that he witnessed a gangland murder and is being pursued by the killer, police, and reporters.

Pages 36/37: *The Good German* (2006) is set in post–World War Two Berlin and shot in black and white, echoing *The Third Man* (1949) and *Casablanca* (1942) in theme and style.

Pages 664/665: In *The Glass Web* (1953), Don Newell (John Forsythe) must write a TV show about a murdered girl he had an affair with.

Page 675: Femme Fatale Robbie Lawrence (Marilyn Maxwell) in *Race Street* (1948).

Pages 676/677: In *Vicki* (1953), Lt. Ed Cornell (Richard Boone) becomes obsessed with the death of supermodel Vicki Lynn.

Page 687: Private detective Chris Conlon (Richard Conte, center) is framed for murder in *The Spider* (1945).

Page 688: Tony Reagan (Scott Brady) is just out of prison, so he is the perfect fall guy in *Undertow* (1949).

Back Cover: The noir cityscape of *Sin City* (2005).

IMPRINT

Copyrights

20th Century Fox 11tl+b, 12tl+b, 39tl, 130–137, 150–155, 178–183, 220–225, 252–257, 300–305, 340–345, 524–529, 652–657, 676/677, 687, A Band Apart 588–595, ABC 78–85, Amazonas 584–587, Aubrey Schenck Productions 14, Bandai Visual 616–619, Brighton Productions 536–539, Buena Vista International 39b, 45bl, 630–637, back cover, CCC Filmkunst 424–429, Ciné-Alliance 70–77, CJ Entertainment 44, Columbia Pictures 2, 13, 16, 20–35, 48, 240–245, 306–311, 430–435, 518–523, 184–187, Concorde Film 568–573, Constantin Film 45t, Enterprise Productions 214–219, Fidelity Pictures 6/7, Films sans Frontières 50–57, First National Pictures 9, Forward Pass Production 602–607, Gloria Filmverleih 440–445, 490–493, Greenwich Film Productions 530–535, Harbel Productions 436–439, Harry M. Popkin Productions 328–333, Hemdale Film 42tr, Helkon Filmverleih 624–629, Highlight Film 620–623, ICI 104–109, IFC Films 44bl, International Pictures 138–143, J.E.M Productions 2, King Brothers Productions 294–299, Les Films de la Pléiade 456–461, Les Films de la Tour 548–553, London Film Productions 282–287, MGM 17l, 41, 124–129, 188–193, 266–273, 312–319, 476–483, 484–489, 494–499, 514–517, 562–567, 574–577, Michael Powell 446–449, Nero-Film 62–69, Neue Visionen Filmverleih 10, New Line Cinema 596–601, Nouvelles Éditions de Films 404–409, Orion Pictures 540–543, Paramount Pictures 8r, 15, 39tr, 46, 118–123, 166–171, 320–327, 346–351, 416–423, 450–455, 504–507, 508–513, Parklane Pictures Inc. 372–375, Pathé Cinéma 334–339, 366–371, PRC 162–165, Reliance Pictures 234–239, RKO cover, 18, 144–149, 172–177, 194–201, 226–233, 258–265, 675, Senator Films 49, Solar Productions 500–503, Studio Canal+ 578–583, The Ladd Company 544–547, Theodora Productions 358–365, Toho Company 470–475, UFA 12, 58–61, 658–663, United Artists 274–281, 376–381, 382–389, 390–397, 398–403, Universal Pictures 6, 7, 12tr, 17r, 47, 48, 98–103, 110–117, 208–213, 410–415, 462–469, 664/665, 688, UPI 638–643, Vera Films 352–357, Warner Bros. 8l, 9–11tl, 36/37, 42tl+b, 43, 86–91, 92–97, 156–161, 202–207, 246–251, 288–293, 608–615, 644–651, Warner-Columbia 554–561.

Images

All posters courtesy **Heritage Auctions/HA.com**
The Alain Silver Collection 113, 153t, 191, 260, 298/299, 308, 317b, 362/363, 384b
British Film Institute Stills, Posters and Designs, London 39tr, 145, 146, 163, 165tl, 235, 236, 237b, 259, 270/271, 314, 315
ddp images, Hamburg 111, 112, 116, 164, 261, 264, 280, 295, 297, 309, 310tl, 311, 318, 330, 335, 337tl, 342, 343tr+b, 359, 384t, 389t, 392, 400b, 402tl, 618, 619, 862–872
The Paul Duncan Collection 1–38, 39tl+b, 4–49, 114, 115, 117, 147–149, 151, 152, 153–155, 165tr, 179–183, 189, 190, 192, 193b, 221–225, 237–239, 262–269, 272, 273, 275–279, 281, 301–305, 307, 310b, 313, 316, 317, 319, 329, 331–333, 336, 337–339, 341, 343–345, 360, 361, 364, 365, 389b, 391, 393–397, 399, 400t, 401, 402tr, 403, 431–435, 471–475, 485–489, 625–629, 664–688
Independent Visions 54/55, 84, 93, 119, 122, 143, 174, 193t, 244, 289, 293b, 310tr, 326, 349, 349b, 353, 356, 356, 357, 374r, 381, 421, 452, 455, 497t, 499, 505, 506t, 511t, 538b, 539, 571, 572, 572, 573b, 575, 577b, 579, 580t
The Kobal Collection, London/New York 617
The Lee Sanders Collection 296

Editors: Paul Duncan and Jürgen Müller
Editorial Coordination: Martin Holz and Florian Kobler, Cologne
Technical Editing: Philipp Bühler, Berlin
English Translation: Ann Drummond in association with First Edition Translations Ltd, Cambridge (introduction by Müller /Hetebrügge and texts from movies released from 2000 onward); Isabel Varea, Caroline Durant, Karen Waloschek and Monika Bloxam, for Grapevine Publishing Services Ltd., London (texts from movies released before 1931); Daniel A. Huyssen, Patrick Lanagan and Shaun Samson for English Express, Berlin (texts from movies released between 1931 and 1990); Deborah Caroline Holmes, Vienna (texts from movies released between 1991 and 2000) and Katharine Hughes, Oxford (captions from movies released between 1991 and 2000)
Production: Ute Wachendorf, Cologne
Design: Sense/Net, Andy Disl and Birgit Eichwede, Cologne www.sense-net.net; Josh Baker, Los Angeles
Final Artwork: Daniela Löbbert, Cologne

Texts: Ulrich von Berg (UVB), Ulrike Bergfeld (UB), Philipp Bühler (PB), Paul Duncan (PD), F. X. Feeney (FXF), Robert Fischer (RF), Steffen Haubner (SH), Jörn Hetebrügge (JH), Douglas Keesey (DK), Katja Kirste (KK), Heinz-Jürgen Köhler (HJK), Oliver Küch (OK), Petra Lange-Berndt (PLB), Jan-David Mentzel (JDM), Nils Meyer (NM), Olaf Möller (OM), Eckhard Pabst (EP), Lars Penning (LP), Anne Pohl (APO), Stephan Reisner (SR), Burkhard Röwekamp (BR), Alain Silver (AS), Eric Stahl (ES), Markus Stauff (MS), James Ursini (JU), Rainer Vowe (RV), Christoph Ziener (CZ)

To stay informed about upcoming TASCHEN titles, please subscribe to our free Magazine at www.taschen.com/magazine, find our Magazine app for iPad on iTunes, follow us on Twitter and Facebook, or e-mail us at contact@taschen.com for any questions about our program. Delve in and enjoy!

© 2014 TASCHEN GmbH
Hohenzollernring 53, D–50672 Köln
www.taschen.com

Printed in China
ISBN 978-3-8365-4356-9